IBIZA '98

IBIZA '98

How far will you go?

LUKE ATWOOD

Copyright © 2021

All rights reserved.

No part of this book may be reproduced in any form or by any electronic or mechanical means, including information storage and retrieval systems, without written permission from the author, except for the use of brief quotations in a book review.

CONTENTS

Foreword	vii
Introduction	ix
Preface	xi
1. The Stolen Fish	1
2. The Interview	5
3. Magaluf: Training	24
4. Sales Training	33
5. Booze Cruise & Buttkiss	60
6. Greased Lightning	85
7. Ibiza: My Arrival	105
8. The Balcony Marauder	121
9. Schoolboy Error	128
10. The Waterpark	133
11. The Distillery	142
12. The Go-Kart Track	150
13. The Beach Party	156
14. Pool Entertainment	160
15. Baptism of Fire	174
16. The Liverpool Connection	181
17. Rep's Cabaret	192
18. Hairbrush horrors	205
19. Moped Tragedy	215
20. Knock-a-Door Smash	222
21. Crime & Punishment	234
22. Dark Times	243
23. Bunny Boiler Barbie	254
24. The Human Squid	278
25. Cereal Killer	306

26. Civilian Life 313
    Epilogue 316

    Acknowledgments 319

FOREWORD

I ducked out of a lads holiday as a 1980s teenager. A previous visit to the island had filled my head with images of fish restaurants, wall lizards and wheezy hire cars; of Ibiza Old Town, Santa Eulalia, coves and harbour lights, all swathed in Mediterranean heat and backed by a philharmonic of cicadas, muffled conversations and music.

The planned revisit would involve drink and sex and not necessarily in that order. I recall the awareness that I would rather rebuild the old Nissan engine lying in pieces at the back of my parents' garage and, having declined the invitation, became concerned there must be something wrong with me, and that evenings spent adjusting valve clearances were not the way most people my age had fun.

I've been curious about the party island ever since avoiding going back there (and having long since come to terms with being a natural introvert). This curiosity is partly because I fell in love with its music; more specifically, the way Balearic beats transport you to San Antonio pre-parties and on to 5am beaches without the need for any literal or figurative baggage. It's also because I believe the life of my extrovert friend Luke, whom I have known for more decades than I would care to admit, was greatly informed by his stint as both supervisor and sales demonstrator of all the happy carnage there.

On his own he is quietly spoken, sharp and polite; the first to listen and to help. To quote Fred Rogers, "When I was a boy and I would see scary things in the news, my mother would say to me, look for the helpers. You will always find people who are helping." The author is one of those people, as a rather tense scene amongst these pages will affirm. But give the man a crowded room and something happens.

I won't waste time describing the transformation because it is laid bare over the course of the book. To summarise, though: I have to believe that a number of years spent herding unruly holidaymakers around - each one preoccupied by where and when the next drink and sex were coming from - has made him both a welcome guest and compère bar none. When it all goes wrong, the person to whom everyone turns to put it right. So I can't think of a more appropriate person to shine a light on what was really going on behind the scenes on the White Island.

11/1/21

INTRODUCTION

I can remember quite clearly when I first decided I wanted to be a rep. It was the summer of '97. I was in Magaluf, on a boys' holiday with my best mate. We were there for one reason and one reason only. To do damage. In the 90s, being a lad and going on holiday to a perfect destination without getting your leg over was an uncontested failure. There was no salvation from Instagram or Facebook. No conciliatory likes or hashtags. There was no such thing as a smashed avocado breakfast, cracked pepper or something drizzled on anything. Burgers were served on plates not on wooden boards, and black surgical gloves were reserved for vets when fisting horses. The only people sporting beards then were foreign footballers, kiddy fiddlers and Hulk Hogan. There were no low contrast filtered photos of my feet in the water, the closest your snaps came to a coloured filter was the little orange date stamp in the bottom right corner letting you know what the date and time was!

It was a different time, with different motivations, and more importantly different degrees of evidence. The aim of

INTRODUCTION

the Balearic holiday wasn't to #livemybestlife or demonstrate how #blessed I was, it was to sleep with more girls than my comrade and it was to drink and dance without puking on myself, and if I was lucky, not lose my wallet, passport or underwear in that order.

PREFACE

For the best part of 20 years I've wanted to write this book. I've been fortunate to sit on many great memories from a different era, long consigned to the nostalgia that accompanies middle age. I've also sat on certain fears that my experiences, accounts and memories would also be chastised if told in today's social climate.

I hope no offence is taken by the contents of this book. Keep in mind we live in a different era now. Behaviour that was normal and acceptable then, might not quite be the case now. That's not to say we weren't liberal then, it's just our liberalism seemed less defining.

Whilst my memories might have dulled over the years, the accounts are truthful, and if these stories are outrageous and unbelievable, that's because to those who've never been to Ibiza, they could well seem it.

As a teenager living and working on the greatest island in the world at the turn of the century, the sheer amount of life experience I gained in that short time opened my eyes and made me who I am today.

PREFACE

Enjoy the book, be open minded, and I hope it raises as many smiles for you as it did for me writing it.

CHAPTER 1

THE STOLEN FISH

We'd arrived in Magaluf raring to go. It was the summer of 1997, peak season. We wanted to nail, so that we could abandon the stigma of "nil points" and then relax for the rest of the holiday knowing that the primary objective had been fulfilled, and the mission was accomplished. The simple fact was as a teenager, if you got your nuts in on holiday, the rest of the plans could go to hell, but you still had a good holiday. If you returned home with a doughnut on the scoreboard, your mates would end up caning you without even knowing it. So, did you get your end away? No? Oh, what happened? Clubs closed? Was the resort full of parents? Bad weather? You guys have a bust up? You get ill or something? This was not a conversation I wanted to have. The alternative was infinitely more appealing. Shag something. Anything. Return home a gladiator. You smash? Yep. Decent? Alright enough, average. Nightlife was awesome. Good lad.

The rep for our hotel must have only been a year or so older than us, but in terms of life experience it could have been a decade. We were like lambs to the slaughter. We bought the full package of trips he was selling. I think I held out for a slight discount out of principle but the truth of the matter was that we would have bought drinks in a free bar. Don't get me wrong, we didn't regret it for a moment, we had an amazing time, but it never really occurred to me to try and get a rep job until our hotel rep swooped in like a pterodactyl and snatched a bird out of my grasp as I was on course to go back to hers. That's right. This lothario from Manchester literally pulled the fish out of my mouth before I had a chance to even nibble. Fair play to him. I mean all's fair in love and muff, but at the time it left a particularly envious feeling in my mouth. It wasn't until my partner in grime suggested that I should apply to be a rep that I started to think about the possibilities. Free drinks, a different girl every week if not more frequently, and to spend the summer getting paid to live in one of Europe's most bustling resorts. What's not to like? Towards the end of the holiday the rep basically told us about this reunion that was taking place in the North of England a few months later. We only needed to put a small deposit down now and then pay the rest nearer the time. It was basically a weekender at Butlins but for all the holiday makers who'd been away with the tour operator over the whole season. The rep basically sold it to us in one or two lines. Imagine all the girls going on this weekend hoping to rekindle their holiday romance and to try and relive their summer holiday over two nights. It would be like shooting fish in a barrel. Done. Sold. Sign me up. Take my money. Despite us both being students and understandably skint, this was something neither of us were going to miss. Even if it meant eating Tesco's value rice and bbq sauce for a few weeks and brewing our own beer so as to save up the rest of the cash to afford entry to the pussy palace.

    We finished out holiday in good spirits. I thankfully,

managed to fall into something on one of the last nights, alas poor Mike, my wingman, only managed a hand job by the fountain. He was the one having to deal with the awkward questions when we got back to uni. Get laid? Nope. Both of you? No, he managed to smash. Why didn't you? Not sure. We'd paid down our deposits and now had a couple of months to save and wait for this big reunion. To be honest, we both pretty much forgot about it.

 University life kicked back in and we were busy chasing skirt there, stealing traffic cones or other peripherals not screwed down, and trying to pass exams. It wasn't until we both received the request to pay the rest of the sum by the end of September, that we started to think about it and look forward to the impending carnage. Time flew and before long we were sat on a coach heading up the M1 drinking cans of cider. The weekend was fantastic. We made friends on the coach, we made friends in the block, we met randoms. Everyone was continually pulling each other, dancing, drinking, pulling some more. Both of us got repeatedly laid, and we were making friends left right and centre. It was as if Carlsberg actually did weekend benders! So buoyant was our mood, that the industrial plastic sheeting covering the mattresses, the non-existent heating, and the rising damp in the rooms seemed to just add character to our cells that were doubling as hotel rooms. At some point on the Sunday just after checkout, it was made known that initial interviews were going to take place for those that wanted to try and get a rep's job. Thankfully, I wasn't that hung over, so I decided to go along and see what it was all about. It was very busy, but they seemed to have reps from every resort so there were more than enough 'hands' on deck to handle the initial questioning. Thinking back, it wasn't so much an interview but an assault. The girl opposite me was flirting outrageously and continually trying to embarrass me. There was an endless stream of innuendo and banter designed to confuse and conquer. I just served the ball back in the manner it was played and after 2-3 minutes of this we began to talk more seriously about why I wanted to work there and what experience did I have. I asked a couple of questions, made a few quips and after a few more minutes of pleasantries I was done. She smiled warmly, shook my hand and I was filing out the side with everyone else. I had no idea if I'd made a good impression or not. I hoped I had, but any thoughts of getting a position soon flew out of my head as I needed to focus on the task in hand. I needed to buy beers for the coach journey home and sneak back to our room to see if Mike had pulled or not, and if so, catch a glimpse of it. Alas, he did manage to slay someone, but she'd already shot off back to the swamp by the time I returned. It didn't perturb me, there were still viable targets on the coach and we both still had a good chance of a feel up before we reached home.

CHAPTER 2
THE INTERVIEW

I remember when the letter arrived. It was some time during the spring of '98. It had been sent to my family's address instead of my address at university. I just thought it was easier to use Mum and Dad as a post box than having to update everything each year as we changed digs at Uni. Mum told me I'd received a letter from a tourist agency. I didn't immediately twig what it was. I mean the interview I had at the weekender was back in October. I assumed it was some invitation to attend a time share pitch or some crappy voucher or newsletter that I'd been sneakily signed up to. I asked her to read it out on the phone. She said I'd been successful in my application to be an Overseas Representative and that I needed to come for an interview in London where they would formally narrow the selection of candidates before making their final selection. I was given a time and a date where the interview was due to take place and also a list of things that I needed to prepare in advance. As she went down the list most of it was pretty standard. Bring a copy of photographic ID, ideally a passport or driving licence, national insurance number, appropriate costumes or props. I interrupted Mum "What do you mean appropriate costumes or props?" she replied "ah, it says here you need to entertain people for 2 minutes." That's ok I thought, I've got a good sense of humour, most people seem to get on with me and often said I'm funny. I can tell a few jokes, and maybe the odd experience and that should be ok. No props needed, sorted! "You can't tell jokes; you can't show any videos." Bugger it, now what will I do? I thanked mum for calling, and said I'd think about it. I'd be down in a couple of weeks anyway and I'd make sure to coincide my trip with the interview in London anyway so I'd kill 2 birds with 1 stone. I didn't really give it much thought. I mean what can I do? I can't sing for shit, I can dance, but I'm going to feel like a complete tool dancing in front of a room full of strangers on my own to some hip hop. I was at a loss. What will everyone else do? What if we end up doing the same? As the interview drew nearer, the pressure started to climb. I spoke with Mike and my flat mates. One of the girls jokingly remarked in her beloved welsh accent, "My dear, it's simple. Do a striptease!" I initially laughed this off, and the rest of the room giggled, but as the laughter subsided, I thought about it a little further. This might work. It's only 2 minutes. It will show I'm not a prude, should get the girls cheering in the group at least, maybe some of the guys depending on whether they like what they see or just want to encourage me anyway. I can make this funny, it doesn't have to be serious or sleazy. Besides, the Full Monty film had just come out fairly recently, and that had gone down really well with the public. It was also very topical, given the holiday reps had to do strips all the time in resort. We hatched out the plan further, choosing the music and costume. I decided that whilst I wasn't particularly bothered about taking my clothes off in front of a room full of strangers, I didn't really relish the idea of going the full hog and showing them mini-me. If I was going to pull this off (pardon the pun) I needed to make it impactful and funny enough that I didn't need to go down to my birthday suit. There was only one option left available for me. My elephant G-string. For my previous birthday one of my flatmates had bought me an Anne Summer's G-string. It was horrific. It was an elephant's head, with big googly eyes that moved around as you gyrated. It had flappy ears, a small tuft of blue hair, and a blue elastic sleeve for a trunk where you'd park your chap. As for the rear and sides, well it was a couple of threads of elastic. It was ridiculous to look at in its box, let alone to wear. If this didn't have people laughing then I didn't know what would. Besides, I deemed it was more preferable for them to smile and point at that, than it was to look at my pipe hanging there flaccid like the last unwanted chicken at Tesco. For the music, I chose 'You Sexy Thing' (I believe in Miracles…) by Hot Chocolate – also a favourite in the Full Monty. I needed an outfit now. I asked mum to sew in some Velcro risers into the sides of an old pair of boxers I still had at home as I wanted to be able to rip these off in one go. My mum agreed, and together with my sister they worked on them for an evening. Pausing only for me to try and rip them off to see how much Velcro to add. I wanted to be able to do it in one go, otherwise I'd look pretty stupid trying a second or third attempt, or God forbid, having to step out of them. Oh, the shame of that. It's one thing to choose a strip tease, but there's no fucking way I am not going to commit to it and do it properly. Thankfully mum's sewing was perfect. There was enough Velcro to keep the boxers together when sat down and without making that scratching/tearing noise, but not enough that I couldn't yank them off with one sharp tug from either side of the hips. I borrowed my sister's ghetto blaster. I had the CD. I was ready.

My mum and dad found the whole thing funny. We've always been an open family, and the thought of me stripping down to the trunk in front of a room full of strangers didn't really phase them or me. My parents' friends on the other hands were shocked. They were asking me things like how are you going to do it? What if it goes wrong? What if the music doesn't work? They were making statements like "Oh I could never do that!" or "I don't know how you can do it; I'd die." Whilst initially I was proud to be doing it, determined to show everyone that I had the guts and didn't care, I must admit after a while this continual negative and pessimistic attitude was beginning to get to me. What if I freeze? What if no one laughs? What if I get thrown out for indecent exposure? What if I humiliate myself? As I began to weigh the gravity of my choices in my head, I suddenly remembered that I'd told all my flatmates and our close circle of friends that I was going to do it, and my family had spent their time on helping to make me a costume. Fuck it. I'm not letting them down and I'm not turning back now. The interview was the next day, I tried not to think about it for the rest of the evening.

The following morning, I was up bright and early. I shot down the gym determined to try a last-minute patch up job for the interview. No time for stretching or cardio, this was beach muscles only. I hit the bench press and sit up machine like a man possessed. Thankfully, due to my staple uni diet of a bag of rice a week and my love of sports, I was already pretty slim with a modest 6 pack and a set of shoulders on me. I shouldn't have worried, but this was all part of my mental preparation for what lay ahead. The interview was at 2pm, I skipped lunch (again, thinking of the belly). I got there at about 1:45, it was being held in a conference room at one of the hotels in King's Cross. I was nervous. I walked in, and there were about 15-20 candidates there all from the ages of maybe 18 to mid-20s. They had travelled far and wide to get to the interview, and they all looked more relaxed than me. I introduced myself to a couple of guys sat in one corner and made small talk until one of the staff members came out to the waiting area, introduced herself and then led us through into the room.

There were flip charts and refreshments at one side, a small stage area and seating on the other, and there were welcome packs adorning every table. As we began to file in and take our places, I realised that the number of candidates that I initially had at max 20, was a gross underestimation. More and more were turning up. Even after they closed the doors others were still rolling through. I reckon the final numbers were nearer 35 -40 including 4 staff members and a couple of hotel staff who presumably were there to assist in the refreshments. As we finally began with the welcome speech, one last figure walked in. A photographer. My heart sank. I couldn't believe it. He was here for their internal magazine and potential publicity surrounding the new intake of reps. It was naive of me to think I'd be able to walk into this hotel in the middle of London, stick on some 70s disco music, rip off my trousers, gyrate my hips to 40 strangers, wave my trunk to the nearest girls in the crowd, and then calmly return to my seat without damage or embarrassment, only supreme confidence. Now I'm fucked. What do I do? I've got no time to make an alternative plan, the room seemed pretty amped up and keen, and I'm competitive. If they've all got these really good acts and I stand up there unplanned, I'm finished. It was a battle of my modesty/photographic exposure versus my pride. It wasn't the only thing that was weighing on my noodle either. Whilst making small talk with the guys outside, one of the guys said that he was going to do a drinking game which he liked to play. Another said he was going to wing it, but the third in the group said he was going to do a strip. Again, I felt a twinge across my chest when I heard this. Fuck, this completely levelled the playing field. He was bigger than me in a rugby sort of way and then I started to doubt myself. What if he goes first, I'm going to look silly coming afterwards, as no one remembers second best? What if he's ripped to bits and the girls go mad? I'm going to look like a twat and the atmosphere will sink quicker than a fart at church. If he manages to get out the traps in front of me and he goes the whole hog, fruit and veg out, then I too will have no choice. The trunk will be but a minor comical distraction, but the reality is, the brooch and earrings are coming out. If he's a foot long making me in turn look like I've been ice diving, so be it. I'll just have to style this out. In fact, if he doesn't go full nude, I'll have to anyway, just to prove that I've got what it takes, and he fell short. Once I gained my composure, I decided it was on. Others might have considered backing out, but there was no way I was going down without a fight. I wanted to do the strip to prove to everyone I could do it and I wanted this job. I wanted to drink for free and to shag every night. This was just another obstacle in the way. I thought to myself, if they want to see a lively character, they're going to get one. If the photographer wants a shot in the company paper, he can get a portrait view of my elephant-sheathed cock complete with google eyes and hair that resembled Marge Simpson's minge.

The next 30 - 40 minutes passed by uneventfully. It mainly consisted of an introduction to the company, what they would expect from us, what we can expect from them and some general ice breaker style introductions from all the candidates, followed by some light hearted banter across the groups to try and warm everyone up for the main event. I, along with the others, made sure I was particularly vocal. This was not a room for shrinking violets. I made a few quips got a few laughs, received some stick from one of the interviewers also, which I thought was a positive sign given the circumstances. All of the interviewers were ex reps themselves and between them probably had enough stories and situations to make a TV series. As we were nearing the end of the current section of the interview, the main guy proudly announced that we were moving on to the entertainment section next and that we had 15 minutes to get a tea or coffee and to get ready. Game time. The level of tension in the room suddenly jumped. Everyone was both nervous and apprehensive but also excited to see what others had prepared. All of a sudden, bags were being ripped open and various props and pieces of clothing were being dragged out of a multitude of plastic bags. I excused myself and went to the bathroom. I started to get into costume. I remember contemplating whether or not to have a wank and try and get some life in the old boy. Nothing wrong with the elephant's trunk being a little heavier than normal I mused. I carried out a risk assessment and the fear of suddenly getting a spontaneous boner outweighed the benefits of extra trunk. Besides, the material was pretty long anyway, so having a semi would hardly make much of a difference. I remember looking down, making sure everything was ok and the boxers were functioning normally. I looked at myself in the mirror for a couple of seconds. This was my Eminem moment. Whatever happened with rugby dude, I was going for it and that was all there was to it. I exited the toilet and then went and sat back in my seat. As we started to sit down the excitement was noticeable higher. I'd kept my ghetto blaster in my rucksack so as not to give the game away, and no one knew I was sporting the latest in penis animal fabrics. I couldn't risk any other guys trying to do the same thing before me.

All eyes were on the main stage and the speaker. He reiterated the rules. We each had 2 minutes to perform, with 1-minute preparation time before we were due to go on. The idea was that we were to get ready whilst the other candidates were performing the second half of the act. We were to do so quietly, and be courteous at all times to those performing. At this stage it felt like we were at a drama school rather than some outrageous holiday company. Again, I slowly started to question my choice of performance again. That wretched thought disappeared immediately when he asked who wanted to go first. I flung my hand in the air like a school nerd competing for the extra star after the teacher asked an easy question. I thrust my hand so high, my triceps felt a pang from the workout I put myself through a few hours earlier. "Easy Cowboy" joked the main man, and he chose a girl who had been smiling at him in the front. "What do you say? Fancy it?" he asked her. She reluctantly nodded and stood up, drawing every pair of eyes in the room on to her. She turned to face the crowd, her cheeks flushing slightly red as she spoke. She said that she was going to sing a song that was close to her heart and that she hoped we would enjoy it. She then began to softly sing this song that I'd never heard before. It reminded me of Aled Jone's Walking in the Air. I remember thinking to myself that she was a decent singer, but also why did she choose this song. As we listened intently for 20-30 seconds, suddenly the compere interrupted her. "Hey there, thanks for that it's really nice, but I have a small request. Can you sing it in Chinese please?" Everyone looked bemused. She replied to him "But I don't know Chinese." Her eyes widening at the thought. "That's ok, nor do we, we'll never know the difference. Go for it!" You could see the redness in her cheeks intensify as her eyes darted around the room desperate for salvation. She found none. In an even softer voice, she slowly started to sing her own variation of mandarin or cantonese, her voice cracking as she went. "Sooo Waaaa Weeeee, Waaaa wuuuuu shuuu…" The audience loved it, everyone in the room was laughing except her. As she saw people were reacting favourably to her efforts she began to sing louder with more gusto. "Wuuuu shi Wuuuu, haaaaaaaaayoooooo…." and people laughed even harder. Thankfully the compere stopped her short of her full 2 minutes, but no one minded. Everyone laughed, and the whole room felt more relaxed. He thanked her profusely, but then pivoted round to the audience, glancing at me as he bellowed "who's next!" Again, my hand shot upwards, but again he teasingly picked someone else. Had he known the severity of his choices I wonder if he would have acted in the same manner. If he inadvertently chose rugby boy before me, that meant there was high chance he was going to be looking at my tea towel holder together with my bald hamster shortly after whatever rugby boy was packing. If he made the smart choice and chose me, then he'd be blessed with a glimpse of Nelly the elephant wearing a coat, and all would be right with the world. One of the female interviewers quipped that I was keen. I just smiled, trying not to show my eagerness. I wondered whether my enthusiasm was going to pay off or if I had hindered myself. It was a balancing act. They could leave me longer down the list now to annoy me and entertain the majority at my expense, or they could just put me out of my misery and choose me next so they could see what I was so eager to show everyone. Only time would tell.

He selected one of the guys I was sat outside with earlier. He stood up and gestured to two hotel staff to bring something over. The staff brought over a table into the middle of the room and he gestured everyone to gather round. He basically tried to cram as much of the audience around the table as possible. In the middle of the table was a long tray full of water. The tray was probably a metre long maybe 50cm wide, and was about 10cm deep. It had been filled with water three quarters of the way to the top. On either end of the tray there were some goal posts that had been crudely made with straws. He asked the audience to split into two and then proceeded to create two teams. He then handed 2 straws to 2 members of each team and pulled a ping pong ball out of his pocket. The aim of the game was to blow the ball into the opposing team's goal. He was adamant that everyone was to get low, but no one could lean over the water. He got everyone to join in for a countdown and then dropped the ball in. Immediately the straw guys started furiously trying to blow across the water from their respective ends. It was quite amusing to watch. I wasn't so close, electing to watch from a few meters away, as I was more preoccupied with being selected next and I was trying to keep my eyes on the prize. After about 30-40 seconds of frantic blowing and cheering on both sides, he started to wind the room up with football style commentary, and he encouraged everyone to lean in and for the rest of the "supporters" to blow towards the ball instead. As the ball started to dart around more frequently everyone began to focus more and more on it. No one saw what happened next. One of the staff members handed him the second tray and he suddenly slammed the second slightly smaller tray hard down into the first tray engulfing all four sides of the table, including himself, with a mini tidal wave. There was not a single dry face around the table. There was a brief pause in the room. You could almost hear the mental reconciliation going on. Then the whole room erupted into laughter and clapping. He was pissing himself. You could see the interviewers were pleased. People sodden with water returned to their chairs wet but happy. The table was removed and the compere stood up. I tried to feign disinterest. "Do I need to ask who wants to be next?" he asked the room. All eyes were on me. "Come on then, show us what you've got!" he gestured to me. Bingo! Finally, here I am. It's funny, I was so pre-occupied with trying to get out in front of any of the other guys that I'd almost forgotten the fact that now I was going to be stripping off in front of 40 strangers and that photographer who up until now had been lurking in the distance like a pervert in the bushes at your local park. I don't know if it was just me, or he'd been encouraged to come closer, but he suddenly found the energy to move forward and sit near the front. Bastard. He's been put up to that was my initial thought, but to be honest, the butterflies in my stomach were pretty much drowning out any thread of rationality.

I grabbed the ghetto blaster out of my bag. I'd previously set it to the exact track and volume and purposefully placed it on the desk nearest the stage area and angled it at the crowd. I strutted over to the centre. I turned to face the crowd. I could see the pervert was already firing off shots. If he's like this now, he's going to be frantic in about 90 seconds I thought to myself. I already knew that there was a 6 - 7 second delay on the track before the first beat drops and before everyone will recognise the song and immediately realise what I'm doing. Still, no turning back now. With a long face, I calmly informed the audience that I was an undercover health and safety inspector and that today there'd already been several violations. I nodded to one of the guys in the crowd who'd previously agreed to press play for me, and he did as instructed. I looked straight into the eyes of one of the female interviewers (the prettiest) and calmly asked if anyone would like any more (violations)? I held her gaze with the utmost confidence. I was like a swan.

Calm and graceful on the outside as I moved around the room, but under the surface, I was kicking like a drowning foal. I was shitting myself. Thankfully everything went to plan, and before she had a chance to respond to the sort of cheesy line only a stripper could mutter, the first beat dropped. This was quickly followed by the second. I broke into a wide warm smile as I switched my attention to the audience, who thankfully, also started to smile back towards me. I began to shake my hips from side to side to the beat of the music as I started to clap in time with the music. Soon enough the audience followed and within a few seconds the whole room was clapping in unison as I was strutting my stuff around the area like a peacock in heat. My initial butterflies were subsiding, and I began to relax, pouting at the photographer and anything else with a heartbeat. Off came the jacket, the shoes were undone loosely. I kicked one off to the side, and one in the direction of the compere. I originally meant to just throw it off to the floor, but as I flicked my leg, the shoe received some lift. Thankfully he caught it and I just winked. It was a brilliant bit of improvisation, but it could have gone so badly. Next was the belt. I ripped that out of the trousers with one tug. I held it aloft like the Sword of Grayskull before pretending to whip myself with it. I threw the belt down. I moved towards the front of the audience with the confidence of a lion. I bellowed at the audience the more they clap the more they see. This seemed to do the trick, even the guys at the back at this point were supporting me. I threw off the socks. One by one, I undid the buttons on my shirt. The girls in the front mockingly reaching forward for a touch. Next it was the trousers. I put my back to the audience and started to slowly tug the trousers down over my behind, and with one full swoop the trousers were dropped. I stepped out of them to the side. I just stood there in my boxers, arms outstretched listening to mainly the girls baying for flesh and a few wolf whistles. I turned around to face my admirers. I had forgotten about the pervert, but as I swivelled, I nearly stepped on him, he'd not only left his front row chair for a closer look, but he'd actually moved into the stage area and had crouched down on one knee firing upwards. I was too far in the 'zone' at that point to care what he was doing. Rather than retire at the unflattering angle he was most probably portraying me in, I thrust my hips forwards to the front of the lens. Take that pervert. You could tell he was up for the challenge, the shutter rebounding furiously as he was trying to max out his roll of film. I thrust again, he backed up a little. I side stepped him and with one last gesture to the crowds, all that was left were the boxers to come off. I teasingly grabbed them. I hadn't even managed to get a proper grip when the compere shrieked "Cut!" He hastily made his way between myself and the photographer. The music was paused, and there was a collective groan from the audience. Mainly the girls I might add. I think the guys in the audience had done their duty by supporting me. I didn't hold it against them that they were not disappointed in not seeing my love muscle. A mix of emotions hit me. I was happy due to the endorphins that were flooding my body as a result of performing itself. I was proud that not only had I carried it out, I'd carried it out confidently, making the holiday company call time. No one could say I didn't have the balls to go the full hog even though I was secretly relieved I didn't have to get mini-me out. I was also struck with disappointment. The highlight of my whole act was the elephant thong. Now no one is going to see it, and I felt that I would look like some self-obsessed weirdo for choosing to show myself off for other people's entertainment. My mind went into overdrive. "You don't understand," I exclaimed "this is the highlight of my performance!" The whole room laughed. "I need to finish" I added, capitalising on the crowd's mood. The compere replied "I'm sure it is very spectacular, but we don't need to see what you're packing." The audience chortled again. He tried to move quickly on asking the crowd who wanted to go next and who could top that. As I gathered my clothes up from the various areas of the stage area, I felt I'd been denied the reaction I so desperately sought. As I crouched down to pick up my belt, I ripped off the boxer shorts as I stood up. Standing there proudly, the whole room roared with laughter. Fingers were pointed, I was met with a barrage of cat calls and clapping. I revelled in it. Even if this meant I wasn't getting the job, no one was going to forget this! The pervert had already retired to the back of the group and was so busy reloading his camera with film after all the shots he had rattled off earlier, by the time he looked up he had missed his window. I was thankful, as it meant he didn't get to frame any of Nelly, nor would I be appearing in any magazine article looking like a prick. The compere scowled at me. "I had a wardrobe malfunction" I muttered, looking down at the little blue trunk. Thankfully rather than stay cross with me, he broke into a smile, shook his head exchanging some comments with his team and then proceeded to select the next act. I gathered up my belongings, dragged my practically naked ass back to the tables and got dressed. I sat back in my seat and noticed the female interviewer was looking at me. I caught her glance and winked. She just smiled before turning to the others. I was on fire. I was elated. Mission fucking accomplished!

I don't really remember what the next act was. I think it was someone else wanting to sing something. They started well, but predictably enough the compere asked the person to sing it in a different language. Instead of choosing

Chinese though, he threw it out to the audience. I think in the end the chosen language was Icelandic. I watched with intrigue, clapped when I should but was generally unwinding. I'd been pretty anxious and wound up before the performance and I could feel the tension dissipate. I then got a nudge from the guy next to me. I turned to him "what's up?" I asked, he just gestured to rugby boy. Rugby boy had caught his attention so he could alert me. "Hey mate, can I borrow your music?" he asked. Fucking cheek. I mean, we're competing here, and there's no way I want to help my competitor. I then proceeded to soften a little. I had managed to go first and I didn't have to go the full hog. It was clear that the company didn't want me to. It's unlikely they'll let rugby boy go further, and I'm sure he's not packing an animal banana hammock, so he won't outdo me. I further rationalised that if he was seen to be borrowing my equipment, he would look less prepared making me look better as well as compassionate. "Sure thing." I agreed. My feelings might reveal me to be an asshole, but this wasn't a leisurely meeting. There were limited places and the competition was strong. As I said before, I wanted that job.

Another couple of acts passed by. People were getting a little tired, and the room needed a break. The compere said we had time for one more act before a break. He chose rugby boy. Rugby boy collected my ghetto blaster and walked over to the stage. I sat there trying to look as relaxed and supportive as possible. I didn't have anything against the guy, despite him borrowing my music. He then turned to the crowd and said "you might have seen something similar before, but this time it's WITH the body!" Some members of the crowd made the sort of whooing noise you do at school when someone called another a dickhead and a fight is about to break out. All eyes were back on me. I just proceeded to stretch a large yawn and patted my gaping mouth slowly, breaking into a warm smile shortly after. Cunt. I understand that he needed an edge or something to help him, after all he was going second, and perhaps he didn't anticipate someone else doing a strip or going for it gangbusters like I had. Since I'd also leant him the ghetto blaster, I didn't appreciate being called out publicly. Thankfully, my irritation was short lived. I hadn't told him what track number I'd used. I didn't know what he wanted to dance to, and I wasn't going to lay it all out on a plate for him. As he hit the play button, he turned the music up but he had the wrong track. It took him a couple of tries to find the right one, but as the music was loud, each time he hit the wrong track everyone knew about it. He asked me what the track number was. I retorted that 'the body' should be able to dance to any of them. Eventually he found it, and a familiar intro started. He'd grabbed a chair and sat on it in a seductive way legs spread wide. I don't know whether it was because the room was tired, they'd already seen one striptease, or he just didn't commit to it fully, but whilst people smiled and supported where they could, the atmosphere was significantly flatter. I think he didn't even manage to get his last shirt button undone when the compere stepped in and called time. I waited with baited breath to see if he was going to make him dance in a funny style, or take his clothes off in a certain way which would make everyone laugh, but thankfully for me, he just quipped that he'd never seen so many candidates trying to get naked and that it was time for a break. Rugby boy a little dejected returned to his place handing me back the ghetto blaster.

During the break he thanked me for lending it to him and he said he wasn't sure what to do beforehand, and only decided on a strip that morning, so he was totally unprepared. He also apologised for mugging me off with the body remark, but said he needed a way in as otherwise it would have been just weird. I completely empathised with him. He was actually a decent bloke, and I began to feel guilty for my previous thoughts and attitudes towards him. That being said, it just reassured me that my initial instinct was correct, and that all the effort in trying to get out first paid dividends. For the next 30 minutes or so everyone was chatting about the various acts and how people had been nervous, or props had failed etc. It was like a gathering of school children just after exams. Stories of triumph and failure and the continued need of reassurance floated about the room.

After the break, we returned to the stage area where we continued to witness another 9 or 10 acts. These pretty much passed by without incident or memorability. Next, we all sat down together and basically had a debriefing from the day's events. Everyone was pretty tired. We were thanked for our commitment and enthusiasm. The interviewers gave us a rundown of qualities that they were looking for, what they'd seen, what they liked, what they didn't like and how we should all be proud to have come this far. I didn't actually realise it at the time, but the next step was basically the selection/deselection process. They had already chosen from this group who was going through and who was going home. We were told that when our name was read out to stand up. For the next minute a barrage of names was read out and one by one people were standing up. I was convinced I smashed the interview, but my heart felt heavy and my pride was being dented by not hearing my name. You could cut the atmosphere with a knife. Had I been too graphic? Had I pissed the interviewers off by being too cheeky? Had the trunk been a length too far? Finally, I heard the words "and last but not least…." The interviewer paused only to then read out someone else's name. As the last person stood up, I was bitterly disappointed. I looked around the room, many of those sat were looking down at their feet, dejected. The compere gathered everyone who'd been called up and asked them to stand together. "Guys, thank you so much for coming today, you've all put in super performances, and should be proud of yourselves. Unfortunately, it pains me to say it, but for this year, your journey stops here and you will not be moving forwards with us to resort. There are only so many places we can fill, but you're all more than welcome to try again with us next year. If you could collect your belongings and go through that door there, you'll be able to grab a tea or coffee before you go, and one of us will be through to chat with you shortly." What the fuck did we just hear? I watched as disappointment began to descend upon those who'd stood up. It slowly began to sink in that I, along with my seated compatriots, had indeed been successful. No one said a word. Out of respect for those who hadn't been so fortunate, everyone remained silent and motionless.

When the last person filed out of the room and the heavy felt-laden door shut behind them, the compere immediately said to us "well you know what that means don't you? I'll spell it out for the slow learners here. You fucking made it! Congratulations to each and every one of you. You, barring any mistakes in resort, are on your way to becoming holiday reps with us!" Everyone started shaking hands and high fiving each other, girls were hugging. He gathered us all around and handed us welcome packs with all sorts of legal papers and general information that we needed to be aware of. He said the next steps were that we were going to be flown out to one of the resorts, most likely, Magaluf or possibly one of the Greek islands, where we'll receive formal training, and meet the other successful candidates who got through in Manchester, and Leeds. As he continued, we all listened intently, but truth be told, the information was going in one ear and out the other. He continued to update us for a further 10-15 minutes before wishing us all well, congratulating us again and dismissing the group. We filed out of the place on a high. Most of us had agreed to go to a bar around the corner where we shared a couple of congratulatory beers before I began to make my way home. I couldn't wait to tell my parents when I got back. They were really pleased for me. I think they were proud that I'd succeeded, and they were clearly happy that I was happy. Did they know what was in store for me? Definitely not. Would they have been so happy had they seen what I was going to be walking into I'm not so sure. I couldn't wait to tell my friends at uni that not only had I gone through with the strip, but I'd gotten the job there and then.

CHAPTER 3
MAGALUF: TRAINING

Mum, Dad and my sister all came to Gatwick to drop me off for my week's training abroad. It was around Easter time and I had taken one of their suitcases which was almost bursting at the seams. It was full of various clothes and props that we were told to collate ready for our week of training. I still don't think that my family really understood what the job was going to entail or what I would actually be getting up to. Hell, at that point, I didn't know what was to come. Both my mum and sister had helped me accumulate the various props I was going to be using. They both gave me a cuddle and a small kiss each as we said our goodbyes. I then turned to my dad, giving him a man hug, where he quietly told me to keep a hat on it with a wry smile. "The chance will be a fine thing!" I proudly responded in front of them all, remembering I had indeed packed my condoms. Mum smacked my dad playfully on the shoulder and told him "not in front of us" (referring to her and my sister), and my sister just rolled her eyes. She quipped that I needed to maintain some standards and not fall for pull-a-pig again. As you can tell we were an open family, and as they laughed at my expense, I retorted "if there's grass on the wicket, let's play cricket!" At that point, Mum told me to behave. I kissed her again, and then proceeded to make my way to the departure lounge. As I walked in, I could hear and see a group of people having fun and generally irritating the surrounding passengers. As I approached closer, I recognised a few of them from the interview. I joined them and we began to immediately get reacquainted.

By the time we'd got on the flight, everyone had already had a few drinks and spirits were high. You could already tell there were some smaller groups forming and some of the lads were already putting the ground work in with some of the girls in the group, myself included. This might have been a "work" event, but in my mind, I was basically on a freebie to Magaluf and indeed if there was to be any grass on any sacred cricket stumps, I was going to do my best to make sure I was out to bat! We'd all pretty much boarded together but we had been seated into smaller groups on the plane. This was basically the worst thing they could have done. Rather than sit us at the back as one unruly group which could still be controlled by a stern air host or hostess, they'd split us into several smaller groups of 5s and 6s. Given the drinks we'd had at the airport and the drinks they were serving us on the plane, the groups were beginning to get rowdy and naturally wanted to banter/abuse the other groups dotted around the plane. Pretty soon people were hollering at each other across 4 or 5 rows in either direction, much to the pain of the other passengers. Every time one of the groups was told to be quiet or to behave, the other groups took the piss even more. By the time we touched down in Palma, you could tell we were the pariahs of the plane. We were met by some of the senior members of the repping team who'd flown out a day or so earlier, presumably to get their plans in order and to work out a game plan about how they were going to control us. As we got to the coach park outside the airport, we were each handed a beer and told to file on to the coach. When everyone was onboard, one of the senior reps took hold of the mic, and preceded to welcome us aboard the "fuck truck" and to ask us to put our hands together for "Manuel" who was going to be leading our merry siege to the hotel which was situated in Arenal a short journey away from Palma. He then roughly went over the itinerary, as well as selectively choosing passengers at will to ask where they were from, and to well, generally abuse them publicly. We didn't care, we were all an open-minded lot, and to be honest, it was just a continuation of the banter we ourselves were already hurling around the group.

We got to the hotel soon enough, and the company did its best to register us through reception as quick as possible. I was fortunate to be in a room on my own. I figured that this increased my chances of getting laid, by not having another cock to block me if I did manage to drag a stray back. I ripped through to the toilet like a Florida tornado, and proceeded to remove as much of the alcohol I'd been lugging since Gatwick. Then as instructed, I dumped my bags down, stopping only for a quick spray of deodorant, and a mouthful of toothpaste. Everyone had been told to meet in the hotel bar as soon as possible, and I was anxious not to miss out on any of the fun nor allow the girls to be paired off before I'd had a chance to try my magic. I walked into the bar and to my surprise there were already 20-30 reps already there, drinks in hand. I was impressed by their devotion to the cause. Most of them hadn't even bothered to go to their rooms, they just left their bags and cases in a heap in the corner of the bar, much to the annoyance of the hotel staff. The next 30 - 40 minutes passed quickly. We proceeded to drink more and more and get acquainted with the rest of the reps. At some point we were joined by more senior reps and then some senior management. I guessed they were management, as they weren't wearing any form of identification, and most of the senior reps were doing their best to converse with them. The newbies (myself included) couldn't have given a fuck. One of the seniors then made his way round the bar explaining that we were to have a quick meeting in the conference room next door which would last about 40 minutes, before we would be left for an hour to get ready for dinner. We were told to finish our drinks and be in the room in 5 minutes. In general, the group was slightly irritated by this. Most of us had forgotten that we were here to work and to learn stuff. We were happy to drink in the open planned bar, looking out to this wide azure blue pool that stood between us and the beach. Begrudgingly, we finished our drinks and filed into the room. I was doing my best to sit next to a group of girls that had been particularly vocal and loud in the bar.

When everyone was sat, we received a formal introduction from one of the senior managers. Whilst we didn't know who he was, his mannerisms, and steely glare was enough to let everyone know that he was funding this gig. The minute he opened his mouth the room fell silent, and he continued for the next 10 minutes undisturbed. One by one, the other members of his team then took over to take their turn in welcoming us and informing us what a good opportunity we were now faced with. They congratulated us on getting this far, throwing stats at us that for every place on the "program" there were 45 - 50 candidates, and so we really had achieved something by making it to the training camp. They of course knocked us back down immediately after saying that we still had to prove ourselves, and that whilst we were being flown to Magaluf and housed on the company's dime, this was anything but a freebie or a piss up. Yeah right. I shot a couple of glances around the room and most were already smirking at each other. We were all on the same page, even if management appeared not to be. The last person to speak was a senior rep. He was southern, possibly Kent or Essex and he had a steel wit and wasn't short on self-esteem. He proceeded to take us through the itinerary for the week and began putting us into smaller groups. As he was reeling through the list of names, a couple of guys at the side decided that they would prefer to chat amongst themselves instead. Much to his annoyance, they failed to heed any warning signs that were being thrown at them. The senior rep broke off from his list, and proceeded to stare at them. These guys were so engulfed in their conversation that they continued, blissfully unaware that their cards were being marked. Such was their ignorance to their surroundings, one of them didn't even pay attention to one of the girls next to him who was trying to subtly elbow him to catch his attention. At that point the rep decided enough was enough. "Hey fuckwits!" he bellowed. The guys stopped immediately and turned to face him. "What group are you wankers in?" He asked them. Even if they'd known, which they didn't, not one of them wanted to draw his attention, and so they remained silent. "Come on dickheads, what groups are you in? Have you decided to make your own group? You've all had a couple of beers and feeling pretty relaxed yeah? I mean you're reps now, you don't need the training do you?" The group (and the room) remained silent. The rep had a point, I mean this wasn't a piss up and the company had spent money to bring us here although I couldn't help but think this was an excuse to drop the hammer as an example to the rest of us. As the room was silent, I thought he'd let up, but he didn't. "You ball-bags are going to come to me after the meeting as

I have something for you to do. Anyone else want to join them?" Clearly no one looked up. He then proceeded to continue listing the remaining names. Jesus, I thought to myself. A couple of reps in front looked at each other and made that movement with their eyes when someone's over reacted. Once he'd finished the list, he then informed the group that for those who didn't remember, or hadn't "fucking listened" the list would be placed on the board by the exit. He went on to tell us about what we would be doing for the next week. Basically, the week was divided into sales training and practical training, with the evenings spent on the entertainment side of things. We were further disheartened when he read out the start and finish times. I mean, we were really going to be working here. You could feel the disappointment in the room as he continued. This together with the dressing down of the other guys had managed to take away the holiday feeling. That being said, I was still determined to party and hook up whilst I was here.

Practical training covered the sorts of things that would occur whilst out in resort. Examples such as what to do if a guest falls ill, misses their flight, loses a passport, gets arrested etc. This sounded pretty uninteresting, but could be useful I thought. I mean even from your own point of view, if something happens to you abroad, it's always good to know how to get yourself out of a situation. Sales training on the other hand sounded absolutely atrocious. I mean who the fuck wants to sit there in a conference room in the sun, in Magaluf, opposite a big bright blue pool and a fully stocked bar, learning how to sell to clients. The very notion of it instantly summoned visions of time share or telephone sales. That feeling you get in the pit of your stomach when a Scouser rings you up and asks if you know what PPI is, or when "Bryan" from Cardiff calls you up and asks if you're happy with your house insurance. Fuck off

Bryan, I'm busy. Anyway, from the looks of it, the sales side of things looked to take up around 75% of the training time. I guess they were serious about bringing in commissions. Whilst I was disappointed, it wasn't the end of the world. I still would be shagging and drinking for free when I got to resort. People always said I had the gift of the gab, so maybe sales wouldn't be so tough anyway.

The entertainment training provoked a lot more interest. We would be splitting into smaller groups for this. We would then be practicing and choreographing various routines. Some were picked by the company, others we would come up with ourselves as a team and we would be performing them at the end of the week in front of the other groups. A kind of talent competition so to speak. They'd already listed the themes when they sent to us our welcome packs and we'd already been collecting the necessary costumes. The themes were Grease (the musical), Cowboys & Indians i.e. western, and the Full Monty (striptease) for the guys, and some kind of burlesque show for the girls. We would be doing rehearsals every day, with some bright spark even setting them for after dinner. This meant the window to try and smash was getting smaller and smaller. The flip side of this was that we would all be spending far more time with each other than initially thought, so maybe that would allow us the opportunity to put in more shovel work, so things weren't all bad.

Once we'd received all the information regarding the week ahead, we were dismissed. We were to meet back up for dinner in about an hour and a half. Most were beginning to tire at this point, with the exception of a couple of lads who proceeded to hammer the bar. I was feeling pretty beat myself and so I retired to my room. I wanted to unpack a little and clean myself up etc. As we left the room, I remember hearing those immortal words "where are the fuckwits?" I couldn't help but laugh. The senior rep was hunting for the guys. Reluctantly they went over to him. I don't know what was said next as I headed up to my room, but I was disturbed about 15 minutes later. It was one of the lads. The rep had basically tasked them with delivering to everyone various items of apparel. This poor sod was lugging around a box that looked like it should have been on a forklift. He asked me what size I was. In his hand he was holding a variety of coloured t-shirts. The company were giving us 3-4 branded t-shirts for the week along with some notepads and small bags to carry them in. All typical team building stuff. My gobby colleague along with the other mouth in his support act were basically delivering them to each trainee. They decided to split the floors up to try and be methodical, but it was a task for sure. I quipped to him about how much of a pain in the ass it must be but he just grinned stating "it is what it is" and went on his way. Am not sure how happy I would have been to be dragging a box that could house three midgets on my shoulder, but then again, I am not stupid enough to sit in the audience and mug a speaker off when he was trying to convey relatively vital information.

Dinner passed pretty much without event. We shared a few drinks before and after but most of the group were knackered at this point. I scouted around the bar after dinner but most of the girls had already retired for the evening. There was one girl sat at the bar being entertained by 3 - 4 guys who were from the midlands and had already began to band together. I thought about joining, but given they were already waist deep in conversation, I was tired. She also had the sort of face only a mother could love so I decided against it. Besides, seeing how badly those other two were punished by the senior rep earlier had me thinking. He was taking us for sales training in the morning and

I definitely wanted to be sharp for it. If I overslept or started fucking up, who knows what he'd have in store for me. Last thing I needed was cleaning toilets or carrying shit around for everyone else. The other two were late for dinner as it was, due to their "chores." I decided to pull the chute, and headed up to my room.

CHAPTER 4
SALES TRAINING

Sales training kicked off at 8:30 sharp. The senior rep Damien who was also our instructor for the morning session was standing there sharp, ready and focused like a drill sergeant waiting to shit on this year's new recruits. "Morning girls" he barked as we filed in. Some were still chewing the last remaining mouthfuls of their breakfast as they reluctantly left the restaurant next door to take their places. It was pretty early for the army routine but no one dared to give him any grief back. We'd all taken our places, and when the flow of bodies stopped at 8:30 sharp he shut the door and pulled the curtain across it. This served two purposes: a) it signalled to us that we were ready to begin and b) it meant there was exactly zero chance of any late comers managing to sneak in unobserved. I mused to myself that he was already selecting the punishments in his head for the next lot to walk through that door. Sure enough, once we'd all taken our seats the first wandered through the doorway and proceeded to struggle with the heavy curtain for the next 10 seconds. Once the fabric barricade was conquered, a smiley face emerged victorious. The girl was from Leeds, and had a huge mane of curly hair lifted in a bun. "Sorry I'm late" she said to Damien. "Doing your hair were you? Making sure you looked good for us eh?" responded Damien. "You needn't have bothered" he followed up with. She just shot him a look of dagger eyes as she tilted her head to the side. Damien broke into a big smile "only joking Moody. Take your seat!" he told her. His voice softening a little. The next victim to fall at the fabric forcefield didn't fare so easily. "Did you never learn how to tell the time when you were at school?" The guy was dishevelled and clearly flustered. He was from a region just south of London. I can't remember where but it was a nice part of the world and he spoke properly. I wouldn't go so far as to have called him posh but having replied "I apologise. I overslept," Damien immediately latched on to his twang. "I guess that posh school you must have gone to had you more preoccupied with playing soggy biscuit and giving the house master hand jobs after supper than learning a clock face." It was brutal. Unexpected but funny at the same time. Most of the room sniggered. Posh boy just remained quiet. "Just take a seat, we need to get started we've got a lot to cover today" instructed Damien. No sooner had posh boy placed himself on his chair when the door burst open again and another walked in. "For fuck sake!" raged Damien. "Has no one got a fucking alarm clock" he hollered in the direction of the doorway. "Sorry mate" said the new target, not expecting to be collared so hard this early in the morning. Damien didn't let up. "Mate? We're not mates yet, but if you're late again the only mate you'll have will be the toilet cleaner! You'll be helping him every day and you can swap life stories whilst cleaning pebble dash from the rims." Again, the rest of us began to laugh. The room was beginning to enjoy the exchanges, and whilst Damien wasn't someone we wanted to cross, his outbursts and confidence were fun to watch. Before the latest serial sleeper had a chance to respond, the next culprit burst through, fighting with the curtain as he knocked into him. "I don't fucking believe it" muttered Damien. He was almost incredulous. We anxiously waited for the next volley of abuse to be summoned, but this time things were different. The next volley wasn't fired by Damien but the newcomer. "Man, what the hell did you guys serve me for dinner? I've had the shits all night!" he announced to the room in a gruff Glaswegian accent. "The bowl has not been cold all evening and I've got ring sting!" The room erupted. Even Damien let out a smile. Clearly for this guy the best defence was offence, but it was pretty funny and his timing was perfect. "Just take a seat let's get going" Damien replied, reluctant to open up a slanging match with the scot so early on in the program. Once we were all finally seated and ready to start, the mood changed to a more studious one. Damien, who by now had been joined with several other reps began to tell us about how the company made money and how we ourselves would be making additional money when we got to resort. He listed the amounts we could expect to earn depended on resort, size of the hotel, number of guests etc. He wasn't very 'salesy.' He didn't try and sugar coat it, he just told it how it was and I think the group respected him more for that. At least I did. He went through sales as a concept before drilling down into various aspects of the process which if mastered, would make closing an actual sale all the easier.

He proceeded to break down the sale into four of the following stages. Subliminal selling, the welcome meeting, the close, and then objection handling. He went to great efforts to convey that the stronger each section was carried out, the easier the next section would be, culminating with the point that if the first three steps were done professionally and successfully, you wouldn't even need the fourth. Now I can't speak for the rest of the group but despite my initial reservations I was fascinated by it all. The thought and prior planning that went into the whole process was impressive. I thought back to how our rep had sold us the package of bar crawls and events in Magaluf. I thought at the time that we chose to go on them purely because it increased our chances of getting laid, but given what I'd just heard it now seemed like we were more than likely going to be paying for these trips regardless. It was just a case of us subconsciously choosing our own reason for pulling out our wallets. My opinion of Damien and the other reps that were assigned to help teach us increased dramatically. This sales stuff was both effective, interesting and self-reinforcing. I'll attempt to give a quick crash course, but keep in mind that we were given the best part of a week to learn this and go through the various scenarios and drills, so you'd be forgiven if you're not entirely convinced after a few short pages.

∽

IT ALL KICKS off with the subliminal selling. This could be something as simple as mentioning something many times over in a conversation but so casually that you begin to plant seeds in someone's mind without them noticing. A more complicated but no doubt effective method employed would be flash up an image in a film or tv show for just a frame or so. It would be too quick for your conscious to acknowledge it, but your brain would have seen and registered it somewhere without you knowing. It's the same on a plane. The air staff serve you peanuts or other salty snacks making you thirsty and then when the drinks cart comes around, voilà. Everyone wants to buy a drink. In this instance, we would effectively take the price of the trip package in local currency and in sterling, and then use both of those numbers as many times as we dared prior to actually mentioning what the price of the trip package was in the close. The idea being that the audience was so used to those numbers that when you actually mentioned the number, it shouldn't come as a shock. In fact, if you asked someone how much did you think the package should be, in an ideal world, maybe the punters would actually volunteer the number themselves. As long as you're not surprised at the price, in your mind you would think it's fairly priced. To give you an example, a 2-week trip package in Ibiza (1998) cost around £130 or 32,000 pesetas give or take. So those that were coming out on holiday with the company for 2 weeks needed to see, hear or think about that number ideally before they even got to the meeting, let alone hear the closing pitch. This meant that we needed to incorporate it in every spiel/speech or publication we would hand out. For instance, when the holiday makers were brought in to resort from the airport on the coach we would tell them about the weather and the resort itself. We'd say that everyone needs to put plenty of sun cream on because yesterday it felt like 130 degrees. You'd find a pale person on the coach, and have some banter. We'd quip that he or she would probably need factor 32,000! We'd say that there are 130 different bars and clubs in Ibiza. If someone was pissed on the coach, you'd probably joke on the mic that I bet they started in the airport in the UK and were asleep by the time the plane hit 32,000 feet. If we were talking about the trips that we were planning as part of the package, we would describe the go-karting track and issue someone a challenge to beat the record on the straight which was 130mph. If they did, they got free drinks for the rest of the holiday. Of course, the go-kart couldn't hit 130mph on the straight. I doubt a formula one car would, but it was all part of the presentation. Now this sounds obvious, but if played with subtlety, no one ever realises that you're using the same numbers. It was a nice idea, in reality most of the reps didn't bother with it, although some (including myself) did, and some scripts that we were given required it. It wasn't just these numbers we needed to contend with. Some people would only be out in resort for a week. The one-week package obviously costing less and so you'd interchange the numbers for both, making it again that little less conspicuous. Some resorts even went so far as to print out flyers or small posters with the numbers incorporated into various slogans or captions. I found this whole idea intriguing, and began to question my own experiences and if someone had done this to us. To this day, I don't recall it being done, but seeing how far ahead these guys were thinking am sure it was, we just didn't know it. Throughout my time in resort, I'd heard many different ways the numbers were incorporated into the various patters. Things like "…and then the DJ will kick it up a notch just before the foam comes on. Imagine the scene, you're dancing to the latest house tunes at 130bpm, and you're hot, but loving it, and then suddenly the signal is given, and the foam cannons kick in and you're suddenly getting drenched with 32,000 litres of foam…" Another one is "this bar stocks over 130 types of different beer. How many of them do you think you can try before you fly home?" or "be careful if you decide to hire a moped whilst you're in resort. Please don't drink and drive, as we have around 130 accidents a week on the island mainly involving holiday makers for one reason or another, and we don't want you to end up spoiling your holiday." The list went on and on.

    This brings us nicely on to the welcome meeting. I'll cover this in more detail later, but the main purpose of the welcome meeting is to get everyone together in one group and attempt to sell to them the package of excursions and club tickets directly. When young people reach these party resorts you really only have one shot at getting them all in one place and together, and that's the first morning. If you don't do it then, you will seldom have another chance. As soon as they touch down, they like to scatter. I mean who doesn't. You're on vacation. You want to go swimming. You want to go on the piss. You want to go to the beach. In Ibiza, some people disappear within minutes of you dropping them off in the hotel, only returning 5 days later in some half-conscious drug induced state. It was one of the hardest things to do as a rep. The whole week's sales figures and therefore the mood of the hotel and the unity among the guests depended on your ability to wake people up, stop them from dissipating, and keep them sober long enough so that you can have an open conversation and tell them about the trips. Normally you would tell the holiday makers, as was initially told to us in Magaluf, that they had to be present at a certain time in the morning or lunchtime with their flight tickets and booking confirmations in order to check and register them for the flight back. Sure, this wasn't strictly true, but we did have to tell them about the resort, point them in the direction of where emergency services were, fire assembly points, and also working hours of the reps, and information about the pickup for their intended departure. As am sure you can imagine though, having just woken up on your first morning on your 'boys' or 'girls' holiday, the last thing you want to talk about is what time and where you're going to be picked up to go home. That being said, on the whole the approach worked. Participation in the welcome meetings was normally 90% and above, which is great. You would hold the largest welcome meetings slightly later on in the day, as there would be more people to herd together, and you would need more reps on hand to attempt to close sales immediately once the meeting finished. To put it in perspective, a large meeting could hold anything from 100-200 holiday makers. In peak season, this could be even more in Ibiza. That's a potentially large amount of revenue. The pressure intensified around such meetings. Once the presentation is given the close would begin. To be truthful, the word presentation doesn't really do it justice. In the bigger meetings, it was more like a performance. Many different reps would be pulled into speaking in front of the room and at times it resembled a cabaret. If you could deliver the message in an enthusiastic and energetic manner with plenty of laughs, light heartedness and some audience participation, the job of closing the sale was that much easier. People remained alert and engaged, and actually began to warm to the idea before prices were even mentioned.

We were taught to flirt outrageously. There was one mindset that stuck with me and I employed it to great effect during my time in resort. If you wanted to get to know someone you needed to break the ice. This could take a certain period of time depending on the environment and persons involved. If you could somehow introduce physical contact into the mix without coming across as creepy or unwarranted this dramatically reduced the time it took to make a bond and break barriers. In sales this is key. It could be something as simple as shaking a guest's hand, or giving a high five, to hugging a guest, or even sitting on a lap. Anything went. It was down to each rep to find their way. We are all different, and each of us has strengths and weaknesses. Every guest was different. In our lives we all know one person who could say literally anything and get away with it, because they're funny and somehow inoffensive. Yet if another friend tried to say the same it would be extremely awkward or cringey. Well this is no different. One friend can put their arm around you and you think nothing of it. It's comforting and reinforces the bond of friendship or offers support if needed. Someone else can do the same but then it instantly feels wrong. Well this was the fine line we were playing with. Get it right and you come across as a natural, and you'll be selling for days. Get it wrong and it can make the whole atmosphere frosty and uncomfortable.

As the welcome meeting was progressing other reps would turn up having concluded their previous meetings. The rep based in that hotel where the meeting was being held would adopt a coordination role. Kind of like a quarterback. As time went on, we got to know each other and the client base. We soon realised that various reps were better suited to different types of people and scenarios. You would normally mix sexes as much as possible. Boys would be better suited to selling to girls and vice versa for obvious reasons. If you were particularly confident and flirty you would normally be tasked with dealing with the larger groups. If you were of a softer more reserved nature (at least relative to others in the group) you could be left dealing with smaller groups and couples etc. It was all thoroughly thought out. If there was a particularly large group you might even assign them a couple of reps. The guests wouldn't even know it, but whilst they were listening to the welcome meeting their rep was standing at the back directing the reps to various individuals and groups. The audience would be completely divided and locations were selected to divide the room up further, allowing us to speak with them quietly without distraction. Once the plan had been laid, we would then infiltrate the crowd and start to warm them up. When we first heard this in Magaluf, I was somewhat sceptical. We were told to flirt outrageously when speaking to people, embrace physical contact. I mean quite frankly, girls had been using this to great effect but now I was being asked to step my game up. It almost feels weird writing this now twenty something years later. Times have changed. Mobile phones are in play now and generally what was acceptable then might not be acceptable now. A good one which used to work would be if there was a group of 5-6 girls towards the back of the room. I would proceed to make my way along the row, disturbing those around. Now when I got to my allocated group, there wouldn't be any seats, so I would just squeeze myself in and practically sit on the closest one's lap. If she protested, or would try and shove me off, I would just stretch myself out like a cat and lay across the laps of all of her friends. This was normally the first time they would have seen me, and so were shocked initially. Such was my confidence and big smile it didn't seem to bother them and any shock or irritation normally dissipated quickly. In fact, if it didn't, usually the rest of the girls would find it even funnier that one of their friends was being wound up. As I'm lying there across the laps of 5-6 girls I'd never met before, I guarantee that one of them will pull a hair off my leg or try to give me a small pinch. On the off chance they didn't, there was always a rep behind or alongside who would encourage them, or step in to do it, making it look like it was one of them who did it. I would feign injury and over react, they would laugh or protest it wasn't them and we would all have a chuckle about it. I wouldn't move though. Sooner or later, after a minute or so, some of the girls would even rest their arms down onto my legs as they continued to watch the welcome meeting. They would become normalised to this stranger laying on them. It's as if they've already processed that I'm harmless, and have moved on to the next stimuli which happened to be the reps presenting. I would continue to distract one or two of the group and tried to encourage them to annoy one of the other reps in the surrounding area. As childish as this sounds, you need to remember this was Ibiza in the 90s, we were all probably 17-22 and everyone was in a holiday mindset. Hormones and expectations were running high.

If I couldn't lay on the laps, then sometimes I just sat on the edges of one of their chairs. Other times I would just start passing fruit out to one in a group. They wouldn't understand what was going on, but I would take fruit from the bar restaurant and continually keep giving it to one or two girls. At first one would take it as if it was a gift, but by the time they'd taken the 10th or 11th lemon they would begin to get flustered much to the amusement of the rest of their group. At a suitable intermission I would then interrupt the flow of proceedings to announce to the room that someone has been suspected of stealing fruit from the restaurant and the police are going to be called. As everyone started to look around at each other, the guest in question would begin to blush and try to hide the lemons. The group would start laughing. I would laugh, and eventually the girl would start to smile once the blushing subsided. When I went to take the lemons back, claiming loudly "I've solved the crime" I would normally get some abuse or even a shove in the ribs or a lemon thrown at me. It was always light hearted. I know it sounds pretty harsh, but it was also funny at the time and always well received. I would then sit next to them and offer my apologies, giving them a couple of candies or whatever I happened to be snacking on at the time as a peace offering. They would take the sweets every time breaking into a smile or even being playful by throwing the wrappers back at me. Either way, we'd have a laugh and then would chat normally about where they're from and what they're doing etc. The whole idea behind this was to try and turbo charge the ice breaking so that by the time we got to sit at that table and talk further, we already had a connection.

As the welcome meeting was pretty much concluding and the jokes/laughter began to subside, they would introduce the close. This could be a different rep or could be that hotel's rep. You would essentially dispense with the silliness and summarise what they'd heard so far on the various trips and events that had just been described to them. The rep would rhetorically ask how much should such a package cost in Ibiza? Before giving anyone the chance to shout something silly and undermine the whole effort, he or she would then proceed to tell the price. Once the price was mentioned the rep would then immediately return to listing exactly what you got for your money. The idea was to focus on the two-week package regardless as that broke down easier providing more value for money. Only at the end of that would you mention the one week. "If any of you are out with us for just a week, unfortunately you won't be able to enjoy the full benefits of the two-week package but that also means you won't be charged for it either. You guys get to pay the lower rate of xyz, which still represents fantastic value for money when you consider that for just under xyz you are getting…" This would normally be followed up with a confident declaration that for the two weeks, this was evidently a no-brainer as you're getting twice the value for only a fraction more than the one weekers. During the close, you would need to appear confident, open and approachable. Body language was key. There was a great deal of emphasis put on this during training. Don't wring your hands together. Keep them out of your pockets. No rocking on your heels and keep your arms open and inviting. Maintain eye contact. Be prepared for heckles and ready with your counters. This was important. Should someone shout something out at an inopportune moment it could destroy any positive momentum and immediately make it harder for the reps to recover once everyone had been split into groups. One of the hardest things to overcome, believe it or not, were drunk people. All the reps would have immediately been warned about anybody who was smashed. In some instances, if people were that drunk, they would be disruptive, even if they didn't mean to be. Not only do you not want a drunk person shouting shit out, but you also don't want them staggering around causing the focus of attention to be moved. Also, no one wanted to sell to a drunk person. Whilst we were there to close sales and bring people out on the trips with us, no one wanted to sell to someone who was pissed. You left yourself open to all sorts of issues if they suddenly got buyer's remorse or made a complaint. You would be hard pressed to defend yourself in this instance, so if a person or group were really hanging, more often than not we would assign a rep to take them out of the equation by offering to drink with them at the bar or by the pool i.e. remove them from harm's way. The hotel rep would then approach them at a later point in their holiday, or just leave them to it. Such was the art of getting the welcome meeting done early on in the day that thankfully this seldom happened. Once the close was given normally the room would fall silent, we would be left paying attention to any tell-tale signs from the holidaymakers. Did any group appear happy or unhappy with it? Who in the group was giving the signals? What was the reaction from the others? We needed to glean as much information as possible in that short space of time so that we could formulate our game plan for the next step.

By the time the welcome meeting and the close had finished, we would walk the guests to a secluded part of the room and begin chatting with them. By now, hopefully the ice would have been well and truly broken. I tended to work with groups of girls better, but the methods described earlier would work the same for the same sex. Often, you'd have teams of lads coming out for a vacation. You'd see them sat together. Rugby boys tended to be more obvious due to their statures, footballers tended to be a bit leaner, and flashier. Either way, you would send in the female reps. They would already know who the perceived ring leader was because their hotel rep would have told them. This information is usually gathered by asking a simple question to the group. Depending on the style of question and the ensuing conversation, you'd find out within a minute or so who was top dog. The female rep, depending on the dynamics of the group, would either sit on the main man's lap and flirt with him or sometimes would sit on another lap flirting with the guys but looking at the main guy at the same time in an effort to provoke competition within the group. The idea being that if she could create an environment where all the lads were lobbying for her, she would be relying on the ring leader to give the approval for the trips and thus gain her admiration. He would thereby reinforce himself as the alpha and win her affections at the same time. Sometimes if the group was too large or weren't particularly warming to their rep enough, they'd send in a second rep of either sex to play back up. This could be a more senior rep, or sometimes just a fresh pair of legs. Sometimes it was good cop bad cop, other times it would be a super flirty one and the other one would be same sex and more down to earth, attempting to 'level' with the group. We'd played out so many different role-plays during the training week that by the time we got to resort, we pretty much all knew the drill and how to handle the various scenarios.

One of the biggest things I took away from the sales training I received in Magaluf was how to close a sale and objection handling. Simple phrases and steps that you could use which could alter the dynamics of a sale were subtle yet effective. Once you'd sit the group down you would start to smile. Naturally when you smile at someone more often than not, they smile back at you. You start to nod slightly, they also nod. It's a strange phenomenon. Try it for yourselves. We would look at the guests whilst smiling, wide eyed and then ask something confirmatory. "How did you like the presentation? I saw you guys laughing during the middle of it." This opener, accompanied with a smile and maybe even a subtle nod, would normally be met with a response like "Yeah it was funny." Or "some of you reps are crazy!" You would smile, and nod causing them to nod back again. Then you would just make a presumption "So you're coming out with us then, yeah?" The 'yeah' at the end, whilst subtle, was designed to help the rep for what came next. Sometimes the guests would say "yeah we're on for it," other times they'd say something like "we don't think so" to which we would always express surprise and immediately ask "why not?" The person speaking on behalf of the group would then express the main reason, which 9 times out of 10 would be the money. It was imperative that you find the reason why they didn't want to come with you and then isolate it. It was important to isolate it because if someone said it was too expensive and you spend 10 minutes overturning that, they can then say, ok it might be affordable, but we can't do it because.... And so, you run around in circles. The theory is that if you can isolate the objection and then overturn it, it becomes very difficult for the person being sold to find another reason why they can't mentally move forwards with the purchase. "So, if it wasn't for the money, you'd be coming out with us then, yeah? You liked what you heard and the package seemed like fun right?" Now most people who initially thought they didn't want to go, would end up grasping that sentence like it was a lifeline. "Yeah, we liked it but it's just the price, we don't have much money." I can't tell you how many times over my stint in Ibiza did I hear this. We had gone through this objection so frequently during training and practice that it was second nature. You would then ask the group "May I ask a personal question?" to which the answer was always "sure, go ahead." "How much money have you guys brought out with yourselves for the holiday?" The girls or guys would normally proudly tell you that they'd brought out maybe £300 or sometimes £400 for their two-week holiday. At this stage you would then ask them to detail what they were looking for from their holiday. Were they looking to party, go clubbing, maybe find love? Most said a mix of the three, nearly everyone said to party and drink. We would then openly ask if they were lightweights or could handle a 'proper' drink. Now no one is ever going to confess in front of their friends to being a lightweight and most responded with enthusiasm about how much they could drink and what they normally would order. They said they wanted to visit the clubs and dance the night away. You could tell from their answer whether they were looking to go clubbing to dance and possibly take drugs, or whether they wanted to go to a night club to drink and meet a member of the opposite sex. Sometimes it was both, it didn't matter. We were prepared for every eventuality. If it was to go clubbing, you would ask them calmly and matter of fact if they took drugs. This normally made them recoil as it's not something you would normally discuss openly with strangers or admit to in such public fashion. They normally said no, to which I answered that I wasn't judging. After all, it's Ibiza, and that it would have been cheaper if they did. I then produced a couple of receipts from Amnesia (Cream) and Privilege (Manumission). For those of you who don't know, these were the largest clubs on the island which hosted the biggest events, attracting the biggest DJs in the world. Entry fee to these clubs back in '98 was approximately £35-50 each for just entrance depending on the night you chose. I then showed them the drink receipts. A bottle of water was ridiculously expensive. If memory serves me correctly, it was something like the equivalent of £5-6 with beer similarly priced. A vodka and red bull which seemed to be the fashion at the time was nearer to £11. I would wait to watch their eyes widen. I then openly calculated that they would probably spend at least 4 if not 5 hours there. I.e. get there for midnight and leave around 5 in the morning. I said after you've spent £50 to get in, you want to get your money's worth. I then would break it down further. I said if you were extremely frugal and chose to have just one drink an hour, and opted for only water. That alone would be £25 for the night. So that one night alone, not including food, a taxi to and from the venue, was going to cost £75 minimum. If they decided to have a couple of proper drinks or got thirstier due to dancing then it could well end up costing significantly more. I would never tell them it wasn't worth it, but when you actually laid the prices out on the table in front of them you could see that their budget of say £300 for the two weeks just wasn't going to cut it. Two nights out in the big clubs would see them spend basically two thirds of their budget. Leaving them £100 to spend for 2 weeks on food and drink. Once this began to dawn on them, it wasn't a case of whether you wanted to come out on the trips with us, it became a case of can you afford not to? Given that we included approximately 4-5 club tickets, a bar crawl, free food and drink on at least two themed nights out, as well as go karting, a water park, a beach party and a big daytime open-air festival we could easily help their funds go further. Now the club passes didn't include the big clubs like Privilege or Amnesia, but we still went to Eden and Es Paradis which still had big name DJs playing there. At this point the group usually decided to go with us. It wasn't a particularly hard sell in Ibiza. Of course, the competition was tough, but frankly speaking, the price point of our trips and the relative value it offered to those on a relatively limited budget was unparalleled. The clubbing objection was pretty easy to take care of, but it wasn't as easy as those who were looking to basically drink themselves silly and go on the pull. If I got the sense that they were on the pull and just wanted to drink and party, I took a slightly different approach. I would ask them outright if they liked a drink and on average how many drinks they would take on a night out. They would normally offer up a number anything from 3-10 drinks depending on the gender, group and part of the world they were from! The higher the number the better, so I would sit back and allow them to boast. Now if they were lads, you would just ask who's looking to get laid? Most would express excitement at the thought and cheer, some even put their hand up like I was a teacher. I then would ask how many nights did they think they'll party on? Of course, the answer was every night. Everyone in the group would laugh at me as if I had just asked the most ridiculous question known to man. This was a good reaction, the stronger the better. I would then dive into my bag and pull out the largest and most childish calculator in the world. It was the same size as a Texas instruments speak and spell, but with about 16 buttons on it only. I don't know what looked more stupid, ET trying to phone home on it, or me trying to do sums as slow as I possibly could, without upsetting those across the table. It really was quite ridiculous, but this was the reaction I wanted. The simpler the calculator, the simpler I looked. The guests needed to think they were one step ahead of me every time. Not that I was lying to them, but when someone reaches their own conclusions supposedly ahead of the salesman, they feel like they've already made the decision of their own accord. They're not "being sold to." I would take the number of drinks they said and multiply it by £4 or £5 pounds. That was the cost per night. I would then multiply that by the number of nights they were here for. I always gave them the benefit of the doubt. I would always take a few drinks less, and give them a night off or so. For example, if they said they have around 6-7 drinks a night (that's one an hour if they started at 8 and finished at 2), I would say let's pretend you only have 5 drinks. Everyone around the table knew the number was going to be far higher, but I didn't need to go this hard. They were here for 2 weeks, which worked out to be 13 nights. Let's say they had 1 if not 2 nights off, that would work out to be 11 nights out, 5 drinks a night at £5 a pop and that's £275 of the budget gone. I purposely then took the remainder which I did on the calculator (unnecessarily). £300 minus £275 = £25.00 over 13 nights = £1.92 a day for food. Obviously, no clubs' entries are included. (if someone said they had a budget of £350-400 I could easily include a club ticket there, but then the drinks receipt comes out and the mention of taxis and expensive drinks also comes into play. I used to round it all off by saying (if they were guys) that if they did want to get laid, and they wanted the attractive girls, then they would also need to buy those girls a few drinks so it might mean some of them would have to do without. Some would remark they would be happy with taking the "minger" or a "large Marge" much to the amusement of everyone else. I would then counter saying that they would probably end up spending more as they would probably end up at a kebab van buying food instead at silly o clock in the morning. With their current budgets it just wouldn't be possible. Even the most hardened party animal understood that they would need to also eat. I'm all for a bit of 'eating is cheating' and student warfare, but after the second night, I need a proper breakfast! Their current budget just wasn't sustainable. At this point if they weren't sold already, I would then relist what the package included. I also slipped in that the girls they were ultimately chasing were more likely to be going on our trips also given their own budget constraints. They would be looking forward to drinking for free as would the guys be. It's not a tough sell. It was a common sense approach. As a rep I was given drinks free wherever I went. I always palmed a few off and gave them to my guests. It was no skin off my nose and the barmen didn't care. When we walked into a bar with 3-400 guests, they were more than happy to service us continually and if that meant giving out a few rounds of free schnapps or a couple of bottles of beer here and there or a fish bowl, so be it.

This exercise I've just gone through above was ground into us continually in Magaluf. It stuck, it made sense. It wasn't rocket science and I think it was extremely successful because of it. The sales conversion rate in Ibiza was extremely high. Now would it have been so high if we were on one of the Greek or Canary Islands? Possibly not, but then I assume their trip package would have been cheaper or they would have to have offered more for it, given the price competition.

For the next few days, we were continually grilled and workshopped various objections. We were all asked to write down as many as we could think of, ranging from the obvious to the most ridiculous. Once we managed to produce a long list, we then opened the forum up to solving the objection. I don't like dance music was an easy one.

You're in Ibiza, you'll be surrounded by dance music anyway. We actually go to the rock bar most nights which is opposite your hotel, and we have a Grease themed night as well as a Cowboys and Indians night which won't have so much dance music. 50s and 60s music as well as a general mix of party music will be played at Grease, and then the other nights we have karaoke as well as a hip hop night and general pop. In fact, compared to the rest of Ibiza, we're probably the least "clubby" out there. I don't like to drink. That was easy too. You didn't have to drink, in fact one of the other guests in the hotel doesn't drink either. You don't need to do anything you don't want to do. The free food and club passes were still great value for money, and you were still getting go-karting, water park, beach club etc., which were all day time events and not everyone will be happy to start drinking so early in the sun, so you'll be able to relax and unwind with them. I have a boyfriend/girlfriend, so am not interested. This was also easy, I mean half of the people on the holiday were with someone, either officially or unofficially. How did having a significant other stop them from dancing and having a good time? The argument dropped away because all the situations that they would be faced with were going to be the same either with us, or without us if they were wandering the bars alone. I heard the package trips were crap, my friend did it. This was slightly harder, but a couple of short questions after and we were normally set. Where did they do it? When did they do it? Usually they did it 2-3 years before, and usually in another resort. You would mainly spend the time comparing and contrasting the program in Turkey or Greece with that of Ibiza. The price comparisons usually clenched that one.

If someone genuinely didn't have the money for the trip and were so skint that you didn't want them to come on it, you would normally leave them there with it to think about. You would then approach them and offer them a cut down deal later on after a day or so, with the permission of the boss. They would have had to have missed some of the bigger events though because if word got out that they were given a deal and didn't pay full price it would have caused problems with the other guests. The trick was to go to them after the others had just come back from one of the big days out. Usually everyone would be hammered and chanting or singing in the hotel pool in unison. People would already be hooking up with each other, and spirits would be extremely high. That was the time then to speak to those to see if they wanted to reconsider. They would already be feeling left out and this would usually work. The objections went on and on, and the more unlikely the objection, the more unlikely the counter. We covered them all anyway just for completeness' sake and to be able to demonstrate to each rep that there really was an answer to everything. In reality, in Ibiza, the main objections were due to not having the money, they came to Ibiza just to go clubbing or they'd been on trip packages before but didn't like them. Out of those three, a good 80-90% were objecting due to the cost.

Once we went through the variety of objections and closes, we took it in turns to role play. One being the seller, one being the guest. This was quite difficult. The guest was one of the senior reps or management. Even Damien took his turn to be an awkward holiday maker, really putting the reps through their paces. He would come out with the most ludicrous objections, but the way in which we approached them was always the same. If it wasn't for 'xyz....', you'd be coming out with us yeah? It soon became second nature to attempt this. You would literally go through the scripts, boxing the objection(s) in and then dealing with them on a case by case basis.

Many reps moved on after their spells in resort to sales roles with some becoming very successful. I've had sales training at many points during my various careers, and none of the courses have ever come even remotely close to what I was taught by the holiday company. It's not about pressure selling, but just the finer points and the mechanisms available to assist you in closing a deal at a price that's right for both parties. Could it really be this easy? Was it really this scientific? It was a real eye opener. Things moved at such a frantic pace though in resort. Turnover during peak season was over 3,000 a week, with two large arrival days, meaning anything from 5 - 7 welcome meetings per day, twice a week, sometimes more. That's anything from 10-15 meetings a week, each week, every week. You soon got into the rhythm and you got the chance to apply your training. You would tweak your methods continually self-evaluating and improving. As the season went on, you began to develop a nose for it. You would see the tell-tale signs. You would instinctively know who was the ring leader, who you could lean on, who you could poke fun at, who you could or couldn't win over. Sometimes if you weren't having much luck and they didn't want to pay for the trips, you would cut your losses and move on. There was always another group or another rep that would need assistance. This wasn't like selling time shares or trying to sell PPI claims. It wasn't pressured. It was always good natured, and most of the time comical (at least with me).

We were told to read various magazines about the UK scene for music and clubbing before we got to resort. Understand the names of the big clubs in every town, try and pick up some of the local lingo, slang for various cocktails and drinks etc. Understand the rugby and football teams in the local towns and who were rivals etc. You wanted anything you could use as a touch point to help form the bond with the group you were sat opposite from. Now in an ideal world, I would be placed with people from similar areas and regions as it would provide more familiarity between us, but in reality, this wasn't always possible. Ibiza was a clubbing destination. There was no point in me speaking to a group from Birmingham about clubs and what they like to do or where they like to go, if I didn't know what Miss MoneyPennys was. You wouldn't ask a group from Liverpool how often they went to Gatecrasher because that was in Sheffield. Cream was the major club in Liverpool at the time. It wasn't just the super clubs you wanted to know either. You also wanted to know the names of the piss up places. You needed to know what was the biggest meat market in Newcastle, or where pull-a-pig was most likely to take place in Kent or Leeds. The more info you could arm yourself with, the more banter you could bring to the conversation and the more regard the holiday makers would hold you in. You needed to become the authority on going out, clubbing and pulling. They needed to feel that you knew how to party and that you knew how to help them party. Now don't get me wrong, we didn't know everything, but we knew enough to have a conversation and not ask a stupid question if we didn't know the answer or we ran out of rope. As time went on in resort, we naturally began to pick up more and more information from the variety of guests that by the time peak season arrived some of us knew more about the social scene in the rest of the UK than we did about our own home towns. In order to demonstrate this, Damien asked the group where everyone was from again. We were a diverse group stretching from Newquay to Aberdeen. As each rep called out their hometown, he responded with the name of the closest night club there and the nearest rugby team. It was pretty impressive. He then asked us how many do we think he'd been to. As we all called out a variety of percentages, he declined to answer. He simply said it didn't matter. All that mattered is that we now thought he knew about clubbing and liked rugby. The truth of it was he was a football fan and had never played or watched a game of rugby in his life and he had 2 left feet and preferred pubs to clubs. This was an extremely effective demonstration of how to increase your standing in the minds of others. Just another tool in our growing sales arsenal.

∽

THIS SALES SESSION went on for most of the day. We broke for lunch but returned to the room to continue with the objection handling later on. In order to get us thinking in a more 'sales' mindset Damien also split us into groups and got us to produce a simple script and presentation about something on the table. For us it was a pen, for others it was a ring binder, a paper clip, a name tag, or a lanyard. It was actually a really useful experience. We were brainstorming, listing down any objections and how we would handle it. The rest of the group were tasked with trying to torpedo the pitch with wild objections which no matter how silly or ridiculous we had to isolate and overcome. Damien revelled in this, as this was his chance to put us on the spot and proceeded to throw in as many eye watering questions as possible. All the presentations were funny and presented energetically. Initially we were a little flustered, embarrassed almost to be presenting such a menial product for sale, but after the first or second presentation was given and insults were traded publicly, we began to relax and the confidence grew from there. I realise now that this was the key. The whole point of this exercise which was repeated several times throughout the week wasn't to spend any serious time on trying to convince someone to buy a highlighter pen or why they needed a folder to keep their papers in order. It was to prepare us for shit. It was to get you used to standing in front of a group of teenage/twenty somethings and handle a barrage of bollocks that was shouted at you designed to throw you off your pitch or to make you look silly. The training was designed to keep you under pressure, but remaining composed, comical and quick witted. The harder the counter, the more the audience would laugh. The more confident you would feel, the more control of the room you had. It was a self-inflicted feedback loop. I remember one of the girls losing it on the first session when she was presenting a paper clip to the audience. One of the senior reps intentionally interrupted her presentation to ask if the paperclip was safe enough to clip to his cock to provide support for him when he was playing football. She just melted. The room roared. She turned crimson and forgot the rest of her pitch which seemed to amuse him even more and encouraged others to bark out other questions designed to embarrass her. Could it fix a damaged foreskin? Would it double as a nipple clamp? Could it stop a duck from quacking if applied to the bill? This was the quality of the commentary from the audience, but it did the job. She folded instantly. Now compare this with the same girl during our last session. She was a totally different character. Not only was she mentally prepared for such shite, she was even actively courting it, picking on select individuals around the room before they even dared to talk. She was presenting a highlighter pen, one of those fluorescent yellow Stabilo ones that everyone seemed to have at school. She began her spiel about how revolutionary the ink was and how it was resistant to drying out when Damien weighed in "is it safe to use on your penis?" She immediately countered "Not only is it safe to use on your dick, but you can use it on your girlfriend. It glows in the dark so she can write some simple instructions on her belly so next time you're 'down there' you won't forget and be a massive disappointment!" without letting up she continued "In fact, you can also use the lid as a measuring device. So, if you're wondering how many cm you are, you can buy 2 of these and line up the lids end to end. These combined are about 5cm, so you'll have a target to aim for! They're small enough to put in your bag too, so you can bring them with you wherever you go." Everyone kept quiet awaiting a response, but there was none. Damien just smiled at her and turning to the other senior rep (football cock) gave a nod of approval. She just continued with the rest of her pitch, unashamed and undeterred.

CHAPTER 5
BOOZE CRUISE & BUTTKISS

When we weren't objection handling or giving sales pitches, we were training on the activity side of things. Early on into the week the seniors and management took everyone out on a booze cruise. This was to serve two purposes. Firstly, it was team building, pure and simple. It was to inject some fun into the week and to break up what until now had been a pretty heavy sales orientated training. Secondly, it was designed to give us a glimpse into how to behave as reps. The senior reps all had several years' experience under their belts already. In any normal job you would still be considered somewhat junior after your first season, but in this industry, considering the amount of life experience you gained in such a short space of time if you were a second- or third-year rep you were a seasoned professional. Unflinching in confidence and experience, with the ability to delete shame, embarrassment and shyness from your persona.

We were all brought to a small local harbour where we proceeded to board a large boat. There were approximately 60 of us including crew on the boat. It reminded me of a typical tourist boat. Too large to be a dive boat, but one of those double decker style boats that would ferry tourists from island to island around the Mediterranean. This would be perfect for something like whale watching or a sunset cruise etc. When we got to the boat, every single senior rep was dressed head to toe as a pirate. Even the senior management looked like sailors on the Black Pearl. We were served drinks immediately which we proceeded to down like Gazza in his heyday. We were given a few words from the big man at the top thanking us again for working hard and nailing the training down. We were told to relax and enjoy the day, but at the same time to watch how the senior reps were behaving, interacting and to take notes. I personally took this as a thinly veiled attempt at asking us not to go wild, but within an hour everyone was pissed.

We moored a short way off the shore. The calm of the crystal blue water was immediately shattered by Brits abroad as one after another jumped over the side. Some were in swimmers, others forcibly chucked in with their clothing. It set the mood early on. The DJ kicked into life, and all of a sudden, an impromptu 'dentist chair' was set up on the top deck. One by one each of us took our turn to kneel down in front of two of the senior reps. Each stood ready with a bottle of drink. One had melon schnapps and the other had hierbas. Now for those of you who don't know, hierbas is a Spanish digestif. I think this is the wrong classification, I personally think it tastes like it's already been digested by someone else. It's a strong alcohol made of wild herbs and supposedly has its roots in the Balearic islands and was originally used by monks for its medicinal properties. In other words, it tastes like absolute shite. As I knelt down and opened my mouth, I prepared myself for this modern-day communion. "Give that wanker extra!" bellowed Damien as the seniors proceeded to fill my mouth with the vilest piss you can imagine, coupled with a drink that's effectively ouzo crossed with rosemary scented petrol. It was all I could do not to throw it backup. I kept swallowing as they were pouring, not wanting to spill it down my front, and also not wanting to look like a pussy in front of my new found team mates or Damien. Eventually my mouth began to involuntarily close at the same time as they began to right the bottles upwards. I didn't even have a chance to finish my gulp when I suddenly found myself launched over the side of the double decker vessel into the waters below with no consideration for who might have been swimming below. There was no pause, the pace was relentless, no sooner had I swum away from the boat another rep came tumbling down. By the time I got back on to the second floor to witness who else was being punished, they were already on the third pair of bottles and things were already getting silly. Some trainees were already on their second 'visit to the dentist' others were ferociously trying to avoid being grabbed by a couple of the seniors who were acting in unison like an eastern European snatch gang. Some of the girls were desperately trying to evade them. Some opting to jump off the side themselves, others looking for a cabin or cubby hole to hide. Each time they thought they'd found one, one of the trainees or crew grassed them up and they were soon scooped out and taken to the altar to receive their liquid blessing. Whilst the pace slowed a little, the action didn't stop there. Next up some of the seniors then turned their attentions on each other. Most people at this point were split across the lower deck and in the waters surrounding the boat. I myself was on the first floor having taken a piss and looking for something to eat to try and soak up the booze. All of a sudden, I heard a huge roar. As I looked in the direction of the stairs, I caught site of a naked body dropping from the floor above. One of the seniors had had his clothes removed and he too had been jettisoned into the azure waters. Everyone laughed. In between laughs he was shouting obscenities at the seniors who did it. Shortly after a pair of pants was thrown over the side, which he gratefully put on as he climbed aboard. Next a couple of female reps were thrown over the side topless. Again, these were seniors, and despite the public protestations they didn't appear to be bothered. As if they'd seen this a hundred times before. One of the girls put up such a meek resistance, I think she secretly wanted to hang her baps out for all to see. Everyone cheered as she held her nose and dropped off the edge.

Everyone was having a good time, the booze continued to flow, and the DJ was actually pretty good. Anyone watching from the shore wouldn't have had a scooby that this was a work event. The intensity of it all began to drop a little as we made plans to return to shore for the next part of the day. The naughtiness might have slowed, but that didn't stop the trainees (nor the seniors for that matter) from pulling back on the booze. Beer after beer, sangria after sangria followed. By the time we docked, everyone was bladdered. Some had even begun to pair off. The trainees were gossiping like old boys on an assembly line. Rumours were flying like crazy. One of the trainees had puked on herself already and was currently having her hair pulled back from her mouth by another. One of the guys had cut his head slipping off the side of the boat being stupid and was needing to go to the local 'Galena' (Doctors) once shoreside. A couple of trainees were snogging and word had it that one of the senior reps had already received a blow job on the boat. On the boat? Are you fucking kidding me! It wasn't even 3pm in the middle of the day, mid week, and one of the lads is getting noshed. This was music to my ears. We celebrated this news with another round of drinks. If this was a glimpse of what life as a rep was going to be like, then this is going to be a summer to remember.

Once back into shore we filed off the boat and walked a short distance along the beach to a venue that had been purposely chosen and set up for the event. As we walked along the beach, we must have resembled a crab race, with some moving more sideways than others. We were in high spirits and good moods. All except the rep with the cut head, he proceeded to receive a couple of quick stitches in the local clinic. He did return an hour or so after, wearing a big bandage making him look like Mr Bump. He received a huge cheer and a bottle of beer to celebrate. The bandage was that large I thought the doctors were taking the piss. It didn't matter to him. He was immediately greeted with the sympathy of some of the female reps. He finished his bottle in one, waving to the crowd like a Roman emperor. Everyone laughed, despite some head shaking from the seniors.

As we walked into the venue, you could see off to the side of the private beach there was an area that had been cordoned off. There you could see some of the staff were tending to long banqueting tables with benches. We had a compere who welcomed us into the venue as we showed up, and waiters were already on the private beach handing us drinks before we were able to put our bags down. One of the senior reps took over on the mic and started to provide commentary on those who were still walking up the beach. He was really funny, announcing everyone as they stepped into the area like you see at posh weddings. Obviously, he was making this stuff up, but he had the whole audience fixated. "Here comes Mr and Mrs Puddlesbury from Grimsby. When Derek is not hanging around the local primary schools and day care centres he likes to tend to his allotment. Carole who once posed for 'readers wives' owns her own hotdog van which is a fan favourite and can often be seen close to the local dogging spots of Grimsby and nearby Cleethorpes." "Following in behind the Puddlesbury family is Mr and Mrs Cunthorpe from Enfield. Ivan Cunthorpe is a retired dildo engineer and now consults for Anne Summers. Wendy Scunthorpe is currently working on an adult film production where she holds the title of chief fluffer, having previously worked extensively on Shaving Ryan's Privates and RoboCock." He went on for ages. He adlibbed the whole thing, not pausing once. It didn't matter who came up the beach.

Once everyone was there and with drinks in hand, he directed his attention to our private beach area. Calling everyone forwards, he began putting us into teams. He randomly split the group in 2 and made us all sit in 2 long rows one behind the other, ideally boy girl, boy girl etc. He then proceeded to ask the remaining seniors to get the drinks ready. Each trainee sat on the sand behind each other (we sat in between each other's legs like a rowing team). We were each given a plastic cup full of sangria and told to hold it above our head. Anyone caught not doing it was threatened with a drinking fine. He proceeded to detail the rules of the game. Basically, the person at the front needed to down their drink, turn around, kiss the person behind them, and then sprint to the back of the row and shout to the front when sat so the next person in front could do the same. The winner was the team that had finished their drinks first and had done a complete lap i.e. the front person who ran to the back was now sat at the front again. Anyone deviating from this plan was going to be given a drinking fine by Damien. Damien piped up that he was going to "fuck someone up" if they cheated. Both rows started to giggle and mutter between themselves. The guys started shooting each other glances and expressions as it dawned on them who they were going to be kissing. I felt a huge double-edged sword in my side. I was sat behind the curly haired girl from Leeds. She was cute, and had a nice figure. Also, as she was going to be going first, it would be her that was the initiator, so this reduced the chance of me being publicly mugged off if I went in for a kiss only for her to turn her head. I also didn't know if this was going to be kisses on the lips or a full-on snog. I was clearly hoping for the latter, but fortunately we were already about 6 or 7 persons back, so we had time to see how things kicked off initially. She didn't look back at me, so I had nothing to gauge her reaction at the news that potentially she might be getting off with me on the beach! Just as she didn't look backwards, nor did I. The other side of the coin was that I was sat in front of a bit of a unit. She was from the midlands, and whilst nice enough, we didn't really seem to hit it off. I found her quite brash and a bit cold. I didn't find her attractive at all, and whilst there wasn't anything to really say about her appearance, it was her demeanour I didn't like. The thought of kissing her wasn't exactly floating my boat. To be fair to it, she was probably thinking the same of me but in order to stay positive, I chose to focus on Leeds for the snog.

There was some commotion behind me with people laughing and protesting. As I looked round, one of the Scottish lads had basically inserted himself in between one of the guys and one of the fittest girls in the group. Much to the annoyance of the guy who was initially sat there lined up for this angel. As he told the lad from Edinburgh to piss off and get back in his spot, he was met by a "Get ta fuck pal." This line can only be delivered by someone north of Hadrian's wall. The initial guy said he wasn't going anywhere, to which Scotty said he didn't give a shit, because if it meant snogging him to get to her, it was a chance that he "cannae pass up." Faced with the prospect of getting tongued by Edinburgh the other trainee, dejected, upped and left and retired to the back of the queue. Everyone laughing at the encounter. The fitty that Edinburgh wanted to snog pretended like she didn't know what was going on behind her. She continued to feign disinterest to maintain her cool stature. The other row of reps had a bit of an issue. There were slightly more lads than girls so that meant that some of the boys would potentially be kissing each other, much to their protestation. The rep on the mic called for some senior "minge" to help calm and fix the situation. A couple of the senior female reps happily inserted themselves in between the boys at the back whilst flicking the finger to the rep on the mic.

At this point everyone was ready, drinks in hand. Tensions were high, most of the guys were raring to kiss or be kissed, some of the girls were clearly happy to get stuck in too, although am sure some in the group had their reservations. No time to think about that time now. "Go!" was bellowed over the mic, immediately causing each row to break out into howls of encouragement and cheering. I could see their row more clearly than ours from my vantage point. The guy who started their side off skulled the sangria in one and then turning around quickly he meekly kissed the girl behind him. It wasn't so much a snog, but more an intense kiss on the lips, as I leaned to the side to focus on my own row's starter, it was a girl from London. Cute and bubbly. She took a little longer to finish her drink but threw the cup to one side and launched herself on to the guy behind her. Not only did she put her tongue down his throat, but basically forced him on to his back and nearly ended up in the girl's lap behind him. Everyone cheered. This girl single handedly set the pace for everyone else. As she picked herself up from the sand and started to sprint past us all to the back of the queue, our number two had finished his drink and was already frenching the Doris behind him. Even their side picked the pace up having witnessed how we were behaving. Some of the girls in both rows didn't want to kiss or be kissed, so they would just turn their cheek or somehow avoid the lips altogether, screwing their faces up into a ball like you used to when you got kissed as a child from someone elderly. As each person downed and kissed their way to the back the cheers and encouragement got louder. Eventually it was the turn of Leeds. She'd full on kissed the guy in front of her and was just downing her sangria. Mic rep was giving all the encouragement he could muster to both teams. Once finished she turned around, looked at me for a split second before tilting her head slightly. Bingo. She dove in. I tried to kiss her softly yet as manly as possible. She didn't recoil, and I wasn't in a rush to start downing my drink. I tried to kiss her for that little bit longer than the others had swapped spit for and in my head I thought I succeeded. In reality it was probably no different to anyone else. We stopped kissing, and without a moment's thought I downed the sangria. Horrible cat's piss. I even inhaled a piece of orange or whatever fruit was left in it. With that done, I turned around to greet sour puss. I lunged forward and stuck my tongue in her mouth with all the romance of a bolt on a garden gate. The tongue went in, once round the garden and out again. Without even giving her a second glance, I was already on my toes and pegging it down to the back of the queue. I smiled at Leeds as I collapsed in the sand behind her. Neither of us said anything, but I sat much closer to her than before. As we both lent backwards propped up on our hands, I noticed her hands were in contact with my legs. Physical contact. This was a good sign

I thought. I didn't really pay much more attention to it as we were busy cheering on our row and just enjoying the spectacle unfolding in front of us. There were a couple more people yet to kiss before they would get to the angel and Edinburgh. Everyone was so focused on what was happening in front of them that no one really knew what was going on behind them.

One of the senior reps decided whilst Edinburgh was funny in what he did, it wasn't particularly a team building move, and decided to even the score. He quietly asked the girl behind him to scoot back a bit and inserted himself into the queue behind Edinburgh. Only this time he didn't sit down. He just stood there with his back to Edinburgh, smiling to everyone in front of him which by now were mainly people who had already done their drink and had their kisses. He beckoned to everyone in both rows not to say a word by putting his finger to his lips. No one knew what was yet to come, but everyone assumed that Edinburgh was going to be on the receiving end of it. The rep on the mic immediately started to ratchet things up, trying to encourage people to drink and kiss quicker. In the same way a horse commentator gets excited on the final furlong he was upping the pace. The angel feigned a quick kiss with the guy in front of her and started to chug the sangria. At which point Edinburgh starts making lewd comments on how she's about to get kissed like never before and she's going to love it etc. He sounds like a prick now, but he was actually pretty funny at the time. Anyway, as soon as she turns around, she tries to kiss him on the cheek. He immediately grabs her and they tussle for a bit (playfully) but the best he manages is a peck on the lip-cheek area. He then proceeds to neck his sangria. Unbeknown to him that the rep behind him loosens his shorts and pulls them down to his knees, holding his carrot as he does, so as to protect the girl in front of him (who would have been the Scot's next kiss) from getting tea bagged. Everyone by now is focusing on this and cheering and whooping. The original guy who got displaced is roaring like it's a cup final. As Edinburgh tosses the cup to one side, the rep bends forwards. Scotty turns around on all fours in one motion without looking first. I guess he wanted to spring on the girl behind and grab the spotlight. He grabbed the spotlight alright, but not in the way he thought. As he turns to face his intended victim, he's instead met by the tea towel holder of the senior rep. He immediately stops dead in his tracks and his face recoils in terror. With perfect timing the rep, still bent forwards, steps backwards. It's a beautiful scene. Scottish nose and chin are immediately wed with the senior's undercarriage. The whole group roars. Edinburgh is trying to push the rep forwards, but he's not on solid footing. The senior continues to back up and almost starts to squat. It was the funniest thing ever. Seeing Edinburgh get to see the inner workings of the senior's balloon knot and the struggle he put up was one of my fondest memories from that trip. Everyone was laughing including the venue's staff. Even girls who would normally shy away from such puerile behaviour were cheering. A split second later, and without a word, the senior simply leant forward and kissed the girl behind him so the race could continue. He then stepped to the side and pulled his trunks up, grabbing his beer. Edinburgh left the game and immediately went to wash his face, calling the senior a "dirty bastard" and other derogatory terms as he went past. The senior just looked at him smiling. One of the other reps pointed to him and told him he deserved it, at which point the Scot begrudgingly agreed and his irritation began to defuse. By the time he returned from the bathroom, the owner of said starfish brought him over a beer and they both had a laugh about it. I don't remember which side finished the race; we were laughing too hard about the ass to mouth action we'd just witnessed. For the rest of the day and evening, 'buttkiss' (as he was affectionately renamed) would be continually ribbed about the incident. On the plus side, he did get a drink for the trainee he'd originally displaced. He realised that what he'd done whilst funny, wasn't particularly helpful to the team spirit of the group, and what had happened to him in return was deserved.

The beach entertainment didn't stop there. Next up was the pole game. Again, we were split in two groups and told to line up. We were first going to be given a demonstration by the seniors. We all intently looked on wondering what was in line for us. Having been fed drinks continually, snogged one another and even witnessed the beginnings of the human centipede, emotions were running high and we were keen to see what would be thrown our way next. Two of the larger framed male seniors were standing next to the pole, with two of the smaller senior reps (one guy, one girl) stood at the front of both rows. The rows were approximately 10m away from the pole, and the reps. The aim of the game was simple. You would run from your row to the reps (approximately 10m) where a glass of sangria was to be necked in one go. You would then move forwards a couple of feet where if you were small enough, you would be hoisted on to the reps' shoulders and spun around in a circle ten times. If you were too heavy for that, you would put your forehead (using your hand as a cushion) on top of a broom stick pole and run around the pole 10 times without breaking contact. Once finished, you would then have to sprint back to your team's row and tag the next rep in a relay style race, where they would repeat the process etc. No one really paid much attention to the fact that we were downing yet more drinks, and this seemed pretty fun and not difficult to grasp. Mic rep gave a quick dummy run for the reps to show us. He shouted "Go" into the mic and the two seniors went bolting over the sand to the reps. They ploughed through the whole glass of sangria like it was a thimble full of water. The larger reps then grabbed them and aggressively spun them round. Of course, both the girls and the guys there had already had years of experience in this, but I got the feeling the spinners were trying extra hard to make them dizzy. It was either that or just simply they had fresh shoulders to spin them on. Everyone was cheering initially but then after 10 spins, they didn't stop. They gave them an extra 5, much to the hollering and shrieking from the girl. We all watched intently for what was coming next. The seniors were put down and off they set, mic rep bellowing at them to sprint. Well it was ridiculous. The girl lifted a foot up an inch off the sand and she immediately face planted. Much to the amusement of everyone. The guy also failed but he managed to take four or five steps. He shot off towards us, but immediately veered off to the side. He was desperately trying to move straight. His head was tilted like a drunk giraffe, but no matter what he did he kept running at a 45-degree angle to the side. After the 4th or 5th step his coordination gave up and he hit the deck also. As he went down our focus switched to the first one. She by this time had picked herself up again, but no sooner had she moved forwards on to her front leg, she came barrelling down again into the sand. This was hilarious.

Eventually after another round of failures, the reps made it back to us, where they both tagged us trainees. As soon as we were tagged in, the memories of failure dissipated and the competitiveness kicked in. One after the other we sprinted towards the sangria. Most of the guys at this point had basically put their head downwards and ran

10 times around the pole. After 4 or 5 people on either side had gone through, they decided to up the ante. They suddenly switched out the sangria for a glass of beer. I hadn't had my go yet, but I guess they must have seen the look on my face as I saw the beer come out. Once I was tagged, I ran towards it like a rabid alcoholic. I chugged this San Miguel down as quick as I could, not wanting to let my team down. I didn't even get a chance to put the cup down or even burp. I was immediately lifted from behind and stuck on a rep's shoulders. It wasn't the usual rep, it was Damien, and for some reason, he had a point to prove. "I'm going to make you puke like an anorexic" he hollered as he proceeded to spin us both. It was all I could do not to spew down his back there and then. The beer had hardly had a chance to hit my stomach and here it was being squeezed back out of my oesophagus via this human centrifuge. "I'm going to puke" I belted out, much to everyone's laughter. This only spurred Damien on more. If being scooped up like a damsel in distress wasn't emasculating enough, being made to puke a beer would have been the icing on the cake. I kept my mouth firmly shut. Soon enough, the beer began to rise. With my jaw clenched shut I swallowed the bile infused beer back down and made my escape from Damien's clutches. As soon as I was back on my feet it hit me. The horizon was one large seesaw swaying from left to right and back again. I took about 2-3 steps forward and had to stop. When I analysed my position, I had effectively walked sideways and not forwards. I was determined not to fall and give the seniors the satisfaction. I was already being abused for not being quick enough, the last thing I wanted to do was face-plant. "Run you twat" was aimed in my direction, along with "forwards you tart" and "no this way you div!" I took 4 more big steps having completely reversed my angle to hopefully bring me

back on track. I was somewhat closer but close wasn't enough. I decided to go for it. I just accelerated towards the next person in the relay team. I immediately started to tilt but my legs didn't let up. I started making ground but the lean was becoming closer and closer to terminal. As I could feel the inevitable happen, I just tried to out-sprint it. Obviously failing, I hit the sand with a thud and took a facial. I was close enough to release the next rep. She shot past me as one of the guys helped me up off the floor. I was still dusting sand and shit out of my ears and nostrils when she made it back to tag our team mate in. I looked up at Damien, he stood there grinning at me. I couldn't help but smile. At that point I was just grateful I didn't throw up on myself. A San Miguel, sand and puke encrusted t-shirt wasn't going to help me get laid and it certainly wasn't going to stand me in good stead, reputation wise, as someone who could drink or handle it.

The final game that was bestowed on us was one called 'stab the crab.' This was a game involving just the lads. They randomly selected approximately 10 guys out of the group and got everyone to make a big circle around us. They then applied makeshift blindfolds out of t-shirts to us and made us lay in the central area. We were told to keep our eyes closed and just imagine we were laying on the beach on a hot summer's day. I was one of those chosen, so I laid there motionless and tried to picture myself laying on a beach in the Caribbean. Mic rep proceeded to detail the scene and had us imagining and acting out certain actions. "Imagine the weather is scorching hot, and you are sun bathing. It's so hot you begin to feel a shiver. Not because of the wind, but because you're beginning to burn a little. You need to grab the sun cream from the small table next to your sun bed and apply it to yourself." At this point, I and the other lads began to rub invisible sun cream on ourselves. We began to stretch out and shiver a little with the heat. "Now imagine you've just ordered a cold beer. You take it from the waiter's hand, holding it to your forehead for a brief moment before you take a long hard sip of that beer, instantly cooling you down and making you feel relaxed." Again, we all continued to play along with the charade. I reached into mid-air, took my bottle of beer and did as was suggested. Some of the audience were laughing at this point. I was blindfolded but assumed one of the lads was being an exhibitionist and was drinking the beer in a funny manner. Maybe he was drinking two, maybe he was stroking his cock as he pretended to down his pint, I didn't know. "Now imagine you're dozing on the sun bed under the intense heat. You've finished your beer and had a quick 30-minute nap. You are slowly coming around but are startled when something runs over your foot and you immediately kick out not knowing what it is." As I began to follow the instructions, I was interrupted by one of the reps. She sat me up and removed my blindfold but signalled to me to keep quiet. As the blindfold was removed, I saw that there were only 3 other guys left, laying there blindfolded. Everyone else had been removed from play, just as I had been. We all watched on in unison as the 3 remaining trainees continued to kick into mid-air, much to the titters and laughs of the others.

One of the reps was massively over egging the improvisations. He was not so much kicking at this creature, but practically trying to kick his jeans off in one motion. This was the sign the reps were waiting for. One by one they removed the other two players from the area, leaving Mr Theatrical to play out the scene on his own. Of course, the rest of us were shown the finger to the lips, and we all remained silent in front of the drama queen. Mic rep continued. "Imagine that the crab has come back and keeps running over your legs. You're annoyed, and you try to kick it away. It jumps from leg to leg. You don't want to sit up though as you're so comfortable. Instead you just lay there trying to remove it from your body with both arms and legs." Drama boy continued to throw his limbs about. Such was his exaggeration; he looked more like he was having an epileptic fit crossed with some mad energetic tribal dance. Everyone laughed, which obviously gave him inspiration to continue acting the fool further. "Now imagine that little crab has managed to somehow climb up under your shorts and is now hopping around in your swimming trunks. You immediately grab the nearest thing to hand which is a cocktail stick from your girlfriend's martini glass. You don't want to touch the crab because he might take your fingers off with his powerful claws. Instead you begin trying to stab him with the cocktail stick." Now we're getting somewhere. Drama boy was laying there in front of everyone with his hand down his shorts trying to make a stabbing motion at this imaginary crab. Everyone was laughing. It looked like he was furiously tugging one out whilst wearing a t-shirt blindfold, that by now looked more like a sandy turban. He's rocking back and forth and stabbing with all the drama of a James Bond fight scene. People are pissing themselves. Remember, as far as he's concerned, he's joined by 9 others of his brethren in the fight against the penis eating crab. He's unaware he's a solo act at this point. Mic rep continues to build the scenario. "As you battle with the crustacean, you begin to hear the sound of distant water. What started off as a light wave crashing on to the beach has begun to intensify. You hear water getting nearer and nearer. You'd normally be concerned; however, the problem is that this little bastard has managed to evade being stabbed so far, he's set his sights on your old boy. The crab is beginning to climb up towards the end of your chap. You must get him before he latches onto the tip. Stab him. Stab him now!" Mic rep did a good job raising the tempo. At this point Drama boy is rolling around on the sand, frantically moving his hand in and out of his shorts. He's literally a poster child at this point for someone with a wank addiction. The whole crowd is laughing at him. Just him. Mic rep doesn't let up. "You nearly got him, keep going, ignore the water, although it's getting closer and closer... that's it, faster, he's cornered, get him before he uses his claws on your chop." At this point, the crowd parts and two of the other reps walk forward with a big plastic bin. It's full to the brim with iced water. It's what was set out earlier for us and it was keeping the beers cold. At this point, we all knew what was coming next. They took their positions. The bin was big. It was like the old plastic barrel sized bins we used to have in the garden as children. Between them they managed to lift it up to chest height. Acting in unison, mic rep continued, his voice noticeably quicker and higher pitched "That's it, you got him, he's wounded. Stab him again, make sure you finish him off. Do it quick! The water's getting LOUDER AND LOUDER, CLOSER AND CLOSER. ALL OF A SUDDEN...." Before he got a chance to finish his sentence the two reps emptied the bin on him as quickly and powerfully as they could. Wallop! Drama boy took the full load to his upper torso. His body recoiled on to the sand and he just laid there rigid, in shock. The whole place erupted. One of the reps quickly removed his blindfold. His eyes quickly darted around the area. As the realisation dawned on him that everyone had been laughing at him and only him, everyone cheered again. The shock on his face due to the freezing water mixed with the embarrassment was a picture. This simple game of improvisation would go on to be played out time and time again when we got to resort. It was one of the most popular games that the reps would play with the guests.

Shortly after the games concluded, we were then called into the main party area for food and more drinks. The rest of the day continued in a boozy fashion. The seniors continued to entertain the trainees and together with the venue staff, they ensured that everyone's glass was permanently full. It was only towards the end of the night that the seniors started to drink and relax more with everyone else. At several points during the evening, management came to us all in our little groups or individually, asking if we were having a good time and to see what we had observed. We discussed the behaviour of the seniors. The games and party tricks they'd shown us, and asked us to come up with words that would describe how they'd made us feel. To be honest, I could have done without the debriefing as I was more intent on getting on to the dance floor to try and strut my stuff and grab a snog. Regardless, the rest of the evening became hazy. We were all tired, weary from drink and overfed. Any thoughts of wanting to hook up were rapidly evaporating. That being said, it didn't stop me from trying to fire into Leeds. Everyone had been sitting together on a long bench table and whilst she wasn't close to me, I caught her glance a couple of times. At some point in the evening we passed each other in the aisle and we stopped to chat. We made small talk. I asked her if she was having a good time. She replied that she thought the whole day had been brilliant. I cheekily said "you're welcome". She asked me what for. I said for making her day being such a good kisser. She blushed but quickly fired back that it was in fact her that was the good kisser and she felt the need to direct me as she thought I wouldn't know what I was doing. I loved it. A girl with banter and a quick wit was always my weak point. After a few more exchanges we were interrupted by a couple of the other trainees who brought us each over a shot of tequila so we could join them. Great I thought to myself. All I need is more drink. At this rate, even if I could get a sniff, I'd probably pass out or fumble the ball. Leeds wasn't mucking about though, she took the shot down immediately, and continued to stare at me. She told me to man up, which resonated with my ego. I nailed mine and gave the empties back to the other two. At which point the reps came over to all 4 of us and told us that the coaches were leaving in 10 minutes, so we needed to get our stuff and be on them.

I tried to stick as close as I could to Leeds on the way out. I didn't want to lose her in the sea of pissheads being herded back to the hotel. As we left the venue, I was surprised to see the carnage that was outside. Several of the reps had been removed either voluntarily or by force and were littered around the fire exit. One was laying on the floor singing. One girl was hugging the bin whilst vomiting profusely, again with a female friend holding her hair back from her mouth which is customary. Another trainee was laying fully outstretched under a bench and was asleep. How he got there I have no idea. The seniors were busy dealing with these casualties of war whilst the rest of us got on the coach. The moods varied between the groups, some people were already asleep on the coach, others were having passionate debates about complete shit. What was noticeable though was that everyone had already formed bonds with each other. People were laying there, arm in arm, slumped together. Some girls were sat on laps. Some had their legs up on each other, and some couples had also blatantly been copping off too. Something I was eager to do. I managed to sit next to Leeds on the coach. We made some small talk about the training course in general. We recounted the humorous events of the day, including stab the crab and also seeing Edinburgh's unfortunate encounter with the rusty sheriff's badge. I was keen to keep talking about the beach games and in particular the boat race as I was hoping subconsciously to keep the thought about us kissing alive. Thankfully she either didn't realise, or was happy to keep discussing it. We continued to talk for another minute or so, but it wasn't long before we were both kissing again. Happy days. We continued to make out in the seats for a minute or so before the lights on the coach fired up and the seniors brought the dregs back on. They'd managed to wake the sleeping giant under the bench, and pukey had stopped for the time being, but she was immediately given the bin at the front of the bus in case she felt the need to volunteer more chunks. Leeds and I both sat there not saying anything as we were counted. They needed to make sure everyone was present and correct before leaving. We didn't really say anything for the rest of the bus ride back. We just sat there, hands next to each other, touching, but not holding. It was enough for me. I'd pulled. It was a successful end to a successful day. I still hoped the night would continue when we got back to the hotel. Unfortunately, the seniors had other ideas.

Once we got back and everyone was off the bus, the seniors called a quick meeting. They basically took the guys into the usual conference room and the girls were taken to another part of the hotel. We were then given a quick run through of what we needed to do the following day, and a debrief of the evening's affairs. Some of the guys got a bollocking for being too drunk. They reemphasised (again) that this wasn't a free for all or a jolly. They wanted us to enjoy ourselves, but if we couldn't be trusted to not get totally shit faced, how could we be trusted to look after holiday makers, who would be getting hammered themselves. Someone needed to stay sober and alert, and unfortunately that would be us, and it was the main reason why we were being paid and put up in resort. A few loose threats were made and we were told that senior management also wasn't impressed to find people incapacitated outside the venue. We were told if that happened again, we would be flown home and our contracts (which hadn't been signed yet for the upcoming season) would be retracted. It was a sobering thought and anyone who was still pissed pretty much reigned it in there and then. Finally, they said they were aware of several inter rep relationships that were already kicking in. They then detailed who they saw kissing, canoodling and where in front of everyone. Leeds and I were mentioned amongst 4 or 5 other impromptu couples. They said that inter colleague relationships were heavily frowned upon and that whilst they do happen, it was in our interests not to get tied up with each other. At the end of the speech, one of the senior reps levelled with the group and said basically that there was no point getting involved with someone on the team because the minute we hit resort we were going to want to fuck around and mess around with the holidaymakers anyway. Why go there with baggage? Why upset the apple cart or limit yourselves? It was this last sentence which really had the most impact and took the sting out of the school teacher dressing down that we'd just had to spend 10 minutes listening to. With that they wished us good night and told us they'd be seeing us bright and early. At this point nearly everyone retired. I say nearly, because I still had other plans for Leeds, and another lad who also got a mention for getting stuck in was also circling around the bar. Both of us trying hard to make it look like we were having a casual conversation. It must have been obvious we were just waiting for the girls to come out of their meeting. When they did, most of the girls retired upstairs immediately. I saw Leeds with one of the older reps. It was as if the older rep was standing guard. I couldn't get to her on her own without being cock blocked. Had she not been there, do I think that Leeds would have been up for an 'after party'? Maybe or maybe not. She kept shooting me 'help me' looks and rolling her eyes whilst gesturing towards her new found chaperone. After about 15 - 20 minutes of idle chit chat, I suddenly felt a breath on my neck. "I thought we told you guys to keep it in your pants. Fuck off to bed already!" was whispered quietly behind us. As I looked round, it was Damien. He was grinning, but he meant it. I looked across at the other guy who was also waiting for cock block to leave. "You too" said Damien as he gestured to my partner in crime. The game was up. We both finished what was left of our drink and left the bar. I wasn't too disappointed; I mean I'd had a good day and managed to get involved. It just meant I was going to have to get sneaky if I wanted to get laid.

The rest of the week passed by at a slightly lighter pace. As time went on, the sales related exercises became less and less frequent. We actually started to learn more about what we as reps would be expected to do and what to do in a variety of circumstances. We were taught what to do in case of emergency. What happens if a guest needs an emergency medical procedure? Who do you call first? Who do you need to notify? What happens if a guest loses their passport? What happens if a guest passes away? What happens if a guest needs the morning after pill? What happens if you lose a guest? What happens if you find extra guests in the hotel? What happens if there's a big fight? What happens if a guest gets arrested? What happens if we get arrested? What happens if a room is burgled? What happens if a guest gets in a fight with another guest? What happens if a rep gets in a fight? What happens if a guest damages their room or the furniture in a room? This was a particularly comical topic as some of the senior reps began to recount stories of what they'd seen some holidaymakers do. You'd be surprised, but more on that later. What could we do if a guest needs medical attention i.e. balancing permissible help versus liability? For example, maybe a guest needs a paracetamol, is that ok to give? Remember we're talking 20 odd years ago and this idea of health and safety regulations wasn't anywhere near as painful as it is today, but even then, there were still limits to what we could do. What happens if a guest has an overdose? What happens if we catch guests doing drugs in the hotel? What to do if a guest's luggage doesn't arrive? What to do if a holiday maker misses their return flight? What to do if there's an accusation of assault or rape? The list went on and on. We were given a complete check list and we repeatedly went through the whole lot. To be honest, aside from the odd funny one, it was pretty sobering. I mean we were only 18-20 somethings ourselves, and having to deal with some of these things on the list would be a stretch for anyone to deal with, especially those of us who were basically students working abroad during the summer holidays! Whenever reference was made to a more serious situation, the trainers tended to use phrases like "in the unlikely event…" or "not that it's likely to happen…" This didn't convince anyone and if anything, reminded us that there'd be a high chance of it happening whilst in resort. The company alone was probably responsible for sending 7-10 thousand horny holiday makers to resorts around the Mediterranean twice a week during peak season, and statistically you were likely to encounter X number of motorbike accidents, fights, overdoses, assaults, burglaries, and furniture destructions. Unfortunately sexual assaults, rapes and deaths were also commonplace. It was a shuddering thought. Going through each and every scenario took time. We basically used up a whole day on it, but it was important. The procedures were drilled into us as to what we should do and who we should call. Once we'd finished this part of the training, we cut for the day and were told to meet by the pool for a sunset drink. Management didn't want to throw anything crazy to do in the evening, and we essentially had an evening off. After the training, most of us we're reflecting on what had been said and everyone was talking to each other about what it might be like handling some of the more serious eventualities. Others recollected situations that they'd been in previously, with some of the senior reps contributing with some of their war stories. Everyone listened to each other intently and spent the time relaxing whilst getting to know each other. It was a very relaxed and low-key evening, with a quiet dinner. No one, myself included, really wanted to party after. Tomorrow was our final day and our last night and we needed to make sure we had plenty of energy left.

CHAPTER 6
GREASED LIGHTNING

The following morning, we all woke up refreshed, and most of us had started to pack. Breakfast was done and dusted quickly and we returned briefly to the room to collect the props that we'd brought out to resort with us. You see today was cabaret day. We met mid-morning at different secluded areas throughout the hotel in our small groups. The plan was to have a practice session before lunch. Grab a bite, and then have a final practice session (with costumes) before heading to the main function room for 3pm. All week we'd been working on various performances and now was going to be the chance to perform and show them off. Everyone was pretty tired by now. Whilst working here in Majorca still beat being back in the UK, we'd had a relatively intensive program and we already had one eye on the weekend. Rehearsals, regardless of the type of event to be performed, are boring. Nevertheless, we continued. I was sent to a small room to join up with the other lads where we were due to perform a Grease dance. We were told that this was essentially a dry run and we would be performing this in resort for the season ahead, and so the more we took away from the practice and performance now the less we'd have to struggle with when we got to resort. We could lark about now, but most reps were going to be in resort only a week before the guests arrived, so you had a relatively short time period to familiarise yourself with the hotel, the resort itself and manage to learn all the dances. The minute the guests arrive and start buying trips, you're performing for real and they need to feel they're getting value for money. The company took this extremely seriously. Each of us had brought out a cheap white boiler suit, and a leather jacket (with the T birds logo emblazoned in white across the back of it). The idea was to essentially re-enact the garage scene from Grease, where John Travolta and his gang of T-birds were finishing the tune up on their car before singing along to "Greased Lightning." We had a choreographer with us and she was taking us through our paces. We'd been learning this short routine throughout the week. Despite never having received formal training, I seem to have been blessed with a pair of hips and could actually move my feet with rhythm. Unfortunately, the same could not be said with some of my compatriots. The routine was simple enough, you just needed to remember the right bars when to kneel, when to spin around etc. We were all going to be in unison, so if someone fucked it up it was going to be obvious. We continually repeated the routine until even the slowest in the group knew what to do (at least theoretically). The problem was getting some of them to remember it. At one point, on maybe the 14th attempt, the choreographer lost her cool. "For fuck sake lads, how can you still be getting this wrong, it's down on the first beat and up on the fourth! Let's take it from the top again." We were all getting tired and a bit ratty with this by now. Those that couldn't get it, were getting more agitated with every failure and those that could get it, were quite frankly getting irritated at having to repeat something relatively simple due to others having lead feet and as much rhythm as a brick. We decided to take a break for 15 minutes.

At this point, we proceeded to sneak off to the bar for some liquid encouragement. One of the gang, a young lad from Bristol, was the first to break silence. "Bollocks to this." He muttered as he reached for his pint. "I didn't sign up to be Michael Fucking Flatley. I can sing. I can tell jokes. I can drink, but let's face it chaps, I can't dance for shit. I'm holding you all up. I'm really sorry." He paused only to take a hearty lug of his San Miguel, before continuing "I reckon they're going to kick me off the program." "Don't be daft, none of us here can dance." I replied. "You just need to work on your timing a bit. Our job is not to be dancers, it's to entertain. Now that could be in any form, right? You just need to make people smile? Clearly, we're not a fucking boy band. What we will be doing though is entertaining. I mean at the end of the day, we're all going to be performing a striptease in resort every week, and the full hog. Now if that's not going to be funny, I don't know what is." The weight on his brow seemed to lighten. I continued "you just need to find your own pace. Count in your head, or make up a rhyme to the music, and whilst you're up there, remember the key words to go down, and when to spin round etc. You'll be fine." "Easy for you to say, you've not cocked it up once." He retorted. "No, he's right!" chimed in one of the other trainees. "You don't need to be a dancer; you just need to be funny. I mean who the fuck pays all this money to go on holiday with the lads or the birds, to places like Magaluf or even Ibiza, the fucking capital of clubbing, to watch a group of lads dance around in leather jackets pretending to be John Travolta from the 50s. It's bollocks. Now if you ask me, what they are paying for is to get absolutely shit faced, get laid and have a laugh whilst doing it. Seeing us knock out a 10 out of 10 performance of Greased Lightning won't win anyone up here a blow job. Now if we go up there and smash it by being funny and making people laugh, well who knows? You might be getting your pickle tickled sooner than you think!" We all chuckled at that. The way he delivered the last line was unexpected. Even Bristol was tittering into his pint. "Don't pay any attention to the choreographer. She's been paid to teach us to dance. Dancing is in her blood. It's her passion. It's her career. Of course, she's not going to be happy if we start to take the piss. The only ones we need to concern ourselves with are those in front of the stage. If we keep the crowd laughing, we're golden." No sooner had the words left my mouth when 5 large cloudy looking shots appeared in front of us. "What the fuck are they? Who ordered these?" We looked at the barman and he just smiled and gestured behind us. As we turned around it was Damien. Unbeknown to us, he'd been watching us from the other side of the bar. "Alright boys. I just spoke to Tanya (the choreographer). She said you lot are absolute dog shit, and the worst excuse for a boy band she's ever seen." She also said "you seem to be that devoid of rhythm she wonders if you can even manage to pull yourselves off." We all began to smirk. "Anyways, fuck her, what does that cow know about being legends. I heard what you girls were whispering about, and I just wanted to add something to it. No one cares if you can dance or not dance. What we do care about is that you give it your all. If people can see that you're trying your best, you will win the support of the crowd, including your managers. Now get these shots down you and get back in there." It was funny. It was the first truly supportive thing we'd heard from Damien and his timing was impeccable. "Are you having one with us

Damien?" One of the others asked. "Fuck no, am not drinking that shit." He bellowed in his raspy voice. "Wankers drink that. Now get it down you and get back to ballet." We all laughed. He took a long sip of his pint as each of us proceeded to take down the shots. It was horrid. I guessed it was hierbas. It looked like a chlamydia-laden specimen and had the delicate texture of sulphuric acid. I shuddered as the cloudy alcoholic urine hit the back of my oesophagus. We finished our beers and returned to class. By the time we'd had a pep talk and Tanya had gone back over the routine, the alcohol was beginning to kick in. No one cared. Rather than focus on our routines and timing, everyone began to ham up their performances. It was as if we all had taken on our alter egos. Gone were the trainees from different parts of the country. Edinburgh had begun to strut around like Mick Jagger, we also had a Steven Tyler, a Michael Jackson, a Robbie Williams and Bristol was pouting like Freddie Mercury. Even Tanya started to laugh when she wasn't barking at Bristol for kneeling when the rest of us were spinning. For the next 20 minutes or so of the practice we were pratting about and trying to outdo each other at every attempt. By the time we got to lunch we were in good spirits and everyone had forgotten the stress and grief we'd had to deal with previously.

Lunch passed quite quickly. Everyone seemed to be preoccupied with the cabaret and what was to come after. You see, once the performances were finished, we were going to be having a debriefing. It was at this point that we would then be told whether we were a) acceptable to the company and moving forwards to become "Overseas Representatives" and b) which resorts we were going to be given. We'd previously been asked which resort would be our first choice and which would be our last. We'd already filled this in on a form we were sent where we also had to list our experiences, talents, short biographies etc. Listening around the tables you could hear that most people were keen to go back to the resorts where they'd first experienced the company and the fun that came with it. I was no exception, first choice for me was going to be Magaluf, but my last choice was going to Tenerife. No real reason for that, I'd never been there, but some of my school friends' parents had time shares there and had been going to Playa de las Americas for Christmas every year for as long as I can remember and as far as I knew, both he and his mate who always went there, were both virgins. It made sense to avoid that resort!

Once lunch was out the way, the last practice session flew past. In fact, we spent more time dicking around with our costumes and props than we did with actually performing any routines. Bristol who was clearly taking the pep talk to heart appeared with a big bottle of coke that he'd bought in the supermarket next door. He brought in some paper cups with him. "Here you go guys," he said "we all need some energy." I tried to refuse him as I was full from my lunch and am not the biggest lover of coke. He just interrupted me. "Trust me, you'll be needing this shortly when you're tired" and his eyes widened in that way when someone is trying to communicate something to you without letting the wider group know. I immediately understood and gratefully took a cup. I took a sip, and immediately felt the taste of Jack Daniels. "Why thank you kind sir" I mused as Bristol immediately turned around to refuel the rest of the T Birds. To be honest, we'd had a small glass of wine with lunch, and coupled with the shit we'd had to drink earlier and the beer, I was already feeling woozy. That aside, Bristol was a legend for doing this. It was almost like he was trying to apologise to the group for making us repeat the routine so many times and also to thank us for trying to help him and keep him positive. Fucking hero. One of the senior reps came into the room and told everyone playtime was over and we needed to bring ourselves and our costumes to the main hall as were about to get started. Everyone was excitedly moving as a herd, arms full of various props and costume pieces, trying to remember various lines, routines, and timings. All except the T-birds. We were too busy trying to find another bottle of Cola. The hotel shop wasn't opening for another 2 hours, and the bar was at the wrong end of the complex and we didn't have time to get there. In the end it was Edinburgh who made a mad dash for glory. He managed to nip past the seniors claiming he'd left part of his costume in his room, and would be back in 2mins. They told him to hurry. He went straight to the bar and ordered a small bottle of coke. He figured if he suddenly came back with three or four, or even two glasses of coke it would look suspect. At least if he came back with a small bottle, he could claim it was in his room. Anyways, he was back a few minutes later. No sooner had his ass hit the seat next to us, Bristol sprang into action. His hands moving under the table smoother than Han Solo conversing with Greedo. He topped it off with as much JD as he dared whilst still leaving the cola looking dark enough that no one was any the wiser. A few short moments (and the odd spillage) later and we were all passing round the bottle. The warmth of this toddy helping to overcome the performance anxiety that I was nursing. As I looked around the table, I marvelled at how close we'd become. It's funny really. This rather unassuming podgy trainee from Bristol who couldn't dance for toffee, had inadvertently brought us all together. The fact that he had gone and bought a bottle of JD to help carry himself and us through the performance as well as inadvertently implicating us in his crime had united the T-birds. We weren't interested in what the other groups were doing. We weren't looking at girls nor were we competing for attention or playing who could be the biggest dickhead. We were just happy with each other's company, sharing a drink and a private joke within the group. I hoped wherever I was posted I was going to be with some if not all of the lads. Pretty soon the performances kicked off. The senior reps went first with an old cabaret sketch called Six by four. This was unexpectedly entertaining and it involved them detailing that if they were not a holiday rep then what profession would they choose to be. They would then utter a random profession with innuendos and sexual references of an activity that they would be doing i.e. a hairdresser would be offering blows or a horse jockey would be offering rides… it all seems rather puerile now, but witnessing it first hand was funny and the reps knew what they were doing and were extremely graphic and vocal. They really set the bar. Then we had the next group. It was a selection of the female trainees. They basically did a Spice Girls' tribute act. All of us were cheering. As cheesy as it was, we wanted to offer them encouragement, and besides… the JD was beginning to settle in nicely. Not to mention some of the reps were fit and what's not to like seeing some of them shoehorn themselves into tight numbers with short skirts. Leeds was there. She was Sporty Spice. Despite her having to wear a Liverpool "trackie" she still managed to squeeze herself into a sporty crop top and was jiggling around all over the place. In fact, whilst I was busy watching two puppies wrestling in a pillow case, I ended up missing my swig of the coke. By the time I realised where it was, the bottle was empty and everyone was laughing at me. Edinburgh piped up "A ya daft bastard, ye put pink before drink, that waz yah first mistake!" – the rest laughed, and pretty soon I was laughing with them. At that point Damien gave us the tap – we were up next.

We made our way back stage. We started to get into our white boiler suits. Our leather jackets were already being strategically placed around the edges of the stage. The intention was that we could just grab them quickly as we stripped out of our boiler suits to reveal tight black t-shirts (sleeves rolled up over the shoulder) and dark jeans. Some of us had cigarettes and others had combs to complete the look. Tanya was present. She was trying to tell us something about the routine and to remember which bars to move on etc. Obviously, we paid her exactly zero attention. Something else had our focus. Damien had another tray of shots. "Oh, for fuck sake! Really?" I moaned. "Yep" he replied. "Only this time there isn't 5, there's 6." Damien's devious expression softened a little. It was as if we'd received his acceptance. We knew he was a good bloke underneath the tough exterior, but it was touching to hear. We all reached forward and took a shot each, leaving the 6th there on the tray for him. At this point, Bristol chirped up "Thanks Damien, really appreciate your support. On three?" "Fuck no!" hollered Damien. "I'm not drinking that shit. Tanya get it down you." She begrudgingly accepted her share of the piss and turned to face us. Damien ditched the tray, grabbed his beer, and said "whatever happens next, whatever the fuck up, whatever the issue, don't stop, smile, try and smile again! Now down that piss you're on in 30 seconds." I'm not sure what hit us more, Damien refusing yet another shot with us or the actual taste of it. The next thing we knew we were being introduced and we filed out to take our place on the stage. The stage went dark and the crowd fell silent as everyone waited for the music to kick in. We all stood motionless and nervous. I tried to recite the routine in my head one last time as I looked down at my feet. I think I got only about 20% of the way through it when the intro kicked in. It was an excerpt from the film Grease. Danny is having a discussion about the race with Kenickie, when one of them mentions Greased Lightning... all of a sudden, the music kicked in, the lights came up and we're in full swing. Everyone remembers their place and the routine begins. Even Bristol seemed to know what he was doing. Well at least I thought he did for the first 10 seconds. The first time we needed to kneel he forgot and was late. By the time he knelt we were already on our way up. When we span to the left, he went to the right. At first, we felt silly. The synchrony and therefore the routine had been effectively ruined but then it dawned on us. The crowd were going mad. They were chanting his name, and cheering. Even the waiters and waitresses tasked with handing out refreshments had stopped and were smiling. It had clearly dawned on Bristol too. I looked across at Edinburgh he looked back at me in disbelief. Bristol had stepped out of the line and was adlibbing. We continued to do the routine as we'd been told. Kneeling and gesturing left to right with our arms. Next, we were up and spinning in unison (minus Bristol of course). Bristol just stood there out front doing a kind of shuffle. At one point he tweaked his own nipples. What the fuck? Did he really just pull his own nipples? I started laughing mid routine. Tanya put her head in her hands but was also clearly laughing. As the music dropped to another excerpt from the film and the light dimmed allowing us to strip out of the boiler suits, one of the lads waltzed over to Bristol to pull him jokingly back into the routine. Boilers off, leathers on, combs out. Such was the buoyancy of the crowd, that we decided it was time to ham it up. Again, Freddie Mercury, Michael Jackson, Steven Tyler, Mick Jagger and Robbie Williams appeared. The more ridiculous we acted, the funnier the crowd found us. The last half of the routine just flew. We relaxed, enjoyed the moment and before we knew it, took a bow. We were elated. People were still cheering Bristol's name as the lights went dark and the curtain closed. Some of the senior reps came around to greet us and to tell us how funny we were. Tanya was hugging all of us. Despite not showing her choreography in the best light, she was still proud of us. Her assignment was complete.

As we stood there revelling in what had just happened the male reps quickly jostled us out from the back of the stage. It was time for the grand finale. The male seniors were going to be doing the final act. We jubilantly took our places back in the crowd. I managed to clock eyes with Leeds as I sat down. She gave me a thumbs up, I shot her a big smile and a wink. The room was already energetic when one of the senior reps took to the mic. She was on the stage thanking all of us for our contributions and asking if everyone was having a good time. Who was glad they came? Who's looking forward to resort? Who wants to see more? The atmosphere was great. It was a like a Toni Robbins seminar. People were whistling and cheering, even when they shouldn't have been (or maybe that was just Bristol- still revelling in the JD infused whisky or the dopamine release he received from tweaking his own man-boobs). "Now who's ready to see how it's going to be done by the seniors?" The crowd cheered. "Keep an eye on this dance guys, you'll be learning it as you get out in resort where most of you will be performing this in front of hundreds if not thousands of guests every week!" At this point the crowd pulled back a little. We were now curious to see what was coming next. No sooner had she said the words, when the lights went dark, and the older male reps all dressed in dark suits took their positions. The crowd fell silent. I could just about make out Damien at the side and a few of the others.

After 10-15 seconds, the first bars of the music kicked in. It was the Gary Glitter number from the Full Monty. We recognised it instantly. The girls went mad. Most of the guys just sat back intently. One by one a spot light illuminated a different member of the group. Once they were all on, they started. For the next 1-2 minutes the reps in unison removed most of their clothing. The girls at this point had gathered around the front of the stage and were baying for flesh. Most of the guys in the audience were cheering and whistling. The seniors were all smiling but professional in their approach. Each knew the routine and all had the correct, matching costumes. I guess there was no way they were going to be outdone by the trainees. As the music began to peak the males were down to thongs and hats. None of us were quite sure how far they were going to take it. Our curiosity was soon answered. The peaked hats were lowered to waist height, and with one full swoop the thongs were ripped off. The whole place roared like a rugby final. The lights then switched to a strobe effect, and with the widest of smiles the hats were flung into the crowd revealing the reps in all their glory. The girls immediately started to point in uncontrollable fashion immediately looking at their sorority sisters to show them what they were witnessing. Although it wasn't as if the girls next to them hadn't already seen the 5 or 6 naked pricks that were hanging literally a foot above eye level on the stage. A short second after and the guys shot off the stage revealing shiny arses that hadn't seen the sun in decades. The girls loved it. They were all giggling and sniggering to themselves. The male trainees just looked at each other. I mean it was good fun and fair play to them for going the whole hog with saveloys out, but there was also this uneasy feeling that we were going to be doing that very thing every single week in front of hundreds if not thousands.

We started to discuss amongst ourselves. We didn't get very far, the DJ put on some music and within a few minutes people were dancing and drinks were being served. This went on for another 20 - 30 minutes. By the time the music had stopped, the big boss was on the stage joined by all of the senior reps. "How are you all doing? Did you guys enjoy that?" he asked. Everyone immediately began to pipe down and sit back in their places. He proceeded to give a quick speech about how well we'd all done and thanked us for our efforts in not just the performance but the week in general. He said it's often difficult to appreciate that whilst it feels like a jolly being flown out to a hotel in another country and being given a good time with drink and food, you are in fact here to work. He said we'd struck the perfect balance and that whilst it was no doubt tiring at times, he'd hoped we had enjoyed it and that we were looking forward to getting to resort. He then went further to remove anyone's doubts about the program. He told us that everyone had passed and that no one was going to be sent home without an offer. I never really took that threat seriously, or at the least ever thought it would apply to me so I sat there motionless, but you could tell some in the room were instantly relieved. He then passed the mic over to one of the other senior reps who then went through the next bit. She was going to read out the resort and then the names of the people who were going there. She said in advance that they had tried to get everyone their first choice where appropriate, but couldn't please everyone. We then got a quick speech about how it didn't really matter where we would end up. It was going to be an experience of a lifetime regardless and she said we should have no hesitation in going to wherever we would be placed. I remember thinking to myself fuck that. I don't want to go to Tenerife if no one is getting laid there. She then read out the first resort… "Bodrum." The whole room fell silent. You could hear a pin drop. One by one she listed those who were going to Bodrum. She then repeated the process with all of the other resorts around the Mediterranean. Faliraki, Kos, Ayia Napa, Malia, Zante, Gran Canaria, Playa de Las Americas… As she went through the lists you would hear the occasional 'Yes!' or the murmurs as people didn't get what they'd hoped for. In general people seemed pretty happy. Neither myself, Bristol nor Edinburgh had received their placements yet. "Next up, Magaluf." Here we go. I was ready. She read out 4 or 5 names, but mine wasn't one of them. Shit. "And last but not least…" I took a deep breath as she read out the next only to hear Leeds name. Leeds was happy enough. The girls sat around her encouragingly touched her on the shoulder. I smiled too, but deep down I was gutted. I really wanted to head there. I'd been there before a few times, knew the score and knew that it was a real shagging resort. I tried to hide my disappointment.

"Which brings me on to the last and largest resort…. Ibiza!" As she finished saying those words, half the group let out a cheer. She read out the names and within the first three or four mine was called out. Followed shortly by Bristol and Edinburgh. Immediately I was being patted on the back and being told we were lucky bastards by some of the guys that had been posted around Greece. I partook in the congratulations but deep down I was still disappointed. I'd never been to Ibiza. I liked to go clubbing and liked house music, so assumed I wouldn't have a problem, but I was longing for Magaluf. That being said, after the 4th or 5th person had told me how lucky I was to be going to Ibiza (despite my brave face masking my irritation), I began to ease off. I mean these guys had gone there, I hadn't. Maybe they knew something I didn't.

We had a further debriefing for about 20 minutes, but most people were already chatting in their groups. The time was about 8'o'clock, but we were told that we had the night off and that if anyone wanted to go out there was a coach going to a local strip of bars at 9pm and returning at 1am. Most of us were flying around midday the following day, so we were told coaches would be leaving for the airport around 9:30. If we missed our flight or our transfer, costs were on us and not going to be met by the company. As soon as this speech was over, the whole place began to clear. Everyone chatted noisily with each other about their respective resorts, anxious to find out who they would be working with. It was agreed we would meet back in the bar 20 minutes later ready to go out. I shot back to the room. I quickly packed up as much as I could so I wouldn't need to bother doing it all afterwards. I was still put out about Magaluf but my disappointment was short lived. I was already back in the hotel bar earlier than most of the others. I started chatting with one of the seniors. He had already spent two seasons in Ibiza and knew I was being posted there. He asked me how I felt. My initial response of Ok, failed to hide my disappointment. He was a little taken back. "Why aren't you happy to go to Ibiza?" He asked. When I told him I'd never been there, and that I really wanted to go to Magaluf, he burst out laughing. This grated on me. I felt he was taking the piss. "Why are you laughing?" I defensively replied. "Mate, Magaluf is shite compared to Ibiza. You were chosen to go to Ibiza for one reason and one reason only. Sales. Everyone can see you can sell, and you're smart, and quite frankly don't give a fuck. We know you're at university, and we know you can do this job standing on your head. We are sending you to

Ibiza because we think you're capable of earning the company and yourself a load of cash. Cash that won't be available to us or you in Magaluf or Greece, or Turkey combined." My stance softened a little. "In fact, you were one of Damien's first choices. Everyone knows he doesn't fuck about, and no one was going to argue against him. The rest of us were well pleased. You're going to love Ibiza. We have several thousand guests a week. You know what that means don't you?" He paused for a moment. "An infinite number of blowjobs, hand jobs, threesomes and cash! You'll not only pay off your student loan, but you'll come back wedged up. Honestly, it's the best resort. Most people who come to Ibiza, can't afford to go to all the big clubs, so we're an attractive proposition. You try selling our packages in Greece or Spain where there's cut price booze, and local bar crawls every night. Trust me. You'll be knee deep in pesetas and minge before you know it." This last line made me chuckle. I began to break into a smile, and my mood lightened. "It's really that good?" I asked. "It is. To be fair, it wouldn't have mattered where you end up, you're going to have the experience of a lifetime, but Ibiza is just awesome. There's a reason why there's three times as many reps there as there are in Magaluf." "Go on" I beckoned. "Simple, three times as much pussy and pesetas. It's not rocket science!" We both had a laugh. Our conversation was cut short by the others who made their way into bar. Bristol and Edinburgh were elated that they got Ibiza. They too helped to suppress my doubts as they recounted stories and experiences, they'd both received in San Antonio, and how they were looking forward to getting stuck in. Everyone seemed to be so enthusiastic about it, I began to forget all about Magaluf. I also knew that my street cred at University would benefit from everyone knowing that I was going to be living in Ibiza over the extended break. I mean, most of us were skint and could barely muster a week away. Some of my friends would end up working in local newsagents and supermarkets, or picking fruit in France over the break. I was going to be working in one of the world's most popular clubbing meccas.

As their comments began to sink in, I soon lost my resistance to the idea, and a wave of positivity began to wash over me. Now, was this the thought of going to Ibiza or was it the beer kicking in, probably a mixture of both. Besides, it was our last night here of course, and everyone was determined to make the most of it. Spirits were high as we finished our drinks and headed for the bus.

When they said that they'd laid on transport for us, we all assumed it was going to be a coach, or something suitable to fit everyone on. Apparently not. The coach was in fact a minibus. I think officially it should probably sit 12, maybe 14 at a push. By the time we'd paid our bill and left the hotel, there were probably nearer 30 people on there. People were sat on laps upon laps. "Fuck that" sighed Bristol. "Yeah, let's just get a cab!" I mused. Within seconds of shouting taxi, several cars pulled up. They were all Mercedes of yesteryear, with big worn leather seats that felt as familiar as your favourite trainers, or your old high school fuck buddy. Each taxi driver was fiercely jostling for our attention. I guess off-peak meant work was in short supply. A few minutes later and we were in a bar. It seemed to be the busiest bar on the strip. In fact, it was the only one with disco lights on. Soon enough the rest of the sardines managed to arrive having extracted themselves from the 14-seater death trap. The bar staff couldn't believe their luck. Everywhere else on the strip was dead, if not closed, and they just landed the biggest if not the only group of young promiscuous pissheads currently on the island. Within minutes of the larger group arriving, there were trays of shots being laid out and some dubious coloured fish bowls with straws longer than most people's arms. I won't go into the details of the rest of the evening, because, quite frankly, I don't really remember it. The bar itself was a dive, but the company was electric. Emotions were on full display. Tears of happiness, tears of sadness, tears of pain. We were a competitive bunch, so any sort of challenge you could think of was being thrown around. Press ups, pint downing, shot downing, breakdancing, karaoke. You name it, it was attempted. By the time everyone ended back up in the hotel, everyone was hammered. Some had lost items of clothing; others had lost decency. I wish I could tell you how I swept Leeds up into my arms and took her back to my hotel room to give her the nailing her sporty crop top deserved; alas it wasn't meant to be. A mixture of poor timing on my part with alcohol causing me to miss signals and poor timing on her part with regards to her being on blocks meant the most we managed was a drunken fumble in the corridor, and some loose intentions of trying to visit each other at University when we got back to the UK. Of course, we never saw each other again, but it was a nice end to a nice week.

The following morning, everyone was hanging. Most people missed breakfast, and the special few that didn't appear to have a hangover proceeded to waltz around the hotel restaurant like Cinder-fuckin-rella. Don't you just hate those people. They took absolute pride in telling everyone how great they felt and how they didn't need any paracetamol. In fact, one went so far as to say he'd been to the gym. Wanker. I could just about manage to hold my orange juice down. We filed on to the coach like zombies. We were shadows of our former selves. By the time we got to the airport, most of us were starting to perk up. A group of reps were laughing really hard amongst themselves. I wandered over out of curiosity and asked what was going on. "Have you not heard?" was the response. "What?" "James threw up and passed out under a shower in someone else's room last night and rather than wake him up and take him to his own room, they let him sleep in the shower cubicle slumped in the corner like something out of the Crying Game." Ok, I thought to myself, but that's not that funny. There must be something else. I didn't have long to wait. "The best bit. Someone had poured Immac on his nut and just left it on there. Spiteful bastards." The rep broke out into laughter again, as did the other two standing with him. I couldn't believe what I was hearing. I had to see it. "Where is he?" The rep pointed to a dishevelled wreck of a man, crumpled into an airport chair with people standing all around him. I approached. As I drew nearer, I could see what everyone was laughing at. This poor guy had a dark, thick head of hair on his bonce the night before, but now he resembled nothing more than a manky old leopard. His hair was patchy, and with every person who ran their fingers through it, it was becoming worse. I couldn't help but smirk. "Are you alright mate?" I asked him. "Yeah, I'll live." He replied. "Bastards! I'll have to shave it all off now. My girlfriend hates skinheads. She's going to be well moody about this. I don't even remember going back to the hotel so I have no idea who even did it." I thought I'd try and make light of the situation and try and console him. "It's not that bad. Besides, your hair will grow back. It could have been worse. It could have been your brows! Imagine losing those bad boys. Your missus would really have issue then." He reluctantly agreed, before he went on to issue a loosely targeted threat "When I find out which wanker did this, he's in trouble." As soon as the words left his lips, the rest of the group started to laugh. I could tell he instantly regretted saying the words out loud and within a few short moments he couldn't help it but a broad reluctant smile broke out across the face of this festering old feline. The rest of the conversation that followed involved a collaborative effort in trying to piece back together the night's events and to formulate a timeline that everyone could somehow relate to. The group dispersed shortly after that, as some were flying to London, Manchester, Edinburgh and even Glasgow. Efforts were made to dispense emails and telephone numbers with promises to keep in touch and suggestions of meeting up again before we all went to resort. Eventually my flight was called and I said goodbye to those that were left and filed on to the plane. I was asleep before we even took off.

CHAPTER 7
IBIZA: MY ARRIVAL

I'm not sure what my parents thought when I first told them that I was going to live/work in Ibiza. I think initially they were proud of me that I had been accepted for the job, but were probably somewhat concerned about what type of trouble I could get myself into whilst there. They knew I was relatively smart and clued up, but at the same time also knew that I was impulsive and usually took the bait on any type of challenge. I think what must have helped ease their concerns was that my parents had their honeymoon in Ibiza and were therefore full of fond memories from yesteryear. When they thought of Ibiza, I like to think they were seeing images of lazy afternoon beach strolls in Portinaxt or dinners in a local restaurant and a stroll along the coastline of Cala St Vicente as opposed to the boozy bar crawls and casual sex of San Antonio or the drug fuelled night clubs littering the main carriageway between San Antonio and Elvissa.

The minute I got back to University after the Easter break, I was immediately envied. My course mates and friends at uni couldn't believe I'd actually got the job and I was actually going to be paid to go clubbing and be given free drinks every night of the week. I was continually baited and abused for it for the rest of the term. One day after lectures Mike took me to one side. "You know what this means?" I looked at him puzzlingly. He quickly followed up. "You need to get yourself in shape. Competition in Ibiza will be tough. Whilst you'll be getting loads of birds, you need to make sure they're quality and not pull-a-pig." I laughed. He wasn't wrong. I hadn't really thought about it until then. "We need to get in the gym and quick smart!" Whilst I wasn't out of shape by any means, I did like a drink and I wasn't exactly built. I trained a couple of times a week but it was more a social thing. I immediately saw that I needed to up my gym game if I was to up my quality out there. For the next 6 weeks it was gym 3-4 times a week. I ate healthier, I ran more, we were hitting the beach muscles most sessions. Typical adolescent males… leg days were skipped continually! One day it was chest and arms. The following session it was arms and chest. Back was thrown in for good measure, and every day was abs day! I had to admit, I was quietly happy with my progress. Nothing moves a guy forwards than the lure of a fit girl. There was no way in the world I, as a rep with a bit of banter, was going to settle for swamp donkeys that I could already nab ten to two at the student union.

The next 6 weeks seemed to flash by. No sooner had I got back to studies and to the gym it was time to start packing for resort. Each of us had been issued with a big welcome pack listing all the things we would need to take with us. There were the Grease outfits, the Full Monty strip show outfits, wacky outfits for bar crawls. Themes like Drs and nurses, porn stars (think 70s lush), sportsmen, and of course usual gear to go out in during the nights when it was "relatively" normal. Every weekend and usually even midweek I could be seen frequenting the local charity shops looking for various outfits and articles of clothing, hoping to save a few quid here and there. Eventually I managed to get everything packed up. Oh, and condoms. Lots and lots of condoms. I think I packed so many prophylactics in my case that should a baggage handler drop the bag it probably would have bounced back off the tarmac. There were high expectations for sure. Not just mine either. My Dad grinned at me and threw me a packet when Mum wasn't looking. Little did he know that I already had enough latex to coat a Concorde! As I left the university digs, I recall Mike and my flatmates all wishing me luck and taking great pleasure in wishing me every STI under the sun. I recall flipping the bird as I left, asking them to save some of that fruit they were going to be picking. My family took me to Gatwick. I was excited but nervous. Not knowing what to expect. We were running a bit late due to traffic, but it probably did us all a favour. By the time we got there, we only had time for a quick au revoir and I was off.

When I finally got to resort, it was late afternoon. Most of the reps had already arrived a few weeks prior, but due to some university assignments, I wasn't able to get out to resort earlier. I was a little irritated by this, as it meant I was starting at a disadvantage. Most of them all started from the same position together and had already started forming bonds with one another, and if truth be told, I felt like an outsider. I wasn't the only one. Another rep was also starting with me, he too had coursework he couldn't get out of, and he arrived a few hours earlier than me. His name was Nigel, and he was from Reading. He seemed cordial and pleasant enough. If anything, he seemed a little quiet, almost retiring. I couldn't really make him out. I was glad he was pretty relaxed though. I was hoping to ease myself into this, and the last thing I needed was a jackass wannabe, trying to prove how reckless he could be and mouthing off. We started to get to know each other. He confided he was a bit nervous and didn't know what to expect. I was relieved to hear it and told him that was exactly how I was feeling. I quipped that we needed to find a few birds to warm up and he laughed. The resort of San Antonio had basically been divided up into areas. We were both assigned to the same area thankfully. We had been told to report to the sales office at 5.30pm. Where we were going to meet the rest of the team etc. The sales office was basically a small room that had been pinned on to the back of a hotel near the maintenance area. The place looked like a bomb had ripped through it. There were flyers, props, promotional t-shirts and just general shit laying everywhere. When they said office, I was expecting desks and monitors, not the remnants of a crack house.

We walked in and were immediately greeted in that familiar abusive voice we both knew and loved. "Look what the cats brought in. Come and grab a seat you pair of tarts!" It was Damien. For one reason or another we'd been assigned to his team, and whilst I knew he was going to be riding us all season, I was kind of glad. I figured at least he was the one constant I could count on as my world was about to get flipped upside down. We both took a seat. We were on time, but the rest of the team were still on their way back. He reached behind his desk and chucked us both a couple of backpacks. I peered inside, mobile phone, emergency contact list, list of everyone in resort (reps and managers), couple of t-shirts, and a pair of large foam hands (for waving like a cock in the airport). He said the phones needed to come back at the end of the season, the rest of the kit was ours.

Damien informed us that for the first two weeks, we weren't going to be working as reps. We would be assisting them during the day time with admin, and in the evening, we would be observing the other reps to see what they were doing, and how they were doing it. We were to officially act as holiday makers, and we weren't allowed to tell anyone we were reps or in training. When he told us initially, I felt a mix of emotions. I was initially relieved, because it gave us a breather and a chance to see how it's done and to know what we were letting ourselves in for, but on the flip side, not starting as reps meant that quite frankly there was a delay to getting into the crumpet. I also figured it wouldn't help us close the gap that was forming between the reps that were already working in resort and Nigel and I the outsiders. Damien reiterated the part about not telling the other holidaymakers we were reps. "If I hear or catch you smashing any of the guests, or using the rep lines, you'll both be bounced out of resort quicker than you arrived! Use this time to observe and learn. You have the rest of the season to get your little shrivelled ends away. Am I understood?" "Yes Damien," we meekly replied. With that, the door burst in and the rest of the wolf pack sloped in. They looked tired and irritable and were collectively whinging about something. Nigel and I looked at each other trying to work out what to make of it all. Damien stepped in with the subtlety of a breeze block. "Shut the fuck up and sit down. You're late and we have a sales meeting to get through. Firstly, I want to introduce you to your new team mates, tweedled dick and tweedled dunce. You should know them already from Majorca. They're going to be assisting you in day to day, but observing in the evening for one complete cycle." "On a jolly? Lucky bastards!" said Terry. One of the reps from Sheffield. Damien immediately squashed that. "It's not a fucking jolly. Besides asshole, you had two weeks at the beginning of season to observe the seniors to see how it's done, so wind it in." That was that. The rest of the team kind of smiled in our direction, but quite frankly, they all looked knackered and I don't think they gave a shit one way or the other.

Damien then proceeded to go through the day's sales, checking off the hotels' commissions versus their targets, his area versus the resort, and individual performances within the team. I have to say it wasn't particularly pleasant, but it was fair. This type of meeting was to be held daily just before dinner, as it gave every rep a chance to turn in any cash or documentation they'd taken as well as receiving an update and an itinerary on the evening's entertainment ahead. They did a quick run through of what was on in the evening. Thankfully it was just a bar crawl, but given the sheer number of potential holiday makers in resort at any one time, they needed to split the group into smaller crawls, and then agree to meet up in a nightclub at a perceived time. I didn't think about it initially as everything was a lot to take in, but I assumed the company as a whole got a decent kick back from the various bar owners and night club owners in the resort. After all, even the mini bar crawls could have anything from 100-400 guests at any moment in time, and by the time we got to the club, it could have been anything from 500-2000 if not more. That's a lot of horny teenagers looking to party and buy drinks! The whole meeting lasted approximately 40 minutes before he cut us loose. Nigel and I specifically were told to go back to our hotel (we wouldn't be assigned flat mates or apartments until the two weeks were up) and be ready to meet at 7.30 in the evening. The minute we left Nigel opened up. "I'm glad we are getting a couple of weeks to settle in. It looks like quite hard work judging by the rest of them!" "Agreed, but am a little disappointed not to be able to tell anyone." I retorted. "I wanted to get started early doors." Nigel had the right idea. He said "We don't have to tell them outright. We could just intimate that we're undercover. Besides, reps or no reps, we've just been given a two-week paid holiday!" Nigel was right. We had essentially been given a life line, and whilst we needed to observe what the reps were doing, it didn't stop us from observing the rest of what Ibiza had to offer. We went back to the hotel, grabbed a quick bite to eat and then got ready for what would be laying ahead.

We met in the hotel bar at 7.30 as requested. The bar was already packed with holiday makers in various states of tan and sunburn. Nigel and I both stuck out like sore thumbs. I hadn't seen the sun in about 3 months due to studies, and Nigel was paler than milk. We walked over to the bar to get a couple of drinks. As we ordered a couple of beers and went to pay, we heard a high-pitched voice come over the bar. "Miguel, those two on my tab please. Remember our little chat earlier?" We spun around to be greeted by Laura, the rep for the hotel. "Are you sure?" I asked. "She said yeah, it's fine, reps don't buy drinks. We all have tabs in our hotels, but as long as the hoteliers see you're doing a good job and you get the punters buying drinks, you won't pay for a thing all season. The same goes for food. It's not official so offer to pay initially, but once they get the measure of you, they'll just add it to some imaginary bill." "Happy days" exclaimed Nigel "So, what's the plan now?" he asked. "Now we're going to wait for 30-40 minutes, until everyone is here and ready, then we're going to hit the first bar. I normally like to spend an extra 10 or 15 minutes in the hotel bar just to keep the owners happy and on my side. Our main job here is to get everyone warmed up and to ensure that all the guests feel comfortable around each other. We'll do a couple of drinking games in a bit and we'll encourage groups to start talking to each other. The more the clients are able to have a good time with everyone else, the easier our jobs will be. Don't worry if it seems a bit overwhelming now. Everyone was like that a few weeks ago, but once you get in the groove, it's great." She was reassuring us but then she suddenly needed to break away as one of the hoteliers needed to speak to her about something.

Nigel and I turned to the bar just as Miguel placed the bottles down. "Hola, soy Miguel. Welcome to our hotel, and welcome to Ibiza." We introduced ourselves in return and thanked him for the drinks and the hospitality. "First time here?" We both nodded. He let out a big broad smile and said in a deep Spanish accent "you guys are going to love it here. You'll have so much pussy you won't know what to do with it." I spluttered my beer, Nigel's eyes widened, and the three of us started to laugh. At that point, Miguel reached under the counter and placed a couple of shots down next to us. "Chupitos for our new reps!" he exclaimed grabbing a third. The three of us took the shot. Fortunately, it was a sickly schnapps. It was sweet and not great, but better than the hierbas shit they'd had us drink before in Majorca. Miguel continued to serve the other holiday makers. Some of whom were already ordering ridiculously strong drinks despite it being early. "I could get used to this" beamed Nigel. At which point, a couple of girls who had been behind us interrupted and asked if we were reps, having overheard Miguel. I just smiled, but Nigel lent over and whispered that we were undercover. He told them that we'd been flown out to Ibiza to observe the reps and to report to management on how things were going. He then asked them not to say anything as only a few knew and it was important that it didn't get out. The girls seemed nice and agreed not to say anything and then started saying how they didn't think they could do the job as they would be too nervous etc. They intimated that we must be super confident and totally crazy and they didn't know how we did it. We just smiled. I couldn't believe it. This stuff was actually working and we didn't even have the tags round our neck yet. Hell, we hadn't even left the hotel bar, on the first day of our first season. We continued making small talk. Whenever we tried to pay for a drink, Miguel insisted on not taking payment. After about half an hour and some pretty basic drinking games, the room was warmed up, people were chatting and it already looked like some couples were pairing up. Laura pointed a few out and said this is exactly what she was hoping for. She then announced to the room that we were moving on to the next bar. She gave Miguel a quick peck, and led us out in the direction of the main strip.

Despite it being early, the strip was awash with neon lights, loud music, and touts trying to pick off the stragglers. Although Nigel and I were already warmed up and trying to stick near to the girls, we made a point of walking alongside Laura. She was doing her best to shepherd the holiday makers through this technicolour jungle. She was pointing out various bars and clubs along the way as we waltzed down one of the main avenues of San Antonio. Outside most of the bars, various touts were beginning to work. They would hang around on the strip and purposely interrupt or block the paths of young holiday makers heading out for the evening. They were paid on the number of people they got through the door and would promise various cocktails and drink promotions to get them into their bars. Two for one, three for one, with two free shots, free fish bowl with every 5 drinks ordered, you name it they went on and on. Whilst they like us were affectionately labelled "workers" there was a complete spectrum of relationships on the strip. As time went on you would work out who were your friends, who were your enemies, and who were absolute shitheads that needed some alone time with security. More on that later. Laura already seemed to know most of them as she was acknowledging and being acknowledged as we reached the first bar. She told us how the touts were one of the biggest issues, and was why the company tended to bring their guests out early on bar crawls. The number of people on the strip began to increase sharply as time went on. If there were 200-300 people on the strip at 8pm, by 9pm, it was 500-600, by 10pm it was probably 1500 and by 11pm it was several thousand. People were also getting progressively more and more pissed as time went on, so you needed to get the guests out and into the first bar early doors to have any chance of being able to lead a sizeable percentage of them to the second bar and the third bar. After that we needed to get them into the club that they'd bought tickets for. It was like moving herds on the Serengeti. In a big group they were strong and safe, but the minute the touts started to intervene they started to scatter with the stragglers being picked off. It wasn't just the touts that would interrupt the procession. The guests themselves would often be having a good time in the first bar, maybe they were being chatted up, maybe they were enjoying their drinks, or maybe they just couldn't be bothered to move on so soon. This was fair enough, but it didn't quite fit our plan, as we had targets to achieve and we needed to make sure that we brought as many of the guests as possible into the second and third bars and finally the club. I presumed the company was being paid commission. Most of the time it wasn't an issue. Our bar crawls weren't exactly small. A large bar crawl would have seen myself and Nigel lead several hundred guests into a bar, where we would also be met with several other reps in our area and their subsequent hotels' guests. In peak season, when our company entered a bar, it could potentially be 400-500 guests or more which was a valuable part of the bar's takings for that evening. Now our company had several 'areas' each with 5-10 reps and 5-10 hotels, so from a bar/club perspective we were good business. Competition for our guests was high.

We entered the first bar. It was like a scene out of Tron. Bright neon lighting with UV light bulbs adorned every wall. When we got there, there were already about 30-50 people there. They were also holiday makers from our company. Laura advised us that it was always better to arrive slightly late if you could withstand the grief from the boss and the bar owner. As I mentioned before, not only did it mean you got your own hoteliers a bit more cash in their bar, which in turn allowed them to look after you better with free food and drink etc., but it also meant that you weren't faced with being the first to arrive at an empty bar. She said it's not the best look to be the first to an empty bar and quite often a lot of the guests will immediately do an about face and leave for somewhere else. She said at least when there's people around the dance floor and there's some life in the place the guests are more willing to give it a go. Besides, within one or two minutes the 30-50 people often become 200-300. This was all valuable advice. One of the lads approached the three of us and said the bar was shit. There was no one there and he didn't understand why we chose this place. Laura without batting an eye lid told him that the plan was to bring us to a quieter bar initially so that everyone could get a drink. She said the second bar is going to be busier, but no one wants to spend the whole night queuing for drinks. She said make use of the time now to get a couple of rounds in before moving on to the main bars. She also added that another rep was currently on route and would be here with another 200 guests, so don't hang about. Upon hearing this, the guy's position softened immediately. He put his arms around her and threw her a big kiss on the cheek. He said she's wasn't just a pretty face and that he was going to be back with a drink for her in a few moments. He asked if we also wanted a drink, to which we declined, before disappearing inside. Despite only having a few weeks head start on Nigel and I, Laura seemed to be a natural. You'd have thought she was in her 2nd or 3rd year of repping.

True to her word, within a few minutes another pair of reps arrived with their guests. What looked like a semi empty bar was now brimming. It wasn't even 9pm yet and the bars were 2-3 people deep. One of the reps took to the mic and did a few shout outs to various towns around the UK to get the crowd warmed up. He encouraged everyone to get a drink and threw a few drink promotions out there for good measure. The rest of the reps, Nigel and myself included, were huddled towards the back. We were introduced to the owner who greeted us enthusiastically. I guess we were walking cash cows. We were talking with the rest of the reps trying to gain any more insights and quizzing them on their experiences. Whilst they were open and warm enough with us, I couldn't help but feel like we were still outsiders. You could see from their body language with each other and the shared experiences they'd already notched up in these few weeks that they were already very close. I was quite surprised at that. I didn't say anything about it, but later on in the evening Nigel also mentioned how he felt like we weren't in the clique. I reassured him and told him I knew exactly what he meant. It wasn't going to take long for us to be assimilated, besides if anything, it just strengthened the bond between Nigel and I.

About 20 minutes later mic rep announced it was last

orders at this bar and that we were all moving onwards to the next one. It was important not to reveal what the next bar was, because then the guests could simply decide not leave now but to catch up with us later or to 'meet us there.' Every rep was tight lipped about this. When it was time to go, each one went to their biggest groups (from their hotels) and basically grabbed them and anyone in the surrounding vicinity and essentially walked them out of the bar and on to the strip, destined for the next one. We watched as the holiday makers were moved onwards despite some playful protesting. Others guests who were more resolute in their desire to stay at that bar found themselves up against the most outrageous flirtation from reps from both sexes. Eventually probably 95% of the people in the bar left and Nigel and I were suddenly part of a huge caravan of people marching to the next watering hole. We were both tipsy at this point and started to relax and forget that we were here to observe.

The next bar we entered was on the corner of the strip. The staff here were extremely friendly with all of the reps. Everyone was in high spirits, and the atmosphere was electric. As the holiday makers traipsed into the venue, there was an immediate roar from the crowds inside. The venue was packed. So much so, some of the guests in Laura's hotel decided to try a different place. Laura, having seen what was going on, grabbed them on their way out. She handed them a couple of drinks vouchers and suggested a bar opposite. She said keep an eye out for when everyone leaves for the club so they could re-join the group. Nigel and I having witnessed this asked her why she did that. She said she felt bad for them not having enough room and wanted to keep them happy. Also, she said she had more chance of getting them to re-join the group which will help us when we descend on the club later for admissions on the door, as well as making it easier for her to sell further tickets to them in the future.

At this point in the evening, Damien appeared. He spent most of his time talking with the bar owner and some of the more senior staff outside than he did with us or mingling with the guests. He spotted Nigel and I and approached. "How are you two bell ends? Pissed yet?" We both protested our innocence, to which he just smirked. "Sure, sure. Just remember that at 2am we have a meeting outside the front of the club! You better be there and not be off your faces or your arses are mine." We just nodded. The minute he left; we went back to the bar. The reps wanted to generally keep a low profile here and again were all huddled over the back. One of the female reps looked like she was struggling. It looked like there were some tears at one point and some general comforting going on. Nigel and I didn't really know anyone close enough and didn't want to intrude, so we opted for the other direction and just started to enjoy ourselves with the other guests.

By the time we had to head over to the club we were both pissed. We needed to be shepherded as much as the guests! In our defence neither of us knew where the club was, but the shots and beers that we were being given for free didn't exactly help to sharpen the senses. We wandered into this cavern of a club that was already jammed with other guests. It must have been just before midnight by the time we got there. Again, super early by Ibizan standards, but the place already looked like a battlefield. There were bodies everywhere. Some were making out on couches. One couple were practically dry humping on the bar. Others were being marched out by security due to their inability to stand up. They would be cut loose about 5-6 meters away from the main entrance to an area already filled with people puking and others sitting on the pavement dazed. It was carnage. Thankfully, Nigel and I weren't that bad, and could still string a sentence together between us, but we knew we had to buck our ideas up. Nigel was covered in glitter and had lipstick on his cheek from a random drive by kiss. I'd snogged someone earlier on the dance floor but then was unfortunate enough to have her spill her drink down my shirt so the pair of us were already beginning to look like extras from the movie The Hangover.

We were both on the dance floor when Laura grabbed us and brought us outside for the rep meet. I was unexpectedly apprehensive. I don't know why, I'd had enough drinks inside of me to do karaoke, but I guess Damien's warning about getting pissed sat at the back of my mind. I needn't have worried. We left the exit and approached the side of the club. The reps were all gathered there with Damien. We were out of sight of any of the guests. There seemed to be a commotion going on and he didn't look very happy. As I glanced to the left, there laying on the pavement was the rep from earlier who had been having a bad time of it. She was absolutely leathered. In comparison to her, Nigel and I could have been sober enough to be pilots. She was at that stage where she was flip flopping from singing to crying and back again. He did his best to ignore her. Am sure it wasn't the first time he'd seen this and it definitely wasn't going to be the last that season. We basically had a quick debrief. He said we'd done well to get the number of people we did to the bars, although the first bar owner was complaining that everyone was late to the bar. He proceeded to run through the itinerary for tomorrow and was checking up on how everyone was doing on their sales targets. 5-10 minutes later it was over. Nigel and I were directed to go to bed and not destroy ourselves and with that he was gone. Most of the reps decided to call it a night. A couple of them volunteered to take home the adult sized rag doll who was at this point sobbing on the pavement. Nigel and I kept our distance, and as soon as everyone had left the area, we went back into the club. Needless to say, neither of us remember getting home. The next morning, I woke up with a serious headache. My tongue which resembled a piece of sandpaper was stuck to the roof of my mouth. Judging by the packaging on the floor by the bin, the only thing I had managed to drag back with me was a burger.

CHAPTER 8
THE BALCONY MARAUDER

Any thoughts Nigel or I had of relaxing during the next two weeks flew straight out of the window. Despite us not being "official" they certainly had us working like we were. Most of our days were spent learning the admin side of the role. Whilst in resort we were obviously selling the trips, but we were also selling tickets to the company's annual weekender that was held back in the UK in autumn. Tickets for this were about £80, but the guests only had to pay a deposit whilst in resort, allowing them time to save up for the remainder. I found selling the weekend party easy, because my prior experience of one to this day still remains one of the greatest weekends of my life. People could tell how impressed I was with it. Besides the deposit was small, so it wasn't a difficult decision. Nigel and I were shown the ropes with regards to form filling, handling cash/credit cards etc, as well as general incident reports and paperwork that came hand in hand with having a hotel under your wing.

When we weren't in the office, we'd be on the roof or in a function room of one of the hotels, learning and practicing the various dances and routines we needed to perform for the nights out. The other reps were particularly prickly about doing this. I think because they were already well and truly in the groove, and we clearly weren't it caused some issues as it was eating into their downtime. It wasn't anything major, but it certainly didn't help to bridge the gap between us and the wider team. Thankfully we picked it up pretty quickly, or rather, didn't care so much about perfecting the routines. Happy to learn on the job, the reps were happy to nick off early where they could for a siesta/shag or whatever else they needed to do.

Nigel would often whinge that this seemed like too much hard work, but the truth of the matter was that we were paid to entertain, be entertained and to party. It was the best job in the world. When we did manage to actually get some downtime during the day, we would head to the pool area to get some sun and to try and make the most of the time we had left before we were dropped into the deep end. What we really wanted to do though was to get stuck in to the girls. Thankfully because we had to shadow the other reps, people were already noticing us. They'd spot us at 2am outside at the nightly rep meeting. They'd see us back stage, or conversing with Damien in areas that were off limits to guests. They'd see that we weren't paying for drinks when we were out and that bar staff and security would be friendly with us. This was magical. We didn't have to tell anyone we were reps, they sensed it, and would come over to us anyway. Despite Damien telling us we would be bounced out of resort if we started trying to capitalise on our yet to be received title, Nigel and I would continually put the spade work in. Guests would outright ask us if we were reps. At first, we'd stick to the undercover line that we'd used previously, so as to try and keep it on the down low, but as time went on and we became more and more visible things became more obvious. We dropped the undercover bit and became more open. We started to tell the guests who asked that we were reps, but just not ready to start. When pushed, we said we wanted a quick break before we started work, especially as we'd both just finished exams at uni. It sounded cooler than "we're trainees and learning the ropes."

It wasn't long before word got round the pool, and guests started to treat us differently. We both sensed it, and our confidence began to grow. The rest of the reps in the area would start to hand off little jobs to us and before you knew it, we were kind of half way in, half way out. Nigel and I would pay attention to what the reps were doing during the evening for about an hour or so, and then we'd both sly off and try to find some action of our own. Thankfully Damien never intervened. He must have known. He wasn't silly by any means, but he didn't stand in our way either. I guess he knew better than anyone that once we had the uniform and the rep tag on, we were his 24/7 for the rest of the season without a single day off so he could afford to let us have these few evenings to try and get into the swing of things.

I clearly remember Nigel was the first to get laid out there between us. She was from a group of girls who were staying in the same hotel that we were both temporarily being housed in. He couldn't wait to tell me, and I couldn't wait to hear the details. Hearing that he'd already lost his "L" plates meant I was all the more determined to lose mine. I'd also been chatting with the group alongside him but I had let booze get the better of me the night before and had missed a few signals, where he had still kept his edge. I wouldn't make the same mistake twice. I ended up putting her friend over the next night. This pattern of behaviour continued for the next week or so. Literally it was the first question we'd ask the minute we saw each other in the morning. We never told anyone else though as loose lips sink ships and we were still trying to escape Damien's watchful eye. Besides, am sure the other reps were already doing far more than we were at that point anyway and would probably have little interest in our activities.

As time went on and we distanced ourselves from our training wheels, we became bolder, more confident. We chased less, but got more attention. We were continuously on the hunt, and learning quickly as we went. Social pressures and stigmas that you grew up around just didn't exist here. No one was unapproachable or unobtainable. Everyone was friendly. Everyone was interesting to us, and we were interesting to everyone there. In reality, clearly that wasn't the case, but it didn't matter, that was how it felt. Every rep felt it. It didn't matter what you looked like, where you were from, what you had or didn't have. Of course, we still had our hang-ups and complexes, but the point was they took a very distant back seat. We would be continually having fun and flirting with guests, plying our trade. You'd learn quickly what was working, what wasn't. What you could get away with, what you couldn't. What lines made people laugh, what lines made them cringe. After 10 days of being continually on the prowl, and striking lucky maybe 40% of the time we began to find our rhythm. Now imagine what that felt like after a month, or two, or five? It was like one giant positive feedback loop. By the time I got back to the UK, I was unrecognisable to my friends back home.

Towards the end of our two-week hiatus I had a few drinks and managed to line up a cuddle after work. We always finished work at 2am (airport nights aside). I had met a girl from Birmingham. Great laugh, good banter and she worked at Miss Moneypenny's as a dancer (you can imagine the moves!). We'd finished our rep meeting, and as per usual, Nigel and I snuck back into the club on the prowl. I caught up with Miss Moneypenny, and within a drink or two we were heading back to my hotel. There was no messing around, good adult fun and giggles all round. As we lay there after, we were just generally chatting. She was telling me about her job and what she wanted to do with her life and travel plans etc. We were just continuing to get to know each other really. She was super cool, and the sort of person you could chat to for hours. All of a sudden there was a huge knock at the door. It was aggressive, I thought it was either the Guardia Civil or her boyfriend. We both looked at each other a little startled. I began to get out of bed and put some jeans on. It wasn't until I got near to the door when a loud but recognisable voice came through from the other side. "Hey, you in there? I can see the light's on. Are you awake?" Shit. It was a girl who'd I been with a few nights before. I'd bumped into her at the club earlier but had thought nothing of it. She was a lively Irish lass, and I can tell you now, if she caught me like this, it would have all kicked off big time. Instinctively Miss Moneypenny began to gather up some of her belongings. This is going to be awkward. She looked at me asking who was it? Rather than man up and tell her the truth, I took the coward's way out and lied, I figured it would be less messy all round. I still didn't have my rep's tag and the last thing I wanted was to rock the boat between guests at the hotel. I told her it was my boss. I told her that I'd forgotten to meet her to collect some paperwork and that she's probably going to drop it off. If she catches me with a guest like this, I'm history. Miss Moneypenny, was cool, she began to get dressed, but neither of us made a sound. I stood by the door quietly, but could hear the other girl knocking on the neighbours' doors to the left and right of me. No one was answering. I half expected her to go and get security to let her in to the room, so I was relieved to see Miss Moneypenny clothed and practically ready to leave. I figured as soon as the coast was clear, she'd slip out and I'd be home free. All the time this girl was knocking and shouting like a mad woman. In fact, it was so ridiculous, I was beginning to think my little story about her being my boss was about to fall flat. I didn't have that much time to think with all the racket this other one was making. Eventually she managed to wake up one of my immediate neighbours. The hotel walls were paper thin, and besides, we were practically standing the other side of the door. She began quizzing my unwitting neighbour as to my whereabouts. He obviously didn't know where I was. In fact, I don't think he even knew who I was. This wasn't enough for her though. She persuaded him to let her go through his apartment as she was coming in over the balcony. As soon as I heard his door close, I knew it was battle stations. Miss Moneypenny knew it too. She started to giggle which then set me off. I literally gave her a quick snog, and jettisoned her out of the apartment at the same time as his balcony door was pulled open. She was still laughing as she scuttled down the corridor. It was like something out of the Benny Hill show. I quietly shut the door behind her, and immediately got out of my jeans and got back in bed, pretending to be asleep. I didn't say a word. All I could hear was "mind how you go love, it's a long way down." Literally within seconds, of hearing that, my balcony door was wrenched open and I found myself being rudely shaken by a tipsy but determined young lady from Cork. Thankfully I got away with it, but it did serve as an early warning. I made sure I was more careful in my venue selection after that. When I told Nigel, he laughed, but he also confirmed my first thought. If Cork had caught me out, I would have been attacked.

This pattern of behaviour pretty much continued throughout the whole season. If anything, it intensified as time went on. By the time both of us were christened with reps' tags, we were well and truly on our way. I wish I could tell you that I found maturity, religion, a steady girlfriend, or a meaningful relationship but I'd be lying. For the next 5 months, Nigel and I tore through San Antonio as best we could. It wasn't just us lads that were misbehaving. The female reps were as bad. They were extremely predatory among the guests. They would often try and hide it initially, but it was obvious, after a few days, they would even tell you which guy they liked and if he was in your hotel, you'd do your best to try and arrange a meet. It was a case of get your end in, get your friend in! Some of the female reps between them also had a thing where they would tease the guys. They would try and get a muff dive without giving anything back and then try and duck out early for some reason or another. If they succeeded they would brag about it amongst themselves. It wasn't until Nigel overheard them and immediately spilt the beans to everyone else that this little charade became infinitely more difficult. On the quiet, we would forewarn the lads in our hotel ahead of time, pretty much putting a stop to that little caper!

Occasionally reps would get together. We were working long hours closely with one another so it was inevitable that some would become items. Sometimes such interactions would be purely physical, other-times it would be more serious, but in general, it was best to try and keep a lid on those feelings, besides, we could all see what everyone was up to. Catching or seeing the opposition playing with others, wasn't always the best basis for starting a relationship.

CHAPTER 9
SCHOOLBOY ERROR

I remember the first time we were asked to take part in a live welcome meeting. I was nervous. We'd been watching the other reps carry it out for a fortnight, so we knew what to expect, but knowing how it should turn out and actually doing it are sometimes two different things. The welcome meeting was supposed to be lively, comical but informative. We'd trained hard for it before we got to resort and now it was sink or swim time. I don't think it would have been so bad had we all started from the same point, but because the others already had the head start and had already become immune to shyness or insecurity, Nigel and I knew that we would end up looking non confident or amateurish by comparison and that just added to the pressure. Thankfully we were eased into it. We were only given small parts initially, i.e. I was talking about the hotel and resort in general, before someone else would step in and talk about the particular trips or bar crawls before someone stronger still would step in for the close. It was pretty nerve wracking to begin with, and it wasn't until my 4th or 5th welcome meeting speech (or performance) that I began to ease into it. You knew the material, you just needed to convey it in a funny and lively way. That's not to say that things always went to plan. Quite often the reps would try and trip each other up with various pranks and heckles. Sometimes the timing was perfect and it added to the overall performance, other times it was just odd and if anything broke the momentum and left guests a little puzzled. It was a fine line that some were better than others at treading. At first the slightest distraction would throw you off keel. It could be anything from something as simple as throwing a paper aeroplane at the speaker to having a bucket of water dropped on their head. The audience would laugh and the rep speaking at the time would do their best to continue despite the rest of the reps taking the piss. It was also common to be flashed from the back. That is, you're standing there speaking in front of 50 - 70 guests only to have one of the reps standing at the back to expose themselves to distract you. After a while though, even that wouldn't phase you and you'd walk around the staging area in full command of your audience.

Pretty early on in my season I remember giving the spiel about the trips and telling people about the day trip. The guests were laughing and hanging on every word I said. I was revelling in the spot light. The louder and more mischievous I became the more they laughed. What I didn't anticipate though, was what was to come next. I made a schoolboy error and one that was fully taken advantage of. I can't remember what came first, the sound of the audience's gasp or the feeling of having the lower half of my uniform instantly removed. I'd forgotten to tightly tie the drawstring at the top of my swimming shorts. One of the female reps decided to try me on, and with a quick yank on either side of my hips, my shorts instantly became ankle warmers. Female rep 1 – male rep 0. I remember looking down in the direction of my feet, noticing that my chap was poking out from beneath my t-shirt. It felt surreal standing there in front of the new arrivals who were only sat a couple of metres away from me. One minute they were listening to how they were going to be chilling out in the water park and a split second later they were looking at my beanbag. The whole audience in unison collectively switched their attention from my bits to my face looking for a reaction. I was dying inside, but didn't want to show it. I looked back at the female rep who was at this point second guessing the deed herself. Out of disgust, I slowly shook my head from side to side and then calmly announced to the room that it was the only way this "moose" was ever going to lay eyes on it. The audience laughed, the female rep blushed, and I then proceeded to carry on with my part. I made no effort whatsoever to pull up my shorts. I was about 70-80% of the way through my section anyway, so they wouldn't have long to wait. When I did eventually sign off, the audience gave me a massive cheer. I'd shown myself as someone who didn't rattle easily (even if just on the outside) and no one ever tried that on me again.

Once the welcome meeting was finished and we were split into groups to close the sale I quickly put into practice what I'd been taught with the objection handling and body language. If I do say so myself, I was a natural. I seemed to get on with everyone and people just seemed happy to pay for the trips. The senior rep in training was correct. Ibiza was so expensive for most that we offered a very attractive proposition. You didn't need to push it at all, and nor would I want to. If people wanted to do their own thing it was fine by me, but most of the time once you pulled out the drinks' receipts, club entry ticket stubs and your Fisher Price calculator, it was a bit of a no brainer. Not everyone went on them, but the vast majority. Such was my confidence when closing the deals, I used to play around with the guests and would try and make the experience more fun for them. No one liked the feeling of being sold to, even if in some situations it was for their own good. I would issue challenges to the guests. If they won, I would pay for them out of my own pocket. If they lost, they would pay there and then no questions asked. These challenges were always tongue in cheek and light hearted. I remember sitting down with a couple of girls from the west country. They were really comical. They gave as good as they got and were here for a good time and didn't care who knew it. As soon as we sat down, they were bantering with me. They were giving me abuse right out of the blocks and I loved it. These were exactly the sort of people the company catered for perfectly. They proudly proclaimed they were here to pull, to drink and to dance. Perfect. I asked them how they were paying? I didn't even bother going through the checklist, such was my belief they were coming with us. Without the blink of an eyelid, the main one replied they weren't. They thought they'd have more fun without us. I was shocked. If ever there was someone the package was designed for, it was this pair. We went through the details of the trip and the breakdown of the costs. The girls seemed like they were interested, but just needed help getting over the line. They were adamant that the "company" couldn't contain them and that they were too wild for our nights out. In reality they were teasing and holding out for a deal I think. I wanted to spice things up a bit. I decided to issue a challenge that would settle it. I asked if they were game for a laugh, looking to party and were easily shocked. They claimed they partied the hardest, were up for anything and nothing ever shocked them. This was music to my ears. I then issued a challenge. I said I could shock them and make them laugh. I was to sit still, keep my hands on the table and I wasn't allowed to shout or interfere with them in any way. If they laughed, they were paying. If they could keep a straight face, they were going for free, which meant that I was paying, because the company didn't do freebies. Challenge accepted. I gave the girls a minute to compose themselves whilst I made some notes of their flight details. After about 45 seconds, I asked if they were ready to begin, and reiterated the rules. I could see they were intrigued. They told me to begin. I looked the main one straight in the eyes and calmly and quietly mentioned this gem of a phrase. "My bollocks are out." I sat there motionless, my hands were on the table, and I just watched for their reaction. Unbeknownst to them, whilst I was writing their flight details down, I had a quick rearrangement down there and managed to hang my bean bag out the side of my shorts. I didn't say anything else. I just waited for what was to happen next. In a strong accent the ringleader questioned me "You what? Your bollocks are out?" I didn't say a word, I just smiled. She was puzzled. Her friend just looked at her equally confused. I'm not sure if they wanted to look under the table or not, but after a few short moments, curiosity began to get the better of them. They slowly leant down together towards the lip of the table and began to pull back the table cloth. Sure enough, there was my beanbag looking back at them. The minute they saw it they both roared of laughter. I mean really laughed. They couldn't believe it. They were shocked. I quickly followed up that if I could provoke that sort of reaction with an old walnut, imagine what fun we could have with a coach load of guests. Without delay, a credit card was placed down on the table in front of me. The girls were fully signed up and had a whale of a time. Both were tearful when it was time to say goodbye.

CHAPTER 10
THE WATERPARK

I had a love-hate relationship with the waterpark. It was always a pain in the arse waking up the guests to get them on the coach for the early kick off. It was like pulling teeth. I understand why. I mean we'd taken them out the night before and dragged them into bar after bar and then to Es Paradis where we left them partying until silly'o'-clock. I myself having finished work at 2am then would usually sly off with one of them for the rest of the evening's entertainment. This would then involve me turfing her out early doors (much to her annoyance) or it would mean I needed to get up even earlier to do the walk of shame back to my apartment to then get my gear on only to return to the hotel to start waking them up. Coupled with the fact that it was airport night the night before that, most of the reps were tired and somewhat irritable. That being said, once we actually got on the coach and on our way, people began to unwind and come round a bit. Of course, there were always a few holidaymakers that were intent on drinking right the way through. They would be swigging straight from a bottle of hierbas or schnapps or some other coloured shite whilst they sat on the coach. Whilst I admired their enthusiasm, experience also taught me that these would be asleep in an hour or so and then we would have some fun with their lifeless slumbering corpses. Depending on how rowdy/playful they'd been, how many were in their group and our relationships with them would determine how much stick they would ultimately be met with. More on that later.

Once we got to the waterpark, which was a 20 or 30 minute drive out of San Antonio, we would take the guests to an area specifically reserved for us all and proceed to park them there on the sun beds. We would usually be there for a couple of hours. Once everyone had arrived, we gathered for a quick rep meeting where we would discuss the plan of action and the general itinerary for the day. Once over we were free to entertain and mingle with the guests. I'd developed the perfect strategy here. Normally there would be a group of girls in my hotel and more often than not someone I had my eye on. I would basically get them all to stick their sun beds together edge to edge and put someone sideways at the bottom of the other beds. I would effectively be making a big square. I would make sure all their towels were basically interlocking. They would always be puzzled by this and would question my intent. Once everything was all locked together and covered over, I would then (when my colleagues weren't looking) duck under the sun beds and make my own little bed under there. Even though it was on concrete, I'd double over the towel and use my bag as a pillow. The guests knew how hard we worked and how tired we were, as they themselves were knackered. I would set my watch for 90 minutes and proceed to get a power nap in. I would always make sure I was under the bed of the girl I liked too, or as close as I could be. You'd be surprised how many times they would peek under to see if you were sleeping (which I normally was). If they did catch me half-awake, we'd normally share a smile but that was rare. I was normally out like a light. Afterwards, I'd often get comments like "how sweet I looked whilst I slept," or "how I snored like an animal!" (not true). Either way, it was more touch points with the girls and something for us to tease each other with after. Often the other reps or managers would be looking for me, but my guests would always cover for me. I don't think even Nigel knew I used to do this, as loose lips sink ships and this 90-minute cat nap was precious to me! I actually looked forward to it. Even the lads who were doing their best to flank us and get involved with the girls themselves would cover for me. This was touching actually. They could have easily grassed me up which would take me out of the picture with the girls for that moment in time as I would inevitably go and have to do something, but they chose not to. This type of behaviour only helped to reinforce the bond I had with the guests in my hotel.

Once the alarm went off, I would sneak out once the coast was clear and jump into the pool (fully clothed or not). This had two effects. Firstly, it quickly woke me up and helped to remove the imprint of the bag I usually would have over my face and secondly it helped me with my story. When I checked in with the other reps, they would have been irritated having to look for me, at Damien's direction. When they asked where I'd been, I would just point to the water slides and say I'd been with the guests. As I was dripping wet, who could argue? By the time I'd met with the guys, the chore or activity that needed to be done had been done already and I was usually left to my own devices for the remaining hour or so. This is where I would put into plan the second part of why I loved the water park. I'd grab Nigel and the pair of us would go and find some girls we were keen on. We did this the first or second time we ever went to the waterpark and we were so pleased with the outcome that we made it a ritual. Once we found the girls that we both had an interest in, we would get them to the top of this water slide. I forget the name of it, but it was probably something like the blackhole or the twister or some other corny generic waterslide name. You had to go down in pairs, and you could only go down on one of those large rubber rings. They were for two and resembled the figure 8. There were two chutes, so two pairs could go down at the same time. We would dress this up as a competition between Nigel and myself. We would already be extremely flirty with the girls, and they would know we were interested in them. They would show interest in us too, and so the stage was set. We would all have been flirting outrageously in the queue and leaning on each other etc., the way teenagers do. When it was time to go, we would sit the girls in the front and the boys in the back. The idea was that by the time we got to the bottom we had to have swapped places. Innocent enough? Nigel and I would be challenging each other as to who was going to win and what the repercussions would be for the losing team. By the time we had the green light from the chute attendant it was on like Donkey Kong. Both teams wanted to win. This was perfect, it meant that the girls were enthusiastic. The minute we were launched (normally other members of the group/guests would each give us a shove to get going) we descended into a dark tunnel. There we would spring into action. I would immediately shift myself forwards from the rear ring into the front ring (squeezing up against the girl in front). She was to then turn around and climb over me to sit in the ring behind me. I was to lie back flat so as to make it easier for her to clamber over. What actually would happen is as she turned around and began to climb, we would normally hit the first couple of twists and drops in the tube and she would more often than not slip on her arms and land on me. If she somehow still managed to keep her balance, then usually I would tickle or outright grab her. As she'd fall onto me, I would seize the moment and grab a quick kiss. This was always reciprocated. After a quick snog she would climb over me and sit in the rear before we emerged from the tunnel arms in the air cheering! It was great fun. Not only was it quite funny and full of banter, but it set the stage for the rest of the day. Having stolen a cheeky kiss when no one was looking helped to cement a bond. Every glance between us after that was loaded with intentions. We would behave normally, but the tension was clearly there. As if in Ibiza you needed any other excuse for two teenagers to get in on!

As the season went on and we got bolder and more confident, we upped the stakes. We started to make the forfeits for the losers bigger and sillier. The losers would have to swap bathing suits with each other, i.e. I would wear her bikini, she would wear my shorts and one of my t-shirts. This was fine for me. It was quite standard. In this role, I was used to looking silly and walking around dressed in fancy dress or as a girl, and it didn't bother me at all. In fact, it was encouraging because again you'd be sharing the experience together and again you would be drawn to each other (she could hardly walk away or try and tap off with other lads whilst I'm wearing her clothes). We also started to get other holiday makers involved. This was great. Not only did it help to hide our lustful intentions of grabbing a snog, but it also helped the guests to mingle with each other. I would actively try and pair up girls and lads with those who I thought had shared interests. I even went as far as to ask the guests who they liked. The lads would often point out directly whilst the girls would rarely answer. Usually they would be relying on their friends to blurt out which one they had her eyes on. If no one was forth coming, I would play match maker anyway. We would run it hotel v hotel or regionally. It didn't matter, any excuse to generate some interaction between the sexes and some healthy competition and banter. It had the knock-on effect of helping couples to pair off earlier in the holiday and to increase the general morale and interaction within the hotel which made our lives easier and quite frankly more fun!

Nigel came up with a great idea. He said that we were to swap over positions like usual, but this time we had to put on the girls' bikini tops. As we were both wearing only shorts, it meant that the girls would effectively be topless. Believe it or not, there were hardly any objections to this suggestion. I think the girls were more concerned about losing the race and the potential forfeits they were looking at. If we were doing the bikini swap as well, then we needed to reverse the seating positions. I would sit in the front, and she would be in the back. All would happen as before, however this time there was more of an urgency about it, because you also had to get a bikini off and back on someone else by the time you hit the pool below. This was less dainty and clumsier, but just as fun. As we hit the darkness I would spin around in my seat and she would normally have her top off ready and passing it to me. I would grab a quick snog and then somehow climb over her with all the agility of a spider but the grace of a donkey. I'd slip the bikini over my head and arms (there was no way it was being done up) and we would wait for the light at the end of the tunnel below. Unbeknown to them there was a slight drop as you came out of the tube. This would catch everyone by surprise, and there was a fixed camera there ready to catch the moment. I was aware of this; Nigel was aware of this. Guess who wasn't! Just before the drop I would put my arms in the air and roar out my hotel's name, which usually encouraged the girl in front to do the same. We were often just in time for the flash of the camera. We would always be met with a massive cheer and laughter all round. We would grab towels and allow the girls to fix their bikinis back before walking to the kiosk opposite to check out the photos. No word of a lie, they were some of the best photos taken at that water park. The broadest of smiles, laughter and cheering captured in one moment (maybe the odd boob)! More often than not the girls would purchase the photos there and then. This would set up a pattern of continual teasing and exchanges of banter going back and forth throughout the rest of the holiday, helping to stoke the tensions.

Once we were finished on the slides, we would try and calm things down a bit and circulate among the guests. We would check that everyone was ok and that they had enjoyed their night out and generally share in the gossip and war stories. Eventually, we would let them know that in about 20-30 minutes we would be leaving, so would begin the task of getting them ready for the next part of their day out. As we walked around our area, we would see the guys that chose to party through. As expected, they were normally totally crashed out. They'd be laying on a sun bed somewhere or asleep on the bar. Normally it was one or two out of a group and more often than not it was lads. We would start to chat with the guys and then between us and the other members of the group we would start to mess with them. Depending on who it was and how bad they'd been, fines would be levelled. We would get a lipstick and get everyone else in the group (guys and girls) to apply it and then proceed to give the "pass out" kisses all over the face and arms. If someone had a blue marker pen, then the guy could find himself getting smurfed (literally coloured in blue). Others would be signed by everyone in the hotel with their name and dates. I remember one group from Scotland had been particularly brutal to a member of their group. One of them had proceeded to annihilate himself on shots and vodka and god knows what. I mean this guy was wasted. He sat in a chair wasted, topless in the sun. I suggested that his friends take him under the shade. Given he was from Scotland, he had more chances of self-combusting in the sun like a vampire than catching a tan. They agreed initially, and I set off to the rep meeting. Unbeknownst to me, they instead decided to recline his chair and move his hand to his chest. They left him there for an hour or so. By the time I returned he looked like a bar of Barratt's Nougat. His back was as white as tip ex, but his front was an angry shade of crimson. On our return, I immediately grabbed his chair with another rep and moved him into the shade. In moving him, his hand slumped by his side, revealing a perfect hand and forearm mark on his chest. The whole place roared. I couldn't help but laugh too. I mean the outline was picture perfect. I couldn't have traced his hand better with a felt tip. It was as if his hand hadn't moved a single millimetre for the entire time. We gingerly woke him up and proceeded to put some Fanta into him and some ice water. When I looked across at his mates, they just said it served him right. Apparently, he'd been too drunk the night before and caused a few of them to lose chances with "lasses" so this was payback. Fair enough. Can't argue with that. It's one thing to be a crap wingman, but it's another to be a social hand grenade.

When it was time to go, we would begin to round everyone up. It was like herding cats, there were always a few that we just couldn't find. So much so, that reps would have to wait behind and continue to search the waterpark until everyone was accounted for. It didn't matter how many announcements you'd put over the loud speaker. No matter how many chute queues you'd go through or toilets you'd be inspecting, some people just had this knack of staying hidden. For the rest of the holiday makers who were back on the coaches, the mood was considerably better and more alive than before. People were refreshed, and looking forward to what was coming next on their day out.

CHAPTER 11
THE DISTILLERY

The next part of their day out was the distillery. This was a short 10-15 minute drive from the water park and basically served one purpose, to get the guests (and us) warmed up for the beach party. The distillery was a small collection of buildings set on a decent plot of land. It looked very traditional. The aim was simple. It was essentially a drive by booze. Each coach that arrived would empty their passengers outside the front of it, and the guests would have 15 minutes to drink what they wanted (or could) on the house. Again, remember times were different then. No one had smart phones or cameras with them. As far as anyone was concerned this was a chance to drink as much as you wanted free of charge. It was student fucking heaven. It was carnage. We would also do a whip round on the coach too. Everyone would put in a few hundred pesetas each and the reps would purchase several bottles of various schnapps for afterwards including a kick back to the driver for putting up with what was inevitably going to be a difficult afternoon ahead! Each guest was supplied with a small shot glass. These weren't your average shot glasses. Probably half or a third of the size. The guests would then wander through the distillery, free to try any drink they wanted as many times as they wanted. There were a hundred or so different varieties of schnapps. Any fruit you can think of, and double the number you can't. The thing needed to work with mathematical precision. We ran the schedule like the opening night at a Disney theme park. Too slow and the guests would start to get out of control and the owner clearly wasn't happy watching his profit disappear among the variety of impromptu dentist chairs that would form! Not to mention the other coach-load would be impatiently waiting behind them. Too quick and the guests would moan they didn't have enough time to sample XYZ. We also didn't want to arrive at the next venue early. It was always better to not be first. That way by the time you arrived there were already guests partying and it was much easier to carry the momentum with your own troop than to create it from a fresh.

The distillery was always one of the more interesting venues we visited. You could people watch for hours, despite only having about 15 minutes. There were different types of groups. You would see those guests that were initially shy and reserved. They would gather together around a barrel, and slowly open the tap and have a sample. Immediately followed by a brief discussion about the taste and then slowly move on to the next one. They would slowly move on in herds. There was hierarchy to it. The same person went first, every time they reached a new barrel. At the opposite end of the spectrum, you didn't have hierarchy, but anarchy. This group tore through the distillery start to finish and back again. Half the time they didn't even bother to shut the tap in between samples so as not to waste a single second of drinking time, despite wasting the alcohol. These were my favourite types of guests. They were hilarious. Not only were they funny to watch with their animalistic instinct and behaviour, but as they always over egged it, you knew you were going to be seeing a lot more from them throughout the day. These were the chosen ones for the games. The ones that would abandon their inhibitions on stage and would help entertain the rest of the group.

Despite us not being allowed to drink at the distillery, this rule was seldom followed. Remember this full day out had followed a night out which had followed an airport night, and keeping the guests entertained was tiring. Why couldn't we get a little boost here or there. Besides, the owner of the venue was also the owner of half the bars in San Antonio, so they knew us all and realised that the happier they kept the reps, the more chances they had to earn off of us. There was also an unofficial shot record that everyone tried to hit. It was set by an unknown rep one of the previous years. It stood at just over 105 shots. Now remember these shot glasses aren't the usual size and the spirits we are talking about are watered down schnapps. Even still, in 15 minutes that's a pretty strong achievement. Us reps would openly challenge each other in the coach park in front of the guests. Guests would ask what the record was, we would tell them, and then watch the carnage follow as they plucked themselves up to take on the challenge. Quite often if there was a decent size group, or a couple of lads interested in measuring up, they would dish out direct challenges to their hotel reps. This happened week in and week out. Most of the time you could side step it. I needed to work, I needed to drive later, I'm not allowed. I'm too hungover etc, but occasionally, just occasionally, the volleyball was just at the right height to be spiked down. Challenge accepted.

It was probably about a third of the way through the

season, peak time. I guess end of June, early July. I had a group in the hotel from Essex. These guys were brilliant fun. They thoroughly loved every minute of Ibiza. They were the first to try any games or challenges, and were infectiously funny to be around. They partied hard, had fun during the day despite the hangovers, and were a big hit with the rest of the hotel and girls alike. Even other reps would comment how good a group I had and how they wished they were staying in their own hotels. On their particular distillery visit, one of the ring leaders fancied his chances and called me out on the coach. "So, you reps drink or what?" He bellowed from the back of the bus. "I think you lot are all mouth…" he followed up with before I could answer his first statement. The whole coach threw out a "wooooooooooo" like you did at school when someone gave backchat to the teacher, and in doing so encouraged the teacher to fire back. We bantered back and forth for a minute or so, before I felt my pride begin to roll down the see-saw towards him. "Ok, Gobby. When we get to the distillery, you make sure you take your skirt off and we'll see who's still standing!" I instantly felt better about myself as the words left my lips. The whole coach began chattering like monkeys. He just smiled at me from where he sat and nodded in approval. I wasn't done though. "What's more, let's make it more interesting. Loser wears nothing but a bikini out tonight?" Suddenly the coach in unison swung around in their seats looking for the reaction of their challenger. I could see the blood drain from his cheeks. There was no way he could back down now with this peer pressure. He pondered for a moment, allowing his friends to interject, coaxing him on, telling him things like he had this, and he could do me. I wasn't going to give him an inch of wiggle room. "What's the matter? You said we were all mouth and couldn't drink? Where's your voice now?

Besides, I think you'd look good in a bikini!" The whole coach continued to look at him. I was standing there with a huge grin on my face. He piped up "Ok rep, you're on! Loser wears a bikini and nothing else."

Whilst I wouldn't normally relish the thought of going out to bars and a night club in just a bikini, the truth is that most of the strip had seen me in worse states and most had seen me semi naked in some form or another. Besides, I was quietly confident I could beat him mentally if not physically. I seized upon the opportunity to buy myself some protection. If I was going to go toe to toe on the booze with one of my guests, I was going to need everything to go like clockwork and for the guests to behave and above all look like they're having an amazing time. Inevitably I was going to get smashed and my boss was going to be hanging out the back of me. Experience had already taught me that it was better to be drunk during the course of your job than to be just drunk on the job. When we got off the coach, I gathered my lot together into a huddle away from the others. I made sure the Essex boys were with me in the centre, such was their popularity, most of the coach gathered with them. "Listen guys, If I go through with this, there's a good chance I am going to get smashed and I'll probably be in trouble later. Can I ask a favour of you?" I purposely paused waiting for the responses "Sure, anything", "of course you can", "what do you need? Name it…." I said to them all "I need to make sure that you are the loudest group here. I need for every other hotel to hear our name and learn how we party. We need to be doing it better than everyone else. Can you do that for me? If they drink, we drink more. If they cheer, we roar." It did the trick. I was met by a wave of expletives in return. "Too fucking right", "they won't know what hit them", "they'll be singing our fucking hotel name by the end of the night." I explained to them that this would be enough to get me off the hook with management and this was just the sort of reaction I needed. Everyone was onboard and the whole group moved to the front of the distillery in unison. The other reps were warned that I was going to be having a go at it, and to help cover me. They obliged. I handed out the shot glasses. Essex boy was next to me grinning. I laughed. "You won't be getting laid tonight, will you?" I mocked. "Why do you say that" he beckoned. "Well if you beat me you won't be able to stand up let alone stand him up, and if you don't everyone's going to think you're a prick." We both laughed as he nudged me in the ribs. "We'll see" he muttered. As soon as one of the other reps beckoned us in, it was on. I confidently strode up to the first barrel and poured us one each. Before I'd even let go of his shot glass in his hand, I'd banged mine down and reached up to the barrel above it, only to repeat the process. I couldn't even tell you what flavour it was. Melon, banana, apple, hierbas (also known as dog shit), coconut, it didn't matter. One after another was slammed. We were already starting to generate a crowd around us. I paused for a moment. "You had enough yet? You want your skirt back?" I teased. I then told everyone else to fill up. I needn't have had to. My lot were already following in our footsteps and were out-drinking the other coaches by a factor of two to one. Both sexes were gunning, and with each slam, the group became bubblier. On we went, barrel after barrel, row after row. Some of the reps began to look on shaking their heads. They knew I would still have the rest of the day to contend with not to mention the state which my guests would be in. we even had other guests from other hotels joining in and getting in on the act. We hit shot 70 and he began to waiver a little. Remember our shot glass was much smaller than a normal one. Now this was a particularly sweet drink that we'd just finished, and his eyes began to glaze. They rolled for a split second. It was quick, but I caught it. "You're gonna spew! If you puke, you're done, and it's bikini night for you." His mates roared at him. "Don't you dare, don't you fucking dare" they hollered. He paused for a moment. One of the other reps had already brought us a bucket. She shoved it in front of his face like it was a horse bag. The whole group cheered us on. Without waiting for the results, I poured myself another and took it down. I was lucky, having been drinking every day and night for the past few months, I'd built up a decent tolerance. If I had tried this 4 months before, I would have been on my back in the foetal position probably puking and shitting like an extra from Trainspotting. Of course, I was feeling light headed, and it was going to hit me hard shortly, but for now, my stomach was as determined as my will. He meekly held out his shot glass for it to be poured. His hands were shaking, and he looked pale. I seized the moment. "Pour me a double of this one please, I like it." I stood there looking at him grinning. The whole hotel was egging him on to go further. He put the glass to his lips and began to drink. You'd think he was being asked to swallow nails the way it seemed to go down. I chuckled, took the shot down again and moved on to the next one and continued. I knew he was done, but I wanted to make sure there were no doubts. I quickened my pace. I was a good 5 or 6 ahead of him now. He was beginning to struggle. One of the other reps told us we had 2 minutes left before we had to leave. I took another 3 or 4 down in quick succession when he raised his hand like a symbolic white flag. I shook his hand, he man hugged me and patted me on the back. As he let go, I drank another 3 shots, smiling at him as I did it. "What am I on?" I asked the group. "82" was the reply. "That'll do for now" I replied nonchalantly. I forget where he stopped, but I think it was low 70s. Everyone was laughing. In the course of watching us go for it, many had lost count of their own intake. We all moved outside to the coach park like a big group of giggling teenagers. 5 minutes later the fresh air hit us, and we moved in unison, swaying like a herd of pissheads. Everyone was congratulating me. I was laughing and joking with everyone. Any thoughts I'd had of working at that point had evaporated. It had been agreed amongst the other reps that I was essentially going to be a liability, and so someone had volunteered to take over for my coach and look after my guests as well as me!

Some of the reps, as planned, had used the proceeds of their whip rounds to buy several extra bottles. They were dishing the juice out to anyone and everyone who even remotely caught their eye or came into their vicinity. I was with the Essex boys trying to put a brave face on it. My opponent was broken. He'd already thrown up in a bush and was being comforted by one of his admirers. She was rubbing his back and trying to feed him water. I was still jubilant. For sure I was pissed, but for now I had full control of my limbs, and most of my speech. The car park was carnage. People were bouncing off one another, singing, laughing, kissing, dancing. If people were going to throw up we always managed to get them to puke in the bushes, so as not to cause issues with the drivers who clearly weren't going to be happy to transport them onwards. That being said, the other half of the whip round was always given to them, and nothing pleased a coach driver more than a fistful of pesetas and an apology in advance. Once everyone had been cleaned up and straightened out, we boarded the coaches where it was time for the next step. Go Karting!

CHAPTER 12
THE GO-KART TRACK

The next part of the day out was always full of adventure. It always got the loudest cheer in the welcome meetings. You would jubilantly boast about how drunk everyone was going to get at the distillery, and then you would ask the crowd loudly, 'what do you want to do when you're absolutely smashed? Yep, you guessed it, Go-karting. We're going drink driving.' This as irresponsible as it sounded, always got the biggest laugh out of the meeting. Even the most stone-cold demeanour normally broke at the thought of this. Just outside of San Antonio, a few kilometres up from Es-Paradis was a go-karting track. We would take coach loads of holiday makers there. Everyone would have been well oiled from the distillery and the reps would be winding them up on the coaches any way we could. The coaches would be full of football and rugby songs, rude chants and general rowdiness that by the time we pulled into the coach park, the guests would be firing on all cylinders. We lead them straight to the bar where the music was banging. Most people at this point of the day didn't want to queue for the go-karts. It took too long to mess around with safety forms, safety clothing, helmets and briefings etc. Most just partied at the large open bar and the terrace which overlooked it. We were there for normally an hour or so. People were more preoccupied with hooking up with each other, recovering from the distillery and just generally relaxing than climbing behind the wheel. That being said, the most competitive guests from the hotels would indulge in the racing with mixed results.

I always remember one guy. He was absolutely plastered. He was from Nigel's hotel. Nigel found me and grabbed me to one side. "mate, you have to see this. This guy is blind drunk but is adamant he wants to have a go at the go-karts." Nigel took me over to see the state of him. He was like a human gyroscope. His hips were rotating a different direction to the rest of him, and he had difficulty staying on his feet. I laughed. "There's no way he's going to be able to drive. We can't let him on." Nigel said "I know, I've tried. Every time you try and tell him he acts up and gets moody. His mates said just let him on, else he'll kick off. Apparently, he's a handful when he's pissed." Fair enough I thought. I didn't like it, but what else are you going to do. Besides, it was Nigel's call. The last thing we want is for a fight to kick off and spoil the party atmosphere. Instead we asked the kart guys to put him in front and stick him in a lower powered/knackered one. He slumped into his kart in pole position. Unbeknown to him we purposely kept the rest of the pack back behind him. The flag was waved, he took off, but no one else did. They all sat in their karts laughing, watching this guy. The track was outdoors, and relatively wide with big run off areas. It resembled something like you'd find in Mario-kart. Nothing too strenuous, and only one tight turn. As this guy shot off down the straight on his own the rest of the place stopped to watch. As he neared the end of the straight, the bend was approaching. He should be turning any time now I thought, only he didn't. Not only did he not turn when he should have, he proceeded to drive straight off the track and through the field. The only thing that stopped him was the tyre wall. He didn't even attempt to turn. It was hilarious. The whole place broke out in laughter. One of the stewards walked over to the kart which was motionless. Apparently, the guy didn't want to get out and so the steward just lifted the front of the kart up, turned it round by 120 degrees in the direction of the next part of the circuit and off the guy set. Watching the guy drive over the grass back on to the tarmac and straight through to the other tyre barrier without the slightest attempt to turn the wheel a second time was even funnier than the first. Everyone was pissing themselves. Even the stewards thought it was funny. The karts weren't powerful to do damage to yourself, and as long as we kept him out there on his own it was ok. The steward walked over again and repeated the procedure. Yet again, after setting off, he didn't even attempt to turn. This whole process was repeated again and again. Eventually the patient but somewhat irritated steward just pointed him in the direction of the finish flag and we all watched him cut straight across the track, cheering for him as he went. Having wiped out for the final time, his mates helped him out of the cart and he rose his hands up in victory, thinking as no one had over taken him he'd won. This just made us laugh all the more. We let the rest of the pack go and things returned to normal.

For those not interested in the racing, there was a pretty cool bar there. The reps would basically mingle with all the guests and keep them entertained. It was also a prime time to go sharking. We'd start to lay the ground work with the girls that caught our eye. We would circle like wolves. It was like a game. It wasn't enough to be on offense, we would need to be defensive in case another rep came sniffing for a girl in your hotel. If you had a fit one in your hotel, you needed to move quickly otherwise the minute your back was turned the hyenas would be on the case. Some of the reps played really filthy. A favourite was to get on the mic, and interrupt the proceedings. "Excuse me ladies and gentlemen, can I have your attention for a moment, I have an announcement to make. Where's Mike? Ah there he is. Mike stand up so everyone can see you. Guys, whilst we know it's important to have a good time and a great holiday, it's also important to remember that it's family that's the real important thing in life. I'd like to propose a toast to Mike who just became a father of a beautiful baby boy, Christian." By the time Mike could say anything in protest, each and every guest was toasting "to Christian." This was a blatant lie. Mike didn't just become a Dad, Mike wasn't even in a relationship. Mike just happened to have got caught sharking in someone else's hotel. Half of the girls there now considered Mike to be out of bounds, and despite his protestations of being single, many wouldn't go near him. Other favourites would be to announce the engagement of one of the male reps to one of the female reps. Everyone would cheer. The female rep would then proudly point and display a ring on her wedding finger to the crowd. Again, another blatant lie. It could have been a Haribo ring let alone a wedding ring, but the damage was done. The go-karting venue was a good place to attack as it was one of the first occasions that everyone was together and the reps actually had some time to sniff around.

I'd been blown up several times after my arrival to the White Island, but I soon discovered a tactic against it. If there was a real fit one in my hotel, I'd often go out on the offensive. I'd pick my moment when everyone was having a good time and was relaxed at the distillery. I'd wait and then take the apple of my eye to one side and flirt. I'd tell her that she's probably going to hear some false things about me later, and not to pay any attention. She would ask what sort of thing, I'd say it doesn't matter, it could be any number of things, but it wouldn't be true. She would then confusingly ask why would someone say it? I would say that the rep in question isn't the nicest and is trying to mess with me. Again, a pretty cryptic answer. She would normally push further, "but I don't understand, why?" I'd then simply say, "because the rep knows I'm fond of you." I would then abruptly need to leave and go and tend to something. We wouldn't say any more of it, but I would shoot a few smiles here and there and would normally receive them back. She would immediately tell her mates, and then everyone would be wondering what was going to be said. When we got to the go kart venue, I'd work out who was my biggest competition among the male reps (it could be the good looking one, or the one that's from the same area as her, or the one that made her laugh the most, whatever) and annoy him. I would purposefully flirt with his hotel guests. Sure enough, he would take the bait, and an announcement would be made about me fathering twins, getting married, coming out as gay, whatever. I would smile and wave at the crowd sheepishly. Things would return to normal and like clockwork within a minute or so, the apple of my eye would find me. "Is that what you meant earlier?" "Yep. I knew he'd do something like that. It's in his nature." She'd agree and say "I think that's well out of order." I'd shrug and say "it's not nice to tease someone because of their feelings towards another." She'd probably blush. I'd smile, and ask her if she's enjoying her holiday, and we'd begin to chat a bit more until I was pulled away or she went to get a drink or something. Sooner or later, the other reps would come sniffing. The mic rep who made the announcement was on a loser before he even started. Her and her mates would usually take an instant dislike to him. That group would then talk poorly of him to other groups. Not only had I just cemented my chances with her, but I'd also torpedoed my competition. To quote Alonzo Harris "This shit's chess, it ain't checkers!" (Training Day) The funny thing about this is that it worked. And if it worked before, it will work again. It became a regular approach. Some of the male reps even thought it was funny to continually name me as the recipient of children, marriages etc… some would even congratulate me on my successful recovery from chlamydia or some other scrape. They had no idea they were hanging themselves in the process. It's funny, even though there were more than enough girls to go around it was really irritating and offensive to find a male rep had been creeping in your hotel. I don't think it was even the fact that they might have been with one you had liked, although obviously that happened. It was more territorial than that. We all felt the same, and the patterns of behaviour became predictable.

After copious amounts of flirting with the opposite sexes, we would then round the guests up again for the final destination of their day out – the beach party. By this point a lot of people were the worse for wear. Most people needed something to eat, and a place to relax. Some were already asleep in chairs, whilst others were continuing to party hard. We rounded them back on to the coach for the final destination.

CHAPTER 13
THE BEACH PARTY

Again, about 15-20 minutes away from the Go-karting track was the beach party. This was a large open-air venue with banqueting tables as well as a large man-made beach area. The whole theme was very reminiscent of what we'd gone through during out training in Majorca. We'd welcome the guests with sangria or beer as they preferred and we'd entertain them whilst everyone arrived. Ideally, we wanted everyone to sit down to eat together, so if reps were late with coaches for one reason or another it really messed everything else up and the seniors would be pissed.

A lot of the guests by now would be flirting heavily with each other and some would be pairing off. It wouldn't be uncommon to find a couple shagging in the toilet, or the odd rep catching some head in the store room! Other guests would be looking for anywhere to have a sleep. When you've ruined yourself too early in the day you'd be surprised where some people would take refuge. We would be digging people out from underneath the benches, under bushes, cuddling toilet bowls. We even had one guest proceed to climb into the luggage area underneath a coach!

It was only by sheer chance that one of the bus drivers was taking a smoke in the shade of the bus that he happened to hear some snoring, otherwise who knows when he would have been found. For those that were still able to party, we would be doing the usual beach games that I'd covered earlier. Stab the crab, boat race, limbo, piggy back races. You name it we would do it. Despite everyone being hungry and battle weary, the games still provided opportunity for match making. I would purposely try and manipulate the teams and queues to put various guests next to each other. Working in peak season you soon developed a radar for knowing who liked who. I would do anything I could to encourage that romance! Although don't think that high of me yet. I also used it to tease and bait my own interests. As reps we would often have to get in the thick of it and show people how it was done. If that meant that we needed to start the snog off in a boat race, well I made sure that I was sat in front of an angel and not a moose. If there was a guest who was particularly keen, I'd tease. Most of the guests didn't know what the game entailed, so we could place them unknowingly into queues as we saw fit. I'd be lying if I said I hadn't placed some guests purposely next to what I will politely term "undesirables." Only to sit back and watch the fireworks as the kissing game began. Just like clockwork, you'd have them come up to you immediately after to give you a faux telling off. A cheeky smile here and there a few choice phrases and that was it. Game on for later It was hilarious. The games would normally go on for 20 minutes or so. We were careful not to over egg it as most of the guests would be needing food and were cloudy from the drink and the last thing we wanted to do was to irritate and for the mood to change. Before long, the rest of the coaches would have arrived and then everyone would be sat down on the long tables according to their hotels. We always tried to keep the groups together so they would socialise more with each other. It made for a better hotel atmosphere and made it easier to keep a good momentum in the hotel.

As soon as everyone was sat, we'd have to spring into action. We would be delivering pitchers of beer and sangria to the tables. They would be drinking them as quickly as we could place them down. Most of the reps would be carrying 3 or 4 2-litre pitchers at a time and we were always short-handed. In hindsight I would have said it was calculated. The more we brought out, the more that was drank. Not only would bringing more out lead to a decrease in profitability, but it probably would have dramatically increased the bad behaviour that we tried to keep to a minimum. We were keen for everyone to have a good time and get their monies worth but no one wanted to be dealing with people vomiting, crying, injuring themselves or fighting. Whilst the venue had its own staff for serving the food, it was our responsibility to keep them watered. On the main stage there would be a comedian and various acts on there to keep them amused. It had already been a long day for most, so things tended to calm down a bit at this point and it was more about enjoying a big BBQ feast in the afternoon sun rather than trying to annihilate yourself on sangria. This was also normally when we were able to eat for the first time that day and to legitimately catch a breather. After an hour or so of relaxing, we would then take the guests back to the hotel. Most of the time we would continue the party at our respective hotel pools. Most people by that point were either dead and crashed out as soon as they got back or ready for round two. We would cater for their endurance as best we could, but we would have to report back for a sales meeting and plan for the night's entertainment.

This was one of the most tiring day's out, but was always my favourite. The guests thoroughly enjoyed the day, and you could see on their return to the hotel how friendly everyone was each other. People had genuinely enjoyed a fantastic day out and the whole group had bonded in one way or another. I often felt sorry for those that chose not to go on the trips, because they were in the minority, and by not going they probably felt left out. This was probably the moment when I imagined they would have felt it the most acutely. You know what it's like yourself. You go on holiday, your other half forces you to book a day trip which you can't be bothered to get up for, but begrudgingly you do it, and surprisingly you really enjoy it. Well this was definitely the case out there. There were usually so many war stories and highlights from the day out it would make us smile for the rest of the week. Guests would be giggling about it for the remainder of their stay. This single day out helped to create a positive vibe across the guests which helped carry the atmosphere of the hotel.

On a side note, it was also normally the first chance we'd have to really zero in on the new arrivals in the hotels. In between entertaining and serving food with alcohol, all of the reps would have been putting the ground work in and all would be keen to see how that ground work played out over the course of the next week or so. A little smile here, a nudge there was often all it took to kick start a cuddle.

CHAPTER 14
POOL ENTERTAINMENT

Now, the day trip aside, most of the focus of the trip and entertainment package was undoubtedly on the evenings. That's not to say we weren't busy during the day. We would normally have a quick work meeting in the morning after breakfast around 9:30. I think it was set this early intentionally to make sure we weren't oversleeping (easily done when you don't have a day off and you're working from 8am until 2am and sometimes longer). We needed to be in the hotel for around 8-8.30 in the morning to be available for guests and to deal with issues that might have come up overnight. The majority of guests at this time were sleeping still, with a minority still at the clubs doing god knows what. Usually I spent the time changing over posters, putting up flight schedules in the reception, and chatting with the hoteliers. Sometimes there would be some paperwork to fill in, as well as reconciliations needed to be completed on passenger manifests. i.e. make sure that the hotel and the company were on the same page with regards to departures and arrivals. I took this part of the job seriously. Nothing upset a guest more than arriving travel weary at silly o'clock in the morning and finding that you don't have a room available, or that you've been moved into a different hotel, which always isn't as good as the hotel you thought you'd booked (regardless of the reality). Not only that, but it often gave those guests such a bad first impression that they were then less likely to take out the entertainment package and less likely to flow with the rest of the hotel. It just made our lives more difficult. Nigel was the complete opposite to me. He didn't give a toss for paperwork and would happily find somewhere to sleep during the morning. Don't get me wrong, I'm not saying I wouldn't nod off from time to time in the reception, but it was never intentional. I'd just close my eyes for a moment and wake up 30 minutes after. Most of the guests were totally understanding, they knew we worked hard around the clock, despite the image of us just poncing drinks and banging the holiday makers. Some of the guests would even take you under their wings. I'd often open my eyes again to find myself surrounded by a few of the guests who would be actively stopping some of the more mischievous guests from trying to fuck with me. It was very flattering actually, and no doubt they'd saved me from being smurfed or worse on many occasions. That being said, it wasn't unknown to be shown a photo of me asleep in a chair with 20-30 of the guests all smiling in the background pointing!

Back to Nigel. He was like an old lazy cat. All he would do is seek out places where he could sleep. You'd find him in store cupboards, in spare rooms, in the swimming pool outhouse behind the boiler. One time he even got onto the roof of his hotel where they had chairs and old sun beds stacked. He had constructed himself a little den and would often disappear up there when he could. Remember this was in the days before mobile phones had really taken off. We had them for emergencies, but hardly ever used them, and most of them were out of credit anyway. You could disappear for hours on end and make up any story you liked. Unless you were spotted, no one was going to be none the wiser. Nigel's ability to sleep under a chair also made him a natural magnet for hotel fuck ups. You name it, it happened to him. Passenger manifests would be incorrect, there would be all sorts of mix ups. Guests would be dropped off in the wrong hotel, guests would miss their departure coach and sometimes even their flight because Nigel forgot to change the notice on the board detailing when they were due to be picked up. He was a complete liability logistically speaking, and everyone knew it, but despite his short comings, he had one quality that saved him time and time again from everyone's irritation. He was hilarious. This guy could pick up a microphone and talk absolute bollocks non-stop and people would love it. He could be talking about anything, and he had people in hysterics. To look at he was the most non-threatening guy in the world. I don't think he could even push a door in the wind let alone a push up, but he had such charisma and a wicked sense of humour that the guests and staff loved him. Oh, and he liked to get naked… a lot. I wasn't so comfortable with the microphone. Sure, I did public speaking, and I've spoken in front of six or seven hundred before without issue, but I always preferred to be more hands on. Something about holding that mic in my hand that I found distracting. I'd sooner shout. This made Nigel a great partner in crime. He would get on the mic and start the crowd off, where as I would be running the pool side antics.

I used to enjoy the time during the day as most people were chilled and happy to chat. The reps tag hanging around your neck meant that you could essentially wander up and talk to anyone without them thinking who the hell are you? Or why are you bothering us? I would go and sit on the edge of the sun loungers and check that everything was ok and they were enjoying their holidays. I would get the war stories, hear things that people had done or didn't do, and just get to know the guests. I often would unintentionally end up swimming. No matter what I was wearing I was shoved/thrown/dropped/tackled into the pool on a daily basis. Didn't matter what time of the day it was. As a rep you soon learned not to walk within 2m from the pool's edge if you had a bag with you. You would hear a table or chair scrape across the concrete suddenly and instinctively you dropped your bag, threw your wallet on the ground and waited for it. I didn't mind this, in fact I welcomed it. I was fortunate to get on well with the vast majority of the guests, there was never any malice, so them dunking me in the pool just provided me with opportunity and targets to fuck with throughout the week. Sometimes some of the guests would try and do it on their own and fail. A quick side step here, a roll and duck there and suddenly the guests would be in the pool with me still standing on the edge, dry as a camel's beanbag. Nothing pleased me more. Not only did the rest of the guests laugh, but my public gloating would encourage other groups to try and shove me in. I did this intentionally. It was all part of the bonding experience. Sometimes the girls would try. This was always hilarious. I'm not particularly big but I'm not that small either. Seldom would they get me in, and if they did, it was normally because she was cute and I wanted us to fall in together to create a touch point for later on in the day/evening. Nigel on the other hand could have been pushed in the pool by the hotel cat if it chose to. The sight of him trying to resist being dumped in the deep end was nothing short of pathetic. He played up to it of course, but even the smallest of girls would be sizing him up to drop his ass in.

We would normally start the pool games around 11am. It wasn't anything formal, it was a much more relaxed affair. We would be socialising with the guests and then gradually increase the circle until we reached critical mass. I was very aware that there's nothing worse than being on holiday and someone is coming around asking if you want to play a game of something when you don't want to. Or worse still, say you agree to a game of volleyball, you then have to stand there like a bell end for 10 minutes whilst the staff try and find 5 other players. We would generally mess around in the pool for a bit and increase our involvement with other groups until people naturally wanted to join in. A good starter for this, would be a Lilo bridge. You'd borrow a couple of Lilos, lining them end to end across the pool. You'd then try and walk/run/crawl across and see how far you'd get. Nigel would go first as athletically he was just shit. Anyone would be better than him so it took the pressure off. No one wanted to come last. Bit by bit, the natural competitive element would rise and more and more of the guests wanted to have a go. It was funny to watch. The only way you were getting across was to be quick but nimble. The minute you paused you were sinking fast. A few of the guests would manage it and start giving shit to the other members of their groups and to the reps. Others would rise to the challenge, and it wasn't just testosterone filled guys either. Both sexes would pitch their agility against the inflatables. Once we had at least 10-15 people engaged, we could then start to do more. We'd have wrestling matches between guests, sexes, towns. You'd basically hoist someone on to your shoulders whilst stood in the pool and the person on top would try and overthrow the opponent off the shoulders of their mule. Again, if we could swing it, we'd make sure we'd do it with the girls on our shoulders, again helping to create touch points for after hours. The flirting would be outrageous. This was comical to watch, and we'd often pit girls versus guys or I'd pair people up. Again, helping to play match maker.

As time went on, more of the guests would gather around the pool edge and become social at which point I'd normally signal to Nigel to grab the mic. I'd then clear an area around the pool for the next event. Belly flops. Whilst I was busy removing chairs and tables from the proposed runway, Nigel would start to challenge the guests. He would select 3-4 guests to be judges and proceed to hand them score cards that we'd made up. I.e. pieces of A4 with numbers marked on them 0-10 in a big black marker. Most of the guests in the pool naturally dispersed to allow us some room to go for it. By the length of the runway I was clearing, they could see I was serious. Together Nigel and I would start to challenge the guests in a public manner. I would target the ring leaders first with some banter, they'd take the bait and then in turn they would drag other members of the group. Nigel would inform the judges to judge on flair, aggression, height and distance. I always made sure I went first. Nigel would announce me as the current record holder and that I was setting the bar to beat. This meant, to quote our American brethren, I had to go big or go home. Everyone would wait to see what I was going to do next. I would wait at the end of this runway as if I was trying to focus on my inner peace. Obviously, it was all for effect. I would set off and sprint towards the water like a seal trying to avoid a club. Silence would set around the pool as they watched intently what was going to happen next. As I got to the edge of the pool, I would launch myself as hard as I could. Arms flung out to the side, feet together chest puffed like a teenager in the gym and chin up. No one could be in doubt of my commitment to the cause. By the time I hit the water I'd covered over a third of the pool's width. I'd smash into the water with an almighty splash, the noise being drowned out by that of the pool's collective "oooooh." There was a method to my madness. You see the trick was to hit the water on your chest first but to enter not just directly down onto the surface but as much forwards as downwards. Kind of diagonally in. This meant that you got the drama of a big splash and a slap as your body hits the surface, but most of your momentum forwards would carry you through the surface normally unscathed. It was a little sore on the neck and upper chest but a fraction of what it would be if I just fell forwards onto my belly from the side. No one likes to do a belly flop. Everyone has childhood recollections of falling on to their stomach or back and can instantly associate the experience with that instant sting that followed. I would triumphantly emerge from the water and immediately lay down the challenge to the rest of the contenders. Nigel would also start to wind the crowd up. As each guest stood up for it, Nigel would introduce them. Their name, where they're from and some random piece of information he'd gleaned from the 15 seconds he spoke to them, or he would completely make something else. A typical example of some of the patter would be "next we have James. James is 19 and from Doncaster. James' favourite phrase whilst making love is you don't sweat much for a big bird!" As uncouth as this sounds in this day and age, back then times were different. Everyone would be laughing. You could see the girls looking at each other in shock assuming this was in fact what James had said. The guys would be laughing, and everyone would be focusing on this lad who was about to show everyone his best belly flop. Naturally, no one wanted to be out done, so the guy would also come enthusiastically running up to the edge, however, there would be one difference between us. I knew to fling myself forwards. He didn't. He would get to the edge, stop and throw himself vertically. Big mistake. He would land square on his front with an almighty whack. You could hear the whole pool grimace. By the time he resurfaced he'd be doubled over. His face gurning like he'd eaten a bag of pills. The next bit was the best. He'd climb the stairs out of the pool revealing a bright red torso. Half the pool would be laughing, the other half would be waiting for the next victim. Any gusto that anyone else had about attacking the challenge began to melt like a child's ice cream. You could see the guys start to look uneasy. Nigel would be all over this. "Now I hope none of you have changed your mind fellas. If I see anyone trying to skulk away there's going to be forfeits. The rest of the pool are watching you." That was that. Their fate was sealed. One by one the lemmings would plunge into the pool, in varying degrees of difficulty, instantly regretting their testosterone fuelled decision to take part. Sometimes if things were waning due to a lack of enthusiasm, I would go again and chuck some banter out at them to try harder. This normally helped pick things up a bit. Eventually I'd swap with Nigel and I'd get him to do one. It should come to no surprise that his attempt was usually pathetic. I'm not sure if he even managed to land on his front or on his knees. It wasn't through lack of trying though. He wasn't trying to escape the pain. It's just he had the coordination of a brick. As always, it didn't matter, people loved him for it.

We'd chill out for a bit after this. We'd start drinking a bit more and would encourage others to follow. We'd dish out some shots or cocktails as prizes for various bits and bobs, and sometimes we'd even dish out some shots ourselves. We would often hold back a bottle or two of schnapps or even buy one from our hotelier. I didn't begrudge spending here, and it paid back in dividends because it was unusual for reps to buy guests drinks and it was unexpected. Once the drinks were flowing, and everyone was loosely relaxed, we'd play the next game. This was always one of the most popular. There were always a couple of guests who were due to pay their forfeit for something they did or didn't do. Remember earlier when I said it was good to have a few on the list to fuck with. We'd grab them off their sun beds and volunteer them for this next one. I'd demonstrate this game with a girl. I'd be sure to pick one who was up for a laugh and not particularly prudish. We had some huge industrial sized bin bags. They were large enough to fit both adults inside them standing up. Nigel would select two couples (including myself and a girl) and blindfold each of us. We would then have the black bags placed over each couple (we were standing close enough together) and the timer would be started. The aim of the game was simple. The winning couple were those who managed to exchange their clothing first, and pull their bag off themselves. Nigel would get the whole pool going with a united countdown, and some appropriate music was played. As soon as he started it was frantic under the black bags. My trunks were down immediately as I stepped out of them, she'd pull her bikini top off and hand it to me as I exchanged it for my t-shirt. I put it on as quick as I could. You had to have some kind of coordination together. The bags weren't that big. If you both tried to bend down to take your bottoms off you were bashing heads. If someone moved left when the other went right, there was a high chance of someone getting some genitalia in the face. You couldn't see what was going on under the black bag, but you could make out various shapes and collisions and everyone was laughing and cheering the couples on. This was a race, not a perve fest. No one was intentionally trying to cop a feel of the other's bits. It did happen on occasion but it wasn't intentional. As soon as she confirmed she's covered, we ripped the bag off our head as quick as we could. You couldn't tell if you were in the lead or not before that point. Everyone would be laughing throughout the whole process. They laughed even harder when the bags came off. My counterpart would be wearing rep shorts and a t-shirt or vest. I would be stood there in a bikini, struggling to contain myself. Now whether we were first or second it didn't matter, the whole thing was great fun. Some people had no idea what they were doing. Some had inadvertently allowed the black bag to rise as they were trying to scramble underneath it, meaning that the rest of the pool were catching glimpses, to which you could hear a mixture of laughter and cheers. Some guys physically couldn't fit into the bikinis. When the black bag was lifted, they were hanging out the side of it. Some people were so uncoordinated that they just started arguing under the bag. There was never a dull moment. After we ran this through a couple of rounds, we would do a final. We would select the quickest times out of the previous heats and run a kind of playoff. Now was the time for revenge. Each couple knew what they were doing by now, and were determined to improve on their times. We would give away some tickets to a club or a bottle of drink to the winners. It was more symbolic really; everyone was just happy to play anyway. We would blindfold everyone and get everyone in their starting positions. Now this was where the prank was played. As the two or three couples stood there in their starting positions, Nigel would be winding up the pool area on the mic. As I was handing out the bags to the couples, I would gesture to the crowd to stay silent with my finger on my lip. The third bag I handed out would be a transparent one that no one had seen until now! I made sure those that had their forfeits were the lucky recipients. As the bags were lowered, the pool counted them down. The participants were oblivious as they had blindfolds on. Everyone was laughing and eagerly waiting as Nigel set them off. The couples immediately started exchanging clothes, but they were met by a massive roar from the pool. Even passers-by would stop and peer through the door way or the fence as the guests cheered them on. The participants were none the wiser and probably just thought it was all part of the "atmosphere." Nigel would crank up the pace and encourage people to quicken up. We would insist that everyone kept their blindfolds on when finished. One by one as the couples raced to take the bag off, I would slowly move the bags behind the couple and have them (whilst still blindfolded) face the crowd. When the final couple finished. We would ask the participants to remove their blindfolds and accept a round of applause from the guests. They would be met with a healthy cheer as we would then hold a vote as to who would win. We always selected the first two couples and they got a reasonable cheer and everyone clapped them. When Nigel highlighted the final couple, the whole place went off like a cup final. The applause was so rapturous that the lucky couple would often turn to face each other bewildered. I would do my best to keep them from looking behind them and would present them with their bottle of plonk, or the tickets to the club etc. Whatever I had on hand really. All the focus was on them. It was at this point we thanked the guests for playing and Nigel asked if they could return their bags to him. Only then did the penny drop. The look on their faces was priceless. At first it was bewilderment, then a small dose of gotcha! They were always good spirited about it. The whole hotel would clap them on. We would always go over to check that they were ok about it and not put out. I normally received a dig in the ribs and small grief, but genuinely they were laughing about it, and would complement us on the setup. It might sound brutal now, but when we were selecting the guests for it, we always picked out those we thought would find it funny. What was all the more amusing was that most of the time the couple that bared all ended up getting together for a holiday romance. I guess it was the shared experience that gave something to work off. I would often tease them about it.

Another pool side antic I would indulge in which was slightly more devious and targeted was that you would pair up with a member of the opposite sex (I'd choose the girl I was most interested in) and then compete as couples in random challenges. It could be anything. The losing couple had to exchange clothes privately and then run down to the town to fetch something from a pre-selected bar or shop. Kind of like a naughty game of orienteering. You would play several games until each couple had failed at something and a random object was selected for them to buy. Things to buy could be toothpaste from the local spar, a plaster from the local surgery, a comb from the hairdresser whatever. Then it was a race. Normally most of the pool would count you down and then wait and see which couple came last. We could always think of a forfeit for that couple. Again, all good spirited, and funny to watch. As we'd shoot down the road cross dressed the guests on their balconies lining both sides of the street would be cheering you on and wolf whistling. Before that though we had to exchange clothes. I'd nip off to the toilet and then tell people to get ready to find somewhere to swap the outfits. It was a race, so as soon as we departed from the pool side it was on. Unbeknown to the others, I'd get myself in the cubicle and start to sort myself out. I wasn't looking for satisfaction, just wanted to wake him up a bit. Once proud, I'd go back to the group and say right, let's swap then. We'd all nip off in pairs to a toilet or a room somewhere and swap the clothes.

I'd have my chosen angel with me. Once we were in the office, store room, pool house, whatever, I'd say right let's go. My top would be off anyway. As she was pondering where to go to protect her modesty, I'd rip my trunks off bold as brass and hand them to her. Taken back, she'd cop an eyeful and then say something like "you're not shy, are you?" to which I'd respond with some corny line like "well is there anything I need to be shy about?" with a big grin naked as the day I was born. I'd then ask for her clothes. Any hesitation and I'd say "relax, you've not got anything I haven't seen before..." usually provoking a cheeky response. I'd then turn my back, give her some privacy and we'd continue the swap. Once we had the clothes sorted, we'd congregate back poolside with the other cross dressed couples. Nigel would count us down and we were off. We'd all bolt straight through the pool area and main reception and make our way towards the strip as quick as we could to the relevant shop to buy our chosen object. Once purchased we'd shoot back. We're talking maybe a kilometre in distance so fitness seldom came into it, but we tried to win. It was good fun. We would always have an unfair advantage because I knew where I was going having lived there, but even still it was a decent run in the heat. People would just laugh and cheer us on as we pegged it past them, the guys would struggle to contain themselves in bikini bottoms and the girls were always encouraging them to run faster. Once back to the pool area the couples were marked down. We weren't always first, but we were never last. Eventually when the final pair got back, we would all have a good laugh about it. There would be some kind of forfeit agreed for them later that evening and then we would reward ourselves with cocktails at the bar. We would normally try and make it coincide with happy hour so the rest of the guests could partake too. The girls would be caught giggling amongst themselves every time you looked over in their direction. Sometimes even comments would be thrown out, usually much to the embarrassment of the girl who had told her friends in the strictest of confidence what she'd seen! I never reacted, but this was exactly the sort of light hearted response I was looking for. After an hour of lounging with everyone, I'd grab my partner and ask to swap back. We'd disappear somewhere quietly and swap back our clothes. You'd be surprised, having been naked in front of each other how your inhibitions were subsequently lowered. As we swapped back, I'd normally complement her on her figure. I'd usually receive a complement in return or at the least a blush, and sometimes we'd even grab a cheeky kiss there and then. Not always, but often. If no dice, I'd give her hand a gentle squeeze as I led her out back to the bar. It set the scene for the evening ahead. She would usually dart straight back over to her friends and more giggling would follow. Nigel and I would then have to report back to the office to get a briefing for the evening's entertainment and sort out any other issues that were present. The other reps did pool entertainment as per their schedules, but Nigel and I preferred to do it more often and on a more relaxed basis. Again, nothing forced. I mean these people wanted to relax on their holiday, not be scheduled. Often reports would get back to other reps and staff that they saw Nigel and I and other guests racing through town and how funny we looked. We liked hearing it. It meant that other people were noticing how much fun our hotels were having and consequently how good a job Nigel and I were doing at keeping the guests entertained.

CHAPTER 15
BAPTISM OF FIRE

Having spent a couple of weeks with Nigel as 'official observers' we were given our rep tags and officially assigned to our own hotels. Nigel was in a bigger hotel than me. It was large enough that there were two reps working it. Lucky bastard. He had someone to share the duties with and someone he could ask for help. We were in the same area, and we were sharing the same pool, which fortunately for us, was huge, so I always had help on hand when I needed it, but I couldn't help but think he got a much easier introduction than I did.

As I was just starting out and very green behind the ears, I'd made the maximum effort to start to get to know the guests. It was important to me that they were having a good time, and they liked me. I wasn't 100% sure on what I was doing, so that made me a little more sensitive I suppose. I was paying attention to everything. Who was friends with who, who was looking to pair up with who etc.? I remember there was a couple of lads from Manchester who had come out for a week. They'd been here before and whilst they were nice enough, they were on a drugs vibe.

Whenever I saw them in the hotel, they always looked like they were on a massive come down or just outright stoned. I wasn't judging, I mean this was Ibiza and was par for the course, but it did strike me as weird. They were perhaps a year or so younger than me, and didn't seem to have any interest in trying to pull, only to get off their face. Fair enough, if we were all the same it'd be boring, but it was this mindset that surprised me to see one of them hook up with one of the girls in the hotel. She was from just north of London. I want to say Barnet or Enfield. I caught her doing the walk of shame one morning when I was replacing posters in the hotel. She wasn't too bothered, we just smiled as she closed his door behind her. They seemed to be getting on well with each other just as any other teenage holiday romance.

On one of our first official nights as reps, we were taking the guests to a venue for a western themed evening. Basically, Cowboys and Indians. Free food and drink, line dancing (yes you read that right), a decent DJ and then on to a club. I was wearing the full cowboy attire complete with Stetson! We were serving everyone with food and drink and I could see that these two (as well as their respective friends) were absolutely smashed. I mean they were really going for it. One minute there's passionate kissing all over the table as if they were the only ones in a room and not actually sat on a banqueting table with 30 other guests next to them. The next minute there were tears and a mini argument. Then kissing, then crying, then kissing, then arguing. I tried to ignore it, but I did make a conscious effort to place the beer and sangria away from them. Literally as soon as the booze was placed, it was snatched up. Despite some protests from other members of their group, I think I did a decent job in helping to channel alcohol around them. Once the food and drink were basically done, the DJ came on and most people hit the dance floor or were lingering around the bars on the edge. Everything was open air so there was no reason for people to gather anywhere else. I was standing by the side of the venue stuffing down some food when the girl approached me. She'd clearly been crying as her mascara was beginning to run. She was the worse for wear drink wise for sure. I asked her if she was ok. She started to sob and she put her arms around me. I consoled her and asked her what the matter was. She said that the guy was an asshole. I asked what the problem was, I thought they were getting on well (just trying to help patch over a pissed-up argument). The next thing she said could have knocked me down with a feather. She tells me he's been forceful. Everything stopped at that moment. I asked her to repeat it clearly, which she did. I then asked her if she meant sexually and she just clammed up. She didn't answer. I said to her that if it was the case that something along those lines had happened, I was going to report it and we needed to make this formal. I was still somewhat surprised with the allegation given what I'd witnessed at the table not 10 minutes before. I couldn't tell if she was just lashing out at him or if something untoward had happened. She stood there sobbing and began to talk incoherently. I suggested we get her friend. I wanted the friend there to keep her busy whilst I reported this to my management. If something had gone down then this needed to be handled with the police, medicals etc.

I began to walk her back to her friend when all of a sudden, another rep grabbed me by the arm and told me that one of my guests was unresponsive and an ambulance had been called. Thankfully her friend was just there, so I walked her over to her friend, told her I'd be right back and immediately left the main venue area and went outside. There was this lad slumped on a bench with a mixture of puke and dribble hanging from his mouth. It was the guy she had just been telling me about. This guy looked like he couldn't even lift an eye lid let alone anything else. I still fully intended to report it, but this looked more serious. As soon as I was there the rep that was sitting next to me said "Thank fuck for that, he's a mess" and began to leave. I said "where are you going?" to which I was bluntly met with the phrase "your guest, your problem. I've got my own to sort out!" An ambulance had been called and I was pretty much left to it. I held his head up and listened to him. He seemed unconscious but he was still breathing. Someone passed a tissue so I was able to wipe all the dribble and puke from his mouth. I sat there with him for about 5 minutes when I heard some commotion. I looked over and the girl from earlier was there with her mate trying to hold her back. She was tearful and by now the fresh air had hit her fully. She was babbling incoherently. She sat the other side of him and put her arm around him, hugging him tightly. I was completely confused at this point. Was this the guy she just complained had been forceful? Was she just hammered and angry? My mind boggled. I was sat here literally a couple of weeks out of university thinking what the fuck have I signed up for. Every time her friend tried to take her back inside, she turned aggressive. In the end it was easier to just leave her sat there. She was nurturing him but I needed to keep an ear out to make sure he was still breathing. Eventually his mate turned up too. "What's he taken?" I asked him. The guy sheepishly replied "nothing, just beer." "Bullshit" I insisted. "What's he taken?" Again, the friend stuck to the story. I was beginning to get irritated. "Don't lie to me, or you can sort out the paperwork with the Hospital and the Police without me." Miraculously the girl who couldn't speak about 2 minutes ago 'fessed up. "It's eccy. We've all took it. He also smoked some weed before we came out."

"Thank you for telling me." Before I had a chance to ask anything else the small ambulance pulled up. The minute the back doors opened, the orderlies were out and lifting the kid onto a stretcher. They weren't messing around. They knew what they were doing. I thought that was it. Then one of the paramedics said "you're going with him." I didn't know if this was protocol or not, but I did as I was told. All of a sudden, the girl leapt in the back too. The paramedic tried to stop her, but she was hysterical. In the end, he figured it was easier just to let her be (as I had found earlier). They shut the doors and off we went. The girl was sobbing in the back of the ambulance the whole way there. She had hold of his hand tightly, and was begging him not to die. I had to keep her from practically laying on him as I wanted to keep checking his airways were clear. The whole situation really pissed me off. I mean what kind of idiot goes on a drinking bender taking in as much sangria and beer as they can physically drink and then decides it's a good idea to drop some pills too. Why you'd be taking ecstasy at a BBQ feast for Cowboys and Indians escapes me. At least do it in the club later! Coupled with that, I'd left my bag and all my belongings back at the venue and I was now dealing with Juliet whining over Romeo.

We pulled up to the medical centre shortly after. We all got out. She did the typical thing you see in films. She was running along the corridor until the orderlies got annoyed and basically bundled her back out of the room. I needed to sign some forms. I still wasn't quite sure how serious it was. I think the receptionist felt my naivety. "Don't worry, he's going to be fine. We'll keep him on a drip to rehydrate him, and we're going to give him an injection in the buttocks to bring him round." I guess adrenaline? I had no idea. She said it happens all the time. She smiled. I tried to make light of the situation. "Is it a big needle? For the backside I mean?" "Yes" she replied. "The biggest." We both had a chuckle, I got a copy of the forms I needed for management, and I was done. She said he would be discharged in the morning, with a sore bum and he'd be about £250 lighter for the privilege. Now all I had to do was deal with Juliet. My annoyance at the whole situation had subsided, and I started to think about what she'd told me earlier. I mean, if something did happen, we were in the medical centre and we needed to get her checked out. I went to her in the waiting room and quietly reminded her of what she'd told me, and that if it was true, we needed to make it formal. I also asked did she want a nurse to have a chat with her. She just glared at me, clearly irritated that I even brought the subject up. "Nothing happened. I was just pissed!" I still couldn't be sure. I mean what if she's just feeling guilty or uncomfortable talking to a guy. I offered again the chance to speak to a female rep. She just insisted she made it up. When I said why would she do such a thing, she said she was jealous of the way he was looking at another girl. She knew it was bad and just wanted me to forget the whole thing. I wanted to reprimand her about it, but I wasn't even sure what to believe now. In the end I just told her we'd say no more about it but if she did want to talk to someone, my door was always open and there were plenty of female reps about if she felt better speaking to a woman. I walked her back to the hotel. I dropped her off and then made my way to the night club to meet the others.

Thankfully, Nigel had found my bag and brought it with him. When I caught up with him, he was pissed. I told him what had happened and all he did was laugh. "It's not funny you cock!" he said "Yes, it is. It's our first week of being official reps. You've had a stalker, a drug overdose, and a trip to the medical centre and now you've got paperwork to do. All I got was a hand job behind the stage after the line dancing. There's no justice." I just grabbed him by the neck and put him in a headlock messing his hair up as I did. It didn't matter, he was laughing too much to care. I was too tired and out of sync with the rest of the group by the time I got my bag back. Defeated I headed home. Nigel on the other hand got laid. He was right, there was no justice!

CHAPTER 16
THE LIVERPOOL CONNECTION

Not everything played out so well for me in Ibiza. I remember one incident in my first season. One of the girls in my hotel had hooked up with a guy the night before, and basically needed the morning after pill. She came to me first thing in the morning. She was discrete, embarrassed (although she needn't have been), and a little panicky. She asked me not to tell her friend she was staying with. Naturally, I agreed. I told her I had a meeting with the other reps first, but then if she met me in 40 minutes or so, I would take her myself to get it. I told her to get some cash out and that I can probably do it outside the insurance so she wouldn't end up paying some ridiculous clinic fee that all medical facilities in the Mediterranean liked to charge young foreigners. She agreed, and as promised, I slipped away for an hour and brought her to the nearest medical facility we used. As you can imagine with thousands of holiday makers every month going through the books, we were continually seeing these people. Everyone was on a first name basis. I was greeted with smiles as soon as I walked through the door. There wasn't anyone else in there aside from one guy, about 6', probably 11 stone or so with bleached blonde hair. I quietly told the receptionist what I needed and asked was it ok to do cash. She just smiled and nodded. I brought in the guest who quietly took a seat next to the counter. She would still need to answer a few questions re allergies etc before they would just hand over the tablet. At that point, the main Doctor walked out. I shook his hand as we greeted each other warmly. He was a lovely Doctor. Probably early to mid 60s. He had a great sense of humour and had seen it all having been based in San Antonio for the best part of 30+ years and we got on very well. I remember needing to take a phone call which was a rarity because my phone hardly ever had credit. I stepped outside, reassuring the guest that I would be literally 1 minute and I would stand by the doorway. The receptionist was very kind and told her not to worry, that she was in good hands and that it wouldn't take long so relax. I stepped outside and took the call. It was something to do with DJs needing to be picked up and ferried to and from a venue we'd booked. I remember agreeing to something and then hung up. As I walked through the doorway and back into the main waiting area. The doctor had his back to us (myself, the guest and this blonde lad) talking to the receptionist. All of a sudden, the blonde lad (we'll call him Asshole from this point on) lunged forwards and punched the doctor in the back twice. He aimed straight at the kidneys. The doctor let out a yelp as he slumped forward onto the receptionist's counter. The receptionist recoiled in shock and Asshole grabbed the prescription book and made a dash for the main doorway. As he passed me and shot to the exit, I instinctively lashed out and swung a punch in his direction. Bingo. I landed it right on the side of his face around the cheekbone causing him to fall forwards, his momentum carrying him out of the door and into the side of the ambulance parked outside. He stumbled on to one knee, but rather than fall over fully, he managed to scramble away together with the prescription book. I don't know why, but I slung my bag to the guest and gave chase. I wanted that prescription book back. Even if I couldn't get any better justice for the doctor, I wanted Asshole to fail. He kept telling me to fuck off as he ran in this thick scouse accent. Undeterred, I told him to drop the book and just fuck off himself. He told me that I didn't know who he was, and that he was going to have me cut and he knew people not to be messed with. Again, I told him to just leave the book and to go forth and prosper. Don't you just love adrenaline fuelled conversations! At one point he stopped in an area where the main fountains were and turned to face me, there was probably about 5m distance between us. I was cautious to go running in and so I too pulled up. We had an exchange of words and then he turned on his heels again, I gave chase, only for him to stop again about 20-30m further up one of the lanes on the strip. He proceeded to throw the prescription book at me. I picked it up and he was off again. At this point I didn't follow. I picked up the book instead. I don't quite understand what happened next. By the time I picked up the book and stood upright, he was only about 10m away from me and was running when all of a sudden, a couple of waiters from the surrounding restaurant intercepted him. How they knew who he was or what he'd done was anyone's guess? He started to whine and struggle like an animal caught in a snare. As he struggled a bit too much, one of the waiters punched him clean in the face. He yelped. Then the other waiter gave him one across the chops and he yelped again. I won't lie, this was great. Another waiter came out and he too proceeded to give Asshole a dig. I was happy to watch. I stood there clutching the prescription book breathing heavily, adrenaline flooding through me not to mention the 3-400m sprint I'd just endured. You won't believe what happened next. As I stood there watching this fuckwit get slapped repeatedly by the locals, a big hand was placed on my shoulder. It frightened the life out of me. As I spun to the side it was the 60 something years old doctor. He too had run after us. He held onto my shoulder as he caught a breath. "Thank you, my friend!" he managed to get out in his deep Spanish accent. "Don't worry, I've got your book Doc." I proudly responded. "You're a good boy." he wheezed. Suddenly he let go of my shoulder, straightened himself and strode over to Asshole who by now was crying out for assistance. The waiters seemed to part to make room for old Doc and I kid you not the Doc threw in an uppercut. It was glorious. It wasn't going to knock anyone out, but it was a punch that only an older person can throw. I thought to myself that serves you right you prick, thinking that would be the end of it. It wasn't. Doc hit him again. And again. And again. I'll never forget the look on Asshole's face as justice was administered to him. Every time a blow was landed, this Scouser yelped. I think after the third or fourth whack they let him go. As the Liverpudlian set off, he was assisted by the boot of one of the waiters who kicked him cleanly in his ass lifting the blonde bastard 6 inches off the floor. He ran off towards the seafront. I turned towards the others but they were all gesturing wildly and conversing in Spanish between them.

I returned to the surgery and placed the book proudly on the desk. The receptionist hugged me. The guest sat there a little dumbfounded. I sat down next to her and tried to play it down. The receptionist asked the guest to come over and after about 2 minutes of questions, gave her the pill with some water. She asked how much do I owe you and the receptionist just smiled and said "Nothing. Thank him for that" and gestured to me. The guest just smiled at me. I won't lie, I felt like a hero. My bean bag felt weighed down by a pair of apples. Again, I just smiled back and said it was nothing. At that point, Doc walked back through the door, his short sleeved, lemon shirt wringing with sweat. He was out of breath. I asked him if he was ok, he said he was fine. He said the coward got him with a sucker punch, but he got his justice. He said the main thing was that I got the book back. I jokingly told him I didn't know he could box, at which point he broke into a broad smile and said neither did he. "Besides, you threw a quick right yourself," he followed up with. At that point he thanked me again, shook my hand and turned to his receptionist who was ready to make a fuss of him. We left the clinic and returned to the hotel. My adrenalin had subsided by that point and I just wanted to check that my guest was ok and she'd taken her pill and she was no longer stressed. She was perfectly calm. She thanked me for looking after her and being discrete, as well as saving her some money. Again, I played it down. I told her we'd speak no more about it. I dropped her off at the hotel and went to find Nigel to tell him all about it. He was equally impressed. We joked that we could get all the STD meds in the world for free now and this was a sign for us to smash the whole of Ibiza. I told him I would be getting them for free, and that I would be selling them to him. He called me a wanker and we continued to chuckle amongst ourselves. About an hour later we headed to the main pool where we found the majority of our guests chilling out. As we walked in, I was met with a round of applause. I was initially puzzled, then I saw my guest just smiling. Apparently, she decided that what I had done was a good deed and that it shouldn't go unnoticed. She'd told a few guys around the pool and before you knew it, it had gone around the whole place. I was repeatedly patted on the back. Everyone was being super nice to me. I won't lie, the feeling was very great. Even the girls were looking at me more intently. Brilliant, I thought. I'll be capitalising on this tonight. Nigel picked up on it too… he kept whispering to me "take your pick, but aim fucking high!"

The rest of the afternoon was a casual affair. We weren't really in the mood for a pool party and the guests seemed happy to have a chilled one. We were all lazily lounging around and sharing drinks with the guests. Just after sunset we went to the rep's meeting. I was intent on not saying anything to the others as I wasn't sure what the reaction would be from Damien and I didn't want to get into trouble. Besides, if they were going to find out about it and praise me, it would look better if they heard it from someone else, rather than me blowing my own trumpet. I needn't have worried. The minute we walked through the door I was met with a barrage of abuse. "You absolute twat." I tried to feign surprise. "What's up?" I protested. Damien was having none of it. "Do you know what you've done?" before I had a chance to respond, Damien hit me with a string of words that I don't ever really want to hear again. "Do you know who he was?" I immediately dropped the act. "Go on…" Damien continued to tear me a new one in front of the others. Apparently, I'd whacked a lieutenant of someone on the island that was well known for supplying various bits and bobs to bars and clubs. He'd gone bleating back to his master and a call had been put in to one of the bar owners looking out for someone fitting my description. The bar owner in turn put a call into one of the seniors that one of theirs was at risk. My heart sank. I was massively out of my depth. I only tried to get back a prescription book, and now I'd somehow gotten myself tangled up in a world I definitely didn't want to be a part of. I looked around the room for answers. There were none. To add to the seriousness, Damien dismissed the rest of the team and told me to take a seat. I was worried. I knew the company had connections. We were one of the biggest tour operators on the island. We worked day in and day out with bar owners and club promoters. I asked Damien what to do. He told me not to worry and that someone was going to be putting a call in to someone somewhere to explain and to try and close this box that I had inadvertently opened. I wasn't convinced. You meet a lot of people in life who tell you they know such and such and they're connected and blah blah bullshit. I wasn't buying any of it. "How quickly can I get a flight if needed?" I asked. "It won't come to that. We'll get it fixed. Don't worry. Just keep your head down. Make sure you stay with the other reps, and no sneaking off for a smash after hours. At least for the next few days." This was hardly reassuring. The last thing on my mind was getting my nuts in. I was more worried about being caved in! Damien could see I was scared. He did say that everyone in the office was proud of me for what I did and that the nurses and Doctor think I'm a hero. He continued that I would probably get free chlamydia medication for life now. We both chuckled. I then left and went back to my apartment.

When I got there, Nigel was waiting for me. He checked I was ok, and asked what Damien had said. I told him the whole story. He tried to reassure me. When I asked what the others had said or thought, Nigel burst my bubble of reassurance with a javelin. Apparently, all the other reps had been told not to let me out of their sight, and that I wasn't allowed to go anywhere alone. Even if I went for a shit, someone had to be with me. If anything happened to me on their watch they were going to be in big trouble. Nervously, I tried to play it down. "Am sure it will be ok. They'll fix it up for me. I'm going to get ready. See you at the hotel in an hour." Nigel said he'd be here for me in 45 minutes. I agreed and we both went to get ready. I didn't get ready. I started packing. I basically packed my whole suitcase and was pretty much ready to go at a moment's notice. Passport, and what little cash I had was all good to go. I took a shower and then started to worry even more. The thing is, we were so visible in Ibiza. Everyone knew us, and on the main strip most of the workers knew me. Whether it was the silly crossdressing relays, the drunken pub crawls, or just me being social. It wouldn't take Sherlock Holmes to work out which hotel I worked, where I was staying etc. In Ibiza, the workers are like a community. I tried to rationalise it in my head. I would be surrounded by other reps and guests, not to mention workers and security in the various places and I was always friendly with them. I didn't want to take any chances. I left the hotel and met up with Nigel who was already waiting for me.

I don't really remember the first half of the evening. I was like a swan, calm on the exterior but under the surface my legs were going ten to the dozen. I was continually glancing around the room and behind me, all the while smiling at the guests and still receiving their praise from what had happened earlier. A couple of the girls were already on my case. One said she wanted to reward my good work and the other was trying to arrange a meet after work. I denied both and said I was on an airport run that evening. This was a blatant lie, but the last thing I wanted to do was get laid. True to their word, everywhere I went members of the team went with me. Every once in a while, one of them would rest a hand on my back or shoulder and tell me not to worry and that management will sort it. It didn't help at all. If anything, it made it worse. It's like when you're a kid and you're not feeling well. Your mum puts her hand on your back and rubs it gently hoping to comfort you when in fact she's coaxing you to puke! I appreciated the gesture none the less, but I was still painfully on edge. Thankfully, aside from me being wound up, the evening passed relatively uneventfully. I was in bed for just after 2:30 which was the earliest I'd been in the sack all season. As I tried to nod off, I tried to focus on the girls that I'd passed over. I figured I'd go creeping in the morning.

I was pretty tense for the next day or so. I tried to surround myself with as many guests and friends as possible. Over time I began to slowly ease off. Damien popped round to the pool to see me. I think I was in the middle of a lilo race or something daft. He pulled me out to one side. He could tell by my face how anxious I was. "Relax soft cock, it's good news." He got straight to it. "The big man has had a chat with one of the club owners about your situation. The club owner has made it clear to the relevant people that you're out of bounds and that by all accounts the guy you hit is a fucking liability for bringing attention to something that's best left in the shadows. The club owner was also disappointed that such a fuckwit would even be in such a position of employment. Not to mention that the doctor is a well-known and well-liked chap." My sphincter began to loosen. He didn't need to spell it out to me. We brought in a lot of money for the various clubs, bars and venues over the season. Some of those guests no doubt contributed more money in different ways than others. I guess the last thing anyone important wanted was for some idiot from Liverpool slapping a 60 year old doctor in public and then making a further spectacle and issuing threats on behalf of someone he shouldn't. "If I was you, I would relax. Take a few hours off. Sort some Doris out and come back for 7:30. No airport for you this week." I could have kissed him. It was the news I was waiting to hear. I gave him a big man hug. He recoiled in agony and called me a nonce. We both laughed. It was like someone had lifted a huge weight off of my shoulders. I practically skipped back to the pool. I grabbed a sheet of paper from the bar and a pen. I quickly scribbled a quick note. 'Sorry about the other night. Your apartment – 10 mins, cuddle'o'clock?' I know it was pure cheese, but this was a dead cert. She was in the pool with her mate talking to a group. I slipped the note under the magazine resting on her sun-bed. With that I went and sat by the bar and ordered a San Miguel. Nigel was already there chatting to the barman. He could sense I was happier. "All sorted?" he quipped. "All sorted. Am in the clear." "I'll drink to that!" he said. I told him about the note and who I was angling for. He laughed and wanted to know who was her mate. I pointed her out and he looked interested. He analysed the situation. I was undoubtedly going to get into her friend. She would immediately spill the beans after I was gone, and her friend will probably feel left out. Therefore, she's going to be looking for a pick me up. That pick me up he calculated should be a piece of Nigel. I laughed. Thing is, his logic was sound. He said as soon as she gets the note, if she leaves, he was going to hit on the other one. We didn't have to wait long. About 10 minutes later, a familiar voice appeared. "Were you reading my magazine earlier?" "I might have been." I teased. "Looking for makeup tips were you?" She bantered. "No, there was a part in there about getting your beauty sleep during the day, and I thought it made sense." Have that I thought to myself. Make or break time. There was a brief silence. "I read that too, I'll have to try that out. Am heading back now, am a bit tired. Catch you later." "Ok, cool" I replied. Nigel couldn't help himself. "Enjoy your nap." Prick. I glared at him, but she just said "I think I will." With a quick smirk and a look, she was off. "What did you say that for you bell end?" Nigel just laughed. He finished his beer and said it was time for him to rescue a damsel. He went straight over to the side of the pool where her friend was chatting and inserted himself into the conversation. I squared away my San Miguel, and continued chatting for another 5 or 10 minutes with some of other guests. I wasn't in a rush to go back. Don't get me wrong, I was horny as hell, and she was cute, but repping had taught me to play the long game.

CHAPTER 17
REP'S CABARET

As a rep, one of the most exhilarating nights out was the cabaret night. It was probably one of the cheesiest nights for the guests, but it was also by far one of the messiest. Right from the off, as soon as it was time to meet in the hotel bar, we would make every effort to get the place rocking early. Court would be particularly aggressive in terms of drinking fines and various drinking games would be played with particular attention to the rules (and rule breakers!). The guests were always up for this, I'd even forewarn them a day or so in advance that this night was going to be painful for those carrying misdemeanours or anyone committing sins within the group. I'd usually receive a continual stream of nominations for fines. I kept a small book in my bag and as soon as someone mentioned the word crime or sin, out it came and details were taken. As authoritarian as this sounds, the guests loved it. Allegations would include puking, taking too long to get ready, too drunk to perform or spilling drinks. Sometimes the guests would be really graphic. One group had gone to the local brothel to help a friend out. The friend had been on at them all night to go there. Every time they were getting close to a group of girls in the bar, he kept blowing it up by proudly announcing where they were off to afterwards. That wasn't the best look, and the girls would quickly move on. Out of irritation they eventually took him to the cat house, only to find out that horny had forgotten his wallet and so the others had to club together for him to pay for his cuddle. If that's not a 4 finger fine of tequila I don't know what is. Another guest had gotten so drunk he decided to relieve himself into the wardrobe in a semi-conscious state. The thing is, it was his mate's clothes that received the shower. That's another Mexican Kitkat in a glass! Anyways, you get the picture. After hearing the accuser and the evidence, you'd ask the defendant. Rarely did they deny it, you'd ask the bar, they'd shout guilty and the drink was given! The stories were always funny and it was a good way to get people down to the hotel bar relatively punctually. If you said normally let's meet in the hotel bar at 8… people would slowly drip in from 8:30 onwards and some would come down literally as we were leaving. This court idea was good fun, and normally people didn't want to miss it, so you'd set a start time and to my surprise, most would be down ready for it.

By the time we would have everyone on the coach some would be swaying. We'd pull up to the venue and get everyone inside. The venue itself was like an amphitheatre. There was a big stage next to the dance floor with seating and tables built up around the edge. The music would already be pounding as the guests arrived, and people would immediately flock to the various bars dotted around the place. The reps would pretty much immediately disappear back stage and start to go through their various scenes and check for props and costumes. The first time I was here I was nervous as hell. I knew the various routines I was going to perform inside out. We'd practiced them in Majorca during training, and during our introductory weeks, Nigel and I had been continually going through them with the other reps. We were up to speed. It didn't stop me feeling nervous though. The rest of the reps went into autopilot. They knew where the props were and who was doing what. I was in over my head. Now cabaret was performed in each area once a fortnight. Due to the large number of guests we had, it meant one area would be doing it this week, and another area would be doing it the following week. What this actually meant was that no one gave a fuck about putting stuff together nicely, or washing the costumes. They were minging. They smelt and were uncomfortable. The Full Monty outfits were the worst. Now keep in mind this consisted of not only a full uniform, but also a bright ruby coloured thong with Velcro holding the three bits of string together at the back. These had been purposely made for the job. They looked like they'd been worn day in and day out for the last 5 years. In fact, they looked so bad, even if you stuffed them with sausages and bacon not even a dog would approach them. As soon as the reps got back stage they made a beeline for the 'props cupboard' and began rifling though the clothing trying to choose the best thongs. I didn't really understand what was going on initially, but by the time I got over to there to pick out my own one, I quickly understood that I'd lost out on the thong stakes. I unravelled this thing with a heavy heart and put it underneath my pile. No one said a word. I managed to cobble together the rest of the costumes and props I needed for the night ahead. We each had our own pile and we laid everything out in order of what we'd need next to ensure a smooth transition from act to act.

Once set, we then went back in to the main hall and interacted with the guests. We would bring out a hypnotist next. Now this wasn't the normal Butlins run of the mill hypnotist. This was an adult entertainer. He was hilarious. He would pick, with our encouragement, randoms from the audience. They would be hypnotised and would then be at his mercy. He would have people simulating sexual positions with an inflatable crocodile lilo. He would make people imagine they were invisible or that their dick had disappeared. He would have girls flirt outrageously with other guests, but would tell those guests the girls were their sisters or mothers. The audience would be in hysterics. If I hadn't seen it with my own eyes, I wouldn't have believed it. Rarely would someone not be able to be hypnotised. If it happened, we would just quietly tap them on the shoulder and then bring them off the stage to leave the rest up there to entertain the crowd. Often when the guests would come out of it, they would have little to no recollection of what had just transpired. We filmed every show, and they were free to watch it afterwards. They would be amazed at what had taken place, although am still not quite sure if it actually triggered any recollection. I always wanted to try and be hypnotised. Several times I've crept up on to the stage to see if he could put me under. Unfortunately, it never worked. I'm not sure whether I'd had too much or not enough to drink, or just couldn't relax enough to have my subconscious pierced. Thankfully, there were plenty of other people who more susceptible. During the hypnotist show, we'd do the rounds, making sure our guests were having a good time and that everyone had a drink etc. We'd often sit and have a few with them to help loosen us up. Then at a certain point towards the end of the show we'd be given the tap and then we'd sneak off back stage to get ready for the main event. A variety of sketches would be performed. I'd already covered a few of them here in Majorca. They were light hearted, and the guests seemed to enjoy them. In between each sketch, the DJ would kick in, so people would then be free to mingle, drink and dance as they wished. It wasn't as torturous as you might think. As the night went on, the crowd would get more raucous. When their reps were on stage, they'd be cheered for, or abused. Often it would be extremely difficult to keep a straight face when some comments were thrown out, and the guests knew it. If they detected a smirk or a snigger, that was your lot. They'd continually heckle you until you broke. Once you started to laugh, they'd cheer and then choose the next victim.

The first time I did the show, I was all over the place. I was rushing to change into the next costume and not miss my cue. It was fun to do, and at the end of each sketch you'd get a big cheer from your hotel which was massaging for the ego. Behind the stage, shots were being handed out like a stag party. By the time we got to the main events, everyone was pissed. It was time for the female reps to get on the stage. They did a Spice Girls tribute act which half way though descended into a burlesque kind of show. One minute, Ginger Spice and her gang were wearing track suits and doing high kicks to Wannabe, and the next they were down to suspenders and little tight numbers rubbing growlers up and down chair backs that just happened to have been placed out front and centre for the crowds. It was soft titillation but the whole room erupted with cheers and unintelligible crowing. It reminded me of the annual Army v Navy rugby match at Twickenham. The girls were well choreographed to be fair. They'd all put in plenty of practice, had infinitely more rhythm than their male counterparts, and well, quite frankly they looked damn good in stockings. They received rapturous applause at the end of their set from pretty much everyone in the room. By the time they got behind stage they were elated, dopamine flooding through them. They quickly got changed into something more comfortable, did another shot with all of us, and went back into the main hall to share a drink with the guests and to get ready for what was to come. Namely, us, naked.

We were getting into our costumes for the Full Monty. Damien appeared behind the curtain. He wanted to wish us well. He warned us not to get overtly naked or there would be airport duty, but told us to give it our all. I was still a little confused by what he'd meant. I asked one of the lads next to me who was swigging a beer. "Basically, don't get your cock out" was the response. I had no intentions of swinging out in front of 800 people if I could help it, but that being said, it was a little counter intuitive. He continued to go through what was to happen after in terms of logistics, which bar/club we were to meet in, and which order we'd pull out of the venue. I wasn't paying attention to any of it. I was trying to readjust my costume. This shrivelled thong was scratchy as hell and I was trying to sort out the Velcro on the side of my trousers to make sure there weren't any gaps. Looking back now, I don't know why I bothered, but at the time I wanted to try and give the best performance I could, and that involved looking the part. I loosened my laces to ensure I was able to kick the shoes off, but tied them loosely so as not to trip my ass up on stage. Just as I was straightening my jacket and tie, I felt something unusual. I couldn't work out what it was. At first it was a tingle, but then after a few seconds it began to get more intense before starting to burn. All I could work out was it was coming from my groin area. I wasn't the only one feeling it either. Nigel, as subtle as ever suddenly blurt out that his dick was on fire. The rest of the lads roared with laughter. I looked at Nigel, he looked back at me with a distressed look on his face. One of the reps then held up the evidence. It was Tiger balm. We'd been well and truly stitched up. For those of you who don't know what Tiger balm is, think of it as a pot of Vicks Vaporub only about 100 times stronger. I think it's originally from China and it's been used as a muscle relaxant for centuries. It heats up the skin really aggressively. That's great if you have a bad back or a muscle spasm, but less than ideal when you've just had your helmet coated in the stuff. By the time it had dawned on us what had happened, my chap was burning big time. We started to fiddle and adjust ourselves, but it made no difference. The more I tried to reposition myself in the ruby banana hammock, the more my boy made contact with more of the balm. Damien looked irritated that we'd interrupted his briefing, but even he was beginning to smirk. One of the reps just said "welcome to the team" and the rest of the group, including Damien laughed again. Nigel was scratching at himself like a crack whore. I was just trying to think about something else, attempting to keep as still as possible. Damien finished what he wanted to say, wished us well and told us not to fuck up. He shot Nigel and I a glance as he finished, shook his head with a grin and disappeared behind the curtain.

By the time we were ready to walk out on to the stage in darkness I couldn't feel the burning any more. In fact, I couldn't feel my penis either. My whole nether region had been numbed. If there weren't any concerns about not being "big" enough for the crowd before, there certainly were now. In the event I did happen to get naked in front of 800 people, the last thing I wanted to show was a bright red speckled egg. Measle cock isn't a good look for anyone. I didn't have much more time to think about it.

We were introduced on stage and we shuffled out in silence, under the cover of darkness. The girls had been encouraged to move to the front of the stage. There must have been 100 crowded up against the edge of the stage. They were cheering us on and ogling. Some were even waving disposable cameras. Thank god this was pre smartphone. The last thing I'd fancy was seeing our little performance going viral on Instagram or TikTok. Even before the music started, the girls refused to stay silent. The music was familiar. It was the same tune I'd performed in my interview, only this time there was no rugby boy to pre-empt. There were 5 other male reps on the stage all in their prime, experienced and ready for what was about to come next. Oh, plus Nigel who was still rubbing himself at the back. We both needed to measure up and quick!

We'd gone through this routine so many times before, it was second nature. As soon as the initial bars kicked off, the spotlights came on and we moved into a V position. Thankfully I was off to the side, so wasn't quite the focus of attention. That honour fell on the most senior rep in the group and he was flanked either side by some of the other reps who already knew what they were doing. We went through the routine as normal. Off came the jackets. Undo the shirt cuffs. Smile at the girls. Belts out. Smile at the girls. Kick your shoes off. Drop to your knees in unison. It was at this point that I felt something give. I tried to subtly look down at my trousers to see if half the Velcro had come undone, but both seams seemed to be holding in. What the fuck was that? Did I just split the ass in them? That didn't really bother me as they were about to be ripped off anyway. What was it? No time to think now. We took off the tie as seductively as we could, before the buttons started to be undone… nice and slow, lots of eye contact! Then in one move, the shirts were undone and thrust down behind us. The girls were roaring… even most of the lads were showing support. We had to wait for the right bar in the song before we straightened up quickly to our feet. Lots of hip thrusting and gyrating. The girls were really digging it as you can imagine. Even if we looked pretty ridiculous, the fact we were trying made it worthwhile for them. In my head I was going through the next steps. We were approaching the point where I needed to rip the trousers off. This would involve leaning forward and bending over whilst wiggling our butts in the air. Then we'd essentially grab the side of our ankles and in one motion rip upwards towards the heavens. If everything went to plan, I would be standing there holding my trousers to the ceiling, with a big smile and a rolled up crusty red G-string hiding my squirrel. Seems easy enough right? Things aren't always so simple. As I'm standing there smiling at the front 2-3 rows of girls gyrating my money maker like Elvis on a pill, something catches one of the girl's attention and she nudges her mate who begins to point down at my feet. I didn't notice this immediately, but within seconds, 3-4 other girls are nudging each other and pointing and within a further 5 seconds, there's 30 pointing and smiling at me. What's going on? Is this another prank? As I look down, my heart sinks. Sitting proudly upon my right foot is a little piece of ruby coloured fabric, which looks like it hasn't been washed in a year. Bollocks. I look up to the sky and eyes closed. You know the feeling you get when you drop your pint and well, today's just not your day. My reaction just made the girls laugh all the more. I refocus and continue to try and style it out. By now the other reps are looking round to see what the girls are pointing at. They notice it and they begin to laugh themselves. I can't believe it. Especially as Damien had said no cocks out. What to do? There's no way I'm not taking my trousers off, but if I go for it, I'm hanging in the wind. If I try and do it one handed, not only will I look like a twat, but then people are going to think I'm embarrassed, and I'll be "that" guy out of the group. The rest will be loud and proud, and I'm going to be the tool at the side battling Velcro one handed, whilst hoping no one gets a glimpse of mini-me. I'm wracking my brains for a solution. I glance at Nigel with a false smile on my face. Hoping for some support or a suggestive glance that might unlock a solution. No chance. He's pissing himself. He's not even moving to the music. He's just roaring at me. Prick. I face forwards again, still smiling. By now the girls are starting to chant "off, off, off!" They know what's coming next. They're all focused on me, smiling, cheering and pointing in unison like you would at a football match. The music's building, the moment is nigh. I look up at Damien, he's already shaking his head. I assumed I'd be doing airport for a month if I flop out here. It was simple. Either cover my modesty and try and get by as best I could, or go for it and take the consequences. We were already all bending forwards wiggling our asses. The music was climbing, it was make or break time. I grasped my trousers with both hands and just paused, bent over waiting for the crescendo to hit. I looked up and was directly in eye line with what felt like the whole audience. The girls were all nodding, smiling and giving me the thumbs up. I was grinning like a naughty lothario. I winked at them, and let out a wide smile. Fuck it. The beat dropped and I ripped that material upwards and behind me in one aggressive fashion. By the time I released the material, the trousers were practically on the guy behind me. I had nothing to lose, and no point in doing it half arsed. The other reps all stood there proudly in there bright shimmering thongs. They tossed the trousers down in front of them, smiling at the audience. All eyes were on me. I stood there wearing just a police officer's cap, arms outstretched like Russell Crowe in the gladiator. I cast a glance up to my Julius Caesar. Damien just put his head in his hands. I looked at where most of my hotel were sitting and the lads were giving me a standing ovation and whistling. I'll not lie, standing there without a stitch on and being applauded by most of the room was electric. I wasn't in a rush for this to finish, but the show had to go on. Together with the other reps we reached up to grab our hats with both hands and then seductively place them down in front of our bits. The other reps were teasing the crowd. I was just smiling at the girls in front of me. They then ripped their thongs off from behind the caps, whilst I just stood there laughing. I was even intimating that this lot were pussies for not going the whole hog. I thought I'd try and capitalise on this moment. Just before the final bars of the song, the lights went into a strobing pattern. Once the signal was given, the hats were then thrown into the crowd and all of us who were all starkers at this point made a dash for the curtain. We brought the house down. They were still cheering when we were getting changed back into our usual attire.

Back stage everyone was laughing. People were congratulating me on going for it. I was beaming. I had loved it. The recognition, the attention, the support, it was addictive. We got dressed quickly into our regular clothes because we were about to be brought out on stage to receive applause. The female reps were on stage receiving theirs and we were to be brought out next. Damien was nowhere to be seen. Probably a good thing. Had he laid into me right now, I think I would have smiled even wider and would have gained an extra month of airport duty. Literally within a minute we were being called back out. I was one of the last to get ready so by the time I was back on stage I was the last in line. As the compere announced each of us and our respective hotels we were representing, the audience would cheer. Obviously, the guests in the hotel the rep was from would be the most enthusiastic in their support. I stood there smiling and clapping politely whilst the rest of them were being announced. Finally, he got to me. I got a massive cheer. Everyone was laughing and wolf whistling. Like a twat, I even took a bow. I looked up to see where Damien was, but the eagle's nest was empty. He wasn't in his normal position (by the mixing deck and lighting rig at the back). We all took a final applause and then left the stage. We threw the props back into the cupboard and filed out to the main hall.

We had about 20 minutes with the guests before it was time to leave and get them on coaches back to San Antonio and into a nightclub. Damien ambushed me as I was leaving the dressing area. He came out of nowhere. "What the fuck was that? What part of no nakedness did you not understand?" I wasn't sure how to play this. I mean was he just winding me up, or was my wardrobe malfunction a serious offence. I wasn't sure of my footing here. I erred on the side of caution. "Damien am sorry, the thong broke as I ripped the trousers off. I didn't feel it come loose." A little white lie, but I didn't want to go down the route of how I tried to save the performance. I was banking on him having not seen the girls' pointing and their reactions and my prior knowledge of what was going to happen. He paused before calling me a twat. I thought now was the time to try and win some favour and I knew just how to do it. "Damien, we both know I'm a bit unlucky when it comes to this sort of thing, but we also both know I'm your favourite salesperson…" "Don't push it!" he interjected "I'm still trying to decide whether to give you extra airports or not." I asked him playfully how much in sales would it need for me to avoid this punishment. Before he could respond, I offered up "5 new packages?" Meaning 5 additional people would sign up to the full package of trips for us, thus helping the hotel average and his area commissions, making him look good in the process. "10" he aggressively countered. I asked him if he was sure. He said I had until tomorrow night to get them. I opened my bag and started to rummage though it. "No fucking way" he said as I handed him a thick brown padded envelope. "There's 12! I managed a quick round this afternoon and hit the football lads from Exeter. It's not the full package, as they've already missed a night, and I threw in some extra drinks tickets, but that's ok right?" I was smiling. He couldn't chastise me any further. I might have been a twat, but I could sell. "You had this all along, didn't you?" he challenged me. "Well I hadn't had a chance to hand it in yet. I only closed them at 6 o'clock." "Fair play. No extra airports. Just do us all a favour and keep your fish finger in your pants next time!" I nodded, we both smiled and I was turned loose into the main hall.

I figured I had about 20 minutes to try and line up some cuddles and try to capitalise on my exhibitionism. I had 20 minutes, but 2 would have been sufficient. As I stood at the bar, a pair of keys were placed in the rear pocket of my jeans. I was already speaking to another pair of girls so didn't do or say anything immediately. I made my polite excuses after a moment and then retrieved the keys. It was my hotel and I knew the room. I approached the culprit by the side of the bar and gave them back to her. I had a skeleton key anyway. "Someone just handed these in, I think you dropped them." "Yeah must have done" she smiled. "Thanks for returning them." I leant in and just whispered 2:30 under my breath. She smiled, and with that I gave her the keys and left.

Cabaret wasn't always as eventful as that, but it never failed to grab a cheer from the guests. It was always a very productive evening in terms of 'after-hours', and it also reinforced our personas as people willing to get naked at any time and who didn't give a shit. We'd ride that wave as best and as often as we could.

CHAPTER 18
HAIRBRUSH HORRORS

I'll tell you a funny story. Peak season was well under way, and Ibiza was heaving. It was around early August. The parties were getting bigger, the crowds were increasing and the vibe was great. We were having an amazing time, and the hotels were packed full of guests looking to party away for 1 or 2 weeks. Everyone was out to play. We had changeover day and some new arrivals came to the hotel. There were a couple of lads, slightly older than the rest but up for it all the same. I spoke with them when they arrived. They saw the welcome meeting, and they loved the sound of it. These were here to misbehave with the opposite sex and drink as opposed to go to the big clubs and see the DJs. They were men after my own heart. They signed up for the package there and then without a blink of an eye. I don't think they even looked at each other for approval. One guy simply said done. The second one handed over a card. I got to know them better over the course of 2-3 days. One guy was a squaddie and had been stationed in Kosovo over the last year, his mate was working at home but they'd been best friends since school.

This trip was as much about reconnecting as it was about getting laid. That being said, I knew the squaddie was going to be roaring. Word got around that he was in the forces, and he had the usual ink to show it too. He would tell stories by the pool about his times abroad. He never went into enough detail to depress anyone, but he told just enough to make you think twice about things and to realise how lucky/sheltered you were. They were very popular. Not only did neither of them give a fuck, they also came across as very genuine and would help with things when needed. Whenever there was some kind of competition either within the guests or between the hotels they would volunteer. Whenever there was some kind of challenge, albeit drink or dressing up, they were doing it. They were 100% enthusiastic and people loved them for it. Needless to say, the other guys in the hotel looked up to them and so did the girls. In fact, the squaddie was doing alright on the quiet. I think by day 5 of his one weeker, he'd managed to score with 3 different girls. His mate had managed a sniff here and there but when quizzed he always just said his love of the booze kept blowing him out. In fact, it was a recurring theme. He'd either get too pissed to perform, or too pissed to speak, whatever came first!

Day 6 came for the pair of them, and it was their last night. You see they were flying home the next day, and both were determined to go out with a bang so to speak. On this particular night it was a Grease themed event. Again, usual scenario, we met in the hotel bar first, had a few sharpeners, before jumping on a coach to a venue for free food and drink, bit of a DJ and then back into a club in San Antonio after. I remember walking into the Hotel bar just before 8 and receiving an almighty cheer. I was dressed as a T-Bird complete with leather jacket, tight drainpipe jeans and slick back hair with enough brylcreem to keep an army of wookies looking shiny. I was sweating my tits off in the jacket. I was about to take it off, when one of the girls I'd been after said she liked it. I laughed it off, but I kept it on. I figured if I ended up hanging out the back of her later and she complained I smelt, she only had herself to blame. It wasn't just her looking to deal too, there were a couple of back up options forming already and it wasn't even 8!

The bar was bustling, and the vibe was good. Drink forfeits were already being dished out for various misdemeanours that had occurred throughout the day. Some of the guests clearly struggled with their left and rights. Within 5 minutes of playing left hand drinking, the hotel bar had emptied a bottle of tequila, and the hierbas was coming out. As I looked around at the bar, I could see most of my guests were either paired up, pairing up, or were about to. It was perfect. The short march to the coach stop was comical with various childish antics and jokes all round. We played a round of confessions on the coach where one by one the guests were encouraged to make a confession to the rest of the group. It was hilarious. I noticed on the coach ride that the squaddie was putting the ground work in with a group of girls. I didn't doubt him for a minute. Even his mate looked like he was capable of scoring. Grease night continued without a hitch. We did our little performance, everyone was dancing, drinking etc. At one point I was talking to some guests when I got hoisted in the air from behind (as they do in rugby when it's a line-out). I looked down and it was the squaddie. At which point the other one threw a can of lager across the bar. I caught it, and proceeded to shot gun it whilst being held above everyone's heads. I managed it with minimal spillage. The guys were having a blast. As soon as he dropped me down, he spun around and snogged the girl next to him. I don't think he even knew who she was. She certainly didn't object. Then it was man hugs all round and he was off into the crowd after another who had dared to look in his direction.

I didn't see much more from the pair until we'd already got back to San Antonio. We'd gone into the night club as planned. I had given my leather jacket to the girl from the hotel bar who had admired it. I thought she could keep that as a trophy for the time being. That was quite common. It usually meant that they wouldn't leave the club without finding you first which meant they were less likely to cop off with someone else. And find me she did. Just as I was finishing work, she approached me near the exit. I came up with some corny line about how great she looked in the jacket and then I asked her what she was up to. She said she wasn't sure, and asked me what I was doing. Green light! I told her to meet me outside up the road away from the entrance and I'd be out in 5mins. I finished my nightly work debrief. As I was sneaking out to meet my angel, I spied the squaddie being led up the road by a girl. She wasn't the smallest and she was literally pulling him by the belt. It made me chuckle to myself. It just made a fitting end to the last night of his holiday. I didn't think anything more about it. I had my mind firmly on other matters. I grabbed the girl and we went to a bar that happened to be close to my place where we made small talk over the smallest beers I could order. We didn't even end up finishing them.

I was running a bit late the following morning as I was up for round 2. I got to the hotel just after 9am. I quickly checked in with the staff to make sure everything was ok and there were no issues from the night before. As I sat down with a cuppa in reception who did I see trotting up the steps but the squaddie. "Oi Oi, you dirty stop out!" I hollered at him from across the entrance. "Don't even go there" he replied with a heavy voice. "What's up? Hungover? Woke up with a beast?" My mind was racing, itching for the story. "None of the above. You won't believe it. I've had a shocker." He slumped down next to me but as he sat down, he grimaced. I guessed this was something serious. I poured him a cup of tea and he began to recount the events of the night before. He basically quickly brushed over the night's events. He went through how much fun he was having, how he was pulling left right and centre and how much he enjoyed the whole Grease night. We were patching a few things together regarding which girl he was with etc, and I told him I remember seeing him being led up the road after the club by a bit of a unit. He laughed at my expression and explained himself. Apparently, he had his heart set on another girl in the bar and he was supposed to go on to another club with her and her friends, as her mate was due to meet up with a fella and she'd promised she'd wing her. He said we were all good, but they ended up losing each other. The girls left whilst he was searching for his mate. By the time he found him, the girls were long gone and he forgot which club they were supposed to meet at. He decided to have a few more drinks, but over did it. He said that was when she pounced. He said she barely said 6 words to him and they were heading out back to hers. He said he thought he'd settle for the easy win given it was his last night, but he also wanted to have one more drink in one of the bars on the way back. He said she immediately ordered a fish bowl and they both got stuck into this rancid multicoloured bowl of hangover. He said they were both hammered and things started to get hot and heavy in the bar. He said there was no way they were going to make it back to hers so they dragged each other into the toilets. He paused as he took a breath and a sip of tea. He sighed.

"This was when it all went wrong!" he continued. She was on her knees giving him a blow job in the toilets. He said it was totally surreal and the culmination of one of the best holidays he'd ever had. He said everything was going lovely (this expression made me chuckle, which I did a poor attempt at stifling), when disaster struck. He said he wasn't sure what happened, but suddenly she either started to choke or she had a fit. He said she made a funny noise and then suddenly bit down on his old boy. "I'm not talking about a playful nip or a fetish/vampire bite, I'm talking a full-on fucking shark chomp." I couldn't believe what I was hearing. "What happened next?" I excitedly interrupted. He said he tried to pull out but she was biting so hard he couldn't move. He said there was so much blood it was horrific. He didn't know if she was crazy and trying to bite it off or she was having a serious bout of epilepsy. He then confessed he had to punch her in the side of the head just to get her off. "I'm not proud of it like, but what else could I do?" You could see he felt bad. He said he hit her and her jaw loosened enough for him to pull out. He said he nearly fell over trying to back away. He admitted he was pissed and a little unsteady anyway, but this was something else. He said she just fell back on her ass and sat there, kind of dazed. She wasn't really looking at him just looking forwards into the room. He said he wanted to check on her, but then he saw how much blood she had all over her blouse. I then looked down and saw the blood coming through my jeans. I knew I was in a bad way, so I pegged it out and managed to find a medical centre. He said he was frantic. They calmed him down, gave him a glass of water and some saline to help rehydrate him and then put him under a local anaesthetic. He said it was like a dream.

When he came back round the Doctor told him he'd had 16 stitches and under no circumstances was he to have sex or masturbate for the next 6 weeks at least. The doc had said if he did, he risked damaging himself further which could affect his ability to get an erection going forwards. My jaw dropped. "I know right!?" he exclaimed. "I know it's shit now, but dude you're lucky. She could have damaged you permanently or even worse!" I tried to console him. "Mate, that's not the worst of it! I'm engaged and my fiancée thinks I'm still in Kosovo. She thinks I'm flying back to the UK in a couple of days. I didn't tell her I was sneaking to Ibiza for a knees-up. Not only will she be pissed that I lied, but how am I going to explain this to her? I've not banged her in over 4 months and this will be the first chance. I won't be able to hide it." Try as I did, I couldn't hold back any further, I started to laugh as the sheer gravity of his predicament began to unfold. Seeing my reaction, he also started to laugh, shaking his head as he did. "The boys on the base are going to love this!" he muttered. We both sat there for a moment in silence. We were like a couple of Eastbourne pensioners looking out to sea on a bench. "I don't know what to do or say!" Suddenly an idea popped into my head. "You need to own up to a little white lie so she's cross and it's more believable. Tell her that you actually went on leave 2-3 days earlier and you and a group of lads from the base went to Belgrade on the piss. After all you're all like brothers over there and you won't be seeing them for ages now. You can say one of the lads had a baby or something like that so you were wetting the baby's head." "Go on..." he said calmly and clearly interested. "Tell her that things got out of hand with some of the locals. Everyone had been drinking all day and someone started a fight. Tell her things got really nasty and you ended up getting glassed in the groin area. Make up some other injuries that some of the other lads got too, so it doesn't look like you were the ring leader. You can comment about how savage they are and don't fight fairly blah blah. Then you tell her you were rushed to the local hospital where they gave you stitches. She'll be so relieved you're ok with no permanent damage that it will soften the blow of you lying about stealing a couple of days away with the lads." He sat back marinating on what I'd just said. It was bullshit, but it was good bullshit. "Brilliant! Mate, you've just saved my bacon. That's spot on there. There's no way she'll be able to not believe a story like that. I mean, I've got the stitches for fuck's sake." After a moment or two, I followed up again "You need to make sure that you have nothing, and I mean nothing that ties you to Ibiza. You can't have flyers, photos, receipts, pesetas at all. Your boy needs to be sworn in too. If she finds one shred of evidence that you've been near the Mediterranean, you're dead. You'll need to remove luggage tags, flight tickets etc when you land." I was beginning to wonder why I was so good at this! "You're right. Good thinking. This is going to be tricky, but I think it can work." His mood seemed somewhat lighter. I don't know if it was the good old PG tips that we kept behind the bar or whether it was this plan that we hatched that was lifting his spirits. "Remember what the main thing is though" he sat forwards waiting for me to complete my sentence. "You have had an amazing time here in San An and have fucked the place royally. You even have the scars to prove it!" He roared of laughter. I didn't let up. "Besides, chicks dig scars!"

Under usual circumstances, I would have felt uncomfortable asking to look at another man's cock, but in this situation, I thought it wasn't entirely inappropriate. I mean it was an awesome story and I wanted validation. I leant across and said to him quietly "You have to let me see it." He laughed but agreed. He had been given some tracksuit bottoms to wear from the medical centre as his jeans were ruined and stained with blood. He leant back in his chair and pulled them down and loosened some bandaging that had been lightly applied. I couldn't believe what I was looking at. It looked like one of those hair brushes that your sister had in the 90s. You know the fluorescent type that had the long black spindles with the small little black balls on the end. The doctor had left the stitches long, I'm guessing at least an inch on each stitch. I don't know if that was intentional but it made it look all the ghastlier. I shuddered as he showed me how the rip had gone half way along the underside of it, and circled just under his helmet. I can only imagine the pain that must have caused, not to mention the shock. I'd be mentally scarred for life. "Mate, it looks like Frankenstein's thumb!" He chuckled as he carefully placed his chap back into his nest of bandages.

Our moment was interrupted by the hotelier who needed me to look at some paperwork for the upcoming changeover day. I left him for what must have been 5 minutes only to return to him telling this belter of a war story to half the hotel. Word had gone round quickly and he was proudly showing off his war wounds to all and sundry. I remember him needing to make the phone call to his fiancée explaining the story. I could tell for all the bravado he was nervous. He slipped away to the phone box. I was already busy with other guests and errands when he returned. His arms were outstretched like a prize fighter, "She only fucking bought it!" I was pleased for him. He gave me a man hug, told me how I'd saved his bacon, and that I was the best rep in the whole of Ibiza. It was quite touching. Then his mate who had since resurfaced told him to stop being soft and get the beers in. They spent the rest of the day mulling around the main reception area waiting for the coach to pick them up and ferry them back to the airport. It was a shame they weren't staying for longer. As they were leaving, he shouted to me from the steps of the coach to thoroughly apologise on his behalf to any big unit I see over the next few days with a black eye. Legend.

CHAPTER 19
MOPED TRAGEDY

Unfortunately, my time in Ibiza wasn't always as happy and pleasant as it could have been. As I alluded to earlier, the sheer number of people coming through our hotels per week in peak season were in the thousands. Statistically speaking, when you consider the general behaviour and potential for disaster with your teenage Brits abroad it meant that a number of people were going to get sick. A number of people were going to have fights. A number of people were going to do too many drugs and drink too much alcohol. A number of people were going to fall off scooters or have car accidents. A number of people were going to meet the wrong person etc. It was the ugly and unfortunate side of life. For 99.9% of those guests on that island it was going to be the time of their lives. For the 0.1% it was going to be life changing but for the wrong reasons. When shit hit the fan, we were the first responders.

When I look back to my days in Ibiza, I mainly remember the crazy times. The silly stuff that I did but wouldn't dare do now. The things I got away with then. The girls I've loved, the girls I've lost. The friends I've made. However, on occasion I also think about some of the people who weren't so lucky. The things I'm about to tell you about are a bitter pill to swallow for most people. They were especially heavy to deal with as a young adult not even in his twenties. I was a student. I was there to party. Unfortunately, fate at times had other ideas.

In our first season, initially, there were no real major incidents in either Nigel's hotel or mine. Some minor theft, some drunk and disorderly, and a few fights outside were about as bad as it got. It wasn't until some way through June that we were told of a problem with one of the other hotels in our area. We both came to a sales meeting and were late for one reason or another. As we walked in we were expecting to get railed by Damien for not being on time. I was quietly confident I'd escape an 'airport' as I'd just closed some more sales in my hotel. In fact, they were the last people in my hotel to sign, so my participation rate was 100%. That was a first all season, especially as peak season was well underway. In my head, I basically thought I'd be walking on water. I was particularly looking forward to Nigel being given some forfeit as he hadn't even managed to get 50% participation. He was going to be doing airports for a month. I figured I would be given nights off. How wrong I was. When we got there one of the girls was in tears. She was being comforted on either side of the chair by two other reps. The mood was sombre. We asked what had happened. Damien then proceeded to take us to one side and fill us in. There were two guys staying in her hotel. They must have both been 17 or 18. They were extremely friendly and funny and were super enthusiastic. Every joke at the welcome meeting they found funny, any volunteers for anything on stage they were game. They spoke to anyone and everyone. I don't think they even cared about pulling, they were just having a great time. You knew you had good guests when the other reps in your area knew of them. Damien went on to let us know that they had basically hired a moped for the week. We'd known this already as they would always toot us up as they passed us on their way to a beach somewhere, and often gave us some stick as they went. They'd had a few drinks and apparently decided they were going to drive back from one of the big clubs just outside San Antonio. No one knew the direct ins and outs of it, but it appeared that as they pulled out from a side road to join the main carriageway, they were struck by a car coming from the opposite direction. Both were taken by ambulance to the main hospital in San Antonio and both were pretty banged up. We were talking fractured arms, legs, ribs etc. Now whilst one of them managed to come round in the morning, albeit with a leg, arm and hand in plaster, and a collar bone sling, his friend had unfortunately never regained consciousness and had lost his life. It was gutting to hear this. This guy was a year or so younger than me and was already done. I felt a huge lump in my throat and Nigel began to well. Damien then told us that both families had been informed. I asked what was to happen next. Apparently, the family of the deceased boy was making arrangements to have their son flown back, but both families had decided they didn't want to tell the other lad whilst he was alone on holiday. They wanted him to try and enjoy the remainder of his days before being given the news back on UK soil. I can't remember what the official line was but it was either that his friend was doing ok and had been moved to a specialist unit somewhere on the island or on the Spanish mainland, or he had been flown back already to have surgery on a nasty leg break. Remember that no one really had mobile phones then so there was no way to really check. We were told that the more fortunate one was going to be in hospital for the next day or so whilst they finalised paperwork and help him to recover but then he was going to spend the next 2-3 days at the hotel before flying back. It was horrible. I really felt for the girl whose guests they were. You develop an attachment to your guests, especially the nice ones. This was a real tragedy. Damien said there wouldn't be a sales meeting now or this evening after hours. He told us once we got the guests to the club we were going to be cut loose for the evening. He told us not to take the piss by getting drunk with any guests and do not under any circumstances mention this to anyone outside of these walls. No reps from other areas, no holiday makers, no hoteliers. No one. He said this was fucking serious, and if anyone slipped up, they were history. Of this we had no doubt. The last thing we wanted to do was to be the ones to inadvertently break this poor lad's heart whilst he was here on his own.

We were dismissed and everyone left the office. The atmosphere was understandably flat and everyone was saddened. Nigel and I decided to creep off to a bar on the outskirts of our area. We knew we wouldn't be bothered there. We shared a beer and tried to take in what we'd just been told. We couldn't believe how young he was, and how only yesterday he was making people laugh around the pool. I know people have a tendency to look fondly upon the deceased, and there's usually a lot of rose tinting to be found at funerals, but this kid really was a good lad, and that's what made it all the worse. We only stopped for one and a chat and then decided to go and get ready. I made sure that I'd already checked through my arrivals and departures with my hotelier because I knew I was going to be in a state the following morning and so was taking a pre-emptive strike at my workload. We met everyone in the hotel bar as usual but you could see that the reps were different. We did our best to keep the guests happy with false smiles, but even they picked up on it. "What's wrong?" "Are you ok?" "Has something happened?" was all I kept hearing. I guess they weren't used to us being quiet or not gobby. All I mentioned to a couple of groups was that I'd received some bad news from home and that whilst everything is ok, it's playing on my mind. People just assumed someone was sick or worse at home. The funny thing is I guess word kind of spread around my hotel and whilst no one actually approached me on it, everyone was being very kind. It was lovely to witness but it made it harder to mask. We took the guests to a couple of bars and then on to the club. I'd already forewarned my lot I was going to be retiring early. One of the reps put a hand on my shoulder and whispered the bar where to meet. I didn't react. We wanted to keep it quiet as we didn't want guests anywhere near there. As soon as we got to the club, we basically abandoned ship. I waited until the last of my guests passed security and I was off. Pass hidden, bag stashed. I wasn't even the first to the bar. A couple were already there and clearly the wrong side of a bottle of vodka and a stash of redbulls. The girl whose hotel the lads were staying in was visibly upset. Again, she was being comforted by others. I just sat into my chair and poured myself a long cold drink. The focus of my thoughts turned from the guy who'd passed to the guy who survived. All I could do was picture his face being told his best mate had died and it just cut me. Once the others arrived, someone brought out some shots and then things just went downhill from there. I don't really remember getting home. I know there were tears, drinks, more tears, hugs… some altercation with some others who weren't in our group, more shots and maybe some vomit.

The next morning everyone woke up hanging. My head was thumping and I felt cloudy for most of the day. The only thing I wanted to do was recover. In a way the hangover helped me from thinking about it. I couldn't really feel anything else except sorry for myself and wanting to go back to bed. It got easier as the day went on, but I distinctly remember still feeling shit the day after. By that time most of us had other things to think about. It was departure day and half the guests were leaving and we had to prepare for the new arrivals. I was on airport duty that night so I knew I wouldn't be getting much sleep. I managed to "find a friend" in the afternoon and managed to steal a couple of hour's kip in preparation. The airport came and went. We dropped the newbies off at the hotels and I managed to get some sleep ahead of the welcome meetings. I had pretty much all but forgotten about everything until I walked into her hotel late morning to take part in her welcome meeting. There at the bar was the guy back from hospital. He looked like something from a Disney film. His leg was sticking straight out in a plaster cast, and one of his arms was in a 90 degree cast all the way to his shoulder. His face was yellow with bruises and there were cuts on his forehead, arms, and the other leg. He was already drinking a beer despite it being 11ish in the morning. As I was looking at him, he caught sight of me and immediately hollered "Oi oi! What's the matter, you never seen handsome before?" I laughed and retorted immediately "state of you, you bell-end. What happened?" I walked over to him. I could have cried, I just wanted to give him a hug. He proceeded to tell me what had happened, well what he could remember of it. He followed up with "if you think I'm bad, you should see the other guy!" and laughed. It was torture. I had to ask though as it would look odd if I didn't. "Where's your boyfriend then? What's happened to your partner in crime?" I teased. He told me he wasn't as lucky and has been kept in to see some specialists. He then joked he'd be trying to molest the nurses and will probably be thrown back out soon enough. I laughed, I put my hand on his shoulder, told him I was glad he was ok and that I'd buy him a beer later. I made my excuses and went back to join the welcome meeting. I tried not to catch any other reps' glances as I went as it would only have made things worse. As the meeting went on, I remember catching a glimpse of the hotel rep. She shot me a false smile but was managing to keep a brave face on it. As the welcome meeting progressed, he was heckling us from the back and throwing out banter. We were dishing it back through our normal interactions, but it was such a shame. Again, I kept picturing his face changing as he was being told. He was due to fly out a few days after on the next turnaround. By all accounts he mainly stayed in the hotel entertaining his fellow guests and the barman during the time he had left.

Nigel and I paid him a visit on his departure day. He was still none the wiser. We made up some bullshit about why we were at his hotel and not ours and we shared a beer with him. When it was time to go, it was man hugs all round and Nigel and I slipped away. We weren't able to dwell on it for long as Nigel was off to the airport himself and I was in charge of taking the remaining guests to a 70s night. The whole team were relieved when he finally left the island. We desperately liked him, but the burden of trying to behave like everything was normal and not letting slip that his best mate had already died several days earlier was proving difficult. We also knew that he would at least be told by his family or friends and that he would be able to grieve with people around him.

CHAPTER 20
KNOCK-A-DOOR SMASH

Nigel and I got on very well in Ibiza. We had a very similar sense of humour and enjoyed each other's company. We were like peas in a pod. We complemented each other well. He would be on the mic, I would be hands on the ground, so to speak. I wasn't too bad at most physical stuff (dancing, sports etc.,) but he was uncoordinated. Although I could speak to large crowds on the stage, he was way more confident and comfortable doing so. We quickly found a good way of working together. Thankfully, we had different tastes in girls. I would go for the extroverted cheeky types, and normally would gravitate to the loud one in a group. For me it was all about banter and the chase. He would normally end up with the quieter ones that were cute and a little mousey looking. We used to joke that they only wanted to mother him. They would take him home to look after him but before they knew it, they'd be getting railed. Both of us were more than capable of grabbing the high-end beautiful girls out here. Unfortunately, we were both equally as capable of taking one not just for the team, but for the league. It didn't matter at all to us then. It was just a game. We were out having a brilliant time for free, partying with like-minded people and drinking like fish. Girls genuinely wanted to sleep with us. I'm no oil painting, although I wouldn't describe myself as a minger either. I guess we were just uber confident (bordering on arrogant) and probably about the furthest thing from desperate you could be. If one didn't want you, there were several others who did.

After a few weeks into the swing, and a few pleasant surprises, we were able to remove those pedal-stools that society would have you sit people on. You could go up to any girl you wanted and start a conversation. Didn't matter how pretty she was, in a group, alone, with a guy. It didn't matter. She saw the rep's tag hanging from your neck like a prized medallion and understood that it was just your 'job' to talk to her or her friends. There was no creepiness involved. In fact, as you were talking to everyone anyway, it would seem strange if you didn't say hello and check in with her too to make sure everything was ok. We must have appeared very cool and fortunate to be living in such a party paradise. Getting into any bar or club we wanted, never buying a drink, knowing everyone from the DJ to the door staff and all the touts walking up and down the strip must have ladened us with credibility. We would get on well with the guys too. We were naturally boisterous, ultra-competitive, keen to drink and so we were fun for them also. Not to mention I would regularly play match maker so I would often help the guests get stuck in to a group of the opposite sex or in such a position that he or she would be given the opportunity to chat with other guests that they liked but were maybe too shy to approach. In general, people were just happy to associate with us, and that made for a lucrative season.

One bad habit that Nigel and I got into was not going

straight to bed when we finished work like the others but pushing on to other bars. Actually, a lot of the time we would lead our own after-hours bar hop with some of the guests. These were much smaller affairs and we'd end up taking maybe 10-20 guests to some dive or karaoke bar somewhere.

At this point, if neither of us was on target we would sometimes quietly disappear to play knock-a-door-smash. I'm not sure who coined this expression. I think it was Nigel. Basically, we would wander back to one of our hotels (normally pissed) and we would play rock, paper, scissors to determine who was choosing a floor. Then we would have a second round to choose a number. So once a room number and floor were chosen, we would head up to the chosen location and knock. We would wait for an answer. We'd already have chosen door or window. If guys opened the door, they would normally see the state of us, laugh and just shut the door on us or invite us in for a drink. Usually they were all still on their balconies having fun and whistling down to anything that even closely resembled a skirt on the bubbling streets below. If girls answered we would ask how they were doing, and almost always got invited in for a drink. We would always check we weren't bothering them but they always insisted. We would then sit down and continue to chat. We would then proceed to charm and hone in on our respective targets. We would ask how the hotel was, were the rooms comfortable, and then Nigel would break out with the phrase about how he hated air conditioning, but liked to sleep by the window because he found it too hot especially during peak season. One or both of them would always agree. He would then ask if that person was by the window too. The girls would then reveal who was by the window and who was therefore by default by the door. In doing so, identifying themselves as targets.

Remember we'd already played rock, paper, scissors for the door or window before we went in. As ridiculous as this seems, it was hilarious to play at the time. You were truly putting your faith in destiny's hands.

We also had additional rules to the game that evolved as the season went on. If we knocked on a girls' room and there were already guys there, we would move onwards to the next immediately. It wasn't worth the grief. We basically wanted to get laid and get some sleep in quick. If there was already a crowd, you knew you were going to be drinking for longer, as it was much more social. There was a high chance that you were going to pass out either through exhaustion or alcohol before getting any action and usually you were going to get fucked with. The last thing you wanted to do was get smurfed, shaved, moved, or stripped in front of the whole party (as often happened to those that overdid it too early). Another rule was that each of you were allowed only one pass per evening. If we entered the room of a pair of horrors either one of us had the right to pull the rip cord. You didn't want to pull too early though in case the next room was even worse. We would wait to find out who had the bed by the window or door before calling time. You could only do it once per evening, and by pulling it, you automatically gave your opponent dealer's choice over door or window in the next round and choice of room number and floor level. It became a total competition of strategy between us. We both agreed early on in the season that we would never break the rules, and neither of us did. It did leave us both open for some awful stitch ups though. More often than not, Nigel would be the first to pull the chute. Often it wasn't because his one was a minger, but because my one most definitely wasn't. If he thought I was getting the sweeter end of the deal by a long way, he would pull out his veto just to spite me. We would make our polite excuses about needing to get up early for work the next day and we would be on our way. The minute the door closed behind us, he would burst into tears of laughter and be met by a sharp punch to his arm or shoulder. "What did you do that for you prick? Mine was an angel!" He would laugh even harder. We would then go a few floors up or down and go again. This time he had no veto left. Quite often it would backfire on him, particularly if it was in my hotel. You see my hotel was smaller than his and I pretty much knew where all of my guests were staying. It was therefore quite easy for me to pitch him against a hound intentionally. It often meant that I would be sabotaging my own evening, but if it meant he took a bigger torpedo than me, it was worth it. More often than not we would both get laid and then make our excuses about work, trying to nip back in the early hours to snatch a quick kip before we had to get up for hotel duties. We would rib each other and laugh about the previous night's events for days to come. You see the banter didn't just stop the next morning. The guests would often come sniffing for round 2 which we would welcome or sometimes try and politely avoid where we could. This would make us laugh. Then there would also be the constant reminder of the fit ones that got away due to being intentionally vetoed. More often than not I would try and follow up with them the following day. Depending on the reaction I would change my pitch. If she played it cool, I would too. I'd check if she had a good night, thank her for the after hours drink and then plainly ask if she was going to such and such bar or club that night. Then I would try and intentionally chat and befriend other girls in her vicinity. It didn't always work, but most of the time it did the trick. That was if she was playing it cool. If she seemed butthurt or irritated that we ran out on them the night before, I had to think more quickly on my feet. My usual line was that Nigel had a dodgy stomach and that whilst we wanted to spend more time with the girls getting to know them, he was super embarrassed about it and didn't want to leave early on his own. I would claim that he really liked her friend and begged me to leave with him. As he was my best mate, of course I agreed. This would normally be enough to soften the icy reaction. She'd often crack a joke about him needing to eat some eggs or brown rice or something similar, and then I would try my luck there and then with a quick invite back to my apartment now or to suggest a secret rendezvous at theirs after lunch. I'd make a point that Nigel wouldn't be with me for her to take the hint and get rid of her mate for an hour. You would be surprised at how frequently this would result in a cuddle. A lot of the time you'd be laughed at there and then but they'd always follow up with an opening. You'd often get "instead I'll see you tonight" or "maybe later if you're a good boy". That sort of thing. This would fill me with warmth for two reasons. First and foremost, it pretty much meant that I was going to be cuddling a fitty and that always made me extremely happy both on the inside and out. Secondly, it meant that I'd just put Nigel into a world of hurt, because I just told her that Nigel really liked her friend and was extremely embarrassed that his sphincter had deserted him. Nigel wasn't an idiot. Even if I was working with quality, unless his wasn't a complete horse, he probably wouldn't have pulled the cord unless he was totally smashed and out to kill my spirit. More often than not, it meant she had to be super rough for him to not only take me out, but make a break for the border himself. Now he'd have Muttley chasing him for the remainder of her holiday.

You can see the potential for banter whilst playing this game. I alluded to it before about how I made sure we kept this quiet. I didn't want other reps in on this. It was our little secret. It kept us continually having something to laugh at between ourselves as well as keeping the other reps guessing why we were always pissing ourselves during meetings. The last thing we wanted is for the other reps to announce to a coach about our little "game" and to spoil it for us. It represented a decent chunk of our cuddling, and we weren't about to lose it.

One occasion sticks out in my mind quite clearly. Both of us had been drinking quite heavily during the day and night. At one point, I think I even started to drink water early in the evening as I could feel my legs getting away from me. This was rare. Anyways, we continued to 'work' throughout the evening and we'd managed to bring several hundred guests between us to a small bar/club called Summum. It was one of those nights where everyone was in a good mood. There were no issues, no fights, no tears, no puking. Just good old-fashioned merry carnage. This was towards the end of the season and a lot of the reps were already tiring. Nigel and I just ploughed on. We were dancing on stage, organising drinking games, dirty dancing, limbo you name it. I think at one point, Nigel even crowd surfed. The managers could see we were hammered, but they didn't seem to mind. The guests were having a great time, spending heavily, and, well, we were quite entertaining to watch. I assumed some of the other reps were probably asleep in the toilet or the cloak room closet (another favourite) so they could hardly complain about us being drunk, given we were actually still working. I don't remember the evening debrief after work. I'm sure we were both hounded and abused for being pissed, but we'd also brought the largest number of guests to the club by far so I doubted we were going to be punished. Whilst my memory is hazy, I do remember us walking along one of the corridors in my hotel. We were playing knock-a-door but this time a familiar voice hollered up the corridor behind us. "Oi oi, where are you two off to?!" We both spun around. I needed to steady myself on the wall. Nigel practically stumbled over. "Oh God, look at the state of you both. Get in here I'll make us some tea." It was one of my new arrivals. Pretty little thing, nice eyes, not so tall. She was from Newcastle if memory serves me correctly. I'd tried talking to her earlier in the evening, but to be honest, it was so loud on the dance floor and I was clearly on the wrong end of a vodka redbull that the conversation was like pulling teeth. Yet here we were being invited in. We graciously accepted her offer. As we were crossing the threshold, under his breath, Nigel muttered "Door" to which I responded "Done!" We slumped on to her sofa as the kettle boiled and we began chatting. She also gave us both a glass of coke each which seemed to perk us up a little. Nigel was brilliant with accents and insisted in speaking to her in Geordie. It was like being in the middle of an episode of Byker Grove. Normally I think this would have pissed her off, but she was relatively cool about it. She could take a joke and was dishing out some stick to us both anyway which I was lapping up. The more Nigel continued to shovel a hole for himself, the better he was making me look so I made no effort to stop him from hanging himself. She came over to the sofa and sat next to me. She didn't sit between us which meant she had to lean across me to speak to Nigel. Which meant she was edging closer as the conversation continued. We began to talk a little bit deeper about things in general (as you do when you're drunk). The tea definitely did the trick. I seemed to lose all sense of my pissed self and discovered coherence again. Nigel was also getting better, albeit not quite at the same pace I was. Nigel could tell that we were pairing up here and he was without. Like a good wingman, he started to make his excuses to leave but she interrupted him and told him to relax. She said her friend was going to be back any minute. Apparently, she'd gone to try and score some weed from some guys in the pub opposite the hotel. We continued making conversation, although we were both mindful not to leave Nigel out this time. She was telling us about Newcastle and we were comparing notes on bars and clubs and where we'd been there. As she spoke, she put her hand on my leg. Green light! Nigel clocked it and caught the glint in my eye. Again, I think he was getting ready to do the off, when her friend came through the door with all the grace of a cow on ice. She was relatively tall and broad shouldered, and looked a bit of a bruiser. My late Great Aunt would say she had a face like a bulldog licking piss of a nettle. She was irritated, she hadn't been able to buy any drugs but she clearly wasn't ready for the party to finish. This was a double-edged sword. On one hand, I was hoping that if she wants to party there's more chance of everyone copping off, however, it also meant that the chances of us ducking off soon to grab a smash were waning. Nigel and I were both tired. Whilst we wanted the flag, we didn't want to drink anything else. Aside from some small talk I sat quietly pondering what to do next. Thankfully Geordie came to my rescue. She announced she was tired and that she was going to turn in. Her mate began to protest that it was still early despite it being 3:30am. I stood to go. I thought that was that. Geordie stopped me and leant in "Don't you want to tuck me in?" Music to my ears. I smiled, calmly put my tea cup on the side and without hesitation or comment proceeded to walk with her to the bedroom. Nigel, faced with the consequences of needing to take down Bulldog tried to throw a veto. "Hadn't we better get back as we have to go to the airport early?" he suggested. I calmly responded "I'm not on airports this week." He tried to continue, but I interrupted. "Do you remember playing rock, paper, scissors earlier?" I questioned him. "No, when did we play, and who won?" a bemused Nigel replied. "That's the point," I continued "we haven't played. All bets are off!" he wrinkled his nose up, defeated. I smiled as I quietly closed the door behind me. The last thing I heard as the door shut was Bulldog bellowing "oh don't mind us will you!"

I stayed over that night and woke up late the next day. I managed to get straight down to reception to change into my spare shorts and proceeded to jump in the pool in lieu of a shower. The only one who clocked me was the hotelier. He just smiled and brought me a coffee. We were having a nice conversation about the hotel and how business was going for him in general this season when Nigel appeared. He looked like shit. We both laughed at him. He slumped down in the chair beside me. The hotelier brought him a coffee too and left us to it. "How did you get on?" I grinned at him, desperate for him to tell me about what happened with Bulldog. He tried to claim that I'd broken protocol by ignoring the veto but I wasn't having any of that. He saw that avenue get closed down immediately and gave in. He began to fill me in. After I'd retired with Geordie, he basically started drinking with Bulldog. He said she seemed to just want to get obliterated. They started with 1 litre bottles of San Miguel that she'd brought from the supermarket earlier in the day and quickly moved through those and on to a bottle of Archers that they'd brought from duty free. That stuff is terrible even with a mixer and they'd been drinking it straight! Nigel went on to tell me that at some point they started to kiss and things unfolded from there. He said his memory was patchy, but they were trying to get it on. He'd drunk so much it was like picking a lock with plasticine. I laughed out loud at that one. He said rather than give him time to gather his thoughts or change tack a little, Bulldog just got more and more aggressive. He said he found himself laying on the cold tiled floor of the lounge, chap in hand, trying to work one up with her sitting on his face grinding him like it was punishment. He said eventually he managed the slightest resemblance of a semi and that was it. She jumped on it like it was a game of whack-a-mole. I was crying as he described her face and the grunts she was making. To anyone else you'd think he was mimicking a silverback. Anyone looking at us would think we were simple. He also confessed to not bagging up which was a cardinal sin out here. He blamed the Archers and said a Jonny would have not only killed his poor excuse for a bone, but he feared she'd get angry. Before I could ask if he got a second wind and went to town on it, he confessed that whatever he did manage to muster fell back to sleep within about 30 seconds and she reluctantly got off him. I was still laughing. He said she made him stay with her until they both fell asleep. I was surprised to hear this. I didn't see him or his stuff this morning when I slid out of the apartment. He said he woke up about 7:30 covered in drool with a banging hangover. He said he wasn't sure if he'd been drooling or it was Bulldog. He needed to leave and quickly. He said he did a runner and threw himself into the swimming pool on his way home. I asked him why the hell did he do that? It must have been cold. He said he didn't care. The pool boy was cleaning it and had just topped up the chlorine and he said given the state of her, he wanted to wash his bits properly and fresh chlorine was probably more potent than any soap or shower gel. He needed to remove any traces of Bulldog, not to mention cleanse his soul. I couldn't believe the words coming out of his mouth. She was that bad he threw himself into a heavily chlorinated pool, totally ignoring the toxicity just to wash his cock. This was priceless. I couldn't stop laughing. He looked at me shell shocked as if he'd suffered a flashback. He told me he'd brushed his teeth three times and still felt dirty. Fucking Nigel! There was no way I was letting anyone else in on this and diluting the comedy value. He then asked me how did I get on. This was my chance to pour a bucket of salt on to his open and festering wound. I told him we'd had a lovely evening. I said she'd already lit some candles and we gave each other a quick massage before sensually making love. I told him I performed like a lion, she was above average, and together we managed a great cuddle. After, we fell asleep in each other's arms. I stirred just before my alarm clock went off and managed to grab a lovely blowjob and she made me a bacon sandwich just before I left for work. His eyes were staring in disbelief. "I don't believe it. You literally hooked up with a palace princess, whilst I had something out of her dungeon." I replied to him "That's karma for being a rat and trying to throw out a false veto!"

CHAPTER 21
CRIME & PUNISHMENT

Several times throughout the book I've alluded to various people falling asleep early or passing out and then being abused. This was and still is common practice among party groups. It happened all night, every night, all day, every day in Ibiza. You can bet your money maker on it. If you overdid it on booze and crashed prematurely, you were targeted. It didn't matter if you were male or female, young or old, in a pair or a team of 10. The punishments were wide and varied. Ranging from the silly to the outright evil. I already told you about the guy at the waterpark who had his hand suntanned into his chest, but things didn't stop there. One time a rep passed out in the sun. He had been goaded into drinking with a big group of lads and he didn't fare too well. He basically went into autonomous mode, found a sun bed and crashed out onto it. Despite it being common to see people practically unconscious after beers during the day, it was extra special for it to be a rep. The guests continued to drink until one bright spark decided it was time to claim their victory over the poor sozzled representative, who at this point was lying diagonally across two sun beds on his face wearing only his shorts. A quick reconnaissance around the pool area allowed them to find a factor 50. Game on. A few went over to the rep and asked how he was doing. No response. Next, they gave him a nudge. No response. They then proceeded to draw a huge cock and balls on his back in suncream. The rep didn't flinch an inch. They drew it reasonably thick, but not thick enough that you couldn't pay attention to the detail, particularly around the helmet and bean bag. It was a masterpiece. The rest of the guests gathered and began to giggle, but no one woke the rep up. He must have crashed out for a good hour or so. Of course, he wasn't wearing any suncream himself (well, aside from his new phallus) and naturally he was pale in complexion. In fact, out of all the reps in our area, if there was one guy always asking around for suncream it was him. You couldn't make this up. Eventually I think one of the girls in his hotel took pity on him and woke him up with a splash of water to his face. He rose to a seating position, groggy as hell. Clearly still wearing the effects of the booze earlier. As he sat up, there was immediate laughter around the pool. As he turned around the intensity of the giggling increased. He switched sides again confused by what people were laughing at. In doing so he showed the penis Picasso to the other side of the pool area who by now were patiently waiting for their own show. It wasn't until the Samaritan who had woken him earlier, told him that it dawned on him what had happened. He immediately went to the bathroom to look in the mirror. As he walked towards the toilet he was whistled and jeered. The rest of his back already crimson would have brought out a reaction as it was, but having this huge white monster of a prick between his shoulder blades deserved special attention. A few minutes later he emerged from the bathroom with a deflated look on his face. He did take it in good spirits, I mean, he overdid it, and that was his mistake, but you could tell he was less than impressed with his new look.

By way of a follow up to this one, I did hear a few years back that he had got married to a local girl and they both took a fabulous honeymoon to the Caribbean somewhere. Apparently, they were relaxing by the pool, enjoying some drinks and crashed out in the early afternoon. She'd managed to sleep underneath some shade, he unfortunately hadn't been so lucky. When he woke up some hours later, he'd burnt himself again. Apparently as the sun began to set, it began to come in through the side of the shade they'd previously been enjoying. Guess what? His Balearic battle scar had come back. His new wife nudged him awake and asked what was on his back. Again, his back had turned red where he'd burnt and his sun tattooed "tool" had reappeared. I'm not just talking about a smudge or a patchy area of paler skin, I'm talking full outline, detail and all. He was gutted. He had to wear a t-shirt on the beach for the remainder of his honeymoon. Let that be a warning to you. What happens on tour doesn't always stay on tour!

Again, I've mentioned smurfing previously where someone essentially has their face coloured in with felt tip. This was always comical to see afterwards. I've seen people smurfed with permanent marker too. That's a special type of evil. Can you imagine how red raw your face must be after you've been trying to scrub that off. We had such markers in reception because when we were writing up notices for the guests you had to make sure you wrote them large enough for them to be seen clearly. I was forever having to buy more of these in the local stationary shop as it was important to have departure notices, meeting points, bar crawl times and such like every day. Like clockwork these would be stolen. I didn't twig at first. I assumed it was the hotelier just borrowing them and forgetting to put them back after. It wasn't until I'd seen a couple of the guests looking like coal miners at breakfast that it clicked. It wasn't just guys doing it either. The girls were equally as guilty of adding some extra ink to their compatriots if they happened to pass out early.

Whilst smurfing is a little on the extreme side, there were plenty of variations of the pen painted punishment floating around. One of the funniest, again with the thicker markers, was the chaplin. I hadn't heard the expression before, but will never forget it. I remember walking into my hotel just after lunch and there was a commotion by the bar. I wandered over to see what was happening, but it was 2-3 people deep. I managed to squeeze myself into the centre and there was a welsh chap, who was absolutely battered, leaning on the bar. He was telling everyone about his night out (he looked like he hadn't been to bed yet) and what adventures he'd been through. The thing is, he had failed to notice that someone had basically inked his face with a wide marker pen. They had drawn a thick moustache on his top lip and increased the size of his eyebrows 2-3 fold. He was completely oblivious. At some point in the night, he must have crashed out briefly and then fell victim. I turned to face his friends. They were sat away from him, laughing and just watching their social hand grenade of a friend hold court with the rest of the guests. "What happened?" I asked with a smirk on my face. One of the lads lent forward and in his finest welsh accent began to fill me in. "Oh man, he was a total fucking nightmare last night. He wouldn't stop doing shots. Every time we got close to some birds he would come over and spoil it. The only thing we could do was take him out. We dropped back by the hotel bar and got him a couple of shots of absinthe. About 10 minutes later he was done. We took him upstairs like, and put him to sleep. We left him to it and went back out. We all came back a few hours later and he was missing. He then rolled up at 10am this morning in a right state. No one told him he's been chaplined and he has been drinking ever since. He's a fucking lunatic." I looked back over at him and shook my head. The boys were chuckling to themselves about the whole affair. "Make sure you get some water and sugar in him soon otherwise he won't be out tonight" I told them. They agreed and I left them to it. As I left even the hotelier and the barman were shaking their head laughing.

Another variant on the same theme, is the Hogan. Hulk Hogan was a big WWF wrestler of the 90s with long blonde, but receding, hair which accompanied a ridiculous beast of a moustache that went from his nose to the bottom of his jawline. It was the sort of moustache I've only seen on Hell's Angels members and Hogan himself. Quite often you'd see people wake up with one of them. Other times I've seen people get signed. Once, one guy passed out in the reception of the hotel. He wasn't even a guest here and I don't think he was actually on tour with our company. He was just a regular dude who overdid it and basically made a beeline for our reception couch to crash on. The night staff had tried their best to wake him up and move him on, but in the end gave up trying to move the lump. Besides, they didn't know if he was a guest here or not. At some point early in the morning, when the night staff came off duty, they just left him to it. The day staff assumed he was a guest. I got to the hotel about 9ish in the morning. As I walked in, a small group of guests were surrounding him and laughing. It was only when I got closer to him that I saw what they were laughing about. They were signing him. Yes, you read that right. He was a human postcard. The guests were taking it in turns to sign any clear patch of skin. It wasn't just their names or drawing dicks, they were actually writing phrases and dating them. They'd written on his face, his hands, arms, neck, everywhere. At one point, one of the girls had rolled his jeans up and pulled his socks down so she could continue the drawing of a butterfly she'd started. When I witnessed one guy trying to sign his nose I intervened. I convinced the crowd it was time for him to go and proceeded to get a pint of water from the barman. Moments later, our postcard was splashed from his slumber and sent on his way. He looked down at his hands briefly, bemused by the multitudes of inky scrawl he was now adorned with but didn't say anything. I can't imagine the look on his face when he would have looked into the mirror to see "Wozza woz 'ere, Ibiza's the bomb!" in half inch script across his forehead.

Unfortunately, it wasn't always just ink that was dished out for a premature crasher. Sometimes the punishments were distinctly longer lasting. Seeing guests missing an eye brow, or only having hair on one leg was a regular occurrence. In fact, a couple of times it happened to some of my colleagues. It's comical for everyone else but an awful thing to be faced with personally. I can imagine waking up with one eyebrow doesn't just leave you feeling mutilated, you're also left with the choice of what to do next? Do you shave the other one off and walk around looking like an alien? Witnessing people reacting strangely to you but they don't know why? You still look humanoid but different. Until it dawns on them that you've got a pale bald patch where your caterpillars used to be? Or do you leave as is. You wait for the other to grow back. You style it out as an Ibizan party scar, but deep down you pray it comes back as it was and doesn't grow bushier and stays a similar size to the other one. The alternative, and probably one that most opted for was to leave it as is, and basically beg steal or borrow an eyebrow pencil from one of the female guests and attempt to draw it on yourself. This was usually done with varying degrees of failure. If it wasn't hard enough to match the shape and density of the other brow, the colour nearly always gave it away. There was no point bothering if you were blonde. You looked even more of a twat with one mousey blonde/brown brow with its partner gunmetal black!

Another weapon used for dishing out punishment was the electric razor. Sometimes the clippers would be used in a jackass fashion i.e. a member of the group would creep up behind another and proceed to mow the back of his head in one swift movement. The faster your reaction the less hair you lost. This was always funny to watch but it always followed the same pattern of events. Each morning as the lads came down to breakfast, you'd see a myriad of tram lines as they'd been repeatedly messing with each other throughout their stay. By the end of the holiday, most usually threw in the towel and shaved the rest off as it looked more preferable to walking around looking like you were recovering from a lobotomy. I remember one season an athletic group of guys were staying at the hotel. They were ultra-competitive and basically, we held a fitness challenge at the hotel involving various sit ups, press ups and running challenges. They were in great shape. I think most of them were semi-professional sportsmen, gymnasts and just naturally ripped. You could tell they looked after themselves. Every time they were in the pool, they were the centre of attention. Every girl was staring, and most of the guys were green with envy. In fact, I think Nigel christened them bench-press club at one point and it stuck. Not that they minded. They revelled in the attention. Anyways, they decided to hold a fitness challenge amongst themselves and anyone else who fancied a go. It was all very public. The catch was the last one to complete the list of challenges was to have their hair shaved like Friar Tuck and to keep it that way until the end of the holiday. The severity of that punishment was initially much softer. In fact, I think it was Nigel or one of the other reps who basically came up with the idea of a tuck cut. The strongest in the group knew they had next to no chance of losing then got behind it, and the whole thing snowballed from there. Once peer pressure was involved and Nigel announced it on the mic, the whole pool turned to them and the wheels were set in motion. The fact that a couple of outsiders fancied their chances too meant that no one from bench-press club wanted to refuse the challenge. Game on. I seized on the opportunity to make a proper spectacle out of it and excitedly cleared a space by the pool side and brought a chair with some clippers out. There was no turning back. Nigel grabbed the mic, rounded up a couple of extra challengers and proceeded to get the crowd going. I can't remember exactly what the challenge was but we managed to insert downing a pint into it, to the surprise of all those involved. We figured this might be the cat amongst the pigeons. Some of the previously confident members of the team suddenly looked a little less sure of themselves. We brought out a tray of San Miguel. The pool counted them down and they were off. It's one thing to be able to do 40 press ups, 40 sit ups, 40 burpees etc in quick succession, but it's another to do it with 500ml of liquid gold at the top of your stomach. It threw everyone off course and made it much more entertaining. Slowly but surely, they started finishing the challenges. Predictably, the biggest and most toned guy came first, with his compatriots quickly finishing after him. A couple of the outsiders were also finishing in quick succession, leaving the last and only place that everyone was focusing on, up for grabs. It was going to be settled between one of their group and an outsider. Everyone was cheering them on. Their peers were piling the pressure on and it really came down to the wire. Eventually, however, the outsider managed to finish a split second before him, meaning that the last member of bench-press club was getting a haircut. Everyone started to cheer and we picked someone out of the group at random to do the honours. It was difficult to find someone who actually knew who Friar Tuck was and was willing to actually inflict such a statement on a fellow human. But this was Ibiza. Soon enough, someone was found and she was handed the clippers. Within a minute or so, the deed was done. It was hilarious. The top of his head had been shaved bald (or as close as we could get it with the clippers) as if someone had sucked the top half off with a bowl. Next a thick belt of hair was left wrapping from ear to ear almost like modern ski wear to keep your ears warm on the slopes. Finally, below this belt of hair, they shaved the back of his neck up to the bottom of his ears. The whole pool was roaring. He looked less than impressed and was desperate to find a mirror. The girl that actually did the shave, was trying to apologise to him, but she was also laughing, so I don't think her sincerity really shone through. The rest of bench-press club were pissing themselves. I reminded Nigel about the rules. Nigel reaffirmed to the crowd that he had to remain like that until the last night before his holiday. When the guy returned from the toilets, he was embarrassed but smiling. He took it in his stride. I think he was more concerned about how he was going to get laid than how he was going to be returning home with a skinhead. He needn't have worried. As much as people would go on to laugh about his situation and his haircut, the girls as always were on hand to provide attention and much needed sympathy, and he was milking that for all it was worth. In fact, given the poor strike rate of some of his chiselled team members, I half expected some of them to follow up and pull a friar voluntarily!

CHAPTER 22
DARK TIMES

Another unfortunate statistic that we were met with whilst in Ibiza were sexual assaults. These varied across the spectrum from random gropes in a club to rape. I daresay way more went on than we realised but were just never reported. It happened to both males and females alike. It happened to guests, it happened to workers, it happened to reps. It was honestly one of the toughest and quite frankly the shittiest things I've ever had to deal with. Unfortunately, it happened more than once in our area. Whilst every case was different, when it came to the most serious of incidents, things always seemed to follow a predictable path. I was called to attend various incidents on several occasions due to me being either somewhat senior to the rep present in the hotel, or down to my experience. Not that anyone can really be experienced at this sort of thing in your late teens. I'd already handled a couple and I knew the motions, so I guess that put me up front. It was a real mix of emotions. It was heart-breaking to find the victim absolutely shell shocked and mentally obliterated. You weren't just dealing with the emotions of the victim but that of the friend or partner too. The guilt experienced by the 'friend' was also very prevalent. The consequences of not 'sticking together' laid bare for all to see. You would then have to try and motivate the victim to seek medical attention, ask awkward questions, be soft yet firm where possible. Be comforting but not too close, it involved walking an extremely fine line. You knew that the incident and the events surrounding it were going to be etched in memory like a horrific tattoo and the last thing you wanted to do was make it worse in any shape or form. I mentioned the mixture of emotions because as well as sorrow and regret, there was also anger. Anger that someone would do this. Anger that the person probably wouldn't be caught and anger that they were probably free to do it again. Sometimes the anger was directed at the reps. I understood this. People were lashing out. We'd often be asked how could we let this happen, or why wasn't there security at such and such a point. You just had to suck it up. Let the people vent. Often it was other guests. They would be present in reception etc, word would get round and when you turned up you were the one to cop it all. I understood their anger. The truth was it seldom happened in the hotel. There wasn't really anything we could do to prevent it. Usually the guests would come and apologise afterwards. The main thing was to work with the actual guests involved and assist them through the ordeal.

I remember one particular tragic case. It was during peak season, and everything was well under way. I remember being absolutely shattered. I hadn't slept properly for 2-3 nights. It was that bad that I managed to bring someone back but was so tired I wasn't interested. I think I drifted off as soon as my head hit the pillow. My phone woke me up about 6am. It was rare for someone to use the mobile phones we were given so I knew this was going to be an issue. It was Damien. He briefly told me that someone had reported being raped near one of our hotels by the beach. The rep in the hotel was on site but she was in a bit of a state herself and he needed me to go down there and provide some support. There was no fucking about. I agreed immediately. I woke my cuddle buddy up and turfed her out. I said something serious had happened and I was sorry but she had to go. She understood from the look on my face and besides, she'd clearly witnessed how tired I'd been literally 2 hours before and could tell this was the last thing I wanted to be dealing with. I got dressed and headed straight down there. As I walked, I was trying to remember my training. I was practicing the conversation in my head and thinking about what to say and what not to say, phrases I would use, actions I would take etc. By the time I got there, I was mentally prepared. I was met at the entrance by the hotel rep. She'd clearly been crying. She gave me a big hug. I reciprocated but only briefly. As harsh as this sounded, this wasn't about her. I needed to find out what had happened and we both needed to attend to the situation in hand. I asked her directly to tell me what she knew, what she'd seen and what she thought. Apparently two girls were staying at the hotel. It was their last night and they'd partied along with some others from the hotel. They came back a bit tipsy but happy. They were all hanging around the hotel bar/reception area playing pool. The hotel overlooked the sea and there was an area opposite the entrance that took you down to the waterline but it was rocky. It wasn't a beach area per se, more a wasteland. Apparently one of the girls literally stepped outside to have a cigarette and got talking to a couple of locals. Now neither of us knew if she willingly went with them or if she was dragged, but ultimately it looked like this poor girl was raped about 50m from the entrance. One of the guys held her down for the other one. This was sickening. I asked if there were any other details but that was all she had. The rep burst into tears again. I told her to clear everyone else from reception, all the holiday makers, other guests and passers-by. It seemed like everyone knew what had happened anyway, so there was no need to be particularly tactful. Especially as some were only just returning from the clubs and so they were loaded with god knows what. I approached the two girls who were stood just off to the side of the pool area. I didn't really know them but they recognised me. As I approached the victim I kind of put my arms forward but sort of open. I guess it was instinct really. I didn't want to embrace her in case it set something off, but I was there if she wanted a hug. To my surprise she reciprocated and she put her arms around me and started to quietly sob. This was super emotional all round and I had to swallow hard not to break. After a minute of comforting her, I took her to one side away from her friend. I asked her friend to give us a minute. We sat at the edge of the pool area away from ears and eyes. I asked her to tell me in her own words what happened. To my shock, she immediately said "Look what they did to me" and she pulled her top down revealing most of her cleavage. On her chest were two dark bruised marks in the shape of hands, where she had been held down. You could even make out the outline of the fingers. I was speechless. It was truly repulsive. I think I muttered something like "bastards…" or words to that effect. I then started to gently ask for other details. Where exactly did it happen? How old did she think they were? Had she seen them before? What did they look like? I wanted to go in softly before asking some of the more difficult questions. I then asked her if she had taken a bath or shower. She didn't answer. I apologised for having to ask such questions, but if we were going to report it, I needed to know. She told me she'd had a long shower already and it wouldn't make any difference if she'd reported it or not. I disagreed and encouraged her to come to the medical centre with me. I said they had female nurses and doctors who'd been through this and would be able to give her a medical check etc and then take her statement etc. She declined again. I told her it was important to report it so that we stood a chance of catching this filth and besides we didn't want them to do this to anyone else. She was absolutely adamant about not reporting it. She said "what's the point? I'm flying back this evening. They're going to ask if I've been drinking. I'll reply yes, they'll think I asked for it." I said that absolutely wasn't the case and that the bruises on her chest will leave no hint of doubt. She countered me immediately. "Ok then, what am I going to say when they ask me what did they look like? I'm going to tell them Spanish. Tanned, average height with dark hair." I fell silent. I didn't really have an answer to this. I just pleaded with her to come with me to the medical centre at least to make sure she was ok physically. She declined again and at that point she started to harden, so I decided to leave it there. I brought her back to her friend and went to fetch a couple of teas for them both. Whilst the barman was making them for me, I was intercepted by some of the other guests who were angry at the situation and demanded to make a complaint against the company. I had the female rep handle them and they were issued with forms. To my knowledge nothing was ever filed. They were just upset that something so vile could happen so close and no one could see or do anything about it. In that, they weren't alone. I brought the teas over to the girls and just sat with them quietly. The friend at this point was more tearful and worked up than the victim. The guilt was piling on to her. We both were saying it wasn't her fault and it could have happened to anyone, but it didn't seem to make much difference. I think I ended up staying with them for a couple of hours in the end. Neither wanted to go to bed and any feelings of sleep my end were long past. We spoke with the hotel and extended their checkout from the usual lunchtime right up until the time of their flight. We also said to her that if she changed her mind and wanted to report it at any time, she just had to tell the hotel to ask for me if they couldn't find their rep and in turn, they would get in contact with the office who would grab me immediately. If they wanted to stay longer here (I know that sounds ridiculous as am sure they just wanted to fly home immediately) we would extend their hotel stay and rearrange the flights for them without cost etc. They thanked me for my help and sent me on my way. As soon as I left them, I made a full formal report in writing with dates, times, potential witnesses and observations. I tried to be as thorough as possible in case it would be used in the future. I was still hoping she'd change her mind and report it, but alas she never did. I did check back in with them later on in the day as they were waiting for their coach to take them to the airport. They were both pretty quiet and exhausted at this point. I just quietly asked if there was anything they needed or if they'd changed their mind to which they both told me they just wanted to get home. I understood, and wished them well. I gave them my contact details in case they needed them for any reason which they took. Unfortunately, I never heard anything more of them. The whole episode was horrible. Sorrow soon turns to anger though. The fact that this filth got away with what they did makes me sick to my stomach. I just hope that karma truly is a bitch and that somewhere along the line they'll get theirs.

It wasn't just that type of assault that was occurring in San Antonio. Fights and skirmishes were frequent. Quite often around the main strip of bars you would see the local police force lining up with batons by their side keeping a watchful eye on everything. Most of the time the strips were a happy and vibrant place. Ibiza was separate to the rest of the resorts in that it had many faces to it. It wasn't a typical place where you just got shit faced on fishbowls and fluorescent coloured shots. It was a clubbing mecca. There was a big ecstasy culture there that didn't really lend itself to violence. It was also a trendy place to be. There was a strong bohemian/hippy vibe, and Ibiza town was extremely gay friendly i.e. tolerant. That's not to say that violence didn't happen, but it just wasn't as frequent as you would have found in say parts of Greece, Majorca or maybe Turkey. A lot of time the main ignition points were small groups of guys competing for the same girls, issues with the "lookie lookie" guys who would frequently rip off drunk holiday makers, or if security had been particularly heavy handed with a drunk member of a group. Like most holiday resorts, the security knew what to look for. Most of the time they were decent. As reps we always tried to stay on the right side of them. They would often give us a heads up if one of the guests was about to be ejected. Depending on who it was and the size of their party we would be able to either get them out quickly and quietly under the pretence of going to another bar or club or if the group was the type to kick off and ruin the atmosphere, we would move the whole group to another bar to avoid a confrontation. I also liked to keep security on my side, because I too liked to party, and like most youngsters in Ibiza there were times when I definitely went sailing past that red line. It could be that I was completely wasted and having issues with balance, but that was rare. It tended to be doing something ridiculous and going too far. Keep in mind we were out all night, every night for the whole season. Again, statistically you could catch the majority of issues before they got out of hand from a security point of view, but you were never going to be able to catch them all. When something was about to go down and was past the point of no return you went into damage limitation mode. If there was trouble at the front of the venue, the security would literally shut and lock the doors behind them in unison and you had to do your best to drag other guests out of the blast zone. Once it kicked off it rarely stopped at a slap. You just got as many guests away from the windows and main area as possible. Without fail bottles would start to go flying followed closely by chairs. Anyone in the remote vicinity ran the risk of getting clobbered by accident, and sometimes did. Most of the time the Guardia Civil (local Spanish police) just stood by and watched from a far. If things got too out of hand, they would casually wade into the mix with pepper spray and watch the strip empty itself immediately. It was always a shame when that happened. A big fight would empty the main area for about 15 minutes before the void would be filled back in with horny holidaymakers. Pepper spray and their presence would clear it for an hour. San Antonio had little pockets of bars outside of the main strip, so if things were naughty on the main strip, people would just divert to the sunset bars (del mar, mambo's etc) or to San Antonio Bay. Sometimes the guests would desert the strip and head straight to Ibiza town reducing every bar and club's takings for the evening. Therefore, it was in nobody's interest to clear the strip from a business point of view.

The Guardia Civil were not always objective in their response either. I don't really blame them. I mean can you imagine patrolling your beautiful island and being witness to 1000s of gringos night after night trashing not only themselves but the place itself. After a certain point it's going to grate. I remember walking back from the strip one night towards my hotel for a rendezvous. It must have been around 3am. I'd finished work and had agreed to a nightcap. I'd had a good evening, had a few drinks in me and was looking forward to a smash. About 50m from my hotel just under some trees there was a bench. An English guy had passed out on it and some local kids were messing with him. They were slapping him across the face trying to bring him round and another was kicking at his legs. There must have been 5 or 6 of them. They were the annoying little bastards that rode up and down the narrow streets on mopeds with the loudest exhausts in the world despite them resembling a smarties tube. They would abuse holidaymakers on one hand, but do anything to try and get laid on the other. They were probably 15-16 years old. As the guy began to come round and sit up, one of the lads hit him a little harder with a clenched fist, although it wasn't quite a punch, more a paw. I quickly inserted myself in between the English guy and these pricks. From what I could gather he was just pissed and had passed out and these cowards were just opportunistically rounding on him. In my broken Spanish I told them he was a pisshead and an idiot and no offence was meant. I didn't quite know what else to say, besides it was 6 on 1. Matey boy behind me couldn't even find his feet let alone self-defence. As he dragged himself to his feet, still dazed, one of the local lads proceeded to football kick him in the thigh and then another stepped forward. Things were escalating. I turned to this guy and told him to run or he was going to get beaten. As he looked at me, I began to shove him out of the circle of knob heads he'd found himself in. He began to break through and run towards the strip. As I turned around to face the group, I was immediately hit in the side of the head with a crash helmet. One of these pricks was holding the chin guard and had swung it. I immediately recoiled into the side of a car that was parked up near the bench. As they came forwards for me, I lashed out and managed to hit the kid who had the crash helmet. I planted one on his temple, pretty much where he hit me on my own face, sending him sprawling into this friends. I quickly backed up around the car and away from the group who were trying to kick at me. They were shouting obscenities at me in Spanish. I backed up a bit more but they were reticent to follow me. I didn't know why, I just kept moving backwards. Eventually when it was clear they weren't going to chase, I turned around, only to see two policemen sitting there perched on the bonnet of their car happily enjoying the show. What the Policia didn't see though was that about 10 balconies worth of my hotel had witnessed me getting attacked and had fled down the stairs to come to my aid. I looked at the Police with contempt but they didn't give a shit. I looked towards the hotel and there were 10-15 lads coming out arms outstretched gesturing to the locals. Obscenities were being offered in both directions now. This startled the policemen and they jumped up quick and pulled out their batons. I immediately tried to usher everyone back in the hotel. The police quickly followed up behind me ready to strike. I thought I was going to get one in the back of the legs or shoulder but they held their nerve. Eventually I managed to drag my guys back into the reception. The Spanish lads had already scarpered on their noisy hairdryers leaving the police to face off with my guests. The police were pointing to the balconies and telling everyone to go upstairs whilst waving their sticks. The guests however were more content on voicing their opinions on the officers' mothers. Eventually the hotel security had a word with the police providing me with the chance to deflate the situation and move everyone upstairs. One of the rooms was open and it was just along from another room of lads who had been down with them so this seemed like a good place to stash everyone. I asked if anyone had a beer and things pretty much settled back down. I shared a beer with them and some other guests from the same floor. Most of the rooms were open with everyone frequenting the hallway, including my planned liaison! She'd heard all the commotion and came to see what was going on. One of the guests told her before I could get a word out, that I'd been fighting. She didn't look impressed. I quickly got my side out that I was just trying to help someone which was immediately backed up by everyone in the room. At this point, I'd started to bruise on the side of my face where I got smacked. She told me I needed to put some cream on that otherwise tomorrow it will look awful. With a glint in her eye, she said she had some in her room. I don't think a single person standing there in the hallway believed she had an anti-bruising cream, but no one made a scene out of it or ratted me out either!

CHAPTER 23

BUNNY BOILER BARBIE

How many of you regularly use the word stalker? How many of you have ever actually had to deal with a stalker? I'm not just talking about a jilted Doris who got railed and then ignored. I am talking about a full-on obsessive. Someone completely devoid of common sense or the ability to reason with? Well if you have, you'll know how stressful and completely helpless it can be. Let me tell you, Ibiza is not without its fruit loops.

I was in my hotel bright and early one morning getting the bar area ready for a welcome meeting. I was lining out chairs and just generally getting the space cleaned up when I heard a commotion just outside of the main entrance. I went to check out what was going on. There was a guy and a girl arguing about something. The guy had his hand on her wrist and whilst she was trying to pull away from him, he refused to let her go. I watched for a moment or two. I didn't want to get involved immediately in case it was a just a typical holiday drunk couple row. The way she was speaking to him though I could tell they weren't together. He started to raise his voice and was telling her to just go with him. I decided to intervene. He was certainly bigger than me, but I felt pretty confident in my surroundings with the various staff and guests potentially behind me if needed. I asked what was happening, and asked them both to calm down. He basically asked me to mind my own business and to stay out of it if I knew what was good for me. It was time to nut up or shut up. I told him to fuck off and leave the girl alone before I brought out half the hotel to straighten him out if I couldn't do it alone. I positioned myself next to the girl and as he dropped her wrist, I moved in between them. He seemed to give up at that point. Trying to drag a girl anywhere against her wishes in public is just stupid. I assumed he was either horny as hell on booze or tripping on something stronger. Either way the dickhead decided it wasn't worth the hassle and slumped off bitching and moaning about her and probably me under his breath.

I shepherded the girl back to the hotel reception area and grabbed her a cup of tea. It wasn't until I actually sat her down that I actually paid attention to how pretty she was. She had blonde hair up in bunches and was wearing all pink. She was slim with a nice figure and was wearing this ridiculous pink crop top and matching pink hot pants. She wasn't particularly tall but she had these wedge shoe things that helped her out. She had a matching pink bag with Barbie emblazoned across the side of it, a pink choker and a pink barbie toothbrush in her hand. She kept chewing on her toothbrush nervously. At this point I didn't know if this was just a barbie themed outfit that she wanted to rock the night away in or whether she was truly weird as hell. Regardless, I asked her if she was ok. She looked at me, and I noticed how big her pupils were. You could hardly see the whites of her eyes. She said she was ok now and thanked me for the intervention. I asked her what she'd taken. She paused initially before confessing to a mixture of a pills and speed. She said she was coming down now but she's still a bit all over the place. I told her to relax here. There was no need to rush. She could spend as much time as she wanted chilling out. I got out of my chair to walk behind the counter. She immediately asked where I was going. "Relax, am not going anywhere" and handed her an orange Fanta I had grabbed from the fridge. "The sugar will help with the comedown." She thanked me and then began to tell me about herself. She was from Manchester, worked in a department store and had saved for ages to be able to afford a couple of weeks out here. I think she said it was her third or fourth evening of clubbing and her and her mate had got separated at Manumission. I joked it was easy to do. Manumission was a night held at a club called Privilege. Privilege (formerly known as the Ku club) was at one point the largest club in the world holding a night with 10,000 guests. Wikipedia lists it as having 70,000 square feet, and I don't doubt it for a moment. Once you get separated from your group there, you're on your own. She said she ended up chatting to this guy in the cab queue and they shared a cab back to San Antonio. That's when he started to hit on her and she felt uncomfortable. As time went on, he got worse. Apparently, that's when I showed up. She said she was a little unnerved. A mix of the comedown and his behaviour had put her on edge. I reassured her again and told her there was nothing to worry about. She wouldn't be seeing him again, and there are plenty of people around to assist. I did say to her that I had a welcome meeting to prepare for so couldn't sit talking for too long and then I would have to present at other welcome meetings around the town but I could find some friendly guests to sit with her if it would make her feel better. She thanked me again and said if it was ok with me, she was just going to unwind here for a bit. Of course, I agreed. I said to her that the staff at the hotel were lovely and that if she needed anything, they would assist her. I put my hand on her shoulder as I walked past her and told her to relax and to drink her Fanta. I smiled and left her to it.

I finished lining out the room with chairs and then began the arduous process of waking up the new arrivals and getting them down for the meeting. I didn't have many, so it didn't take long. Within 30 minutes, I had about 20 bleary eyed pale new arrivals sitting in front of us. Other reps from the area were arriving on cue and between us we performed the welcome meeting. It went well, everyone was laughing and soon it became obvious that they were going to be taking out the package with us. As my various colleagues did the paper work and took the money in, we began to make a move for the next hotel. One of the female reps came up to me and asked me who my secret admirer was. I didn't know who she was talking about, but obviously I wanted to know who my next potential target was. "Who?" I immediately inquired. She just smiled and quietly told me that Barbie sat in reception hadn't taken her eyes off me from the moment she arrived at my hotel. I didn't really have time to bother with her once the welcome meeting got underway. You see each rep is responsible for their hotel's figures. Poor welcome meeting attendance and Damien is up my ass. Poor sales figures and Damien is up my ass. Poor bar turnout and Damien is... well, you get the picture. I looked across and sure enough there she was just looking at me. I smiled at her and she smiled back immediately. I was pleased. She was fit, albeit quirky and I'd already inadvertently put the ground work in, so I assumed this was going to be a quick hunt. The rep teased me about it. Not that it bothered me. Why would I be teased that someone might fancy a slice of the big fella? If anything, it emboldened me more. I shooed the rep away and with the others we left for the next hotel and the rest of the welcome meetings.

I didn't really give it much thought for the next few hours. I was busy performing, selling and handling the financial side of my job. It wasn't until I returned to my hotel in the afternoon to issue tickets and welcome packs to the new arrivals did it dawn on me that something might not be quite right. I walked into the hotel greeting everyone as I did. There in reception was Barbie. She was still as I left her. I asked her how she was feeling. I was somewhat surprised to see her there still. My ego was telling me that she was definitely going over and she must have been clearly impressed the way I got rid of the other man but something in the back of my head was sending me warning signals. In a normal situation out here, I would suggest that we find a place to have a quiet drink, or jokingly suggest that I might kidnap her for a cuddle or something equally as cheeky. Not this time. I didn't even tell her she looked better or that her eyes had stop resembling those of a playful gremlin and her pupils were actually normally sized again. She just looked at me, clutching her barbie toothbrush, smiling. I made my excuses and continued to go about my duties. I hung around the pool for a while. Nigel joined me, he too remarked about Barbie. I told him what had happened, he just said she's probably just shell shocked from the drugs and maybe this guy really scared her. He followed up with this marvellous phrase of reassurance. "She might be a nutter, but she's fit. You definitely should smash it. Imagine she's normal. It would be a waste." Nigel always managed to make me laugh. He saw the potential in every situation. The last thing I needed was any situation messing up the good thing I had going on here, but even with that said, I definitely didn't want Nigel or any other rep taking a dip. If Barbie was going to be getting any Ken, it was my Ken. Nigel and I messed around the pool for a bit. We entertained the guests in general and got to know some of the new arrivals. As we were working the pool area I was trying to work an angle with a group of girls from Brighton. There was one there that I really fancied and she knew it. I had practically told her it, besides she was stunning. The girls were all happy to flirt with us, but I wanted to put a plan in motion and set the ball rolling. As she walked towards the bar, I made my excuses to leave the others and intercepted her on her return. We stopped to chat and I jokingly asked her what outfit did I need to wear for her to take me seriously as a potential partner and cuddle buddy. She laughed and thought I was being silly, but I was deadly serious, well at least about being her cuddle buddy. She told me she always had a thing for a gladiator. They always looked so tough and protective. I managed to get her to expand on the subject a little. We briefly discussed the Romans as a whole and I ended up getting her to agree that the Romans were basically cool and would make suitable playmates. I told her I would not disappoint and that I would be seeing her later. She teased that she'd hold me to that. Game on.

I left Nigel at the pool as the sun was setting and left to get ready for the night's entertainment. On my way out, Barbie was nowhere to be seen. I was kind of relieved. It would have been even more weird to see her still sat there. I didn't really think about too much else except meeting Brighton later and making good on my plan. I was looking for a bush with thin leaves and vine like branches. I was going to go out on a limb here and turn up to the bar in fancy dress. Whilst I didn't have a gladiator's costume on hand, one thing I did have was a fresh white sheet. The apartment's linen always made excellent togas. All I needed now was a small leafy vine I could make a wreath with and bingo, one horny Julius Caesar. I had it all set up in my head. This was out there. She would be shocked and initially embarrassed by the attention I was going to pour on to her. She'd love the attention really, but would hide it. We'd flirt, then I would just party away with everyone else. People would laugh, people would try and grab me under the sheet. It would be fun. I'd be the life and soul of the party. By my calculations she would be impressed by how much I didn't give a shit and we would end up horizontal at some point over the next few days. The other reps would be wearing the promoter's t-shirts we were told to wear. I was going to disobey that. Damien would call me a cock but my sales were the highest in the area so he wasn't going to be too pissy with me. The only thing I needed to do was to make sure I had my best fitting underwear on. There was high chance I'd be stripped of the toga out there and the last thing I wanted was to pull a Bridget Jones and be left on the dance floor with some skanky undercrackers on. I only had one clean pair and they weren't the best. I opted for my tried and tested Armani boxers my sister bought me as a going away present. Problem was they weren't clean and looked like they could walk out of the apartment on their own. I chucked them in the washing machine. After 30 minutes or so they were clean but wet. I hung them out to dry but as the sun had gone in, it was pointless. Thankfully we had a microwave. I slung them in there and repeatedly put them on for 10 seconds at a time. I only wanted to dry them out. After three or four goes we were golden. I slipped these puppies on and then proceeded to adorn myself in this double sized sheet. We'd done toga parties quite a bit over the season already so I already knew how to do one and tie it off properly. The last thing I wanted was to look like Casper the friendly ghost with a twig on my head. Thankfully, the toga sat perfectly. The wreath was a bit makeshift, but I figured that would be stolen as someone's trophy within minutes anyway. I had some sport sandal things anyway to complete the look. There was only one thing left. Aftershave. They say less is more, and that might well be so, but in the sweat filled halls of some of Ibiza's clubs sometimes you need to be a little more defensive. There was a knack to this though. Your average guy would spray some on his neck or cheek and be done with it, or if they were old school and didn't use the Eau de Toilette, they'd pour some into their hand, clap them together and rub their necks. This might be ok if you're good looking, but if you're really looking to make the difference, here was a tactic keenly employed by some of my more successful mates. Quick spray each side on the jawbone. That's just to cover the bases. Next, spray a liberal amount on each arm just on the inside of the wrist. I'll get on to why in a minute. Thirdly, spray a little amount on your fingers and rub them behind and just underneath the back of the ears. This sounds ridiculous to read, and almost as silly to write, but the method behind the madness was as follows. Everyone wants to smell nice, but no one wants to smell as strong as a whore's handbag. So, a quick splash either side of your mush is acceptable. The wrists are for when you're in a club or a loud bar and you can't hear what someone is saying, you can put your hand up close to the girl's face/head so as to bring her closer in. You don't have to touch her, but the gesture is normally enough for her to come in closer. Her nose will be approximately 3-4 inches away from your wrist. Or maybe you might want to move an out of place strand of hair or catch an invisible insect that's close to her head. Either way, the scent will catch her The icing on the cake is just behind the ears. You and your potential suitor are speaking close to each other but something distracts you and you just need to turn to the side a little. You don't want to be too keen so you always need to look like you're not fully engaged, but you also want her to catch a whiff too. Anyways, these were tried and tested tips. Brighton was in trouble.

As soon as I left the apartment block, I was getting attention in the toga. Some local girls hollered out "Hola guapo!" which basically translates as hello sexy or hello handsome. I blew them a kiss which sent them all tittering away. Some lads were laughing as I walked past them. One said brilliant, the other followed up with 'fair play'. By the time I got to the hotel I was 20-30 minutes late. I was hoping Brighton and her friends would be there already. I strolled into the bar like something out of a film. I walked in head held high with a pair on me that would rival the jolly green giant. As soon as I walked through the door, people started to laugh and cheer. I walked straight up to Brighton and her pals in the corner. The conversation stopped instantly when they saw me. They all laughed. I looked straight into Brighton's eyes and told her 'a Roman you wanted, a Roman you got! I'm not messing around.' She blushed, I grinned, and the rest of the group told me I looked great and we all had a photo. We were joined by the rest of the guests and the drinking and party continued. I didn't speak again to Brighton for the next hour or so, although I'd smile, every time I caught her looking. I thought I'd let the idea soak in for a bit. Besides, I was having a lot of fun with everyone else. Some of the lads in the hotel loved the idea and to my surprise and the hotelier's horror they too emerged at the hotel bar fully laden in white sheet toga's. I told the hotelier I would pay for any damage or loss of sheets. I also informed the guys that if they lost them, they were paying for them but they did look cool. Before I knew it, another 15-20 lads also had togas. This was brilliant. Not only did I look like I didn't follow the rules, but I was also a trendsetter! Spirits were high and the atmosphere jubilant. I was in a great mood. Fancy dress always made me happy, and I was pretty certain Brighton was on my case. At least judging by the mates' reactions and giggling between them every time I walked past. After a few drinking games and the day's forfeits had been dished out, it was time to leave for the first bar.

As I got everyone mobilised and ready in reception, I heard a familiar voice. "I love your outfit!" It was Barbie. I was a little taken back. She still had her hair in bunches, but had changed out of her pink ensemble to something equally as glittery but dark and shiny. She had another crop top and shimmering dark trousers with heels. She looked good. If she looked like an anime dream this morning, now she looked pretty sophisticated. I asked her how she was doing and if she managed to get some sleep. She apologised for the state of herself in the morning and again thanked me for looking after her. She gave me a hug. Normally I would have reeled this in all day long but it was somewhat awkward. The reception was full of guests waiting to go to the first bar and all eyes were on us. The fact that Barbie clearly wasn't staying in the hotel or was even on one of our tours was painfully apparent. She asked us where we were going, I replied nonchalantly that we were going on a bar crawl. I didn't ask her where she was going as that would invite the possible response of 'no plans' or 'can I tag along.' Again, normally I would be all over this, but there was still something off about her and besides, I had Brighton hot to trot no more than 4 metres behind me. I apologised that I couldn't talk longer with her, and gestured to the merry band of horny togas behind me and told her I was working. She understood, hugged me again and we proceeded to march out. I must admit I was a little torn. She seemed perfectly normal, pretty, and pleasant. In fact, I felt like a bit of an asshole for being somewhat short with her. I tried to reason in my head that I was working and she would have seen that and it's not like I was rude to her, but I still felt awkward.

The walk to the bar was eventful. The guys in togas really got into persona. You'd think they were members of the senate about to throw an orgy. They were trying to get involved with anything and everything in a skirt. Including some in trousers. It was amusing for everyone. One of them held me back and took me to one side. "I think that bird wanted a bit of you." He told me directly. "Which one?" I feigned ignorance. "The fit one in reception. Why didn't you invite her along? Are you mad?" I knew that the rest of the group were within earshot. I had to think quick on my feet. I didn't want to lose street cred, but I also didn't want my ego to blow me up with Brighton. "To be honest mate, she is really fit. Normally she'd be right up my street. Thing is, there's someone else am early stages with and I'm kind of into them right now. Hopefully I'm not making a prick of myself." There. If she's in earshot, that should do the trick. I was hoping the guy would leave it there and basically change the subject. Before I could ask about his endeavours and swiftly swap the spotlight on to his misdemeanours, he threw me the best pass anyone could wish for. This guy essentially crossed the ball in front of an empty goal. "I would have been up her like a rat in a drainpipe. I guess this girl must be pretty awesome for you to pass up that. I hope it works out for you man." This was the volleyball set up… the ball was hanging waiting to be spiked. "Me too dude, me too." I glimpsed across at Brighton who heard everything. Check mate.

Predictably as we got to the bar there was Damien outside talking to the bar owner. I was at the back of the group making sure we kept hold of everyone, much to the touts' annoyance. He stopped talking once he started to see the lads walking in wearing togas. Nigel was already there and was counting them in at the door. The minute he saw me, Damien face palmed. "You absolute cock. What do you look like?" he berated me. "Julius Caesar" I retorted. "Funny cunt. You were supposed to be wearing the Es Paradis t-shirt." He persisted. I wasn't particularly bothered by this, but didn't want to get into a slanging match in front of the guests, nor try and ridicule him otherwise he would have my ass on airport duty for a month. "I can go and change if you really want? I was just trying to spice things up a bit. Besides, given I've got 100% of my hotel here and it's their first night out I wanted to promote some unity among the group." His stance softened. "I see what you did there. You just reminded me that you're a great salesman, especially when compared to this useless minge next to you." He gestured to Nigel. "Only the facts" I grinned. I stopped short there. I sensed I was winning. "Seriously. If you want me to change, I'll nip back now." I offered, knowing full well that wouldn't be necessary. "Just get in there you bell end. Don't let me catch you copping off with any of the guests otherwise you'll be the office bitch, sales or no sales!" I just smiled and walked in. As I passed him Nigel got in on the act "I'm not that bad Damien, you're just not managing me right," I chuckled as the words left his mouth. "Get in the bar before I put you on airports for a fucking month you helmet." Nigel followed me in. The minute the door closed behind us and we were out of earshot we laughed. "Love the toga big man" he told me. "Cheers dude, I'm pulling the stops out to close Brighton." I continued to tell him what had happened with Barbie but how I was determined to sort out Brighton. I did tell him I still had an interest in Barbie though in case he had any ideas. To be fair it wouldn't have bothered me much if Nigel did have a go. We were close, but Nigel was also good at cock blocking, and not always accidentally. If he saw another guest make a play for a target, he was pretty good at taking that person out of the equation. Normally we would do it in the form of drinking games. You would just issue a drinking challenge, make sure the guy sniffing around the girl we deemed off limits was involved and just make sure he got extra pissed. It worked every time. By the time we were done we might have been pissed too, but he was literally obliterated. I guess after doing this day in and day out, without rest, we had gained some sort of tolerance or immunity to most of the effects of the booze. Also he wasn't the only one who could take a player off the board. I was pretty ruthless at it. Rather than see it as a necessary evil to help a friend or my own interests, I would often not just put the guy out of the race but out of the game. That being said, no one was ever forced, and I never let anyone drink something that I wouldn't drink myself first. The other way to do it was to appeal to someone's ego. You'd basically whisper in his ear that you'd heard a group of girls saying how fit they thought he was and how by the pool they were debating whether they would sleep with him or not. We would then point to some random decent looking girls and just point him in their direction. If he was just looking for action most of the time he'd immediately go after them thinking he was on a certainty. If he had higher aspirations and was chasing the same as us, out came the drinking hat and he was going to be going either home alone or with some beast that would put up with him in such a state. This might not have been fair, but these were the rules we played by.

Once in we grabbed some drinks and went straight on to the dance floor. Most of my lot were already warmed up and dancing. Everyone was having a good time. The lads who were in togas were revelling in them. They were attracting a lot of attention and making the most of it. The girls were having fun with them and taking pictures etc. The other hotels' guests looked quite conservative by all accounts. I liked this feeling. If I noticed it, others did too. At one point, Brighton came up behind me and told me my bum looked big in the sheet. This was an opening pass and only acted to boost my confidence. It was loud, so I pulled her in close and told her it wouldn't matter if I was wearing a dress or a sack, she'd still fancy a go. Have that. Shots fired. She blushed and then grinned. I asked her if she was having a good time in general out here. She teased me further, remarking that the place was great, the bars and clubs were awesome, but the staff and reps were awful. I bantered back and forwards with her like this for about 20 minutes. We were interrupted by Nigel. He told me it was time to go to the next bar and we had to round everyone up. At that point I thanked her for a thoroughly boring conversation and wished her well in her hunt for someone who wouldn't fall asleep on her. As I said it, I started to grin. She punched me on the shoulder and abused me back. This was perfect. The stage was set. I needed to make sure that I didn't get hammered and I needed to make sure she didn't get hammered (it was her holiday after all). I also just needed to make sure none of my guests caused any issues or fights or anything silly and I was home free. The rest of the evening went like a charm. No issues, no fights, no puking, no stress. My debrief was at 2am. At 1.50 I asked her what she was up to. She told me she didn't know and asked what I was up to. I told her I'd meet her in 15 minutes outside the club opposite a bar that we had walked past earlier. I was jumping inside. Back home she'd be a 9+ out of 10. Here she was messing with me. I couldn't wait for Damien to finish the meeting. He slung shit my way about the togas. It didn't even register. No retort. No quips. No demonstration of my wit or mental prowess. I was happy to confess to being a prick whatever, just finish. I had a date with an angel. He sensed I just wanted to go and asked me to stay behind to help with something. Bastard. He was just playing with me. He wasn't silly. He knew what and more importantly who I was on for. As soon as the meeting ended, he pulled me to one side. I was waiting for the lecture about not sticking to the appropriate attire or fraternising with the guests etc, but he threw me off keel. "Listen, I know you're about 10 minutes away from smashing the granny out of the fitty staying in your hotel, and quite frankly all the reps are jealous about it. I also know that's why you wore the toga. One of her friends was talking to me earlier on about you and spilled the beans. I just wanted to say that you're doing a fantastic job as a rep, and the whole office knows about you and your sales. Keep it up. You got a bright future with us! Fair play on the toga too. I would have worn a kimono and heels if I thought it would help me squeeze into that!" I couldn't believe it. I was being praised for my efforts on top of hopefully getting laid with Brighton. "Thanks Damien, I really appreciate it. I know I can be an ass at times, but my heart's in the right place. I do try" He put his hand on my shoulder looked me in my eye and said "Stop being a bender, get to the bar, get her done, and I want to see you at lunchtime by the earliest. Oh, and if any of your mates lose their sheets, you're paying for them!" Wow. Damien had effectively given me the morning off. They really must be happy with my sales numbers. This just confirmed one thing. She was coming back to mine. I didn't want to go back to hers and be woken up early by hungover roommates and deprived of hopefully round 2. This equation took me all of about 10 milliseconds to solve. My place + smash now + smash in the morning + lay in =

bliss. I gave him a man hug. He squealed and wriggled like it was his first night in prison. I gave him a big kiss on the cheek, he called me a cunt, I bid him farewell and I was off like a shot. I covered the distance to the bar in a time that would have Usain Bolt blushing. I shot inside to see her by the bar being chatted up by some Adonis of a man. I mean this motherfucker was handsome. He was tall, chiselled, in shape, well dressed, tanned, and looked like he owned a small country. Bollocks. She was clearly entertained or at least was happy being chatted up. I felt my tablets began to shrink a little. How am I going to fix this? I mean if she was a 9+ on the UK scale, this manimal was clearly a 9+ too. There's only one thing for it. Blitzkrieg. No way was I going to entertain a three-way conversation to give her the chance to weigh up Adonis the retired Olympic champion son of a billionaire shipping magnate against a geezer dressed in a toga. Anyone who knows me will appreciate that whilst I might not act with surgical precision, I am effective. I decided to rush the show. I bowled over as quick as I could without running. To an outsider I was probably walking like someone who had just sharted and was going to the loo for a check. I interrupted the conversation. You could tell she felt awkward, but I didn't have time to think about her feelings. "Adonis, nice to meet you. Thank you for looking after my sister in my absence." He didn't really know what to say. Not only was he surprised that his patter had been interrupted so abruptly, but he also seemed to be confused by my toga. I quickly looked at Brighton "Agatha, mum and dad are outside. We need to go, they're really pissed." Before she had a chance to reply, I grabbed her by the hand and ripped her out of there. As we left, he muttered "But I thought your name was…" We didn't give him a chance to finish. Before she knew it, she was outside the bar on the street. I was laughing. She started to laugh too. I seized the initiative. I snogged her. I grabbed her by the waist. She reciprocated. As soon as we stopped, I laid it out. You're the best-looking girl on the island right now. There is no way I am losing you to that specimen. Besides, he looks like he couldn't string a sentence together without memorising it first." I know this was a) cheesy and b) unfair on him, but I needed to score some points quickly. She just laughed and threw her arms around me again. She pecked me on the lips and said "where to next, Julius?"

We went to a couple of bars on the strip. I don't know why but given that Damien knew about my interest and was almost giving me his blessing, I was happy to relax in public with her. Normally there would be something more clandestine about messing around with the guests, but on this occasion, I was happy to just unwind wherever. It didn't not help that she was gorgeous, and I was happy to let the bar staff and touts know who I was with. We had a blast. We went into my usual haunts, where the staff were happy to accommodate Brighton and myself. There was some karaoke involved, some shots, half a fish bowl, and lots of salsa / Spanish style dancing. By the time we were heading home both of us were merry but happy. I probably needed the sleep more but there was no chance I was letting this chance slip through my fingers. We'd been walking hand in hand, arm in arm from the strip. Giggling and talking loudly as drunk people do. As we got to my apartment block, I was fumbling with my keys when I heard that familiar voice. "You alright?" we both turned around. It was Barbie. "Oh hi, what are you doing here?" I stumbled. "Oh, I was just in the area and thought I'd see how you are? Have you had a good night?" Before I had a chance to answer, Brighton found her voice. "Yeah it was brilliant. We've been to all these bars and special little places I never would have found if it wasn't for Julius. He's great." Shit.

This is awkward. I hadn't even begun to think about how she knew where I lived, or what or why she was outside my apartment. I was pretty drunk and still on target for Brighton. All I could come up with in that split second was that we were tired and that maybe I'd see her tomorrow if she's around. With that I opened the main entrance to the apartment block and Brighton, giggling, bundled me through before the door was fully open. Once the door had shut behind us Brighton asked me who was that. I told her the story of how we met and that I thought she wasn't stable. I probably spoke too much, but Brighton just laughed and quipped that both Barbie and Adonis had lost out tonight. I chuckled at this as we entered the apartment.

It was a lazy but 'productive' morning. I hadn't had a lay in for months. I was in no rush to get out of bed. Eventually when the pair of us did surface we got ready and left for the hotel. I devised a plan to walk with her most of the way but made up needing to run an errand in Nigel's hotel. His hotel was close enough to mine that she wasn't going to feel abandoned and would continue on her own, yet it was far enough away to give me some cover. Whilst I was proud, I didn't really want my hotel seeing us walk in together. Besides, I couldn't wait to fill Nigel in. As we paused to split, I gave her a snog, thanked her for a lovely morning and said I'd see her by the pool shortly. She just smiled and quipped about this not meaning we were engaged or anything. I laughed. She was caning me and I loved it. I didn't retort, I just smiled. I thought best to let her have the banter victory. As she continued on, I practically skipped across the street into Nigel's hotel. As I waltzed in some of Nigel's boys came out. They were heading to the pool. They must have seen us let go of each other across the road. "Oh my god, did you nail that? You did, didn't you. Lucky bastard." He'd asked and answered the question before I could deny. I just shot him a grin. They were laughing. I didn't stop to answer anything. I made a beeline for Nigel. He was sat in reception talking to some of his guests whilst hanging posters. I couldn't wait to tell him. He saw me but before I got a chance to unleash the pride, he got in there first. "Mate, brace yourself!" He threw me. "What? What's happened?" he took me to one side. I was concerned. "Is everything alright?" I asked again. He led me to an area at the back of the bar that was seldom populated. "Mate, I don't know how to tell you this. You've got a bunny boiler!" He stopped. "What are you talking about?" I failed to grasp the fatal attraction reference initially. "Man, you got a stalker, big time." I instantly knew who he was talking about. "Barbie?" "Exactly. What happened there? Did you do her in the end? She's been to the hotel 2 or 3 times already asking for me just to ask where you were. I figured you'd overdone it or were smashing into fitty somewhere." I sighed. "Fuck sake. All I did was help this girl out of a tight situation with some drugged-up asshole and now she's on my case. I haven't touched her or gone anywhere near her. I was nothing but a gentleman. In fact, I thought she'd get the hint as she was waiting outside my apartment last night when I rocked up with the Doris. It was obvious we were not just friends. We were practically holding hands as it was silly o'clock." Nigel could sense my irritation. He tried to make light of the situation. "Can you imagine what would happen if you nailed her? She'd be looking for marriage. She'd probably cut your cock off if you even looked at another girl!" We both chuckled. I told him that in order to save my manhood and not get my throat cut, if Barbie did try anything on with me, I was going to tell her that I was gay and that Nigel was my partner. Before Nigel could say a word, I added that I was going to be the husband in our relationship. We continued to laugh. Nigel then changed the subject. "So, what did you want to tell me? Catch an angel, did we?" I suddenly remembered why I'd gone over to see him in the first place. I started to tell him all the details. I was jabbering on with excitement. He could tell I was pleased with myself, and also that I liked this girl a lot. "So, when's round 2?" he asked me with a smile. I corrected him. "Round 3 will be later on this afternoon or tonight with any luck! She'll need some time to recover otherwise it will look obvious she got railed within an inch of her life!" We both laughed. "Well you better make sure the stalker doesn't catch you, otherwise you might find yourself within an inch of your life!" I just sighed.

I left Nigel there in the bar and proceeded to check in at my hotel. I needed to make sure everything was ok, and no one had done anything stupid like launch a bed into the pool or break a sink from shagging. I was trying to work out what to do next with the girl. I didn't want to come across as too keen, but I was also painfully aware that she was only here for a week, so it's not as if time was on my side. I was also weighing up what to do re Barbie. I'd already told Brighton all about it, and she'd witnessed her first-hand last night. I wanted to make sure there was absolutely nothing that could fall back on me, I mean it was pretty unusual to have a girl go batshit on you for no real reason. Especially as Barbie was attractive too. It would be an easier sell if she was a swamp donkey and was just infatuated by me, but as she was decent, surely, I must have done something to encourage her right? I decided I was going to play on her being a nutter and it was better for me to just smile and continue being polite. I mean she hadn't actually done anything she was just coming across as weird or a bit needy. I didn't want to cause a scene and the last thing I wanted was for there to be any conflicts in the hotel.

I didn't want to over egg it or give any excuse for Brighton or her mates to involve themselves, so I was going to try and walk a thin line. As I walked into the hotel, Barbie was sat there in reception waiting for me. "Hello stranger, what time do you call this?" she asked. I just smiled and told her I had a few things to take care of. As I got closer, I could see that Barbie had been partying. She was wearing hot pants, a flimsy thin low-cut top and a pair of funky anime style trainers. She was clutching a bottle of water like it was a life line. I went to the reception desk to check the incident book and as I stopped to check to see if there were any entries, Barbie gave me a hug from behind. It was awkward. The receptionist made the 'loco' expression with her finger and just shook her head. It was like being hugged from behind by your kid sister. A few of the other guests were close by and it was attracting attention. I tried to make a joke out of it by wriggling around and turning myself towards her, putting her head on my chest. She didn't let up one bit. I then began to literally stroke her on the head like a dog, ushering patronising phrases like "there, there" and "There's nothing to be afraid of anymore." She laughed and eventually she let go and sat down next to me. I could see her pupils were wide again, so I assumed she was high. I asked her if everything was ok. She just smiled like she always did and replied everything was fine. I didn't really want to engage any more at this point. I wasn't sure what was going on in her loaf, so made my excuses and left her at reception. I had a quick scout round to make sure neither Brighton nor her mates had witnessed our impromptu hug. Thankfully the coast was clear. A couple of lads gestured to me that I should "take care of her", I just smiled and rolled my eyes.

I made a point of not going through the reception area for the rest of the afternoon, so I couldn't tell you how long she stayed there if at all. I found the whole thing rather confusing. We were on such different wavelengths. I mean, I know people say that about exes after they've broken up and try to explain what happened to others. Most of the time what they really mean is they didn't fancy their partner anymore or they found someone else they fancied more. Or maybe one was abusive or just outright boring. There was normally at least some common ground. Here I really meant it. I didn't know if Barbie wanted to bang me with her body, or bang me with a cricket bat. Did she fancy me? Was I just a big brother for her? Had I inadvertently created a safe space at my reception area where she felt she could go and unwind after a night of disco biscuits and marching ants? To this day, I still have no clue. She was harmless enough, in fact she was very warm and friendly, not to mention fit, but that only distracted me more. It's not like I was Robert Redford and girls were throwing themselves at my feet. Well definitely not ones that looked like this. Other holiday makers began to pick up on it. Over the next few days, I was being continually asked what's up with that blonde bird in reception? Or lads would shout the stalkers back and then start doing the jaws music as the shark was closing in on its prey. It was funny initially, but it became tiresome.

I hadn't spoken about her publicly to anyone other than Nigel and Brighton. I didn't want the guests being horrible to her. Over the next few days, the pattern continued. I would wander back to my apartment (more often than not with Brighton in tow) and she would be there waiting at the door. We would say hi to her, ask her how her night was and then proceed to go inside. In the morning, I would walk back to the hotel with Brighton, pausing to split just as we got to the hotel, and Barbie would be there waiting for me to say hi and give me a hug. Sometimes she would stay in the hotel reception, other times she would immediately disappear. If I wasn't at the hotel within an hour or so, she would seek out Nigel asking where I was. At one point I think Nigel got fed up with it and when asked where I was, he told her 'probably banging the back doors off one of the guests.' Apparently, Barbie just smiled and told him she'd wait for me at the hotel.

We managed to sail through the rest of her stay on the island with no incidents or issues, aside from her checking up on me and resting in reception during the mornings. Brighton had already flown back, and we'd had a new wave of arrivals. On Barbie's last night she came into the hotel bar where we were getting ready to leave for a bar crawl and asked if she could speak with me outside. I agreed and followed her outside the bar. I generally hated these situations because it was always in full view of the public and even if the conversation was harmless enough, it didn't look harmless, and these were the sorts of things that the other girls specifically picked up on. No matter how subtle you tried to slide out the door, you were always spotted. As we walked out of the bar towards the exit at the side of the hotel Barbie put her arms around me and told me she was going to be leaving for the airport in a few minutes and just wanted to say good bye and to thank me for looking after her on her holiday. She said she'd had an amazing time and that she would never forget Ibiza nor me. She hugged me tighter. To be honest, they were nice words to hear but I was relieved that she was going back. Not that I didn't enjoy being hugged by a pretty member of the fairer sex, but I wanted things to return to normal around the hotel in terms of my extra-curricular activities. I was also quite proud of myself for showing restraint and not allowing the little brain to take over the big brain and get myself in trouble. It was definitely a missed opportunity. Barbie was fine, but the risks were too great. I remember standing there just hugging. When she suddenly looked up at me. It was a classic move. She was a bit shorter than me, and by looking upwards, she put herself in the kiss zone. I saw it all unfold in slow motion. Don't do it. Don't kiss her. She'll ignore the flight and then you'll have problems. Someone else will see. She'll fly back out. You'll lose your job. It was like I was trying to 'close' myself. Every time I came up with a reason not to, I was objection handling myself. There was no end to the objections, but equally no end to the answers. We were still for a few seconds. I somehow managed to remain emotionless. At least from the neck up. My fella, however, betrayed me. At the same time as she pulled me just a fraction closer, I must have felt a twitch. The next thing I knew we were kissing. It lasted for a few seconds. I can't remember who broke off first. She just smiled, handed me a sheet of paper with her email address and disappeared out the side door of the hotel. My mind was all over the place. I was sure it was a mistake and one that could end up proving costly. Thankfully, she must have made her flight and for the rest of the season, the hotel reception area resembled more a front desk and less like a chill out zone.

CHAPTER 24
THE HUMAN SQUID

Not every cuddle had a happy ending. Towards the middle of peak season Nigel and I fell into the trap of playing knock-a-door-smash a little too often and we got comfortable. We got sloppy. We would continue to party hard with the guests after hours and we were drinking like fish. It didn't matter whether we pulled or not we had a backup plan. If I think back now, half the time we both had girls ready and waiting to leave with us in the bars and clubs, but we were too busy knocking back ridiculous drinks and being too boisterous to even notice. I think it was the fact that we didn't give a shit that set us apart from most of the other guys who would be stalking around the club looking to hook up. Just as a guy who doesn't care or chases can be attractive to the opposite sex, that only works for so long and half the time the girls got bored, gave up and went off to pull others. We did not care one bit. As far as we were concerned there were plenty of fish in the sea, and we had big catching nets.

One night in particular was extremely messy. We found

ourselves in a dive of a bar with a good group of guests. There were a couple of big groups and a several smaller ones too. Everyone was getting on like a house on fire. Half the groups were already intertwined, but no one was looking to sly off anywhere for cuddles, they were too busy having fun in the bar. We were on the dance floor and it was carnage. There was dirty dancing, limbo and even impromptu breakdancing competitions. Nigel had challenged a guy to a pint race and subsequently vomited on the floor half way through. I was trying my hand at Latin dancing before losing my balance and wiping out a table of drinks that were poised ominously at the edge of the dance floor. We weren't in our usual 'company' bars so it would have been easy to get into trouble with other groups, security etc, only there were so many of us in comparison, that people just accepted we were pissed and left us to it. Well almost. Nigel needed to get a mop and bucket and clean his own sick up otherwise we were all getting thrown out. Even that was funny and passed by without a hitch.

Eventually we all started to get a bit battle weary and we all made tracks towards the hotel. There was no way Nigel and I were going to make it back to our apartments and no way we weren't playing knock-a-door-smash. We sat in the hotel bar and ordered a couple of drinks. Most of the group had already dispersed with each other, and those who were still able to drink, pulled up some chairs with us and continued. It was already probably 3.30 in the morning and some of the clubbers were beginning to return in various states. We were all talking complete shit, sharing war stories, and spilling the beans on various incidents etc. At some point, I began to nod off. Nigel saw it and quickly sprang into action. He kicked me in the leg causing me to wake up and basically made excuses for us both and dragged me upstairs in the hotel. Despite my protestations of being too tired and incapable he bundled me into the lift. As soon as the lift doors shut, I went into overdrive. Without hesitation I blurted out "5" to which he replied "12". We were practically holding each other up as we mooched along the corridor to 512. He confidently knocked at the door and as we heard the chain slide off the rail, he whispered "window" in my ear. The door opened and to our surprise (and delight) it was one of the girls who had been in the bar earlier with us. Her and her friend didn't want to drink downstairs and hadn't copped off with anyone so decided to hit the hay. She found it funny that we were both a little unsteady on our feet and invited us in. She was already in her pyjamas. As we sat down in the living room her mate came out also in her pjs. She laughed as soon as she saw us. They poured some more drinks and we all sat down together. We were initially just chatting but then started to play cards. I began to get a second wind, but Nigel wanted to up the ante, so he proposed that we play strip poker. I kept quiet at this point. I wasn't sure how that was going to go down. The girls had been massively flirty with us earlier on in the evening, but if the truth be told, everyone had been flirting with everyone anyway, so I wasn't reading too much into this. The girls whispered a few things in each other's ears and there was lots of giggling going on. This was a good sign. They then confidently told us "it's on" and that we should prepare to get naked. Awesome. Green light. They then went into the bedroom to change into something more comfortable. At which point Nigel just smiled across at me. When the girls emerged, they hadn't just put something on more comfortable, they put on something much, more threatening. Layers, and lots of them. They'd each put on extra socks, t-shirt and a cardigan on top of their pyjamas. Despite Nigel's weak protest, the girls just laughed and told us a deal's a deal.

Undeterred we began to play. Now given how much booze we'd had, the fact that I can't bluff for shit, and Nigel has the numerical accuracy of a sloth, we began to lose and badly. I think after 10 minutes, Nigel was in his pants, I was topless in jeans and one sock, and the girls had managed to lose just a few socks between them. Within 15 minutes, Nigel was sat there naked, I was in my undies, and one of the girls was back to just her pyjamas, the other was in her bra and knickers. We were all having fun and the drinks continued to flow. It was inevitable that something was going to happen between us all: I didn't know if that meant Nigel and I would be swapping, or the group would couple off. Eventually, one of the girls lost and that meant her top came off. She was sat closer to Nigel and she was by far the prettier one out of the two. As she took off the bra she flicked it at Nigel. Nigel not one to miss a sign, picked it up and put it on himself. Everyone was laughing. He strode over to the full-length mirror in the bathroom naked as the day he was born (except for the bra) to admire himself. He made a cheeky comment about it fitting him better than her, she sprung up to give him a dig in the ribs. He asked her to undo it for him. Both girls took the piss out of him for not knowing how to undo a bra, but Nigel was one step ahead. As soon as she stepped into the bathroom to help him, he closed the door behind her. We could hear the pair of them kissing through the door. Normally, this would have been really awkward had it been at home, but this was Ibiza. All it had done was settle the question of who's with who. I think we poured another drink without them, but after one or two sips, we were both kissing too. A minute or so later, Nigel and his one passed through the lounge straight into the bedroom, closing the door behind them. Nigel did throw me a solid favour though, just before walking into the bedroom he managed to turn the lounge lights off, leaving us to make out in the dark. That was a cool wingman move. I mean no one is going to object to that and it just paved the way for the night ahead. I say night, it was probably 5-5.30 at this point and everyone was drunk and tired. I wish I could tell you that I performed like a lion and that even her friends would get to know my name back home, but the truth of the matter was it was a drunken fumble. It was hard enough just to be able to stand up and when that little layer of numbing rubber came into play a couple of times it was a case of man down. I'm not even sure we fancied each other, but those were the cards we'd been dealt. I seriously doubt I did much for her, and she wasn't exactly doing it for me. At one point, I was at the back and I think I managed to rock myself to sleep. I only came back round when she asked why I stopped. I think in the end we just gave up and crashed out.

Nigel woke me up in the morning – we were both late for work and he needed to get home and get changed. I was fortunate in that I had my emergency bag with spare uniform stashed at the hotel, and so I would be ready in about 5 minutes. I just needed to hover near the pool long enough (30 seconds or so) for someone to rugby tackle me in and that was the shower taken care of. I had tooth paste and hair gel etc also stashed. Nigel wasn't so forward thinking and so that meant he was going to be late for the sales meeting. As we left, we thanked the girls for a nice evening and tried to get a move on. As we left, I told Nigel how bad the fumble was and how I was surprised I even managed to hold wood. Nigel just laughed confessing that I did better than him. He said it was ridiculous. He couldn't stand up for more than a few seconds. He said you'd have better luck trying to pick a padlock with plasticine. I asked if she was upset, he said not sure. Probably not, allowed her to get some more sleep. I loved Nigel's sense of humour. He truly didn't care. As we were parting, he started to laugh. "What's funny?" I asked. Apparently when I used their loo, shortly after arriving, he'd asked who was sleeping where. My one answered by the window. He said he took one look at her, and decided he was going to switch and so practically begged the other one to sit by him. He said his one was by far the prettier, and that's what made him break the rule. I punched him on the shoulder. Was it not enough for him to know that I ended up with the rough one? He had to tell me he broke code too? What a wanker. Soon we were both chuckling. We parted ways, I headed to my hotel, he bolted home.

I quickly went through reception, grabbed my bug out bag and went into the toilet. Within a minute I was changed, and sprayed with deodorant, but I still looked dishevelled. I left the loo and hovered by the pool. Literally within seconds I was rugby tackled into it, and emerged from the pool, wet, but relatively clean. I walked into the sales meeting a few minutes later dripping wet. Damien was unimpressed. I told him I'd be bundled into the pool by 5 guests who dragged me through reception. What could I do? Besides, I wasn't the highest on his shit list. Nigel was late and his sales figures were languishing in last place. Damien quizzed me on his whereabouts? I said nothing. Only that I hadn't seen him. By the time Nigel showed up, the meeting was practically finished. As he walked in flustered, Damien asked him where he'd been. Nigel lied and said he'd been at the clinic helping a guest out who had fallen over and hurt their wrist. Damien called his bluff and informed him that he'd been in the clinic getting some tablets for gastroenteritis and he hadn't seen him there. Clearly, Damien was lying, but Nigel folded. He admitted to being late for oversleeping and in return was rewarded with airport duty for the next couple of nights. As we left the room, Nigel was bitching. I was laughing, claiming it was karma for him pulling a switcheroo and leaving me with the hound.

Over the next day or so we saw the girls by the pool and in the hotel bar and everything was cool. We were all friendly and from time to time a bit flirty etc. There were a few cracks appearing though, and I could already tell that this was going to become an issue. Nigel's one, the prettier one of the two, had developed a serious crush on him and wherever we went she would sit there just staring at him. He liked her, but wasn't that bothered, and wasn't showing her that much attention. This meant that there were some tears from time to time and awkward conversations. You know the sort, when a girl says "can we talk a minute?" Nigel was pretty good at staying aloof though and so whilst it was an issue, he somehow managed to keep it low key, allowing him to continue to party with others. My one on the other hand, well she was of a different breed. In the first day or so after that evening, we were chatting and laughing together like nothing had happened and how things were before that fateful game of poker. She even laughed about her friend getting all googly over Nigel, as if she was being dramatic and naïve. I liked this though. I thought mine was cool, knew the score and I was comfortable around her, but oh how I got that wrong. As time went on, she began to change. I was very discrete with my extra curriculars, so as not to upset anyone else or rub anything in anyone's face, so she hadn't caught me with anyone else or anything like that, but something had clearly begun to offend her. As I'd walk round the pool, I'd ask how they were doing? Are they enjoying the holiday? etc, you know rep stuff. The other one would always ask how is Nigel? Where is he? What time is he going to be at the bar? She'd at least feign a conversation with me. My one, however, would just give me daggers. The longer the time went on the worse it got. We'd be in the hotel bar and I'd be arranging some drinking games, or holding court with a group of guests and she'd continue to snipe at me and make sarcastic comments. I was continually heckled and singled out. Even some of the other guests would quietly come up to me and ask me what her problem was, so it wasn't something in my head. It got to a point where it became totally toxic. Any fun and happy vibes I was creating in the bar were being challenged by grumpy tits. I needed to do something about it. One particular comment she made was about me being a shit rep. I laughed it off, and brushed over it. I wasn't bothered by it, but it was becoming an issue. I pulled her to one side and just asked her what I'd done that had offended her so much. She stayed silent. I asked her if it was down to poker night? She kept quiet. I asked her was it because we stayed over and hadn't spent the night since? I know that sounded egotistical, but I needed to create a reaction just to try and engage in a conversation. I wanted to squash whatever this problem was so it didn't continue to spill out. When she heard the last line, it was like lighting a match. She went off at me. Telling me that us reps were dogs, we'd behaved badly. We were stringing girls along. I kept quiet, choosing to soak it up instead. I let her berate Nigel and I for a minute or so, saying very little. When she'd lost the wind in her sails, I asked her to tell me what was really the problem. A gamble on my part I might add, but given how relatively cool she'd been for the first few days, I figured there was more to this than what had happened (or hadn't) between us. She paused before getting tearful. I comforted her, and told her to let it out. She began to pour out her heart. It wasn't to do with me at all. She was pissed with her mate for falling for Nigel. Despite their disastrous encounter, she really liked him and wanted more. She'd spent the whole time talking about Nigel, planning nights out around where he was going to be, and asking continual questions to my one about whether Nigel would like her outfit, or what he would think on this or that, or anything else. I sympathised with her. She said she came away to relax and have fun, but she says all they're having is discussions about him, and by extension me, and it's upsetting her and causing frictions between them. Eventually her watery eyes cleared, she composed herself and then she apologised to me for being a bitch. She said she was lashing out, and as I was the only other person really 'known' to her, I was receiving the brunt of it. I told her it didn't matter and that as long as she was ok that was the main thing. I asked her if she'd like me to introduce the pair of them to some other groups to try and dilute her friend down a bit so she could talk about stuff other than Nigel. She laughed and said that would be helpful. She gave me a hug, straightened herself out, and then we both went into the bar. I immediately arranged a drinking game and set up a couple of teams. I paired the girls up with one of the larger groups of guys as well as a couple of really friendly girls also staying at the hotel. After a few minutes they were all chatting together nicely and I didn't think anything of it. Part of me was relieved by this. I did feel sorry for the situation, but was glad to know that she wasn't just uber pissed at me. In this job, we were always going to have certain situations etc, and bed hopping was par for the course, but you never wanted to upset anyone. I was also pleased that there wasn't going to be any more nastiness in the hotel between us. As I've written previously, once you build a good momentum in the hotel, it's imperative to maintain it. It really helps to keep everyone smiling and having a good time, which was good for the atmosphere, good for the mind, and good for the sales. Whilst I needed to have a chat with Nigel (who was on airport duty) to make him aware about his one, I felt pleased I'd settled the issue. Or so I thought.

The rest of the evening went off without a hitch. We even exchanged some smiles between us. I got their group some free drinks in various bars and I continued to lead the pack along the strip. I was having a good night, despite being tired. I think I must have spoken at one point to every group in the club. Ensuring all was good, they were having fun and no issues. At 2am after the final meeting of the day, I went back in to the club to get my bag and stopped to get a cup of tea at the back of the bar. Cup of tea, right? Hardly rock and roll. The bar staff all knew us well as we saw them practically every other night and at various other events the company organised, so they were really friendly with us. They were more than willing to get me a cuppa and some of them sat and chatted with me for a bit whilst I unwound. We even shared a laugh about my missing partner in crime Nigel who was sitting there at the airport waiting for a 4:45am flight to come in. One of the girls in my hotel who I'd been flirting with, approached us and joined a conversation. She completely took the piss out of me for drinking tea, but when the barman asked her what she was having, she just pointed at it and said the same. We all had a laugh about it. I liked this girl, she had good banter, was relaxed and seemed like an older head on young shoulders. She was attractive, mousey blond shortish hair, quite tall, and athletic looking. She pulled up a pew next to me and we began to chat. After about 20 minutes of putting the world to rights she leaned in, putting her hand on my leg, and asked me what I'd done to that girl to make her so pissed with me. I was a little taken back by her directness, and quite frankly, was too tired to be polite or elusive. "We shared a night after some drinks, and it was a mistake all round. She's pissed off at me because her friend likes my mate, and he's not interested, and so she's bored of hearing about it." The girl took it all in her stride and didn't bat an eyelid. Out of nowhere I decided to play the advantage… "Plus I look terrible naked. Like really terrible, and she can't get the image out of her mind. She hates me for poisoning it." The girl pissed herself laughing. "I can imagine you do" she retorted. Here we go… one-way train to Bantsville. I decided to up the ante. "As if you look any better with no slacks on. You probably got a massive wookie and a hairy stomach!" She kicked me immediately "You cheeky bastard! I got a good mind to…." I intercepted. "Prove it!" She playfully kicked me again. "If you think I'm going to show you my lady garden right here, there must be something in your tea, because you've lost it!" She was still smiling though. Unbeknown to her, her friends were approaching from behind and I knew they were going to party on. I was shattered, so decided to play my parting shot before they got here. I leant in and beckoned her closer. "Listen, even if you do have a baby Chewbacca down there, it doesn't matter to me. You have a wonderful personality and that's what counts." Before she could say anything further, I picked up her hand and kissed her on the wrist. "I bid you farewell." She didn't know what to say. I just stood there grinning. "You're unbelievable." She laughed. I told her I was going home to sleep, but if she was out tomorrow night, I looked forward to seeing her. She just laughed. At that moment her friends sat down and I made a move. I thought I'd played that quite well and it set the stage for tomorrow. As I was leaving the club, I saw the rest of my guests having a good time. I even saw Poker Night having fun with her friend and they were dancing with some of the lads from the hotel. I was so tired, I couldn't even face walking back through the strip. I hailed a taxi. I couldn't wait to get into bed.

The next day was arrival day. Nigel looked like he hadn't had a wink of sleep. I mercilessly teased him about how I was asleep by 2am and I slept solidly through on clean fresh cotton sheets. He was unimpressed. We had full welcome meetings from 9am through to 1pm. Once finished we returned all cash we'd collected with documentation to the office and then headed to the pool. I'd told Nigel already about his one from Poker Night being obsessed with him. All he could muster was that a night with Nigel would leave any girl hanging for more. Again, did not give a shit in the slightest. We got to the pool area and after a quick bite we begun to hang out with the guests. I made a beeline for Chewie. She was sitting with her friends chatting pretty close to some other lads from the hotel who were sniffing about. "Hi guys, girls, Chewie, how you doing?" Chewie rose to the occasion and smashed me immediately. "Bastard, if we're going to be Star Wars characters you can be Yoda. Not because of your admittedly big hairy ears, but because you're hung like him!" her group laughed. I loved it. Again, not wanting to punish, I left things alone right there "touché." I sat on the foot of their sun beds and started chatting with everyone. It seemed like everyone had a good time and there were no casualties or collateral damage. One of the lads was in conversation with me about hiring mopeds when Poker Night passed me. I smiled at her and said hi, but she just gave me the filthiest look and walked past. I was surprised, but mainly disappointed. I thought we'd squashed this shit, and here we are back to toxic. Everyone picked up on it. I was a little embarrassed. Chewie piped up "Must be seriously bad in the buff." I smiled. "You have no idea. Shouldn't you be getting back to your Millennium Falcon?" She gave me a playful dig in the leg. The others were bemused by this exchange, but we continued to chat as before.

After a while I made my excuses and started talking with other holiday makers. I approached Poker Night and their new friends to check they were ok, and if am honest wanted to see if she was going to continue to act shitty with me, or if maybe I just read her wrong. Nope. I read her correctly. She was an asshole. I asked if they had a good time, but all she could say was that the club was shit. The music was poor and the whole place smelt. I tried to soften her. "Hopefully you'll like tonight better we're going to…" She interrupted me. "We're probably not going out with the reps tonight. We want some real fun." It was a little public for my liking, but I didn't bite. "Ok. We're meeting at 8:30 in the bar if you guys change your mind." I swiftly retreated. I'd gone from being concerned and maybe feeling a little guilty about what had happened to being pissed off with her. I wasn't about to allow this little madam to mug me off in front of my guests and ruin the good vibe I'd worked hard to create and maintain. I thought about telling Damien what had happened in order to pre-empt any possible complaint that was going to be made about me, either here or when she got back home. I decided against it. I was still the number one salesman in the area if not the resort, and everyone was getting on well with me aside from this ass. Nigel popped over and I told him how she was being. He said just ignore her. After a San Miguel in the sun, I began to come round to his way of thinking. We did some pool entertainment, finished some admin, and then spent an hour watching the sunset with some more beer with some of the guests. We were in good spirits. As I was leaving to go home to get changed, Chewie asked me if I was off to break some mirrors. I laughed. I told her that if I do, I'll bring one of the sharper fragments back and we can have a go at her bikini line. Seeing as conventional scissors aren't sharp enough. She was impressed with the wit, but she came up close and told me not to keep telling everyone she had a wookie. People will think it's true. I only smiled and told her it's as true as me looking terrible naked. She just said "we'll see..." I smiled and left.

By the time I got back to the hotel I was buzzing. All thoughts of Poker Night had disappeared. I was in a good mood, well rested and happy with the day's sales. I'd had a good intake at my hotel, everyone was friendly and tonight we were going to one of my favourite clubs, and I was still on course for a dalliance with Chewie. As I walked into the hotel bar the atmosphere was electric. As everyone knows, the first night of the holiday is always aggressive. Most of the hotel were already drinking shots. I began to get to know the new guys. I got them some drinks, introduced them to some of the guests who I already knew and tried to create a more inclusive atmosphere. I figured the harder I worked at this now, the sooner everyone would mix and feel comfortable. I also informed the new arrivals about court. Court was something that was held nearly every evening and basically involved a drinking fine for the guests that had carried out various misdemeanours. Some of these were straight forward, like drinking with your right hand if we're playing left hand, or someone not finishing a drink and moving on. Other forfeits would be dished to those who had lost a bet, spilt a drink, etc. It was all very light hearted and everyone was a willing participant. Fines would be measured in fingers, i.e. two fingers of tequila or sambuca or whatever. There was already a fair few of the guests in court, including myself. I'd been caught out a few times left-handed drinking instead of right etc. I was getting 4 fingers of tequila as a double punishment, because not only did I break the rules, but they were my rules, so that deserved extra. I took it without objection or hesitation. As others were lining up to be sentenced with their various crimes being read out, everyone was having fun and laughing. Everyone except Poker Night. She had a face like a bulldog chewing a wasp. She was shooting permanent dirty looks at me, and just muttering continually under her breath about how pathetic it was and this was a waste of time. Even the one Nigel banged seemed to be having a good time which made it all the more apparent. I was beginning to lose my rag. I kept quiet initially and carried on with the rest of the gang. I didn't want a scene, particularly in front of the new arrivals. Chewie and her friends arrived late and at the insistence of the crowd they were given fines, which they drank without objection. Chewie even got me to do one by saying I gave them the wrong time. I wasn't going to argue with her. Poker Night continued to bitch and moan during the whole thing, even when one of the guests was telling the rest of the crowd what his mate had done the night before and why he was nominating him for a fine, she was making sarcastic comments whilst the guy was speaking. Eventually my patience wore thin. I think she was moaning about something else and then I heard the word prick uttered. That was it. I issued her a fine for insubordination. Under normal circumstances she would have just told me to fuck off or ignore me, but here with peer pressure her card was marked and she knew it. She rolled her eyes and said big deal. Like two fingers of tequila was going to make a difference. I suggested we could always up it to 4, she said only if I drink it too. I gracefully accepted. I was hoping this would be enough to wind her neck in. I drank the tequila down. Thankfully, tequila isn't an issue for me, I've always liked it and so it wasn't so much a punishment for me, but more an aggressive drink. She didn't fare so well. Eventually she got it down her and then returned to her seat. You could tell she wasn't impressed, but she'd stopped shouting shit out at everyone, so it worked, at least for now. Next the guests decided to play Russian roulette. This involved filling up several shot glasses of warm water with a few filled of vodka. You play opposite the group in front of you and there were usually 10-12 glasses in the middle. You all take it in turns to pick shots out and you drink them. For additional risk, you are supposed to keep a straight face when you drink regardless of water or vodka. At any time, another player in front of you can accuse you of drinking a vodka. They smell the glass after. If it's true and you did take a vodka then you have to take another. If it's false and they misread you, they take a shot themselves. This was incredibly fun to play and it always went down well. It was also incredibly risky. If you had a couple of players intent on trying to wipe each other they would normally succeed in a short period of time. False accusations would fly, and the longer it went on for, the harder it was to hide your reaction to getting the Russian bullet. Even I needed to focus on keeping a straight face if I ended up downing one. That being said, I had a talent for faking it too, so guests also used to end up having a drink themselves against me. On this occasion the game was in full swing. We were pulling out 15 shots at a time, and instead of 2-3 being vodka, it was more like 4-5. I didn't know the exact number as I myself would be playing, instead it was the barman that would choose. A few rowdy players began to face off against each other and the number of shot forfeits were increasingly rapidly. It might have only been 4 or 5 out of 15 but such was the aggression of some of the players trying to call each other out, I think there was easily 10-15 shots being taken per round. We would play 2-3 rounds with various guests and then a decider. Nigel's poker girl wanted to play, but wouldn't play on her own, thus dragging her miserable witch reluctantly into the arena with her. It was as much as she could do to look at me, but when I tried to step out, she became vocal and wanted me in the game. I guess she thought she was going to stitch me up and have me drink. That was her first mistake. I poised for a moment, irritated that she was still out for me, and concerned that if I did drink again (I was already going to be in the next final round) I might push it too far and end up shit faced and in trouble. The last thing I wanted was Damien wearing me like a glove and putting me on airport duty for the next week, especially as I had built up good momentum through the sales. That said, I also hoped if she did manage to get me a few drinks she might feel a little less toxic towards me and maybe her quest for vengeance might be partly satisfied.

As I was weighing this up, she took the decision for me. "Come on rep, don't be a total twat." The bar fell silent. "Wooooooo" was the hive's response. On top of all the shit I'd already had from her, I wasn't having that. The balls on her! She wasn't even a good lay. I casually agreed, much to the delight of the others who also fancied their chances of getting the rep battered. We began slowly at first but then things began to pick up. I was the first to go as always. Thankfully it was just water. I grimaced ever so slightly. I think I twitched the corner of my lip and held my breath ever so slightly to make my eyes bulge. The poker night pair fell for it hook line and sinker! "Vodka!" they both excitedly hollered, along with another innocent bystander. I proudly handed the glass over for them to smell it. Three shots of vodka promptly followed for them to enjoy. Enjoy it they did not, but I did. We played on. A few more took their turns some successfully called out, others not so successful. Next it fell to the witch. She took a glass and quickly banged it down. She tried to act nonchalant, but I could tell she was hurting. I was going to take the higher ground, but at the last moment the devil won. "Vodka." I calmly purred. Her face was a picture. She slowly held out the glass for us to smell and indeed it was vodka. The barman handed her a shot. If she wasn't irritated before, she sure as hell was now. I tried not to make eye contact to antagonise her further, but deep down I was smiling. Next it was her mate's go. She got lucky and also managed to pull a water. She acted normally. Just when I thought it was the next turn, her friend, her rock, her Ibiza-sister claimed vodka. I was surprised. If I had been her, I would have kept my mouth shut and tried to regain my composure. Her friend was a little bemused that her mate had tried to call her out, but equally satisfied that it was indeed just water. Everyone laughed, as the witch was handed another vodka. I didn't dare look. We played on. It got back to me for the second and final time of this round. Unfortunately, it was a vodka. I took it in my stride. Didn't bat a lash. No one called me out on it. They assumed it was just water and onwards we went. Thankfully most of the vodka had already been taken out by the previous turns so most just sipped the water and moved on. As we finished the round, we agreed we'd have a break for 15minutes before playing the final. Everyone was in good spirits, a few were drinking water or coke trying to remove the after taste of vodka from their palettes. I quickly got away from the girls. I could see that they were already having a few words and didn't look too happy. I think Nigel's one was irritated that Misery had tried to stitch her up, and also concerned that her wingbird was getting too pissed too quickly. I didn't want to be any part of that. She'd already made her bed, the question was how quickly would she be lying in it.

The break passed quickly. We were already running a bit late, so we decided to do a speed round. 12 contestants,

12 shot glasses, 6 water, 6 vodka. The winner was getting free drinks tickets in the club we were going to. We quickly started. Thankfully Poker Night wasn't in this one. She was still having words with her mate at the back of the bar when we started playing. Predictably, the game got messy. Several false accusations of vodka, as well as general stitch ups were going through. All good fun. Thankfully I managed somehow to miss out on some shots, and I certainly wasn't trying to call someone's bluff on it. My head was already beginning to cloud and we hadn't even made it out the bar yet. By the time everything was all said and done, everyone was in the mood. There were already a few people unsteady on their feet, and the new arrivals were mixing nicely with the existing guests. Chewie was smiling at me and her mates giggling with her, so that was going well. So far so good. We made our way to the first bar. I got a bollocking for being late. The rep already there had been in charge of counting, and whilst moaning at me for making her wait outside, did remark that we looked like we were having a good time though. I took that as a compliment and meekly apologised for being late. Poker Night walked in with her mates and the neighbours. They seemed ok. I smiled at them both. Nigel's one smiled back. Happy chops just glared and walked past me. I was beyond caring at this point. I walked into the bar, found Nigel and some of the other reps and started to unwind. At some point, Nigel's one walked over to him and they started talking. You could tell she was into him, and Nigel wasn't exactly fending off her flirtations. I think this really irritated her ice-cold friend. It was as if he was recharging her for another few days of "do you think Nigel…" and she headed off to the bar. I stepped back a bit to give Nigel some space to talk with his and I just paused for a minute to 'people watch' and take it all in. As I stood there looking at all the guests,

someone flicked my ear hard. I turned around to see Chewie smiling at me. "What was that for?" I asked. "For telling everyone I had a wookie!" She replied. I started to chuckle. Of course, I hadn't told anyone else that, it was our little joke, but the fact that she made reference to it, meant she wanted to continue the topic. "Well until you prove otherwise, I'm afraid the people are going to make up their own minds. As I said before, it's not an issue, you have a nice personality." I cast that line out deep into the lake. She not only bit, but she was being reeled in. "I'll have you know I'm shaved down there thank you very much. Maybe you'd get to see it if you weren't so cheeky." She feigned irritation. I didn't let up. "Maybe I'd let you show it to me, if you weren't so physically abusive. My ear is hurting." She laughed. "You look like you can take it." Bingo. "Only one way to find out. Let's meet up later and go to your Millennium Falcon." I was banking on her knowing her Star Wars films. I mean everyone knows who Chewbacca is, but not everyone knows the name of his space ship. She just laughed, shaking her head. "Ok." She said, and turned and left me to it. Happy days, I thought to myself. I didn't want to chase after Chewie, or be seen to be chasing. I moved on to a group of lads in my hotel and started to chat with them.

The night continued as planned, and after an hour or so it was time to move on to the next bar. One of the reps got on the mic and the rest of us ushered the guests out and started to walk them to the next bar up the road. As they were filing out, one of the reps grabbed me by the shoulder and told me that there was some trouble forming with some girls from my hotel. I got the details and wandered around until I found them. It was Poker Night. She was ruined. She was swaying on her feet and arguing with bouncers that had been trying to move her on. Her friend was trying to calm her down, but she too was getting flustered by it all.

The lads from next door weren't really doing much, just casually observing. I tried to insert myself into the situation to be the buffer between security and the girls. Security backed up and let me do my thing, but it was like pulling teeth. Poker Night was literally spitting with anger. I managed to coax/march her outside where she went from angry to tearful in a split second. She threw her arms around me and just sobbed. It wasn't down to any kind of affections she had or didn't have for me, she was just upset and very drunk. I could feel her swaying from side to side and at one point she leant to one side so much she nearly took me down with her. I started trying to comfort her gently and tried to encourage her to take a seat and get some water, but her mood swings were almost violent. One minute she was apologising for being such a bitch and the next she was calling me a cock and saying nasty things. I went from being gentle to showing tough love and telling her she would be arrested for drunk and disorderly if she didn't calm down. After about 10 minutes of this her mate blew up. You could tell she was irritated that her night was being ruined and she was making a massive scene. That's when the fireworks really started. They started to argue and square up to one another. It was at this point that I figured there was only one option. Without saying a word, I grabbed her and put her over my shoulder into a fireman's lift. She was dangling behind me helpless. She was screeching at me and using every swear word she could think of as well as making some new ones up. I told her firmly I was taking her back to the hotel to cool off and then we would go back out again. Still she hollered. Thankfully she was very light and slim and the hotel wasn't far otherwise I'd have struggled. Her mate and some of the lads from next door came back with us. I don't think they knew what to do, and didn't want to get in my way so left me to it.

About two or three minutes later we were back at the hotel. I put her to her feet at the reception and we all went up into their room. She'd calmed down, and was just sobbing. Her balance was completely gone, and as soon as the door opened she basically laid on the bed. I got her a glass of water and put the kettle on for some tea. I didn't know if she was going to be able to go back out or not and suspected that she'd be crashing out. I didn't want her to think that though in case she got her "second wind" and started to act up. By the time the kettle was boiled she was asleep. Her friend was pissed off with her, accusing her of spoiling their night out and being a dick. I tried to calm her and made her a cup of tea. The lads next door also tried to be the voice of reason. Clearly, they were sniffing around to get laid, but they were helping all the same. After 10-15 minutes, we started to laugh about it. I told her to get plenty of water ready for her in the morning and get some paracetamol or something because she was probably going to have a blinding hangover. Everyone agreed, and an action plan was laid out. Shortly after that, I made my excuses and left. I had to get back to the bar as technically I was still working, and besides, I wanted my lightsabre played with. I felt partially responsible for encouraging, or at the very least not preventing Happy chops from drinking so much, although I've no idea what she drank after. I checked to see if there was anything else that I could do or if they needed anything, but they were all cool. Nigel's one apologised to me for her behaviour, and thanked me for getting her back to the hotel safely. I told her not to leave her friend alone because she was super pissed, likely to be super confused, and that there were lads around it was better to keep an eye on each other. I don't think she'd thought about that side of things, but agreed and thanked me for reminding her. I slipped out and left them to it.

I couldn't wait to get back to the bar. I went back to the bar on the schedule only to find that they'd already been moved on and were now in the club. I rushed to the club only to be met at the door by Damien. "Where the fuck have you been?" he inquired in his usual cheerful manner. I told him the story and one of the other reps vouched for me too, which broke his mood. We all went into the club. It was Es Paradis, one of my favourite clubs in the world. Es Paradis was beautiful. It was a big white pyramid with a roof that slid down to allow the sun to come in. Within the club there were trees and greenery dotted around it. All the guests were always impressed by this, and we took the new arrivals there early on in their itineraries and it would blow them away. The club was very light, not the usual dark studio or brick-walled warehouse. It was a bright, white fancy looking club with strong lighting. You could see everyone and everything, and so it was great for flirting at a distance. It was like eye fuck central. The only issue was it was big. If you spied a hottie and fancied your chances it could take you 10 minutes to find a way round the bar or up and down the various platforms and podiums to reach them. At that point, as was often the case, they would have moved on already, and you would spend the next 30 or 40 minutes looking for them like a goose. As we went in, I tried to slip off to one side to hunt for Chewie, only to be foiled by Damien. He wanted to drink with the team and that meant we all had to go to one of the VIP bars at the back of the club. Normally I wouldn't have minded, but I was on a cert and didn't want to miss out. Plus, at this point in the season us reps became somewhat full of ourselves and when everyone hung out together, it became a bit much. People were trying to outdo one another in terms of drink (or drugs) or showing off about this girl or that etc. They were trying too hard to be the most outlandish. All I wanted to do was have fun with the guests and smash. That being said, I really liked Damien and wanted to drink with him. I followed behind them but my eyes were on stalks hoping to catch a glimpse of Chewie. I wanted to signal to her where to meet, or at the very least make sure she wasn't being pulled by someone else. Alas she was nowhere to be seen. We got to the VIP area and a big bottle of vodka was pulled out from behind the bar and a bucket of redbulls. Everyone tucked in and things got lively, quickly. Nigel was particularly pissed and was fumbling on the sofa with a couple of the other female reps. Everyone had already seen him naked many times throughout the season, but apparently he'd somehow managed to convince them that neither of them could give him a hard on, so they were taking it in turns to touch his old boy and try to make him stand. They were trying to be subtle about it, but everyone was just laughing. Damien was sharing some war stories with some of us from his earlier repping years and others were just drinking and dancing in the area. It was a fun time, but I wanted to be on the pull and whilst I appreciated the bonding, this was heavily eating into my hunt in terms of energy and time.

After about an hour and too many vodkas, I was nudged by one of the barmen. He took me to one side and pointed across the bar to another barman at a different bar who then pointed to a girl who was waving at me. It was Chewie. Somehow, she hadn't been grabbed by another and I was still able to walk, so I took this as a good sign. I looked across at the rest of the reps. Nigel and the two girls either side of him were asleep. Damien was trying to light a cocktail but couldn't even hold the glass next to the flame, and various other reps were dribbling into each other's ears about this and that and god knows what. I took the opportunity to quietly slide away. Thankfully I'd already dumped my bag back at the hotel reception when I took back Poker Night, so I slid off quietly into the crowd. I could see Chewie was having a good time and had clearly been drinking as much as I had. The minute I got close to her we practically pounced on each other. I didn't even try to be subtle. I went in for the kiss at the same time we did and we clashed teeth. Not my finest moment, but hey, a snog's a snog. We laughed about it, and then snuck off to a bar the opposite end of the club. We basically sat at the bar, ordered a drink and made out like a couple of teenagers for 20 or 30 minutes or so before we left. Her girls had decided to return to the apartment early as their feet were hurting and some lads had gone back too for a balcony party. We settled on going back to mine.

The following morning, I had to get up bright and early, so didn't really have time for round 2 and both of us were feeling hung over. I quickly made Chewie breakfast which involved a piece of bread with ham and cheese and a pint of water with an Alka-Seltzer and we made tracks. As always, I needed to "see Nigel" and we parted ways before we got to my hotel. Nigel was nowhere to be found however, and so I just hung out for 5 minutes or so until the coast was clear. When I got to the hotel, there was all sorts of rubbish in the reception area. Some of the posters had been torn down, and people had basically scrawled all over the guest book. At first, I thought it was just usual mindless shit some random had done, but on closer inspection, I could see one or some of the guests had done it. They were specifically mentioning me. Phrases like I was a shit rep, I loved cock, I had no friends, I loved myself. It was weird. I won't lie, it irritated the shit out of me. I might not have been a prince, but I wasn't an asshole either. Deflated, I took all the defaced posters and papers away and put them in the bin. It wasn't until I got to the pool area that things started to become more apparent. Some of the lads were hanging out by the pool. I approached them and asked how they were doing but they seemed to brush me off. I couldn't work out why. I wondered if one of them was on for Chewie and they'd seen me bag her. I asked if I'd done anything to upset anyone or if there was a problem and then eventually one of them spilled the beans. It was to do with Poker Night. It turned out that after I left their room to return back to the bar, some of the neighbours came in with some drinks and started to have a party. Due to no one wanting to wake Poker Night up, her mate (Nigel's one) basically popped next door to the neighbours and partied on with them. She was in there for about an hour or so drinking and dancing along with some girls from the balcony above. When she returned to her room a short while later, she could see that Poker Night was in a bad way. Apparently, Poker Night had shat herself uncontrollably and it was everywhere. We're not just talking a loose stool; we're talking human squid. She was still asleep, but unbeknownst to her, she'd shit not only her clothing, but the bed, the sheets, part of the wall, the floor. Nigel's one was mortified. One of the neighbours popped back with her to check in and so he saw it too, so there was no chance of keeping this quiet. He volunteered to help clean up with her whilst Poker Night slept. He said they'd been scrubbing for hours. I wanted to laugh when I first heard this, but managed to keep tight lipped. I could see that he and his friends were holding me responsible for it. I guess part of me was in some way, but that didn't really make me feel guilty. She'd been riding me all week long making me feel uncomfortable, so I didn't feel that much remorse. I didn't really know what to say to the lads, so thanked them for telling me and went back to reception. I went to the laundry room and collected a new set of sheets, covers with towels etc and also grabbed a couple of sachets of resolve and a bottle of coke. I knocked on their door prepared to face the music. Poker Night opened the door, she looked rough. I walked in and quietly put the linen on the chair without saying a word. I handed her the coke and the medicine and asked how she was feeling. You could tell she was mortified. She just said that she'd had better mornings. I just advised her to drink the coke and take the sachets. The sugar would help and to get a decent lunch in if she can eat. I asked how Nigel's one was (she was in the shower at the time). She just said she wasn't talking to her. I told her not to worry, she'd come round, she was probably tired and hungover herself. I said nothing else, she thanked me for the items and I left. You could tell she was wounded. We've all been there. I began to feel bad a bit more, but then I saw Nigel. He'd come over to talk to me and tell me what had happened with him and the other two reps in Es Paradis. I laughed and told him I know what happened, because the whole club witnessed him trying to get a boner. He just grinned, not in the slightest bit bothered. I told him I landed on Chewie, but focused more about what had happened here with Poker Night. I instantly regretted telling him. He roared of laughter like Father Christmas in a children's film. You'd think I'd given him 3 litres of laughing gas. When he finally managed to catch a breath, instead of inhaling, he roared "Shitter" at the top of his voice. He was loving it. I tried to stifle him. I was concerned that there still might be some blowback on me if a complaint was made. I mean clearly the lads by the pool were put out. I showed him some of the posters I'd fished out of the bin. I told him I was worried but he consoled me. That at least took some of the sting out of his merriment. We spoke for a few minutes more and then he went back to his hotel. Not before shouting "shitter" as he left. I can still hear him laughing now in my head. The girls only had a couple of nights left on their holiday. I just acted normally like nothing happened. Nigel's one was still following him around like a lovesick puppy, but thankfully for me, Bertie Squirty opted to keep a low profile. Can't think why!

CHAPTER 25
CEREAL KILLER

Even now, despite it being some 20+ years on, I can still clearly remember a lot of the guests that stayed in my hotel. I have many fond memories and photos that still make me chuckle today. I remember one big group of girls from Scarborough. They were an absolute scream. I think there were 8 or 9 of them. They were partying hard with us and had taken out the trip package. They'd been misbehaving from start to finish. They had big characters and were popular around the pool. I'd been flirting outrageously with all of them. I had my eye on a couple of them as did Nigel. They were really homely. They would cook meals in the apartment to save a few quid and always had balcony parties late at night when their feet began to hurt from dancing. I'd scored a cheeky snog here and there with one of them. She was full of banter and great fun to be around. In fact, they all were.

It was during peak season, I had near on 100% participation on the trips and it was bar crawl night. It felt like my whole hotel was out on the town with us. Everyone was having a fantastic night, when a couple of the girls wanted to nip home and change shoes or something. It was only when they got back to the hotel that they had discovered that unfortunately someone had broken into their room and some money had been taken. They alerted the hotelier, and whilst one stayed back, the other came to find me and the rest of the girls to let them know. We all went back to the hotel. It looked like someone had gotten in via the balcony and gone through some drawers. Someone had left some money on the side and that had obviously been taken as well as a small camera. Thankfully the girls had mainly been using the safes in their room and passports, travellers' cheques and other cash they had was well locked up. Obviously, they were pissed that this had happened, but in the grand scheme of things, they'd gotten off lightly. Together with the hotelier I checked the balcony doors in both of their apartments and they were secure. It just looked like they'd left it open. It felt like it was an opportunistic theft and so as irritating as it was, everyone was relatively benign. I produced a full written report for them for their insurance so they would be able to claim back what was missing anyway when they got back. The girls didn't feel like going back out that evening, and I didn't blame them. As far as anyone was concerned, I was dealing with the break in and the reports etc, so I was free from bar crawl duties. It wasn't long before the drinks came out, the music was turned on, and one of them decided to cook up some grub. I was invited to stay and share in a drink and some food. I graciously accepted, but made some excuses and nipped out.

I went down to the hotel bar and grabbed a couple of bottles of schnapps and several large bottles of San Miguel. I wanted to try and get them a little something. I felt kind of responsible for the break in as it had happened on my watch, and besides, it was the least I could do as I was going to be getting fed! When I reappeared with the drinks, I got a very warm reaction. I got a hug and a kiss from several of them. I was sat at the end of the table and served a bowl of macaroni cheese and some beer. It was a far cry from the noise of the bars and the clubs that were less than 300m away from the hotel. I began to unwind and we all got to know each other a bit more. One of the girls who I'd shared a quick snog with came and sat next to me. Every time, I was teased, she came to my defence. It was nice actually, and we all chatted for ages. The girls were keen to hear more about repping and some of the things that had happened to me out here. I opened up about some of the things, not just the good but also the bad. Some of them were shocked. It also shocked them how little sleep did we all get, i.e. working for months on end with no days off, late finishes, relatively early starts and adding airport duties on top of them, they collectively didn't know how we did it. As time went on, I began to get a bit sleepy, but truth be told, I was having a really nice relaxed evening with them. I felt myself yawn a few times, and some of the girls were already getting ready to go to bed. I began to make my excuses, when my defender stepped the game up. She told me I could crash out here with them. I wasn't sure initially; I mean it was a little too open with 4 others sharing the apartment. As I hesitated, one of the others insisted, said it was no bother at all. I agreed, but was thinking what was going to happen as regards the sleeping arrangements? The couch and the pull-out bed were already being utilised. I was hoping to cuddle in with my one, but again, I didn't want to be presumptuous, nor make it weird. Within moments, she came to my aid once more. "You can crash with me. You don't snore do you?" "Like a dying mule!" I responded, trying to make light of the situation. As the girls got ready for bed they shared the bathroom and there was plenty of giggling. This was a good sign. One of them told me I better not keep them awake with any funny business. I just laughed and told them to use ear plugs. I waited outside on the balcony for everyone to sort themselves out and turn in. I was called in shortly after and I slid into her bed alongside her. It was like something out of the Waltons. People were saying goodnight to each other, pissing themselves, and then saying it again. After about 5-10 minutes people stopped talking. I already had my arm around her, and we'd shared a couple of snogs as quietly as possible. To be honest as much as I didn't want to keep her mates awake with the sounds of us carrying on, I found the whole thing awesome. It was naughty, and we needed to be clandestine. This was floating my boat. Unfortunately for me, I was also shattered. Within a minute or two of the general chat finishing, I think I managed to squeeze one boob before I was in the land of nod.

The following morning, I woke up pretty early. I was a bit hungover and in unfamiliar surroundings. As I looked around the dimly lit room, I could see 5 familiar faces all asleep. I reached down to scratch myself and that was when it hit me. I'd been fucked with. Someone had pulled off my pants and had wrapped a feather boa around my boy. Not only that but I was wearing a second one around my neck. I confusingly pulled them off and threw them out of the bed. I was racking my brains trying to remember what had happened before I went to sleep. I was hungover, but not majorly and didn't recall getting naked with her before crashing out. I wasn't too alarmed, I found it pretty funny. Nothing could prepare me for what happened next though. As I scratched myself further, I found bits on my bits. On closer inspection, it appeared to be cereal. It didn't stop there either, I reached down under the arch and found even more cereal under my bag. No way, surely not! I reached further round and there was even more in the crack of my ass. What the hell? Who had loaded my Gary Glitter with fruit loops? This was comical but too weird for me to let sleeping beauty lie next to me undisturbed. I didn't want to wake the room as I was still hoping to try and give her one on the quiet but I needed to know who had tried to impregnate me with rice crispies. I wrapped my arm around her waist and cuddled up right behind her. She stirred but not enough. I put my other arm under her pillow and around her. She lent back into me and wrapped her arm around the rear of me. I pressed myself against her, causing her to push back slightly on me. I lightly whispered into her ear "why have I got cornflakes in my ass?" She stopped what she was doing, and immediately turned around to face me. I guess that wasn't what she remembered first when she stirred. She looked at me and with a huge grin told me that was punishment. There was not even a hint of denial. She said she was horny as hell the night before and as I crashed out on her, I was getting the treatment. When I asked who did it, she just replied they all had and started to grin wider. I couldn't believe it. As unnerving as it should have been, this just made me start to laugh and like the group all the more. Before I had a chance to ask any more questions, she put her tongue down my throat and started to touch me up. We didn't get very far. We must have woken one of the others up and she loudly told us to knock if off which woke the rest of them up. There would be no cuddles that morning. I came out on the offensive. "Who molested me with cereal then?" I asked the group who were now stirring like vampires at dusk. They all started to giggle. The ringleader told me it was my fault and that no one falls asleep on a Scarborough girl! The girls laughed even more with some adding their agreement. Not one single ounce of shame amongst them. I loved it.

After laying there for a further 20 minutes or so fiddling and being fiddled with, it was time to get up and get ready for work. I thanked them for a nice but unusual evening and slipped out. It wasn't until I got to reception that more of my punishment was revealed. "What the fuck do you look like?" "What the hell happened to you?" were two comments I received on entering the reception. "Have you seen yourself in the mirror?" was the next line to hit my ears. I instinctively reached up to my eyebrows. They were still both there. Thank God. I went into the toilet. I couldn't help but laugh. Not only had the girls wrapped my cock up in feathers, put cereal in my asshole and continued to drape shit around me, but they'd also given me a full make up session. I looked like a drunk drag queen. There was mascara all over my face, bright red lipstick and my cheeks had been coloured in pink making me resemble a cross between Daryl Hannah in Bladerunner and Aunt Sally from Worzel Gummidge. What I found even funnier, was not only did I not know, but I'd been getting stuck in to my girl earlier, looking like this. What must that have been like for her. My admiration for these girls continued to climb. I scrubbed my face until most of it was off. As I emerged from the loo Nigel was there. He couldn't believe what had happened and was laughing. We grabbed a bite to eat in my hotel bar and just had a quick catch up. After about 30 minutes most of the Scarborough girls appeared. They just smiled at me as they passed through to the pool. The ringleader asked if I had enjoyed my breakfast and started to giggle. Before I had a chance to respond, she asked me to pop up and see her friend (my cuddle buddy) as she was having an issue with the insurance forms. She told me she was waiting alone up in the room. I took the hint. Nigel couldn't believe my luck. He already liked them as a group, but having heard about their banter and antics, he liked them even more. I knew exactly how he felt. I don't think the girls had even managed to clear the steps outside the hotel and I was already in the lift, keen to pick up where we left off.

CHAPTER 26
CIVILIAN LIFE

All good things in life come to an end, and our season in Ibiza was no different. We stayed as late as was realistically possible. I was having so much fun out there that I even chose to miss the beginning part of term at University. I figured with some graft, I'd be able to catch up what I had missed. Weeks out here repping were easily worth months of party back home. Just as we'd arrived together, we decided to leave together. Nigel and I scheduled our return flights back for the same evening. By this point we were thoroughly exhausted. I mean fall asleep standing up exhausted, but the experience and the memories that we had obtained were priceless. I remember our final night. It was very emotional. Some of the team were still staying out, some had already left, but such was the bond between everyone at this point there wasn't a dry eye in the team as we hugged and shook hands before jumping into a taxi. What didn't make things easier was the fact that we were both smashed, having chosen to spend our last afternoon on the lash with some of the guests rather than go for a nice closing evening meal and choosing some souvenirs for friends and family back home. By the time we landed in Gatwick the hangovers were kicking in. Nigel and I gave each other a big hug before leaving to continue our journeys to our respective home towns. My parents had come to meet me, and whilst I was really pleased to see them, I don't think Dad had even managed to pay for the parking before I was asleep. In fact, I took an extra week off before going back to University. I basically spent the week in bed, catching up on months and months of missed shuteye. I don't think my Mum could quite believe it. I would be asleep before 10 and would surface just before lunch time. In fact, even when I was back at University, I could still be found napping from time to time for the first month or so, such had been the impact on me.

The transition to civilian life was a weird one. It was very strange. I was single and happy to continue going out on the prowl, but I was operating at a different wavelength to everyone else. I found this quite difficult to contend with. If the pub shut at 11, I wanted to go to the bar or club. It didn't matter that it was a Monday or a Tuesday, or that I had lectures in the morning. If there were a group of girls in our vicinity, I wanted to go roaring in. I needed wingmen to help me. A lot of the time those wingmen weren't there. With the exception of Mike. He was my best friend at Uni. He was always up for the challenge, but sometimes I wasn't always out with him, or we needed more than just the two of us. I can only imagine what people must have thought of me when they first saw me back on UK soil. They must have thought I was off my head, or the most arrogant thing in the room. Truth be told, I was really struggling with the social scene at University. Having been given a turbo charged block of life experience and a wealth of knowledge and new social skills, being suddenly dropped back into the normal Friday night pub routine was excruciating.

Everyone was so reserved. They were so nervous to talk to people they didn't know. They were so shy to tell someone they were interested. I couldn't understand it.

My confidence and lack of inhibition definitely helped me at University, but things rarely reached the plateau of Ibiza. That's not to say that I didn't have an absolute ball when I got back, but I was sorely missing the White Island. Nigel felt exactly the same. It was therefore a great weight off our minds when we both received letters inviting us back for the following season…

EPILOGUE

When I started writing this book, the goal was simple. I wanted to give you the reader, an inside look into what life was like working as a rep in Ibiza at the end of the 90s. I've put my memories down on paper as best I could, and have tried to convey how outrageous and fun it was then. The thing is, what started out as a non-fiction biography of sorts, could just as well now be interpreted as a work of fabricated fiction. You see, the Ibiza I knew, loved, lived and worked in no longer exists. Behaviours and trends change. What was acceptable and fashionable then, definitely isn't now. I returned to Ibiza in 2017, nearly 20 years after. I was shocked. What used to be Space, arguably one of the coolest (and messiest) clubs on the face of the planet and absolutely iconic for the time period, has become a concrete jungle now housing Glitterbox with Ushuaia (try pronouncing that after a couple of shots) across the road. I took my other half around San Antonio to where I used to live, where I used to drink and where we generally used to unwind. We took a stroll down to watch the sunset outside Café del Mar and Café Mambo. The plan was to grab a couple of beers and sit on the rocks and watch the sky turn different hues of red and orange with Café del Mar playing something subtle as it changed. The scene I have just described is something that had played out many times before. Sunsets were a big thing there. We would sit and watch them with hundreds and hundreds of people. They would gather out of nowhere for 20-30 minutes, and then disappear as suddenly as they assembled. When we got there, I was dismayed to see that they'd built a boardwalk stretching right across the whole beach line, and each beach bar had basically been turned into a restaurant. In fact, it was so commercial, if you didn't look out towards the sea, you could have been in Brighton Marina. I was gutted. Clearly nostalgia tints the spectacles, and time waits for no man, but the whole experience in general was a shadow of its former self.

We were staying in a villa in Santa Gertrudis, but stayed in San Antonio long enough to see the lights come on along the strip and to see things start to wind up for the evening's entertainment. Again, the bars all had different names (and probably new owners), but the buzz just wasn't there anymore. Bars that had been previously open-fronted with big social terraces, had been glazed over with any outdoor seating needing to be removed by 11pm. The whole area just looked tired. Some of the bars had been converted into tourist shops selling various shite with the words "Ibiza" plastered everywhere. I suppose it was inevitable given the various drives over the years to clean the West End up and to try and remove the "booze culture" from San Antonio. Just to give you a further illustration, booze cruises have been outright banned. Happy Hours have been prohibited, and shops can't sell alcohol from 9:30pm at night until 8am the following morning. Can you imagine, if those rules had been in place when we'd been there, Nigel might actually have managed to avoid getting sexually assaulted by Bulldog! Even pub crawls, the bread and butter of our world, have been banned. Clubs in the West End now have to close by 3am. Now clearly, at 40-something, I am not the target audience. If I am being truthful, I don't remember the last time I saw the inside of a club after 1.30am. The thought of barrelling through a bottle of vodka and redbull or getting stuck into a fishbowl fills me with a sense of uneasiness and fear of the impending three-day hangover that will follow. That being said, I can't help but feel saddened that the next generation won't get to revel in debauchery and the crazy antics that we used to experience. Then again, they have smartphone cameras with instant evidence! #Blessed

ACKNOWLEDGMENTS

Time flies, pain heals, chicks dig scars, but glory lasts forever! Whilst it was more than half of my lifetime ago, the friendships that were forged on the White Isle cannot be forgotten.

Glowworm, Doc, Starfish, Big Fella, Newmans, Balloon Knot, Ginger Spice and Danny: You maybe out of sight, but never out of mind! x

I'd like to thank Adam and Phil for their assistance in helping me put everything together. Your advice as always was precious.

Printed in Great Britain
by Amazon

Printed in Great Britain
by Amazon

OXFORD MONOGRAPHS ON LABOUR LAW

General Editors: PAUL DAVIES, KEITH EWING,
MARK FREEDLAND

Welfare to Work

OXFORD MONOGRAPHS ON LABOUR LAW

General Editors: Paul Davies, Cassel Professor of Commercial Law in the London School of Economics; Keith Ewing, Professor of Public Law at King's College, London; and Mark Freedland, Fellow of St John's College, and Professor of Employment Law in the University of Oxford.

This series has come to represent a significant contribution to the literature of British, European and international labour law. The series recognizes the arrival not only of a renewed interest in labour law generally, but also the need for fresh approaches to the study of labour law following a period of momentous change in the UK and Europe. This series is concerned with all aspects of labour law, including traditional subjects of study such as collective labour law and individual employment law, but it also includes works which concentrate on the growing role of human rights and the combating of discrimination in employment, and others which examine the law and economics of the labour market and the impact of social security law and of national and supranational employment policies upon patterns of employment and the employment contract. Two of the authors contributing to the series, Lucy Vickers and Diamond Ashiagbor, have received awards from the Society of Legal Scholars in respect of their books.

Titles published in this series

Freedom of Speech and Employment
LUCY VICKERS

International and European Protection of the Right to Strike
TONIA NOVITZ

The Law of the Labour Market
SIMON DEAKIN AND FRANK WILKINSON

The Personal Employment Contract
MARK FREEDLAND

The European Employment Strategy
DIAMOND ASHIAGBOR

Towards a Flexible Labour Market: Labour Legislation and Regulation since the 1990s
PAUL DAVIES AND MARK FREEDLAND

EU Intervention in Domestic Labour Law
PHIL SYRPIS

Regulating Flexible Work
DEIRDRE McCANN

Welfare to Work

*Conditional Rights in
Social Policy*

AMIR PAZ-FUCHS

OXFORD
UNIVERSITY PRESS

OXFORD
UNIVERSITY PRESS

Great Clarendon Street, Oxford ox2 6DP

Oxford University Press is a department of the University of Oxford.
It furthers the University's objective of excellence in research, scholarship,
and education by publishing worldwide in

Oxford New York

Auckland Cape Town Dar es Salaam Hong Kong Karachi
Kuala Lumpur Madrid Melbourne Mexico City Nairobi
New Delhi Shanghai Taipei Toronto

With offices in

Argentina Austria Brazil Chile Czech Republic France Greece
Guatemala Hungary Italy Japan Poland Portugal Singapore
South Korea Switzerland Thailand Turkey Ukraine Vietnam

Oxford is a registered trade mark of Oxford University Press
in the UK and in certain other countries

Published in the United States
by Oxford University Press Inc., New York

© Amir Paz-Fuchs, 2008

The moral rights of the author have been asserted

Crown copyright material is reproduced under Class Licence
Number C01P0000148 with the permission of OPSI
and the Queen's Printer for Scotland

Database right Oxford University Press (maker)

First published 2008

All rights reserved. No part of this publication may be reproduced,
stored in a retrieval system, or transmitted, in any form or by any means,
without the prior permission in writing of Oxford University Press,
or as expressly permitted by law, or under terms agreed with the appropriate
reprographics rights organization. Enquiries concerning reproduction
outside the scope of the above should be sent to the Rights Department,
Oxford University Press, at the address above

You must not circulate this book in any other binding or cover
and you must impose the same condition on any acquirer

British Library Cataloguing in Publication Data

Data available

Library of Congress Cataloging in Publication Data
Paz-Fuchs, Amir, 1971–
Welfare to work : conditional rights in social policy / Amir Paz-Fuchs.
  p. cm.
Includes bibliographical references and index.
ISBN 978–0–19–923741–8
 1. Welfare recipients—Employment—Law and legislation—Great
Britain. 2. Welfare recipients—Employment—Law and legislation—
United States. 3. Welfare recipients—Legal status, laws, etc.—Great
Britain. 4. Welfare recipients—Legal status, laws, etc.—United
States. 5. Public welfare—Great Britain. 6. Public welfare—United
States. I. Title.
KD3009.P39 2008
362.5'84—dc22   2007048427

Typeset by Newgen Imaging Systems (P) Ltd., Chennai, India
Printed in Great Britain
on acid-free paper by
Biddles Ltd., King's Lynn

ISBN 978–0–19–923741–8

1 3 5 7 9 10 8 6 4 2

With unbounded love to Nimrod and Amitai, our children,
who share the burden of correcting our faults.

General Editors' Preface

In the prefaces to previous books in this series we have stated it as our objective to publish works which are, on the one hand, of the highest quality of scholarship and, on the other, innovative, seeking to expand the boundaries of the subject and to bring new methodologies to bear on established areas of discussion. The present work can be placed firmly in that canon.

This study is an analysis of welfare-to-work programmes—not just in the United Kingdom—and thus crosses the boundary into what used once to be thought of as the separate area of social security law. However, as employment lawyers have increasingly become interested in the process by which aspirant workers seek to obtain employment, the line between employment law and social security law has become blurred, to the point, perhaps, of disutility. The set of incentives, positive and negative, which operate on the workless to seek and obtain employment are to be found in both in both these areas of law.

However, we commend this work not simply for crossing a boundary line which employment lawyers should now seek to ignore, but also for the strength of the theoretical analysis the author brings to bear on the subject matter. Dr Paz-Fuchs not only delves below the detail of the various programmes so as to identify the 'best fit' in terms of the policy rationales and objectives of the governments which have introduced welfare-to-work programmes, but in an important addition to the existing literature also brings to bear concepts of political philosophy to sustain his critique of these programmes. In particular, his detailed account of the transformation of social contract theory from an abstract political philosophy to a set of practical social policy imperatives lays the groundwork for his later theoretical analysis of the reasoning underlying the welfare-to-work policies.

That later theoretical critique touches on issues of human rights, on the distinction between economic and social rights and on ways of reconciling notions of equality and responsibility which, we are sure readers will find stimulating and provoking. So we warmly welcome this latest addition to our series.

Paul Davies
Keith Ewing
Mark Freedland

Preface

This book examines welfare-to-work programmes in United States and Britain and develops a normative perspective to analyse and critique the theoretical and doctrinal justifications for welfare-to-work programs. The book sheds light on the contractual paradigm that is advanced both as a new interpretation of citizenship and as a jurisprudential mold for the configuration of the relationship between rights and responsibilities. It is submitted that the two aspects of contractualism, just noted, are related. Viewing rights as demanding responsibilities carries the threat that rights will lose their strategic role in practical reasoning. When this conceptualization is couched in social contract rhetoric that putatively implies a continuous contract between citizens and the state, a vast array of conditions on welfare are supposedly legitimated. These conditions include workfare; the obligation to accept any job offer; and the variety of moral and social preconditions that are based on a vague notion of reciprocity. It is shown how the phenomenon has exacerbated over the last decade in social discourse in general, and in the field of welfare unemployment in particular.

Following a critique of the prominence of the contractual conceptualization, I move to suggest a structure of legitimate conditions on welfare benefits. This structure takes account of the contemporary appeal of personal responsibility, and reconciles it with the traditional fidelity that is owed to equality in the welfare state ideal. It is shown that equality's concern for the worst-off supports a recognition of a strong legal right to welfare. The book concludes by showing that rather than undermining social inclusion and labour market integration, strengthening welfare rights and relaxing preconditions on entitlement would serve the very objectives that welfare-to-work programmes are supposed to advance.

Acknowledgments

A few years ago, a series of peculiar events drew me to the eye of the storm that, in unprecedented fashion, brought welfare reform to the centre of legal, social, economic and political debate in Israel. I took that interest with me to Oxford and, following my doctoral work, continued to investigate the philosophical underpinnings, the doctrinal provisions and the empirical consequences of welfare reform. Though I realize that I am not the first to express this sensation about my work, I cannot help but feel that welfare reform is unique in its interdisciplinary range. Indeed, journal volumes and conferences in economics, philosophy, political science and law have already been dedicated to the matter. The topic can be addressed by focusing on its effect on human rights, the low wage labour market, privatization and regulation, minorities and women, enforcement of morals, poverty and equality, and many, many more.

This is why I feel more than lucky, first, to have stumbled upon this most interesting and important arena and, moreover, to have benefited from the guidance of two superb and generous scholars, Mark Freedland and John Gardner, who patiently harnessed my tendency to go astray, and showed the astounding ability, time and time again, to show me what I was trying to say all along. My debt to them is beyond words. After reading through my full draft, Denis Galligan and Lord Raymond Plant challenged me to improve, tighten and elucidate my argument. Lucy Williams' comments helped me to add critical depth to the manuscript, and Anne Daguerre's excellent suggestions finally showed me how to merge and associate the arguments throughout the book into one that is hopefully both coherent and important.

Along the way, I was privileged to belong to an extraordinary community of scholars and friends in an environment that surpasses even its own exceptional image. Loren Goldman, Jane McAdam, Ben Saul, David Tester and Ekow Yankah have not only been splendid companions in the long journey, but have also generously taken the time to read portions of this work along the way. Penny Analytis added excellence to grace by offering to edit the work towards its final stages, just when one would have thought that her dinner parties were a sufficient reason to keep her in close contact.

My thanks go to my parents, Camil and Ilse Fuchs, and my sister Ofri, who provided endless words of confidence and enthusiasm that were invaluable during the rough stages along the way.

Lastly, it is difficult to imagine embarking, let alone finishing, this project without the intellectual and emotional support, often undeserved, from my partner Tzili. Without reading a word of the manuscript, her astute observations on the subjects during our long evening walks found their way into the arguments. This is as good a time as any to declare my love and endless gratitude.

Table of Contents

Table of Treatises and Statutes	xv
Table of Cases	xix
Introduction	1
1. The Social Contract of the Modern Welfare State	**10**
A Welfare-to-Work Programmes in Modern Welfare States	10
B Welfare *Rights*?	18
1 Co-dependence 20	
2 A True Divide? 21	
C Social Contract: Tradition and Manipulation	29
1 Social Contract Objectives and Typology 29	
2 Rights, Obligations and Welfare in Social Contract Theory 33	
3 Two Different Intersections of Social Contract and Welfare State 38	
4 Manipulation 42	
D Conditioning Welfare	49
1 The Theoretical Background 49	
2 Rights, Reciprocity and Collective Interests 53	
3 Constructing Welfare Rights as Conditional 57	
4 The Consequences of Conditionality 62	
E Conclusion	64
2. Welfare-to-Work Programmes Under the Poor Laws	**66**
A Antecedent Themes in Welfare-to-Work Programmes	68
1 The Administration of Relief 68	
2 The Beneficiaries 72	
B Setting the Poor to Work—The Conditionality of Welfare	75
1 Conditioning for Deterrence 77	
2 Conditioning for Social Control 80	
3 Conditioning for Efficiency 86	
4 The Narrow Contract—Quid pro Quo 89	
C Conclusion	92
3. Contemporary Welfare-to-Work Programmes	**94**
A Legislative Background	98
1 The American Programmes: AFDC—Operation and Termination 98	
2 The British Programmes: Beveridge and Beyond 102	

    B Themes and Provisions in Current Welfare-to-Work Programmes   107
        1 United States: PRWORA and TANF   110
        2 New Deal, New Ambitions, New Contract for Britain   122
    C Conclusion   130

4. From Equality to the Right to Welfare   132

    A Equality—A Very Short Introduction   133
    B Equality, Choice and Responsibility   137
        1 The Incentive Role of Responsibility   138
        2 The Agency Approach to Responsibility   141
        3 Reasonable Responsibility   146
    C Conditioning Rights—the Case of Welfare Benefits   152
        1 Substantive Equality   155
        2 Germaneness   159
        3 Fundamental Rights   161
        4 Conditioning Rights and Reasonable Responsibility   162
    D Deriving the Right to Welfare from Equality   163
    E Conclusion   170

5. Welfare, Work and Social Inclusion   172

    A Why Social Inclusion?   173
    B Social Inclusion Between Equality, Choice and Responsibility   177
    C Social Inclusion, Social Contract and the Duty to Work   181
    D Social Inclusion, Poverty and Welfare Rights   194
        1 Basic Needs and Social Inclusion   194
        2 Welfare Rights as Strategies Towards Social Inclusion   196
    E Conclusion: Social Inclusion and Conditionality in
        Welfare-to-Work   199

6. Conclusion   201

Bibliography   206
Index   223

Table of Treatises and Statutes

International Covenants and Declarations
Limburg Principles on the Implementation of the International Covenant on
  Economic, Social and Cultural Rights..................................... 25
Maastricht Guidelines on Violations of Economic, Social and Cultural Rights. 25

South Africa
South African Constitution...................................... 22
  Art 26 22

United Kingdom
1576 Poor Law Act (UK) 18 Eliz 1 c 3 82
1601 Poor Relief Act (UK) 43 Eliz 1 c 4................................. 67–70, 80, 86
  s 1... 67, 69, 70
1662 Settlement Act (UK) 13 & 14 Cha II c 12.................................. 71
  s 1 70
  s 19... 69
1696 Poor Relief Act (UK) 8 & 9 Will III c 3
  s 2... 73
1824 Vagrancy Act (UK) 5 Geo IV c 34
  s 3... 90
1834 Poor Law Amendment Act (UK) 4 & 5 Geo IV c 76 .... 77, 78, 80, 81, 85, 88
1905 Unemployed Workmen's Act (UK) 5 Edw VII c 18............................ 102
1909 Labour Exchanges Act (UK) 9 Edw VII c 7 102
1911 National Insurance Act (UK) 1 & 2 Geo V c 55 104
1920 Unemployment Insurance Act Amendment (UK) 10 & 11 Geo 5 c 30
  s 7(iii), (iv) 103
1921 Unemployment Insurance Act (UK) 11 & 12 Geo V c 1
  s 3.. 103
1924 Unemployment Insurance (No 2) Act (UK) 14 & 15 Geo 5 c 30................. 103
1930 Unemployment Insurance Act (UK) 20 & 21 Geo 5 c 16
  s 6.. 103
1945 Family Allowances Act (UK) 8 & 9 Geo VI c 41............................. 105
1946 National Insurance Act (UK) 9 & 10 Geo VI c 67 106
  s 11(2)(a)(i)... 106
  SI 1955/143 106
1948 National Assistance Act (UK) 11 & 12 Geo VI c 29 106
1966 Social Security Act (UK) (Supplementary Benefit Act)..................... 106
1971 Social Security Act (UK)
  s 11... 106
1986 Social Security Act (UK) c 50 106
  s 20 106
1988 Social Security Act (UK) c 7 106
  s 4 107
1989 Social Security Act (UK) c 24 107
  s 2 107

Table of Treatises and Statutes

s 10 . . . . 103, 107, 127
ss 12, 13 127
1992 Trade Union and Labour Relations (Consolidation) Act (UK) 52
s 288 52
1995 Jobseekers Act (UK) c 15 . . . . 95, 122, 126, 128
s 1 . . . . 44, 128
s 3 124
s 6 . . . . 126, 163
s 7(3) 127
s 9(6) 128
s 13(2) 124
s 14 161
s 19 . . . . 128, 129
s 35(1) 124
SI 1996/207 reg 5A 128
SI 1996/207 reg 8, 9, 13, 16 126
SI 1996/207 reg 16(2) 126, 163
SI 1996/207 reg 18 127
SI 1996/207 reg 20 . . . . 126, 163
SI 1996/207 reg 31 . . . . 126, 128
SI 1996/207 reg 72 128
1996 Employment Rights Act (UK) c 18
s 203(1) 52
1997 Social Security Administration (Fraud) Act (UK) c 47 125
1998 School Standards and Framework Act 1998 (UK) c 31 60
1999 Youth Justice and Criminal Evidence Act 1999 (UK) c 23 60
2000 Child Support, Pensions and Social Security Act (UK) c 19
ss 109A, 109C 125
sch 6 125
2001 Social Security Fraud Act (UK) c 11
ss 1, 2 125
SI 2002/817 125
2003 Anti-social Behaviour Act 2003 (UK) c 38 60

United States of America

1935 Social Security Act PL 74–271
42 USC ss 601–617 98
1961 Social Security Act Amendment PL 87–31
42 USC s 607 99
1962 Social Security Act Amendment PL 87–543
42 USC s 602 98
42 USC s 1315 99
1977 Food Stamp Act PL 95–113 110
7 USC s 2014 . . . . 110, 111
7 USC s 2015 111
1981 Omnibus Reconciliation Act PL 97–35 101
1988 Family Support Act PL 100–485 . . . . 101, 102
1996 Personal Responsibility and Work Opportunity Reconciliation
Act PL 104–193 . . . . 11, 58, 96, 110, 111, 113, 114, 116, 117, 118, 120, 121, 122
s 101 113
s 103 117

s 114	121
s 115(a)	117
s 401(b)	119
s 402	116, 122
s 402(a)(1)(A)(ii)	120
s 402(a)(1)(A)(v)	116
s 402(a)(6)	113
s 402(d)	118
s 402(e)(1)	121
s 403	122
s 403(a)(1)(E)(2)	116
s 407(c)(1)	118
s 408(a)(1)(B)(2)	116
s 408(a)(4)	115
s 408(a)(5)	115
s 408(a)(7)	119
s 408(a)(8)	113
s 408(b)	44, 122
s 409(a)(9)	119
s 409(a)(4)	113
s 415	116
s 510	116
s 815(a)	120
s 824(a)	120
2006 Deficit Reduction Act PL 109–171	97, 116, 118
s 7102(a)	118
s 7103	116

Table of Cases

Canada
Belczowski v The Queen (1992) 90 DLR (4th) 330. 60
R v Morgentaler [1988] 1 SCR 30. 22
Sauve v Attorney General of Canada (No 2) [2002] 3 SCR 519. 60
Schachter v Canada [1992] 2 SCR 679 26

European Courts
BECTU v DTI Case C-173/99 [2001] ECR I-4881. 63
Hirst v United Kingdom (No 2) (2004) 38 EHRR 40 60
Z v United Kingdom (2001) 34 EHRR 97 [73] 22

Israel
HCJ 4541/94 49(4) *Miller v Minister of Defense* 94. 23

South Africa
CCT 11/00 *The Government of the Republic of South Africa v Grootboom* 2001(1)
 SA 46 (CC) 20
CCT 32/97 *Soobramoney v Minister of Health (Kwazalu-Natal)* 1998(1) SA 765 (CC) 20

United Kingdom
Bowmaker Ltd v Tabor [1941] 2 All ER 72 52
Butler v Fife [1912] AC 149. 53
Cutler v Wandsworth [1949] AC 398. 53
Lewisham Union v Nice [1924] 1 KB 618 90
Philips v Brittania [1923] 2 KB 832 53
R v Newton (1864) 28 JP 725 75
R(U) 5/80 127
R(U) 7/86(T). 127

United States of America
Alcozer v North Country Food Bank 635 NW2d 695 (2001) 157
Bagley v Washington Township Hospital District 421 P2d 409 (1966) 161
Berkemer v McCarty 468 US 420 (1983). 152
Bowen v Roy 476 US 693 (1986) 157
Califano v Boles 443 US 282 (1979) 101, 157
Dandridge v Williams 397 US 471 (1970). 25, 157
Frazee v Illinois Department of Employment Security 489 US 829 (1989). 157
Frost & Frost Trucking Co v Railroad Commission of California 271 US 583 . . . . 7, 154
Goldberg v Kelly 397 US 254 (1970) 58, 101
Harper v Virginia State Board of Elections 383 US 663 (1966). 155
Harris v McRae 448 US 297 156
Hobbie v Unemployment Appeals Commission 480 US 136 (1987) 157
Jefferson v Hackney 406 US 549 (1972) 113
King v Smith 392 US 309 (1968). 101
Lawson v Housing Authority 70 NW2d 605, cert denied 350 US 882 (1955) 159

Loving v Virginia 338 US 1 (1967) 134
Lyng v Castillo 477 US 635 (1986) 120
Lyng v International Union 485 US 360 (1988)............................. 120, 155, 157
McAuliffe v Mayor of New Bedford (1892) 29 NE 517................................. 153
McDonald v Board of Election Commissioners (1969) 394 US 802 155
McInnis v Shapiro 293 F Supp 327 (1968).. 24
NB v Sybinski 724 NE2d 1103.. 116
New York State Department of Social Services v Dublino 405 US 413 (1973)............... 100
Patterson v Industrial Commssion of Ohio 672 NE2d 1008 (1998)....................... 157
Richardson v Ramirez 418 US 24 (1974) 60
Rosado v Wyman 397 US 397 25
Saenz v Roe 526 US 489 (1999)... 122
Shapiro v Thompson 394 US 618 (1969)... 62, 122
Sherbert v Verner 374 US 398 (1963) 62, 153, 157
Speiser v Randall 357 US 513 (1958)... 101, 153
Stansbury v California 511 US 318 (1994).. 152
Tennessee v Lane and Jones 541 US 509 (2004) 158
Thompson v Keohame 516 US 99 (1995).. 152
United States Department of Agriculture v Moreno 413 US 528 (1973).................. 101
Wyman v Jones 400 US 309 (1971) 162
Zablocki v Redhail 434 US 374 (1978)... 156, 191

Introduction

A survey of the literature on welfare-to-work programmes[1] published over the past decade could justifiably lead to the conclusion that these programmes have been attracting penetrating public and academic interest to a far greater extent than ever before.[2] Their significance is unquestioned; these programmes constitute the seam between the welfare realm and the low-wage labour market and assist the long-term, able-bodied unemployed to enter the job market. But it seems that the reason that so many scholars and policy-makers are addressing welfare-to-work schemes is found beyond this narrow objective, however important. Indeed, these programmes force us to reassess our philosophical commitments and to revisit their justification within a liberal framework.[3]

Peter Townsend defined social policy as 'the underlying as well as the professed rationale by which social institutions and groups are used or brought into being to ensure social preservation or development'.[4] This book suggests that the programmes' novelty lies in their bias towards one such dominant rationale, a reigning paradigm of conditionality and reciprocity. The two terms signify a different focus, rather than a different philosophy. While conditionality encapsulates the legal attitude towards entitlement ('one is entitled to benefits if and only if...'), reciprocity offers the political philosophy that supports the approach. Activation policies that underlie welfare-to-work programmes are routinely justified through reference to a conception of fairness that is instilled in the notion of reciprocity. Within this paradigm, responsibilities and obligations counter-balance rights.

The chief role of conditionality in the analysis of welfare-to-work programmes indicates that these programmes provide a fine case for the study of contemporary social contract theory. Thus, if social contract theory as understood by some scholars provides a sound paradigm for social citizenship, and if the rationales behind welfare-to-work programmes can legitimately refer to this version of social contract, it may be asserted that these programmes are justifiable. But by the same token, serious objections directed towards the structure of the programmes

---

[1] I shall prefer the more cumbersome term, welfare-to-work, and shall use the term 'workfare' to designate one feature of the programmes, namely the requirement that recipients work in return for benefits.
[2] I Lodemel and H Trickey 'A New Contract for Social Assistance' in I Lodemel and H Trickey (eds) *'An Offer You Can't Refuse': Workfare in International Perspective* (Policy Press: London, 2000) 1, 4.
[3] J Moss 'Introduction' (2004) 21 J App Phil 239.
[4] P Townsend *Sociology and Social Policy* (Penguin: London, 1975) 6.

could have an impact on the philosophical and legal approach that purportedly supports the programmes. And if, indeed, 'contemporary western society is in the grip of contractual thinking',[5] as many academics and policy makers seem to hold, there is ample reason to conduct a serious investigation of its theoretical background and doctrinal implications. And nowhere are these implications more apparent that in contemporary welfare-to-work programmes.

Welfare-to-work programmes have been implemented in numerous Western countries over the last decade. The popularity of the programmes suggests that different nations share common ideologies, objectives and economic concerns including, for example, increasing the flexibility of the labour market, eliminating dependency and tackling social exclusion. These agendas arguably support implementing certain schemes that are compulsory, work-based and targeted towards a population that faces serious barriers to work. But notwithstanding these common features, the programmes realized by different nations are not identical. Both the common elements and the different solutions reflect the shared suppositions amongst countries as well as the diverse forces and ideologies that are present within particular societies. In the process, the programmes raise an array of fascinating theoretical issues, some of which are the focus of this book.

The sphere of welfare policy and legislation is vast and almost impossible to address within the confines of one work. It is important, therefore, to first distinguish clearly between 'welfare' as used here and its employment by philosophers who use the term to refer to 'well-being', as in discussions for and against 'equality of welfare'. Indeed, if welfare were to designate well-being, one would hardly need to look far to find reasons for welfare. Thus, the task of Robert Goodin's important book, *Reasons for Welfare*, is to investigate 'arguments for and against "the welfare *state*" '.[6] As Goodin notes, the definition, boundaries and institutions of the welfare state are the subject of significant disagreement. And yet, it can be agreed that the welfare state is a political artifact that seeks to 'limit the domain of inequality'[7] in a given society by providing certain public services to all its members, irrespective of their financial abilities. But not even this narrow interpretation (nor, surely, the idea that welfare is akin to well-being) was at the core of President Clinton's plan to 'end welfare as we know it'.[8]

Though education, health care, public housing and provisions for the disabled are undoubtedly programmes identified with the welfare state, 'welfare reform' has come to denote a more limited target. The programmes targeted under welfare

---

[5] V Held *Feminist Morality: Transforming Culture, Society, and Politics* (Chicago UP: Chicago, 1993) 193.

[6] R Goodin, *Reasons for Welfare* (Princeton UP: Princeton, 1998) 5 [emphasis added].

[7] ibid 8.

[8] For a depiction of the political history of this prominent phrase see J De Parle, *American Dream: Three Women, Ten Kids, and a Nation's Drive to End Welfare* (Viking: New York, 2004) 101–4.

reform are those that deliver financial aid to unemployed families. The most common objective of welfare reform, then, is to increase self-reliance by moving individuals off welfare rolls and into the labour market. While acknowledging the central role that health, education and housing programmes contribute to a viable welfare state (and, indeed, to many people's well-being), the focus placed on welfare-to-work programmes in this book permits, and perhaps demands, confining the discussion to welfare provision for the unemployed.

But even this aim carries the risk of being over-inclusive, since a significant number of welfare programmes (such as programmes for detached youth, the disabled or for former convicts) view inclusion into the labour force as a prime solution when addressing certain social and economic issues. What, therefore, distinguishes these schemes from welfare-to-work programmes addressed here? The discussion of welfare-to-work programmes to this point already permits identifying two of their significant features. First, the programmes view work as a prominent vehicle for dealing with economic problems such as poverty, and social problems such as exclusion. Second, they focus on the lowest social and economic tiers. But to these two, a third feature should be added. Indeed, this third facet is probably the reason that these programmes have attracted attention from scholars well beyond those normally interested in social security policy and legislation. The new programmes are perceived to supplant rights-based entitlements that have characterized the welfare state for decades, with *conditional* rights, that is rights that are dependent on the fulfillment of obligations. This new type of social contract between the claimant and the state carries with it *a new construction of rights and responsibilities*. Thus, the British government declared that 'it is the Government's responsibility to promote work opportunities' and that it is 'the responsibility of those who can take them up to do so'.[9] The critical assumption is that welfare dependency and unemployment can be substantially reduced by improving the employability of working age benefit recipients and by connecting them more proactively to the labour market through attaching certain conditions to the benefits they receive.

Here we encounter the first, and probably the most important, ambivalence inherent in such a strategy. Policy makers from Elizabethan times to the present acknowledge that a humane society must make sure that its members do not suffer the indignity of extreme, let alone life-threatening, poverty due to circumstances beyond their control. The criterion of 'beyond their control' could not be more significant to the understanding of the motivation behind the programmes. From very early on, a central pillar of the welfare-to-work structure has been the need to distinguish between deserving and undeserving poor: between those who are entitled to unconditional benefits solely due to their mental or physical situation and those who are judged to be doing less than enough to achieve a life

---

[9] DSS, *New Ambitions for Our Country: A New Contract for Welfare* (Cm 3805, 1998) 23, 31.

of productive work and self-reliance.[10] Since the Poor Law era, the mechanism designed for supporting the poor and creating incentives for them to leave state assistance has been inseparable from the criteria that distinguish deserving from undeserving poor.

The book opens with an overview of the central theoretical argument that is expanded in subsequent chapters. Specifically, chapter 1 focuses on the intersection between the two fundamental pillars under investigation: the social contract and the welfare state. At present, the social contract provides the normative platform for conditionality as it is expressed with respect to the relationship between the individual and the state. This investigation is imperative if one wishes to assess the recurrent justifications for welfare-to-work programmes that refer to a concept of fairness which, in turn, is based on an idea of reciprocity amongst individuals and between individuals and the state. But, moreover, it is already possible to detect how this discourse affects other realms of social and economic policy, and even in realms further afield.

But the conditionality in welfare-to-work programmes is expressed not only in the realms that concern the reciprocal relationship between citizen and state. Chapter 1 continues with social contract implications that are more jurisprudential in nature, to wit rights and the legitimacy of placing conditions upon them. It also suggests that a new perspective regarding the way rights are understood is already in the making. This new construction has the potential to make a significant impact on the value ascribed to rights in society. The critiques that the choice and interest theories of rights have levelled against each other are helpful in introducing this point. More specifically, choice theorists warn that rights under the interest theory are prone to the danger of being reduced to convenient titles for what is actually a result based on the assessment of interests that is reached with no regard (or without sufficient regard) to the weight rights should carry in society. The fear is, then, that rights will be seen to reflect no more than the aggregate of interests in a particular context, leaving them conceptually redundant. In the context of welfare-to-work programmes, this warning could hardly be more fitting.

It is impossible to understand and assess social policy programmes without the necessary familiarity with their context, on the one hand, and their details, on the other hand. The context is provided by the historical developments that lead to current arrangements. Providing the historical background is no mere academic exercise. In fact, contemporary programmes are replete with themes and rationales that are similar to those of the Poor Law era. Many scholars have highlighted these similarities, and an outline of the historical background serves as a useful introduction to welfare-to-work programmes. This is done in chapter 2, which deals with Poor Law policy and legislation, and in the

---

[10] D King, *Actively Seeking Work* (Chicago UP: London, 1995) 23; G Standing, *Global Labour Flexibility* (Macmillan: Basingstoke, 1999) 227.

first section of chapter 3, which describes the immediate legal background to welfare-to-work programmes in the United States and Britain.

Compressing 350 years of legal history, albeit limited to one field, carries the inherent risk of a presentation which is more anecdotal than instructive. For this reason, chapter 2 should be read less as a comprehensive analysis of the socio-legal history of the time, and more as an introduction to the institutions, themes and rationales, descendants of which may be detected today. Since it is presumptuous to claim definitively, for example, that Labour Yards have been transformed into Community Work schemes, the historical analogies are constructed on a thematic, rather than on an institutional, level. It is argued that at different points in time (and sometimes simultaneously), four different rationales can be detected in Poor Law programmes. These four rationales are deterrence, economics, morality and quid-pro-quo. The rationales as stated do not exclude one another, and certain schemes and provisions are supported by more than one rationale. And yet, each rationale derives from a distinct vision of the relationship between the individual and the state and thus has a different impact on the emphasis of welfare programmes. References to each can be found both in primary and in secondary historical material that engage with Poor Law policy and legislation.

Those details are described under the headings of the aforementioned rationales. And yet, the rationales which explain the provisions are themselves subcategories of a common mechanism: that of conditionality. The expressions of this mechanism and its normative assessment are left for the chapters that follow. In this sense, chapters 2 and 3 are descriptive in nature, drawing attention to the existence of the conditional attribute of welfare programmes by outlining the rationales motivating each type of conditioning.

These four rationales are revisited in chapter 3, which introduces contemporary welfare-to-work programmes in the United States and Britain. Despite the similarities in the titles of the rationales, due caution should be employed before shifting our analysis from one time frame to another; first, because the Poor Law era allows one to pick and choose institutions and commentary over a vast time frame, while contemporary programmes supposedly express, at least to some extent, all these rationales at a given point; second, it may be argued that titles such as 'morality' or 'economics' have referred to radically different ideologies over time, thus making such time-spanning assessments a futile exercise. An explanation for the reasons that these two chapters were constructed as they were may serve as a response to both these concerns.

Welfare-to-work programmes, as mentioned, are characterized by the conditioning of benefits upon obligations. Chapter 2, then, outlines some of the obligations that beneficiaries were required to honour during the Poor Law era and highlights the motivations behind them. At a proper level of abstraction, it should not be problematic to view these motivations as transferable to the present. It is indeed the case, for example (and as chapter 3 notes), that the moral issues that policy makers have been concerned with have changed over time. This does not diminish the importance of addressing the justifications for and against the use of the mechanism of welfare-to-work programmes to advance, for example, a particular moral agenda, whatever it may be. Similar contentions are applicable for the employment of other rationales (deterrence, economics and quid-pro-quo) as well.

One introductory note is relevant at this point. There are various types of conditionality and some are more problematic than others. Though a broad range of conditions may fit into an 'if...then' clause, this book will not deal with those conditions that refer to one's immutable status, such as 'if a person is a woman, then she is entitled to special fringe benefits'.[11] Rather, the crux of welfare-to-work programmes, as one may have inferred already from the emphasis on the deserving/undeserving distinction, is that they deal with individuals who are deemed capable of changing their situation. Therefore, conditions are employed as a means to change priorities and influence behaviour. At times, the objective is straightforward, such as 'if you overcome your substance abuse, you will be eligible for benefits'. On other occasions, influencing behaviour is achieved through the process of establishing eligibility, including the forms and declarations one is required to submit and the level of benefits one will enjoy. All these, as will be explained, have an impact on the decision whether to claim benefits. Therefore, the line between legitimate and illegitimate conditions for benefits in such cases is significantly more difficult to draw. I suggest such a structure and explain its application in chapter 4.

The feature of reciprocity, as noted, governs the approach behind welfare-to-work programmes, from the level of a political philosophy to the practical interactions between government agencies and welfare claimants. But it is important to note that despite being a general principle, reciprocity does not have the same impact on all individuals in society. As mentioned in the opening paragraphs, one of the defining traits of the programmes is that they target the lowest social and economic tiers in society. This conclusion, as chapter 4 argues, would mean that the government is not living up to its duty to treat all individuals with equal concern and respect. Reciprocity may be understood in various manners. Different people may uphold the importance of reciprocity in society and still support different institutions and arrangements. One reason for this phenomenon is the way reciprocity relates to the ideal of equality.

In the context of welfare-to-work programmes, egalitarianism is often seen as opposed to reciprocity because of the different attitude that each expresses towards the idea of *personal responsibility*. In effect, while egalitarians are perceived as emphasizing society's duties which are justifiable notwithstanding the individual's failure to take responsibility for her own life choices, some

---

[11] R Wintemute, *Sexual Orientation and Human Rights* (OUP: Oxford, 1995) 174–77; J Gardner, 'On the Grounds of Her Sex(uality)' (1998) 18 OJLS 167, 169–74.

proponents of welfare-to-work programmes offer a conception of fairness that places government duties as contingent upon the fulfillment of personal obligations. Only recently has this divide been bridged. Ronald Dworkin has been credited for performing for egalitarianism 'the considerable service of incorporating within it the most powerful idea in the arsenal of the anti-egalitarian right: the idea of choice and responsibility'.[12]

This is, undoubtedly, an important move for those who care about equality and are not willing to dismiss other aspects of human interaction, such as respect for one's choices and the importance of personal responsibility. The terrain has now been significantly changed, and many writers are now trying to build upon Dworkin's project and to fit responsibility within the egalitarian paradigm. However, despite the sound objective, it seems that in the process of incorporation, the new element has overpowered the baseline imperative of equality. This phenomenon is especially apparent when egalitarian writers such as Rawls, Dworkin and GA Cohen explain how their theories apply to welfare-to-work programmes, thus making the scrutiny of their positions all the more timely. Chapter 4 suggests a different model than the one offered by contemporary egalitarian writers; one, it is argued, that fulfills their objectives better than their own proposals.

Following the discussion of equality and responsibility, it will be possible to offer a tailored structure for the analysis of conditions, legitimate and illegitimate, in welfare-to-work programmes. This customized theory provides the tools for assessing the conditioning of benefits on obligations that vary from the signing of loyalty oaths, through directives that concern the structure of the family household and on to obligations to accept any job offer. And though the approach was developed with welfare-to-work conditions in mind, it is highly probable that this construction could be employed in other arenas as well. Even if governments refuse to recognize welfare interests as rights, they are not free, it is argued, to subject *other* rights to be 'manipulated out of existence'.[13]

Finally, it is important to examine whether a right to welfare should be recognized within the legal framework of liberal societies. Chapter 4 ends with an egalitarian based argument in favour of the right to welfare. A serious appreciation of welfare rights would provide a domain of practical choice, a normative allocation of freedom 'within which the choices made by designated individuals (and groups) must not be subject to interference'[14] and would thus provide protection for the exercise of other rights as well.

The book concludes by bringing together the abstract concepts of social contract and equality and rejoining them with the socio-legal methodology that

[12] GA Cohen, 'On the Currency of Egalitarian Justice' (1989) 99 Ethics 906, 933.
[13] *Frost & Frost Trucking Co v Railroad Commission of California* 271 US 583, 594 (1926).
[14] H Steiner, 'Working Rights' in M Kramer, N Simmonds and H Steiner, *A Debate Over Rights* (Clarendon: Oxford, 1998) 233, 238.

opened the discussion. This is done through the employment of the concept of social inclusion. Social inclusion discourse has been attracting attention at an exponential rate that is, not coincidentally, parallel to that of welfare-to-work programmes. Legal scholars have recently begun to respond to the effort to supplant the place that equality held in government decisions with rationales stemming from social inclusion objectives.[15]

But just as responsibility does not necessarily stand in opposition to equality, neither does social inclusion. The final chapter of the book introduces the significant potential that social inclusion discourse holds for the analysis of welfare-to-work programmes. Originating as a concept that was used in the *critique* of existing social programmes, it has been co-opted as a measure that justifies even more coercive programmes. This is not, however, a deterministic path. Rather, the roots of social inclusion discourse include a serious regard for equality as well as for personal choice, and express the fluidity and flexibility that takes into account agency as well as structure. These theoretical issues, along with the fact that social inclusion is naturally associated with matters that can be addressed from social, economic and moral perspectives, probably explain why social inclusion is increasingly mentioned as one of the main motivations for welfare-to-work programmes.

The problem with the move from the promise of social inclusion policies to the practice of welfare-to-work programmes is the quick analogy that is made between *labour market* inclusion and *social* inclusion. As chapter 5 shows, coercive inclusion into the workforce may result not only in social *exclusion*, but even in exclusion *within* the labour market. Social inclusion does carry the potential to account for contemporary values and policies that are popular, such as reciprocity and social contract. Its origins, however, demand a critical perspective when examining the degree of choice that is given to the individual, the extent of personal responsibility that it is fair to expect citizens to carry and the contribution that a right to welfare can offer to the realization of true inclusion. Understood properly, social inclusion manifests the practical meaning of the imperative that requires treating every person with equal concern and respect and ties together the issues that were discussed throughout this book.

Lastly, though this book has a different focus than the one stressed by Frances Fox Piven and Richard Cloward's most important *Regulating the Poor*, I feel comfortable signing up to their disclaimer:

> ... relief-giving is partly designed to enforce work. Our argument, however, is not against work. We take it for granted that all societies require productive contributions from most of their members, and that all societies develop mechanisms to ensure that those contributions will be made. In the market economy, the giving of relief is one such mechanism.

---

[15] H Collins, 'Discrimination, Equality and Social Inclusion' (2003) 66 MLR 16.

But much more should be understood of this mechanism than merely that it reinforces work norms.[16]

Indeed, a vast terrain lies between basic, unconditional income policy and some of the conditions incorporated in modern welfare-to-work programmes. It is the purpose of this book to assess the fairness of these conditions in light of background justifications, and to question whether the results of a policy that advances such conditions will be equitable.

---

[16] FF Piven and RA Cloward, *Regulating the Poor* (Updated Edition Vintage: New York, 1993) xix.

1
The Social Contract of the Modern Welfare State

A Welfare-to-Work Programmes in Modern Welfare States

Welfare-to-work programmes in modern welfare states are a peculiar blend of old and new. As described in the following chapter, antecedent themes of current programmes are patently detectable at least from early 17th century Poor Laws. On the other hand, in some ways the modern welfare state has changed the context, form and structure of the programme in a manner that demands at least a fresh look. This new perspective places welfare-to-work programmes within welfare state theory and explains the traits that fit (at least certain types of) welfare states. In addition, it demands asking whether some of characteristics of contemporary programmes promote an ideology that is foreign to welfare state fundamentals.

In addition to the welfarist model, the other conceptual pillar on which welfare-to-work programmes rest consists of the ideological, rhetorical and legal matter that form the concept of the *social contract*. Over the past decade or two, political philosophy, social policy and legal relations between citizen and state have been caught 'in the grip of contractual thinking'.[1] In many cases, welfare-to-work programmes are but the foremost derivatives of the contractual paradigm. Indeed, the intersection between welfare state theory and social contract philosophy is a fascinating one, and welfare-to-work programmes offer, as we will see, the necessary doctrinal material for the investigation.

But if a careful investigation of doctrinal material is necessary to establish the theoretical claims in this book, it is clear that a comprehensive survey of all welfare-to-work programmes is not manageable. Indeed, even a focus on contemporary American welfare reform unveils a body of research 'unprecedented in comparison with any prior era of welfare reform'.[2] It is thus important to clarify that this book will not contribute substantially to the volume of literature that

---

[1] V Held, *Feminist Morality: Transforming Culture, Society, and Politics* (Chicago UP: Chicago, 1993) 193.
[2] National Research Council, *Evaluating Welfare Reform in an Era of Transition* (National Academy Press: Washington DC, 2001) 2.

deals with the direct social and economic effects of welfare reform programmes on recipients. This literature focuses on caseload expansion or contraction, income levels, poverty rates, family structure and so forth. While reference will be made to such studies, it is important to note that they will necessarily give an incomplete picture, not necessarily covering the whole range of the population affected by the programmes. Thus, harsh conditions may induce an individual to leave a programme earlier than he or she would have done prior to the reform. The analysis does not necessarily follow his or her life pattern following that decision. Moreover, a particular programme may actually deter eligible recipients from applying, and thus they will not be directly affected by the programme's structure. And, lastly, welfare-to-work programmes place downward pressure on wages in the secondary labour market. Workers in those markets are not obvious candidates for a research that focuses on welfare reform.[3]

In addition, the task of circumscribing the relevant policies that fall under the welfare-to-work rubric is not an easy one. One policy that is highly relevant to the study of efforts to induce transitions from welfare to work is the 'negative income tax', which provides refundable tax credits to families with low earnings. These policies, known as Earned Income Tax Credit (EITC) in the United States and Working Tax Credit (WTC) in Britain, are not only much larger in scale than mainstream income support programmes such as Temporary Assistance for Needy Families (TANF) (spending on EITC is three times greater than spending on TANF),[4] but may also significantly alter the incentives and disincentives of individuals who calculate the economic consequences of leaving the welfare rolls and entering the labour market. However, their structure does not include the difficulties raised by the programmes discussed here, and therefore they will receive little mention. The same may be said about child care and health insurance policies. While they may figure in a broad definition of welfare reform, they do not reveal the tensions usually attributed to such programmes.

One minor exception to this rule concerns the greater attention given to the American Food Stamps programme. Formally, this is done because the statute that is responsible for the most revolutionary welfare reform in decades, the Personal Responsibility and Work Opportunity Reconciliation Act 1996 (PRWORA),[5] also reformed the Food Stamps programme. This reason, of course, is not sufficient by itself. More important is the change proposed by the statute. In essence, the rationale governing the changes in the Food Stamps programme is identical to the one governing welfare reform. It is an ideology of 'work first' and an effort to reduce dependency. However, while work tests were implemented

---

[3] A Weil, 'Assessing Welfare Reform in the United States' in N Gilbert and A Parent (eds), *Welfare Reform: A Comparative Assessment of the French and U.S. Experiences* (International Social Security Series vol 10, Transaction Publishers: London, 2004) 145, 149.

[4] J Handler and Y Hasenfeld, *Blame Welfare, Ignore Poverty and Inequality* (CUP: Cambridge, 2007) 81.

[5] Pub L 104–193.

in an 'evolutionary' fashion where income support was concerned, conditioning Food Stamps on work tests involved a significant change in approach. And, indeed, the convergence of rationales guiding the two forms of benefits has led to similar effects (such as reduced participation rates) amongst recipients of both schemes.[6] As the analysis below shows, this result is far from surprising.

So instead of addressing a wide range of policies and populations, the analysis in this book addresses a matter that is of particular concern with respect to welfare-to-work programmes, and with respect to social policy in general: the ease in which rights, in this case the right to welfare, have been transformed to 'negotiated claims'. Instead of having a lasting effect on social and economic policy decisions, these rights are viewed as 'contractual'. It is not always clear what this last term refers to, and it is very likely that different people mean different things by it. At times, it is meant to refer to *social contract* ideology. And even here, there is much to be explained. Is the social contract meant to serve as short-hand for values such as autonomy and choice, individualism and responsibility, or is it an abbreviated reference to justice and equality, citizenship and social rights? At the other end of the ideology-doctrine spectrum, the contract has much more tangible manifestations. The most obvious one would be the agreements recipients are required to sign as a condition for receiving benefits. In essence, the relationship between the (poor) individual and his or her state or society is transformed into one which is based on contractual terms. The ramifications of this change may be profound. And, as noted below, it is becoming clear that welfare-to-work programmes are serving as an *avant-garde* to social policy programmes that are already evolving in other realms.

Within this narrower range of interest, it is possible to offer a comparative perspective. The choice to focus on the United States and Britain and to add only occasional references to other countries derives both from the characteristics of the welfare state that these countries embody and from their attitude towards contractual ideology. When investigating both these facets, which are central to the foregoing analysis, one finds that the United States and Britain exhibit very important similarities in a manner that justifies a common theorization. On the other hand, where differences exist, the peculiarities permit an interesting comparison without casting too wide a net. The ambivalent attitudes that concern the cultures and politics of the two nations divided by a common language are well noted not only in popular writings but, insofar as social and economic policy is concerned, rest on a strong academic background as well.

Indeed, the two countries share the same group in four dominant welfare state regime typologies. In Esping-Anderson's well known *The Three Worlds of Welfare Capitalism*, both countries are categorized as 'liberal' welfare states. The social policy advanced by such countries includes no full-employment element, caters mainly to low-income individuals, is predominated by means-tested assistance,

---

[6] Weil (n 3 above) 156–57.

modest benefits, strong incentives to opt for work instead of welfare (the principle of 'less eligibility', discussed below), and entitlement that is associated with stigma.[7] Remarkable similarities between the policies in the two countries are also found when analyzing the conditions for entitlement.[8] In both countries, Esping-Andersen concludes, such traits lead to a 'stratification profile' in which the poor are primarily dependent on stigmatizing relief; the middle class are predominantly clients of social insurance; and the privileged group derives its welfare from the market.[9]

But even the typologies developed largely as a reaction to Esping-Andersen's reach a similar conclusion with respect to the relative position of the United States and Britain.

In Liebfried's typology, both countries are grouped as 'Anglo Saxon' welfare states, which hold the role of the state as compensator of last resort and tight enforcer of work in the marketplace while at the same time guaranteeing a right to income transfer.[10] These countries fall clearly within the 'residual' welfare model of social policy that Richard Titmuss identified.[11] This model is based on the premise that individual needs are properly met through the private market and the family. Only when both these institutions break down or fail to function properly should welfare institutions come to play, and then only temporarily. Titmuss rejects this model, in favour of the 'integrative' or 'institutional-redistributive' model of social welfare. Under the integrative system of social welfare, fundamental needs 'are characterized not so much by exchange in which a quid is got for a quo' as by universal, unilateral transfers.[12] In the Anglo-Saxon model, entry into the labour market is facilitated more by force than by training or subsidization. Selectivism reigns through means-testing, distinguishing these countries (in addition to the USA and Britain, Australia and New Zealand fall in this category) from the Scandinavian countries, which promote universalism, and where the basic income debate is more than an academic issue.

Siaroff's gender oriented typology focuses on the reality of female work-welfare choice by comparing employment conditions and benefit structures in different welfare states.[13] He classifies both countries as 'Protestant Liberal' welfare states, in that they place relatively high currency on the importance of gender equality

---

[7] G Esping-Andersen, *The Three Worlds of Welfare Capitalism* (Polity: Cambridge, 1990) 26–28, 42–43.
[8] ibid 48–52.
[9] ibid 64–65.
[10] S Leibfried, 'Towards a European Welfare State: On Integrating Poverty Regimes into the European Community' in Z Ferge and J Kohlberg (eds), *Social Policy in a Changing Europe* (Westview Press: Boulder, 1992) 245, 252–53, 264 n 42.
[11] R Titmuss, 'Developing Social Policy in Conditions of Rapid Change' in B Abel-Smith and K Titmuss (eds), *The Philosophy of Welfare: Selected Writings of Richard Titmuss* (Routledge: London, 1987) 254, 262.
[12] ibid 263 (quoting Kenneth Boulding).
[13] A Siaroff, 'Work, Welfare and Gender Equality: A New Typology' in D Sainsbury (ed), *Gendering Welfare States* (Sage: London, 1994) 82.

in the labour market while guaranteeing rather minimal family benefits. Women in these countries thus have both a direct and an indirect incentive to work. First, due to the relatively egalitarian nature of the labour market and, second, because of the commodified nature (i.e. earning related) of welfare benefits.

Lastly, the analysis offered by Castles and Mitchell is especially instructive in light of the fact that the they take special issue with Esping-Andersen's treatment of benefits related to unemployment, and because they place the two countries in different groups.[14] And yet, the differences between the two groups are at the same time both slight and mostly irrelevant for our purposes. Thus, while they view the United States as a 'Liberal' welfare state and Britain as a 'Radical' welfare state, both types are characterized by low social spending and the adoption of equalizing instruments in social policy. Both countries have seen long periods of political dominance by right-wing parties. According to this typology, the difference between the two groups exists in the effort to achieve pre-tax, pre-transfer income equality, especially through the labour movement. This trait characterizes Britain more than the United States. While the role of equality in social policy and welfare reform is central to the analysis that follows, the issues of trade union density and the role of the public sector, along with their impact on redistributive social policy, will not figure in the discussion.

In addition to their welfare state regime, the centrality of contractual ideology in both countries in political rhetoric, policy jargon and academic analysis is highly apparent and well documented. While the Republicans in the United States accomplished an overwhelming victory in the 1994 Congressional elections under the banner of a 'Contract with America', Tony Blair's government chose the title of 'A New Contract for Welfare' for several social policy proposals during 1998–1999.[15] But more important than political rhetoric is the significant supply-side emphasis in current policy programmes, an abandonment of structural explanations in favour of individualistic, behaviour modification arrangements and a reconstruction of the jurisprudential nature of welfare (and perhaps other) rights as 'contractual'. The latter characteristic, central to the thrust of this book, implies that because the citizen is viewed as engaged in contractual relationship with the state, his or her rights are reframed as dependent on obligations.

One curious trait of welfare-to-work programmes concerns their immediate political background. The structure and basic provisions of the programmes that are in place in Britain and in the United States were proposed by the Conservatives, in the former case, and by the Republican Congress, in the latter

---

[14] F Castles and D Mitchell, 'Worlds of Welfare and Families of Nations' in F Castles (ed), *Families of Nations: Patterns of Public Policies in Western Democracies* (Aldershot: Dartmouth, 1993) 93, 104.

[15] DSS *New Ambitions for Our Country: A New Contract for Welfare* (Cm 3805, 1998); DSS *A New Contract for Welfare: Principles into Practice* (Cm 4101, 1998); DEE *A New Contract for Welfare: The Gateway to Work* (Cm 4102, 1998); DSS *A New Contract for Welfare: Children's Rights and Parents' Responsibilities* (Cm 4349, 1999).

case. One may wonder how can the ideology of the minimal state, the trademark of these parties, correspond with such aggressive social policy measures, which have a dramatic effect on the labour force and the market in general?[16] Undoubtedly, one may reply to this query by suggesting that in advancing these programmes, Conservative parties have swayed from their traditional libertarian platforms and have incorporated other objectives. To an extent, certain provisions, explored in subsequent chapters, support this explanation.

A more general response, however, posits the incentive for welfare-to-work programmes as part of a general explanation for the erection of welfare state institutions and state intervention. Thus, structuralist theory, which seeks to capture the logic of development holistically, explains how the rise of social mobility, individualism and market dependence made pre-industrial modes of support such as the family, the church, *noblesse oblige* and the guild inappropriate. Esping-Andersen explains that the 'crux of the matter is that the market is no adequate substitute because it caters only to those who are able to perform in it. Hence, the "welfare function" is appropriated by the welfare state'.[17] Welfare-to-work programmes, then, have the dual role of offering support to those who are most in need while constantly emphasizing the link between relief and participation in the market. By preserving labour power while enhancing the 'commodification' factor in society, eg the dependency of individuals on the market, these programmes are far from antagonistic to Conservative ideology.

Welfare-to-work programmes touch on another matter that raises similar political sensibilities. The relevance of the distinction between the private and the public is almost implied by the programme's title. 'Welfare' is obviously associated with government institutions, interests and regulations. The institutions relevant for 'work', on the other hand, are the market and family. Both of these are perceived as 'prior to' and independent of state power, a 'discrete and bounded sphere of social and economic activity in which participants are fully and exclusively engaged'.[18] The fact that these programmes distribute government aid through statutory criteria and regulations is expected, if not welcomed. The legitimacy of the impact that the programmes have on the low-end labour force and on the intimate decisions of poor members of society, however, is questionable.[19] Moreover, it is all the more curious that such a significant effect on labour market interactions and family life would be advanced by political parties that favour 'night watchman' governments.

---

[16] I thank Professor Lord Raymond Plant for raising this matter with me in discussion.
[17] Esping-Andersen (n 7 above) 13.
[18] J Conaghan, 'Women, Work and Family: A British Revolution?' in J Conaghan, R Fischl and K Klare (eds), *Labour Law in an Era of Globalization* (OUP: Oxford, 2002) 53, 56; L Williams, 'Beyond Labour Law's Parochialism: A Re-envisioning of the Discourse of Redistribution' in J Conaghan, R Fischl and K Klare (eds), *Labour Law in an Era of Globalization* (OUP: Oxford, 2002) 93, 94.
[19] For a narrative description of such an impact see J De Parle, *American Dream : Three Women, Ten Kids, and a Nation's Drive to End Welfare* (Viking: New York, 2004).

Plausibly, in light of the above, one may ask whether welfare-to-work programmes should be viewed as antithetic to the foundational elements of the welfare state, or as one of their integral and logical elements. To answer this most basic query, one must supply an accepted working definition of the welfare state. Surprisingly, no such definition exists. It is clear that the welfare state should secure basic needs for its citizens in core areas such as unemployment insurance, disability benefits and old-age pensions. But should the goal of welfare state policy reach beyond staving off poverty to realms such as redistribution and promoting equality? Should it aid the market process or emancipate individuals from market dependency? And how are 'basic needs' to be identified and quantified?

I have already mentioned Titmuss's distinction between residual and institutional welfare states.[20] The residual welfare state intervenes as a mechanism of last resort, when family and market fail. It thus limits its intervention to marginal and 'deserving' groups. The institutional welfare state is universalistic in nature and thus extends its commitments to all citizens in a greater variety of social welfare areas. These two models, though ideal types by nature, may helpfully explain certain transitions in the provision of relief to able-bodied unemployed throughout history. Though the distinction between 'deserving' and 'undeserving' poor was never absent from these programmes, the conditions placed on eligibility to benefits became increasingly strict in contemporary programmes, means-testing became a serious obstacle to receipt of relief and the programmes became significantly less universal in nature. When these traits are combined with low benefits and social stigma, relief indeed becomes the safety net of last resort, thus increasing commodification and compelling all but the most desperate to participate in the market.[21]

Within this rudimentary typology of welfare state concepts and features, the phenomenon of unemployment is especially challenging. Indeed, it is not insignificant to note that only in the 1880s was the concept itself, *unemployment*, recognized in Britain as a structural phenomenon, 'signifying an abstract, impersonal, amoral condition, in contrast to the older word "unemployed"'.[22] Then as now, in other words, it has never been quite clear what obligations are to be shouldered by the state to alleviate the harsh consequences that are associated with unemployment. Herein lies the importance of the ubiquitous distinction between the deserving and the undeserving poor.

Measures of public policy necessarily rely on distinctions. In the welfare realm, it is routinely claimed that the state cannot afford to provide everyone with the same material assistance. In addition, it is added, arguments of fairness also support certain distinctions, such as those based on merit, desert, need or similar denominators. Desmond King suggests distinguishing between three categories

---

[20] Text to n 11 above.
[21] Esping-Andersen (n 7 above) 13.
[22] G Himmelfarb, *The Idea of Poverty* (Faber: London, 1984) 13.

of unemployed individuals.[23] The first category consists of those normally in employment but made unemployed due to seasonal or cyclical trends. The magnitude of this group may change in periods of economic growth or recession.[24] The second category includes the unskilled, long-term unemployed and people who have never worked, all of whom have difficulties obtaining work. The third category is occupied by welfare recipients who may or may not have worked previously and are receiving welfare benefits. In terms of public perception, it was suggested that a fourth category, though obviously not part of welfare-to-work programmes in the strict sense, was important in forming the images of the various groups of the poor and the distinctions between them. This is the group of the working, or 'labouring' poor. It is routinely argued that the existence of the working poor undermines the justification for granting provision that places the able-bodied pauper at a material position that is overly advantageous.

Returning to social policies that relate to unemployed individuals, it is apparent that those in the first category, ie who are only temporarily unemployed, elicited the greatest sympathy. Unsurprisingly, provision for their maintenance was made available in many Western countries in the early 20th century, decades before income support was offered to long-term unemployed. This support was conditional upon proof of past employment and was depedendent on monies deducted from workers' salaries while they were engaged in the workforce.

However, this book, while focusing on social *assistance* programmes, will touch upon unemployment (or social) *insurance* (UI) programmes only in passing. The distinction between the two is quite interesting in light of their obvious similarities, just noted. First, functionally, both provide subsistence to unemployed individuals. And second, rhetorically, both are often grounded in contractarian language. However, analysis of UI rules resorts to contractual terminology *strictu sensu*: an individual receives in direct proportion to his or her deposit. Greater salaries during employment lead to greater deposits which, in turn, lead to more substantial UI payments at times of unemployment. Conversely, social assistance programmes are discussed in contractual terms only in a metaphorical sense. Eligibility, rates and exceptions are decided on a statutory level. The two programme types, it has been argued, are not only dissimilar, but actually reify the borders between workers and non-workers.[25] Social insurance programmes for (ex) workers are typically financed by employer-employee contribution schemes and entitlements are perceived as obtained as a matter of (contractual) right. They are thus 'meshed with the political culture's emphasis on individual effort and

---

[23] D King, *Actively Seeking Work* (Chicago UP: London, 1995) 3–4.
[24] Though, contrary to King's straightforward (inverse) link between economic growth and unemployment, 'in most European countries, the proceeds of economic growth in the past 20 years have not been used to generate new jobs (in net terms), but have been appropriated by those who have remained in employment'—P Ormerod, 'Unemployment and Social Exclusion: An Economic View' in M Rhodes and Y Meny (eds), *The Future of European Welfare: A New Social Contract?* (Macmillan: Basingstoke, 1998) 23, 31.
[25] Williams (n 18 above) 102.

(labor) market exchange... [and are thus] less controversial entitlements in our culture than welfare entitlements'.[26] Social assistance programmes, on the other hand, are designated for 'non-workers', are financed from the general revenue, are less generous and are highly stigmatized. Eligibility is based on need, and not on earning history or prior contributions.

Notwithstanding the distinction just noted, the fact that both programmes provide relief for unemployed individuals merits a separate investigation of the relationship between them. Thus, Lucy Williams notes how 'UI rules exclude many low-waged workers, particularly women and people of colour, from the definition of "employee".'[27] This is done by instituting minimum requirement earnings for UI eligibility that disproportionately affect those marginalized groups. Clearly, if this charge is true, such policy choices will increase the dependency of members of these groups on social assistance programmes.

So while the logic of UI programmes, like all insurance programmes, is to provide relief for contingencies that are not the result of personal choice, but rather a consequence of 'brute luck',[28] social assistance programmes present a greater ideological challenge. Understood minimalistically, the long-term unemployed are eligible for material support only when they have done all that is in their power to attain gainful employment. And so the line between the deserving and the undeserving poor is redrawn to indicate the distinction between those who are making a genuine effort to enter the labour force, on the one hand, and the 'scroungers' who are exploiting the system, on the other hand. Understood liberally, however, social assistance programmes are intimately connected to one of the main aims of the welfare state: the de-commodification of labour relations and the lessening of individual dependency on labour-market contingencies. This position, if entertained, would have to create conditions that would make an individual's choice to enter the labour force more attractive, and to accept as justifiable her right not to enter the labour force on any terms.

B Welfare *Rights*?

Welfare rights, like all social and economic rights, have the potential to support de-commodification. In the absence of such rights, and barring extreme need, one's attainment of material well-being relies on one's ability to acquire basic goods, such as education, health care and income, from the market. Recognition of comprehensive welfare rights, on the other hand, would require that governments grant certain benefits to all, irrespective of contribution or performance.

---

[26] L Williams, 'Welfare and Legal Entitlements: The Social Roots of Poverty' in D Kairys (ed), *The Politics of Law* (3rd edn, Basic Books: New York, 1998) 569, 572
[27] Williams (n 18 above) 104.
[28] R Dworkin, *Sovereign Virtue* (Harvard UP: London, 2000) 287.

Prominent examples of such a model in many Western countries are children's benefits, paid maternity leave, universal pensions and so forth. Recognition of welfare rights, however, *need* not lead to such precise policies and social structures.

And yet, as argued below, serious recognition of welfare rights should have significant implications.[29] For example, they should support a decent minimum level of provision, and one that includes fair and acceptable conditions of access. If benefits fall significantly below normal earnings that permit an adequate standard of living in a society, the effect would be to drive the recipient immediately back to the workforce, as soon as possible. In addition, such rights also place limits on eligibility rules and restrictions on entitlements. By doing so, they create an emancipatory detachment between livelihood and the market. Moreover, such a system supports equality of status and promotes social inclusion by moderating the dualism that exists between those who rely on the market (commonly identified with the rich) and those who rely on the state (commonly identified with the poor). Incidentally, it should be noted that when factors such as tax breaks and subsidies are taken into account, this dualism often appears overblown, at the very least.

Of course, different jurisdictions recognize different welfare rights to different degrees. Just as freedom of speech in France is not as authoritative a right as it is in the United States, so various countries may find certain welfare rights more attractive than others. This trivial insight, however, assumes that welfare rights, and social and economic rights in general, are conceptually equivalent to civil and political rights. Though it has been repeatedly asserted that arguments against recognition of social and economic rights have been effectively answered,[30] this premise is still the cause for explicit and implicit objections, especially when the issue of welfare rights is raised.

As noted below, the analytical arguments in favour of the distinction between social and economic rights and civil and political rights are far from convincing. Both 'types' of rights guard essentially the same essential human interests, and in many cases social and economic rights do so better than civil and political rights. And to argue that social and economic rights demand a radically distinct set of obligations on the part of the state is to entertain a superficial and stereotypical perspective of each type of rights.

So if the argument here is a cogent one, and the analytical challenges against welfare rights are not convincing, the political explanation comes to the fore. In other words, if social and economic rights are not conceptually different from

---

[29] R Gavison, 'On the Relationship Between Civil and Political Rights and Social and Economic Rights' in JM Coicaud, MW Doyle, AM Gardner (eds), *The Globalisation of Human Rights* (United Nations UP: Tokyo, 2003) 24. For a discussion regarding the implications the right to welfare should have on welfare reform see C Wellman, *Welfare Rights* (Rowman and Allanheld: Totowa, 1982) 183–215.

[30] J Waldron, 'Introduction' in J Waldron (ed), *Theories of Rights* (OUP: Oxford, 1984) 1, 11.

civil and political rights, it would be fair to suggest that the arguments for and against the former are, in essence, arguments for and against their expected consequences. A right to welfare is 'a right to be provided with cash or material goods or services either without charge or at a subsidized rate below their market value'.[31] As such, it may 'limit the domain of inequality',[32] serve as an obstacle to the commodification of the labour relationship and reduce reliance on market contingencies. Arguments in favour of welfare rights are, therefore, arguments in favour of a different welfare state model than the one that is currently in place in many Western countries. This is not the place to defend this claim, let alone to investigate its implications. This section will address only the first part of the argument, seeking to refute the alleged distinction between welfare rights and civil and political rights. The second part of the argument will have to be discussed at a separate occasion.

1 Co-dependence

On the theoretical level, most civil and political rights rely, as a background assumption, on social and economic rights for their implementation. For what can the right to privacy mean in the face of homelessness?[33] And what would the freedom to express oneself in writing mean to the illiterate?[34] Links between access to adequate health services and the right to life hardly require elaboration.[35] Indeed, it may well be that social and economic rights are *more fundamental* to a person's welfare:

A life of struggling to subsist offends the notion of human dignity much more than a life in which one's freedom to speak is curtailed... Some forms of adequate standards of living may be necessary background conditions for exercising civil and political rights.[36]

In addition, the right to equality serves as a bridge between the two branches. Quite often, when courts were unwilling to accept an argument on the basis of the recognition of a social or economic right, they accepted the challenge on the basis of the right to equal treatment:

---

[31] A Buchanan, 'Deriving Welfare Rights from Libertarian Rights' in PG Brown, C Johnson, P Vernier (eds), *Income Support* (Rowman and Littlefield: Totowa NJ, 1981) 233, 235. Similarly, it has been suggested to view welfare rights as the right to a certain minimal level of well-being. See, eg, AI Melden, 'Are There Welfare Rights?' ibid 259, 273.

[32] R Goodin, *Reasons for Welfare* (Princeton UP: Princeton, 1998) 8.

[33] CCT 11/00 *The Government of the Republic of South Africa v Grootboom* 2001(1) SA 46 (CC).

[34] P Schneider, 'Social Rights and the Concept of Human Rights' in DD Raphael (ed), *Political Theory and the Rights of Man* (Macmillan: Basingstoke, 1967) 81, 92.

[35] DD Raphael, 'Human Rights, Old and New' in Raphael (n 34 above) 54, 63. For an interesting case regarding access to adequate health services in South Africa see: CCT 32/97 *Soobramoney v Minister of Health (Kwazalu-Natal)* 1998(1) SA 765 (CC).

[36] Gavison (n 29 above) 32. See also J Waldron, 'Liberal Rights' in J Waldron, *Liberal Rights* (CUP: Cambridge, 1993) 1, 8; A Gewirth, *The Community of Rights* (Chicago UP: Chicago, 1996) 53.

The equal protection clause is the constitutional text which most naturally suggests itself to one who would claim a legal right to have certain wants satisfied out of the public treasury, insofar as he means to found his argument upon a comparison of burdens and opportunities which must otherwise accrue to the relatively rich and the relatively poor.[37]

Indeed, as argued in chapter 4, equality plays an important role in the justification of the right to welfare.

2 A True Divide?

Some writers have argued for a distinction between social and economic rights and civil and political rights. In this section I examine the theoretical and pragmatic claims that wish to establish a barrier between these two forms of rights and argue that close inspection finds such claims wanting.

a) The Theoretical Dimension

As mentioned, rights serve as grounds for duties. One may suggest, then, that if we find a significant difference between types of duties, we may conclude a meaningful difference between the corresponding rights. This is how some have argued for a distinction between the types of rights. 'Positive' rights establish a duty upon another *to act*, and thus entail allotment of funds to carry out the duty.[38] These rights were seen as synonymous with social and economic rights. In contrast, 'negative' rights, which entail a duty *to refrain from action* and hence (according to this argument) pose no financial burden, were perceived as synonymous with civil and political rights.[39] However, such a link between the duty to act (or to refrain from action) and the categorization of rights seems tenuous. Each branch of rights internalizes both positive and negative elements.[40] In fact, three aspects

---

[37] F Michelman, 'On Protecting the Poor Through the Fourteenth Amendment' (1969) 83 Harvard L Rev 7, 11.

[38] P Rosanvallon, *The New Social Question* (Princeton UP: Princeton, 2000) 74.

[39] Though the dichotomy between 'positive' and 'negative' liberties is often attributed to Isaiah Berlin in his 'Two Concepts of Liberty' in *Four Essays on Liberty* (OUP: Oxford, 1969) 118, it is important to note that Berlin speaks of a different distinction. For Berlin, 'positive' liberty involves the idea of being 'truly free' to realize one's potential, as opposed to being free from negative constraints. Indeed, Berlin later admonished 'the failure of such systems to provide the minimum conditions in which alone any degree of significant "negative" liberty can be exercised by individuals or groups, and without which it is of little or no value to those who may theoretically possess it'—'Introduction' in *Four Essays on Liberty*, ibid 45, 53. See also Waldron (n 30 above) 6–7.

[40] R Plant, 'Free Lunches Don't Nourish: Reflections on Entitlement and Citizenship' in G Drover and P Kerans (eds), *New Approaches to Welfare Theory* (Elgar: Brookfield, 1993) 33, 36; H Shue, 'Mediating Duties' (1988) 98 Ethics 687, 689; J Waldron, 'Rights in Conflict' (1989) 99 Ethics 503, 510–11; G Mundlak, 'Social-Economic Rights in the New Constitutional Discourse' (2000) 7 Labor Law Yearbook 65 [in Hebrew].

can be identified in social and economic as well as in civil and political rights, namely: respect, protection and realization.[41]

i) Respect: This facet refers to the negative aspect of the right, *prohibiting the state* from acting in a given manner. Thus, the negative aspect of the right to life would mean that the state should not kill its citizens, the negative aspect of free speech would prohibit censorship by the state, and so forth. However, a negative aspect exists also in relation to social and economic rights.[42] In the realm of labour relations this facet includes the right of workers to obtain and retain remunerative work, to form a union, to engage in collective negotiation, to demonstrate and to go on strike without being harassed;[43] the negative facet of the right to housing would include the right not to be evicted by the state;[44] and from the negative aspect of the right to health one may infer that the state should abolish criminal restrictions on abortions, for example.[45]

ii) Protection: Even when a state is not an instigator of human rights violations, it may not be an indifferent bystander when such violations are perpetrated by third parties. Hence, we deduce that civil and political rights are respected when the state not only refrains from acting, but also positively acts to protect them. Respect for the right without guaranteeing protection would render it almost meaningless. This is why Bills of Rights as well as international conventions emphasize both these aspects. For instance, Article 6 of the ICCPR states that 'Every human being has the inherent right to life. *This right shall be protected by law*. No one shall be arbitrarily deprived of his life'. Indeed, courts have made clear that governments should 'provide effective protection' so that individuals within their jurisdiction do not suffer ill-treatment 'including such ill-treatment administered by private individuals'.[46] In many cases, this would mean that states should provide funds such that individuals may make use of their civil and political rights. This is because all rights, from voting rights to enforcement of contracts, from protection of speech to protection of property, entail costs and require

---

[41] See P Macklem and C Scott, 'Constitutional Ropes of Sand or Justiciable Guarantees: Social Rights in a New South African Constitution (1992) 141 U of Pennsylvania L Rev 1, 74; similarly Gewirth (n 36 above) 35.

[42] Brian Barry places a strong emphasis on this understanding of rights even with respect to education and health, for example: B Barry, *Why Social Justice Matters* (Polity: Cambridge, 2005) 25–26.

[43] Gewirth (n 36 above) 217–18; R Ben-Israel, 'The Ramifications of the Basic Laws on Labor Law and Labor Relations' (1997) 4 Labor Law Yearbook 27, 36 [in Hebrew].

[44] eg Article 26(3) of the South African Constitution: 'No one may be evicted from their home, or have their home demolished, without an order of court made after considering all the relevant circumstances. No legislation may permit arbitrary evictions'.

[45] *R v Morgentaler* [1988] 1 SCR 30.

[46] *Z v United Kingdom* (2001) 34 EHRR 97, [73].

taxpayer support.[47] It goes without saying that protection of social and economic rights also requires funding,[48] but the special reservation that courts exhibit when those rights are concerned is contestable.

iii) Realization: Though the distinction between 'realization' and 'protection' is not always clear, there is an important difference between the two. The protection of a right implies that the state has a duty to provide the 'infrastructure' necessary to enable others to take advantage of the right. The state is not expected to organize a demonstration, but it should enable it to be carried out by others. Similarly, the state may be obligated to build youth centers, so that third parties may carry out extra-curricular activities. But when the state is obligated to realize the right to education, it cannot satisfy itself with merely building the schools. Instead, the state is also expected to pay teachers, to set up a curriculum and to supervise the administration. The state's duty is to see an end-state realized: to ensure, for instance, that citizens will not be found wanting of food, shelter, health services and education. When the court is involved in decisions on such matters, it is seen as acting on the most activist level possible, and thus feared by those who oppose the acknowledgement of social and economic rights. But such is the case also when we turn our attention to civil and political rights. Thus, for instance, the state organizes and funds public elections, and even sees to it that the elderly and people with disabilities are able to cast their votes

How does this analysis contribute to our understanding the reluctance to recognize social and economic rights as being on a par with civil and political rights? Scott and Macklem are probably right to suggest that civil and political rights are deemed easier to implement due to the comparison of the first level (respect) of the former to the third level (realization) of the latter. And yet, one must not disregard the fact that the nature of the different types of rights may have an impact on such an invidious comparison. Thus, while legislation prohibiting the eviction of a person from her house does not fulfill the right to housing, some advocates for a strong right to free speech would ask for no more than an absolute disempowerment of government censorship. Social and economic rights, Gavison argues, 'require a richer range of human and social interaction' because sanctioning speech may require much less of a social effort when compared to 'ensuring that a black child in the south receives proper

---

[47] S Holmes and C Sunstein, *The Cost of Rights* (WW Norton: London, 1999) 44; R Plant, H Lesser and P Taylor-Gooby, *Political Philosophy and Social Welfare* (Routledge: London, 1980) 76; Gavison (n 29 above). In one Israeli case, dealing with a decision barring women from entering a pilot course, the court declared that 'the protection of human rights costs money, and a society that protects human rights should be ready to withstand the financial burden'—HCJ 4541/94 49(4) *Miller v Minister of Defense* 94, 113.

[48] GJH van Hoof, 'The Legal Nature of Economic, Social and Cultural Rights' in P Alston and K Tomasevski (eds), *The Right to Food* (Dordrecht: Boston, 1984) 97, 107.

education'.[49] However, as Gavison immediately clarifies, this is not a conceptual distinction, let alone one that has conceptual consequences to the disadvantage of social and economic rights. For if it were a conceptual claim, such an argument would have to explain why civil and political rights that have a dominant realization element, such as the right to vote, are not seen as less worthy, while social and economic rights are deemed vulnerable for that reason alone.

b) The Pragmatic Dimensions

Before examining the merits of the pragmatic arguments against social and economic rights, attention should be drawn to two introductory issues. First, it is important to assess these claims with the background of the theoretical dimension in mind. If the theoretical distinction between social and economic rights and civil and political rights does not hold, a significant onus lies on one claiming that pragmatic arguments alone are sufficient to deny social and economic rights, while maintaining the force of civil and political rights.[50] Second, due to the nature of the pragmatic arguments discussed below, their acceptance would move society dangerously close to barring the courts from adjudicating matters such as claims against social security agencies, Home Office directives or regulations brought forth by the Ministry of Education.

The pragmatic rationalizations lodged against social and economic rights are vagueness; separation of powers and competency of the courts; financial burden and applicability; and universality.

i) Vagueness

The argument, in principle, states that social and economic rights deal with goods whose criteria for distribution are vaguer than those offered for civil and political rights. It is maintained that while the decision whether or not to allow a demonstration presents a yes/no dichotomy, one cannot as easily evaluate proper education and sustainable environment. Thus, the United States Federal Court declined to enforce the spending of funds for 'educational needs' due to lack of 'discoverable and manageable standards by which a court can determine when the Constitution is satisfied and when it is violated'.[51]

Yet while civil and political rights require us to constantly define the scope of the right and the scope of its protection, it is the social and economic sphere that is opulent with criteria and indices for a minimal standard of living, a reasonable standard of income, and so forth.[52] Among these one can refer to studies

---

[49] Gavison (n 29 above) 37.
[50] For a similar line of thought see B Ackerman, *Social Justice in the Liberal State* (Yale UP: New Haven, 1980) 233–34.
[51] *McInnis v Shapiro* 293 F Supp 327, 335 (1968); also see M Walzer, 'Philosophy and Democracy' (1981) 9 Political Theory 379, 391.
[52] C Fabre *Social Rights Under the Constitution* (OUP: Oxford, 2000) 155; D David, P Macklem and G Mundlak, 'Social Rights, Social Citizenship and Transformative Constitutionalism: A

combining estimates of the costs of a nutritious diet and expenditure surveys,[53] international standards such as the 1987 Limburg principles[54] as developed in the 1997 Maastricht Guidelines on Violations of Economic, Social and Cultural Rights[55] or those compiled by international organizations such as the United Nations, the ILO, the UN Committee for Economic, Social and Cultural rights, and the poverty lines in each country.[56] Such precise criteria often present the court with instruments to expound a rational, informed decision in a manner that is not readily available when dealing with other rights. Furthermore, some cases in the field of social and economic rights may pose a yes/no dichotomy, for example: is an immigrant entitled to health care; should a convicted felon be denied public housing, and so on. Of course, questions regarding the quality of health care and size of the public housing apartment would be open to debate. But such is the situation when discussing the implications of other rights as well. Lastly, the vagueness encountered in the field of social and economic rights can be also attributed to the courts' reluctance to deal with such rights and to propose rational doctrines, as opposed to their eagerness to do so when dealing with civil and political rights.[57]

ii) Separation of Powers and Competency of the Court

Since the realization of social and economic rights entails substantial public funds, it has been argued that the recognition of social and economic rights will result in the transfer of authority from parliament and government to the courts, thus encroaching on powers held by other branches of government. Further, the courts, which hear cases on an individual basis, are not disposed to deal with issues that require a broader view. The House of Lords has been characterized as holding 'a deeply embedded judicial conviction that matters of public finance are the preserve of the elected branches of government and not of the courts'.[58] Similarly, the United States Supreme Court remarked that 'the intractable economic, social, and even philosophical problems presented by public welfare assistance programs are not the business of this Court'.[59]

Comparative Assessment' in J Conaghan, R Fischl and K Klare (eds), *Labour Law in an Era of Globalization* (OUP: Oxford) 511, 518–19.

[53] WH Simon, 'Rights and Redistribution in the Welfare System' (1986) 38 Stanford L Rev 1431, 1489; The United States Supreme Court in *Rosado v Wyman* 397 US 397, 413 saw the state standard of need as an important factor in its decision.

[54] *The Limburg Principles on the Implementation of the International Covenant on Economic, Social and Cultural Rights* UN Doc E/CN.4/1987/17 published at (1979) 9 Human Rights Q 122.

[55] *The Maastricht Guidelines on Violations of Economic, Social and Cultural Rights* UN Doc E/CN.4/1987/17.

[56] For a critique of the measuring of poverty lines, see BH Barton, 'Law and Equality' (1996) 94 Michigan L Rev 1993; Handler and Hasenfeld (n 4 above) 5–7.

[57] Mundlak (n 40 above) 96–99.

[58] E Palmer, 'Resource Allocation, Welfare Rights' (2000) 20 OJLS 63, 74.

[59] *Dandridge v Williams* 397 US 471, 487 (1970).

One may recall that the same court did not shy away from 'social, and even philosophical' problems such as abolishing segregation in the public school system, allowing abortion, reviewing decisions concerning public prayers in schools, and checking affirmative action programmes, to name but a few. Moreover, as noted, social and economic rights are not unique in requiring funds for their realization. As the Canadian Supreme Court noted, 'any remedy granted by a court will have some budgetary repercussions, whether it be a saving of money or an expenditure of money'.[60]

There is room, indeed, for due care when courts review decisions that were made by competent authorities that exercise legitimate powers and are (unlike the courts) accountable for their decisions. But this caution should not imply that the courts should refrain altogether from judicial review in this sphere.

A related argument is that since courts hear cases on an individual basis, they cannot assess the social and economic environment from which the case stems and which is affected by the decision. Though courts should not be dismissive of the fact that the individual case they are addressing may have repercussions for others whose claim is not heard, it should also be recalled that courts deal, on a daily basis, with intricate economic problems that have serious ramifications in trade, business, monopolies, taxes, and similar realms. This is done, of course, with no qualms regarding competence.[61] It is obviously undesirable that the modern welfare state bureaucracy will be permitted to act outside judicial supervision. Further, the court does not have the option of 'not intervening' in the sense of 'not making a statement' with respect to a case presented. Not intervening, in such cases, would usually mean embracing the highly controversial baseline of the market.[62] Though this is occasionally a legitimate option, it should be one that is preferred on the merits of the case rather than for questionable worries that relate to the court's aptitude.

iii) Financial Burden and Applicability

This argument is particularly common in discussions regarding welfare rights, as governments constantly refer the public to the rising costs of welfare benefits. The theoretical support for this political argument suggests that rights that are regarded as impractical should not be recognized:

If it is impossible for a thing to be done, it is absurd to claim it as a right. At present it is utterly impossible, and will be for a long time yet, to provide 'holidays with pay' for everybody in the world. For millions of people who live in those parts of Asia, Africa, and South America where industrialization has hardly begun, such claims are vain and idle.[63]

---

[60] *Schachter v Canada* [1992] 2 SCR 679, 709.
[61] F Michelman, 'In Pursuit of Constitutional Welfare Rights' (1973) 121 U of Pennsylvania L Rev 962, 1006.
[62] A Sen, *Inequality Reexamined* (Clarendon: Oxford, 1992) 100–1.
[63] M Cranston, 'Human Rights, Real and Supposed' in Raphael (n 34 above) 50.

In the above passage Maurice Cranston raises two distinct claims: the first deals with an inability to give effect to the duty that a right imposes. The second relates to the universal dimension of a right and will be dealt with below.

We may, on a charitable interpretation, hope that Cranston is not ridiculing the real universal interest manifested in Art 24 of the UNDHR that he quotes from. This provision articulates the obvious importance in having periods of respite away from the business of subsistence.[64] As such, it is a human interest that should be attended to seriously. Cranston's fear, however, is probably that the recognition of one type of right (social or economic) to which one cannot give effect may lead to a derogation of the status of rights in general and to the state's commitment to the protection of rights.[65] But there is no reason to assume that advocates of the right assume that it is an absolute one, or that the state is under a duty to invest all its resources in one right or another. As Joseph Raz notes, the tendency to portray support for certain rights as espousing a position in favour of absolute rights amounts to a 'simple mistake' which is more common than what would be expected:

> The fact that a given right can be overridden by moral considerations, just like the fact that it can be overridden by another legal right, shows nothing except that it is not an absolute right which defeats all contrary considerations. But legal rules rarely, if ever, have absolute force.[66]

Though different countries do have different budgetary capabilities, there is a difference between recognizing a right and realizing it to the fullest. If a full realization of the right to health and education would require that everyone be able to enjoy free comprehensive health services on demand and free education to her heart's content, it may well be that no country will ever have the financial capabilities necessary to hold up to such a standard. This does not imply, however, that within the domestic legal system these rights carry no weight, and surely does not demand the conclusion that they are not rights at all. Despite attempts to dismiss rights that correspond to 'imperfect obligations' (used here to refer to obligations that cannot be addressed in full),[67] the feasibility of enforcement of rights is not a criterion (or at least not an overwhelming criterion) when dealing with the question of recognition of rights. Just as one would not say that a creditor has lost her right to repayment solely because she is faced with a bankrupt debtor,[68] no right comes 'complete with extensive enforcement mechanisms'.[69] Since rights cost money, the decision to realize civil and political rights by policing political

---

[64] Waldron (n 30 above) 13.
[65] For a similar argument see LW Sumner, *The Moral Foundations of Rights* (Clarendon: Oxford, 1987) 16.
[66] J Raz, 'Legal Rights' in his *Ethics in the Public Domain* (Clarendon: Oxford, 1994) 238, 257; A Gewirth, 'Are There Any Absolute Rights? (1981) 31 Phil Q 1.
[67] R Epstein 'The Uncertain Quest for Welfare Rights' 1985 DYU L Rev 201, 204
[68] Wellman (n 29 above) 37.
[69] Gavison (n 29 above) 34 (discussing *human* rights); also Plant (n 40 above) 38.

demonstrations that people find offensive, for example, may divert funds away from building hospitals. Such a decision, in other words, is a political and not a conceptual one.[70]

iv) Universality

There are, in essence, three ways to understand this argument.[71] First, as an assertion that a right should be *relevant* to all human beings; second, as a claim that all rights are rights that impose themselves on all of humanity; and third, that rights have to have equal effect around the globe and across borders.

In terms of the first claim, it is argued, for instance, that social rights of workers are not relevant to all humans, but only to those who are not self employed or are unemployed.[72] But the right to a fair trial is relevant to an even smaller portion of mankind, to wit—those facing criminal charges, and this does not bear on the force of this fundamentally important right.[73] The second claim of universality evokes the debate regarding positive and negative rights. Such an argument states that while negative rights impose a duty on all of humanity, positive rights are substantially different, imposing duties only on public authorities. But since positive and negative elements may be identified in both social and economic rights and in civil and political rights, such a claim would problematically challenge both 'types'. Lastly, the distinction between states is not alien to the nature of civil and political rights, and the third 'universality' argument breaks down when one bears in mind that the right to vote, the nucleus of political rights, clearly distinguishes citizens from residents who are not citizens, and that different states attach different rules of eligibility to the whole array of civil and political rights.[74]

This section sought to establish that welfare rights are indeed 'rights a just society, given its concrete conditions of production and so on, must guarantee',[75] by arguing that general objections to social and economic rights, including the right to welfare, do not withstand criticism. Social and economic rights are at least as instrumental in advancing the same values that civil and political rights promote. In addition, social and economic rights are so closely connected to civil and political rights that no argument manages to target the former while absolving the latter. These objections were important to address since they are at present directed more often towards the right to welfare than towards any other second-generation right.

Within the general structure of the book, this section supplies a fundamental building block. If welfare-to-work programmes are argued to be endangering

---

[70] Dworkin (n 28 above) 137.
[71] For a discussion of some of these arguments see Gewirth (n 36 above) 63–70.
[72] Cranston (n 63 above) 51; M Cranston 'Human Rights: A Reply to Professor Raphael' in Raphael (n 34 above) 95.
[73] Fabre (n 52 above) 26–27.
[74] Raphael (n 35 above) 66.
[75] R Peffer, 'A Defense of Rights to Well-Being' (1978) 8 Phil and Pub Affairs 65, 82.

basic constitutional rights by transforming them into 'contractual' rights or 'negotiated claims', it first has to be shown that the rights in question are *indeed* rights to begin with. Within the context of these programmes, welfare rights are particularly relevant. The 'positive' task of arguing in favour of a right to welfare is left for chapter 4. This section clears out of the way recurring obstacles en route.

To this point, the chapter has introduced aspects of welfare-to-work programmes that are relevant to the welfare state. I now turn to explain how the concept of the social contract has been resurrected and employed to support particular social policy measures in general, and welfare-to-work programmes in particular.

C Social Contract: Tradition and Manipulation

1 Social Contract Objectives and Typology

What is the allure of the concept of the contract, and the social contract in particular, that has granted it such prominence in social policy discourse? To fully answer this question, one must distinguish clearly between early and modern social contract theory, since the two have very different objectives. Early social contract theories, such as those proposed by Hobbes,[76] Locke[77] and Rousseau[78] are centrally interested in investigating the ideas of social co-operation and, to a greater extent, of political obligation. As far as these writings are concerned, moral theory, which is concerned, inter alia, with the balance of rights and obligations and the logical hierarchy between them, seems to be a subset of such political theory and to derive from it. This may explain why, when compared to the vast amount of literature on the social contract, relatively little attention has been granted to the logical extensions of the early contract theory to areas that concern rights and obligations.[79]

Modern social contract theories, on the other hand, take the existence of the modern state as a given. The social contract, then, is employed as a mechanism for identifying proper social institutions and policies that reflect justice as the basic virtue in society.

In light of these differences, what do these theories have in common that merits a common title—social contract theories? It would seem that the central attribute of social contract ideas is to perform an important *legitimating* function. It is of fundamental importance here that contractual terminology is employed. Indeed,

---

[76] T Hobbes, *Leviathan* (CUP: Cambridge, 1992). Hobbes is considered to have offered the first exceptional argument in the social contract tradition: M Lessnoff, *Social Contract* (Macmillan: Basingstoke, 1986) 13; J Hampton, *Hobbes and the Social Contract Tradition* (CUP: Cambridge, 1986) 3.
[77] J Locke, 'The Second Treatise' *Two Treatises of Government* (CUP: Cambridge, 2000).
[78] JJ Rousseau, *The Social Contract* (Wordsworth: Ware, Hertfordshire 1998).
[79] AJ Simmons, *The Lockean Theory of Rights* (Princeton UP: Princeton, 1992) 3.

if one inspects the preconditions required for a legitimate *commercial* contract (eg full information, no coercion, etc) one finds that when they are fulfilled, the contract should be executed and enforced, even when a contractor regrets having signed the contract. In other words, signing the contract, under designated background conditions, gives a sufficient reason to viewing its enforcement as legitimate. And yet, though some have argued that 'the general social contract cannot be completely dissociated from private labour contracts',[80] the role that choice and individual consent play in our understanding of social contract theory cannot stem from our perception of ordinary contracts, for:

> the social contract is always a distinct and special contract, which cannot and must not be put on a par with the everyday contracts of buying and selling with which everyone is familiar... Ordinary contracts leave the personality of the contractors intact... The social contract... aims always at giving practical effectiveness to a common will regarding the fundamentals of human coexistence shared by the contractors.[81]

The question, then, remains: to what extent are the basic features of the commercial contract transferable to the *social* contract? For some early contractarians, justifying social co-operation and political obligation through a contractual mechanism is possible if it can be shown that a *historical* contract to that effect actually existed,[82] or if it is possible to discover an *implicit* contract that mandates such schemes.[83] These theories portrayed a certain 'state of nature' as a starting point for the theory, and suggested that citizens of the time contracted, or should be seen as if they contracted, an understanding to which they can and should be held to. The very different characterizations of the state of nature in Hobbes, Locke, Pufendorf and Rousseau indeed lead them to very different conclusions as to the expectations from the state, the conditions for rebellion and the rights of individuals.

The problems associated with the idea of an historical or implicit contract are now well known. First, no account of such historical contract (where *all* agreed to the terms[84]) was ever recovered. Second, even if such an account were recovered, one would still have to address the problem of demanding obligations from future generations on the basis of the supposed historical consent of their ancestors. As David Hume mockingly notes, 'But were you to ask the far greatest part of the nation, whether they had ever consented to the authority of their rulers or promised, they would be inclined to think very strangely of you'.[85]

---

[80] Rosanvallon (n 38 above) 65.
[81] M Forsyth, 'Hobbes's Contractarianism' in D Boucher and P Kelly (eds), *The Social Contract from Hobbes to Rawls* (Routledge: London, 1994) 35, 39.
[82] Locke (n 77 above) §99, §101, §138; JD Mabbott, *John Locke* (Macmillan: Basingstoke, 1973) 151. See J Waldron, 'John Locke—Social Contract versus Political Anthropology' in Boucher and Kelly (n 81 above) 51.
[83] Rousseau (n 78 above); Locke (n 77 above) §119; See A Ripstein, 'The General Will' in C Morris (ed), *The Social Contract Theorists* (Rowman & Littlefield: Oxford, 1999) 219, 231–35.
[84] Waldron (n 82 above) 58; Lessnoff (n 76 above) 87.
[85] D Hume, *Treatise of Human Nature* (OUP: Oxford, 1978) Bk III, c II s viii.

And as for the implicit contract, proponents of these theories suggested that tacit consent is implied from the acceptance of benefits from the regime. The problem is that such a position would rob the contractarian argument of any power to make 'free consent' the source of one's allegiance to government, for such consent would imply that one is able to refuse the benefits offered by society.[86] Locke seems to reply that one may withdraw tacit consent by leaving the country. To this Hume offers the following rejoinder:

Can we seriously say that a poor peasant or artisan has a free choice to leave his country, when he knows no foreign language or manners, and lives from day to day, by the small wages which he acquires? We may as well assert, that a man, by remaining in a vessel, freely consents to the dominion of the master; though he was carried on board while asleep, and must leap into the ocean, and perish, the moment he leaves her.[87]

And so, following the penetrating critique of Hume and Bentham in Britain,[88] along with the influence of Hegel in the continent,[89] many had thought that the era of contractarian methodology had come to a close. Bentham observed, 'As to the Original Contract... I was in hopes... that this chimera had been effectively demolished by Mr Hume. I think we hear not so much of it now as formerly'.[90]

In fact, the critique only brought the tradition to rest for two centuries, to be resuscitated by John Rawls's *A Theory of Justice* in 1971.[91] Indeed, the latter part of the 20th century has witnessed a tour de force of social contract theory in areas spreading from constitutional theory, civil society and morality itself. This phenomenon, no doubt, owes a great deal to John Rawls's *A Theory of Justice*, which relies heavily on traditional contractarian theory and Kantian insights. Rawls and his followers made the social contract a powerful platform for the construction of rights and responsibilities in the modern welfare state. Even if 'we are now well beyond the stage when "political philosophers now must either work within Rawls's theory or explain why not"',[92] Rawls is credited not only with reviving the social contract tradition, but also with refocusing the objective of political philosophy to 'social justice—the way in which the major social institutions distribute fundamental rights and duties and determine the division of advantages

---

[86] Hampton (n 76 above) 267; J W Gough, *The Social Contract* (OUP: Oxford, 1957) 139.
[87] D Hume, 'On the Original Contract' in *Essays Moral, Political and Literary* (Liberty Classics: Indianapolis, 1987) 475.
[88] D Gauthier, 'David Hume—Utilitarian' (1979) 88 Philosophical Review 3; D Castiglione, 'History, Reason and Experience—Hume's Argument Against Contract Theories' in Boucher and Kelly (n 81 above) 95.
[89] GWF Hegel, *Elements of the Philosophy of Right* (CUP: Cambridge, 1991) §72–81; B Haddock, 'Hegel's Critique of the Theory of Social Contract' in Boucher and Kelly (n 81 above) 147.
[90] J Bentham, 'A Fragment on Government or a Comment on the Commentaries' in JH Burns and HLA Hart (eds), *Collected Works of Jeremy Bentham* (Athlone Press: London, 1977) 393, 439; see D Boucher and P Kelly, 'The Social Contract and its Critics' in D Boucher and P Kelly (eds), *The Social Contract from Hobbes to Rawls* (Routledge: London, 1994) 1, 21.
[91] J Rawls, *A Theory of Justice* (Revised Edition, Harvard UP: Cambridge MA, 1999).
[92] T Pogge, *Realizing Rawls* (Cornell UP: Ithaca, 1989) 2–3 citing R Nozick, *Anarchy, State and Utopia* (Basic Books: New York, 1974) 183.

from social cooperation'.[93] Moreover, Rawls's concern with the 'worst-off' or 'least advantaged' members of society, tentatively identified as the 'unskilled worker',[94] goes to the heart of the subject matter of this work. Lastly, Rawls's merger of two prominent values in his theory—the public virtue of equality and the individualistic notion of self-respect—is not only highly significant but will also have important implications to the study of welfare-to-work programmes. And so, writing in 1957, JW Gough observed that Kant 'brings us within the end of the history of contract theory'.[95] Half a century later, contract theory has gained such a formidable stature that history may well have to be rewritten.[96]

Rawls explains that the original position, his version of the state of nature, 'is understood as a purely *hypothetical* situation characterized so as to lead to a certain conception of justice'.[97] From here on, be it through the metaphor of a veil of ignorance, a desert island,[98] a spaceship approaching an uninhabited planet[99] or, indeed, a 'view from nowhere',[100] social contract methodology revolves around counter-factual thought experiments. Philosophers and policy-makers suggest an ideal construct from which legitimate decisions may be derived, and translate these conclusions to non-ideal scenarios by assessing current practices or offering new ones.

However, it has been noted that such a hypothetical contract cannot easily justify political institutions for it 'is not merely a pale form of an actual contract; it is no contract at all'.[101] This argument presents the more serious version of the quip according to which a hypothetical contract is not worth the paper that it is not written on. Though theories of an explicit or implied contract are prone to difficulties of their own, they enabled the contract itself to serve as a separate justification for demanding obedience. But when we place an ideal contract in place of an actual one, we are also substituting idealized (free of coercion, endowed with full information, etc.) contracting agents for the actual consent of individuals. And, of course, the most difficult part is what one may call the de-idealizing stage—expecting the consent of the idealized individuals to bind the actual individuals. This is what Rawls referred to as 'the problem of stability'.[102] The problem of stability is indeed a problem, D'Agostino explains, because an idealized social and political theory is based on a state of affairs that is somewhat

---

[93] Rawls (n 91 above) 6.
[94] ibid 84. For a critique arguing that this agenda, desirable though it may be, does not flow from his Rawls's theory see B Barry, *The Liberal Theory of Justice* (OUP: Oxford, 1979) 57.
[95] Gough (n 86 above) 183.
[96] Castiglione (n 88 above).
[97] Rawls (n 91 above) 11 [emphasis added]; also p 104.
[98] Dworkin (n 28 above) ch 1 and (though reaching a radically different conclusion) D Gauthier, *Morals by Agreement* (Clarendon: Oxford, 1984).
[99] Ackerman (n 50 above) 24, 168.
[100] T Nagel, *The View from Nowhere* (OUP: New York, 1986).
[101] R Dworkin, 'The Original Position' (1973) 40 U of Chi L Rev 500, 501.
[102] J Rawls, *Political Liberalism* (Columbia UP: New York, 1993) 14–15.

different from the one that exists at the moment.[103] However, if there is too great a distance between the psychological, ideological or moral construction of our idealized surrogates and that of actual stakeholders, we risk creating a form of 'puerile utopianism'.[104]

Moreover, if the metaphor of a contract is employed simply as shorthand to judge whether social institutions or conventional morality itself are just (and by that it is meant to ask whether they are rational, egalitarian and publicly defensible) why not inquire if they *are* rational, egalitarian and publicly defensible, avoiding the problematic use of the contractarian terminology altogether?[105]

It has been suggested, therefore, that 'hypothetical' contractarianism constitutes such a clear retreat from genuine consent theory that it should be categorized differently, as 'quality of government theory', for example, since its objective is not to base duties on an individual's actual choice, but rather to observe if governments are sufficiently just, good, useful or responsive.[106] Can one conclude, then, that a methodology that is based on the hypothetical contract is not contractarian at all?

Despite suggestions to the contrary,[107] Dworkin does view Rawls's choice of a contractarian methodology as significant. According to Dworkin, Rawls understands the contract to indicate a halfway point in a deeper rights-based political theory, envisaging the argument as going *through* rather than *from* the contract.[108] The hypothetical original position suggests a situation where all parties have veto power over decisions that are to be reached. It is true that in that position parties may impose duties on each other or choose to adopt certain goals in the exercise of their judgment of their own self-interest. But this is very different from a supposition that a theory is duty- or goal-based. Contract theory, Dworkin concludes, 'seems a natural development of [a rights-based] theory'.[109]

2 Rights, Obligations and Welfare in Social Contract Theory

Early contract theory gives very little attention to moral theory and the implications on rights and duties. The little that may be deduced from the writings, however, suggests problematic consequences for the marriage of rights and social contract theory. While men in Hobbes's state of nature enjoy 'naked

---

[103] F D'Agostino, 'The Promise of Social Welfare: New Foundations for the Social Contract' (draft, copy with author 2007).
[104] ibid.
[105] T Nagel, 'Rawls on Justice' (1973) 82 Philosophical Review 220, 224.
[106] AJ Simmons, 'Political Consent' in Morris (n 83 above) 121, 133–34; also Hampton (n 76 above) 273; H Pitkin, 'Obligation and Consent—I' (1965) 59 Am Pol Sci Rev 990; B Barry, *Justice as Impartiality* (Clarendon: Oxford, 1995) 56.
[107] Hampton (n 76 above) 4.
[108] Dworkin (n 101 above) 519; but cf J Rawls, 'Justice as Fairness: Political Not Metaphysical' (1985) 14 Philosophy and Public Affairs 223, 236.
[109] Dworkin (n 101 above) 526.

liberties' (ie rights not paralleled by duties of others to respect or facilitate the choices made[110]) the concept of obligation is introduced with the creation of society, through the act of renouncing or transferring the right.[111] When the act is completed, rights in Hobbes are 'mere shadows of duties'.[112] Gauthier goes as far as asserting that 'Law and duty, not right, is the foundation of Locke's ethics',[113] and Simmons, while sympathetic to this position, prefers to envisage rights and duties in Locke as 'roughly coextensive'.[114]

Similarly, after declaring that 'in the state of nature...I owe nothing to those to whom I have promised nothing', Rousseau asserts that justice is achieved when convention and law allow 'to unite rights with duties'.[115] If understood literally, this would indeed imply 'no private wills to "reconcile" to the common interest...and thus *no need of consent, no need of contract*'.[116] This is directly linked to Rousseau's (perhaps notorious) suggestion that forcing one to obey the general will is tantamount to forcing one to be free, and that is done through the contract.[117] Such a position compelled a sympathetic Benjamin Constant to concede that Rousseau has thus unwittingly 'provided the theoretical support for despotism'.[118]

Moving closer to the central theme of this book, particular reference should be made to the attitude of one of the prominent social contract scholars, John Locke, to the issue of poor relief. Despite the fact that not all social contract writers have published manuscripts on welfare programmes, there is reason to view Locke's 1697 'Proposal for Reform of the Poor Laws' as more representative than anecdotal. The document, referred to as 'appalling'[119] and 'draconian'[120] by contemporary writers, blames poverty on 'the growth of the poor' and 'the relaxation of discipline and corruption of manners'. The proposal adds that provision for able-bodied poor should be granted only after children over the age of three will be separated from their families, so as to allow both mothers and children

---

[110] A Harel, 'Theories of Rights' in M Golding, W Edmundson (eds), *Blackwell's Guide to Philosophy of Law and Legal Theory* (Blackwell: Oxford, 2005) 191.
[111] Hobbes (n 76 above) ch 14; See Hampton (n 76 above) 51–56; D Gauthier, 'Hobbes's Social Contract' in Morris (n 83 above) 59.
[112] H Warrender, *The Political Philosophy of Hobbes* (OUP: Oxford, 1957) 19. For a critique of Hobbes' concept of obligation see Hampton (n 76 above) 55; D Gauthier, *The Logic of the Leviathan* (OUP: Oxford, 1969, repr OUP: Oxford, 2000) 60–61.
[113] D Gauthier, 'Why Ought One Obey God?' in Morris (n 83 above) 73, 79.
[114] Simmons (n 79 above) 68.
[115] Rousseau (n 78 above) II.vi.
[116] P Riley, 'A Possible Explanation of Rousseau's General Will' in Morris (n 76 above) 167, 175 [emphasis added].
[117] Rousseau (n 78 above) I.vii, II.iv.
[118] Cited in J Jennings, 'Rousseau, Social Contract and the Modern Leviathan' in Boucher and Kelly (n 81 above) 115, 118.
[119] M Cranston, *John Locke* (Longmans: London, 1957) 425.
[120] G Parry, 'Individuality, Politics and the Critique of Paternalism in John Locke' (1964) 12 *Political Studies* 163, 175.

to work. Locke's view of poverty as connected to moral depravity, as opposed to economic causes, may be seen as a precursor to some contemporary views.[121]

I suggest that this position, though extreme in its manifestation, is but a natural consequence of the juxtaposition of 'natural' individualism and equality along with 'civil' duties and responsibilities, two features that characterize social contract theories.[122] The union of the two justifies harsh consequences on the poor by blaming them for their own condition. The reference to natural equality of all people leads to the conclusion that, for Locke, if 'virtuous citizens seem to prosper; the poor, then, must be mostly vicious'.[123] This starting-gate equality 'cloaks the status quo with legitimacy through a process of mystification'.[124] If the poor require something from society, the axiomatic equality would show its harsh side,[125] requiring that responsibilities be levelled equally too. The emphasis on obligations and duties throughout made this final theoretical phase possible.

How much of this analysis remains true when considering contemporary social contract theory? For John Rawls, for example, the principles of justice that are the object of the original agreement govern the assignment of rights and duties but 'must not be confused with the principles which apply to individuals and their actions in particular circumstances'.[126] This 'statement of purpose' is of importance when one is confronted with attempts to rely on contractarian methodology to justify conventional reciprocity. Rawls distinguishes the question of a theory of justice from the secondary question of morality, ie how actors, from individuals to governments, may and should act within an ongoing scheme and how we are to assess their conduct and character.[127]

It is becoming clear, then, that a strict balance between rights and duties cannot be derived from an ideal, Rawlsian-style contractarian theory. Rawlsian methodology does not suggest a background mechanism that pairs rights and responsibilities in day-to-day decision-making. Rather, it places the contract as an investigative tool that assesses the principles governing institutions and disappears once rights and duties are in a place that is deemed just. In other words, contractarian thinking comes into play in a much earlier (logical) stage, and does not offer a guide to policy-making at administrative levels. Distancing himself from the idea of seeing rights as dependent on obligations, Rawls unequivocally states that he views individuals as 'self-originating sources of valid claims' who 'have weight apart from being derived from duties or obligations specified by the political conception of justice'.[128] But what 'valid claims' do individuals have, and what obligations can legitimately be demanded from them?

---

[121] CB Macpherson, *The Political Theory of Possessive Individualism* (OUP: Oxford, 1962) 222.
[122] For a similar position see Parry (n 120 above) 175.
[123] Simmons (n 79 above) 334–35.
[124] Barry (n 42 above) 40.
[125] J Dunn, *The Political Thought of John Locke* (CUP: Cambridge, 1969) 227.
[126] Rawls (n 91 above) 47.
[127] Pogge (n 92 above) 22–26.
[128] Rawls (n 108 above) 242.

According to Rawls, justice as fairness starts with the premise that all primary goods are to be equally distributed. This situation serves as a 'baseline' for assessing the justice of institutional arrangements. By granting the first principle of equal liberty logical priority over the second, difference principle, Rawls asserts that men are not permitted to improve their socio-economic situation by surrendering fundamental liberties. Thus not only slavery is forbidden (even when one wishes to sell oneself to an owner) but also the selling of voting rights, for example.[129] This claim may be seen as an abstracted version of the 'illegitimate conditions' doctrine that will be discussed below. Within Rawls's theory it creates a hierarchy: basic liberties may be constrained only when they conflict with other basic liberties, while other primary goods must give way for the sake of those basic liberties.

It is not entirely clear what liberties should be included in the list of basic liberties and, as noted below, some have suggested including the right to welfare in its ambit. Rawls himself, in his *Political Liberalism*, suggests that 'free choice of occupation and a social minimum covering citizens's basic needs count as constitutional essentials',[130] the implication being that these goods are to be regarded as primary goods that cannot be distributed differentially amongst individuals.

It was argued above that contractarian methodology may support non-egalitarian consequences through reference to a state of nature that included an egalitarian premise. Rawls's construction, however, differs substantially by not abandoning the ideal of equality at the original position.[131] The justice of any social institution is ascertained by regarding equal liberty as a substantive, as opposed to an historical, baseline. Indeed, Scanlon argues that Rawls's acceptance of equality as the first solution to the problem of justice suggests that the difference principle marks the limits of acceptable inequality.[132] As equal participants in a system of social cooperation, the members of society have a prima facie claim to an equal share of the benefits that society creates.[133] A serious onus is thus placed on those advancing a structure which exhibits non-egalitarian foundations.

When compared to the abundance of writing on Rawls's treatment of equality, it is surprising to note how little attention is given to the notion of self-respect which is central both to Rawls's theory and to the arguments regarding the possibility of advancing an argument in favour of a strong right to welfare. Rawls states that self-respect is 'perhaps the most important primary good'.[134] It has been suggested that the good of self-respect is a central element in the theory of

---

[129] Rawls (n 91 above) 55.
[130] Rawls (n 102 above) 230.
[131] Dworkin understands equality in Rawls's theory to be a precondition of the contract and not, like other rights, a consequence of it. He states that though Rawls's basic assumption may be contested in many ways, 'it cannot not be denied in the name of a more radical concept of equality, because none exists'—Dworkin (n 101 above) 532–33.
[132] T Scanlon, 'Rawls's Theory of Justice' (1973) 121 U of Pennsylvania L Rev 1020, 1064.
[133] T Scanlon, *What We Owe to Each Other* (Harvard UP: Cambridge MA, 1998) 228.
[134] Rawls (n 91 above) 386.

justice as fairness and principles advanced by the theory are but means towards enhancing that objective.[135] Self-respect is understood by Rawls to encompass both individual and societal features. Indeed, it is woven together with equality through the conceptualization of the contract:

> On the contract interpretation treating men as ends in themselves implies at the very least treating them in accordance with the principles to which they would consent in an original position of equality... The contract view as such defines a sense in which men are to be treated as ends and not as means only.[136]

So would the principles governing the distribution of rights and duties by social institutions favour a right to welfare? In similar vein to arguments presented in the previous section, it has been argued that the interpretation that rejects social and economic rights from the principles of justice is an 'arbitrary exclusion of economic factors from constraints definitive of liberty' and one that is contradicted by Rawls's own theory.[137] Indeed, Rawls notes that the 'parties in the original position would wish to avoid at almost any cost the social conditions that undermine self-respect'.[138] This leads Frank Michelman to argue that welfare rights should not only be considered as primary goods guaranteed under the difference principle,[139] but can also be included as part of the right to equal liberty.[140]

Though the contractual methodology may find difficulties accommodating a multivalued analysis of deprivation (especially noted for the lack of attention granted to people with disabilities),[141] it is often more helpful, especially along the Rawlsian trajectory, when having to address matters of income and wealth. At the very least, in this respect the Rawlsian version of the social contract meets welfare state theories. D'Agostino suggests a process that is not too distant from Rawls's 'reflective equilibrium', the dynamic that is to repeatedly link the ideal, hypothetical contract with the real world:

> No contract legitimates unless it delivers, for those who do not already have it, the social-contractual capacities on which the legitimacy of its terms in fact depends. This means that it is the responsibility of the state to ensure that those social circumstances are progressively realized in which all those capacities which are directly involved in public reasoning about the terms of a just social arrangement are themselves progressively delivered to its citizens.[142]

---

[135] Michelman (n 61 above) 990; Barry (n 94 above) 31.
[136] Rawls (n 91 above) 156–57.
[137] N Daniels, 'Equal Liberty and Equal Worth of Liberty' in N Daniels (ed), *Reading Rawls* (Blackwell: Oxford, 1975) 253.
[138] Rawls (n 91 above) 386.
[139] Michelman (n 61 above) 976–88.
[140] ibid 989.
[141] M Nussbaum, 'Beyond the Social Contract' 24 *Tanner Lectures on Human Values* (University of Utah Press: Salt Lake City, 2004).
[142] D'Agostino (n 103 above) 11.

On this interpretation, social contract philosophy should not reach conclusions that are dramatically opposed to the capabilities approach, for example, which is often suggested as its preferable alternative.[143]

Thomas Pogge advances the same agenda from a different angle. Recognizing the difficulty of going against the grain of an established Anglo-American tradition that denies the plausibility of positive obligations, Pogge suggests that individuals have a negative claim not to be made victims of unjust institutions. He asserts that laissez-faire institutions prior to the New Deal were unjust since they engendered severe disadvantages, resulting in people being 'impoverished (rather than merely poor) [and] were starved (rather than merely starving)'.[144] More than a sophisticated terminological restatement, Pogge's claim should be understood as a call for a more developed awareness. In their seminal article, Felstiner, Abel and Sarat tagged this stage as 'blaming'. It is preceded by 'naming'—the task of saying to oneself that a particular experience has been injurious.[145] Due to a myriad of external factors, they explain, many shipyard workers did not attribute their asbestosis to their place of work. When public perception changed, asbestosis 'became an acknowledged "disease" *and* the basis of a claim for compensation'.[146] They tentatively suggest that the 'cult of competence [and] individualism' has slowed the process that consists of recognizing the blame that may be attributed to the acts of other individuals and social institutions.[147] When one moves to blaming, the perceived injurious experience is turned into a grievance and, moreover, one that targets an individual or a social entity. If one recalls how, after years of accepted practices, blame was suddenly attributed to (and converted into legal charges against) power plants, cigarette companies, segregated schools, slum landlords and police searches, it becomes patently clear that the attribution of blame changes with new moral colouration, insights and information, and Pogge's assertion is suddenly seen as following an already familiar path.

3 Two Different Intersections of Social Contract and Welfare State

To what extent is social contract methodology reconcilable with traditional welfare state tenets? Some have argued that welfare conditionality can be understood to complement the way TH Marshall conceived welfare state social

---

[143] ibid; also R Salais, 'Towards a Capability Approach' in J Zeitlin and DM Trubek (eds), *Governing Work and Welfare in a New Economy* (OUP: Oxford, 2003) 317. For a capabilities approach critique of the social contract see Nussbaum (n 141 above).

[144] Pogge (n 92 above) 35; Incidentally, Rawls mentions that he does not wish to take part in the debate between proponents of positive and negative liberty—Rawls (n 91 above) 176.

[145] W Felstiner, R Abel and A Sarat, 'The Emergence and Transformation of Disputes: Naming, Blaiming, Claiming...' (1980) 15 L and Soc Rev 631.

[146] ibid 636.

[147] ibid 652.

citizenship and state obligations.[148] Against this, critics have objected that welfare contractualism leads directly to a moralistic political discourse that violates the rights of the vulnerable and the socially excluded in a discriminatory fashion. They have noted that the concept of 'contract', which implies negotiation, real choice and consent, is inapplicable in these cases and serves solely as a guise for a disciplinary social policy that too readily employs sanctions. These sanctions find putative justification in the language of reciprocity and responsibility. The Marshallian model of welfare, it is thus argued, was based on citizenship entitlements and the principle that protection and security should be provided according to need. The new welfare arrangement, by contrast, entails the progressive displacement of citizenship rights by entitlements contingent upon reciprocal obligations.[149] The result is that current debates on welfare are conducted in a language alien to traditional welfarist social policy analysis — dependency instead of poverty and inequality, with a focus on changing people's behaviour rather than altering the distribution of resources in society.[150]

While it is probably true that Rawls is responsible for the renewed interest in contractarian methodology, this does not imply that all subsequent commentators followed his lead. Hampton rightly recognizes two distinct strands of modern contractarian writings, each identifiable with a different ancestor. While writers including Rawls and Scanlon refer to Kant's approach, Gauthier[151] and Buchanan[152] are heavily influenced by Hobbes.[153] All are bound together by the understanding that 'the first order of moral business is the definition of social justice',[154] but their approaches can hardly be more distinct. I shall focus here on Scanlon and Gauthier as offering representative theories of each type and, more specifically, on one element that is both fundamental in their writings and will lead to the discussion in the following section. I refer to the problem of the baseline.

Scanlon, following Rawls, understands morality as a constructivist endeavour that seeks to derive a set of rules from a fair procedure. This fair procedure includes the equality and fair placement of the parties in relation to one another, representing their equal intrinsic value.[155] Scanlon accepts the Rawlsian idea

---

[148] TH Marshall, 'Citizenship and Social Class' in *Class, Citizenship and Social Development* (Doubleday: New York, 1964) 65; S White, 'Social Rights and the Social Contract' (2000) 30 British Journal of Political Science 507; A Deacon, 'An Ethic of Mutual Responsibility? Towards a Fuller Justification for Conditionality in Welfare' in C Beem and L Mead (eds), *Welfare Reform and Political Theory* (Sage: New York, 2005) 127.
[149] ibid 240.
[150] P Vincent-Jones, *The New Public Contracting: Regulation, Responsiveness, Relationality* (OUP: Oxford, 2006) 231.
[151] Gauthier (n 98 above).
[152] JM Buchanan, *The Limits of Liberty* (Chicago UP: Chicago, 1975).
[153] J Hampton, 'Two Faces of Contractarian Thought' in P Vallentyne (ed), *Contractarianism and Rational Choice* (CUP: Cambridge, 1991) 31, 51–52.
[154] Rawls (n 91 above) 47.
[155] ibid 51–2.

that emphasizes the connection between self-respect and the requirement to treat individuals as ends, but suggests that such an objective would be better served under a different formula.[156] But though Scanlon is at pains to distinguish his Rescue Principle from Rawls's Difference Principle,[157] it would be surprising if the two would yield different results. The reason for the common conclusions lies in their common premises—the priority given to the worst off and their egalitarian baseline. And, indeed, while Scanlon differs from Rawls in preferring that individuals choose just principles while holding full knowledge of their situation, he balances this fact with the requirement that just principles must be chosen from an impartial standpoint and requires individuals to look at matters of social justice from another person's point of view, as a remedy to their own bias.[158]

These constraints are quite foreign to David Gauthier. Gauthier agrees with Rawls that principles of social justice are reached through a process of rational choice,[159] but finds inspiration for his theory of morality in Hobbes's version of self-interested rational choice. Gauthier refers to the concept of a baseline as an initial bargaining position. Recognizing the proper baseline for Gauthier is understandably of utmost importance.[160] Gauthier agrees with the claim made by another Hobbesian contractualist, James Buchanan, that 'absent such a starting point, there is simply no way of initiating meaningful contracts actually or conceptually'.[161] This baseline incorporates the Lockean proviso that 'enough and as good left in common for others'. Gauthier understands the proviso to mean that the situation of others *must not be worsened due to one's interaction with them*.[162] The proviso for Gauthier is the kernel from which stem not only moral theory, but also the structure of rights themselves.[163] And we can learn more about Gauthier's (and Buchanan's) approach when considering what is absent from it—the idea of equality. Famously (and controversially), Gauthier states that:

The rich man may feast on caviar and champagne, while the poor woman starves at his gate. And she may not even take the crumbs from his table, if that would deprive him of his pleasure in feeding them to his birds. Distressing as this situation may seem, we must not be mislead by it. We think of rich and poor in a social context, and we think that his wealth and her poverty are in some way related.[164]

---

[156] T Scanlon, 'Contractualism and Utilitarianism' in A Sen and B Williams (eds), *Utilitarianism and Beyond* (CUP: Cambridge, 1982) 103.

[157] ibid 226–8.

[158] Scanlon (n 156 above) 117.

[159] Gauthier (n 98 above) 5.

[160] Stephan Holmes and Cass Sunstein argue that Gauthier's thesis must justify or assume the starting point from which the bargaining parties set out. The failure to do so, they claim, is 'an enduring problem for those using social contract theory to demonstrate their moral conclusions'—S Holmes and C Sunstein, *The Cost of Rights* (WW Norton: London, 1999) 177 n 2.

[161] Buchanan (n 152 above) 24.

[162] Gauthier (n 98 above) 203.

[163] ibid 209.

[164] ibid 218.

And it is quite clear that Gauthier *does not* view the rich man's wealth and the poor woman's poverty as related and therefore finds that there is no violation of the proviso. Notions of solidarity and equal citizenship do not enter the analysis.

It may be worth noting that such an approach is diametrically opposed to the position proposed by Pogge and Scanlon, for example. Scanlon notes that:

if you are presented with a situation in which you can prevent something very bad from happening, or alleviate someone's dire plight, by making only a slight... sacrifice, then it would be wrong not to do so. It is very plausible to suppose that this principle, which I will call the Rescue Principle, is one that could not reasonably be rejected.[165]

Gauthier's stance is in line with his critique of Rawls's egalitarian construction. While Rawls's methodology separates an individual's contribution and her expectation to any return from society, Gauthier's different choice of a baseline leads him to a different conclusion altogether. Since we determine if one's position has improved or worsened by comparing it to a situation where the other party to the interaction was absent, Gauthier finds no reason *not* to assess one's contribution when determining one's entitlements.[166] This conclusion is a direct result of Gauthier's insistence on the market as the moral-free zone that serves as the conceptual starting point for the analysis.[167] As in Hobbes's *Leviathan*, Gauthier's baseline for analysis of the principles of justice is the state of nature and therefore a similar conclusion is reached, one that can be characterized (though Gauthier would probably object) as 'justice is nothing but the advantage of the stronger'.[168] Thus, Gauthier's only constraint on the potentially predatory features of the market is the proviso, which is indifferent to matters of social and economic inequality.[169]

The implications of Gauthier's methodology on the limits of conditioning welfare rights should be apparent. Gauthier finds that 'animals, the unborn, congenitally handicapped and defective fall beyond the pale of a morality tied to mutuality' because there is no 'expected benefit' from them.[170] Those who benefit from the principles of justice in a particular society are expected to give in return. Due to the fact that in the absence of the state (or the social security system) welfare beneficiaries would have been worse off, *any* conditions attached to welfare benefits are legitimate. This is, of course, an analogous claim to the market-based argument that individuals always have the option of rejecting the offer (of benefits along with their conditions) and thus they would not be worse off when compared to the situation that no offer was made. Reciprocity here is

---

[165] Scanlon (n 133 above) 224. For Pogge's position see text to note 144 above.
[166] Gauthier (n 98 above) 258–9.
[167] ibid 106 ff.
[168] Barry (n 106 above) 39–42.
[169] P Vallentyne, 'Gauthier's Three Projects' in Vallentyne (n 153 above) 1, 7.
[170] Gauthier (n 98 above) 268.

seen as exemplified in a form of economic exchange.[171] Again, Rawls's rejection of a theory of strict compliance leads him to a different conclusion:

> It is sometimes contended that contract doctrine entails that private society is the ideal, at least when the division of advantages satisfies suitable standard of reciprocity. But this is not so, as the notion of a well-ordered society shows.[172]

Though this sub-section was intended mainly to portray the difference between egalitarian and non-egalitarian contractarian theories, one remark may be offered as a contribution to the substantive debate. Gauthier simply assumes that the rich would be better off and that the poor would be worse off in the absence of the welfare state, but that is far from obvious. Ironically, Gauthier's reliance on Hobbes should be expected to lead him to view the alternative to the state as a war of all against all, where the rich have much more to lose.[173]

4 Manipulation

The controversial title of 'manipulation' for this sub-section does not suggest a diversion from some putatively 'true' contractarian theory. Rather, it addresses a transformation in the usage of social contract theory from a highly abstract, open-ended political philosophy to a controversial, concrete social policy.[174] The first of these two approaches may be characterized as the 'macro-level' social contract, while the second may be referred to as the 'micro-level' social contract.[175]

Macro-level social contracts have been the object of interest for most of the chapter to this point, employing the idea of a hypothetical agreement as a mechanism to legitimize social structures and institutions. In a sense, the macro-level contract serves as shorthand for the *kinds of argument* that can be justified, and the categories of principles that may be referred to. But due to its diffuse nature it may lead, without compromising its premises, to an almost indefinite number of distinct conclusions. Therefore, the debate that is held at this level of abstraction is only of limited interest to our present study. It is when contractarian methodology is applied in a more contextualised fashion that it begins to interest lawyers in general and those concerned with welfare legislation in particular. For when the macro-level contract paradigm is reshaped towards a micro-level contract that presumes to encapsulate the relationship between public authorities and their clients, the specific and concrete obligations that are seen as evolving from the contract draw attention and criticism.

---

[171] cf A Gewirth (n 36 above) 75.
[172] Rawls (n 91 above) 458.
[173] L Murphy and T Nagel, *The Myth of Ownership* (OUP: New York, 2002) 15–16.
[174] N Fraser and L Gordon, 'Civil Citizenship Against Social Citizenship? On the Ideology of Contract Versus Charity' in B van Steenbergen (ed), *The Condition of Citizenship* (Sage: London, 1994) 90.
[175] See M Freedland and D King, 'Contractual Governance and Illiberal Contracts' (2003) 27 Cambridge J of Economics 465.

This transformation has become quite popular, perhaps due to the close relations between the macro-level and micro-level social contract paradigms, and has become especially interesting with the incorporation of the notion of reciprocity. Reciprocity refers to the idea that something should be received in return for something given, whether in the immediate or in the more distant future, as long as there is 'a proportionate return for goods received'.[176] As noted, reciprocity is a fundamental notion in modern social contract writings as well as in welfare-to-work debates.

And yet, it should be made clear that this approach is relevant to the study of the relationship between the welfare claimant and the state (or state agency) only by analogy. Thus, Philip Selznick, while stressing the importance of values such as reciprocity and interdependence, makes clear that their implications must be open-ended.[177] Gutmann and Thompson point to reciprocity as a central norm in regulating public reason.[178] But when discussing workfare schemes, the authors reject the possibility of applying principles of individual responsibility and reciprocity on a localized and temporal basis. Problematically, however, when advancing their own position for 'fair workfare', the authors suddenly adopt a much narrower view of reciprocity, one that is more concerned with people's 'obligation to contribute their fair share'[179] than with reasoning on mutually accepted terms. This position leads them to suggest that a policy that forces parents to work, even if they forego welfare benefits, is justified despite being 'close to forced labor'.[180]

What, indeed, is the impact of social contract theory on the format of welfare-to-work programmes? Social contract has clearly become a dominant social policy paradigm both in America and in Britain, especially in the field of welfare reform.[181] Even the rhetoric is indicative of this prominence. Thus, in Britain, Frank Field, Minister for Welfare Reform until 1998, identified the source of discontent over welfare programmes as the rupture in Britain's shared moral framework, characterized as 'a breakdown of a contract'.[182] Consultation over welfare reform began with the 1998 Green Paper 'New Ambitions for Our Country: A New Contract for Welfare' which, indeed, expressed the future relationship between state welfare and individual entitlement as 'a new welfare contract'.[183] This was followed by Command Papers entitled 'A New Contract for Welfare'.[184]

---

[176] A Gutmann and D Thompson, *Democracy and Disagreement* (Harvard UP: Cambridge MA, 1996) 55, Rawls (n 91 above) 88–90.
[177] P Selznick, *The Moral Commonwealth* (U of California: Berkeley, 1994) 362.
[178] Gutmann and Thompson (n 176 above) ch 2.
[179] ibid 300.
[180] ibid.
[181] L Lundy, 'From Welfare to Work? Social Security and Unemployment' in N Harris (ed), *Social Security Law in Context* (OUP: Oxford, 2000) 291, 293.
[182] F Field, *Making Welfare Work* (Institute of Community Studies: London, 1995) 26.
[183] DSS, *New Ambitions for Our Country: A New Contract for Welfare* (n 15 above) ch 11 para 5.
[184] DSS, *A New Contract for Welfare: Principles into Practice* (n 15 above); DEE, *A New Contract for Welfare: Gateway to Work* (n 15 above).

And the House of Commons Employment Committee perceived the Jobseeker's Agreement as a 'formalised contract [between the claimant and] the *taxpayer*'.[185] In the United States, as mentioned, the welfare reform campaign started with the Republican proposal named 'Contract with America'. But the contract, which suggested cuts in Medicare, Medicaid, food stamps and Earned Income Tax Credit was 'signed' with the American poor rather than with the general populous.[186]

Welfare policy was portrayed as faced with a dichotomy of contract versus charity, 'discrete contractual exchanges of equivalents, on the one hand, and unreciprocated, unilateral charity, on the other',[187] and was thus coerced into a contractual cast. Contractual ideology is cited as a justification for harsher conditions on welfare programmes because, paradoxically, only this paradigm relieves the stigma of charity and the receipt of 'something for nothing'.[188]

In similar vein to the House of Commons Employment Committee Report mentioned above, Eugene Bardach observes that 'behind the welfare reform thinking of the past decade is an implicit belief that recipients made a social contract'.[189] In both we can detect how the macro-level contract and the micro-level contract are fused. On the one hand, Bardach's use of the term 'social contract' and of fictitious methodology ('an implicit belief') implies that we are not concerned with real contracts, but rather with some form of hypothetical contract. And yet, a micro-level contract construction is implied by the fact that only welfare recipients are mentioned and that they are assumed to have 'made' a social contract for the purpose of receiving benefits. Likewise, Vincent-Jones sees the importance of the contractual paradigm in drawing attention to the quality of the relations 'between government and the governed',[190] but also goes on to discuss the use of the regular, legal contract as a technique of behavioural control, as in the case of the 'jobseeker's agreement' that claimants have to sign with the employment office.[191] The contractual approach to welfare reform, especially in the field of unemployment, is thus manifested in macro-level and in micro-level formations. From Contract with America to an Individual Responsibility Plan,[192] from the various New Deals to the Jobseeker's Agreement[193]—the contractual pronouncements are widespread. What are the themes that are emphasized as a result of adopting this contractarian welfare policy?

---

[185] House of Commons Sessions 1995–6, Employment Committee Second Report *The Right to Work/Workfare* (HMSO: London, 13 Feb 1996) xxiv cited in D King, *In the Name of Liberalism* (OUP: Oxford, 1998) 248.
[186] C Noble, *Welfare as We Know It* (OUP: Oxford, 1997) 124–5.
[187] Fraser and Gordon (n 174 above) 91.
[188] Handler and Hasenfeld (n 4 above) 168.
[189] E Bardach, 'Implementing a Paternalist Welfare' in L Mead (ed), *The New Paternalism* (Brookings: NY, 1991) 251, 259.
[190] P Vincent-Jones, 'Contractual Governance' (2000) 20 OJLS 317, 332.
[191] ibid 345–7.
[192] PRWORA s 408(b). See discussion in Chapter 3, section B.1.d.
[193] Jobseekers Act 1995 s 1. See discussion in Chapter 3, section B.2.b.

The Social Contract of the Modern Welfare State 45

An overarching theme is that of individualism, the 'personalisation of risk rather than its collective assumption by the state'.[194] Quite evidently, individuation of the problem of unemployment and poverty fits well with a contractual welfare approach. Transforming the traditional relationship that was based on the concept of citizenship to one associated with consumerism, or 'consumer-citizenship'[195] brings to the fore values such as choice, responsibility and reciprocity. Pierre Rosanvallon, a prominent French advocate of contractarian social policy, also encourages dispensing with statistical categories such as income level, cultural capital and professional status. He explains that 'it is no longer collective identities that have to be described, but individual trajectories'.[196] As Vincent-Jones rightly notes:

> The use of contractual mechanisms both draws upon and reinforces these notions of agency and choice... contracts render individuals responsible for their predicament... in ways that differ significantly from the governance of relations by hierarchal authority.[197]

But this approach leads to policies that are incongruent with welfare state principles and, indeed, are not dissimilar to those outlined as characterizing poor law programmes.[198] These traits of current welfare-to-work programmes will be discussed at some length in the upcoming two chapters. I close this chapter by briefly introducing them, and the impact that contractual welfare has on these themes.

i) Deserving and Undeserving Poor

The American TANF programme has been praised as the 'triumph' of the familiar distinction between deserving and undeserving poor.[199] The characterization of an individual as deserving or undeserving is seen as crucial for targeting the proper approach to each individual. In general, the deserving are those who, like the retired elderly, are now legitimately excused from the labour force. The undeserving are the able bodied adults who are expected to work.[200] But while the contractual policy prides itself on granting treatment to individuals and not to categories of people,[201] the most fundamental categorization—that

---

[194] T Carney and G Ramia, *From Rights to Management: Contract, New Public Management and Employment Services* (Kluwer Law: The Hague, 2002) 165; H Adriaansens, 'Citizenship, Work and Welfare' in B van Steenbergen (ed), *The Condition of Citizenship* (Sage: London, 1994) 66.
[195] N Harris, 'The Welfare State, Social Security and Social Citizenship Rights' in Harris (n 181 above) 3, 27.
[196] Rosanvallon (n 38 above) 209.
[197] Vincent-Jones (n 150 above) 233.
[198] Even Lawrence Mead recognizes the similarity, though he emphasizes the differences— L Mead, 'The Rise of Paternalism' in Mead (n 189 above) 1, 6–11.
[199] A Wax, 'Something for Nothing' (2003) 52 Emory LJ 1, 2.
[200] Handler and Hasenfeld (n 4 above) 70.
[201] See DSS, *A New Contract for Welfare: Principles into Practice* (n 15 above) ch 3.

which distinguishes those who 'can' from those who 'cannot'—is retained and, moreover, becomes central in the modern agenda of reciprocity.[202]

A fascinating, though anecdotal, similarity to poor law policy is revealed in this context. Joyce Appleby cites the motto for the workhouse policy as 'work for those who can labour; punishment for those who will not; and bread for those who cannot'.[203] Tony Blair, a few centuries later, repeated this statement in almost exact form, minus the middle phrase, when he stated: 'work for those who can, security for those who cannot'.[204] It is open to investigation, however, if this omission is also manifested in the policy itself. Tocqueville expressed his reservations about an endeavour that presumes to detect 'nuances that separate unmerited misfortune from an adversity produced by vice',[205] and, if the public debate concerning the sincerity of claims for disability benefits is any indication, it would seem that the force of this observation has not diminished over the years.

ii) Detecting Fraud

The perennial problem of combating fraud has received a central platform in contemporary welfare reform. Governments drafted lengthy reports and papers on combating fraud as an integral part of the welfare structure.[206] Mass advertising and media campaigns against fraud reinforced the negative image of recipients and the benefit system. Freefone services were offered to report cheats. It should be noted that the factual basis for government focus on benefit fraud has already raised some concern, and some commentators have assessed the government's use of evidence on fraud as fraudulent itself.[207]

On the ideological level, reciprocity is posited as the normative base for a structure that should deter freeloaders, thus returning to the ethos of deserving and undeserving to determine who should be outside the circle of cooperation and exchange.[208] Contract here encapsulates, identifies and justifies the rules of the game as well as the interaction between the state and its citizens. Thus, the British government celebrated an 'enhanced sense of responsibility that lies at the heart of the new welfare contract, with people not only taking more personal responsibility... but also more collective responsibility for policing the new system and preventing fraud'.[209] Furthermore, the traditional libertarian characterization of

---

[202] A Wax, 'A Reciprocal Welfare Programme' (2001) 8 Va J Soc Pol 477, 512.
[203] J Appleby, *Economic Thought and Ideology in Seventeenth Century England* (Princeton UP: Princeton, 1978) 131.
[204] T Blair, 'Introduction' in *A New Contract for Welfare: Principles into Practice* (n 15 above) 1. Rosanvallon (n 38 above) 13–14.
[205] A de Tocquevile, *Memoirs on Pauperism* (1835 rpnt, Dee: Chicago, 1997 tran S Dreshcer) 56.
[206] See DSS, *Beating Fraud is Everyone's Business* (Cm 4012, 1997).
[207] A Sinfield, 'The Goals of Social Policy: Context and Change' in J Andersen and others (eds), *The Changing Face of Welfare* (Policy: Bristol, 2005) 15, 16.
[208] Wax (n 202 above) 483–84.
[209] DSS (n 206 above) ch 11 para 6.

the interaction between the state and citizen has been associated with suspicion on the part of the citizen towards government, not with such a government attitude towards its citizens. But if relationships are based on a market-model, one who does not expect the worst from her partner to the contract is failing a duty of care and responsibility. Indeed, 'in a society all too ready to translate political difficulties into psychiatric problems and to see human intercourse as a variant of economic exchange... consent theory fits comfortably: too comfortably'.[210]

iii) The Quid-pro-Quo Relationship

The strict contractual relationship between the employment service and the claimant is almost a natural consequence of contractual welfare. Reciprocity-based policies are a sine qua non in most welfare-to-work programmes, clearly exhibited in workfare schemes. The first scheme that earned the appellation 'workfare' the Community Work Experience Program in the United States was introduced as part of the JOBS programme, justification of which, in turn, was presented in the language of contractual obligation.[211] In Britain, the Employment Committee indicated its support for workfare measures, declaring it appropriate to expect reciprocal activity from benefit recipients on contractual grounds.[212] And Peter Lilley, then Secretary of State for Social Security, stated unequivocally that 'those who think that this is a "something for nothing" society can forget it'.[213]

The jobseeker's agreement is, indeed, a 'tangible manifestation'[214] of contractual welfare. Criticisms were lodged against the ceremonial signing of an agreement by the employment agency and the claimant, thus creating the pretence that the agreement exhibits more 'a meeting of minds' than 'take it or leave it'.[215] The options offered are limited, training is poor or non-existent, choice is limited or restricted to the extent that claimants may be compelled to accept unpopular placements.

iv) The Moral Contract and Behaviour Modification

The Poor Law concept of 'residuum', like that of the present day 'underclass', views causes of unemployment and poverty as related to behaviour and morality.[216] A contractual model is beneficial to organs that have in mind behaviour modification as it converts 'diffuse, non-specific expectations into more specific and concrete obligations'.[217] Following the logic that the contract is the foundation of

---

[210] J Euben, 'Walzer's Obligation' (1972) 1 Philosophy and Public Affairs 438, 444.
[211] King (n 185 above) 275.
[212] King (n 185 above) 239.
[213] DSS, *Press Release* (6 Oct 1993) cited in C Jones and T Novak *Poverty, Welfare and the Disciplinary State* (Routledge: London, 1999) 97.
[214] Lundy (n 181 above) 304.
[215] J Fullbrook, 'The Jobseeker's Act 1995' (1995) 24 ILJ 395, 400.
[216] Jones and Novak (n 213 above) 73.
[217] Freedland and King (n 175 above) 468.

the rules, and that rules dictate behaviour,[218] governments turned to inspect what rules are needed so as to change behaviour of asocial welfare claimants. Thus, social conservatives in the United States argued that since AFDC caused women to have children out of wedlock and families to break-up, the 'Contract with America' needs to fuse a work-oriented agenda with a behaviour-modification agenda.[219] Social welfare can, under this paradigm, demand claimants to change their values, attitudes and behaviour *in return* for assistance.[220]

The danger, of course, is that the rules of welfare-to-work programmes will be exploited to control the behaviour of claimants in fields that are only tangentially concerned with employability. Indeed, Field declared that 'welfare should openly reward good behaviour and it should be used to enhance the roles the country values' since welfare's role is also 'to reward and to punish', replacing 'Christian morality... by affirming right and wrong conduct'.[221]

This danger has materialized in practice with the emphasis on disciplinary elements in welfare-to-work programmes. Amy Wax, arguing for strict reciprocity in welfare schemes, states that governments cannot run welfare programmes without making 'convention based judgments... grounded in how most *ordinary people* are expected to behave and how they do behave'[222] and that:

perhaps potential welfare recipients are *finally getting the message* that they are expected to do anything they can to lift themselves out of poverty, which includes entering the workforce, forswearing drugs and crime and avoiding potentially costly childbearing.[223]

This position, then, would justify procedures that target asocial individual behaviour using the contractual paradigm.[224] Focusing on the narrower point of benefits, we come full circle with the assertion that welfare recipients should be 'deserving' in the eyes of the taxpayer whom they contract with. The lines between deserving and undeserving poor are constantly redrawn, however. In this case, they are constructed on the basis of claimants' behaviour and attitude, rather than on evidence of their capabilities and need.[225] And closely related, it has been suggested that the affirmation the poor are required to receive from the 'taxpayer'[226] may be explained by the fact that 'poor people cannot be trusted to spend money that isn't "theirs"'.[227] This assertion leads us to a discussion regarding the nature of rights involved, to which we turn in the following section.

---

[218] C Murray, *The Emerging British Underclass* (IEA: London, 1990) 25.
[219] Noble (n 186 above) 127.
[220] Jones and Novak (n 213 above) 80.
[221] F Field, 'A Rejoinder' in A Deacon (ed), *Stakeholder Welfare* (IEA: London, 1996) 107, 111.
[222] Wax (n 202 above) 500 [emphasis added].
[223] A Wax, 'Welfare Rights' (2000) 63 Law and Contemporary Problems 257, 285 [emphasis added].
[224] Freedland and King (n 175 above) 472, 476.
[225] L Howe, 'The "Deserving" and "Undeserving"' (1985) 14 J of Soc Pol 49, 68.
[226] See Mead (n 198 above) 13.
[227] J Handler, 'The Coercive Children's Officer' cited in Jones and Novak (n 213 above) 84.

D Conditioning Welfare[228]

Some authors have suggested a clear divide between the Poor Law's construction of duties owed to the indigent and the post-war agenda of welfare rights. And yet, welfare reforms of the past two decades have managed to change the character of welfare rights in a novel way that is increasingly represented as 'contractual' in nature, and has perhaps even 'changed the[ir] fundamental legal basis'.[229] This change has led some authors to ask, somewhat dramatically, if the era of the welfare state and social justice is drawing to a close.[230] Though this may not be the case, two modest insights seem beyond dispute; first, that recent reforms have constructed behavioural requirements as preconditions of eligibility, and, second, that such preconditions have changed the way we conceive of rights and duties in state welfare provision.

The relationship between rights and duties is complex. The political philosophy that was prominent in the first few decades of the welfare state was that one's rights are grounded in one's 'social citizenship' and that they provide a strong reason to place a duty on the state. But this consensus, if indeed it existed, was short-lived. To an increasing degree, an alternative ideal is being advanced by parliaments, administrators and academics. This ideal of 'no rights without responsibilities' is nowhere more apparent than in contemporary welfare-to-work programmes. This section investigates this claim and suggests that welfare rights under current welfare-to-work programmes are constructed as relying in a strong sense upon the fulfillment of duties.

1 The Theoretical Background

Some duties derive from, and are a consequence of, rights. My right to walk at leisure unimpeded in the city centre is the source of your duty not to stop me from doing so. My right to have the furniture that I paid for delivered to me is the reason the store has a duty to do so. So far this is familiar territory. But as Austin and Bentham have stated, and few have contested,[231] rights are not the only source of duties. Following their terminology, we should distinguish

---

[228] For an expanded version of this section see A Paz-Fuchs, 'Rights, Duties and Conditioning Welfare' (2008) 21 Canadian J of Law and Jurisprudence.
[229] N Harris, 'The Welfare State, Social Security and Social Citizenship Rights' in N Harris (ed), *Social Security Law in Context* (OUP: Oxford, 2000) 3.
[230] D Miller, *Principles of Social Justice* (Harvard UP: Cambridge MA, 1999) 2.
[231] M Kramer, 'Getting Rights Right' in M Kramer (ed), *Rights, Wrongs and Responsibilities* (Palgrave: Basingstoke, 2001) 28, 43 for example, states that 'rights and duties are indeed correlative in the sense that the existence of a right entails the existence of a duty *and vice versa*' [emphasis added]. In another paper, Kramer argues that rights and duties are correlative *by definition*—M Kramer, 'Rights Without Trimmings' in M Kramer, N Simmonds and H Steiner, *A Debate Over Rights* (Clarendon: Oxford, 1998) 7, 24.

between *absolute* duties, that have no correlative rights, and *relative* duties, which do.[232] The theory of restricted correlativity suggests, therefore, that every right is a basis for a duty, but only some duties imply a right.[233] Further, while the duty is a ground for action, the rights serve as a ground for the duty.[234] Therefore, by being closer to the acting agent, one identifies the duty that serves as a reason for an action before identifying if it is grounded in a right. So we may know that people have a duty not to burn the national flag or harm their dogs, but does this mean that others have a right that flags not be burnt or that dogs have a right not to be harshly treated? Not necessarily. We should be asking, therefore: if not all duties correlate with rights, what are the criteria for deciding that a specific duty is grounded in a right? And in relation to our present issue: assuming that it is not contested that, under the poor law or welfare state regime, one can identify a duty towards the poor, how may we deduce whether a right to welfare was the source of this duty? Two general approaches address this sort of question—the interest (or benefit) theory of rights and the choice (or will) theory of right.[235]

i) The Interest theory

A simple account of the interest theory holds that Jack has a right that Jill perform A, and hence Jill has a duty towards Jack to do A, if and only if Jill has a duty to do A *and* performance of A by Jill would benefit Jack.[236]

HLA Hart famously criticized the interest theory on the following grounds:

if to say that an individual has such a right means no more than that he is the intended beneficiary of a duty, then 'a right' in this sense may be an unnecessary, and perhaps confusing, term in the description of the law; since all that can be said in a terminology of such rights can be and indeed is, best said in the indispensable terminology of duty.[237]

This critique suggests that, irrespective of its merits, the interest theory is not always helpful in identifying whether or not a right underlies a duty in general, and a duty to provide the material goods necessary for sustenance, in particular. It also illuminates the most formidable advantage of its rival theory—the choice theory of rights.

---

[232] J Austin, *Lectures on Jurisprudence* (Murray: London, 1880) 161–62 (Lect XII); H Kelsen, *General Theory of Law and State* (A Wedberg (tr) Harvard UP: Cambridge MA, 1949) 85–86; J Bentham, *An Introduction to the Principles of Morals and Legislation* (Clarendon: Oxford, 1996) 265.
[233] J Raz, *The Morality of Freedom* (Clarendon: Oxford, 1986) 186.
[234] ibid 180.
[235] Harel (n 110 above) 191.
[236] J Raz, 'Promises and Obligations' in PMS Hacker and J Raz (eds), *Law, Morality and Society* (Clarendon: Oxford, 1977) 210, 213.
[237] HLA Hart, 'Bentham on Legal Rights' in *Oxford Essays in Jurisprudence* (2nd Series, Clarendon: Oxford, 1973) 171, 190.

ii) The Choice Theory

According to this theory, a right is identified as the grounds for a duty not when the purported right-holder benefits from the duty, but rather when she has 'control over the incidence of the duty'.[238]

The advantages of this theory are clear: both in law and in morals the fact that one benefits from a duty does not imply that one holds a right to the benefit. The examples of charity and mercy are helpful. It is not only that 'there is something indecent in making a claim to beneficence'.[239] The fact that charity or mercy may not be *demanded* or imposed upon us seems like an important fact of their character. Indeed, as Shakespeare's Portia reminds us, 'the quality of mercy is not strained'.[240] And this is highly related to the fact that to speak of a *right* to charity or to be treated with mercy seems like a misnomer. Hart, when discussing moral rights and duties, stresses that one's promise to a friend to take care of the latter's mother makes the mother the beneficiary, but not the right-holder.[241] In other words, the choice theory captures an intuition that escapes the interest theory: if a substantive degree of discretion is granted to the duty-holder as to the execution of the duty and, consequently, the beneficiary holds no power to enforce the duty, we are less inclined to speak of a right being held. Conversely, the more discretion granted to the putative right-holder at the expense of the duty-holder, the more we perceive the former as holding a right.[242] However, the focus placed on discretion (or control over the duty) is not only an asset but also a serious challenge for the choice theory.

Hart argues that an important feature of rights as understood under the choice theory is the right-holder's ability to waive the duty and release from obligation.[243] However, in numerous cases we do, in fact, recognize rights that do not include the right-holder's power to waive the correlative duty. Indeed, these are often occasions where the rights under consideration are the most valuable for the right-holder's interest. So valuable, in fact, that we are not willing to grant even the right-holder the power to waive the duty. It is true that we do not, in these cases, grant the duty-holder the discretion whether he will supply the goods or not. But discretion is not a zero-sum phenomenon. We normally argue that children have

---

[238] Kelsen (n 232 above) 81; D Miller *Social Justice* (Clarendon: Oxford, 1976) 62.

[239] W D Ross, *The Right and the Good* (2nd edn, Clarendon: Oxford, 2002) 48–56.

[240] W Shakespeare, *The Merchant of Venice* (Penguin Shakespeare: London, 1600 rpnt 1995) 138.

[241] HLA Hart, 'Are there any Natural Rights?' in Waldron (n 30 above) 77, 81; and see similarly Miller (n 238 above) 62; PS Atiyah, *An Introduction to the Law of Contract* (5th edn, Clarendon: Oxford, 1995) 355. But cf Raz's reply in 'Rights and Individual Well-Being' in *Ethics in the Public Domain* (Clarendon: Oxford, 1994) 44, 50.

[242] Incidentally, this focus on individual choice has, interestingly enough, led some writers to suggest a strong connection between the choice theory and social contract theories: See eg J Finnis, *Natural Law and Natural Rights* (OUP: Oxford, 1982) 208; I Shapiro, *Evolution of Rights in Liberal Theory* (CUP: Cambridge, 1986) 105.

[243] Hart (n 241 above) 81; Hart (n 237 above) 192; For a (problematic) implementation of choice theory to workfare see G Standing, *Global Labour Flexibility* (Macmillan: Basingstoke, 1999) 317.

not only a right, but also a duty, to receive education, without viewing the duty as depriving the right to education of the title. Similarly, an employee cannot release her employer from certain duties through the employment contract.[244] The paradox is, therefore, per the choice theory, that strengthening rights in a manner that lessens control over them would supposedly move them 'outside the genus of rights'.[245]

So the problem for choice theory lies in its inability to take due account of the role that fundamental rights hold in practical reasoning.[246] Rights are not recognized or denied because the individual has a certain power (eg to waive the duty), but rather because it is deemed just that she hold the right.[247] The power to control the incidence of the duty derives from the assertion that the right exists, not vice-versa.

iii) Interest Theory and Choice Theory—the Synergy

Where does this analysis lead? Neither the interest theory nor the choice theory manages to fully explain the concept of legal rights in a manner that would allow one to extract a clear criterion for distinguishing absolute duties from relative duties. Though it is not my purpose to offer here a full-fledged list of criteria, a synthesis that focuses only on the stronger points of both theories would allow moving to questions of analysis and implementation: the interest theory provides the substantive element, while the factors focused on by the choice theory provide helpful evidentiary indication.

The ability to waive the duty is indeed, in many cases, an important *attribute* of a right, a consequence of it. So much so, in fact, that such power serves as evidence for the existence of a right. The converse, however, as we saw, is not true. Control over the incidence of the duty is a sufficient, but not a necessary, condition of a right.[248] Indeed, courts often decide whether a right exists (by ascertaining who the statute is to benefit) primarily in order to decide whether

---

[244] The Employment Rights Act 1996 (UK) c 18 and the Trade Union and Labour Relations (Consolidation) Act 1992 (UK) c 52 are two key statutes guaranteeing a 'floor of rights' from which 'any provision in an agreement...is void in so far as it purports to' derogate from the rights granted under the relevant acts: ERA 1996 s 203(1); TULRCA 1992 s 288. See also *Bowmaker Ltd v Tabor* [1941] 2 All ER 72, 76.

[245] N MacCormick, 'Rights in Legislation' in Hacker and Raz (n 236 above) 189, 195.

[246] R Dworkin, *Taking Rights Seriously* (Duckworth: London, 1977) 365–66; Raz (n 233 above) 166; J Finnis, *Natural Law and Natural Rights* (Clarendon: Oxford, 1980) 205.

[247] Hart, along with other choice theorists, were aware of this problem: Hart (n 237 above) 201; N Simmonds, 'Rights at the Cutting Edge' in Kramer, Simmonds and Steiner (n 231 above) 112, 141–44; See also N Bamforth, 'Hohfeldian Rights and Public Law' in Kramer (n 231 above) 1.

[248] I use 'condition' here very loosely since, as indicated, control over the duty is actually a *consequence* of a right and therefore cannot logically be its condition. Kramer states that one's competency to waive enforcement is neither a sufficient nor a necessary condition of holding a right. But his only example of such a case—the right to be betrayed—is not only bizarre but also far from convincing—Kramer (n 231 above) 62–63, 98. For a critique see H Steiner, 'Working Rights' in Kramer, Simmonds and Steiner (n 231 above) 233, 296.

the putative right-holder has control over the duty, not the other way around.[249] In such cases the courts stated that a right is recognized if the reason for the duty was that it would *protect the interests of the plaintiff*.[250]

This, however, leaves intact a significant critique highlighted earlier. The weight of the interest theory's analysis of rights and duties suggests a strong relation between legal analysis and social and ideological facts as well as a danger that rights-discourse would be supplanted with a construction that views rights as dependent on duties. This threat is arguably realized in the novel construction of contractual rights.

2 Rights, Reciprocity and Collective Interests

The claim that the idea of contractual rights is 'novel' should be immediately qualified. Rousseau insisted that justice could be achieved only by uniting rights and duties.[251] Similarly, John Finnis notes that in certain African tribal regimes, 'right' and 'duty' are terms covered by a single word, normally translated as 'ought' or 'due'. Finnis explains that this phenomenon has its cultural source in the approach that emphasizes 'duty and obligation, rather than the nuance of modern Western society, with a stress on rights'.[252] So, instead of claiming that the ideas themselves are in any way novel, it would be more accurate to state that it is their prominence in modern, Western legal and political thought that deserves investigation. Where, then, lies the explanation for the rise of this agenda? In social, political and philosophical discourse, the influence of conservative communitarian scholars has been acknowledged.[253]

Communitarians have been advancing the claim that 'rights presume responsibilities' for over a decade.[254] In addition, communitarian theory places a strong emphasis on reciprocity,[255] a concept which has already proven central to the analysis to this point. Indeed, communitarian arguments that focus on social and cultural 'problems' have been incorporated in suggestions for welfare reform.

---

[249] *Butler v Fife* [1912] AC 149, 165; *Philips v Brittania* [1923] 2 KB 832, 841; *Cutler v Wandsworth* [1949] AC 398, 416–17.
[250] Raz (n 233 above) 166. Also in A Gewirth, *The Community of Rights* (Chicago UP: Chicago, 1996) 8–12.
[251] JJ Rousseau, *The Social Contract* (Wordsworth: Ware Hertfordshire, 1998) II.vi.
[252] M Gluckman cited in Finnis (n 246 above) 209.
[253] R Levitas, *The Inclusive Society?* (Macmillan: Basingstoke, 1998) 122–25; Deacon (n 148 above) 132–34; J Conaghan, 'Women, Work and Family: A British Revolution?' in J Conaghan, R Fischl and K Klare (eds), *Labour Law in an Era of Globalization* (OUP: Oxford, 2002) 53, 54. The communitarian church is a big one. Philip Selznick, for example, shares some communitarian tenets while placing a stronger emphasis on the aim of social justice. See his 'Social Justice—A Communitarian Perspective' in A Etzioni (ed), *The Essential Communitarian Reader* (Rowan and Littlefield: Oxford, 1998) 61; also Gewirth (n 250 above) 6–8.
[254] A Etzioni, *The Spirit of the Community* (Fontana: London, 1995) 9–10.
[255] ibid 24; M Freeden, 'The Ideology of New Labour' (1999) Political Quarterly 42, 45–46, 49; J Peck and N Theodore, 'Beyond Employability' (2000) 24 Cambridge J of Economics 729.

Social and economic rights may be demanded and received under a communitarian paradigm,[256] but they may also be conditioned on the duty to refrain from asocial behaviour or to exhibit an appropriate attitude.

In similar vein, Lawrence Mead argues that civic virtue and civic behaviour can be achieved also through the welfare system of rights and obligations.[257] Amongst important obligations he names the duty to support one's family, to stay in school and to learn English.[258] And Frank Field, while discussing 'the breakdown of a contract' within the analysis of welfare reform, declares that 'all societies require a shared ideology, containing an agreed moral framework'.[259]

This claim is part of a larger argument in favour of reciprocity. In fact, Field, like other progressive welfare reformers, identified a problem that is separate from that of fiscal and moral issues already mentioned. The problem is that dropping support and political legitimacy for income provision cause a 'legitimacy crisis'.[260]. Saving the system, it is argued, can be done only if the tax paying public can identify with the people whom they are supporting. And this objective entails enhancing reciprocity and strict work requirements. This argument, however, seems to rely more on intuition than on empirical data. In fact, it has been argued that such requirements encourage a perception of 'us and them' and undermine 'a principle of citizenship, which is that everybody should be treated on an inclusive, equal basis'.[261]

Making rights conditional upon duties, however problematic, is not an uncommon legal phenomenon. But linking rights to responsibilities through a '*vague* sense of reciprocity'[262] allows institutions to set conditions on rights that are unjust and thus constitutes a further threat to the role rights should hold in practical reasoning. It may be remembered that Ian Macneil explained why discreteness is a fundamental trait of contractual relationships.[263] Linking this argument to the present context, one may indeed suggest that 'in the absence of discrete norms, any appearance of relationality is illusory'.[264] Positing vague demands for reciprocity against the Beveridge insurance paradigm, Plant notes that for Beveridge:

it is a specific kind of contribution which creates the right—namely, a contribution to National Insurance. The right to benefit is correlated to a specific form of contribution.

---

[256] MA Glendon, *Rights Talk* (Free Press: New York, 1991) 76–108; Selznick (n 253 above).
[257] L Mead, *Beyond Entitlement* (Free Press: London, 1986) 87.
[258] ibid 242–43. And see similarly E Wyne, *Social Security* (Westview: Boulder, Colorado, 1980) 142.
[259] F Field, *Making Welfare Work* (Institute of Community Studies: London, 1995) 26. Field, formerly Minister of Welfare Reform, was described as the 'most forceful advocate of the moral dimension to social citizenship in recent years'—Harris (n 229 above) 29.
[260] Standing (n 243 above) 229; also Rosanvallon (n 38 above) 43.
[261] Standing (n 243 above) 326.
[262] Etzioni (n 254 above) 145.
[263] I Macneil, *The New Social Contract* (Yale UP: New Haven, 1980) 59–64.
[264] Vincent-Jones (n 150 above) 263.

This, however, is not the government's view, despite its emphasis on obligation. The contribution is a much more generalized one.[265]

An example of this danger may be given through Hillel Steiner's argument that we find it absurd that a person may request leniency on account of him being an orphan after killing his parents because 'the set of entitlements should reflect the requirement that persons be held *responsible* for the adverse consequences of their own actions'.[266]

But if the phrase 'set of entitlements' is to indicate the total array of *rights* (Steiner uses rights and entitlements interchangeably in his essay) that the individual is endowed with, this would seem an untenable statement. It would be a harsh position to take if one were to say, even about a person who has committed such a heinous crime, that he has thus waived his rights to counsel, to due process, to freedom of speech and so forth. More tenable, then, would be to claim that *particular* entitlements, more germane to the act itself, may be affected. Thus, what may be considered is that the individual's active role in bringing about his orphanhood may mitigate (though, I would argue, not necessarily nullify) his entitlement to leniency. But it should be noted that though the *decision maker* may consider the individual's responsibility, the *right to request leniency* should not be impacted. And herein lies the flaw in Steiner's argument. It is quite peculiar that Steiner, as a choice theorist,[267] suggested leniency as an entitlement that may be affected. For leniency, as an act that cannot be demanded or waived at will, does not figure in a choice theorist's conceptualization of rights (and for good reason) and thus does not support the general claim that responsibility has an impact on entitlements. Indeed, it is submitted, it is precisely because there is no *right* to (extra-legal) leniency that the decision maker may reasonably take into account, inter alia, a person's behaviour and responsibility.[268]

This discussion brings us back to the jurisprudential analysis that ended the previous subsection. It has been suggested that the interest theory as presented by Raz and MacCormick leads to a situation whereby 'rights become illusory' since rights would 'extend only to the point where our actions ceased to make a contribution to the collective project'.[269] Since the interest theory offers a better understanding of the concept of rights, and since we shall soon turn to inspect precisely similar charges that convey a sense of diluted rights, it is of import to investigate whether this critique points to a key explanation. Nigel Simmonds points out that under Raz's scheme, a right is an interest that justifies holding others to a duty, and that conclusion is reached only 'if not counteracted by

---

[265] R Plant, 'Citizenship and Social Security' (2003) 24 Fiscal Studies 153, 161.
[266] H Steiner, 'Choice and Circumstance' in Kramer (n 231 above) 225, 226.
[267] Steiner (n 248 above) 233.
[268] See similarly the example of moral goodness in R Plant, H Lesser and P Taylor-Gooby, *Political Philosophy and Social Welfare* (Routledge: London, 1980) 57.
[269] Simmonds (n 247 above) 113, 145. For a similar critique see J Chan, 'Raz on Liberal Rights and Common Goods' (1995) 15 OJLS 15.

conflicting considerations'.[270] MacCormick, similarly, is understood to offer a concept of a right that serves as a place holder for forms of protection, but those should be 'balanced against countervailing considerations, so that the protections that finally result are the outcome of this calculus of conflicting interest'.[271] In short, it is argued that rights under the interest theory cannot be entrusted with the task of protecting the individual's sphere of autonomy against collective social goals because these goals are incorporated in the right itself.

If accepted, this is a serious charge. I would suggest, however, that even if the interest theory grants the interests of other people (or society in general)[272] a role in grounding rights, this does not require that 'the rights or the interests of right-holders play no *strategic* role in moral and political affairs'.[273] Such a claim ignores a necessary separation between two phases of investigation. In the first phase rights are recognized and acknowledged. At this phase, rights are seen as legal rules that exclude certain considerations that would have been relevant were we required to make a 'particularistic'[274] decision, that is—a decision that has no regard for the legal rule. As Friedrick Schauer shows, rules are not subject to 'continuous malleability'. They create a temporal gap between the moment of crafting and the moment of applying rights to a particular situation, thus 'resisting current efforts to mould them to the needs of the instant'.[275] Recognition of a certain right changes the balance of reasons (absent the right).[276] Thus, once the right to privacy is recognized, it would not be helpful to argue, or even to prove, that crime would be reduced if cameras were placed in every person's home. Of course, this does not mean that rights prevail all things considered. Such a conclusion would require viewing all rights as absolute. This cannot be true, if only because rights conflict amongst themselves (consider the right to free speech and the right not to be defamed).

Rights do, however, place restrictions on measures that can be taken. Indeed, Boltanski and Chiapello define 'strengths' as those qualities of beings which are 'displaced in the absence of constraints of a normative, conventional or legal kind—that is to say, doing without categorization'.[277] And they continue to ask:

For what purpose do rules and rights serve? How do they increase the strength of the weak? They set constraints on tests in such a way as to limit the displacement of strengths and make visible—hence controllable (or punishable)—alterations which, induced by a multiplicity of local displacements, modify the field of forces.[278]

---

[270] Raz (n 233 above) 171.
[271] Simmonds (n 247 above) 160, criticizing MacCormick (n 245 above).
[272] Raz (n 241 above) 52–55.
[273] Chan (n 269 above) 29.
[274] F Schauer, *Playing by the Rules* (Clarendon: Oxford, 1991) 77–78.
[275] ibid 81–84.
[276] J Raz, *Practical Reasons and Norms* (Clarendon: Oxford, 1975) 39.
[277] L Boltanski, E Chiapello, *The New Spirit of Capitalism* (G Elliot—tr, Verso: London, 2005) 321.
[278] ibid 323.

At the second stage the right is given its proper weight and value in the particular context. Different cases will be affected by particular rights in different ways. Though the right may seem to take account of collective interests yet again, their place in the analysis is now distinct. Once recognized, rights have an a-contextual force that may pull towards decisions where 'no other political aim is served and some political aim is disserved thereby'.[279] It is true that the (first stage) process of recognizing rights also takes into account social goals, but this would not render the second stage analysis superfluous. For if it were found that the public interest would be served by recognizing an individual right to freedom of religion, the *particular* balance that should be reached when this freedom is confronted with a collective interest in, say, public order, is not predefined. The right now stands on its own, somewhat oblivious to its parentage.

This is, it should be acknowledged, a narrow escape from a serious charge. For though it is possible to insist on this strict separation between the two stages, Simmond's argument could, at the very least, be understood to proclaim that interest theory jurisprudence is much more *vulnerable* to a diluted idea of rights, one that has more room for incorporating the common good at distinct stages (such as identification and balancing). Simmonds is right to point out that under the interest theory's own 'terms of engagement', a significant degree of 'semantic autonomy' is compromised if identifying the right-holder depends on the purpose supposedly served by the law.[280] Such a procedure would necessitate 'an unavoidable embrace of a conception of the "good"'.[281] This is not an insignificant cost to pay in any sort of analysis, especially if one thinks that the criterion for identifying a concept should ideally be independent of the criteria for assessing its goodness or badness. But the moral and social weight attached to rights, their 'familiar role in ordinary thinking',[282] requires that an account of collective interests be taken both in the first (identification) and in the second (balancing) stages.

And yet, following Simmonds' arguments, we should be aware of the possible social, legal and political implications of working within the interest theory. We are now in a position to understand how this insight is manifested insofar as welfare rights and welfare reform are concerned.

3 Constructing Welfare Rights as Conditional

Proponents and opponents of welfare reform, as well as the courts, accept that recognizing a legal right to welfare would limit the conditions that may be attached

---

[279] Dworkin (n 246 above) 91; A Harel, 'What Demands are Rights?' (1997) 17 OJLS 101, 111.
[280] Simmonds (n 247 above) 197. Kramer states that 'one scarcely should be surprised by the general fact that we have to interpret each norm before we can decide who (if anyone) holds right under it'—(n 231 above) 85.
[281] Steiner (n 248 above) 293.
[282] Steiner (n 248 above) 236–7; Raz similarly emphasizes the importance of following 'the usage of writers on law, politics and morality who typically use the term'—J Raz, 'On the Nature of Rights' (1984) 93 Mind 194.

to welfare benefits.[283] Thus, when the American administration of welfare relief sought to reduce expenses on welfare relief by enhancing its 'deterrent effect', it was suggested that waiting periods be extended to create a backlog so applicants would be discouraged from applying; that welfare centres should be consolidated into smaller offices; and that new applicants would be required to frequently sign at the employment agency. These procedures, it was clear, could be implemented only if the present system would be 'more selective in offering welfare as a right'.[284] This insight should not be dismissed as mere policy jargon. Indeed, the Special Task Force to the Secretary of Health, Education and Welfare wrote in 1971: 'It is not even clear that anyone other than the mother has the legal or moral right to make that decision [whether or not to accept a job offer—APF] or that anyone other than the mother can make the decision that is best for her and her children'.[285] Arguably, the reservation from such conditions was attributed to a serious regard for equal citizenship and welfare rights. Since rights, if taken seriously, limit the conditions that may be placed between the individual and the interest that the right serves, efforts to impose harsh conditions had to be quickly abandoned.

Indeed, Lucy Williams rightly relates the power to attach conditions to benefits with the nullification of a right to AFDC payments that was previously part of federal law. To permit behavioral conditions on eligibility, she explains, the United States Department of Health and Human Services had to waive the entitlement provisions under 42 USC. §1315.[286] And later she argues correctly that 'the importance of the PRWORA is its repudiation of the concept of entitlement in welfare jurisprudence'.[287] But, notwithstanding their important policy and doctrinal implications, these claims also rest on a sound jurisprudential base. Steiner states that the job of rights is:

to demarcate *domains*—spheres of practical choice within which the choices made by designated individuals (and groups) must not be subject to interference—and to specify those demarcations without reference to the content of the choices to be made within those spheres. It thus requires no very extended argument to show that rights, so conceived, amount to *normative allocations of freedom*.[288]

---

[283] Mead (n 257 above) 2, 9, 206; Wyne (n 258 above) 145; R Plant, 'Free Lunches Don't Nourish: Reflections on Entitlement and Citizenship' in G Drover and P Kerans (eds), *New Approaches to Welfare Theory* (Elgar: Brookfield, 1993) 33, 45; *Goldberg v Kelly* 397 US 254 (1970); LA Sobel (ed), *Welfare and the Poor* (Facts on File: New York, 1977) 122–4 cited in Mead (n 257 above) 119.

[284] Budget Bureau Recommendations for Savings in the Welfare Budget, cited in FF Piven and RA Cloward, *Regulating the Poor* (Updated Edition, Vintage: New York, 1993) 161 n 20.

[285] Cited in Gewirth (n 250 above) 128 n 27.

[286] L Williams, 'The Ideology of Division: Behavior Modification Welfare Reform Proposals' (1992) 102 Yale LJ 719, 721; L Williams, 'The Abuse of Section 1115 Waivers: Welfare Reform in Search of a Standard' (1994) 12 Yale L and Policy Rev 8.

[287] L Williams, 'Welfare and Legal Entitlements: The Social Roots of Poverty' in D Kairys (ed), *The Politics of Law* (3rd edn, Basic Books: New York, 1998) 569, 570.

[288] Steiner (n 248 above) 238. Hart views rights as 'legally protected choices' and tends to regard constitutional rights as primarily creating immunities—Hart (n 237 above) 197.

Now, it is widely acknowledged that the new welfare-to-work regime represents a 'fundamental change in the balance between rights and obligations in the provision of assistance'.[289] Alan Gewirth suggests that 'positive rights *require* personal responsibility on the part of the would-be recipients of help'.[290] Anthony Giddens follows in similar vein, envisaging no less than 'a redefinition of rights and responsibilities'. Giddens condemns 'old style democracy' for treating rights as 'unconditional claims' and asserts that 'unemployment benefits should carry the obligation to search for work, for example'.[291] Giddens is sensitive to the charge that welfare rights have been singled out in this construction, and makes clear that as 'an ethical principle "no rights without responsibilities" must apply not only to welfare recipients, but to everyone ... otherwise—the precept will be held to apply only to the poor or to the needy'.[292]

Giddens's categorization of 'no rights without responsibilities' as an *ethical* principle brings to mind moral theories such as those offered by David Gauthier and James Buchanan, which reside on a contractual platform. In non-legal discourse, one may understand the notion that 'rights presume responsibilities' to resemble the idea of *noblesse oblige*, that inordinate privilege, wealth or power should motivate an urge to 'repay' society. But this is not the meaning usually attributed to the doctrine of 'rights and responsibilities'.[293]

It seems that there is good reason that neither Giddens nor Gewirth supply us with a parallel example involving a more established right (eg speech, privacy, political participation) that is contingent upon fulfillment of duties. It is difficult to conjure up such a sentence. 'Freedom of religion should carry the obligation to ...'—what? One cannot finish this clause by stating something along the lines of 'avoiding harm to others'. Such a claim would simply state the *limits* of the right, not the behavioural conditions for eligibility. We do not say that someone has a right to free speech only if she refrains from drug abuse any more than we say that someone loses his right to property if he lies on his tax statement. Contrariwise, established rights were declared inalienable, natural, sacred and equally deriving from one's personhood. If Giddens claims that a different construction for *all* rights is warranted, it would be a dramatic suggestion indeed—a 'reformulation of the social contract'.[294]

---

[289] Fafo Institute for Applied Social Science, *Workfare in Six European Nations* (Norwegian Ministry of Health and Social Affairs Oslo 2001) 46 in J Handler, *Social Citizenship and Workfare in the US and Western Europe* (CUP: Cambridge, 2004) 144; Also C Jones and T Novak, *Poverty, Welfare and the Disciplinary State* (Routledge: London, 1999) 143; Mead (n 257 above).
[290] Gewirth (n 250 above) 42 [emphasis added]. Gewirth explains how the unfairness of receiving 'something for nothing' supports a duty to work—pp 223, 231–35. This position is somewhat softened elsewhere in the book—p 121.
[291] A Giddens, *The Third Way* (Polity: Cambridge, 1998) 65.
[292] ibid 65–66.
[293] Barry (n 42 above) 144–51.
[294] Rosanvallon (n 38 above) 28.

This paradigm is already being implemented in realms other than welfare provision. Contractual social policy, enforced with concrete agreements (not always legally enforceable) is implemented in additional areas where 'acceptable behaviour contracts' are perceived as beneficial means to a social policy end. British policy and legislation offer several recent examples. First, under the Youth Justice and Criminal Evidence Act 1999, Youth Offender Panels are under duty to reach a 'programme of behaviour' agreement with the offender, the principal aim of which is the prevention of re-offending. Second, following the 2002 White Paper *Justice for All*,[295] 'acceptable behaviour contracts' may be drawn up between a young person, his parents and a representative of the local authority housing department together with a police officer. Their purpose is to create a less severe alternative to dealing with the behaviour of young persons. Third, Home-School Agreements under the School Standards and Framework Act 1998 require governing bodies of maintained schools to adopt a 'parental declaration' which is to record parents' acknowledgment of the school's aims and values and the parental responsiblities that derive from the school's expectations from its pupils. Lastly, perhaps a combination of the aforementioned, is the Parenting Contract under the Anti-social Behaviour Act 2003.[296] This contract is unique in that the parents of child whose behaviour is deemed anti-social or criminal are a direct party to the contract and are perceived as holding direct responsibility for the child's actions. Such contractual policy measures have already raised serious questions with regards to the applicability of the contract mechanism as an appropriate method for the constitutionalization of relationships between the state and vulnerable citizens.[297]

By focusing on the ideological (as opposed to the concrete) contractual facet of these arrangements, one may notice where the danger lies for a strong sense of legal rights. Thus, it has been judicially suggested that prisoners should lose their right to vote because committing a crime is tantamount to violating 'civic responsibility...which safeguards the social contract'.[298] This conclusion rejects the need for a rational link between the act and the punishment and rests on a general paradigm that sees rights as contingent upon fulfillment of obligations. It resonates with Steiner's suggestion, discussed above, that one's entitlements should reflect one's actions. It also employs the concept of the social contract in a manner that restricts, rather than expands, access to entitlements. As the contract mechanism is being used increasingly in the regulation of social relations between citizens and the state,[299] conditions on rights unrelated to the benefit

---

[295] White Paper, *Justice for All* (Cm 5563, 2002).
[296] Anti-social Behaviour Act 2003 (UK) c 38.
[297] Vincent-Jones (n 150 above) ch 9.
[298] *Sauve v Attorney General of Canada (No 2)* [2002] 3 SCR 519, 570 (Gonthier J, minority opinion). For similar remarks on this matter see *Belczowski v The Queen* (1992) 90 DLR (4th) 330, 336; *Richardson v Ramirez* 418 US 24 (1974); *Hirst v United Kingdom (No 2)* (2004) 38 EHRR 40 para 33; see Barry (n 42 above) 102.
[299] Vincent-Jones (n 190 above) 319.

may 'curtail the rights in question to such an extent as to impair their very essence and deprive them of their effectiveness'.[300]

Welfare reforms have arguably created such an effect on welfare rights. Years of small austerity measures and changes in programme eligibility have shifted the post-war emphasis on universal entitlement towards an adoption of reciprocity as the unifying, central principle of social welfare. In the process, they have transformed welfare rights (and perhaps social rights in general) to 'negotiated claims'.[301] Governments have been 'trying to reconstruct social exchange on an increasingly individualistic basis, implementing a contractual reciprocity on a territorial level, and leaving aside universal rights'.[302] When announcing the new Jobseeker's Allowance policy, the British government stressed the link between the right to benefits and claimants' responsibilities, and stated that the latter would take concrete form in the obligation to take up work.[303] Emphasis was placed on fulfillment of duties as a precondition to welfare rights while the government 'reformulated welfare as mutual individual responsibility'.[304] This curtailment of the social citizenship ideal is detected both in American and in British welfare reform,[305] and has led social security law scholars to ask if the welfare state should be seen as merely a phase in the evolution of social policy, and one which is nearing conclusion.[306] Stuart White identifies the contractual paradigm as the dominant theme in both American and British welfare reform:

> ... access to welfare benefits is one side of a contract between citizen and community which has its reverse side various responsibilities that the individual citizen is obliged to meet; as a condition of eligibility for welfare benefits, the state may legitimately enforce these responsibilities, which centrally include the responsibility to work.[307]

White realizes that welfare contractualism violates the traditional understanding that rights 'have the quality of unconditionality'[308], where 'unconditionality' implies that *access* to the rights is not conditional upon fulfillment of

---

[300] Hirst (n 298 above).

[301] R Cox, 'The Consequences of Welfare Reform' (1998) 2/ J of Soc Pol 1, 12; See Plant (n 265 above) 155; A Wax, 'Something for Nothing' (2003) 52 Emory LJ 1, 3.

[302] G Procacci, 'Against Exclusion' in M Rhodes and Y Meny (eds), *The Future of European Welfare: A New Social Contract?* (Macmillan: Basingstoke, 1998) 63, 74.

[303] DSS, *A New Contract for Welfare: Gateway to Work* (n 15 above); A Bryson, 'The Jobseeker's Allowance: Help or Hindrance to the Unemployed?' (1995) 24 ILJ 204.

[304] Freeden (n 255 above) 49. The Labour Commission on Social Justice rejected the idea of an unconditional basic income and preferred a model that offered an 'ethic of mutuality' that had at its centre 'a balancing of rights and responsibilities'—*Social Justice—Strategies for National Renewal* (Vintage: London, 1994) 232; P Dwyer, *Welfare Rights and Responsibilities* (Policy: Bristol, 2000) 5–8; Harris (n 229 above) 28.

[305] Jones and Novak (n 289 above) 195–96; J Fullbrook, 'The Jobseekers Act 1995' (1995) 24 ILJ 395. Even prior to the JSA, John Major's *Citizen's Charter* stated that 'citizenship is about our responsibilities... as well as our entitlements'—Cabinet Office *The Citizen's Charter* (Cm 1599, 1991).

[306] Harris (n 229 above) 3.

[307] S White, 'Social Rights and the Social Contract' (2000) 30 British J Political Science 507.

[308] ibid 509.

responsibilities. Though he avoids the implications of this new construction in the ensuing discussion, it is important to note that this construction is not only theoretically striking, but that it also affects the conditions that may be legitimately placed on benefits.

4 The Consequences of Conditionality

It has been argued that this construction of welfare rights as conditional has led welfare debates to be conducted and decided as matters of policy[309] or politics[310] rather than rights. However, these realms are not usually seen to exclude consideration of rights. On the contrary, principles establishing rights 'may be among the fundamental principles governing all political action'.[311] So what seems to underlie this concern is that debates over welfare reform are held without granting weight to considerations that should emanate from rights such as the right to welfare and the right to work.[312] This is done, I suggest, by embracing a 'more discursive view of rights ... rather than by appeal to fixed principles'.[313]

Hence, welfare rights do not figure as an independent consideration that should have an effect on policy decisions, but rather as a *reflection* of the policy, or philosophy, already established. Welfare rights reflect the balance of interests instead of having a significant impact this balance. For example, it has been argued that the 'entitlement on which the right is based falls within a calculation of reciprocity and compensation. Thus, the disabled veteran or the war widow can be said to have a claim on society since they have, in fact, given something for it'.[314] It may be implied here, then, that a needs-based claim (due to disability or poverty) would be weakened if nothing was given in return.

Ronald Dworkin views this 'balancing' model as 'indefensible' since it '*threatens to destroy the concept of individual rights*'.[315] The European Court of Justice reached a very similar conclusion. The ECJ stated that British legislation that made the right to paid annual leave conditional upon 13 weeks of employment with the same employer amounts to an impermissible precondition on access to the right:

although they are free to lay down, in their domestic legislation, conditions for the exercise and implementation of the right to paid annual leave, by prescribing the specific circumstances in which workers may exercise that right, which is theirs in respect of

---

[309] K Puttick, 'Social Security 2020: A Welfare Odyssey' (1999) 29 ILJ 190, 195
[310] J Handler, *The Poverty of Welfare Reform* (Yale UP: New Haven, 1995) 94.
[311] Raz (n 233 above) 217. Also R Dworkin, 'Rights as Trumps' in Waldron (n 30 above) 153.
[312] This is also made clear, paradoxically, by the fact that the most important decisions protecting recipients have centered on the violation of other established rights, such as freedom of religion (*Sherbert v Verner* 374 US 398 (1963)) or freedom of movement (*Shapiro v Thompson* 394 US 618 (1969)).
[313] Cox (n 301 above) 10.
[314] Rosanvallon (n 38 above) 79.
[315] Dworkin (n 246 above) 199 [emphasis added] see also p 92.

all the periods of work completed, *Member States are not entitled to make the existence of that right*, which derives directly from Directive 93/104, *subject to any preconditions whatsoever*.[316]

The contractual discourse manages to create a unique 'is-ought' reposition, namely: 'if this *is* what policy makers have decided to demand from beneficiaries, it is doubtless what *ought* to be demanded from them. This is, *ex hypothesi*, what their welfare rights entail'. Instead of operating in an a-contextual, rule-like mode, welfare rights operate in a 'variable, contextual, particularistic manner'.[317] This position, if left unchallenged, would leave the use of rights 'conceptually redundant'.[318] It has been suggested that this reconfiguration of rights reflects on the concept of social citizenship itself, which is comparably changed 'from status to contract'[319] and, more ominously, that once rights 'lose their unconditional quality, the door is open not just for the invisible hand of the market… but above all for the visible hand of rulers who tell people what to do when'.[320]

It is noted that this modification also bears on the possibility of external (judicial or other) review. Richard Epstein suggests, and proceeds to deny, that the logical conclusion of a contractual construction of welfare programmes is that they are beyond review.[321] Epstein's suggestion, however, is more convincing than his rebuttal. If benefits are understood simply as a contract between the state and (some of) its citizens, how can any external criteria be relevant? The state offers the benefits, and the potential beneficiary may accept or reject them, along with the conditions attached. And, indeed, Mead candidly states that:

both states and recipients… need not accept the grants, but neither may they demand them without conditions… This strong constitutional position has meant that requirements like work tests are difficult to challenge in court.[322]

What we lack, therefore, is a substantive baseline. Market-based negotiations amongst members of the community require only a thin baseline which would not permit enforcing contractual terms that are, for example, illegal, immoral or exploitative to an inordinate degree.[323] From this outset it is natural to conclude that a person's entitlement corresponds to her contribution. Moreover, the market-based paradigm would morally permit that those with extensive

---

[316] Case C-173/99 *BECTU v DTI* [2001] ECR I-4881 [53] [emphasis added]; see H Collins, KD Ewing and A McColgan, *Labour Law—Text and Materials* (Hart: Oxford, 2001) 399–403.
[317] Harel (n 279 above) 111.
[318] K Campbell, 'The Concept of Rights' (DPhil Thesis: Oxford, 1979) 74.
[319] Handler (n 289 above) 203.
[320] R Dahrendorf, 'The Changing Quality of Citizenship' in B van Steenbergen (ed), *The Condition of Citizenship* (Sage: London, 1994) 10, 13.
[321] R Epstein, 'The Uncertain Quest for Welfare Rights' (1985) BYU L Rev 201, 212.
[322] Mead (n 257 above) 170–71.
[323] Atiyah (n 241 above) 265–81, 341–44; L Murphy and T Nagel, *The Myth of Ownership* (OUP: New York, 2002) 15–16; cf Miller (n 230 above) 104.

economic resources may purchase exemptions from social obligations.[324] It is submitted here that adherence to a traditional conceptualization of rights which derives from values that are unrelated to behaviour would yield a different set of conditions than those exhibited in current welfare-to-work programmes.

E Conclusion

This purpose of this chapter was multifold. First, it sought to introduce the basic concepts and fundamental structures that the book will address. Significant amongst these are the basic welfare state tenets; the role of rights in general, and welfare rights in particular, within the modern welfare state; and social contract philosophy and policy. In addition, the chapter showed how welfare-to-work programmes form a conceptual field that is affected by trends and variations within the manner that the above concepts are constructed. Lastly, and very much connected to both these aims, the chapter introduced a set of policy decisions and distinctions, such as the focus on entrance to the labour market, changes in the way rights are perceived and the division of the deserving and undeserving poor, to name but a few. These changes are often justified through reference to the social contract, while having a significant impact on welfare state fundamentals.

This chapter showed that general objections to social and economic rights, including the right to welfare, do not withstand criticism. Social and economic rights are at least as instrumental in advancing the same values that civil and political rights promote. In addition, civil and political rights are so closely connected to social and economic rights that no argument manages to target the former while absolving the latter.

The exposition of early and modern social contract theories was also introduced with the aim of elucidating the way the structure of a philosophical argument may impact policy decisions. With the focus on individualism, the strong connection between rights and duties and the potentially problematic role for equality (as a justification for further duties, rather than stronger rights) it is almost natural that the social contract would serve as an influential platform for welfare-to-work programmes.

And yet, as no argument was offered for or against a contractarian approach in general, it is significant that the final subsection dealing with the social contract is (controversially) entitled 'manipulation'. By choosing such a heading, I referred to the transformation that an approach that is dominant in justifying liberal philosophy has undergone at the hands of academics and policy-makers. No claim was made as to which theory is closer to the core ideal of social contract methodology, even assuming such core exists and, similarly, the question of whether a social contract agenda is *inherently* problematic to the less fortunate members of

---

[324] Cox (n 301 above) 12.

society was left open. Rawls, probably the most important figure within the modern contractarian tradition, has put much effort into constructing a highly egalitarian theory that would reject this assertion. And yet, some indication that this may be the case is offered earlier in the chapter, with the description of Locke's impatient attitude towards the poor and Gauthier's conclusions that are a result of his 'baseline' approach.

The approach to rights and duties marks a significant convergence point between welfare-to-work programmes and contractarian approaches, since both address the conditions that may be legitimately attached to rights. This final section of the chapter showed that the relationship between rights and duties, though complex and changing, cannot be used in a manner that detracts from the place that rights hold in social debates and legal decisions. The strengths and weaknesses of the interest and choice theories offered a useful starting point for the investigation. As even Hart accepted, the flaws of the choice theory bar it from serving as a general platform for the analysis of rights and duties. And yet, its critiques of the interest theory remain. Noteworthy amongst these critiques is the fear that rights and duties are brought too close together. This is done, first, by turning to collective interests when deciding what rights exist and, second, by incorporating the idea of duties in the definition of rights. The threat is, then, that the independence of rights and their role practical reasoning may be undermined. This, it was stressed in the first two sections, is not a necessary character of the interest theory, but may well be an explanation for the current popularity of the idea that there are 'no rights without responsibilities'.

2
Welfare-to-Work Programmes Under the Poor Laws

Current debates on welfare-to-work programmes may leave the impression that the problem of the unemployed who depend on public assistance for their material well-being is a welfare state phenomenon. But the problem, the proposed solutions and the rationales underlying those solutions can be identified well before the 21st century. The inherent value placed in work along with contempt for those living at public expense echoes through the ages. And yet, alongside such sentiments, we find calls for compassion and structural explanations for the poor person's predicament. Indeed, one can trace similar arguments, in only mildly different attire, throughout history. In doing so, however, one should be wary not to dismiss significant changes that have taken place. The establishment of the modern welfare state and the launching of insurance schemes for unemployment benefits (alongside health and pension benefits) changed, to a large degree, the context of the discourse, if not the arguments themselves. This dramatic evolution, overshadowing many others, makes thematic analogies between earlier and contemporary programmes all the more difficult. And yet, a panoramic view, spanning centuries of 'definitive solutions' to the problem of the unemployed, is extremely valuable. It places current arguments in their proper historical context, demonstrating continuity in welfare issues from early modernity to the present. This chapter, therefore, will outline the main features of welfare-to-work programmes leading up to the 20th century and, at the same time, will introduce some of the theoretical issues that will be developed in subsequent chapters.

The chronological and geographic borders of such an endeavour need to be stated. An historical overview of welfare-to-work programmes must begin with England and, furthermore, it must begin with the English Poor Laws. Gertrude Himmelfarb states that 'England served as a social laboratory for other countries...Just as America was the exemplar of democracy, so England was the exemplar of social welfare—and in both cases, for both good and ill'.[1]

It is fitting to set the beginning of this exploration at the start of the 17th century as until then 'it cannot be said that Poor Laws, in our sense of the word

---

[1] G Himmelfarb, *The Idea of Poverty* (Faber: London, 1984) 5.

(ie measures for the relief of destitution) existed at all; they might more fittingly be called laws against the poor and the rights of labour'.[2] Indeed, though the Poor Relief Act of 1601,[3] (commonly know as the Old Poor Law) was, in effect, a consolidating measure, it has grown to be viewed as 'the history of the country's social conscience'.[4] American programmes, for their part, followed British ideology in spirit and form well into the 20th century. Desmond King, in his studies of programmes targeting impoverished members of societies in Britain and the United States, concludes that 'the principal characteristics of the Elizabethan Poor Law of 1601 ... were adopted by the American states both during and after the colonial period'.[5]

In fact, the importance of the Poor Laws in British social and economic history is so well recognised that some historians consider the Old Poor Law to be a turning point in British economic history, as it created a *right to welfare relief*.[6] A full assessment of this claim requires a jurisprudential and historical analysis that would take us well beyond the scope of this book. However, it should be clear from the analysis provided in the first section of this chapter that, on the basis of the structure and administration of the Poor Laws, no such conclusion can be reached. Rather, the duty of Poor Law officials (known as Overseers) to distribute 'competent sums of money for and towards the necessary relief of the lame, impotent, old, blind, and such other among them, being poor, and not able to work'[7] is phrased as a duty, and not as a right bestowed upon the beneficiaries.[8] Indeed, while a legal right to subsistence may have 'relieved the poor of the obligation to work',[9] the able-bodied had only the choice between work, on the one hand, or confinement and punishment as 'sturdy beggars', on the other hand.[10] And, as already noted and as will be discussed below, a right to welfare necessarily limits

---

[2] TW Fowle, cited in S Webb and B Webb, *English Poor Law History: Part I—The Old Poor Law* (Cass: London, 1963) 397. Thus, the famous Statute of Labourers 25 Ed III c 3 stated:

And because many sound beggars do refuse to labour so long as they can live from begging alms, giving themselves up to idleness and sins, and, at times, to robbery and other crimes—let no one, under the aforesaid pain of imprisonment presume, under colour of piety or alms to give anything to such as can very well labour, or to cherish them in their sloth, so that thus they may be compelled to labour for the necessaries of life.

[3] 43 Elizabeth I c 4 (Old Poor Law).
[4] HL Beales, 'The New Poor Law' (1931) 15 History 308, 309.
[5] D King, *Actively Seeking Work* (Chicago UP: London, 1995) 224 n2; also D King, *In the Name of Liberalism* (OUP: Oxford, 1999) 258–65.
[6] Himmelfarb (n 1 above) 149 argues that 'By guaranteeing to all the means of subsistence as a legal right, England has relieved the poor of the obligation to work'.
[7] Old Poor Law s 1.
[8] Webb and Webb (n 2 above) 397, arguing that the 'English Poor Law at no time gave the destitute a personal 'right' to relief... What was enacted was not a right at all, but an obligation'. Others hold more ambivalent positions on this matter. See eg R Cranston, *Legal Foundations of the Welfare State* (Weidenfeld and Nicolson: London, 1985) 31; S Deakin and F Wilkinson, *The Law of the Labour Market* (OUP: Oxford, 2005) 112–13; L Charlesworth, 'The Poor Law' (1999) 6 JSSL 79, 80.
[9] Himmelfarb (n 1 above) 149.
[10] Himmelfarb (n 1 above) 25.

the discretion granted to officials and the conditions that may be legitimately placed on benefits.

A Antecedent Themes in Welfare-to-Work Programmes

As Deakin and Wilkinson have recently noted, though the 'context of those statutory provision had completely changed... there were many continuities in the transition from the poor law to social security'.[11] And so, instead of attempting in a quixotic way to tackle the overwhelming range of texts and analysis found in Poor Law material, the current chapter will address only those ideas that carry into or have analogies in contemporary programmes. In the process, it would be useful to distinguish between the various features by virtue of their perspectives: those that refer to the administration of relief, on the one hand, and those that govern the way that the beneficiaries are viewed, on the other hand.

1 The Administration of Relief

Identifying the family, church, community or the state as the primary organ in charge of relieving material distress has considerable implications when seeking to elucidate the prevalent understanding of the provision of welfare at the time. The two extremes lie between a concrete institutional duty on the part of the state to satisfy a right to welfare held by an individual, and the belief that while acts of charity are to be praised, it is so because they are, quite literally, 'above and beyond the call of duty'.

i) Public and Private Responsibility

From a social, as well as a legal, standpoint, the Poor Law of 1601 is no less than a watershed in the provision of poor relief. Himmelfarb explains that while 'the old kind of charity left it to the individual to alleviate, according to his means, the suffering he saw about him', the Poor Law transformed relief of material want into 'a matter of social action rather than public virtue'.[12] The bureaucracy erected under the Poor Law mandate was the basis for a less instinctive, more rational and systematic form of relief. It is important, however, not to overstate the implications of this bureaucracy. Though it does demonstrate a break with the past, Poor Law legislation and administration codified many of the prevalent practices of the time.

---

[11] Deakin and Wilkinson (n 8 above) 110; see similarly FF Piven and RA Cloward, *Regulating the Poor* (Updated Edition, Vintage: New York, 1993) 11; J Handler and Y Hasenfeld, *Blame Welfare, Ignore Poverty and Inequality* (CUP: Cambridge, 2007) 154–55; W Quigley, 'Backwards into the Future' (1998) 9 Stanford L and Society Rev 101.
[12] Himmelfarb (n 1 above) 148–89.

Thus, despite the formation of the new administration, it was seen as necessary for the Poor Law to state that it is the family that holds the legal obligation to 'relieve and maintain' its constituents.[13] This responsibility preceded the duty held by the state, and had practical implications for the administration of the Poor Law. For example, after concluding that a man was to be recognized as the father of a child (typically, this situation became contentious when a child was born out of wedlock), the court would order that he, and not the local authority, be charged for the maintenance of the child.[14] Furthermore, under the Old Poor Law, the parish was empowered to seize the goods and chattels of a father or mother who has abandoned his or her children to cover the expenses of the children's maintenance.[15] This idea, of the primacy of family responsibility, is resonant in contemporary welfare reform, as one may deduce from the policy of refusing lone mothers' claims on the basis of insufficient efforts to locate the father.

The administration of the Poor Laws further weakens the notion that a serious, public responsibility was established. A ubiquitous feature in the administration of the Poor Law, bitterly termed 'farming of the poor',[16] requires mentioning, as it carries on to present day programmes. This term refers to the privatization or 'contracting out' of various public duties, predominantly (but not solely) the administration of the workhouse. Two approaches were exhibited. Less popular was a system based on granting the contractor a small sum for every pauper who resided in the workhouse, thus creating an immediate incentive for the operator to see to it that the workhouse was as occupied as possible. This method was not widespread and for good reason: it could not guarantee the object for which the workhouse was founded—reducing the funds spent on relief. Much more popular was the lump-sum approach, whereby the contractor received a certain sum to maintain the poor, and he was free to distribute it as he pleased. Under this system it was in the contractor's interest to have as few inhabitants in the workhouse as possible. Thus, workhouses were run with the harshness that made them 'Houses of Terror' and earned the contractor the reputation of a 'slave-driver of the worst description'.[17]

ii) Local Control and Discretion

Why is the issue of local control at all relevant to the normative assessment of a given system? Under certain circumstances, it may indeed be irrelevant. For example, the control of a school's governing body over the days that each of its teachers is employed would not, barring extraordinary circumstances, affect our

---

[13] Old Poor Law s 1; See Deakin and Wilkinson (n 8 above) 144.
[14] J Ely, 'Poor Laws of the Post-Revolutionary South, 1776–1800' (1986) Tulsa L J 1, 15.
[15] 13 & 14 Cha II c 12 (Settlement Act) s 19.
[16] Webb and Webb (n 2 above) 412–13; See also D Marshall, 'The Old Poor Law 1662–1795' (1937) 8 Economic History Review 38, 46.
[17] Webb and Webb (n 2 above) 412.

conclusion that children of different schools have (or do not have) a right to be educated. But if the school exerts control that enables it not to accept children with disabilities, for example, we would be forced to reconsider the vitality of such a right in the particular jurisdiction. A standard limiting this control and forbidding such considerations to be taken into account would thus promote the children's right to education and to equal treatment. We find, therefore, that the administrative issue of local control should be assessed while coupled with another factor—that of discretion.

The relationship between discretion and welfare rights is an interesting one, and has not been ignored.[18] The traditional position argues for an inverse relationship between individual rights and administrative discretion—the weaker the former, the more the individual is at the mercy of the latter.[19] In the context of the Old Poor Law, the discretion granted to Overseers to distribute 'competent sums of money for... the necessary relief of the lame, etc.'[20] had to be extremely strong for the Poor Law to be accepted as legitimate.[21] However, the result was that the corresponding entitlement could be no more than a trivial one: to receive whatever support the administrator decided to bestow. Contrariwise, as Goodin notes:

The distinctive feature of rights is that they constitute control from below.... Rights thus constitute one clear way of diminishing the discretionary power of state officials, by giving those subject to their authority a certain measure of legal control over them.[22]

This phenomenon was not limited to the Poor Law primary legislation. Himmelfarb notes that the use of open-ended concepts was rampant throughout the administration, noting that the two (discretion and rights) are closely related:

The frustration was all the worse because the 'right' was couched in language that was so vague, all those denominated 'poor' being told that they had a 'right to a "*reasonable* subsistence," or "a *fair* subsistence" or "an *adequate* subsistence." '... The alternative to this *vacuous notion of right* was the idea of 'contract'.[23]

---

[18] J Handler, 'Discretion in Social Welfare: The Uneasy Position in the Rule of Law' (1983) 92 YLJ 1270; WH Simon, 'Legality, Bureaucracy and Class in the Welfare System' (1983) 92 YLJ 1198.

[19] M Adler and S Asquith, 'Discretion and Power' in M Adler and S Asquith (eds), *Discretion and Welfare* (Heinemann: London, 1981) 9, 12. But some have observed that welfare interests require a certain degree of administrative discretion: N Harris, 'Welfare State and Social Citizenship Rights' in N Harris (ed), *Social Security Law in Context* (OUP: Oxford, 2000) 36; CA Reich, 'The New Property' (1963) 73 YLJ 733; WH Simon, 'Rights and Redistribution in the Welfare System' (1986) 38 Stanford L Rev 1431, 1489; R Goodin, *Reasons for Welfare* (Princeton UP: Princeton, 1998) 190.

[20] Old Poor Law s 1.

[21] Deakin and Wilkinson (n 8 above) 117.

[22] Goodin (n 19 above) 211.

[23] Himmelfarb (n 1 above) 161–62 [final emphasis added]; similarly see S Deakin, 'The Capability Concept and the Evolution of European Social Policy' in M Dougan and E Spaventa (eds), *Social Welfare and EU Law* (Hart: Oxford, 2005) 3, 6.

While Himmelfarb concludes that this vagueness offered claimants an opportunity to fill the open-ended terms with their own 'desires and imaginations', Cranston argues that this framework allowed the administration of the poor law to act in a manner that was arbitrary, discriminatory, arrogant, 'and in some cases downright cruel'.[24] Contemporary critics of welfare-to-work programmes similarly suggest that in order 'for there to be rights *in fact*... eligibility has to be fairly clear-cut, with a minimum of field-level discretion'.[25] Indeed, when the power to distinguish between deserving and undeserving poor was transferred to private and charity organizations, such as the Christian Organisation Society (COS), the bureaucracy of relief became entangled with social control and families were seen as undeserving 'by reference to the qualities of temperance, cleanliness and thrift'.[26]

Complementing the discretion granted to officials, the issue of local control or, in Poor Law jargon, the concept of 'settlement' is central to the understanding of the system. It has been argued that 'poor law was largely settlement law, and settlement law provided the rights and obligations which underpinned both the right to poor relief and the duty to provide it'.[27] Though the opening statement of the passage quoted may claim too much, it nonetheless indicates the centrality of the organizational feature of distributing relief solely through the mechanism of the local parish. Under the Act of Settlement, local justices had the power to remove 'any Person or Persons that are likely to be chargeable to the parish [that they] shall come to inhabit'.[28] The use of such discretion was perceived, even by those who were unsympathetic to any form of relief, as 'contradictory to all ideas of freedom' and 'as a most disgraceful and disgusting tyranny'.[29] The situation of paupers was made all the more difficult by the fact that the administration accentuated the harsh provisions of the Act of Settlement with even harsher practices, ignoring even the few safeguards that the law supplied.[30] This was partially because each parish operated separately with considerable legal discretion, exercising a degree of freedom that 'led to increasingly idiosyncratic methods of distributing poor relief'.[31]

In addition to the evident effect on the situation of claimants, such an extreme degree of local control and discretion has also been considered to be an ill-founded mechanism in dealing with the causes and symptoms of unemployment:

It can only be concluded that 'the elementary lesson that effective treatment of the Unemployment problem is utterly beyond the power of Local Government has not been

---

[24] Cranston (n 8 above) 30.
[25] J Handler, *Social Citizenship and Workfare in the United States and Western Europe* (CUP: Cambridge, 2004) 248.
[26] Deakin and Wilkinson (n 8 above) 148.
[27] Charlesworth (n 8 above) 80.
[28] Settlement Act s 1.
[29] TR Malthus, *Essays on Population*, cited in M Rose, 'Settlement, Removal and the New Poor Law' in D Fraser (ed), *The New Poor Law in the Nineteenth Century* (Macmillan: Basingstoke, 1976) 25.
[30] Such as the requirement to obtain judicial order before removal—Cranston (n 8 above) 24.
[31] Charlesworth (n 8 above) 85.

learned'. Even with regard to the provision of maintenance, the government refused to realise 'the difficulties inherent in the use of a local system of relief to cure a depression national in its scope, and due to causes that are national and even international rather than local in their character'.[32]

Nonetheless, we find contemporary programmes following similar paths. Though some aspects of welfare programmes are directed by central government, the emphasis on local control continually resurfaces in present-day programmes.[33] Indeed, it has been argued that, like settlement policy, contemporary residency laws 'cement the relationship between a regional welfare system and a regional economy' and thus to maintain a low wage labour pool in the locality.[34] Moreover, states and municipalities have a strong fiscal incentive to reduce expenses so as not to deter business and wealthy individuals from residing there, even if the factual basis for this fear is highly disputed. Along with the noticeable hesitation of local public officials to assist disenfranchised, unpopular constituencies, granting authority on welfare programmes to state and local governments has led to harsh conditions and lower rates. Indeed, this rationale formed an important part of the reason that the American benefit programme was nationalized in 1935.[35]

2 The Beneficiaries

Conditions for entitlement spread on a continuum between two poles: at one extreme, one finds conditions that target groups of people who are entitled to relief solely due to circumstances beyond their control (such as age and disability). At the other extreme, the individual is eligible for welfare provision only if he or she abides by certain behavioural requirements. Needless to say, such conditions assume the individual's ability to do so. Whether unemployment is more a matter of circumstances beyond one's control or a direct consequence of one's behaviour has been the subject of major controversy for centuries. As this section shows, the rationales and distinctions behind the provisions of Poor Law provisions exhibit a very clear position insofar as this debate is concerned.

i) Deserving and Undeserving Poor

The importance of this distinction in contemporary welfare policies has already been noted in the previous chapter, along with the difficulties of drawing an

---

[32] S Webb and B Webb, *English Poor Law History—Part II: The Last Hundred Years* (Cass: London, 1963) 708 (footnotes omitted); for a similar sentiment see Deakin and Wilkinson (n 8 above) 193–99.
[33] D Finn, 'Welfare to Work' (2004) 13 Benefits 93, 95; Quigley (n 11 above) 106–7.
[34] Piven and Cloward (n 11 above) 144 and generally ch 4.
[35] L Williams, 'The Abuse of Section 1115 Waivers: Welfare Reform in Search of a Standard' (1994) 12 Yale L and Policy Rev 8, 32–36.

acceptable line between the two. Himmelfarb finds that this sentiment was central in the reasoning of the Poor Law Commission of 1832–1834:

> To this end, the 'dispauperizing' of the poor, the commission sought to create a 'broad line of distinction between the class of independent labourer and the class of paupers'. The whole of the report was, in effect, an exercise in definition and distinction, an attempt to establish that line theoretically and to maintain it institutionally... The heart of the matter was in the distinction between pauper and poor. Once that was conceded, the rest fell into place.[36]

'Badging the poor' was therefore merely a crude, physical manifestation of this distinction. Under the *Poor Relief Act* of 1696, a person receiving alms was to wear a badge on their right shoulder bearing the letter 'P', joined with the initial of his or her parish.[37] But the ability to distinguish between the working poor and the pauper was probably secondary to the hope that by making the identity of paupers known it would be more difficult for them to make false claims undetected. 'Then as now', observe the Webbs, 'those concerned to promote economy entertained exaggerated hopes of the savings which weeding out malingerers might achieve.'[38]

In terms of the structure and rationale behind welfare-to-work programmes, however, this distinction between labouring poor and able-bodied paupers is of negligible importance, especially when contrasted with the distinction between the able-bodied unemployed and the 'impotent' (aged and infirm) unemployed.[39] The reason for this seems plain, for it is this latter distinction that discriminates clearly (at least theoretically)[40] between those who cannot gain subsistence due to their own fault or choice, and those who had fallen victim to ill fate. Incentives and disincentives could target those whose personal capacities enabled them (again, in theory) to work, thus eliminating the category of 'undeserving poor'— those able to work but refusing to do so. Therefore, this distinction was also central to the Quincy Report:

> The poor are of two classes: first, the impotent poor, in which denomination are included all who are wholly incapable of work, through old age, infancy, sickness or corporeal debility; second, the able poor, in which denomination are included all who are capable of work of some nature or other...[41]

---

[36] Himmelfarb (n 1 above) 163.
[37] 8 & 9 Will III c 3 s 2.
[38] G Oaxley, *Poor Relief in England and Wales 1601–1834* (David & Charles: London, 1974) 55.
[39] D Macarov, *Work and Welfare—The Unholy Alliance* (Sage: London, 1980) 35–37.
[40] Liverpool philanthropist William Rathbone saw this effort as futile and its consequences potentially disastrous:

> It is beyond the omnipotence of Parliament to meet the conflicting claims of justice to the community; severity to the idle and vicious and mercy to those stricken down into penury by the visitation of God...

LGB *Third Annual Report* Appendix 247 cited in D Fraser, 'Introduction' in Fraser (n 29 above) 13.
[41] *Committee on Pauper Laws* (1821) cited in King, 1999 (n 5 above) 263.

According to the report, assisting the poor would diminish the work ethic by 'destroying the economical habits and eradicating the providence of the laboring class of society'.[42] We find, then, that the necessity to distinguish between the deserving and undeserving poor motivates a practical element of Poor Law schemes, that of 'less eligibility'.

ii) The Principle of Less Eligibility

The ideology behind the principle of less eligibility tied, in clear terms, welfare provision to market wages. In doing so, its architects sought to limit social protection only to those who could not function in the labour market.[43] Explaining the practical implications of this approach, the Royal Commission could not have been clearer than when it stated that:

The first and most essential of all conditions... is that [the able bodied person's] situation, on the whole, shall not be made really or apparently so eligible as the *situation of the independent labourer of the lowest class*... Every penny bestowed, that tends to render the condition of the pauper more eligible than that of the independent labourer, is a bounty on indolence and vice.[44]

Of more acidic nature is Thomas Carlyle's dictum: 'if paupers are made miserable, paupers will decline in multitude. It is a secret known to all ratcatchers'.[45] It should be noted that the concept of less eligibility applied not only to decisions regarding rates of relief but was also used to justify poor conditions in the workhouse. For example, when asked to comment on the report that, on average, three workhouse inmates were assigned one bed, one administrator replied with a question, asking 'whether or not, in the houses of the poor, they did not average more than three to a bed?'.[46] The Webb's Minority Report concluded that 'the premises, the sleeping accommodation, the food and the amount of work exacted, taken together, constitute a treatment more penal and more brutalizing than that of any gaol in England'.[47] Glancing back to the debate mentioned above, the bare standards that result from the principle of less eligibility serve as an indication that the reality of the Poor Law 'was far removed from the idealized picture of a "right to poor relief"'.[48]

This section surveyed the major themes of Poor Law programmes that are exhibited in contemporary programmes. Due to this restriction, other interesting

---

[42] *Committee on Pauper Laws* (1821) cited in King, 1999 (n 5 above) 263.
[43] G Esping-Andersen, *The Three Worlds of Welfare Capitalism* (Polity: Cambridge, 1990) 146.
[44] *Report from His Majesty's Commissioners for Inquiring into the Administration and Practical Operation of the Poor Laws* (1834) [hereafter *Poor Law Report*] 228 cited in Webb and Webb (n 32 above) 62 [emphasis added].
[45] Cited in Beales (n 4 above) 316; Himmelfarb (n 1 above) 163.
[46] Cited in D Ashforth, 'The Urban Poor Law' in Fraser (n 29 above) 128, 140.
[47] S Webb and B Webb, *The Public Organisation of the Labour Market: Being Part Two of the Minority Report of the Poor Law Commission* (Longmans, Green and Co: London, 1909) 79.
[48] Cranston (n 8 above) 32.

features have necessarily been omitted, including the lack of a right to appeal against decisions not to grant relief[49] and the administration's power to recover the cost of relief from beneficiaries if a poor person came into money or security or died leaving money or property.[50]

But one feature has been omitted from the above discussion for a different reason altogether. The conditioning of welfare provision on the duty to work not only did not disappear, but gained such prominence that it is difficult to envisage a welfare-to-work programme in any jurisdiction that is absent of such a feature. This pervasiveness merits special consideration and is taken up in the following section.

B Setting the Poor to Work—The Conditionality of Welfare

Conditioning benefits upon the beneficiary's behaviour and inclinations is a central feature in the typology of welfare-to-work programmes.[51] One may even argue that the precise nature of the conditioning gives welfare relief programmes their specific character. Thus, for each programme, the following questions have to be addressed: *Who* is subject to conditioning? *What* is demanded? *Why* are these conditions put forth (that is, what is the rationale underlying the conditioning of welfare relief)?

Only the first question receives a simple answer insofar as this essay is concerned, for amongst those subject to various kinds of conditioning, the poor, able-bodied unemployed stand out mainly because they are seen as able to change their predicament and to cease living on state aid. The subsequent questions broaden the horizon of issues that may be dealt with, for demands from the unemployed may be as amorphous as 'being responsible for their family's well being' or as concrete as 'accepting any job offered to them'. The rationales and motivations underlying these requirements are similarly spread across a broad continuum, as will be explored below. This section will focus on conditions that concern the attitude and behaviour of the poor towards the labour market, though other forms of conditioning will be mentioned to complete the portrayal.

The conditioning of relief upon work requirements seems natural to a 21st century student of social welfare policy and legislation. It is actually the prospect of unconditional benefits that seems a peculiar suggestion.[52] Though a deeper historical perspective may conceivably yield a different conclusion, it is clear that by the 17th century, welfare and work could no longer be viewed as separate.

---

[49] *R v Newton* (1864) 28 JP 725 in Cranston (n 8) 32; Charlesworth (n 8 above) 88.
[50] Cranston (n 8 above) 32. This transformed the duty to relieve the poor to something that was more akin to a loan.
[51] C Grover and J Stewart, *The Work Connection* (Palgrave: Houndmills, 2002) 23.
[52] Macarov (n 39 above) 11.

Prominent amongst the conditions of the Poor Law programmes is the idea that able-bodied poor will receive only 'Indoor Relief' within the confines of the workhouse. Latter day political and institutional contingencies required a revision of this condition and alternative measures were suggested. Significant amongst them was the Labour Yard, in which the poor would be set to outdoor tasks, often motivated by the desire to occupy the claimants. 'Relief Work' or 'Made Work' projects that benefited society were orchestrated in several regions. Occasionally, the poor were 'set to work' within the confines of the free market, whether through the requirement that they accept any offer of work, or by ensuring that they 'actively' or 'genuinely' seek work on their own.

Different rationales could be seen as dominant in the analysis of welfare-to-work conditions. Moreover, more than one agenda motivates or advances certain programmes and certain provisions within programmes. The text of the legal provisions cannot be expected to offer a straightforward position on the matter, and different approaches may be supported. Thus, Piven and Cloward go to great lengths to show that even when certain policies 'may be justified in the language of moral virtue... their economic effect is to ensure a pool of marginal workers'.[53] And, when Louisina dropped 30 per cent of the cases (of these 95 per cent African American) because the children were born out of wedlock, state officials 'agreed that their law was as frankly directed towards saving public funds as it was toward improving family morals'.[54] This conflation of motivations is quite natural, of course, as 'not every social practice can be interpreted in the sense of discovering its underlying social vision'.[55] Finding an unequivocal interpretation to the social vision of the programmes, therefore, is not the task at hand. Instead, it is important to map out the rationales motivating welfare-to-work programmes in general. Such a platform will also assist in comparing, contrasting and evaluating different programmes and their different emphases. I identify four rationales as especially relevant in the workings of Poor Law and contemporary welfare-to-work programmes:

(1) Deterring applicants from claiming relief by conditioning relief payments upon harsh requirements.
(2) The moral argument extending from the view that work enjoys an inherent moral value to various mechanisms of social control.
(3) The utilitarian or fiscal rationale, emphasizing that resources should be used efficiently and that public costs kept to a minimum.
(4) The contractual, quid-pro-quo understanding of relief that requires clients to give something in return for the benefits received.

---

[53] Piven and Cloward (n 11 above) 127, and see generally chs 4 and 5.
[54] Cited in Handler and Hasenfeld (n 11 above) 165.
[55] H Collins, *Justice in Dismissal* (Oxford: Clarendon, 1992) 74.

A brief defence of this list may be called for. Many authors describing Poor Law programmes focus on their deterrent nature, while appraisers of contemporary programmes tend to identify a shift to a contractual discourse. The two perspectives, however, are not as far apart as this description implies. If contractual discourse is understood as encompassing all forms of conditioning, then it indeed contains all the ideologies and rationales listed above, including the deterrent aspect, as explained below. If, on the other hand, the contractual rationale is an independent ideology that focuses on the reciprocal, quid-pro-quo attribute of human relations, then it stands distinct not only from a deterrent approach, but also from those approaches that highlight, inter alia, fiscal or moralistic explanations.

It is hardly contested that the rationales listed above are not independent of each other. Different ideologies may be invoked to bring about similar consequences while certain institutions may be seen to reflect more than one rationale. And yet, there are significant differences between the motivations, as each reflects a different perspective on human interaction, free will, the image of beneficiaries, and various social and legal institutions. Therefore, though the categorizing of a specific feature of the programmes under one rationale and not another is not incontestable, this thematic portrayal helpfully maps the dominant rationales and the provisions that they inspire. I now turn to outline several of the manifestations of these attitudes as exhibited in poor relief programmes prior to the welfare state.

1 Conditioning for Deterrence

For many commentators, conditions for relief under the Poor Laws, and especially those applied under the New Poor Law of 1834,[56] are driven by the desire to deter claimants from applying for benefits.[57] But if that is indeed the case, why not opt for the 'Alexandrian solution' and cut the knot that is impossible to untangle? Indeed, for some 'abolitionists' during the Poor Law era, lowering the number of applicants was seen as an end in itself, and the existence of a system of relief was viewed as a concession. Furthermore, these views clearly crossed the Atlantic as well as the threshold of the 20th century. Josephine Brown writes about welfare provision in the United States during the Great Depression:

The conviction still prevailed generally that relief should be made so disagreeable to the recipient that he would be persuaded or forced to devise some means of self support in order to get off the list as swiftly as possible.[58]

---

[56] 4 & 5 Geo IV c 76.
[57] See eg King 1999 (n 5 above) 240; Webb and Webb (n 2 above) 243; Webb and Webb (n 32 above) 132–39, 347; Piven and Cloward (n 11 above) 33–36.
[58] J Brown, *Public Relief 1929–1939* (Holt: New York, 1940) 17.

But for others, and they seem to be in the majority, deterrence was seen as the negative corollary of the provision of relief. Relief should be given only to those who are in material dire straits. Those who have other options, whatever they may be, should prefer them. Charity was to be provided under conditions so detestable that 'persons not in danger of starvation will not consent to receive it'.[59] The persistent concern of welfare programmes with the issue of fraud finds a place here, for those who *do* have other feasible options but choose to receive benefits are viewed as fraudulent claimants. These claimants, then, should be deterred by the harsh conditions attached to benefits.

We find, then, that deterrence is connected to conditional benefits via the mechanism of needs-testing. Thus, one of the recurring themes in texts of the Poor Law era is the view that the relief of destitution serves, and should serve, as a test for destitution. The understanding of this mechanism may help explain the seemingly incoherent packaging of a contractual or conditional approach with the emphasis on deterrence. Under the more moderate approach to deterrence (ie distinct from the position that wishes to empty the welfare roles entirely) only the seriously destitute would accept the terms of the 'deal', thus creating a mechanism that would separate the deserving (here meaning the 'truly destitute') from the undeserving (ie the fraudulent claimants). However, the irony is, as Robert Goodin notes, that the more successful deterrent measures are, the fewer 'undeserving' claimants remain on the welfare roles. A successful mechanism would thus lead to a situation where those truly deserving of unconditional relief would be subject to the harshest measures.[60]

The rationale of deterrence is most directly exhibited in the English institution of the workhouse. The Poor Law Commissioners in 1834 stated unequivocally that:

Into such a house none will enter voluntarily; work, confinement and discipline will deter the indolent and vicious; and nothing but extreme necessity will induce any to accept the comfort which must be obtained by the surrender of their free agency and the sacrifice of their accustomed habits and gratifications.[61]

The workhouse was meant to eradicate all forms of outdoor relief, that is relief granted to the poor while they could reside at home. Permission to erect the first workhouses was granted in the early 18th century, but they became a ubiquitous phenomenon after becoming a compulsory mechanism under the New Poor Law.[62] Under the New Poor Law poor families were forced to enter the workhouse, sometimes as a whole unit, but on occasion men women and children

---

[59] Cited in A Stanley, 'Beggars Can't Be Choosers' in CL Tomlins and AJ King (eds), *Labor Law in America* (Johns Hopkins UP: Baltimore, 1992) 128, 137.
[60] R Goodin, 'Social Welfare as a Collective Social Responsibility' in D Schmidtz and R Goodin (eds), *Social Welfare and Individual Responsibility—For and Against* (CUP: Cambridge, 1998) 97, 173–74.
[61] *Poor Law Report* (1834), Part II, Section 2, para 29.
[62] Himmelfarb (n 1 above) 26.

were put in separate institutions.[63] Cranston views even the workhouse's name as misleading, as it served 'not as a source of employment but as a test of destitution itself, a medium for relief and a form of social control'.[64] And Derek Fraser sees the workhouse as the mechanism that set the principle of less eligibility into practice.[65] The principle of less eligibility places relief and wage work on a continuum, so by making the first as unattractive as possible, through the workhouse, potential claimants would opt for the latter. And so, he concludes, the workhouse 'was not intended to reduce poverty but to deter pauperism'.[66] Or, as described by one official of the period: 'The advantage of the workhouse to the parish does not arise from what the poor people can do towards their own subsistence, but from the apprehensions the poor have of it'.[67]

In a similar vein, Sidney and Beatrice Webb argue that the utility of the workhouse test lay in the fact that 'except in the very direst necessity' a person would prefer not to willingly admit himself.[68] The deterrent nature of Poor Law programmes is central to the Webbs' analysis. So much so, in fact, that they find that just as the prospect of successful deterrence was the driving force behind institutions such as the workhouse, the main reason for the demise of such institutions lies in their *in*ability to furnish sufficient deterrence. As political and institutional developments forced changes on the intolerable nature of the workhouse, the workhouse no longer deterred a significant portion of the populous from entering. Thus, a London Inspector in the early 19th century observes that 'the Workhouse is attractive to paupers...there are many persons to whom the Workhouse furnishes no test of destitution'.[69] At the same time, it became clear that a complete ban on outdoor relief was impractical to implement, and so in some cases outdoor relief was permitted, but subject to a strict work test. Over the years the work test was implemented in an increasing number of unions and, by the early 20th century, unions representing three-quarters of the national population had some form of labour test in place.[70]

It may be suggested that the institution that was established to supplement the workhouse suffered a similar fate for similar reasons—lack of deterrence. The Labour Yards were to fill in the gap left by the slow termination of the Workhouses and to reduce the costs of full-time maintenance of the poor by enabling outdoor relief while the men were employed at various tasks. Tasks such as stone breaking, wood cutting or oakum picking were assigned 'purely for deterrence'.[71] And, once

---

[63] The variations depended on time and place, as various workhouses had different policies at different times: Webb and Webb (n 32 above) 132–33.
[64] Cranston (n 8 above) 42.
[65] D Fraser, *The Evolution of the British Welfare State* (3rd edn, Palgrave: London, 2003) 48.
[66] ibid 50.
[67] M Marryot, cited in Webb and Webb (n 2 above) 244.
[68] ibid 248.
[69] ibid 376–77.
[70] Deakin and Wilkinson (n 8 above) 137–38.
[71] MA Crowther cited in King 1999 (n 5 above) 240.

again, the Royal Commission of 1905–1909 saw no reason to maintain the system that had obviously failed its purpose, since 'there grows up a nucleus of loafers, who have found the stoneyard under lax supervision an easy way of earning a scanty living'.[72] It is illuminating to note that, then as now, a perspective that idealized the value of work for work's sake was prevalent. It is thus interesting why those who participated in physical tasks for the most negligible compensation are admonished for 'earning a scanty living'. Is it because they are willing to accept the conditions that were to deter them? If so, this attitude reveals that the more cynical version of contractual deterrence, that saw lowering the number of applicants as its main concern, was more firmly established than what one may have been initially inclined to believe.

Harsh conditions for benefits, some of which will be discussed in the following chapter, were also introduced as measures to combat fraud in early welfare-to-work programmes. Instrumental in this process was the categorizing of all paupers as fraudsters. The low rates of relief at the time of the Poor Law ironically served as a basis for such a broad generalization. Thus, the Local Government Board of 1881 deduced that since the rates of benefits were so minimal, the poor must be working while receiving relief and 'the old abuse of relief in aid of wages must largely prevail in some form or other'.[73] And the leading economist at the time of the enactment of the New Poor Law explained the severe proposals of the Royal Commission as emanating from the failure of the Old Poor Law to eradicate cases of abuse and fraud. His conclusion supports the estimate that deterrent measures to welfare relief are a compromise between those who support the need for such a system and those who would like to see it abolished:

The Commissioners, with very few exceptions, appear to have set out with a determination to find nothing but abuses in the Old Poor Law, and to make the most of them; and this was no more than might have been expected, seeing that this was the most likely way to effect its abolition.[74]

2 Conditioning for Social Control

A reasonable guess would be that ever since the first institution (municipality, church, etc) distributed relief to the poor, it was relief with strings attached. Moreover, those strings probably always had to do with some form of behaviour modification. The public that grants the funds has some expectation that the poor will amend their ways, tidy their linen shirt and refrain from alcoholic beverages. What is the justification for placing such extra-labour conditions on benefits? From an intellectual point of view, a less 'interesting' rationale would be the idea that giving money to the poor grants the benefactor the necessary moral

---

[72] Webb and Webb (n 32 above) 203–4; King 1999 (n 5 above) 231.
[73] A Digby, 'The Rural Poor Law' in Fraser (n 29 above) 149, 158.
[74] JR M'Culloch, cited in Webb and Webb (n 32 above) 84n.

standing to lecture the beneficiary and indeed—to demand that he or she live a proper and decent life, as the benefactor defines it, of course. A more complex notion of social control is exhibited on a national scale where conservative, and even Fascist, regimes were ready to grant social rights that were conditional upon loyalty and morality, thus seeking to nurture the workforce while reinstalling the principle of moral desert.[75]

But there are other approaches which, at least facially, seek to connect moral and cultural norms to the task at hand, namely moving the able-bodied unemployed into the labour force. The importance of these approaches lies in the way they connect popular perceptions on poverty and the reasons for unemployment to the collective response in the form of institutionalized welfare systems.

The first approach views work itself as a moral endeavour, as a 'normalcy' or normative attitude,[76] sometimes even endowing it with reverent religious attributes, 'the power to save the soul'.[77] A second approach perceives the culture of unemployment as the cause for unemployment, and therefore justifies the conditioning of welfare benefits on moral behaviour. The third approach views the culture of unemployment as the *result* of unemployment, and addresses asocial behaviour through conditioning relief.

Though quite clear in theory, the distinction between the first and second approach breaks down when analysing the legislation and policy. Both approaches concentrate on the moral attributes of the unemployed and view a productive life as morally superior to a life of 'indolence and vice'. It is difficult to identify whether the moral authority of a life of gainful employment is seen as deriving from the paramount value of work as an end in itself or as the natural consequence of living a decent (ie productive) life. The two approaches will therefore be addressed under one heading. This section concludes with a significant and distinguishable moral agenda—the paternalistic attitude towards welfare recipients. Though it may have much in common with some of the other approaches (such as the clear concept of the good life that one should strive towards) its peculiarities merit separate exploration.

i) Moral Correction as the Avenue to Work

This perception views a productive life as one of the important common traits of a decent citizen in a decent society. The claimant is said to possess a different set of moral and cultural values and this is what explains his or her reluctance to accept an offer of work.[78] Thus, the New Poor Law sought to modify the behaviour of the poor and unemployed by holding them to a strict disciplinary regime within the workhouse, justified on the basis that 'it has been found that the pauperism of

---

[75] Esping-Andersen (n 43 above) 40.
[76] Handler (n 25 above) 22.
[77] J De Parle, *American Dream: Three Women, Ten Kids, and a Nation's Drive to End Welfare* (Viking: New York, 2004) 162; Macarov (n 39 above).
[78] Macarov (n 39 above) 124; Quigley (n 11 above) 105–6.

the greater number of [able-bodied individuals] *originated in* indolence, improvidence or vice, and might have been averted by ordinary care and industry'.[79] For those who were previously employed, it seemed even clearer that 'their way of life had been anchored in the discipline of work, and so that discipline had to be restored'. The way to do so was to shift 'from direct relief to work relief'.[80]

The moralistic practice during the workhouse era was quite crude: the pauper was to be taken away from his corrupting 'natural' environment and moved to an environment that would build a character that is conducive to society. He would be subject to a system of labour discipline and restraint that, even when not inhumane, had to adhere to the principle of less eligibility and thus be less attractive than the life of the independent labourer.[81]

The moral agenda of the Poor Law included the idea of enhancing male responsibility and punishing ' "intemperate" marriages and births outside wedlock' that were seen as 'responsible for overpopulation and the pauperization of the labouring classes'.[82] But within this practice of removing paupers from their home one notes a clash amongst the rationales that supposedly underpin Poor Law policies. Some regions adopted policies such as sending men to one institution and women and children to another.[83] Children above the age of five were required to work so as 'to prevent an idle, lazy kind of life, which if once they get the habit of, they will hardly leave'.[84] It was important to ensure that 'youth may be accustomed and brought up in labour and work'.[85] However, this policy is troubling since, then as now, those who explain unemployment through reference to moral and cultural norms consider the break-up of family ties to be intimately linked to problems of poverty and unemployment. Indeed, it has been observed that 'life in the workhouse was the antithesis of the domestic ideal: families were fragmented, women worked and men did not provide for their families'.[86] One may wonder if the modern 'man in the house' rules, which deny aid to a mother who is associated with a man in any way, do not have a similar negative effect. Dealing with unemployment by forcibly breaking up families adds more than a sense of irony to the programmes.[87]

---

[79] *Poor Law Report* (1834) 264 cited in King 1999 (n 5 above) 228 [emphasis added].
[80] Piven and Cloward (n 11 above) 80–81.
[81] Deakin and Wilkinson (n 8 above) 141.
[82] ibid 145.
[83] Digby (n 73 above) 153–4. In fact, such a policy was actually prescribed by the Poor Law Commissioners of 1832–1834, and those regions that applied the 'mixed workhouse' scheme did so knowing that they were deviating from that standard. The Webbs view the prevalence of this deviation as one of the reasons the system as a whole was eventually abandoned: Webb and Webb (n 32 above) 376–7.
[84] Cited in J Appleby, *Economic Thought and Ideology in Seventeenth Century England* (Princeton UP: Princeton, 1978) 141.
[85] Poor Law Act (1576) 18 Eliz 1 c 3.
[86] M Levine-Clark, 'Engendering Relief' (2000) 11 J of Women's History 107, 122.
[87] A more sinister suggestion is that poor men and women were segregated to prevent the 'unfit' from having children—B Barry, *Why Social Justice Matters* (Polity: Cambridge, 2005) 135.

The idea that destitution may be attributed to personal irresponsibility, a central facet of modern welfare reforms,[88] was employed to justify poor law measures, including the workhouse.[89] Then as now, the beneficiary was understood to lack the aptitude that enables his fellow man to assume responsibility for himself and his loved ones. Thus, the offer of the House compelled 'the able-bodied [man] to assume responsibility for the able-bodied period in his life'.[90] The role of personal responsibility in welfare reform is revisited in chapter 4.

ii) Addressing the Symptoms

It has been repeatedly noted that unemployment carries with it unfavourable symptoms such as social exclusion, lower levels of education, vagrancy, alcoholism and drug abuse. Conditioning welfare, then, may serve as leverage to modify this behaviour in favour of a good life that society wishes to advance. This approach can charitably be perceived as paternalistic, as society employs an existing mechanism to reach out to groups that suffer from social exclusion and to improve their condition. A more cynical interpretation would view this approach as concerned more with 'social control and the moral improvement of the lower orders',[91] concluding that 'the poor law pamphleteers of the early nineteenth century thought instinctively in terms of controlling the lives of those beneath them'.[92] Indeed, Piven and Cloward advance an even more troubling thesis, arguing that though social control is a foundational explanation for the institution and expansion of public relief, it is social control driven by fear of revolt. In this they cite the Hammonds:

> If compassion was not a strong enough force to make the ruling classes attend to the danger that the poor might starve, fear would certainly have made them think of the danger that the poor might rebel... Thus fear and pity united to sharpen the wits of the rich, and to turn their minds to the distresses of the poor.[93]

The attempt to change the social attitude and behaviour of beneficiaries through contractual arrangements, seen as 'the problematic marriage of social engineering with individual freedom',[94] did not cease with the passing of the Poor Laws. While the 18th and 19th centuries saw vagrancy as one of the main social issues to be dealt with, loose sexual conduct and the break-up of families

---

[88] Mead argues that the 'social contract' entails viewing responsibilities as being on a par with entitlements: L Mead, *Beyond Entitlement* (Free Press: New York, 1986).
[89] Deakin (n 23 above) 8.
[90] T Mackay, cited in Webb and Webb (n 32 above) 441–2.
[91] K Lawes, *Paternalism and Politics* (Macmillan: Basingstoke, 2000) 66.
[92] D Roberts, *Paternalism in Early Victorian England* (Croom Helm: London, 1979) 61–62.
[93] Piven and Cloward (n 11 above) 20–21 citing J Hammond and B Hammond, *The Village Labourer 1760–1832* (Longmans, Green and Company, 1948) 118.
[94] P Vincent-Jones, *The New Public Contracting: Regulation, Responsiveness, Relationality* (OUP: Oxford, 2006) 265.

are viewed today as matters of social concern.[95] The following chapter discusses at length some of the moral facets of contemporary welfare-to-work programmes. Though the significant differences between the societies should be taken into account, it is noted that both Poor Law and contemporary schemes tackle moral issues through the vehicle of welfare reform. In a similar vein, contemporary supporters of such conditions argue that 'the distribution of welfare is one of the great teaching forces open to advanced societies'.[96]

It is not always easy to elucidate whether the process of moral correction is done with the purpose of social control in mind, or for the bettering of lower orders themselves. Thus, the Medical Assistant Commissioner, after reporting the grave hygiene conditions that the poor experienced, opined that 'beneficiaries must be compelled to obedience alike in their own and in the public interest'.[97] A similar ambivalence is found in President Roosevelt's Congressional Address, when explaining why direct relief should be abolished in favour of work relief. Moving between the concern for the individual and the interest of the nation, he explained:

Continued dependence upon relief induces a spiritual and moral disintegration fundamentally destructive to the national fiber... We must preserve not only the bodies of the unemployed from destitution but also their self-respect, self reliance and courage and determination.[98]

This approach bridges the current perspective with a motivation that is more paternalistic in nature.

iii) Paternalism

Since the Poor Law era, the paternalistic approach to income support has viewed the good intentions of support policies as paving the road to increased misery of the poor while only seeming to alleviate their dire conditions. Under this 'perversity thesis',[99] such policies 'increase dependency, erode the work ethic and reinforce the social pathologies associated with poverty'.[100] But, more important for present purposes, paternalism has been viewed as 'the most straightforward justification for conditionality'.[101] The uniqueness of the paternalistic approach lies in its attitude to welfare claimants. In a sense, paternalism may be understood as a concrete policy that does not conflict with reciprocity, but rather

---

[95] Charles Murray wrote that 'illegitimacy is the single most important problem of our time [because] it drives everything else'—cited in A Deacon, *Perspectives on Welfare* (Open UP: Buckingham, 2002) 42.
[96] F Field, 'A Rejoinder' in A Deacon (ed), *Stakeholder Welfare* (IEA: London, 1996) 107, 111.
[97] Ibid; See further A Deacon, 'The Case for Compulsion' (1997) 98 Poverty 8–10.
[98] Cited in Piven and Cloward (n 11 above) 94.
[99] AO Hirschman, *The Rhetoric of Reaction: Pervisity, Futility, Jeopardy* (Harvard UP: Cambridge, 1991) 7–11.
[100] Handler and Hasenfeld (n 11 above) 2.
[101] A Deacon, 'An Ethic of Mutual Responsibility? Towards a Fuller Justification for Conditionality in Welfare' in C Beem and L Mead (eds), *Welfare Reform and Political Theory* (Sage: New York, 2005) 127, 131.

manifests 'the value of reciprocal relations and mutual obligation translated into a holistic, great chain of being'.[102] Indeed, leading up the early 20th century, Poor Law authorities habitually instructed claimants not only how to spend the money granted to them, but also how to conduct other aspects of their lives as well:

The principles of 1907 embody the doctrine of a mutual obligation between the individual and the community. The universal maintenance of a definite minimum of civilized life... becomes the joint responsibility of an indissoluble partnership, such as the duty to treat the sick and educate the children. The inevitable complement of this corporate responsibility is placed on the individual to keep her children in health and send them to school.[103]

This attitude may be understood as almost directly opposed to the efficiency approach that immediately follows. First, while an efficiency approach assumes the existence of and grants credence to one's ability to act rationally, ie in accordance with economic incentives, paternalism sees its justification *precisely* on the grounds that such is not the case. Emphasizing incentives and disincentives is a futile endeavour, for it will not manage to sway people to change their behaviour. Incidentally, the paternalistic approach gains some support from studies that reveal that unemployed men and women exhibit attitudes favourable to wage labour at least to the same extent as working people, and often to a greater extent.[104] Second, the two approaches support opposing views on the attitude towards the unemployed and consequently on the policy suggestions. If the person embracing the efficiency agenda blames the unemployed individual at all, she does so only implicitly. Indeed, she may actually be damning the unemployed with faint praise, congratulating them on their rational behaviour, on their ability to take advantage of the gullibility and naiveté of the state, while the state itself is ridiculed for creating such a moral hazard, encouraging the behaviour it was expected to suppress.[105] The paternalists, on the other hand, will make an effort to assist the unemployed to act on their true will and escape their predicament.

A paternalistic attitude forms part of the motivation for conditioning relief. The Poor Law Commissioner's report of 1832–1834, which provided the basis for the New Poor Law, described the impact the workhouse has on the pauper. The workhouse is seen as infusing

new life, new energy into the constitution of the pauper; *he is aroused like one from sleep*, his relation with all his neighbors, high and low, is changed; he surveys his former employers with new eyes. He begs a job—he will not take a denial.[106]

---

[102] Lawes (n 91 above) 48.
[103] S Webb and B Webb, *English Poor Law Policy* (Cass: London, 1963) 270 and see Webb and Webb (n 32 above) 613–4 for a critique of the parental responsibility policy in the beginning of the 20th century.
[104] E Anderson, 'Welfare, Work Requirements and Dependant Care' (2004) 21 J of Applied Philosophy 243, 249–50; A Alstott, 'Work vs. Freedom' (1999) 108 Yale LJ 967, 992–93.
[105] G Standing, *Global Labour Flexibility* (Macmillan: Basingstoke, 1999) 254, 321.
[106] *Poor Law Report* (n 44 above) 228 cited in King 1999 (n 5 above) 227.

King overlooks the paternalistic undertone of the passage and characterizes the attitude as one of deterrence. But such is not the case. It is on a par with the view advocated by Mead, the contemporary proponent of a paternalistic approach to welfare. Mead views the poor as 'dutiful but defeated'. Though they are naturally inclined to work, they are exposed to a system that leads to 'the degradation of the character of the labouring class'.[107] Instead, the system should create incentives to work through conditioning of benefits.[108] Both Mead and the Poor Law Commissioners convey a 'presumption of innocence' towards the unemployed. Like children, the poor are to be shown the right path. Devoid of the ability to assess their options rationally, they almost demand authority to be imparted upon them. GWF Hegel endorsed this approach:

...society has the duty and right to act as guardian on behalf of those who destroy the security of their own and their family's livelihood by extravagance, and to implement their end and that of society in their place.[109]

Ross Cranston identifies under the Old Poor Law 'the idea of a paternal ruling class which regarded the maintenance of the poor as part of their duty'.[110] He recounts the case of one William Amarys who, as he 'hath behaved himself very rudely and irreligiously in the church',[111] saw his weekly sums cut by half. The similarity to an adult granting a child allowance, and then refusing to pay because the child 'behaved badly', can hardly be more straightforward.

3 Conditioning for Efficiency

No account of historical or contemporary welfare-to-work programmes could be complete without a consideration of the fuel that drives the machine: money. In fact, just as some Poor Law measures were not effectively implemented 'as a result of the excessive costs of making the necessary arrangements',[112] spiralling costs provide a major motivation for contemporary welfare reform. Arguments that are of interest in this subsection may be termed interchangeably as 'efficiency', 'utilitarian', 'fiscal' and 'economic', all to denote an approach that focuses on the rational and efficient use of resources, monetary as well as human.

In identifying the themes that convey an economic notion as motivating the conditioning of welfare benefits, one may differentiate the micro level from the macro level. On the micro level, beneficiaries are perceived to be motivated predominantly by pecuniary incentives and disincentives. This line of thought has

---

[107] The 1824 Select Committee, cited in Deakin and Wilkinson (n 8 above) 133.
[108] L Mead, 'Welfare Employment' in L Mead (ed), *The New Paternalism* (Brookings: Washington DC, 1997) 39; Deacon (n 95 above) 49–63.
[109] GWF Hegel, *Elements of the Philosophy of Right* (HB Nisbet—tr, CUP: Cambridge, 2000) §240; and see similarly JS Mill, *Principles of Political Economy* (CUP: Cambridge, 1977) 758.
[110] Cranston (n 8 above) 35.
[111] ibid 36.
[112] Deakin and Wilkinson (n 8 above) 113.

grown in popularity over the decades, and has culminated in a contemporary discourse that warns policy-makers against granting benefits that would lead to an 'unemployment trap'. The implication is that as long as benefits remain above a certain level, the unemployed, behaving rationally, would never enter the labour force.[113] Values, stigma and social exclusion are set aside from the analysis as far as this discourse is concerned, and the position that 'people conduct their lives not only according to legal and pecuniary sanctions, but also according to social sanctions'[114] is dismissed as romantic naiveté. Thus, one 17th century writer protested that 'the Poor, if Two Dayes work will maintain them, will not work three'.[115] The Poor Law principle of 'less eligibility', that requires one to compare the unemployed to the 'independent labourer of the lowest class', naturally emanates from such a paradigm.

On the macro level, the economic rationale views with concern the waste of human resources that are not used in a manner that will increase society's wealth. Joyce Appleby finds that welfare reform policy in 17th century England did not focus on the loss that the national economy accrued due to the sums paid from the public purse, but rather on the fact that the able-bodied individuals were not included in the labour force. She states that viewing the poor as a source of labour 'represents the infusion of the outlook of those who had embraced the productive ideal into public thinking on charity',[116] and finds:

compelling evidence of the existence of a vision of economic growth and development that took precedence over immediate concerns with the distress of the poor or the exactions of the poor rate... Idle, able-bodied English men and women presented themselves to entrepreneurs as two separable qualities: persons capable of work and idle persons, and more often than not they chose to affirm the value of increasing the national labor force and focus reforming attention upon the idleness.[117]

Amongst examples of economic measures in Poor Law programmes the most straightforward are the public works schemes, which were formed to enable the poor to be 'encouraged, and mercifully dealt with, and kindly used'.[118] Appleby notes the wide range of projects embarked upon with poor relief money, including 'a fishery, the draining of fens, clearing of wastelands, working up of flax or spinning the wheel by thousands of poor whose misery could be exchanged for a supportive competence'.[119] Even more impressive were the accomplishments of the Work Progress Administration under the Roosevelt New Deal. These included, within a

---

[113] H Collins, KD Ewing and A McColgan, *Labour Law—Text and Materials* (Hart: Oxford, 2001) 466.
[114] H Michener and JD Delamater, *Social Psychology* (3rd edn, Harcourt: Orlando, 1994) 512; See also C Jolls, C Sunstein and R Thaler, 'A Behavioral Approach to Law and Economics' (1998) 50 Stanford L Rev 1471.
[115] Cited in Appleby (n 84 above) 145.
[116] Appleby (n 84 above) 151.
[117] ibid 140.
[118] ibid.   [119] ibid.

five year span, 'the construction or renovation of 110,000 buildings, 600 airports, 600,000 miles of roads and 116,000 bridges and viaducts'.[120] At times, this logic was taken to its extreme, as when parish children were seen as 'an ideal labor source for new manufacturers' thus creating a system of '"free" child labor'.[121]

However, the synthesis of wage labour and relief was subject to criticism from both sides of the political sphere. Those prone to laissez-faire ideology had their own qualms about Public Work schemes. Not only were they more expensive, but they also extended the range of government activity into areas traditionally preserved for private enterprise.[122] A more principled argument stressed the fact that wages and relief are governed by two different rationales. While the wage labourer was seen as entitled for compensation for his daily toil, relief claimants were to be offered assistance on the basis of their need, even if they were workhouse inhabitants who were assigned labour.

Another form of work-benefits fusion was the famous Speenhamland system. Under this structure (in its 'roundsman system' variant) sub-minimum wages in the labour market were complemented with parish funds. The parish would send the pauper to a farmer and pay the difference between the wages the pauper received and the allowance he was entitled to.[123]

From a modern perspective, Speenhamland is generally viewed as a failed experiment. Some stress the fact that it generally benefited employers, depressed wages while 'increas[ing] the attraction of pauperism precisely at the juncture when a man was straining to escape the fate of the destitute'.[124] Others have judged the system as espousing 'principles of pre-commidification since it... [was] designed to establish market hegemony in the distribution of welfare'.[125] Be that as it may, the Speenhamland system was in place until the New Poor Law's Labour Test Order (1842) and Relief Regulation Order (1852) directed that no relief should be given to a person who is employed.[126]

It should be noted that charity organisations such as the COS also noted their disapproval of the Speenhamland system:

Labour... is an excellent thing... But it must be labour subjected to the true conditions of labour... Charity is also an excellent thing, but... when... labour and charity are mixed up together, great abuse and demoralisation are always engendered.[127]

With such a rare historical consensus in mind, it is interesting to note that numerous Western countries are experimenting today with initiatives that combine work and benefits.

[120] Piven and Cloward (n 11 above) 97.
[121] Piven and Cloward (n 11 above) 28.
[122] Piven and Cloward (n 11 above) 82.
[123] Deakin and Wilkinson (n 8 above) 128–29.
[124] K Polanyi, *The Great Transformation* (Beacon: Boston, 1944) 99.
[125] Esping-Andersen (n 43 above) 36.
[126] Deakin and Wilkinson (n 8 above) 138.
[127] Cited in Webb and Webb (n 32 above) 643; Deakin and Wilkinson (n 8 above) 130–31.

Using beneficiaries for public works schemes, as well as in the public services, also had immediate implications on the level of wages in the labour market. The consequences of 'creating a cheap pool of forced labour'[128] have not escaped proponents and opponents of welfare reform programmes. Opponents argue that such programmes do not only have negative effects on beneficiaries, but also that they increase the polarization of the labour market by harming the negotiating position of low-wage workers and by depressing wages. Proponents of the programmes respond that all the resources that may be used to increase the ability to compete with foreign markets should be exploited. Ross Cranston notes that this line of thought goes back to the erection of the poor houses in the 17th century, inspired by the need to compete with Dutch commerce through the use of low wages.[129]

4 The Narrow Contract—Quid pro Quo

We have now reached what I find to be the most interesting rationale underlying historical, as well as current, welfare-to-work programmes. This is conditioning for the sake of conditioning. By this I do not mean that no ideology can be identified as motivating the conditioning of welfare relief,[130] but rather that the discourse may be simply and purely a contractual one. The mechanism of conditioning here is not used as a vehicle for moral betterment of individuals, efficiency or deterrence. Rather, the contractual discourse embodies the ideology of reciprocity, offering the notion that a 'something for nothing' attitude is immoral and unjust. Instead, the guiding principle is that 'those who willingly share in the social product have a corresponding obligation to make a reasonable (albeit proportional) productive contribution to the community in return'.[131]

Human interaction is perceived through a quid-pro-quo lens, elevating market intuitions to public policy principles and implying not only that imposing duties upon right holders is feasible and efficient, but also that it is morally just to do so. Appealing to our market intuition that suggests that we would not enter a contract that offers nothing for something, this proposition suggests that the same is true for all human interaction and for the welfare sphere in particular.

Furthermore, the idea that unemployed men and women should receive assistance solely on account of their condition is neither accepted nor rejected as such. The assertion is that given the fact that relief is granted, the question to be answered is what the beneficiaries of relief are to do in return. One of the most

---

[128] National Urban Coalition, cited in King 1995 (n 5 above) 159; Piven and Cloward (n 11 above) chs 4 and 5.
[129] Cranston (n 8 above) 41.
[130] M Freeden, 'The Ideology of New Labour' (1999) Political Quarterly 42 [arguing, inter alia, that there is no 'neutral' ideology].
[131] S White, 'Social Rights and the Social Contract' (2000) 30 British Journal of Political Science 507, 513.

straightforward replies to this quandary was that the claimant should take care of himself before he expects assistance. This might mean that the recipient must accept any offer of employment. In fact, the Vagrancy Act 1824[132] stated that wilfully refusing employment, even when the wages offered were inadequate or below the accepted rate, is a criminal offence punishable by one month's hard labour.[133] Only in the early 20th century did the English courts begin to place constraints on the conditions of the work that must be accepted, if offered.[134]

The quid-pro-quo rationale has reached such prominence in contemporary policies that many writers propose the term 'contractual welfare'[135] as the governing approach for all welfare policies.[136] Sometimes exploiting the concept of a 'social contract', proponents of this view celebrate the advantages that a contractual relationship between the citizen and her government, based on reciprocal rights and duties, has to offer. On one level, the quid-pro-quo ideology is somewhat similar to the economic approach. Individuals are presumed to have the same bargaining power as the state, thus able to accept or reject offers given to them. The problems of poverty and unemployment are individualized, so contracting with individuals is offered as a natural practice to deal with issues of public policy. It was already noted that for the better part of history people were merely unemployed, while the phenomenon of unemployment was not recognized. Thus, it would seem that the individualized approach was never seriously contested. As King states, policy in the United States operates under a similar paradigm:

In the U.S., apart from brief exceptions in the 1930s and 1960s, unemployment and welfare dependency have been viewed as problems of individual indolence rather than as structural manifestations of an industrial economy.[137]

But the quid-pro-quo rationale also adds a normative perspective. The argument is that it is intolerable that the poor should lay about while receiving monies. This kind of understanding would therefore justify 'occupying' the poor in any manner possible. The idea, now referred to as 'workfare', is that the poor should 'work for their benefits'.[138] Yet this attitude is distinguished from a deterrent or an economic approach. The work demanded is not meant to be a deterrent because it is not (at least not intentionally) meant to be repulsive enough to deter

---

[132] 5 Geo IV c 34 s 3.
[133] Deakin and Wilkinson (n 8 above) 139.
[134] *Lewisham Union v Nice* [1924] 1 KB 618 [conviction for refusing to work at less than trade-union rates quashed].
[135] 'Contractual welfare' should not be confused with 'welfare contractualism', which refers to the idea that agents agree that well-being provides a canonical reason for action—O O'Neil, 'Constructivism v. Contractualism' (2003) 16 Ratio 319, 329.
[136] White (n 131 above); P Vincent-Jones, 'Contractual Governance' (2000) 20 OJLS 317, 344; cf M Freedland and D King, 'Contractual Governance and Illiberal Contracts' (2003) 27 Cambridge J of Economics 465.
[137] King 1999 (n 5 above) 258.
[138] A Deacon, 'Welfare and Character' in Deacon (n 96 above) 60, 67.

the poor from applying for relief. But the work also falls short of being economically conducive to society's wealth, and demands laid upon inhabitants of the workhouses were, at times, more costly than any profit gained. Under the English Poor Laws, initiatives such as Relief Work or Employment Relief sought to put able-bodied men to work in local authorities or charitable donations, for sums that were on a par with the relief already granted to them, and well below the market rate.[139]

Notwithstanding some of noted accomplishments of the New Deal scheme known as Made Work, it is clear that at times benefits were conditioned upon fulfilment of almost useless tasks. Josephine Brown describes work projects under the New Deal as 'invented as an excuse for work, obviously made for the purpose of creating means whereby recipients of relief could make some payment for what they received'.[140] But she collapses the distinction between an economic motivation and a quid-pro-quo rationale when she states that:

Wide differences in philosophy were in the back of this method of helping the unemployed. Many people who were not willing to give outright relief to the needy, believed in making them work for what they received, so that the community would have a return for the money expended. They even insisted that the needy should 'work', although this might mean no more than putting them through the motions, as was the case on many a 'leaf-raking' project.[141]

Though, as it was made clear above, there will always be borderline cases that are affected by more than one rationale, the 'leaf-raking' projects seem to be paradigmatic examples of conditions for the sheer purpose of requiring individuals to 'do something' rather than providing a 'return for the money expended'.

The Labour Yards, discussed above, may also be seen as a manifestation of the quid-pro-quo perspective, especially when one considers the type of work demanded from the poor. Indeed, while the most repulsive and humiliating 'occupations' had a distinct deterrent facet, and others, initiated after the publication of the Chamberlain circular, had some economic merit,[142] the poor were also required to take on odd jobs such as cleaning, painting and decorating Poor Law Institutions. It is difficult, in these cases, to avoid the sensation that the motivation behind employing the poor in this manner fits the quid-pro-quo analysis. As we shall see in the forthcoming chapter, current programmes proudly manifest workfare and the 'obligation to volunteer' (oxymoronic as that phrase may be). Like many others, these features, it was shown here, are far from novel.

---

[139] Webb and Webb (n 32 above) 642–43.
[140] Brown (n 58 above) 238.
[141] Brown (n 58 above) 239.
[142] Webb and Webb (n 32 above) 367.

C Conclusion

History does, indeed, repeat itself. Welfare-to-work programmes are not an exception to this rule. In reviewing the publicly administered assistance programmes of the Poor Law era, I highlighted several important themes that serve as the foundations of current welfare-to-work programmes and will be revisited throughout. In doing so, the breadth of the Poor Law era permitted collecting examples that were, at times, centuries apart. This shows, of course, that this chapter is not meant to be an exhaustive historical tract. Rather, the purpose of the chapter was to introduce several themes that had a role, at one point or another, in the construction of historical welfare-to-work programmes. More importantly, these themes, along with the four rationales that governed Poor Law programmes—deterrence, morality, economics and quid-pro-quo—inform, in varying degrees, programmes that are in force today in different jurisdictions. A construction that follows these rationales will be employed in the following chapter, which describes in detail the programmes that are in place today in the United States and in Britain. It is important not to lose sight, however, of the fact that in both chapters these four rationales serve as sub-categories for the governing structure of welfare-to-work programmes: the idea that relief is conditional. These sub-categories, therefore, seek to explain the motivation behind different cases of conditionality. The scrutiny of the idea of conditionality itself is taken up in subsequent chapters.

In addition to these four rationales, other elements were mentioned in the discussion of Poor Law programmes. These features are still, somewhat surprisingly, as central to the discussion surrounding welfare-to-work programmes today as they were in the earlier history. Not all of them can be developed within the confines of this work. For example, the bias towards local control and privatization of welfare services cannot be discussed at length here.[143] Other characteristics, however, are central to the forthcoming analysis of contemporary programmes. First, we find the contractual discourse and the acceptability of conditioning relief upon certain requirements, just mentioned. In the following chapters I shall argue that, as a general attitude, contractual discourse of the kind exhibited during the poor law era is revisited, instigated perhaps by welfare state fatigue.

Second, the elusive distinction between deserving and undeserving poor resurfaces along with the principle of less eligibility. A consensus as to the criteria for becoming 'deserving' (for benefits) has never been reached, though it is probably the case that paradigmatic instances of deserving poor are those who are physically unable to accept any offers for employment and those who are seen to have

---

[143] For recent assessments of privatization in contemporary programmes see Deakin and Wilkinson (n 8 above) 142–43 and D Finn, 'The Role of Contracts and the Private Sector in Delivering Britain's "Employment First" Welfare State' in E Sol and M Westerveld (eds), *Contractualism in Employment Services* (Kluwer Law: The Hague, 2005) 101.

done their utmost to secure employment, but have been unsuccessful. The exemplary undeserving claimant, on the other hand, is one who is work-shy and prefers living at public expense rather than accepting appropriate job offers. Between these two, of course, are the majority of the unemployed population, as well as the most challenging cases.

Third, personal responsibility makes an appearance not only in Conservative critiques of welfare state programmes, but also in mainstream approaches to the Poor Laws. Moralistic agendas, which advanced the notion that the problem of the poor is their lack of responsibility, are detected during the workhouse era along with schemes that were to instill a sense of responsibility in the pauper. Nowadays, however, the concept of personal responsibility must be reconciled with basic human rights and fundamental welfare state intuitions.

All these, along with the important matter of a right to welfare that was only alluded to in this chapter, are issues that are central to the understanding of contemporary welfare-to-work programmes. We now turn to a close look at the details of the programmes in two countries—Britain and the United States.

3
Contemporary Welfare-to-Work Programmes

Welfare-to-work programmes throughout ages and jurisdictions necessarily exhibit similar traits, in form as well as in substance. They all have the following three features in common: first, they view work as a mechanism to deal with economic problems, such as poverty, and social problems, such as exclusion; second, they focus on the most impoverished members of society; and third, they offer benefits as a conditional entitlement, mainly on various work related obligations. The significant importance awarded to work, then, is a common feature, making the programmes a more or less coherent collection of schemes designed to move individuals from the welfare rolls into the labour market. Thus, it should not be surprising that, as the first chapter of this work intimated, on an appropriate level of abstraction, some of the ideas informing current programmes are detectable in programmes implemented centuries ago.

But alongside these common elements, variations also exist. One of the greatest changes took place at the beginning of the 20th century, with the shift from the poor law emphasis on the duty to work at market wages to policies of social insurance, full employment and access to wages that at least support subsistence. These policies, combining collectivist values with legal entitlements, were seen to contain 'the germ of the idea of social citizenship',[1] challenging the Poor Law notion that the poor were responsible for their own plight, and bringing structural explanations to the fore.

Over the past decade a second change occurred, and numerous Western countries introduced significant changes in welfare policy.[2] In more ways than one, these changes constitute a reversion to the latter days of the poor law, based on 19th century economic theory that viewed the market as central in determining wages and employment.[3] Unemployment benefits became increasingly more targeted and less universal, thus reinstating the importance of the distinction

---

[1] S Deakin and F Wilkinson, *The Law of the Labour Market* (OUP: Oxford, 2005) 150.
[2] These include Australia, Belgium, Britain, Canada, France, Germany, Holland, Ireland, Israel and the United States. See B Swirski, *From Welfare to Work—Government Plan to Reduce Income Support Benefits* (Adva: Tel Aviv, 2000).
[3] Deakin and Wilkinson (n 1 above) 176.

between deserving and undeserving poor. Instead of a demand-side emphasis on full employment at decent wages, policy was directed towards supply-side measures of activation that would contribute both to labour flexibility and to the integration of excluded groups into the labour market.[4]

This does not imply, however, that the arguments advanced here are not relevant to the assessment of programmes in other jurisdictions as well. The reason that so much attention has been given to welfare-to-work programmes over the past decade is not because of the fact that these issues are new, or even because the measures applied are ground-breaking. I argue that the change in the structure and character of welfare-to-work programmes indicate a more general shift in the relationship between the state and the impoverished members of its society. The shift may be perceived as a change within the nature of the welfare state or as the complete abandonment of the concept, in favour of a different model: a contractual relationship between the state and its members. Though antecedent themes of this format were exhibited throughout history, the dominance of this perspective, especially in a period that follows the establishment of the welfare state, is indeed a remarkable phenomenon. As noted, this sea-change has significant implications for the jurisprudential discourse concerning rights and duties. And as chapter 4 will show, fundamental welfare-state ideals such as equality are sidelined in favour of alternative values such as responsibility and reciprocity.

When comparing the development of welfare-to-work programmes in the United States and Britain, one finds serious dissimilarities alongside the common threads. Most of the dissimilarities are substantive, drawing from each country's different normative emphasis. This conclusion will be apparent following the exposition of the details of the two programmes. The comparison of the programmes' immediate backgrounds, however, exhibits interesting similarities. In Britain, the welfare reform programme was a major part of the New Labour platform for the 1997 elections, a Minister for Welfare Reform was appointed immediately following the elections and a series of government papers were published, spurring a lively debate. Though heavily reliant on the Conservative Jobseekers Act 1995 (JA 1995),[5] the New Labour Government revamped the British welfare-to-work policy to fit its agenda. Turning our attention to the United States, we find that the three decades prior to 1996 were characterized by such a patchwork of federal and state legislation that commentators were concerned that by the time lawmakers agree on a plan for welfare reform, they might no longer recognize the system they wished to reform.[6] This does not imply, however, that welfare reform programmes were ever far from the public interest or from governmental and congressional initiatives. Senate hearings and

---

[4] ibid 185–92; L Boltanski, E Chiapello and G Elliot (tr), *The New Spirit of Capitalism* (Verso: London, 2005) 217–18.
[5] Jobseekers Act 1995 c 15.
[6] S Bennett and K Sullivan, 'Disentitling the Poor: Waivers and Welfare "Reform"' (1993) 26 U of Michigan J of L Reform 741.

Presidential State of the Union addresses that dealt with welfare were not uncommon during this period.[7]

The American and British processes started to tread a strikingly similar path in the 1990s. President Clinton's declaration to 'end welfare as we know it' ignited an informed debate that led up to a single moment that encapsulated the beginning of a new era: the promulgation of the Personal Responsibility and Work Opportunity Reconciliation Act 1996 (PRWORA).[8] Interestingly, as in Britain, it was a Democrat administration that followed a Republican lead, both implementing agendas that were 'on the table' at the time, and leaning heavily on bi-partisan support.[9]

A problematic aspect for one who wishes to analyse American programmes is the fact that an important part of the 1996 reform is their defederalization. Though the federal PRWORA is a lengthy and elaborate document, important features of the programmes are detailed in state, and not in federal, statutes. Indeed, one may argue that no 'American' programme, per se, actually exists and that the focus should be on programmes in 50 states, or even 3000 counties, each exhibiting local variations.[10] Moreover, as noted in the previous chapter, the issue of local control over relief giving is not incidental, but rather a central policy decision. It is quite often the case with public relief that after a period of federal rule-making, implementation is left to the states 'to adopt any level of benefits they wished, to set any waiting periods and to fix the maximum period of benefits'.[11]

And yet, it may well be the case that 1996 signified a unique point in time, where significant elements of American programmes were in fact mandated by federal legislation. Indeed, it has been noted that PRWORA 'did not simply devolve functions to states; it established specific funding and policy rules, requirements, and signals to encourage and discourage particular state action'.[12] This is because the most significant and fundamental policy decisions have already been dictated at the federal level, while state discretion is largely located at the level of implementation.[13] This conclusion is strengthened following the

[7] D King, *Actively Seeking Work* (Chicago UP: London, 1995) 113–202.
[8] Pub L 104-193.
[9] Another curious link between the implementation of the two programmes is that both administrations granted highly reputed intellectuals the authority to implement their agendas regarding welfare reforms. But after David Ellwood, Mary Jo Bane and Peter Edelman (in the United States) and Frank Field (in Britain) learned that only the harsh measures of their policy would be implemented they resigned their posts.
[10] J Handler, *Social Citizenship and Workfare in the United States and Western Europe* (CUP: Cambridge, 2004) 81.
[11] FF Piven and RA Cloward, *Regulating the Poor* (Updated Edition, Vintage: New York, 1993) 114 and also ibid 94.
[12] M Greenberg, 'Welfare Reform and Devolution: Looking Back and Forward' (2001) 19 Brookings Review 20, 21.
[13] C Hoke, 'State Discretion Under New Federal Welfare Legislation' (1998) 9 Stanford L and Society Rev 115.

reauthorization of TANF as part of the Deficit Reduction Act (DRA) of 2005, which extends funding and authority for the programme through 2010.[14] For example, federal rules have substantially increased the proportion of recipients who must participate in work activities for a specified number of hours a week; the twelve categories of work that may count towards work participation are now clearly and narrowly defined in the Code of Federal Regulations;[15] states are now subject to a five per cent reduction in their block grant if they fail to implement procedures and controls consistent with the HHS Secretary's regulations; and states are now forbidden from counting basic education or education towards a Bachelor's Degree as vocational skill training.

The analysis of the substantive provisions of local programmes shows a striking degree of similarity in policy (e.g. residence laws that deny payments for recipients who have not lived in a certain locality over a certain period) even when the particulars (e.g. the extent of the period in the example above; different payment levels) may differ substantially. Quite related, it is noted that since state practices are subject to state and federal judicial scrutiny—as long as they are not struck down (let alone when they are explicitly upheld by the Supreme Court) federal acquiescence may be seen as implied. We can therefore, for our purposes, consider defederalization of the programmes to be a means to an end, and assess the substantive features of the American programmes at face value.

The first section of this chapter highlights relevant legislation and programmes in force during the second part of the 20th century, leading up to current welfare-to-work programmes. The period between the birth of the welfare state in the mid-20th century (thus ending the poor law era) and the implementation of current welfare-to-work programmes was characterized by thriving legislation in the welfare realm in general, and in the field of social security and unemployment in particular. The first part of this period is referred to by historians as the 'classical' era of the welfare state, ending in the late 1970s. In the 1980s and early 1990s significant achievements of the welfare state were uprooted in a steady process. When examining these changes, special attention will be given to conditions for the receipt of benefits, including means testing, work-tests, community work and implicit moral values underlying the programmes.

The second section of the chapter thematically outlines the characteristics of contemporary welfare-to-work programmes in the United States and Britain. While these programmes are often presented through the use of contractual rhetoric, their provisions are in fact motivated by deterrent, moral, fiscal and strict contractual (or 'quid-pro-quo') rationales, as introduced in the previous chapter. The caveat mentioned there is as relevant here: though the provisions will be presented under the distinct thematic headings, this is not meant to imply that other rationales are not also advanced by a certain provision. After all, welfare-to-work programmes are governed by an overarching objective: to

---

[14] Pub L 109-171 (2006).   [15] CFR s 261.2.

integrate the unemployed into the labour market. For each policy-maker and administrator, the motivation underlying this objective may be different, be it the inherent value of work, the public expenditure, social inclusion, a certain conception of fairness or an interest in impacting the low-wage labour market. Thus, support for each provision is plausibly based on more than one rationale. And yet, one may identify a rationale that most significantly advances each major feature of the programmes. The presentation of the provisions through the aid of rationales is advantageous if one wishes to map the matrix of principles that underlie the contractual rhetoric and to compare the different emphases of each programme.

A Legislative Background

1 The American Programmes: AFDC—Operation and Termination

There seems to be a consensus amongst students of social policy, including those who agree on very little else, that the enactment of the PRWORA signifies the most important moment for the American welfare system since 1935.[16] It is worthwhile, then, to provide a brief overview of the major developments in social security law within the American system that preceded this legislation.

The Aid to Families with Dependant Children (AFDC) programme was enacted as Title IV of the Social Security Act (SSA) 1935[17] and was the central pillar of the American public assistance system for decades to follow. It also generated most of the controversy and disagreement. AFDC was constructed as a joint federal-state programme that supplied cash benefits on a needs basis. Originally entitled Aid to Dependent Children,[18] the programme sought to realize President Roosevelt's 1909 vision according to which children who could not be supported by their widowed, disabled or deserted parent would not be institutionalized. Instead, the mother would receive aid that would allow her to take care of them at home.[19]

Some critics have found the ideology behind ADC to be tainted with questionable motivations. White widows, then seen as 'deserving poor' by virtue of their status, were helped, while the 'vast majority of poor mothers and their children' who were 'divorced, deserted, never married, of color, or engaged in

---

[16] See eg D King, *In the Name of Liberalism* (Oxford: OUP, 1999) 277; H Karger 'The International Implications of U.S. Welfare Reform' (1999) 55 Social Security 7; Ronald Dworkin states that 'the 1996 Welfare Reform Act was a plain defeat for social justice'—*Sovereign Virtue* (Harvard UP: London, 2000) 320.

[17] Pub L 74-271, 42 USC ss 601–617.

[18] The programme became Aid to Families with Dependent Children through the 1962 amendment to the Social Security Act Pub L 87-543, codified as 42 USC s 602 (1970).

[19] I Lurie, 'Major Changes in the Structure of the AFDC Program Since 1935' (1973) 59 Cornell L Rev 825, 826.

questionable behavior' were denied aid.[20] The moral elements of the Poor Laws were incorporated into ADC (and later—into AFDC) legislation and practice in a way that was only superficially race-neutral. Notable amongst these were 'suitable home' laws that conditioned benefits on proof that the mother was morally 'fit' to raise her children, according to prevailing community standards.[21] In many cases, this requirement offered a mother a 'choice' between keeping her 'illegitimate' children or receiving benefits. Staff members, especially (but not exclusively) in Southern states, simply assumed that more work was available for African American single mothers and, with an eye on influencing the supply and demand of the low-wage labour market, intentionally excluded them from receipt of benefits.[22] And yet, it is noted that the AFDC introduced concepts of fairness in substance and in procedure, including the principles that children should not be penalized for the behaviour of their parents, that administration should be uniform within each jurisdiction; and that sanctions should be governed by a fair process.

The 1961 amendment to the SSA marked a conceptual shift. While eligibility prior to that stage depended on physical incapability to support the family, the 1961 amendment[23] permitted (though it did not require) states to provide aid to families of children who were poor due to *unemployment* of a parent.[24] Unemployment thus became a structural condition that, like single parenthood, justified state assistance.

Matters began to change in a different direction the following year, with the 1962 'Service Amendments'. On the one hand, these amendments provided significant federal funding to recipients. However, the funding was directed towards social services to accompany the financial assistance. As Neil Gilbert notes, 'the implicit view here was that poverty stemmed from individual deficiencies'. And so, it signifies a change from a time when welfare recipients were considered 'victims of external circumstances'.[25]

One such amendment to the SSA empowered the Secretary of the Department of Health and Human Services to waive state compliance with AFDC statutory requirements to allow the state to run demonstration projects.[26] The original

---

[20] J Handler, *The Poverty of Welfare Reform* (Yale UP: New Haven, 1995) 25; J De Parle, *American Dream: Three Women, Ten Kids, and a Nation's Drive to End Welfare* (Viking: New York, 2004) 86–87.

[21] J Handler and Y Hasenfeld, *Blame Welfare, Ignore Poverty and Inequality* (CUP: Cambridge, 2007) 157.

[22] W Bell, *Aid to Dependent Children* (Columbia UP: New York, 1965) 29–41; Piven and Cloward (n 11 above) 139–43.

[23] Pub L 87-31, codified as 42 USC s 607.

[24] The 1967 amendment restricted this provision to cases of unemployment of a father.

[25] N Gilbert, 'Welfare Policy in the United States: The Road from Income Maintenance to Workfare' in N Gilbert and A Parent (eds), *Welfare Reform: A Comparative Assessment of the French and U.S. Experiences* (International Social Security Series vol 10, Transaction Publishers London 2004) 55, 56–57.

[26] Pub L 87-543, codified as amended 42 USC s 1315 (1988).

intent of the bill, and indeed the practice over the first two decades following the legislation, was to discover ways to improve services to beneficiaries, and not to reduce costs or to implement behavioral conditions.[27] However, beginning in 1981, the Reagan administration granted states waivers to overcome the entitlement provision guaranteed in federal statute and thus permitted them to condition benefits on employment related activities such as job search and community work. The waiver requests were examined with leniency, usually approved with impressive expeditiousness and soon expanded to cover the field of welfare.[28] I return below to the measures implemented under some of these schemes.

In 1968, Congress reacted to the expanded AFDC caseload by amending the SSA and establishing the Work Incentive (WIN) programme, thus providing the legal platform for one of the most important changes in the character of the welfare system, though its real effects were postponed for 20 years. The move has been characterized as a change from 'soft' rehabilitative services to a 'hard' work oriented approach.[29]

The WIN programme changed the ideological foundations of programmes. Welfare mothers, who were previously required to raise a family, now were required to be self-sufficient.[30] The WIN programme required states to refer all 'appropriate' recipients to a WIN programme for education, training or to accept a job. However, only one-quarter of claimants who were assessed were found 'appropriate' for referral, and even fewer were actually referred.[31] Even so, the mandatory work requirement that is so central to contemporary programmes was established in the United States under the WIN scheme.[32] In rejecting the challenge to the work requirement, Justice Powell stated, in a manner that corresponds with distinctions between deserving and undeserving poor, that welfare is intended for those who are 'genuinely incapacitated and most in need',[33] thus reaffirming the rationale behind work requirement, not far removed from the workhouse test: the offer of work is to serve as the test for relief.

Alongside work requirements, welfare programmes in the United States such as AFDC routinely included moral conditions. These conditions, in many cases carried into current programmes, signify the limited weight of the right to assistance, on the one hand, and the potential to manipulate the plight of the poor by laying down conditions that are not related to work or self-reliance, on the other. Leading up to the early 1980s, only the Supreme Court stood in the way of the

---

[27] For the historical background and consequences of this enactment see L Williams, 'The Abuse of Section 1115 Waivers: Welfare Reform in Search of a Standard' (1994) 12 Yale L and Policy Rev 8.
[28] Bennett and Sullivan (n 6 above); Williams (n 27 above) 24–27.
[29] Gilbert (n 25 above) 58–59.
[30] Handler and Hasenfeld (n 21 above) 179.
[31] Lurie (n 19 above) 834.
[32] King (n 7 above) 141.
[33] *New York State Department of Social Services v Dublino* 413 US 405, 413 (1973).

administration's innovative restrictions on entitlement. Thus, the court objected to a requirement that veterans claiming benefits need to sign an oath stating they did not intend to 'advocate the overthrow of the Government of the United States or State of California by force or violence or other unlawful means'.[34] A 'substitute father' regulation that disqualified children otherwise eligible for benefits if their mother 'cohabits' with another man was struck down.[35] And the court found that an amendment to the 1964 Food Stamp Act that rendered an individual ineligible for welfare benefits if he or she had no familial ties to any member of the household amounted to illegal discrimination of unpopular groups (so-called 'hippie communes').[36]

It has been argued that these Supreme Court decisions, alongside a few others,[37] had a lasting jurisprudential effect. They designated welfare as a right, rather than merely a privilege, and were translated into federal regulations and emboldened anti-poverty legal advocates.[38]

Califano v Boles[39] marks a change in the Supreme Court's attitude towards greater acceptance of moral conditions on welfare, as Justice Rehnquist rejected the charge brought by a mother of an 'illegitimate' child who was not deemed eligible for benefits granted to widows and divorcees.

After his election in 1980, President Reagan vowed to implement the same strict welfare regime that he spearheaded as governor of California. Shifting further towards state initiative in the field of welfare reform, the Omnibus Reconciliation Act (OBRA) 1981[40] authorized states to replace federal WIN programmes with 'experimental, pilot or demonstration' initiatives. By the time the 1988 Family Support Act (FSA)[41] was passed, thirty states responded favourably to this opportunity.[42] And by 1996, forty-three states had waiver-based programmes.[43] Amongst the various state schemes, the Community Work Experience Program (CWEP) was highly popular. According to the Committee of Ways and Means of the House of Representatives, these programmes, now frequently termed 'workfare':

required adult AFDC recipients to perform some sort of community work, such as park beautification or as a teacher aide, in exchange for the AFDC benefit. The individual does not become a paid employee but, instead, works off the AFDC benefit. The number

---

[34] *Speiser v Randall* 357 US 513 (1958).
[35] *King v Smith* 392 US 309 (1968).
[36] *United States Department of Agriculture v Moreno* 413 US 528 (1973).
[37] Notably *Goldberg v Kelly* 397 US 254 (1970).
[38] L Williams, 'Welfare and Legal Entitlements: The Social Roots of Poverty' in D Kairys (ed), *The Politics of Law* (3rd edn, Basic Books: New York, 1998) 569, 574; Piven and Cloward (n 11 above) 374; Handler and Hasenfeld (n 21 above) 167.
[39] 443 US 282 (1979).
[40] Pub L 97-35.
[41] Pub L 100-485.
[42] Bennett and Sullivan (n 6 above).
[43] Handler and Hasenfeld (n 21 above) 181.

of hours a person works may not exceed their AFDC grant divided by the applicable minimum wage.[44]

CWEP was supported both as a means of 'deterring employable people from going on or staying on welfare' and on strict contractual grounds, as 'providing services of value to local communities in return for their expenditures on welfare'.[45] Such state schemes inspired the 1988 FSA and its Jobs Opportunities and Basic Skills Training (JOBS) Program. JOBS mandated federal welfare-to-work programmes, thus turning from principle into practice the WIN commitment to make welfare conditional upon work. The rhetoric of the time reveals a budding contractual discourse balancing rights and responsibilities. Thus, the National Governors Association wrote in support of the reforms:

> The principal responsibility of government in the welfare contract is to provide education, job training and/or job placement services to all employable recipients... The major obligation of the individual in the public assistance contracts we propose is to prepare for and seek, accept and retain a job.[46]

The FSA already distanced itself from the social rights concept that underlay the 1935 legislation. Behavioural requirements and harsher conditions for benefits attracted significant political support, as the 1994 elections saw Newt Gingrich's 'Contract With America' lead a Republican majority into both houses of Congress. A significant portion of the new 'Contract with America' included a rigourous reform of the welfare system. For example, teenage mothers with children under three were required to stay in school and live with their parents or in some other form of adult-supervision living arrangement; single mothers were obliged to establish paternity and to hold fathers responsible for child-support. These changes reflected a new philosophy of 'emphasized civic duties and social obligations that accompany welfare entitlements more than the right to income maintenance'.[47]

The stage was now set for the 1996 Clinton reforms.

2 The British Programmes: Beveridge and Beyond

One may identify three distinct periods in British modern welfare history. The first is the beginning of the end of the workhouse era, establishing the basic structures that would govern welfare-to-work policies throughout the 20th century. The Unemployed Workmen's Act 1905[48] and the Labour Exchanges Act 1909[49]

---

[44] Cited in King (n 7 above) 186.
[45] N Rose, *Workfare or Fair Work* (Rutgers UP: New Brunswick NJ, 1995) 135.
[46] National Governors Association cited in King (n 7 above) 175; see also King (n 16 above) 276.
[47] Gilbert (n 25 above) 60.
[48] 5 Edw VII c 18.
[49] 9 Edw VII c 7.

marked not only the state's commitment to an active role in the organization of the labour market in a manner that would increase efficiency and the flow of information between employers, workers and the unemployed. It also encapsulated 'the first legislative acknowledgment that central government must intervene in tempering the effect of an economic phenomenon that was beyond the power of the individual to control'.[50] Relief commissions were set up to deliver whatever assistance was needed, thus circumventing the various labour tests that existed at the time. However, some basic conceptions of the Poor Law era held strong. The basic framework underwent revision, not abolition. Thus, though it was still necessary to distinguish between the deserving and the undeserving poor, the labour exchanges were to take the place of the workhouses in doing so. Winston Churchill, when introducing the Act of 1909, proclaimed:

it is not possible to make the distinction between the vagrant and the loafer on the one hand and the *bona fide* workman on the other, except in conjunction with some elaborate and effective system of testing willingness to work such as is afforded by the system of labour exchanges.[51]

Though some association was made between placement and benefits with the establishment of the labour exchanges, it was not until the 1920 Unemployment Insurance Act Amendment[52] that exchanges were required to ascertain whether claimants were 'capable of and available for work' and 'genuinely seeking work but unable to obtain suitable employment' as a condition of distributing benefits.[53] Following the economic collapse and mass unemployment, the 'genuinely seeking work' clause was abrogated in March 1930[54] to be revived only in 1989.[55] However, the policy of the exchanges, which were in charge of distributing benefits throughout that period, was such that a claimant could lose entitlement if he or she refused a *suitable* job offer or did not comply with a direction from the labour exchange.[56] This usually meant that a claimant could refuse work at wages below those previously received or below standards set by collective agreements in the district.[57]

In a manner not far removed from the American CWEP, British 'test-work' during the 1920s supplemented 'availability' conditions on entitlement for benefits by sending recipients to tasks not dissimilar to those popularized by the

---

[50] W Cornish and G de N Clark, *Law and Society in England 1750–1950* (Sweet & Maxwell: London, 1989).
[51] Cited in King (n 7 above) 19.
[52] 10 & 11 Geo V c 30 s 7(iii), (iv).
[53] Unemployment Insurance Act 1921 11 & 12 Geo V c 1 s 3(3)(b), The text is as amended by the Unemployment Insurance (No 2) Act 1924 (UK) 14 & 15 Geo V c 30.
[54] Unemployment Insurance Act 1930 (UK) 20 & 21 Geo V c 16 s 6.
[55] SSA 1989 c 24 s 10, requiring recipients of unemployment benefits to be 'actively seeking employment'. See text to n 219 below.
[56] Cornish and Clark (n 50 above) 460; King (n 7 above) 81.
[57] S Deakin, 'The Capability Concept and the Evolution of European Social Policy' in M Dougan and E Spaventa (eds), *Social Welfare and EU Law* (Hart: Oxford, 2005) 3.

Labour Yards: stone-breaking, oakum-picking and road making, along with gardening and boot repairing. An obvious measure of deterrence, it now also aroused anxiety amongst trade union members as test-workers worked side by side with ordinary wage earners, for an amount of relief that 'bears no necessary relation to the rates of wages paid for ordinary employment'.[58] The increased resentment towards this measure led to the gradual termination of test-work, a process that was completed in 1945.

It may be unjust to view the reform that followed the Beveridge Report of 1942[59] solely as a 'second stage' in a series of reforms, but though Beveridge called for a revolution in social provision, his plans are not unrelated to the foundations that he had helped lay since 1905.[60] Be that as it may, his own perception of the Report was not predisposed to understatement. Speaking to Harold Wilson shortly after its publication, Beveridge stated: 'this is the greatest advancement in our history. There can be no turning back. From now on Beveridge is not the name of a man; it is the name of a way of life, and not only for Britain, but for the whole civilized world'.[61]

And, indeed, although government involvement with social insurance had been part of British law since the National Insurance Act of 1911,[62] the significant change was in the mindset: social insurance was to become an encompassing feature, covering all members of society, from the cradle to the grave, in all spheres of life, a manifestation of the 'political ideal of social citizenship'.[63] There are numerous particulars in the report and only some highlights can be offered here. I shall focus on those elements that exhibit the author's perceptions on welfare and work, as they bear on the future development of the programmes under the newly developed welfare state.

First, it is noted that for Beveridge the concept of social insurance was not only an instrument for ensuring subsistence and eradicating poverty in an economically feasible manner, but also a realization of his conception of fairness. He saw the insurance principle as the only means of enabling the distribution of benefits as of right. Further, exhibiting what may be perceived as a contractual outlook, Beveridge rejected the suggestion that contributions to the scheme would be progressive or gradual, while benefits would be flat rate. He condemned such a proposal as the epitome of a 'Santa Claus state', and added: 'I believe there is a psychological desire to get something for which you have paid…You do not like having to pay more than your neighbours'.[64]

---

[58] Cited in King (n 16 above) 242.
[59] W Beveridge *Social Insurance and Allied Services* (Cmd 6404, 1942).
[60] For a similar view see Cornish and Clark (n 50 above) 465.
[61] Cited in H Wilson, *Memoirs: The Making of a Prime Minister 1916–1964* (Weidenfeld & Nicolson: London, 1986) 64.
[62] 1 & 2 Geo V c 55.
[63] Deakin and Wilkinson (n 1 above) 175.
[64] J Harris, *William Beveridge—A Biography* (Clarendon: Oxford, 1977) 416.

Second, Beveridge outlined three 'Heads of Scheme' for the report that 'no satisfactory system of social security can be devised' without. Important amongst them, for present purposes, is the assertion that the state should employ 'full use of powers...to maintain employment and to reduce unemployment to seasonal, cyclical and interval unemployment'.[65] Third, and closely related, Beveridge recommended incorporating training benefits in the programmes.

Since benefits were to be paid with no time limit (reducing benefits simply because one was out of work for a long period of time was simply 'wrong in principle') there was a danger that 'men might settle down to them'.[66] Beveridge thus suggested training or work requirements that would unmask malingerers and those claiming benefits while working. But while Beveridge agreed that 'the only satisfactory test of unemployment is an offer of work', he made clear that 'this test breaks down in mass unemployment'.[67] This, of course, is a crucial element, since contemporary social policy has all but abandoned completely the Beveridge commitment to full employment.[68]

Fourth, despite his aversion to means-tested benefits—he proclaimed that 'no means test of any kind can be applied to the benefits of the Scheme'[69]—Beveridge recognized the necessity of implementing a safety net under a social insurance based platform. But since the Social Scheme was to be comprehensive, the means tested programme could be reduced in scope, and its conditions could be made more severe.

Finally, Beveridge's reluctance to dictate people's behaviour through the vehicle of the welfare system gave way when confronted with an issue that disturbed him greatly: that of the falling birth rate in the years before the war. Beveridge recommended a series of grants, including a marriage grant, maternity benefits and, perhaps most importantly, family allowance, all to 'put a premium on marriage, instead of penalizing it'.[70] Further, the complex issue of benefits for women—employed and unemployed, single, married, divorced, separated and deserted—all had to be structured in a manner that would take into account 'vital work' that housewives as mothers have to do 'in ensuring the adequate continuance of the British race and British ideals in the world'.[71] Accepting this view, the Labour Government of 1945 introduced a truly universal child benefit, contingent neither on contributions nor need.[72]

---

[65] W Beveridge, 'Heads of Scheme' (1941) recounted in N Timmins, *Five Giants—A Biography of the Welfare State* (Fontana: London, 1995) 20.
[66] Timmins (n 65 above) 60.
[67] Beveridge (n 59 above) 57–59, 163–64.
[68] G Esping-Andersen, *The Three Worlds of Welfare Capitalism* (Polity: Cambridge, 1990) ch 7.
[69] Timmins (n 65 above) 21.
[70] ibid 55.
[71] Beveridge (n 59 above) 53.
[72] Family Allowances Act (UK) 8 & 9 Geo VI c 41.

The National Insurance Act 1946[73] offered a modern, comprehensive form of social insurance that extended to the employed, the self-employed and the unemployed, thus coming 'close to realizing a model of employment-based social citizenship'.[74] The unemployed were required to be 'available for employment' as a condition for receipt of benefits.[75] This provision was interpreted in a manner that allowed claimants to define the work for which they considered themselves to be available. Regulations were later introduced to limit the restrictions an unemployed person could place on his or her availability.[76] The National Assistance Act 1948 formally abolished the Poor Law and its remnants,[77] and was followed by the SSA 1966[78] that changed the title of the programme to Supplementary Benefit. Ogus and Wikeley find that it was this act that 'conferred a *right* to benefits in the circumstances set out in the legislation'.[79]

During the 30 years that followed the birth of the welfare state in 1948, it became clear that Beveridge's view—according to which the bulk of benefits could be supplied by the insurance mechanism through flat-rate contributions and benefits—was to be disproved. Means-tested benefits, originally structured as a safety net, *became* the welfare state, constituting an integral part in over 40 different categories of benefits.[80] Beveridge's rejection of the distinction between short-term and long-term benefits was not adhered to, and the division became paramount, reviving old moralistic views on deserving and undeserving poor. Fraser argued that by 1978 'what historians are now calling the age of the Classic Welfare State was clearly coming to a close'.[81]

By her own account, Margaret Thatcher was highly influenced by Victorian values that distinguished between deserving and undeserving poor and by American conservative writings on the 'underclass', fighting 'dependency culture' and implanting ideals of individual responsibility.[82] Thatcher's 1980 budget introduced reductions in social security benefits for the first time in generations. This was quickly followed by the Fowler Reviews of 1984 which led to proposals that were implemented in the SSA 1986, replacing Family Income Support with Family Credit, and Supplementary Benefits with Income Support.[83] Following the 1988 amendment, only young people over the age of 18 were entitled to

[73] 9 & 10 Geo VI c 67.
[74] Deakin and Wilkinson (n 1 above) 164.
[75] National Insurance Act (UK) 9 & 10 Geo VI c 67 s 11(2)(a)(i).
[76] SI 1955/143. See N Wikeley and AI Ogus, *The Law of Social Security* (5th edn, Butterworths: London, 2002) 343.
[77] National Assistance Act 1948 (UK) 11 & 12 Geo VI c 29.
[78] Later renamed the Supplementary Benefit Act 1966—SSA 1971 s 11(1)(c).
[79] Wikeley and Ogus (n 76 above) 274; Derek Fraser takes the same position—D Fraser, *The Evolution of the British Welfare State* (3rd edn, Palgrave: London, 2003) 276.
[80] A Sinfield, 'The Goals of Social Policy: Context and Change' in J Andersen and others (eds), *The Changing Face of Welfare* (Policy: Bristol, 2005) 15, 17.
[81] Fraser (n 79 above) 280.
[82] M Thatcher, *The Downing Street Years* (HarperCollins: London, 1993) 625–27.
[83] SSA 1986 (UK) c 50 s 20(3)(d)(i) and s 20(4), respectively.

income support.[84] Further measures were implemented in the 1989 amendment: first, the strict contractual perception was exhibited in a manner that echoed poor law initiatives, demanding repayment of contributions where earnings increased.[85] Second, as mentioned, the requirement on the part of recipients of (unemployment or income support) benefits to be 'actively seeking employment' was restored for the first time in almost 60 years.[86] And third, a person would be disqualified for benefits if a he or she refused any, and not just suitable, employment.[87]

The final reform of the Conservative government, the Jobseeker's Act, was embraced by the Labour Government following the 1997 election, and will be dealt with in the following section.

B Themes and Provisions in Current Welfare-to-Work Programmes

Welfare-to-work programmes currently in place in the United States and Britain are characterized by themes that are akin to those introduced in the previous chapter. While the rhetoric of an overriding construct of a (social) contract is sometimes employed, the elements of the programmes reveal different underlying ideologies, not dissimilar to those identified when outlining Poor Law programmes. In exploring these programmes I shall therefore make use of the headings that are already familiar: the deterrent rationale, the fiscal rationale, the moral rationale and the strictly contractual rationale. But since the content of contemporary rationales may be somewhat dissimilar to those of the Poor Law era, the exposition requires unveiling and restructuring some of the themes. A brief explanation of the rationales in a modern context may be helpful.

As noted, the strictly contractual rationale heading refers to the idea according to which one cannot expect something for nothing and that rights have to be balanced with responsibilities. Workfare, one of the prominent features of modern welfare-to-work programmes, has such a distinct quid-pro-quo nature. Workfare schemes require welfare recipients to work in return for their benefits. The opposing views as to the beneficial or deterrent consequences of workfare are but natural if one acknowledges them as a side effect of the scheme's main purpose, which is to provide 'services of value to local communities in return for their

---

[84] SSA 1988 (UK) c 7 s 4. An exception to this measure was added in the Act, in the case 'severe hardship will result...unless income support is paid...'—s 4(A).
[85] SSA 1989 (UK) c 24 s 2. adding subsection (gg) to Schedule 1 para 6(1); see R Cranston, *The Legal Foundations of the Welfare State* (Weidenfeld and Nicolson: London, 1985) 33–34. For a similar approach in Denmark see Esping-Andersen (n 68 above) 43.
[86] SSA 1989 (UK) c 24 ss 10, 13.
[87] SSA 1989 (UK) c 24 s 12(1)(b).

e on welfare'.[88] In effect, the services are not given 'in return' in any
real sense. Claimants are required to do *something*, unproductive and even futile
it may be, that will express an effort on their part. Work-tests, unlike
work, do not demand *actual* work contribution but rather test the claimant's
willingness to work by demanding that she actively seek employment or that she
participate in training schemes.[89] Work-tests will also be examined under the
strictly contractual heading. The reason is that work-tests are understood to separate the deserving from the undeserving, assuring that those receiving benefits
have acted responsibly by pursuing all available alternative routes. Handler and
Hasenfeld describe this approach:

> Citizens have *responsibilities*, not entitlements, some conservatives said. This is the social contract; it was a matter of fairness, of equity. The 'truly needy' deserved to be helped, but they must also contribute to society by supporting themselves and their families if they can.[90]

The argument that aspires to link desert and responsibility is revisited in chapter 4.

During the 1980s a consensus seemed to develop around the notion that welfare payments have led to a fiscal crisis and thus to a need for reform that involves reducing the level and duration of benefits, raising contributions rates and tightening conditions for entitlements.[91] The fiscal rationale refers to the goals of the programmes that include reducing the number of the unemployed claiming benefits, reducing the budget expenditure spent on welfare payments, increasing the flexibility of the local labour market and exploiting the human resources that are available.

When compared to the analysis of Poor Law measures, the moral rationale and the deterrent rationale have to be understood in a more flexible and complex manner. Unlike during the Poor Law era, current programmes are judged in the context of human rights and the welfare state. This does not necessarily mean that the objectives and motivations are radically different, but mainly that exposing them is less straightforward. For while past programmes could demand a strict moral regimen for all paupers as a prerequisite for assistance, current programmes, under stringent judicial scrutiny, cannot. They may, however, condition assistance upon matters wholly unrelated, or at most only tangentially related, to work and self-maintenance. Such conditions will fall under the broadly construed moral rationale.

The deterrent rationale requires even more elaboration, as its nature has departed in great measure from the treatment that the poor were subjected to in

---

[88] Rose (n 45 above) 135.
[89] P Bou-Habib and S Olsaretti, 'Liberal Egalitarianism and Workfare' (2004) 21 J of Applied Philosophy 257, 258.
[90] J Handler and Y Hasenfeld, *We the Poor People* (Yale UP: New Haven, 1997) 9; cf L Mead, *Beyond Entitlement* (Free Press: New York, 1988).
[91] G Standing, *Global Labour Flexibility* (Macmillan: Basingstoke, 1999) 228, 253.

the workhouses and labour yards. Deterrent provisions will, therefore, be identified by their motivation to alter the potential claimant's sense of priorities and to sway him or her into choosing other means of maintenance. This objective is less trivial and more problematic than it may initially seem. When programmes drift from a universal to a selective criterion for entitlement, policy-makers should address at least two kinds of efficiency matters:[92] first, and obviously, a policy should be vertically efficient. This means that those it reaches are those in the target group. This objective is advanced by means of procedures to eliminate fraud. But, second, a policy should also be horizontally efficient. This means that a policy should try to reach a high percentage of the target group. The decision to put a programme into practice is a statement that the administration prefers eligible candidates to, in the now-popular vernacular, accept the 'terms of the contract', presumably because the government either views entitlement to the programme under the prescribed conditions as just and fair or because it fears that if claimants do not take part in the programme, they will resort to other measures that will leave society (and conceivably, but not necessarily, claimants themselves) worse off. A low rate of take-up, therefore, creates a moral hazard and consequently a problem that governments should address. Indeed, it has been noted that the purported educative objective of the programmes—to inculcate work skills and proper work attitude—is incompatible with their deterrent and punitive measures.[93]

Recent research has identified several features of social programmes as deterring eligible recipients from claiming benefits to which they are entitled. These include means testing,[94] vagueness and complexity of eligibility rules,[95] a low benefit rate, a structure that binds together service and fraud surveillance,[96] a stereotypical and derogatory perception of the clients and the requirement to periodically renew an application for eligibility.[97] These traits, along with remarkably high rates of eligible individuals who are not aware of their rights (and are not informed by the administration) were characterized as 'a bureaucratic design in deterrence'.[98] The conclusion that these elements have a deterrent effect has been corroborated by subsequent research in several countries, including Britain.[99] Critics have asserted that policy-makers use such methods as a deterrent so as to

---

[92] Standing (n 91 above) 259.
[93] A Gewirth, *The Community of Rights* (Chicago UP, Chicago, 1996) 129; see similarly D Finn 'The Role of Contracts and the Private Sector in Delivering Britain's "Employment First" Welfare State' in E Sol and M Westerveld (eds), *Contractualism in Employment Services* (Kluwer Law: The Hague, 2005) 101.
[94] W van Oorschot, *Realizing Rights* (Avebury: Aldershot, 1995) 17–33, 215.
[95] van Oorschot (n 94 above) 32; A Corden *Changing Perspectives on Benefit Take Up* (HMSO: London, 1995) 14.
[96] van Oorschot (n 94 above) xi, 8; also Handler and Hasenfeld (n 21 above) 170–71; A Bryson, 'The Jobseeker's Allowance: Help or Hindrance to the Unemployed' (1995) 24 ILJ 204, 208.
[97] Corden (n 95 above) 22; van Oorschot (n 94 above) 88–94.
[98] Piven and Cloward (n 11 above) 152.
[99] Corden (n 95 above) 7; Standing (n 91 above) 266.

reduce the costs of the programmes.[100] The low take-up rate, however, has been seen to run contrary to the 'integrative aims of social policy'[101] and to lead to social exclusion. It is important, therefore, to inquire to what extent contemporary programmes implement measures that deter eligible claimants from applying for benefits.

We turn now to describe in detail the features of contemporary welfare-to-work programmes, first in the United States and then in Britain. As mentioned, the elements of the programmes have been grouped together under what it seen as the principal rationale: deterrent, fiscal, moral or strictly contractual.

1 United States: PRWORA and TANF

As aforementioned, the 1996 PRWORA that implemented the Temporary Assistance for Needy Families (TANF) programme is considered to be the most important legislative measure in the field of social welfare in America in decades and is now the chief assistance programme to families with children. The legislation itself is a slightly changed version of the Republican-initiated Personal Responsibility Act, a significant element in the 'Contract With America' platform.

In addition to the introduction of the TANF programme, the PRWORA amended one of the most important social assistance programmes in America—the Food Stamps Program.[102] The purpose of the FSP is to permit low-income households a more nutritious diet and to provide families the opportunity to purchase food supplies at retail stores, as an alternative to receiving meals at soup kitchens or religious institutions. In addition, food stamps may be perceived as a critical source of financial assistance to those in need, increasing household income by over 40 per cent.[103] Even prior to the 1996 reform, food stamps were inextricably linked to income support as 87 per cent of AFDC recipients received food stamps.[104] PRWORA made this link a formal and legal one by stating that participation in TANF serves as passport eligibility for entitlement to food stamps,[105] so the majority of single-parent households that receive food stamps also participate in TANF.[106]

---

[100] C Jencks, *Rethinking Social Policy* (Harvard UP: Cambridge MA, 1992).
[101] W van Oorschot and J Schell, 'Means-testing in Europe: a Growing Concern' in A Sinfield and others (eds), *The Sociology of Social Security* (Edinburgh UP: Edinburgh, 1991) 187, 192 cited in Corden (n 95 above) 16.
[102] Food Stamp Act Pub L 95-113 (1977) as amended.
[103] E Bolen, 'A Poor Measure of the Wrong Thing: The Food Stamp Program's Quality Control System Discourages Participation by Working Families' 53 Hasting LJ (2001) 213, 216.
[104] S Page and M Larner, 'Introduction to the AFDC Program' (1997) 7 The Future of Children 20, 22.
[105] Pub L 88-525, codified as 7 USCA s 2014.
[106] L Castner and R Rosso, *Characteristics of Food Stamps Households—Fiscal Year 1998* (USDA: Washington DC, 2000) xv–xvi.

a) The Deterrent Rationale

The American government states that one of the primary means by which the success of the programme is measured is the degree of take-up, or in American terms—participation, of eligible recipients in the programme.[107] However, an analysis of participation in the FSP reveals that between 1994 and 2000 the percentage of eligible participants for food stamps who participated in the programme dropped from 71 per cent to 59 per cent despite the fact that a fairly consistent number of people remained eligible throughout the 1990s.[108] Recent figures show that only 40 per cent of families eligible for food stamps receive them.[109] The declining levels of participation by eligible households may help explain the puzzling trend that, despite the booming economy at the time, the income of the poorest families actually declined between 1995 and 1999.[110] There are several explanations for this trend.

i) Means Tests

Both TANF and Food Stamps programmes require household income tests. Under FSP rules, a household is defined as a group of individuals who live in a residential unit and purchase and prepare food together. The PRWORA enlarged the scope of the household, now including children under 21 who are married or have children. The eligibility standards for food stamps are incredibly complicated and extensive.[111] Application forms to claimants have to mirror, at least in some respect, these provisions.[112] Bolen notes that:

The average length of an application is 12 pages, though it runs over twenty pages in ten states, and reaches thirty-six pages in Minnesota. In fact, the average food stamp application is six times longer than the federal application for a firearms permit and three times as long as the federal home mortgage loan application.

The demand for documentation to verify the details in these forms is appropriately daunting. The complexity of the application process may be seen as a form of red tape deterrence and its effect on potential claimants is manifest and well documented.[113] In addition, the household must essentially reapply at least once every six months and, if the state agency demands, every month.[114]

---

[107] USDA *Food Stamp Participation Rates and Benefits* (May 2003) 1: <http://www.fns.usda.gov/oane/MENU/Published/FSP/FILES/Participation/PartDemoGroup.pdf> (2 July 2003).
[108] A Schirm and L Castner, *Reaching Those in Need: State Food Stamps Participation Rates in 2000* (USDA: Washington DC, 2002): <http://www.fns.usda.gov/oane/MENU/Published/FSP/FILES/Participation/Reaching2000.pdf> (2 July 2003).
[109] Handler and Hasenfeld (n 21 above) 63.
[110] Bolen (n 103 above) 217.
[111] 7 USCA s 2014.
[112] Bolen (n 103 above) 218.
[113] See the illuminating narrative in Piven and Cloward (n 11 above) 298 and in the chapter added to the updated version on 374–76.
[114] 7 USCA s 2015(c)(1)(A).

ii) Low Rates of Benefits

By way of background to the TANF reform, it is noted that AFDC benefits lost half of their purchasing power between 1970 and 1992.[115] This was somewhat offset by the fact that food stamps maintained their purchasing power, leaving the rate of the combined reduction in purchasing power at 27 per cent.[116] This changed following the 1996 welfare reform.

Though obviously leaving room for alternative explanations, it is a suggestive fact that while Food Stamps benefit rates decreased between 1997 and 1998 by 14 per cent in the United States, participation in the Food Stamps programme decreased by 13 per cent.[117] While families in dire poverty (below 50 per cent of the poverty line) received almost 66 per cent of their income from means tested programmes in 1995, this percentage plummeted to 53 per cent in 2001.[118] During that period, TANF benefits in most American states fell below the corresponding 1994 AFDC level.[119]

After adjusting to purchasing power, TANF and FSP offer single individuals benefits at a rate that, at $125 per month, is higher only than Korea and Hungary (and by a small margin) amongst all OECD nations.[120] For the sake of comparison, Netherlands offers $962, Denmark grants $900, and Luxembourg $881.[121] Provision for couples and lone parents is only marginally more generous, in comparison. Granting $982 for couples and $788 for lone parents, the United States ranks at number 20 out of 28 OECD nations. Acting mainly as a replacement for income, benefits may alternatively be compared through the use of the Net Replacement Rate (NRR) as a percentage of the wages of the Average Production Worker. Esping-Andersen refers to the replacement rate's 'singular importance... for people's welfare-work choices'.[122] In these terms, the United States rates second lowest for NRR for single persons (seven per cent) and among the five lowest rates for benefits granted to couples with no children (12 per cent), couples with two children (46 per cent) and lone parents with two children (38 per cent). Amongst countries that enable young people to apply for benefits (France and Luxembourg have an age limit of 25 and 30, respectively), the United States' NRR rate for young people (seven per cent) is higher only than Korea's (six per cent).

iii) Stigmatizing attitude towards recipients

Stigma, on the one hand, and attitude, on the other hand, are difficult traits to quantify. However, it should be noted that these open-ended terms may and

---

[115] Page and Larner (n 104 above) 24.
[116] Piven and Cloward (n 11 above) 372.
[117] Castner and Rosso (n 106 above) xv.
[118] Handler and Hasenfeld (n 21 above) 55.
[119] ibid 62.
[120] OECD, *Benefits and Wages—OECD Indicators* (OECD Publications: Paris, 2002) Table 2.12.
[121] ibid.
[122] Esping-Andersen (n 68 above) 54.

have been empirically attached to material factors. Thus, van Oorschot shows how Dutch housing benefits were not associated with negative stigma partly because one could earn 150 per cent above the minimum and still be entitled to the benefit, thus leading to a substantially higher level of take-up.[123] Similarly, it has been established that American localities that had higher benefit support rates also showed a lower degree of personal stigma towards recipients.[124] The converse is also true, as governments are far more inclined to cut benefit rates for unpopular programmes whose recipients are stigmatized.[125]

iv) Abolition of Fraud

In order to receive grants under TANF, the state must establish and enforce standards and procedures to combat fraud and abuse.[126] If the state does not participate in the Income and Eligibility Verification Scheme, designed to reduce fraud, the federal Family Assistance grant to the state will be reduced by up to two per cent.[127] The legislation provides that a person found to have fraudulently misrepresented residence in order to obtain assistance in two or more states will be denied assistance under TANF, Medicaid, Food Stamps, or SSI programmes, for a period of 10 years.[128]

b) The Moral Rationale

The moral agenda of American welfare-to-work programmes is quite explicit. Indeed, the PRWORA *opens* with the following surprising statement:[129]

Sec. 101 Findings
The Congress makes the following findings:

(1) Marriage is the foundation of a successful society.
(2) Marriage is an essential institution of a successful society which promotes the interests of children.
(3) Promotion of responsible fatherhood and motherhood is integral to successful child rearing and the well-being of children.
(4) ...
(5) The number of individuals receiving aid to families with dependent children (... AFDC) has more than tripled since 1965.... Eighty-nine percent of children receiving AFDC benefits now live in homes in which no father is present.
(6) The increase of out-of-wedlock pregnancies is well documented...

---

[123] W van Oorschot, 'Troublesome Targeting: On the Multi-Level Causes of Non-Take-Up' (1999) 56 Social Security 193, 201–2 [Hebrew]. Some French benefits are also characterized by high ceilings of means testing—P Rosanvallon, *The New Social Question* (Princeton UP: Princeton, 2000) 49.
[124] Piven and Cloward (n 11 above) 289.
[125] *Jefferson v Hackney* 406 US 549, 575 (Marshall J, dissenting).
[126] PRWORA s 402(a)(6).
[127] PRWORA s 409(a)(4).
[128] PRWORA s 408(a)(8).
[129] PRWORA s 101.

(7) ...The increase of teenage pregnancies among the youngest girls is particularly severe and is linked to predatory sexual practices by men who are significantly older.

(8) The negative consequences of an out-of-wedlock birth on the mother, the child, the family and society are well documented...

As for the amendment to the Social Security Act (SSA) itself, section 401(a) of the Act now reads as follows:

Sec. 401 Purpose
  (a) The purpose of this part is to increase the flexibility of States in operating a program to
  (1) Provide assistance to needy families...
  (2) End the dependence of needy parents on government benefits by promoting job preparation, work, and marriage.
  (3) Prevent and reduce the incidence of out-of-wedlock pregnancies...
  (4) Encourage the formation and maintenance of two-parent families.

The background for the above declarations is quite obvious: from 1960 to 1996 the rate of birth to unmarried mothers increased six-fold, from 5.3 to 32.4 per cent of all births. Teenagers account for a third of all births to unmarried women. Fascinatingly, however, during the exact same period, labour force participation of single mothers increased by almost exactly the same margin to 61.7 per cent in 1995.[130] Incidentally, single women's participation rate continued to climb to 75 per cent in 2006, creating an exception to the trend of reduced labour participation amongst women in general.[131]

On the one hand, there is now compelling evidence that married families are less poor than single-parent families. However, it is far from clear that marriage reduces the adverse economic consequences of non-marital birth.[132] Rather, studies have found a reverse cause and effect, namely that the employment status of the father is the most important factor on the future of the family structure.[133] Handler and Hasenfeld conclude that 'despite its rhetoric, PRWORA does not encourage couples to stay together and get married'.[134]

And so, reading through the PRWORA provisions and, moreover, examining the measures that certain states have taken to take account of these targets, the charge that 'only those women who conform to majoritarian middle-class values deserve government subsistence'[135] seems far from overly judgmental. Indeed, it should not be surprising that some conditions for benefits do not address unemployment benefits or work requirements at all, but rather strictly moral

---

[130] Gilbert (n 25 above) 56.
[131] E Porter, 'Stretched to the Limit, Women Stall March to Work' New York Times (2 March 2006).
[132] Handler and Hasenfeld (n 21 above) 286–89.
[133] ibid 299–301.
[134] ibid 301.
[135] L Williams, 'The Ideology of Division: Behavior Modification Welfare Reform Proposals' (1992) 102 Yale LJ 719, 721.

matters. In some states, such as New Jersey and Wisconsin, 'wedfare' programmes encourage claimants to 'feel responsible' for their children by offering supplementary allowances if parents get married.[136] Under the considerable influence of writers such as Charles Murray,[137] unemployment was construed as a moral and cultural matter, rather than as a social and economic phenomenon. Lawrence Mead writes: 'most poor people are needy because of illegitimacy, family breakup and inability to hold available jobs'.[138] The target of the measures outlined below is the non-normative, and especially the single parent family, and their objectives are mainly to re-establish a particular idea of the family as the preferred domestic structure. Work, then, would 'transform family structure, community life and... would restore the social fabric'.[139] In addition, other provisions refer to the non-normative and asocial behaviour of recipients in general, behaviour that is not directly (or at times not at all) related to employment.

i) Minor Parent not in School

A certain variation of what was known as Learnfare programmes is established under TANF. Under this provision, the state will not grant assistance to an individual who is under the age of 18, unmarried, has a minor child at least 12 weeks old and has not successfully completed high school or its equivalent, unless the individual participates in either educational activities directed towards attainment of a high school diploma or its equivalent, or in alternative education or training schemes approved by the state.[140] Evaluations of such programmes suggest that their impact, if it existed, was moderate. In Wisconsin, for example, where Learnfare was first initiated, the programme had no effect on improving school attendance.[141]

ii) Minor Parent in Adult-Supervising Setting

The state may not grant TANF funds to provide assistance to an unmarried individual who is under the age of 18 and is caring for a child if the minor parent and child are not residing with a parent, legal guardian, or other adult relative of the individual, subject to limited exceptions.[142] The research on the living arrangement provision is limited and mixed. Alongside evidence that teen mothers who lived with their parents obtained more schooling, other studies have

---

[136] P Rosanvallon, *The New Social Question* (Princeton UP: Princeton, 2000) 102.
[137] C Murray, *Losing Ground* (Basic Books: New York, 1984). For the impact of the book see K Mann and S Roseneil, 'Some Mothers Do 'Ave 'Em: Backlash and the Gender Politics of the Underclass Debate' (1994) 3 J of Gender Studies 317, 321.
[138] Mead (n 90 above) 48.
[139] Piven and Cloward (n 11 above) 392–93.
[140] PRWORA s 408(a)(4).
[141] J Levin-Epstein and J Hutchins, *Teens and TANF: How Adolescents Fare Under the Nation's Welfare Program* (Kaiser Family Foundation, 2003) 4. <http://www.clasp.org/publications/Teens_TANF.pdf> (28 July 2007)
[142] PRWORA s 408(a)(5).

shown a decrease in enrolment and graduation and an increase in depression amongst teens living in a three-generation household.[143]

iii) Illegitimacy

The federal government requires states to establish goals and take action to prevent and reduce the incidence of out-of-wedlock pregnancies, with special emphasis on teenage pregnancies, for the calendar years 1996 through to 2005.[144] In addition, bonuses are granted to states that demonstrate a net decrease in out-of-wedlock births.[145] The SSA provides that $50 million per year will be allocated to the states for a period of five years for abstinence-only programmes for teens and unmarried adults.[146] Moreover, the reauthorization of TANF, under the DRA of 2005, includes $150 million per year (2006 to 2010) to promote responsible fatherhood.[147]

iv) Penalty for Non-Cooperation in Obtaining Child Support

If the state determines that an individual is not cooperating with the state in establishing paternity or in establishing or enforcing a support order with respect to a child of the individual with no good cause, the state will deduct from the assistance that would otherwise be provided to the family of the individual no less than 25 per cent, and may deny assistance altogether under any state programme.[148]

v) Family Cap

One of the more popular, and more controversial, measures enacted by state legislatures under the previous waiver system was carried into the framework of the PRWORA. The family cap, sardonically termed 'contraceptive welfare laws',[149] denies lone mothers benefits they would have been entitled to due to the birth of a new child, if they gave birth to the child while on welfare. This measure exhibits the most direct manifestation of the public perception of the lone mother on welfare who engages in illicit sexual relations and 'gets herself pregnant' so as to receive benefits. Though the federal law makes no mention of family cap schemes, it permits states to continue to implement the welfare programmes that were in place under the waiver scheme.[150] Many legislatures saw this as a green light to carry on with such policies as the family cap.[151]

---

[143] Levin-Epstein and Hutchins (n 141 above) 3.
[144] PRWORA s 402(a)(1)(A)(v).
[145] PRWORA s 403(a)(1)(E)(2).
[146] PRWORA s 510.
[147] DRA s 7103.
[148] PRWORA s 408(a)(1)(B)(2).
[149] D Roberts, 'The Only Good Poor Woman: Unconstitutional Conditions and Welfare' (1995) 72 Denver L Rev 931, 932.
[150] PRWORA s 415.
[151] See *NB v Sybinski* 724 NE2d 1103.

As with learnfare, there is no data to show that states that have employed family cap schemes under the waiver system have seen a drop in the size of AFDC families. Furthermore, such families have substantially decreased in size during the twenty years prior to the implementation of the schemes. In 1969, 32.5 per cent of AFDC families had four or more children, while only 9.9 per cent had four or more children in 1990. The average AFDC family in 1990 had 2.9 members (including adults) and 72.5 per cent of AFDC families had one or two children. Moreover, studies have shown that the ability to receive benefits had no effect on AFDC mother's decision to have a child.[152] As such data has accumulated, a number of states have either eliminated the family cap or are beginning to phase it out.[153]

vi) Drug Use

The PRWORA added a provision permanently denying cash assistance and food stamps to anyone convicted under state or federal law of a felony offense that 'has as an element the possession, use, or distribution of a controlled substance'.[154] If the individual is part of a family that receives TANF assistance, the amount of assistance that would otherwise have been provided will be reduced by the amount that would have otherwise been made to the individual recipient. A similar provision is detailed in relation to the food stamp benefits. As the connection to the work market is, at best, tenuous, and the deterrent effects of such a provision are questionable,[155] it would seem that a moralistic approach guided the insert of the provision. It is 'an insistence on moral accountability for one's own past actions' that guides the provision, and not 'an exhortation to future praiseworthy conduct'.[156]

c) *The Fiscal Rationale*

Under previous legislation, states were reimbursed for expenses undertaken with regard to AFDC, AFDC Administration, JOBS and Emergency Assistance programmes. The structure of TANF is substantially different. TANF consolidates and replaces these programmes granting each state an annual sum ('block grants') calculated according to its total expenses under the four programmes in previous years.[157] The result is a simple economic incentive: 'states make money

---

[152] L Williams (n 135 above) 737–40 citing Staff of House Committee on Ways and Means, 102d Congress, 2d Session *Overview of Entitlements Programs: Background Material and Data on Programs Within the Jurisdiction of the Committee of Ways and Means* (1992) 669 [hereafter: 1992 Green Book]
[153] J Levin-Epstein, *Lifting the Lid off the Family Cap* (CLASP, 2003) 4 <http://clasp.org/publications/family_cap_brf.pdf> (28 July 2007)
[154] PRWORA s 115(a).
[155] Note 'Recent Legislation' (1997) 110 Harv L Rev 983, 988.
[156] ibid 986.
[157] PRWORA s 103.

when clients are dropped from the rolls'.[158] Moreover, even though inflation has been relatively low over the last decade, by 2007 the purchasing power of block grants has declined by 23 per cent since 1997.[159]

i) Participation Rates

Under PRWORA, states had to meet an escalating work participation rate for all families, which would reach a level of 50 per cent for all families and 90 per cent for two-parent families by 2002.[160] States received a 'caseload reduction credit' that reduced their target by one percentage point for each percentage point reduction in the TANF caseload since 1995. Following the reauthorization of TANF in the DRA of 2005, adjustments to participation rates are based on caseload reductions after 2005 (which saw an historic low level of caseloads), rather than 1995.[161] As a result of these new provisions, states needed to clear or, perhaps, 'cream' the roles from those who could be put in employment. This would mean, however, that those who remained on TANF face serious barriers to employment, including physical and mental health problems, substance abuse, learning disabilities and low cognitive funcitioning. This conclusion reminds one of Goodin's insight, noted in the previous chapter, that the more successful programmes are, the fewer 'undeserving' recipients remain on the roles.[162]

The federal rules governing the activities that count towards these work participation rates are detailed and complex, and include education, job search and training programmes. For example, recipients in single-parent families with a child under six must participate for 20 hours per week; other single parent families must participate for 30 hours a week; a two parent family not receiving federal funded child care must participate for 35 hours per week, and, if they do receive child care, for 55 hours per week.[163] At least 20 hours per week under the all-families rate and 30 hours per week under the two-parent rate must be attributable to one of 12 enumerated occupations. The DRA limited the range to nine 'core' occupations, and three 'non-core' occupations.[164] The latter may be assigned to participants only under certain conditions. The core occuptions are: unsubsidized employment, subsidized private or public sector employment, on-the-job training, job search and job readiness assistance, community service programmes, vocational educational training and

---

[158] Handler (n 10 above) 58.
[159] Center on Budget and Policy Priorities, *Implementing TANF Changes and the Deficit Reduction Act* 110 (2nd edn, Washington DC, 2007) <http://www.cbpp.org/2-9-07tanf.pdf> (10 July 2007).
[160] Handler (n 10 above) 27.
[161] DRA s 7102(a).
[162] Ch 2 above, text to n 60.
[163] PRWORA s 407(c)(1); 42 USC s 607(c).
[164] 42 USC s 607(c)(1), narrowing the terms set in PRWORA s 402(d).

child care services to an individual who is participating in a community service programme.

ii) Time Limit on Eligibility

States may be penalized for failure to comply with a new 60 month limit on assistance.[165] According to the measure, a state may not use any part of the grant to provide assistance to a family that includes an adult who received assistance under any state programme for 60 months (whether or not consecutive) after the date the TANF programme commenced. While states may exempt up to 20 per cent of individuals on their caseload from this requirement, they may also choose to enforce even more stringent time limits and, indeed, six states imposed lifetime limits of less than 60 months and 11 states imposed a fixed-time limit of 24 consecutive months within the 60 month period.[166] Undoubtedly the most controversial measure in the programme, the idea of a time limit on welfare was originally proposed by David Ellwood,[167] who later was asked to join the Clinton administration, and worked to implement the concept. A decade after the proclamation of time limits, research of Wisconsin TANF has found that in the sixth year of leaving TANF, only 16 per cent of families have earnings above the federal poverty line, while 60 per cent were defined 'extremely poor', with earnings below 25 per cent of the federal poverty line.[168]

Directly related is the proclamation that no individual or family has any entitlement for assistance.[169] This assertion, although stated in dramatic form, can also be derived from the state-focused and consequentialist-oriented perception. If a state fails to reach prescribed goals it loses funding. When individuals reach their five-year limit they lose their eligibility even if their situation and needs did not change. Unlike critics that view these measures as a deterrent,[170] I do not see how they can be understood to have a potential impact on the incentives or disincentives that individuals have vis-à-vis applying for benefits. For if individuals lose entitlements simply because they expired, the personal cost-benefit analysis was evaded completely. Rather, the emphasis is placed here on the grand scheme of things, on the desire to reduce expenses. The proclamation that Americans are no longer entitled to benefits, however, does have rhetorical value. Elimination of federal entitlement 'implies greater discretion with regards to services and supports provided, expectations placed on clients and application of sanction policies'.[171]

---

[165] PRWORA s 408(a)(7), s 409(a)(9).
[166] Handler (n 10 above) 47.
[167] D Ellwood, *Poor Support* (Basic Books: New York, 1988). See n 9.
[168] See Center on Budget and Policy Priorities (n 159 above) 27.
[169] PRWORA s 401(b).
[170] eg King (n 16 above) 278.
[171] A Weil, 'Assessing Welfare Reform in the United States' in Gilbert and Parent (n 25 above) 145, 159.

d) The Strictly Contractual Rationale

Some provisions of the TANF programme exhibit a distinct quid-pro-quo rationale:

i) Work-tests

Recipients are required to accept any work offered to them, with no exceptions made as to prior work experience, prior earnings, education or training. Though the concept of 'willingness to work' was always present in the background of Food Stamp Act amendments,[172] the PRWORA signaled a break with tradition by establishing formal work requirements for FSP participants. The law now states that able-bodied adults without dependants are subjected to the new work requirements. In order to fulfill the work requirement, an individual must register for employment every 12 months. An individual will lose entitlement in any of the following cases: if she refuses to participate in an employment and training programme without good cause; if she refuses without good cause to accept an offer of employment at a wage not less than the applicable minimum wage; if she refuses to provide information required to determine employment status or job availability; or if she voluntarily and without good cause quits a job or reduces work effort to less than 30 hours per week.[173] In addition, adults not engaged for at least 20 hours or more per week in work, training or workfare schemes had their eligibility for benefits limited to a maximum of three months in any 36-month period.[174]

Unlike Britain, the requirement to actively seek work has not become part of the legislative framework that governs the American programmes. In practice, however, the situation is not much different. In fact, in many cases applicants are required to conduct independent job searches while the application for benefits is *pending*. This period can range from two to six weeks, and claimants are sometimes required to contact up to four employers per day.[175]

ii) Work-Related Activity

As part of the 'work first' ideology, welfare recipients must be engaged in some kind of work-related activity (as defined by the state) when they are ready for work or after 24 months of coming on assistance, whichever is earlier.[176] However, it is not clear how this requirement may be satisfied. For example, the federal mandate does not explain whether self-employment, volunteer work or other form of

---

[172] See *Lyng v Castillo* 477 US 635 (1986); *Lyng v International Union* 485 US 360, 371 (1988)—disqualification of strikers from receiving food stamps. Cf G Weber, 'The Striker Amendment to the Food Stamp Act' 22 Ga L Rev (1988) 741.
[173] PRWORA s 815(a) amending 7 USC s 2015(d)(1).
[174] PRWORA s 824(a) amending 7 USC s 2015(o)(2).
[175] Handler (n 10 above) 49.
[176] PRWORA s 402(a)(1)(A)(ii).

non-gainful employment will satisfy the condition.[177] Though participation in the workplace is assumed to nurture and expand aptitude to enter the paid labour force, this often was not the case. Some of the jobs that recipients were sent to required no skills at all, and did nothing to develop hidden aptitudes. In one well-known case, women were required to sort coin-sized toys into piles of different colours. When they finished, a supervisor reshuffled the pile and the next crew began anew.[178]

iii) Workfare

Unless the state opts out, it must require a parent or caretaker receiving assistance who is not exempt to partake in community service employment after two months of receiving assistance, with minimum hours per week and tasks to be determined by the state. For the first time, the PRWORA also introduced workfare requirements to participants in FSP. Subject to the exception detailed below, states are required to penalize individuals if they refuse to engage in work required. The penalty may be in the form of a pro rata reduction of assistance otherwise payable to the family with respect to any period in which the individual so refuses, or by completely terminating the assistance. In addition, a measure that did not exist under the AFDC was added: a state may terminate Medicaid (health insurance for poor individuals) for recipients (though not for their children) if their cash assistance has been terminated.[179] The state may exempt individuals if they show good cause or under other exceptions that the state establishes.[180] The state may not reduce or terminate assistance to a single custodial parent caring for a child who is under six years of age if the individual proved inability to obtain needed child care due to unavailability of child care within reasonable distance, unavailability or unsuitability of informal child care by a relative or under other arrangements or the unavailability of appropriate and affordable formal child care arrangements.

iv) Individual Responsibility Plan

States are to devise an individual responsibility plan for any individual who is over 18 years of age or has not completed high school or obtained an equivalent certificate and is not attending secondary school. The plan will set an employment goal for the individual, a general scheme for moving the individual into private sector employment and the obligations of the individual during that time. These may include attending school, maintaining grades, keeping school age children in school, immunizing children and undergoing appropriate substance abuse treatment. The plan is to be constructed within 90 days (and in certain cases within 30 days) of the receipt of assistance. The individual's failure to comply with the

[177] Gilbert (n 25 above) 61.
[178] De Parle (n 20 above) 168.
[179] PRWORA s 114.
[180] PRWORA s 402(e)(1).

responsibility plan may, in addition to any other penalty, result in a reduction of benefits.[181] Problematically, however, recent studies show that the personal responsibility plan is a contract by name only. In fact, agency workers construct the terms of the welfare contract while excluding the client from the process and recipients have little recourse in getting the welfare department to meet its part of the contract.[182]

v) Residency Laws

The PRWORA makes immigrants with resident status ineligible for Food Stamp benefits, subject to certain exemptions.[183] The amendment also adds a waiting period of five years during which immigrants who enter the United States after the enactment of the PRWORA are not eligible for any means tested benefit.[184] As this new restriction is predicted to result in most immigrants losing their benefits until they become citizens,[185] it conveys the limited scope of the putative social contract, covering some residents, but not all. In the past, similar state enactments that included residency requirements as a condition for benefits were challenged successfully,[186] but it is doubtful that judicial review of residency requirements in a federal act would provide similar results, especially under the ideology currently prevalent in the American Supreme Court.[187]

2 New Deal, New Ambitions, New Contract for Britain

The Conservative government that promoted the JA 1995 saw it not only as a vehicle for producing a more rational or modern form of benefit, but also as an opportunity to restrict expenditure on benefit through tightening criteria on entitlement and strengthening measures to combat fraud, especially with regards to measures claimants must take to find work.[188] As of October 1996, a tripartite structure was established between Income Support, income-based Jobseeker's Allowance (JSA) and contribution based JSA. Only claimants for Income Support, such as the disabled, are not subject to labour market conditions. Both Income Support and income-based JSA benefits are means-tested, and the rules governing them are basically identical, apart from the demand that JSA claimants must

---

[181] PRWORA s 408(b).
[182] Handler (n 10 above) 85.
[183] PRWORA s 402 amending 8 USCA s 1612.
[184] PRWORA s 403 amending 8 USCA s 1613.
[185] T Cosenza, 'Preserving Procedural Due Process for Legal Immigrants Receiving Food Stamps in Light of the Personal Responsibility Act of 1996' (1997) 65 Fordham L Rev 2065, 2080.
[186] *Shapiro v Thompson* 394 US 618.
[187] It should be noted that the provision that permitted states to provide new state residents (who are U.S. citizens) with benefits equal to the amount offered in their former states was declared unconstitutional by the Supreme Court—*Saenz v Roe* 526 US 489 (1999).
[188] IT Smith, *Industrial Law* (7th edn, Butterworths: London, 2000) 543; Deakin and Wilkinson (n 1 above) 178–79.

fulfill the labour market conditions. No means tests are applied for contribution-based JSA. Following a series of government papers dealing with welfare reform (and entitled, tellingly, A New Contract for Welfare[189]) the Labour government moved towards implementing its agenda for welfare-to-work programmes.

As for the construction of this section: for reasons that merit investigation beyond the scope of this book, British programmes do not explicitly advance economic or moral agendas that are so prominent in American programmes. It is not disputed that conservative American commentators have acquired respect and attention with British think tanks and policy makers.[190] Moreover, there is anecdotal, field-level evidence that 'the individual focus of the New Deal was giving way to an increased emphasis on... performance targets'.[191] So even when British governments have declared that they would seek significant cuts in public expenditure and, specifically, in social security spending,[192] it would seem that cultural and sociological differences precluded the use of the vehicle of welfare reform to advance conservative platforms that legislate budgetary or case-load targets at the expense of claimants' particular needs. Similarly, one does not find in the British legislation any proclamations that blatantly profess the superiority of the nuclear, heterosexual family. Moreover, studies have shown that the British are much less likely than the Americans to find that the poor are to *blame* for their predicament. The idea that poverty is 'the result of personal behaviour and shortcomings of the poor themselves',[193] while identifiable in other Western countries, prevails most amongst Americans (including the poor themselves) and is most like attributable to the American ideology of individual achievement and equal opportunity.

In sum, then, the focus of this section will be on the deterrent and the strict contractual aspects of the British welfare-to-work programme. A third section will offer a possible critique of the hidden moral agenda that may exist in the programmes.

a) The Deterrent Rationale

Dean and Taylor-Gooby identify three themes in British employment and social security policy over the last decade, highlighting the connections between the

---

[189] DSS, *New Ambitions for Our Country: A New Contract for Welfare* (Cm 3805, 1998); DSS, *A New Contract for Welfare: Principles into Practice* (Cm 4101, 1998); DEE, *A New Contract for Welfare: The Gateway to Work* (Cm 4102, 1998); DSS, *A New Contract for Welfare: Children's Rights and Parents' Responsibilities* (Cm 4349, 1999).
[190] C Murray, *The Emerging British Underclass* (IEA: London, 1990); C Murray, *Underclass: The Crisis Deepens* (IEA: London, 1994); and see text to n 82 above.
[191] D Finn, 'The "Employment First" Welfare State: Lessons from the New Deal for Young People' (2003) 37 Social Policy and Administration 709, 715.
[192] S Deakin and F Wilkinson, 'Labour Law, Social Security and Economic Inequality' (1991) 15 Cambridge J of Economics 125, 130–31.
[193] W van Oorshcot and L Halman, 'Blame or Fate, Individual or Social' (2000) 2(1) European Societies 1, 7.

three variables that figure in the deterrent approach of the New Deal: less eligibility, targeting and eradicating fraud.

> ... to strengthen the work incentives, which means to widen the gap between benefit levels and earnings; to direct spending accurately to defined groups of needy people, which means greater use of means-testing and of restrictions on entitlement; and to simplify administration of the system, while intensifying the measures to stop fraud and regulate claimants' lives.[194]

As a preliminary remark, it should be noted that Britain stands out in the amount of research that has been conducted recently within the academia, welfare organizations and most prominently by the government, in the field of non-take-up. This effort includes creating a division within the Department for Work and Pensions, entrusted with the task of studying and tackling non-take-up. The motivation driving this effort has been to keep numbers of recipients from falling and to maintain caseloads.[195] The need for intervention has been clear for some time, as past measures have resulted in low levels of take-up rates in general and for single females in particular. It seems that the effort has been successful. The figures for the year 2004–5 show a take-up rate of between 90 per cent and 97 per cent by expenditure (between 82 per cent and 96 per cent for single females) and between 83 per cent and 94 per cent by caseload (between 76 per cent and 92 per cent for single females).[196] These figures show a remarkable 15 to 25 point rise when compared to the years 2000–1.[197]

i) Means-Testing

In order to be eligible for benefits under the income-based Jobseeker's Allowance, a claimant's family[198] income is aggregated and checked, in a series of complex rules and regulations as to income and capital[199] to assure it does not exceed the applicable amount.[200] If a claimant has income below the applicable amount, the income will be deducted from the benefit. This would mean an effective withdrawal rate of 100 per cent.

ii) Less Eligibility

In comparison with other Western countries, Britain ranks relatively well in terms of benefit rates. For example, when comparing Net Replacement Rates,

---

[194] H Dean and P Taylor-Gooby, *Dependency Culture* (Harvester: New York, 1992) 55.
[195] A Doron and J Gal, 'The Israeli Income Support Program in a Comparative Perspective' (2000) Social Security 5 [in Hebrew]; Corden (n 95 above) 25.
[196] DWP, *Income Related Benefits: Estimates of Take Up of Benefits in 2004–2005* (HMSO: London, 2006).
[197] DWP, *Income Related Benefits: Estimates of Take Up of Benefits in 2000–2001* (HMSO: London, 2002).
[198] Defined as a married or unmarried couple and, if relevant, any child that is a member of their household and for either one or both are responsible—JA 1995 s 35(1).
[199] SI 1996/207 chs IV (Income), V (Other Income) and VI (Capital) and VII (Liable Relatives) and Schedule 1 (Applicable amounts).
[200] JA 1995 ss 3, 13(2).

the United Kingdom is ranked amongst or just outside the top five OECD nations for benefits for single recipients (46 per cent), couples (57 per cent) and couples with children (80 per cent). Benefits for lone parents and young people are also relatively generous in the United Kingdom, with NRR of 71 per cent and 42 per cent, respectively. It is all the more disturbing, then, that even in Britain evidence abounds that benefits are insufficient to meet the basic day-to-day needs of recipients. The Poor Law tradition of less eligibility is revisited in the ideology of a yawning gap between wages and benefits, forcing claimants to work while receiving benefits so as to make ends meet.[201] This brings us to the issue of anti-fraud measures.

iii) Fraud and Abuse

An increasing level of public anxiety over the issue of benefit abuse and fraud since the 1970s has culminated in the 1997 Green Paper dedicated to the matter[202] and in the Social Security Administration (Fraud) Act 1997 that immediately followed. The SSA(F)A marked the opening of a new era in government determination to eradicate fraud and abuse. The Act empowered officials with greater authority and changed the balance between the public interest in detecting fraud and abuse, on the one hand, and claimants' rights to privacy, on the other hand, in a manner that has been criticized as inappropriate.[203] Despite the fact that the DSS research report stated that the 'common view was that most of those who committed fraud were ordinary people who committed it on a small scale because of need',[204] the government emphasized increased vigilance and reduced tolerance towards fraud.[205] The government not only dedicated a separate government paper to the issue of fraud but, amongst the papers dealing with welfare reform, it was also by far the lengthiest of them all. Subsequent legislation further extended the powers granted to inspectors (now named 'authorized officers') to seek information.[206] In addition, the Social Security Fraud Act 2001 broadened the list of bodies that may be approached for obtaining information on claimants and expanded the range of situations in which these powers may be used, now including situations where a person either has committed, is committing or intends to commit a benefit offence *or* is a member of such person's family.[207]

---

[201] G McKeever, 'Fighting Fraud: An Evaluation of the Government's Social Security Fraud Strategy' (1999) 21 J of Social Welfare and Family Law 357, 366.
[202] DSS, *Beating Fraud is Everyone's Business* (Cm 4012, 1997).
[203] G McKeever, 'Detecting, Prosecuting and Punishing Benefit Fraud' (1999) 62 MLR 261.
[204] K Rowlingson and others, *Social Security Fraud: The Role of Penalties* (DSS Research Report 64, London 1997) 4.
[205] DSS, *A New Contract for Welfare: Safeguarding Social Security* (Cm 4276, 1999); McKeever (n 201 above) 357.
[206] Child Support, Pensions and Social Security Act 2000 c 19 ss 109A, 109C, sch 6. For criticisms of some of the provisions see McKeever (n 203 above) 265–66.
[207] ss 1, 2 of the SSFA 2001 c 11 ss 1, 2, SI 2002/817; Wikeley and Ogus (n 76 above) 171.

b) *The Strictly Contractual Rationale*
i) Work Requirements

The JA 1995 differs from its American counterpart in the level of detail that links welfare to work—the work requirements.[208] While the American programme leaves much room for state regulation and agency discretion,[209] the British legislation codifies the terms and conditions of the contract between the agency and the claimant. Two significant ingredients constitute the work test: the requirement to be available for work, and the requirement to be actively seeking work.

As described above, the requirement that claimants be available for work has already almost a century's worth of history. Its main function is to distinguish between those who are voluntarily unemployed and those who are involuntarily unemployed or, in other words, between deserving and undeserving recipients. A person is available for work if 'he is willing and able to take up immediately any employed earner's employment'.[210] Though the provision states that a person must accept *any* employment, other provisions narrow the scope of this requirement. During the 'permitted period', which lasts between one week and 13 weeks,[211] a claimant may limit availability to his usual occupation and/or the level of remuneration he is accustomed to receive.[212] After the permitted period ends, a claimant must seek and accept any job offer. The regulations that supplement the JSA provide the criteria that determine the length of the permitted period, including the type of usual occupation, the duration of last occupation, the length of training the person has undergone and the availability and location of employment in that occupation.[213] Though an effort is made to maintain a delicate balance between satisfying the claimants' employment aspirations and practical limitations, it is clear that in case the two cannot be satisfied, the former will have to be compromised.

In addition, the legislation states that regulations may provide conditions under which a person may limit his or her availability and not lose entitlement in certain cases. Restrictions are acceptable if the claimant can show that she has reasonable prospects of securing employment notwithstanding these restrictions.[214] In addition, acceptable limits on availability may include, for example, restrictions due to conscientious or religious convictions, mental or physical disabilities and caring responsibilities.[215] In the latter case, primary carers may reduce their availability to less than 40 hours a week as long as they are available for as many hours as their caring responsibilities permit and in any case for no less

---

[208] Wikeley and Ogus (n 76 above) 337–51.
[209] Handler (n 10 above) 45, 81–82.
[210] JA 1995 s 6(1),
[211] As detailed in the jobseeker's agreement—SI 1996/207 reg 31(f).
[212] JA 1995 ss 6(4), 6(5), 6(6), SI 1996/207 reg 20.
[213] SI 1996/207 reg 16(2).
[214] SI 1996/207 reg 8.
[215] JA 1995 s 6(2); SI 1996/207 reg 13(2), 13(3), 13(4).

than 16 hours. Restrictions may be made as to the nature of employment, periods of availability, terms or conditions of employment and localities. Lastly, claimants may place restrictions on the level of pay for a period of six months.[216]

The 1988 Government White Papers[217] dedicate an entire chapter to the question of availability for work and construct the requirement as one that targets fraud and abuse.[218] Again, such a construction perceives work requirements and abuse detection as governed by the same rationale. As a measure that would supplement the availability requirement, the government resurrected the 'genuinely seeking employment' requirement that was in force between 1921 and 1930.[219] And thus, Beveridge's hope that 'the test had gone and may it never rise from its dishonoured grave'[220] went unfulfilled. Indeed, as tribunals were reading it into the 'availability' requirement for at least a decade prior to its formal return into primary legislation, the test was already looming in the background. In a dictum that was routinely referred to when denying benefits to claimants, the Commissioners ruled that 'availability implies some active step by the person concerned to draw attention to his availability: it is not a passive state in which a person may be said to be available provided he is sought out and his location is ascertained'.[221] This assessment represents a dominant 'active over passive' discourse that is both mistaken and misleading. It is mistaken because, as argued below, the benefit system may promote activity while labour market policies may work against employment activity. It is misleading because enforcing 'activity' discourages systematic consideration of the form and extent of activity achieved.[222]

In a different case, the Commissioners also denied a claimant eligibility on the ground that there was 'no evidence that he took any steps during the period to try to get a job, as by perusing newspaper advertisements, going for interviews, etc.'.[223] According to the regulations, steps a claimant may reasonably be expected to take include oral and written applications, seeking information, appointing a third party to assist in finding employment and registration with an employment agency, while normally one step would not suffice. Measures taken may be disregarded if a person's behaviour or appearance is understood to intentionally spoil the opportunity of securing employment.[224]

If a claimant refuses or fails to apply for a job offered to him by an employment officer without good cause the sanctions levied are potentially substantial, ranging

---

[216] SI 1996/207 reg 9.
[217] DoE, *Training for Employment* (Cm 316, 1988); DoE, *Employment for the 1990s* (Cm 540, 1988).
[218] N Wikeley, 'Unemployment Benefit, the State and the Labour Market' (1989) 16 J of L and Society 291, 299.
[219] SSA 1989 c 24 s 10.
[220] Cited in L Lundy, 'From Welfare to Work? Social Security and Unemployment' in N Harris (ed), *Social Security Law in Context* (OUP: Oxford, 2000) 291, 300.
[221] R(U) 5/80 para 14 cited in T Buck, 'Social Security' (1989) 18 ILJ 258, 259.
[222] Sinfield (n 80 above) 18–19.
[223] R(U) 7/86(T) para 21 cited ibid.
[224] JA 1995 s 7(3), SI 1996/207 reg 18.

between a disqualification period of one week to 26 weeks.[225] Regulations provide that claimants have a good cause for declining a job if it, inter alia, involves less than 24 hours of work per week.[226] In contrast to the situation prior to 1989, however, any matter relating to the level of remuneration may not be considered automatically as 'good cause'.[227] Other claims that would not be considered good cause include the case where the recipient would be financially worse off if he were to accept the position[228] and an argument based on the distance to work, if it takes normally less than one hour each way.[229] Finally, the regulations also detail factors that are 'relevant' in considering good cause. These include significant harm to health, serious religious or conscientious objection, caring responsibilities and expenses that constitute an 'unreasonably high proportion' of expected earnings.[230]

ii) Jobseeker's Agreement

In terms of British labour relations, the Jobseekers' Agreement is an innovation of the JA 1995. Though employment plans existed prior to the legislation, the JA 1995 elevated the agreement to the level of a mandatory condition for the receipt of benefits.[231] Obvious concerns were raised as to the degree of true voluntariness exhibited in the contract. Thus, one Member of Parliament characterized it as 'an abuse of language in an abuse of power'.[232] Indeed, recent field research suggests that notwithstanding the individualistic premise, employment contracts are not tailored for the specific needs of the claimant, sessions are strikingly brief and the jobseeker simply agrees to the terms set before her.[233]

The Jobseeker's Regulations prescribe the content of the agreement and this includes the date, the name of the claimant, restrictions on availability for work, the description of the work sought, actions that the claimant would take to seek employment and the duration of 'permitted period'.[234] The employment officer may, and on the claimant's request must, refer the agreement to the Secretary of State to determine whether it satisfies the conditions of availability and actively seeking employment.[235] In addition, a person must sign on at a job centre every fortnight and discuss available vacancies with an adviser. Longer interviews are held every six months. If a claimant refuses, without good cause, to carry out a reasonable direction from the employment officer the claimant will be

---

[225] JA 1995 s 19(6).
[226] SI 1996/207 reg 5A.
[227] JA 1995 s 19(9).
[228] SI 1996/207 reg 72(6)(a).
[229] SI 1996/207 reg 72(6)(b)—this does not mean that if it takes more than one hour good cause is established.
[230] SI 1996/207 reg 72(2), 72(3).
[231] JA 1995 s 1(2).
[232] *Hansard* col 600 (26 June 1995).
[233] Handler (n 10) 200.
[234] SI 1996/207 reg 31.
[235] JA 1995 s 9(6).

disqualified from receiving benefits for a minimum period of one week, and for a maximum period of 26 weeks.[236]

c) A Hidden Moral Rationale in the New Contract?

In no place in the British legislation can one find a pronounced moral agenda akin to the American emphasis on family and marriage.[237] Indeed, the British government has repeatedly pronounced its commitment to change workplace practices in order to facilitate the successful combination of work and parenting.[238] However, it is undeniably true that, like other European nations, Britain employs authoritative mechanisms through welfare-to-work programmes to address broader social problems than long-term unemployment. The heading often used for this agenda is 'social inclusion', and the idea is that those currently seen as undeserving should be integrated into normative structures such as the labour market and the family.[239]

However, the New Deals for Young People and for Lone Parents are arguably advancing a latent moral agenda that is not remote from the pronounced American one. The New Deal for Lone Parents (NDLP) offers parents to children in school age counseling and assistance in matters such as job search, training and caring for children. While completely voluntary in origin, the Department of Work and Pensions introduced compulsory elements to the NDLP. In particular, as of April 2007, lone parents with a youngest child aged five to 13 are required to attend a Lone Parent Work Focused Interview (LPFWI) every six months as a condition of receiving income support. The requirement will apply to lone parents with children aged 0 to four years as of April 2008. The purpose of the LPWFI is to encourage lone parents to seek work.

The New Deal for Young People (NDYP) offers unemployed people aged 18 to 24 six months of benefit, after which they enter a 'gateway' of intensive counseling with a personal adviser for a maximum of four months.[240] During this period they should be placed in a job in the private market. If this prospect does not materialize, the claimant may choose one of four options:[241] a subsidized job with a regular employer at six months subsidy of £75 per week; work experience in the voluntary sector, receiving an added £15 to the benefit previously received; work experience in an environmental project, receiving an added £15 to the benefit previously received; or full-time vocational education, receiving regular benefit.

---

[236] JA 1995 s 19(2).
[237] A Deacon, 'An Ethic of Mutual Responsibility? Towards a Fuller Justification for Conditionality in Welfare' in C Beem and L Mead (eds), *Welfare Reform and Political Theory* (Sage: New York, 2005) 127, 132.
[238] J Conaghan, 'Women, Work and Family: A British Revolution?' in J Conaghan, R Fischl and K Klare (eds), *Labour Law in an Era of Globalization* (OUP: Oxford, 2002) 53.
[239] Standing (n 91 above) 29; Handler (n 10 above) 144.
[240] For a relatively positive assessment of the NDYP see Finn (n 191 above).
[241] See T Boeri, R Layard and S Nickell, *Welfare-to-Work and the Fight Against Long-Term Unemployment* (Report 206, Department for Education and Employment, 2000).

These schemes have been criticized as seeking to reinstate the traditional roles in the family and to re-establish the prominent role a normative family should have in society.[242] The critique outlines two possible scenarios that the programmes putatively address, both stemming from the lone mother's refusal to marry the father of her children. Her refusal is justified because the financial incentives to marry are missing, on the one hand, and because the male in question is not an attractive prospect, on the other hand. He is, according to conservative writings, a 'barbarian', pure and simple. The first scenario, then, views the welfare system as instrumental in 'taming barbarians': transforming them into potential, attractive and worthy partners. As Murray intimates, 'young males are essentially barbarians for whom marriage—meaning not just the wedding vows—is an indispensable civilizing force. Young men who don't work don't make good marriage material'.[243] Taming the barbarians and socializing young men into their pre-ordained roles in the workforce and in society is seen as the moral notion underlying the NDYP.[244]

The second scenario recognizes that such social engineering may not always succeed. The alternative is to assure that the lone mother will take up functions traditionally associated with the male role model. Sociologist AH Halsey explains that this is because:

...the very, very important ingredient of a role model of a working man, a person who goes to work and comes back and does all sorts of DIY and is a responsible adult person is missing. And that seems to be a way of making sure you don't have barbarism.[245]

If rising rates of divorce and 'illegitimate' births cannot be controlled, pressure can be mounted so the child will see the mother leaving for work on a daily basis. This may be viewed as the hidden agenda underlying schemes such as the NDLP.[246]

C Conclusion

All welfare-to-work programmes view inclusion into the labour market as preferable to reliance on welfare benefit. That much they have in common. Furthermore, we find an array of more specific common features as well. Amongst these, of noteworthiness are means tests, rates of benefits that are kept below labour market rates, emphasis on fraud detection, work tests, special concern with single parents and young adults and even the ceremonious signing of a

---

[242] C Grover and J Stewart, *The Work Connection* (Palgrave: Houndmills, 2002), especially ch 7.
[243] Murray 1990 (n 190 above) 23.
[244] Grover and Stewart (n 242 above) 96–112.
[245] Cited in Mann and Roseneil (n 137 above) at 323.
[246] Grover and Stewart (n 242 above) 55–57, 76–86.

contract between the agency and the claimant. Chapters 2 and 3 have shown significant divergence may exist amidst this common ground.

Four formidable rationales exert weight towards placing a different emphasis on the precise character of the programmes. These are the deterrent rationale, the fiscal rationale, the moral rationale and the strictly contractual rationale. Different jurisdictions, at different times, place more emphasis on some and less on others. Thus, from the survey of programmes that are currently in place, it is clear that while the deterrent and moral rationales are granted considerable authority in American programmes, their importance is negligible in British welfare reform which emphasizes the strictly contractual, or quid-pro-quo, rationale. And yet, both programmes, like numerous others today, have retracted from egalitarian ideals that are exhibited in state involvement in the labour market and in policies of full employment. In so doing, policy-makers have preferred Poor Law philosophy over continuing the welfare-state project. As Deakin and Wilkinson conclude, 'it is in precisely those periods when a belief in the "natural" properties of the market is at its strongest, that the administration of social welfare is at its most repressive'.[247]

Amongst values governing public governance and able to mitigate its potentially repressive power, one of the most important is that of equality. The following chapter, then, takes us from equality to the right to welfare. In doing so, however, the putatively opposing value of responsibility, that has been omnipresent throughout this thesis, has to be addressed and its implications for the analysis understood.

---

[247] Deakin and Wilkinson (n 1 above) 199.

4
From Equality to the Right to Welfare

As noted, in 1996 President Bill Clinton, wishing to live up to his declaration that he would 'end welfare as we know it', signed legislation that signified, for better or for worse, the most important moment for the American welfare system since 1935.[1] It is quite telling, however, that the title of the legislation does not include the word 'welfare' at all. Rather, it is the Personal Responsibility and Work Opportunity Reconciliation Act 1996 (PRWORA).[2] Both within and outside the United States, personal responsibility has everything to do with (the debate over) welfare reform. One of the touchstones of arguments against state benefits, let alone welfare *rights*, is that they undermine one's need to account for her acts since they do not only support those who suffer from unfortunate luck, but also allow people to take irresponsible risks. In response, others have expressed the worry that responsibility is supplanting the welfare state's traditional devotion to equality. The role of this public norm is expressed by altering patterns of extreme social inequality and making accessible basic interests such as health, education and subsistence.[3] This emphasis on equality, it is argued, has been missing in recent welfare reforms that have been advanced by some Western countries.

If true, part of the reason for this unfortunate phenomenon may be attributed to the fact that equality and responsibility are seen as opposing concepts. The most prominent amongst contemporary egalitarian writers adopt what I shall term an 'agency' conception of responsibility which claims, in essence, that equality 'stops at the gate of individual responsibility'.[4] I argue, however, that this approach is misguided, and that the two concepts supplement one another. Furthermore, if my argument is persuasive, I believe it has serious practical implications with respect to certain provisions of welfare-to-work programmes. I begin, then, by outlining the importance of equality within a general theory

---

[1] See eg D King, *In the Name of Liberalism* (Oxford: OUP, 1999) 277; H Karger, 'The International Implications of U.S. Welfare Reform' 55 Social Security (1999) 7.
[2] Pub L 104–193.
[3] TH Marshall, 'Citizenship and Social Class' in *Class, Citizenship and Social Development* (Doubleday: New York, 1964) 65, 101–109; TH Marshall, 'Social Selection in the Welfare State' ibid 235, 237; J Waldron, 'Social Citizenship and the Defense of Welfare Provision' in J Waldron, *Liberal Rights* (CUP: Cambridge, 1993) 271, 280; R Gavison, 'On the Relationship Between Civil and Political Rights and Social and Economic Rights' in JM Coicaud, MW Doyle and AM Gardner (eds), *The Globalization of Human Rights* (United Nations UP: Tokyo, 2003) 24, 43.
[4] P Rosanvallon, *The New Social Question* (Princeton UP: Princeton, 2000) 32.

of justice and then move to discuss how the concept of responsibility fits into an egalitarian approach. The third section considers some of the efforts to map a theory of 'illegitimate conditions'[5] insofar as they relate to conditions placed on welfare benefits through welfare-to-work programmes and offers a contextual, normative framework for the analysis of conditions prevalent in welfare-to-work programmes. The concluding section explains how, notwithstanding the emphasis on personal responsibility, a true understanding of equality supports the recognition of a legal right to welfare.

A Equality—A Very Short Introduction

Thomas Scanlon views 'equality as the first solution to the problem of justice'[6] Axel Honneth argues that 'every conception of justice must have an egalitarian character from the start'.[7] Communitarian Philip Selznick finds that 'moral equality is at the heart of justice'.[8] And Thomas Nagel concludes that 'Up to a point, more equality makes it harder for anyone to object'.[9] The importance of treating all people with equal concern and respect is central to the theories of Ronald Dworkin and Brian Barry, while a foundational element in John Rawls's is the construction of a theory of justice around the idea of individuals as free and equal citizens. What is the appeal of equality that makes it such an important pillar in a theory of justice?

The answer probably lies in the fact that, at its most abstract level, the idea of equality overlaps with the ideal of justice itself.[10] This, of course, does not mean that equality is the sole objective of justice or that the overlap is perfect.[11] However, a strong relationship exists. Prior to inserting substantive criteria that are central to questions of distributive justice, equality basically demands to know if one person's advantage over another is based on proper criteria, in other words—if it can be justified. This enterprise is essentially similar to the task that engages moral philosophy.[12] Theories of equality, mentioned below, offer reasoned standards that purport to justify the focus placed on equalizing certain facets (welfare, opportunity, resources, etc.) and not on others. At a proper

---

[5] The terminology is my own. In American jurisprudence the doctrine is termed 'unconstitutional conditions'.
[6] T Scanlon, 'Rawls' Theory of Justice' in N Daniels (ed), *Reading Rawls* (Blackwell: Oxford, 1975) 169, 199.
[7] A Honneth, 'Redistribution as Recognition: A Response to Nancy Fraser' in N Fraser and A Honneth, *Redistribution or Recognition?* (Verso: London, 2003) 110, 176.
[8] P Selznick, 'Social Justice—A Communitarian Perspective' in A Etzioni (ed), *The Essential Communitarian Reader* (Rowan and Littlefield: Oxford, 1998) 61, 63.
[9] T Nagel, *Equality and Partiality* (OUP: New York, 1991) 67.
[10] HLA Hart, *The Concept of Law* (2nd edn, Clarendon: Oxford, 1994) 159–67.
[11] J Finnis, *Natural Law and Natural Rights* (Clarendon: Oxford, 1982) 173.
[12] T Scanlon, 'Preference and Urgency' (1975) 72 J of Philosophy 655; See also his *What We Owe to Each Other* (Harvard UP: Cambridge MA, 1998) 171–77.

level of abstraction, then, embracing equality implies setting out baseline rules of public governance. One could say that these rules, if they are to fit any theory of justice worthy of its name, should apply *equally* to everyone.[13] In this narrow sense, however, equality is employed in a rhetorical fashion and would mean only that each person should count as one and only as one.[14] This is probably what Dworkin means by arguing that utilitarianism, for example, 'owes whatever appeal it has to what we might call its egalitarian cast'.[15]

Equality's impact on a theory of justice could mean that such a theory should be guided by general principles and should avoid the use of proper names or clear references to individuals. But these restrictions, of generality and universality respectively, are only two formal restrictions that apply to *any* theory of justice.[16] A principle that distributes reward according to race or creed manages to fly under the radar of these restrictions and would still be far removed from an *egalitarian* theory of justice.[17] And yet, the fact that even such immoral theories of justice may be dressed in egalitarian clothing (as expressed in the phrase: 'every person is equally entitled to marry within his or her own race'[18]) would attest to the rhetorical power of the concept. When moving to a theory of justice that is committed to a substantive idea of equality, however, we may have to part from some who share this broad common ground. Though some inequalities may be legitimate, the commitment to equality of all human beings would reject principles that are biased towards a particular race, caste, or those that are unnecessarily favourable to a particular conception of the good life.[19]

Before addressing serious questions that concern the nature and interpretation of a concept such as equality, one needs to be clear about the general idea of what is implied by the term. In the case of equality, philosophers and lawyers sometimes use the term to refer to different notions, mainly because equality may be employed on two distinct levels of concreteness.[20] On an abstract level, it serves as a check on institutions and principles that society is governed by, 'a test to be applied to the moral and legal rules of a society: one which asks about their acceptability among free and equal people'.[21] This primary level of equality is the

---

[13] HLA Hart, 'Positivism and the Separation of Law and Morals' (1957) 71 Harvard L Rev 593, 623–24.
[14] R Goodin, *Reasons for Welfare* (Princeton UP: Princeton, 1988) 53.
[15] R Dworkin, 'Rights as Trumps' in J Waldron (ed), *Theories of Rights* (OUP: Oxford, 1984) 153, 154.
[16] J Rawls, *A Theory of Justice* (Revised Edition OUP: Oxford, 1999) 113–16.
[17] R Dworkin, *Freedom's Law* (Harvard UP: Cambridge MA, 1996) 9.
[18] *Loving v Virginia* 338 US 1 (1967).
[19] B Barry, *Justice as Impartiality* (Clarendon: Oxford, 1995) 8; R Dworkin, 'Liberalism' in *A Matter of Principle* (Clarendon: Oxford, 1986) 181, 191–92; S Fredman, 'Equality: A New Generation?' (1999) 30 ILJ 145, 154.
[20] Similar ideas have been suggested: Honneth (n 7 above) 110, 182; Barry (n 19 above) 227; Rawls (n 16 above) 447; R Dworkin, *Law's Empire* (Hart: Oxford, 1986) 184–86.
[21] Barry (n 19 above) 194. See also B Barry, *Why Social Justice Matters* (Polity: Cambridge, 2005) 23.

type that Rawls, Dworkin and Barry, for example, refer to in their writings.[22] The idea stems from a view that all individuals are entitled to equal concern and respect and to have their needs, expectations and aspirations considered without bias. Understanding equality as a fundamental political ideal would mean that a just government cannot consider my life as a priori more important than yours.[23]

This abstract conceptualization of equality should be distinguished from a second understanding of the concept. Quite often, in referring to equality, legal professionals are concerned with the distribution of goods without bias. On this subordinate level, equality serves as 'a maxim of behaviour in everyday life'[24] and is connected to the notion of equal treatment. When engaging issues that give rise to claims of equality, legal discourse is chiefly concerned with the application of the principle of non-discrimination. Contrariwise, the primary level of equality is interested in the implications that derive from a theory of justice that is concerned with viewing individuals as free and equal persons and treating them with equal concern and respect.[25] Indeed, there have been recent attempts to distinguish between egalitarian principles (here referred to as the primary level of equality) and non-discrimination principles (here referred to as the secondary level of equality) on a conceptual level.[26]

Furthermore, it has been argued that the primary level conceptualization of equality exploits solely the rhetorical value of equality, while in effect the concept is superfluous to the norm advocated. In other words, if what we mean by equality is captured by the claim that all should be treated with equal concern and respect, could we not drop the 'equal', thus requiring that all should be treated with due concern and respect? Surely, the equality of treatment would follow, even without demanding it explicitly. This view, which may be termed the 'humanitarian' objection to egalitarianism, is very persuasive.[27]

I cannot offer here an extensive reply worthy of the debate, but it is possible to say the following. While the requirement to treat people with concern and respect necessarily plays a major role in a theory of justice, it leaves unanswered a substantial degree of problematic discretion if equality is not added. Imagine a situation where it is decided that treating all homeless individuals with concern and respect requires offering them reasonable public housing. However, it

---

[22] For the claim that Rawls and Dworkin do not differ greatly in their proposals for a basic framework of distributional equality see L Jacobs, 'Realizing Equal Life Prospects' in G Drover and P Kerans (eds), *New Approaches to Welfare Theory* (Elgar: Brookfield, 1993) 49, 51.

[23] R Dworkin, *Sovereign Virtue* (Harvard UP: London, 2000) 128; Selznick (n 8 above) 63.

[24] Dworkin (n 23 above) 128.

[25] A similar distinction is proposed by Hugh Collins, in 'Discrimination, Equality and Social Inclusion' (2003) 66 MLR 16.

[26] E Holmes, 'Anti-Discrimination Rights Without Equality' (2005) 68 MLR 175.

[27] See eg J Raz, *The Morality of Freedom* (Clarendon: Oxford, 1986) ch 9, esp 240–44; Gavison (n 3 above) 43; Holmes (n 26 above) 188 n 21. But cf A Gewirth, *The Community of Rights* (Chicago UP: Chicago, 1996) 71–74.

is mandated that while all apartments should be decent and livable, white homeless people are to receive apartments that are slightly larger (say, by five square meters) than non-white homeless people. How can we phrase our objection to this situation without resorting to equality? Of course, one may argue that discrimination of this kind means that we did not *truly* treat some of the individuals with concern and respect. This, however, would mean that concern and respect essentially means *equal* concern and respect, and our task would be done.

This reply suggests that the legal principle of non-discrimination is but one manifestation of the more general requirement of viewing all individuals as holding equal moral worth. Thus, one may understand the shift in legal discourse from formal equality to substantive equality as governed by a more fundamental move towards a deeper, multifaceted approach to what the requirements of equal moral worth actually entail.[28] Indeed, Barry states that 'it is a fallacy that there is any free-standing concept of equal treatment at the first-order level'.[29] Be that as it may, it is the primary level of equality that has provided many commentators with 'the most fundamental justification for the welfare state',[30] and it is this level that we shall turn to when asking what norms, rights and obligations may be legitimately derived from the ideal of egalitarian justice. Therefore, this debate need not be addressed here in full, though some aspects of the issue will be present throughout the chapter.

Following the preliminaries that offer some understanding of equality's initial appeal, we may turn to the more substantive question known as the 'currency' of egalitarian justice or, as Amartya Sen neatly phrased the question, 'Equality of What?'.[31] Contemporary literature on this matter finds me in a peculiar situation: while the intense disagreements amongst the prominent writers who are interested in these matters are of minimal practical relevance insofar as my interest lies, the one point where these authors (and several others) converge is also the single point where I find myself in disagreement with them all. For, though the debate between proponents of equality of opportunity, resources and welfare is indeed intriguing, the differences between the various suggestions may be quite minimal in theory, let alone in practice. This increased convergence renders 'the distinction between [equality of] preferences and [equality of] resources

---

[28] S Fredman, *Discrimination Law* (Clarendon: Oxford, 2001) 92ff; N Fraser, 'Distorted Beyond all Recognition: A Rejoinder to Axel Honneth' in Fraser and Honneth (n 7 above) 198, 231–32.

[29] Barry (n 19 above) 227. Barry's use of first-order and, especially, second-order levels of equality has a different objective that my own, but in this case the terminology is transferable.

[30] Goodin (n 14 above) 51. Goodin goes on to argue that one *cannot* ground the welfare state on the egalitarian ideal. In doing so, however, he refers predominantly to the principle of equal treatment, identified here as the subordinate level of equality. His support of *impartiality* as an ideal rule is not far removed from what I termed the primary level of equality.

[31] A Sen, 'Equality of What?' in *Choice, Welfare and Measurement* (Blackwell: Oxford, 1982) 353.

extremely hazy'.[32] Furthermore, since we lack the information necessary to ascertain which benefits result from talents, which from cultural endowments and which from personal motivation, not to mention the perfect willingness to follow the egalitarian norm that would ideally be chosen, the practical differences between the various proposals seem difficult to discern.

So, if one considers how divergent the positions presented are with regards to the question of what constitutes an equal (or unequal) distribution, it is surprising to witness the consensus on the fundamental issue that may have a serious impact on actual policy decisions. I refer to the place that choice and responsibility hold in a theory of equality.

B Equality, Choice and Responsibility

Since responsibility is a prominent consideration in welfare-to-work programmes, it is important to investigate the relationship between responsibility and equality within this context. As mentioned, equality is a central value of public governance, of how society should treat each individual. Individual responsibility, then, addresses the counterpart: it begins with the individual and assesses his or her relationship with other individuals and with society at large.

As simple as this relationship may seem, its importance has not been clear to writers concerned with equality until recently. Ronald Dworkin is credited for this transformation, as he 'has, in effect, performed for egalitarianism the considerable service of incorporating within it the most powerful idea in the arsenal of the anti-egalitarian right: the idea of choice and responsibility'.[33] The two notions are distinct, however. It is true that a common line of thought suggests that 'because this is a choice by individual women, each individual is responsible for the consequences'.[34] But while responsibility encapsulates the normative assessment of an individual's attitude towards himself and towards others, choice refers to one's ability to act or to refrain from acting. Its relationship to responsibility is contingent, and dependent on the general approach.[35] For example, one may argue that particular choices are so fundamental to an individual's autonomy that his or her decision should be supported, *whatever the choice may be*.[36]

We may say, then, that while choice plays an important, albeit illusive, role in understanding the approach that an egalitarian theory should take towards

---

[32] J Roemer, 'The Mismarriage of Bargaining Theory and Distributive Justice' (1986) 97 Ethics 88, 107; Cohen expresses a similar view: GA Cohen, 'On the Currency of Egalitarian Justice' (1989) 99 Ethics 906, 921. Brian Barry is even more acerbic—Barry (n 21 above) 22.

[33] Cohen (n 32 above) 933. Also J Roemer *Theories of Distributive Justice* (Harvard UP: Cambridge, MA 1996) ch 7; G Standing, *Global Labour Flexibility* (Macmillan: Basingstoke, 1999) 339.

[34] S Fredman, 'A Difference with Distinction' (1994) 110 LQR 106, 122.

[35] Barry (n 21 above) 136–37.

[36] J Gardner, 'On the Grounds of Her Sex(uality)' (1998) 18 OJLS 167, 171 n 9.

personal action, it is the concept of responsibility that takes centre stage. Responsibility serves as a convenient intermediate point, bridging the abstract notion of equality and the pragmatic manner that governs our assessment of an individual's behaviour. Three approaches offer different ideas as to the way that responsibility should be imported into egalitarian theory. I refer to them as the Incentive Role of Responsibility; the Agency Interpretation of Responsibility; and Reasonable Responsibility. While the first is problematic as an approach to both equality and responsibility and can be relatively easily dismissed, the Agency Interpretation of Responsibility is now considered to be the governing approach to the way the two concepts should be investigated. I find it unsatisfactory, however, and offer Reasonable Responsibility as a more promising approach.

1 The Incentive Role of Responsibility

The Incentive Role of Responsibility approach highlights the relationship between equality and responsibility in a somewhat formalistic fashion. What is implied by equality here is the requirement to grant the same rights and obligations to all. Once the appropriate link between rights and obligations is created, individuals (insofar as equality is concerned) are left to their own devices and, in the case of welfare programmes, to choose whether or not to demand their rights (by accepting the correlative obligations) or to forego both the sting and the honey.[37] A cursory glance at this approach may find it peculiar that it is offered alongside more clearly egalitarian proposals. And, indeed, this construction may be more akin to theories usually referred to as 'anti-egalitarian' rather than as egalitarian theories. This approach is discussed here, however, on account of its influence in the critique of generous welfare programmes, on the one hand, and its role in the formulation of contemporary welfare reform, on the other hand.

The incentive-based approach to responsibility emphasizes the requirement to treat all people alike and entails respecting their choices, including choices not to work, as choices made by rational people.[38] If equal concern and respect for each person is a cornerstone of liberal theory, it is argued, then 'denigrating a person's autonomy and prime responsibility for his actions is a risky line to take for a theory that otherwise wishes to buttress the dignity and self-respect of autonomous beings'.[39] Since no-one compensates the working population for their ill-founded choices, requiring other citizens to compensate the unemployed individual for his or her choices discriminates against the tax-paying public.

This line of thought has been highly influential in the early days of welfare reforms and is still quite resonant in conservative critiques. Thus, Lawrence Mead

---

[37] L Mead, *Beyond Entitlement* (Free Press: London, 1986) 12.
[38] C Murray, *Losing Ground* (Basic Books: New York, 1984) 222.
[39] R Nozick, *Anarchy, State and Utopia* (Basic Books: New York, 1974) 214.

asserts that a 'substantial class of non-working adults simply violates the American idea of equality'.[40] It is not only the peculiarity of suggesting that there is a distinct *American* idea of equality that causes some dismay. It seems more pressing to ask: how can a large class of non-working adults be construed as a violation of *any* kind of equality? On a charitable interpretation, it is possible to understand the egalitarian paradigm advanced here as a derivative of classical liberal thought, where universalism and equality live in harmony with minimalist social policy of laissez-faire.[41] However, judging by the general thrust of Mead's book, it would seem that this statement implies that some individuals are not living up to their obligations as citizens, while others are. Responsibility is thus reconciled with equality by understanding the latter as *equality of responsibility*.[42]

This manner of incorporating responsibility into equality is problematic on several levels. First, it has been forcefully argued that, in fact, governments do *not* hold both rich and poor to the same responsibilities in areas such as 'sobriety, sexual "morality" and frugality'.[43] Second, characterizing all violations of our obligations (eg under the criminal law) as primarily a violation of equality seems artificial, if not simply bizarre. Third, the most elementary obligations we have as citizens are, first and foremost, duties not to harm others.[44] It is surprising that the obligation that is singled out in the case of welfare-to-work is an obligation *to act*. Welfare recipients, on the other hand, are to accept prevailing employment conditions as given and are judged harshly if they refuse jobs offered to them.[45] Lastly, and most fundamentally, the way equality is employed here is quite distinct from the notion of treating all individuals with equal concern and respect. The latter is offered as a fundamental, preinstitutional baseline to assess social institutions and policies. The former, at most, takes current power relations as a given and proposes 'equal treatment' by requiring the same from all people, regardless of their social or economic situation. Such a thin baseline is required to support a normative claim such as Nozick's famous argument that 'taxation of earnings from labor is on a par with forced labour'.[46] It would almost amount to intellectual negligence if we were not to bring forth here the sardonic advice 'to labour in the face of the majestic equality of the law, which forbids the rich as well as the poor to sleep under bridges, to beg in the streets, and to steal bread'.

---

[40] Mead (n 37 above) 240.
[41] G Esping-Andersen, *The Three Worlds of Welfare Capitalism* (Polity: Cambridge, 1990) 62.
[42] For a similar idea see L Williams, 'Beyond Labour Law's Parochialism: A Re-envisioning of the Discourse of Redistribution' in J Conaghan, R Fischl and K Klare (eds), *Labour Law in an Era of Globalization* (OUP: Oxford, 2002) 93, 108.
[43] Barry (n 21 above) 133.
[44] B Williams, 'A Critique of Utilitarianism' in JJC Smart and B Williams, *Utilitarianism: For and Against* (CUP: Cambridge, 1973) 93–118.
[45] For a similar structure of argument, concerning the relationship between socio-economic rights and property, see J Waldron, 'Liberal Rights' in Waldron (n 3 above) 1, 23.
[46] R Nozick, *Anarchy, State and Utopia* (Basic Books: New York, 1974) 169.

It is not only the use of egalitarian terminology in this approach that begs for close scrutiny. Perhaps more importantly (because less discussed), the meaning that individual responsibility denotes here proves to be problematic. Despite routine references to reciprocity in the justification of welfare-to-work programmes, no corresponding state responsibilities figure into the equation here. There is no mention of the state as an employer of last resort, of extensive child care, health care or transportation that would help the individual integrate into the labour market. Brian Barry views this format, exemplified in the American PRWORA, as 'personal responsibility with a vengeance'.[47] Moreover, he notes how this notion can be detected in other fields, such as public health, where duties traditionally shouldered by the state have been shifted to the individual, in a transition justified via the deployment of personal responsibility arguments.[48]

The incentive approach to responsibility also suggests that, if all are equal, it is unjust that some care for others' material needs. The claimant's refusal to accept job offers renders her un*deserving* of the fruit of others' toil. Scheffler identifies the crux of this critique as deriving:

> from the fact that the policy in question assigns important benefits or burdens on the basis of considerations other than those of individual desert. In order to reconcile these policies with ordinary notions of responsibility, what liberals would need to argue is... that ordinary principles of desert, properly understood, do not have the policy implications in these cases that critics of liberalism suppose them to have.[49]

At first glance, it seems almost natural that Scheffler shifts between the concept of responsibility and that of desert. This, however, is an unfortunately popular equivocation.[50] It not only leads to 'implicit incoherence'[51] by confusing what people are responsible for in the normative sense with the idea of how prudent or deserving they are. More problematic is the attachment to the notion of desert.

Desert has been convincingly dismissed as a foundational element in a theory of justice by liberals and critics of liberalism alike (despite some efforts to the contrary[52]) because it 'presupposes the existence of an ongoing cooperative scheme and is irrelevant to the question' of whether the scheme itself is just.[53] But unlike desert, responsibility is budding as an important concept that grants depth to egalitarianism.[54] Linking responsibility to desert would only serve to

---

[47] Barry (n 21 above) 149.
[48] ibid 157.
[49] S Scheffler, 'Responsibility, Reactive Attitudes and Liberalism in Philosophy and Politics' (1992) 21 Philosophy and Public Affairs 299, 303–4.
[50] S Hurley, *Justice, Luck and Knowledge* (Harvard UP: London, 2003) 191–201. Though Hurley highlights this equivocation, later (233–34), she is guilty of exactly the same (if not more serious) equivocation when expressing her support for the 'incentive parameter' role of responsibility.
[51] ibid 192.
[52] Scheffler (n 49 above); D Miller, 'Distributive Justice: What the People Think' (1992) 102 Ethics 555.
[53] Rawls (n 16 above) 89; Goodin (n 14 above) ch 10.
[54] S Holmes and C Sunstein, *The Cost of Rights* (Norton: London, 1999) ch 9.

insert through a window a concept that could not enter the door, and thus undermine egalitarian ideals before they leave the starting-gate. As we shall see below, responsibility can take account of individual choice and behaviour in questions of distributive justice within the context of egalitarian theory. Contrariwise, desert takes current structures and entitlements as a given and inquires what individuals may justifiably expect, on the basis of their behaviour. While this may be for some a reasonable basis for a theory of justice, it is no way a promising platform for an *egalitarian* theory of justice.

2 The Agency Approach to Responsibility

This approach is held by most of today's prominent egalitarian theorists, thus comprising the dominant approach to responsibility in contemporary egalitarian thought. We would do well, then, to understand its features. Unlike the previous approach, egalitarian theories refuse to accept the existing situation as a normative baseline from which judgments of desert and responsibility derive. Instead, they offer a baseline of equal concern and respect as one that, at the pre-institutional stage, is insensitive, or blind, to certain circumstances. These circumstances may include talents, capabilities, physical endowments and the like. And notwithstanding the connotations implied by the term 'baseline', it is crucial to note that this is, in effect, a 'moving baseline'. As such, it is distinguishable from non-egalitarian, starting-gate theories[55] that are content with a rudimentary hypothetical egalitarian structure which allows for serious inequalities when met with market forces. The moving baseline, on the other hand, demands adherence to egalitarian criteria at any point in time, irrespective of demographic, technological, environmental or other changes that may be experienced.

One common thread that binds together all the theories grouped under this approach is the presupposition that *luck* should be as minimal a factor as possible in determining one's life plan. It is morally wrong if people are worse off than others through no fault of their own.[56] Now, of course, there is only a limit to what a theory of distributive justice can be expected to do. It cannot salvage a person who was a victim to a direct hit by a fatal flash of lightening. It should, however, structure institutions so that a person who was born to a poor family, or suffers from a handicap, or was orphaned at a young age, will be compensated in such a manner that his potential life prospects would be equivalent to others who have not suffered similar misfortune. *What* exactly constitutes the circumstances that

---

[55] The term is borrowed from Dworkin (n 23 above) 89. In an earlier essay, Dworkin refers to the starting-gate theory of justice as 'the ideal fraudulently called "equality of opportunity": fraudulent because in a market economy people do not have equal opportunity'—'Why Liberals Should Care About Equality' in *A Matter of Principle* (Clarendon: Oxford, 1986) 205, 207; also Sen (n 63 above) 118.

[56] D Parfit, *Reasons and Persons* (Clarendon: Oxford, 1984) 26; L Temkin *Inequality* (OUP: Oxford, 1993) 13–17, 101; Roemer (n 12 above) 8.

should be equalized, what are the criteria to differentiate talents from tastes and from handicaps? All these lead to the differing positions regarding the 'currency' of equality. But, as noted in the previous section, these disagreements have but minimal practical impact, at least for present purposes.

Of immense practical significance, however, is the manner that choice and responsibility are incorporated into egalitarian theory. In addressing the importance of this project, Ronald Dworkin is quite aware that the shift from the traditional split between egalitarian and conservative notions of responsibility towards 'a unified account of equality and responsibility that respects both' is not unrelated to the shift in political agendas in Western countries. He states: 'If that is the third way then it should be our way'.[57] The motivation for such a transformation is clear and, perhaps, even justified. Just as liberalism had to make room for culture and community because of their importance to the life of the individual,[58] it also has to take account of the consequences of an individual's life choices. The question is, however, *how* are choice and responsibility incorporated in egalitarian theses? We find that agency conceptions of responsibility view a person as responsible for *whatever she brings about*.[59] In replying to critics of his 'What is Equality?' essays, Dworkin clarifies that choice and responsibility play an important role in his theory:

We distinguish, for a thousand reasons, between what part of our fate is open to assignments of responsibility, because it is the upshot of someone's choice, and what part is ineligible for any such assignment because it is the work not of people but of nature or brute luck.[60]

This theme is, predictably, highly influential in his chapter which is dedicated to the implications his theory has on the assessment of welfare reform.[61] From this quote (and the conclusion is reinforced by others[62]) the following statements can be inferred to delineate the relationship between choice, responsibility and equality in contemporary egalitarian theory: first, that choice is easily identifiable, descriptively distinguished from and normatively opposed to luck; second, that the responsibility for a certain state of affairs is similarly identifiable as it corresponds to choices that people make; and third, that egalitarian theories aim to neutralize differences due to luck, for which people are not responsible, while choice-based end-states do not give rise to claims of inequality and are not, properly speaking, the subject of distributive justice theories. I would like to contest all three statements.

---

[57] Dworkin (n 23 above) 7.
[58] W Kymlicka, *Liberalism, Community and Culture* (Clarendon: Oxford, 1989).
[59] A Ripstein, 'Justice and Responsibility' (2004) 17 Can J of L and Jurisp 361, 362.
[60] Dworkin (n 23 above) 287.
[61] Dworkin (n 23 above) ch 9.
[62] See, eg, Cohen (n 32 above); R Arneson, 'Liberalism, Distributive Subjectivism and Equal Opportunity for Welfare' (1990) 19 Philosophy and Public Affairs 158.

First, as to the distinctiveness of choice. Amartya Sen, one of prominent advocates of the agency approach, finds choice to be a driving force in any theory of justice. 'Choosing is part of living', Sen writes, explaining that this is why starving is fundamentally different from fasting.[63] But a theory that emphasizes the importance of choice to such a degree must provide clear criteria to distinguish choice-based end-states from luck-based end-states. How much of this choice, then, is our own? It is clear that 'choices' that result from undue influence or coercion are not worthy of their name. On the other hand, it is conducive to the debate to concede that there is a moral difference between a physical assault that is the result of criminal intent and physical harm that results from one's losing his balance, even if the results are the same.[64]

And yet, a variety of free-will objections may hold firm. We can expect serious disagreements as to what constitutes choice and what constitutes circumstance (or, in some versions, luck).[65] Thus, one's lucky talent may be exemplified in the ability to choose rationally, reasonably or in a manner that would gain him the greatest degrees of benefits.[66] But where does that leave the impoverished individual who has similar aspirations but manages to constantly *choose wrongly*? Choice, we can sense, is not an analytically clean concept, distinct from social and natural factors the results of which should be equalized in egalitarian theories. This conclusion brings to mind Tocqueville's remark, noted above, that concerns the inability to distinguish between 'nuances that separate unmerited misfortune from an adversity produced by vice'.[67]

Sen warns that claims concerning inequality can be rejected only after concluding that the individual enjoyed 'effective choice'—that is, after taking into account all social and psychological barriers to actual choice. My response to this reconfiguration is better placed when addressing the last part of the three-prong argument identified above. For now, suffice it to note that choice is better viewed as a matter of degree than as a yes/no dichotomy. This may not only allow us to escape the 'morass of free will problems' but also to 'reduce the dependency of political philosophy on metaphysics'.[68]

Even if individual choice could be isolated and identified within a series of events, would that be a sufficient justification to connect choice and

---

[63] A Sen, *Inequality Reexamined* (Clarendon: Oxford, 1992) 52; for an application to welfare and work see R Salais, 'Towards a Capability Approach' in J Zeitlin and DM Trubek (eds), *Governing Work and Welfare in a New Economy* (OUP: Oxford, 2003) 317, 325.

[64] Barry (n 21 above) 137–39.

[65] Cohen (n 32 above) 932; Arneson (n 62 above); Hurley (n 50 above) 141; Dworkin (n 23 above) 207.

[66] M Dan-Cohen, 'Responsibility and the Boundaries of the Self' (1992) 105 Harv L Rev 959, 973. Rawls is equivocal on the matter. On the one hand, he states that 'it is assumed that the members of society are rational persons able to adjust the conception of the good to their situation'— Rawls (n 16 above) 80. On the other hand, he accepts that social circumstances affect even one's ability to try and take advantage of opportunities open to her—ibid 74, 177, 274.

[67] A de Tocquevile, *Memoirs on Pauperism* (1835 rpnt, Dee: Chicago, 1997, tran S Dreshcer) 56.

[68] Cohen (n 32 above) 934.

responsibility? This is the argument offered by the second statement. Of course, a metaphysically neat identification of choice would lead, if the argument put forward by the second statement is accepted, to a metaphysically neat identification of responsibility. This, clearly, is needed in order to identify the boundaries of egalitarian interest under the agency approach and to assess, for example, if one is responsible for his poverty or his unemployment. It has been argued, however, that 'the notion of the responsibility [for an outcome] is a piece of metaphysical nonsense'.[69] Indeed, if the task of delineating the metaphysical boundaries of choice ran into serious obstacles, the chances that a moral and political concept such as responsibility could be detached from its immediate social context seem even less promising. But even if both choice and responsibility could, arguendo, be properly identified in some morally-neutral manner, and even if this identification would establish the move from choice to responsibility, a case still has to be made for the claim that choice and responsibility serve as an exclusionary mechanism within a theory of equality.

So while Sen views the task that egalitarians face as identifying the social and psychological barriers for 'effective choice', I suggest that we should be searching for a theory of choice that is, to borrow a phrase, political, not metaphysical.[70] A metaphysical stance towards responsibility 'assumes that there is a fixed matter about what it is to be a responsible being'[71] that can be brought to light through discovery and analysis. And so, by 'not metaphysical' I refer to the fact that the emphasis should not be, as Sen suggested, on the effort to try and develop a theory of effective choice which sees all attribution of responsibility as resting on discoverable criteria. At most, this part of the theory should serve as a preliminary check so as to assure that the choice is worthy of its name, that our normative conclusions are based on facts that correspond with the way we normally live our lives and assess them. Such assurance, however, clearly lies outside a theory of equality.

What *is* required from a theory of equality is an outline of what constitutes 'protected choice'.[72] A theory of protected choice has to rest, in the far background, on the general theory of justice that is advocated for and, in the immediate background, on the proposed theory of equality. Choice should not serve as a safety valve for the egalitarian theory. Rather, it is part and parcel of that

---

[69] JJC Smart, 'An Outline of Utilitarian Ethics' in Smart and Williams (n 44 above) 54; Rosanvallon (n 4 above) 32.

[70] Susan Wolf advocates a shift 'from a view that takes the problems of responsibility and free will to be purely metaphysical problems...to a view that takes these problems to be inextricably bound to metaethical, and perhaps also ethical, commitments'—*Freedom Within Reason* (OUP: Oxford, 1990) 71.

[71] Wolf (n 70 above) 17.

[72] Waldron's use of the term, which I discovered after choosing it, is slightly different than my own: J Waldron, *Law and Disagreement* (OUP: Oxford, 1999) 250.

theory.[73] Indeed, certain cases that exhibit inequalities that are a result of a choice made by an individual may give no rise to egalitarian interventionism. After inspecting the 'metaphysical' aspects of the choice and concluding that the inequality rises from, say, an individual voluntary choice, no prima facie cause for compensation should be acknowledged *unless the choice in question is a protected choice*. Now, 'protected' here does not indicate that other choices are necessarily immoral, irresponsible or blameworthy. It simply denotes that within the current theory of justice, of which the theory of equality is part, the consequences that result from an unprotected choice do not merit further transfers. The choice in question could even be commendable, such as the case where one invests all her money in her education or even donates it all to the Red Cross, and still not trigger the exception.

As several authors have noted, egalitarian writers tend to associate responsibility with factors germane to *blame*, on the one hand, and *excuses*, on the other hand.[74] But excuses serve as the filter to avoid legal sanctions or moral chastisement. This is a very important feature of some types of responsibility, but those are quite remote from the kind of responsibility sought after when constructing a theory of distributive justice. As Susan Hurley argues:

> What makes a view correct as a view of responsibility does not necessarily make it appropriate to use as a filter on the currency of distributive justice. This may not be the right way to give responsibility a role in distributive justice or in egalitarianism in particular.[75]

But why is this indeed the case? Understanding choice as the *control* that the individual had over the object is central to responsibility when the latter serves as a factor in matters of retributive justice.[76] In such cases the concern is about the relationship between the individual and the object or position in question. As such, it says almost nothing about the relationship between his position and the position of *others*[77] and so includes no inherent limits on the range of

---

[73] See similarly Barry (n 21 above) 136. It is conceivable that Dworkin sees his theory, which views equality as the 'sovereign virtue' that governs a theory of justice, as immune to such a charge. I would argue, however, that his position is less 'integrationist' than he may have preferred. Dworkin may prefer that the normative surrender of equality to individual choice (in cases where choice, properly identified, has been made) be understood as an adequate amalgamation of the two. I find it difficult to avoid the conclusion that equality, under this theory, stops where choice begins. The concept of protected choice, I believe, fulfills Dworkin's objectives to a greater degree than his own proposals.

[74] A Ripstein, *Equality, Responsibility and the Law* (CUP: Cambridge, 1999) 289ff; Dan-Cohen (n 66 above) 960.

[75] Hurley (n 50 above) 228.

[76] Barry (n 21 above) 140; see Sen (n 63 above) 148.

[77] Hurley (n 50 above) 229. But cf Roemer's suggestion that responsibility (say, for smoking) should be judged according to the individual's performance within his respective social and economic group, that is comprised of factors over which he has no control (family wealth, education, parent's attitude, etc.)—J Roemer, 'Equality and Responsibility' *Boston Review* (April-May 1995) <http://bostonreview.net/BR20.2/Roemer.html> (30 July 2004).

responsibility the agent may assume.[78] This is not a promising feature for a concept that purports to play a central role in distributive justice and equality. The number of cases where a person lacks total control over the choice that she faces may be very limited. What we should be looking for, instead, is a concept of responsibility such that a person is relieved of responsibility not because she lacks control, but 'rather because the choice is too much to ask of that person'.[79]

3 Reasonable Responsibility

Theories of responsibility have much in common. They all involve one being 'regarded as an appropriate object of a certain range of attitudes and judgments and as a legitimate participant in a certain range of practices'.[80] However, as noted above, when applied to a particular normative theory—whether retributive, corrective or distributive—it is quite natural that different attributes of responsibility should come to the fore, while others would seem of less import.

To recap: contemporary egalitarian theories suggest that distributive justice should compensate those who suffer from brute luck or unfortunate circumstances. However, their individualistic predisposition demands holding people responsible for actions that express their individual freedom and choices. But while it is clear that people should not be deemed responsible for matters which are attributed to brute luck, it is not the case that equality should stop where choice begins. These theories problematically develop a concept of choice that would serve as a filter, or a safety-valve, from the requirements of equality, while disregarding the crucial factor that both equality and the supposed 'filter' serve the same objective: the determination of who should bear the costs of a person's decision and who should reap the benefits. In other words, matters of distributive justice demand a social conceptualization of responsibility, one that determines which choices lead to an affirmation of responsibility that rejects allegations of inequality, and which choices leave such charges intact.[81]

In moving towards articulating a theory of responsibility as part of egalitarianism, we would do well to return, once again, to Rawls. It is true that Rawls's attitude to responsibility is complex,[82] but this need not mean, as some have argued, that the place that responsibility holds within Rawls's theory is difficult to reconcile with his support for egalitarianism.[83] Rawls argues that, as 'free and equal moral persons', individuals assume responsibility for their ends and this

---

[78] Ripstein (n 59 above) 363.
[79] Ripstein (n 74 above) 292.
[80] Wolf (n 70 above) 3; See also Dan-Cohen (n 66 above) 962.
[81] cf Goodin (n 14 above) 305. A different set of considerations is relevant when considering allocating other 'types' of responsibility (eg criminal)—Wolf (n 70 above) 19.
[82] Hurley (n 50 above) 134.
[83] Cohen (n 32 above) 914.

affects how their claims are assessed.[84] But this statement should not be taken at face value. Rawls here is responding to the argument that egalitarianism implies compensating people for their expensive tastes. Not only is this an important challenge for egalitarians in general, but an aspect of this argument helps clarify a principal point in my argument. I shall therefore pause here and address it.

Both Dworkin and Rawls may be arguing that the decision not to accept a demeaning job offer, for example, would be categorized as an 'expensive taste'. Rawls, in the course of addressing the expensive taste argument, states that 'as moral persons, citizens have some part in forming and cultivating their final ends and preferences'[85] and Dworkin is even more explicit in arguing that if one 'chose not to work or to work at less remunerative jobs than others chose, then his situation is the result of choice not luck, and he is not entitled to any compensation that would make up for his present shortfall'.[86]

Many egalitarians have conceded that the expensive tastes objection requires a serious revision of egalitarian theory, and I do not intend to turn back the wheel on this repositioning. The juxtaposition of the general expensive taste objection to the decision not to accept any job offer, however, requires more than an appeal to the reader's intuition. Thus, despite Dworkin's statement quoted above, his general argument is more equivocal on the matter. Indeed, it would seem that his final position regarding one's rejection of a job offer should be open to empirical persuasion. Dworkin explains that, for equality of resources, the expensive tastes objection means that 'people decide what sorts of lives to pursue against a background of information about the actual cost their choices impose on other people and hence on the total stock of resources that may fairly be used by them'.[87]

Though Cohen and Dworkin spend much effort questioning whether expensive tastes are deliberately cultivated or are part of a person's constitution (and thus beyond her control), I find this matter of less importance. What is of interest is that the reliance on market contingencies reveals that expensive tastes, like scarcity itself, is society-based. As Cass Sunstein explains, one's socioeconomic background has an important role in developing individual preferences.[88] A person may attach little value to an opportunity simply because it is not a realistic option for him. A child who must work to provide for his family and thus cannot attend school constructs his preferences in terms of possible income, and not academic achievement.[89]

---

[84] J Rawls, 'Justice as Fairness: Political Not Metaphysical' (1985) 14 Philosophy and Public Affairs 223, 243.

[85] J Rawls, 'Social Unity and Primary Goods' in A Sen and B Williams (eds), *Utilitarianism and Beyond* (CUP: Cambridge, 1982) 159, 168.

[86] Dworkin (n 23 above) 287.

[87] Dworkin (n 23 above) 69. Also his 'What is Equality? Part 3: The Place of Liberty' (1988) 73 Iowa L Rev 1, 26–29.

[88] C Sunstein, 'Preferences and Politics' (1991) 20 Philosophy and Public Affairs 3, 8–9.

[89] A de Vita, 'Individual Preferences and Social Justice' (2000) Brazilian Review of Social Sciences 95.

We can take this insight further: it is not only that society plays a central role in the cultivation of individual taste. The combination of rules and policies (along with the state of the economy, cultural norms, social psychology and the like) is significant in defining what is and what is not an expensive taste altogether. This is a consequence of society's determining what goods should be considered scarce goods and what society considers to be an unreasonable burden.[90] Society decides whether a person's insistence on retaining her job while refusing to enter into an intimate relationship with her employer constitutes an expensive taste. Similar things can be said about one's *choice* not to accept life-threatening employment.[91] Before accepting an expensive taste objection in a certain instance, it is necessary to assess if this preference indeed *is* an expensive taste, by identifying the truly scarce good in question and the social context within which the decision is made.

In response to objections that his focus on primary goods (as an alternative to utility or subjective welfare) entails inequitable treatment of people with similar capacities but different attitudes to work, Rawls amended his position and was willing to add *leisure* to the list of primary goods subject to the difference principle. This would entail that 'those who surf all day off Malibu must find a way to support themselves and would not be entitled to public funds'.[92] This assertion derives from the dominant liberal economic model which assumes that work competes with leisure. However, the background structure is, as ever, extremely important to Rawls. Thus, he makes clear that the previous statement holds true only under the assumption that 'positions or jobs are not scarce or rationed'.[93] But here, of course, lies the rub.

Consider a situation of severe unemployment where some unemployed people make bona fide efforts to find jobs that suit their skills and capabilities. Now assume that one such individual refuses to accept a low-paying job offer that does not make good use of a person's talents and, furthermore, inhibits her chances of escaping poverty. Under Rawls's qualification, such a predisposition should not be categorized as an expensive taste. Furthermore, if such a decision does *not* impose on other people's stock of resources then Dworkin who, as mentioned, sees the normative decision as turning on the question of social costs, should also be reluctant to see such a predisposition as an expensive taste.[94] Philippe van Parijs takes this argument further by suggesting that in a 'non-Walrasian economy' (a labour market that does not clear) there will be many people who would like to hold a fulfilling job which makes the most of their skills and capabilities. People

---

[90] Elizabeth Anderson, for example, gives the example of subsidies to farmers who, 'far from being stigmatized as welfare dependants, they are lionized as icons of self-reliance'—'Welfare, Work Requirements and Dependant Care' (2004) 21 J of Applied Philosophy 243, 248.

[91] Gewirth (n 27 above) 237–38.

[92] J Rawls, 'The Priority of the Right and Ideas of the Good' (1988) 17 Philosophy and Public Affairs 251, 257 n 7.

[93] J Rawls, *Political Liberalism* (Columbia UP: New York, 1993) 182 n 9.

[94] A Wax, 'Something for Nothing' (2003) 52 Emory LJ 1, 53–56.

holding such jobs, then, are those who should pay 'employment rent' which would be collected to provide a universal basic income for all.[95] The justification for such a measure lies in the fact that, in addition to talents and wealth, one should include the holding of a job as a type of resource. Seeing his suggestion as more faithful to Rawls's original construction, van Parijs views Rawls's inclusion of leisure to the list of primary goods as an afterthought, artificially 'postulated to be equivalent, at any particular time, to the income enjoyed at that same time by the least advantaged full-time workers'.[96]

The details of both sides of the argument for and against basic income for surfers (or others who refuse to work at all) need not detain us here. It is important to remember, however, that the attitude towards work is rich with myth, ceremony and intuition that are best avoided.[97] While leisure may be a scarce commodity to many, there are also numerous others who are very grateful to have, and would never consider giving up, their fulfilling, engaging and challenging career, despite (or, perhaps, because of) the magnitude of stress and lack of leisure.[98] And while many are work-shy and prefer to stay away from the labour market, others spend a lifetime trying to get a foothold in an environment where a job, and not leisure, is a scarce resource.[99] It would seem then, that we need to supplement the discussion regarding scarce resources and expensive tastes with a more focused, substantive discussion that considers the decision itself, within the context that it is being made in.

For this we need to return to the idea that people should be treated 'as free and equal moral persons'. This phrase may be understood, I believe, in more than one fashion. One interpretation would be to say something along the lines of the incentive approach to responsibility: 'if we truly believe that people are free and equal—that would entail respecting them and their choice, including their bad decisions'. Yet, another interpretation seems as plausible, and is supported by Rawls's writings.

A central feature in Rawls's doctrine of 'responsibility for ends' is that the attribution of responsibility comes into play 'only on certain assumptions',[100] namely the existence of 'just background institutions and the fair provision for all of a fair index of primary goods (as required by the principles of justice)'.[101] By demanding this normative platform, Rawls's position allows responsibility to fulfill an

---

[95] P van Parijs, 'Why Surfers Should be Fed' (1998) 20 Philosophy and Public Affairs 101, 122ff; P van Parijs, *Real Freedom for All* (Clarendon: Oxford, 1997) 92–130.

[96] Van Parijs, 1998 (n 95 above) 111; also Wax (n 94 above) 41–42.

[97] J Handler, *Social Citizenship and Workfare in the US and Western Europe* (CUP: Cambridge, 2004) 12.

[98] D Attas and A de-Shalit, 'Workfare: the Subjection of Labour' (2004) 21 J of Applied Philosophy 309, 314; A O'Connor, 'Cracking Under the Pressure? It's Just the Opposite, for Some' New York Times (10 September 2004).

[99] Barry (n 21 above) 37.

[100] Rawls (n 85 above) 169.

[101] J Rawls, 'Kantian Constructivism in Moral Theory' (1980) 77 J of Phil 545, see Scheffler (n 49 above) 320.

important role within an egalitarian theory, without compromising its foundations. In similar vein, Barry suggests that only when opportunities are truly equal, 'it is possible for differential outcomes arising from choices made among a common set of options to give rise to just inequalities'.[102]

So we find that while most egalitarians associate responsibility with control and (factual) choice, some of their pronouncements reveal a degree of ambivalence when confronted with concrete matters of policy. Thus, Sen suggests a counter-factual test for 'effective freedom'. A counter-factual choice is the choice one would have made if one enjoyed a more favourable background of facts or policy.[103] This position, in effect, asks us to *ignore* the fact that a certain choice has been made and to ask what choice *would* have been made had the situation been ideal.[104] And Dworkin, in a chapter that applies his hypothetical insurance scheme to unemployment benefits, says something quite similar. An undeniable tenet of fairness, he states, is 'that a society comes closer to treating people as equals when it adds to the choices they have choices *they would have had* were circumstances more nearly equal'.[105] This fits well with his outline of equality of resources, where he emphasizes the importance of retaining 'considerable freedom of choice about the character of work and the mix of work and labor and additional consumption'.[106] So while Rawls is concerned with providing a blueprint for a well-ordered society, Sen and Dworkin may be suggesting that in a society that is less than well-ordered, choices that individuals make cannot be judged at face value, as the incentive approach to responsibility may suggest. Rather, we would be advised to consider what choices a well-ordered society would have offered the individual and to translate her behaviour in that context.

The most developed approach along these lines, and the one that seems most attractive to me, employs a useful tool, familiar to lawyers—the 'reasonable person'. The reasonable person exemplifies the objective, public standard that is sought after, and thus is valuable to the effort to assess situations that are not clear-cut. The reasonableness standard allows one to *assess* the choice made, rather than employing a 'strict liability' rule of responsibility simply because there *was* a choice that was made. As Meir Dan-Cohen puts it, 'the assumption and the ascription of responsibility is mediated by the existence of widely shared social conventions regarding the attribution of responsibility...the reasonable person standard helps us assess *responsibility*'.[107] Indeed, the reasonableness standard

---

[102] Barry (n 21 above) 42.
[103] A similar emphasis on true freedom to make fundamental choices leads Philippe Van Parijs to favour an unconditional basic income scheme—'Basic Income Capitalism' (1992) 102 Ethics 465. And see also B Barry 'Social Exclusion, Social Isolation and the Distribution of Income' in J Le Grand (ed), *Understanding Social Exclusion* (OUP: Oxford, 2001) 13, 14.
[104] See similarly Barry (n 19 above) 51; H Steiner 'A Liberal Theory of Exploitation' (1984) 94 Ethics 225.
[105] Dworkin (n 23 above) 334 [emphasis added].
[106] Dworkin (n 23 above) 98.
[107] Dan-Cohen (n 66 above) 970, 995.

should not be seen as a ready-made blue-print for the good life. Rather, it is 'one of law's clever devices to reopen a bit of space for ordinary moral reasoning in a rule that would otherwise be apt to level it away'.[108] When considering matters of distributive justice, the reasonable person serves as a helpful metaphor for 'the person whose actions display appropriate regard for both her interest and the interests of others'.[109] It encompasses social norms that are rooted in the consensus and offers a platform for the assessment of social responsibility.

Indeed, the idea of reasonable responsibility seems attractive most of all because it permits the most 'social' perspective to matters of social policy. While Cohen and Dworkin insisted on paradigms that focus on the individual's choice in the face of a given social structure, this approach recognizes that society does, and should, constantly reassess the status quo. In the mutual effort of reaching beneficial end-states, individuals make choices and society evaluates them. Some pursuits should be endorsed and funded (through positive measures or by avoiding sanctions) while others should not. The immediate worry that comes to mind—that of a theory that is based on perfectionism or moralism—is misplaced for the same reason that understanding provisions against rape as an illegitimate (because perfectionist) form of intervention seems ludicrous.[110] It is much more natural, especially under the egalitarian paradigm, to assert that society should ensure people the equal ability to promote their ideals of the good life.[111] This position is quite consistent with a rejection of perfectionism. Not all values are ultimately reducible to (and best describable as) individual pursuits. Even a liberal society cannot be agnostic about *social pursuits* such as integration of disabled individuals into the society, assisting lone parents in entering the job market, and social inclusion of disadvantaged groups. Though a liberal agenda must sometimes settle for stipulating the *reaction* of social policy to choices made by individuals, it should not hold an arbitrarily neutral position that does not engage with choices made.

To contrast this approach with the agency approach described above, we may illustrate each approach as cutting across each other, creating four quadrants based on two variables: chosen/not-chosen and reasonable/unreasonable pursuit. Both approaches agree that unreasonable choices from a society's perspective (gamble away all the money) should not be compensated for by virtue of an egalitarian ideal (though other considerations, such as charity, may apply) and that unfair, non-chosen states (disadvantage due to disability) allow for compensation. However, the approach guided by reasonable responsibility adds another

---

[108] J Gardner, 'The Mysterious Case of the Reasonable Person' (2001) 51 University of Toronto LJ 273, 299; See also Hart (n 10 above) 132–34.

[109] Ripstein (n 74 above) 192. This is also a reference to Rawls, who finds both reasonableness and reciprocity central to the formation of the fair terms of cooperation Rawls (n 84 above) 232.

[110] See generally Jacobs (n 22 above); On neutrality in workfare see S White, 'What's Wrong with Workfare' (2004) 21 J of Applied Philosophy 271, 272; But cf J Wolff, 'Training, Perfectionism and Fairness' (2004) 21 J of Applied Philosophy 285, 286;

[111] Raz (n 27 above) 110–33; Barry (n 19 above) 144–45; Gewirth (n 27 above) 162–64.

quadrant that requires compensation—that of situations that are the result of reasonable choices.

One may object that we have substituted a relatively precise standard (choice) with a notoriously malleable one (reasonableness). This, of course, cannot be a sufficient reason to retract our suggestion. If the choice standard does not capture the complexity of the situation, while the reasonableness standard does at least begin to address the relevant considerations, there is reason to prefer the latter, despite its open-endedness. We may, however, see this charge as a challenge for a more concrete understanding of the criterion that is offered. And so, taking stock of the argument to this point, we should see what the combination of reasonableness and equality brings to bear. The reasonable person standard already refers to some heavily developed doctrine. Of import for present purposes is the idea that the standard combines both objective and subjective elements or, in the phrase often used by the United States Supreme Court, places 'a reasonable person in the defendant's shoes'.[112] Deployment of equality further limits the terrain in a manner that befits matters of welfare and distributive justice. Equality should thus serve as foundational pillar in a structure that would assist in identifying reasonable choices and legitimate conditions. I now turn to suggest such a structure.

C Conditioning Rights—the Case of Welfare Benefits

As Charles Reich noted in his important article on the 'New Property', the welfare state's increased involvement in civil society results in a parallel dependency of individuals on its wealth.[113] The danger, then, would be that government would 'buy up people's liberty'.[114] Since welfare clients are more vulnerable to economic sanctions, the risk to their individual liberties is proportionately greater.

The importance of a carefully tuned test for the legitimacy of conditions placed on access to benefits cannot be overstated. Indeed, it has been argued that 'a society...may be defined by the nature of the tests it sets—tests through which social selection is performed—and by disputes over the more or less just character of these tests'.[115] The level of social control exerted by a government, the level of commodification exhibited in requiring the individual to keep returning to the deregulated market, the arbitrariness of the demands a community may legitimately place on welfare relief—all those mirror society's approach towards those

---

[112] *Berkemer v McCarty* 468 US 420, 442 (1983); *Stansbury v California* 511 US 318, 324 (1994); *Thompson v Keohame* 516 US 99, 112 (1995).
[113] C Reich, 'The New Property' (1963) 73 Yale LJ 733; cf J Harris, *Justice and Property* (OUP: Oxford, 1996) 153.
[114] K Sullivan, 'Unconstitutional Conditions' (1989) 102 Harvard L Rev 1413, 1494.
[115] L Boltanski, E Chiapello and G Elliot (tr), *The New Spirit of Capitalism* (Verso: London, 2005) 313.

living on the margins of the labour market. The level of scrutiny placed on such conditions thus signifies its corresponding values and ideals.

The vast breadth of situations that a doctrine of illegitimate conditions covers could 'literally suggest a unifying theory cutting across all of constitutional law'.[116] In effect, *all* rights that are not absolute may be limited upon implementation. Thus, Justice Holmes cleverly asserted that a policeman's discharge for political speech was justified on the grounds that, though he 'may have a constitutional right to talk politics...he has no constitutional right to be a policeman'.[117] But the shrewdness cannot obscure the conclusion that, justified or not, the plaintiff was sanctioned for exercising his right to free speech. Hence, an absolute right to free speech, for example, would not allow such sanction, regardless of the plaintiff's right (or lack thereof) to be a policeman. So we find that even the 'classic', uncondition*al* rights (ie not subject to behavioural preconditions), may be condition*ed*, or limited, when conflicting with other social interests. We may say that the general formulation may be stated as follows:

X is entitled to a benefit (B) subject to condition (C) that relates to his right (R).

The more that B is perceived as conditional the fewer conditions placed upon it are subject to review insofar as the *benefit* is concerned. And yet, what of the other half of the formulation—the unconditional, uncontroversial right (R)? While the entitlement to welfare benefits in itself may permit, arguendo, a wide array of conditions, requiring the claimant to declare that she does not, for example, intend to overthrow the government by unlawful means,[118] to forsake her day of rest,[119] to refrain from joining a demonstration or to continue to work even when the union was on strike,[120] may prove to be an illegitimate restriction on the right to free speech, or to freedom of religion, or on labour rights, respectively.

To make matters clear, we should distinguish the situation under investigation from several similar, but distinct, legal dilemmas.

First, we find the situation where X is entitled to enjoy a right (R1) subject to the condition (C) that relates to *another* right (R2) that he is normally entitled to. Thus, we may imagine a situation in which the right to vote is subjected to a loyalty oath. This situation is distinct from the one under discussion because the doctrine of illegitimate conditions is concerned with areas where a government

---

[116] WP Marshall, 'Towards a Nonunifying Theory of Unconstitutional Conditions' (1989) 26 San Diego L Rev 243, 244; Cass Sunstein, in similar vein, remarks that: 'anything so general as the unconstitutional conditions doctrine is likely to be quite unhelpful'—C Sunstein, 'Is There an Unconstitutional Conditions Doctrine' (1989) 26 San Diego L Rev 337, 338.
[117] *McAuliffe v Mayor of New Bedford* (1892) 29 NE 517.
[118] *Speiser v Randall* (1958) 357 US 513.
[119] *Sherbert v Verner* 374 US 398 (1963).
[120] L Williams, 'Poor Women's Work Experience: Gaps in the Work/Family Discussion' in J Conaghan and K Rittich (eds), *Labour Law, Work and Family: Critical and Comparative Perspectives* (OUP: Oxford, 2005) 200–1.

is *permitted* to act but is *not required* to do so.[121] Contrariwise, in the case just introduced, it would be necessary to place under scrutiny *both* the fact that the right to vote is subject to a condition *and* the fact that a loyalty oath is demanded. Indeed, if welfare rights are seen as fundamental legal rights, a similar analysis would have to take place in this case as well. However, if, as in our original formulation, the right R1 is actually a discretionary benefit B, a different range of considerations apply.[122]

Second, it should be emphasized that when considering conditions (Cs) placed on rights, we are dealing with behavioural conditions. In other words, these are conditions where the individual has a *choice* whether to act in one way or another.[123] So while X's right (to free speech, to freedom of religion) is under threat, X may *refuse* to relinquish the right and thus (if the condition is legal) to forego the benefit related to it. Contrariwise, a benefit granted only to members of a certain race, sex or nationality may be considered by certain accounts to be 'conditional' and presumably a violation of an individual's right to equality and dignity.[124] In sum, antidiscrimination doctrine is concerned with who you are; unconstitutional conditions doctrine is concerned with what you do.[125] And so, matters concerning the immutable status of individuals, and distinct from their choices, do not figure in the analysis presented here. One may argue that the decisions that welfare claimants are required to make are choices 'between the rock and the whirlpool'.[126] For the purpose of the following analysis, however, the physical possibility of making a choice should be a sufficient reason to examine the condition placed on the benefit within the general scheme. Indeed, 'a choice between evils, however undesirable, is not by itself coercive'.[127]

Elsewhere I explained why the two original attempts to propose a theory for a doctrine of illegitimate conditions, along with a more contemporary approach, contain fundamental flaws that render them inapplicable in any context.[128] I referred to these three as the Greater/Lesser approach, the Direct/Indirect distinction and the Threat/Offer distinction. I shall focus here on the strengths and weaknesses of three other approaches that, though perhaps not compelling in all realms of law, may be utilized when considering the conditioning of welfare

---

[121] L Alexander, 'Understanding Constitutional Rights in a World of Optional Baselines' (1989) 26 San Diego L Rev 175; Sullivan (n 114 above) 1422.

[122] cf P Westen, 'Incredible Dilemmas' (1980) 66 Iowa L Rev 741; WV van Alstyne, 'The Demise of the Right-Privilege Distinction in Constitutional Law' (1968) 81 Harvard L Rev 1439.

[123] Sullivan (n 114 above) 1426.

[124] M McConnell, 'Unconstitutional Conditions' (1989) 26 San Diego L Rev 255, 260.

[125] L Baker, 'The Prices of Rights' (1989) 75 Cornell L Rev 1185, 1189.

[126] *Frost & Frost Trucking Co v Railroad Commission of California* 271 US 583, 593 (1926); for other examples of such impossible choices see J Brown, L Williams and P Baumann, 'The Mythogenesis of Gender: Judicial Images of Women in Paid and Unpaid Labor' (1996) 6 UCLA Women's LJ 457, 501–2, 533.

[127] Sullivan (n 114 above) 1436.

[128] A Paz-Fuchs, 'Rights, Duties and Conditioning Welfare' (2008) 21 Canadian J of L and Jurisprudence (forthcoming).

benefits. These are the Substantive Equality argument, the Germaneness requirement and the Fundamental Rights consideration.

The proposed structure to dealing with this matter is composed of three elements. As a first analytical stage, substantive equality should be used as a principle for evaluation of the condition. The germaneness requirement is offered as the second element, directing the proper level of suspicion as to the legitimacy of the conditions inspected. And, finally, the nature of the fundamental rights that are affected and the severity of the impact should be considered as a safeguard mechanism.

1 Substantive Equality

It may be worth rehearsing that a condition that disqualifies persons based on their immutable characteristic, as opposed to presenting a choice of action, is related to the present discussion by name only.[129] Such conditions are more naturally discussed within the confines of equality and discrimination in the strict sense. Conditions investigated here presume the existence of a choice open before the individual—to act in one way or another. What, then, could be the place of equality in this analysis? Kathleen Sullivan, for example, states that all conditions 'necessarily discriminate facially between those who do and those who do not comply with the condition'.[130] In effect, equality meets the illegitimate conditions doctrine at two intersections: the first concerns the distribution of the right and the second concerns the distribution of the benefit.[131]

First, one may argue that all conditions on a certain right are discriminatory, since they violate the equal distribution of the right (or the sanction) amongst members of the society.[132] So denying food stamps from striking workers discriminates against workers who are in need and thus cannot afford to strike without the benefit of a safety net.[133] Access to the right to strike, then, is not distributed equally.

This approach, however, is not unproblematic. When dealing with benefits that have an important economic value, the argument that conditioning rights *indirectly discriminates* between those who 'have' and those who 'have not' draws the line of economic means. This argument has not gone well with the courts.[134] It is difficult for the judiciary to quash social programmes that, due to *background*

---

[129] For such conditions see Baker (n 125 above) 1189.

[130] ibid 1490–99.

[131] Sullivan (n 114 above) 1490–99; K Sullivan, 'Unconstitutional Conditions and the Distribution of Liberty' (1989) 26 San Diego L Rev 327, 331–32. This distinction is sometimes overlooked: McConnel (n 124 above) 259–60.

[132] Barry (n 21 above) 152–53.

[133] The US Supreme Court did not accept this argument: *Lyng v International Union, UAW et al* 485 US 360 (1988).

[134] For two exceptions in the United States see *Harper v Virginia State Board of Elections* 383 US 663 (1966) [poll tax struck down] and *McDonald v Board of Election Commissioners* (1969) 394

economic inequality, will lead to different people being treated differently.[135] If taken ad absurdum, such an extreme proposition would demand that all public, and some private, commodities be distributed free of charge, thus creating not only a legal obligation for free education and health care but also the platform for an argument that an individual's unique financial power to publish a newspaper is a violation of the distribution of free speech; and that one's capacity to travel abroad while others cannot leave their own city should be analysed in terms of distribution of the right to travel. But, despite the fact that such an argument should be employed cautiously, the extreme examples should not obscure the danger of creating a 'constitutional caste'[136] of poor individuals who 'may have nothing to trade but their liberties',[137] while these rights are enjoyed by more affluent members.[138]

The second perspective focuses on the equal right to enjoy the benefit. Even without categorizing the benefit as a right, it may be argued that once the government decided to grant the benefit, it created a new baseline, and distinctions between beneficiaries should be strictly monitored.[139] This approach seems more promising, since the relevant individuals share a common economic background. Therefore, the purported distinction between members of this group is based not on their different economic situation but on other features, such as marital status. These features are more controversial when suggested as relevantly distinguishing between individuals. So the state may be understood to be saying, in essence, that all impoverished individuals are entitled to benefits, *apart* from those cohabiting without marriage, for example. One may then argue that a public policy that distinguishes between recipients of benefit on such a basis violates the obligation not to promote any particular comprehensive doctrine.[140]

The latter approach leads to the methodological conclusion that instead of searching for an equality-based approach to the whole range of illegitimate conditions, one should try and find how the principle of substantive equality may be implemented to particular contexts such as public assistance cases. In doing so,

US 802, 807, where the court stated in *dictum* that 'a careful examination on our part is especially warranted where lines are drawn on the basis of wealth or race'.

[135] Baker (n 125 above) 1219.
[136] Sullivan (n 114 above) 1497. See Justice Marshall's emphatic dissent in *Harris v McRae* 448 US 297, 338 where the challenged legislation was described as 'the product of an effort to deny the poor the constitutional right recognized in *Roe v. Wade*'.
[137] Sullivan (n 114 above) 1498.
[138] *Zablocki v Redhail* 434 US 374 (1978).
[139] For a similar line of argument see M Tushnet, 'State Action, Social Welfare Rights and the Judicial Role: Some Comparative Observations' (2002) 3 Chi J International L 435, 442.
[140] J Rawls, 'The Priority of Right and Ideas of the Good' (1988) 4 Philosophy and Public Affairs 251, 262–63; R Dworkin, 'Liberalism' in *A Matter of Principle* (Harvard UP: Cambridge, 1985) 191; Raz (n 27 above) 114–15; P van Parijs, 'Basic Income Capitalism' (1992) 102 Ethics 465, 474.

Lynn Baker argues that one needs to look no further than court practice in the United States.[141]

Baker argues that if the court finds a constitutionally protected activity to be affected by the condition, it checks if the condition discriminates persons unable to earn subsistence income by comparing them to similarly situated individuals earning subsistence income.[142] Thus, a maximum grant regulation which imposed a ceiling of a monthly amount that one family could receive (family cap) would arguably impact the right to procreate by reducing the per capita income each family member receives.[143] But the condition was upheld since this per capita reduction would also be experienced by a family whose income depended on a subsistence wage earner's income. Similarly, the Ohio Supreme Court compared workfare participants to workers and found an equal protection violation in the state's refusal to grant workers' compensation to a widow whose spouse died from an illness contracted as a result of exposure to pigeon droppings in the course of his workfare assignment.[144] Conversely, in a series of 'free exercise of religion cases'[145] the court overturned decisions to deny benefits from unemployed individuals who refused to work on their Sabbath, supposedly because these decisions were discriminatory when compared to similarly situated people earning subsistence income, since the latter are normally not required to relinquish their entire income if they wished to practice their religion.

The explanatory force of Baker's theory, however, is not convincing. Clearly, there are cases that do not support this conclusion,[146] and the explanation for others is sometimes tenuous. It is true that the doctrine's normative basis offers a feasible formulation that allows comparisons between similarly situated individuals without ignoring the particular traits of a market economy. It thus has the advantage of transforming equality from a vague baseline to a working legal principle. Nevertheless, the theory still problematically ignores the wider social, economic and legal background. Thus, certain conditions relating to marital status, for example, may prove non-discriminatory when a comparison is made between welfare beneficiaries and wage earners at subsistence level. But they still distinguish between women who, for example, chose to marry the father of their children and those who chose not to do so,[147] while taking no account

---

[141] L Baker, 'The Prices of Rights' (1989) 75 Cornell L Rev 1184.
[142] Baker (n 141 above) 1217.
[143] *Dandridge v Williams* 397 US 471 (1970) and the discussion in Baker (n 141 above) 1235–36.
[144] *Patterson v Industrial Commission of Ohio* 672 NE2d 1008 (1998); M Diller, 'Working Without a Job: The Social Meaning of the New Workforce' (1998) 9 Stanford L and Society Rev 19, 28.
[145] *Sherbert v Verner* 374 US 398 (1963); *Hobbie v Unemployment Appeals Commission* 480 US 136 (1987); *Frazee v Illinois Department of Employment Security* 489 US 829 (1989) discussed in Baker (n 141 above) 1243–45.
[146] eg *Bowen v Roy* 476 US 693 (1986); *Lyng v International Union, UAW* et al 485 US 360 (1988); *Alcozer v North Country Food Bank* 635 NW2d 695 (2001).
[147] *Califano v Boles* 443 US 282 (1979) discussed in Baker (n 141 above) 1232–35.

of background circumstances that are already in place. This omission may be perceived as the result of treating equality as a principle of non-discrimination instead of viewing it as an ideal that requires treating each individual's choice with equal concern and respect.

An example may be helpful to explain this point. Imagine that Ron is an unemployed person who is bound to a wheelchair.[148] Ron is offered a job by the Employment Service at an office building and, though the building itself has an elevator, the entrance to the building is comprised of a long flight of stairs. Ron refuses the job offer, arguing that he does not want to be dependent on the goodwill of passers-by to assist him every morning. His claim seems quite justified, but how is it explained by the theory proposed? First, it should be clear that Ron's refusal is a choice that he made. It is obfuscating this important factor to state that the *circumstances* of his disability made the job offer a difficult one.[149] His condition, or circumstances, is not the object of our assessment and judgment. His choice is.[150] What would be the substantive approach to this problem?

Here the substantive egalitarian baseline comes to the fore. Though the importance of responsibility is not dismissed, we should start by 'reasserting ideas of the respect due to each individual...in a society of equals, and then fit in issues of responsibility only where there is room for them consistent with these ideas'.[151] Rawls's idea of primary goods or Sen's preference for capabilities may be considered as an index for equality. Arthur Ripstein, for example, argues that only 'once primary goods are equally distributed, the particular risks a person takes...are that person's risks to bear'.[152] Since mobility (or equal access) is an obvious example of primary goods, it is clear that in this case the preliminary requirement has not been satisfied. Ron cannot be expected to bear the cost of his decision not to accept the job because the offer, on those terms, should not have been made to him in the first place. It is true that this would mean that society would have to bear the costs of an individual's independent, rational decision, and one that he identifies with.[153] No such 'safety valve' exists under this theory. If Ron would have been offered the equal treatment he deserves, manifested here in an equal opportunity to access a place of employment, the same decision on his part may well have been judged differently, and he may have been required to bear the costs of his choice.

---

[148] This example is an expanded version of the one given in Ripstein (n 74 above) 275. It became surprisingly relevant when a court reporter who is wheelchair bound filed suit because she was not able to access her place of employment: *Tennessee v Lane and Jones* 541 US 509 (2004).
[149] cf Ripstein (n 74 above) 266.
[150] Dworkin (n 23 above) 323.
[151] Wolff (n 110 above) 288.
[152] Ripstein (n 74 above) 274.
[153] cf Dworkin (n 23 above) 293, offering identification with the act as a criterion for the attribution of responsibility.

2 Germaneness

The equality principle and the constitutional protection of fundamental rights are referred to regularly in legal discourse. But the uniqueness of the illegitimate conditions doctrine requires a factor that addresses its particular traits: a government activity that is constitutionally permitted but not required; a choice given to an individual between holding on to his rights or taking advantage of the benefit; and most importantly, the fact that these options are proposed by the government, and not by individuals.[154]

The germaneness requirement addresses these traits.[155] When compared to other approaches,[156] germaneness proposes a legislative check that is more attuned to the context and particularities of public (and sometimes—private[157]) law. The flexible nature of public law in thus manifested in the formulation: 'the more germane a condition to a benefit, the more deferential the review; nongermane conditions, in contrast...trigger closer scrutiny'.[158] Such a requirement is flexible enough to uphold a loyalty oath requirement in public employment situations that involve national security matters while striking down the same requirement in the context of public housing.[159]

Furthermore, the germaneness requirement seems particularly applicable in the welfare-to-work context. As indicated, such programmes (not unlike other welfare programmes) often include conditions for entitlement that are only tangentially, if at all, related to the declared objectives of the programmes. These objectives are, essentially, quite clear: to provide financial aid for those in need while assisting able recipients to enter the workforce. The conditioning of benefits creates an opportunity for governments to overreach and to circumvent constitutional safeguards, as in the case of the Louisiana policy to cut off aid to needy children in all cases where the mother gave birth to an illegitimate child after going on the relief rolls, except where she could prove she had subsequently 'ceased such illicit relationships'.[160] This is where the advantages of the germaneness requirement are evident.

Two rationales support this approach: a check on the legislative process and a check on state power. As a check on legislative process, the germaneness condition limits irresponsible (and corrupt) 'logrolling' and strategic voting—the

---

[154] W V van Alstyne, 'The Demise of the Right-Privilege Distinction in Constitutional Law' (1968) 81 Harvard L Rev 1439, 1489.
[155] R Goodin, 'Support With Strings' (2004) 21 J of Applied Philosophy 297, 301.
[156] Paz-Fuchs (n 128 above).
[157] Workers at one Peugeot factory were required to sign the organization's Ten Commandments as a condition for participation in a prestigious three week training course—Boltanski and Chiapello (n 115 above) 285.
[158] Sullivan (n 114 above) 1457
[159] RM O'Neil, 'Unconstitutional Conditions' (1966) California L Rev 443, 466; *Lawson v Housing Authority* 70 NW2d 605, cert denied 350 US 882 (1955).
[160] Cited in C Reich, 'Individual Rights and Social Welfare' (1965) 74 Yale LJ 1245, 1247–1251.

practice of trading votes that leads to seemingly irrational conditions, unrelated to the benefits.[161] As a check on state power, the germaneness requirement limits the range of legitimate conditions that may be attached to benefits and thus controls the range of potential encroachments on fundamental rights. And so, the implication of the theory is not that germane conditions are inherently benign,[162] but rather that they are less likely to be malign.

These rationales are particularly relevant in the social and economic realm. First, legislation in this area should be handled with special prudence, since the combination of myriad factors leads to unexpected consequences as a matter of course. Thus, for example, provisions that aim to encourage marriage and enforce child support have been shown, in many cases, to have the opposite effect.[163] Allowing conditions to be tacked on to programmes that are intended to deal with discrete social matters decreases the chances that legislatures would be allowed a serious study of the expected results. The danger would be that the symptom, rather than the cause, would be dealt with.

Second, conditions attached to welfare-to-work programmes target, by nature, a particular group and would therefore have an uneven effect on different members of society (in a manner not necessarily caught by the equality analysis above). Therefore some conditions would adversely impact welfare claimants but not wage earners. And what of conditions that are said to benefit welfare claimants and their families, such as Learnfare? This is a policy that, according to its own rationale, allows the truant children of wage earners to be worse off simply because they cannot be targeted by this policy.[164] Indeed, empirical data shows that Learnfare, first established in Wisconsin, did not lead to any discernable differences when comparing AFDC teens to non-AFDC teens. It did manage, however, to penalize AFDC families for truancy of young parents much more than it penalized middle-class and working-class families with truant children.[165] If, however, this mechanism did not exist, policy-makers would, presumably, have to find an alternative that would include all children in its range.[166] This characteristic of social control contracts may be indicative, leading Vincent-Jones to question whether such arrangements 'are capable of advancing the government's intended policy objectives'.[167]

---

[161] Sullivan (n 114 above) 1469–73.
[162] cf Sullivan (n 114 above) 1476.
[163] J Handler and Y Hasenfeld, *Blame Welfare, Ignore Poverty and Inequality* (CUP: Cambridge, 2007) 294.
[164] cf Barry (n 21 above) 152.
[165] L Williams, 'The Ideology of Division: Behavior Modification Welfare Reform Proposals' (1992) 102 Yale LJ 719, 726–734.
[166] See similarly L Williams, 'The Abuse of Section 1115 Waivers: Welfare Reform in Search of a Standard' (1994) 12 Yale L and Policy Rev 8, 18: 'Rather than establishing proven support programs to keep children in school, Learnfare punished welfare families whose kids were truant or dropped out'.
[167] P Vincent-Jones, *The New Public Contracting: Regulation, Responsiveness, Relationality* (OUP: Oxford, 2006) 32.

It is true, however, that there may be conditions that pass the germaneness requirement, and yet still place an undue burden on fundamental rights. It is for this reason that the fundamental rights criterion is added as a safeguard.

3 Fundamental Rights

Though the main concern raised by illegitimate conditions situations is that rights would be manipulated out of existence, one must consider the unique structure of these problems, as the previous two requirements do. Yet, we find that some cases pass the scrutiny of the first two tests and still yield results that are problematic from a human rights perspective. Consider, for example, the ineligibility of households of striking workers to benefits during the time any of its members is on strike.[168] It would seem that applying the equality criterion does not yield a conclusive answer in this case. As for the germaneness requirement, the United States Supreme Court in this case found that a rational link exists between the benefit and the condition, one that advances the goal of distributing funds to those who are truly in need.[169] A serious consideration of the rights involved (labour rights and the right to family life[170]) may have turned the decision to one that would have favoured the unions. The court dismissed this argument, in a decision criticized as 'baffling'.[171] And still, consideration of fundamental rights has proven central in other cases of illegitimate conditions:

> Not only must the conditions annexed to the enjoyment of a publicly-conferred benefit reasonably tend to further the purposes sought by conferment of that benefit but also the utility of imposing the condition must manifestly outweigh any resulting impairment of constitutional rights.[172]

This statement must be somewhat qualified, however, if the unique structure of situations that involve illegitimate conditions is to be taken seriously. Unlike direct infringements of fundamental rights, these situations present at least a formal choice that allows one to avoid relinquishing her rights at all. However, following the two stages described, the constitutional analysis may come to the foreground. One should consider the degree of available choice, the rights involved, the impact the condition has on them, and the alternative measures that the government may employ. Thus, Piven and Cloward note that:

> A central feature of the recipient's degradation is that she must surrender commonly accepted rights in exchange for aid. AFDC mothers, for example, are often forced to

---

[168] *Lyng* (n 146 above), discussed in R Epstein, 'Foreword'(1988) 102 Harvard L Rev 5, 6–13, 96–102. The same arrangement is exhibited in the British Jobseeker's Act 1995 c 15 s 14. See S Deakin and G Morris, *Labour Law* (3rd edn, Butterworths: London, 2001) 992–93.
[169] *Lyng* (n 146 above) 369. But cf the Justice Marshall's dissent (p 377), arguing that the strikers and their families *are* truly in need.
[170] It was argued that union members may be forced to move out of their households so that their families may receive benefits.
[171] Sullivan (n 114 above) 1438.
[172] *Bagley v Washington Township Hospital District* 421 P2d 409, 415 (1966).

answer questions about their sexual behavior..., open their closets to inspections... and permit their children to be interrogated.[173]

The courts, including the Supreme Court, routinely accepted these practices, categorizing them as irrelevant to the claimant's right to privacy, since he or she could always refuse to allow the social worker in the house and thus 'agree' not to receive benefits.[174] Yet it is clear that the social worker acts in this case as the long arm of the authority, investigating and collecting information.[175] It would be preferable, then, to ask if the violation of the right to privacy is justified, rather than to dismiss altogether the fact that a violation of the right occurred.

For some readers, such dilemmas may be reminiscent of general theories of inalienable rights.[176] Such theories, indeed, are important reminders that illegitimate conditions formulations may have an adverse impact on fundamental rights despite the fact that they managed to sift through the safeguards presented above. However, illegitimate conditions present a unique problem with respect to the general theories of inalienable rights. They require 'not a general theory of blocked exchanges, but a particularized theory for determining when to block surrender of preferred constitutional liberties to government'.[177] In such cases, courts have focused directly on the suppression of fundamental rights using traditional constitutional law approaches.[178] And, indeed, it is important to allow a theory investigating the structure of illegitimate conditions to also inquire directly what impact they have on fundamental rights.

4 Conditioning Rights and Reasonable Responsibility

We are now at a position to see how the idea of reasonable responsibility introduced in the previous section completes the structure offered here. The importance of treating each claimant with equal concern and respect is the driving force behind the reasonable responsibility approach. This approach demands consideration of the social, economic and legal background of each claimant and granting equal regard to his or her choices and aspirations. It is conceivable that legitimate reasons will stand in the way of pleasing all such aspirations. The danger

---

[173] FF Piven and RA Cloward, *Regulating the Poor* (Updated Edition, Vintage: New York, 1993) 166.
[174] *Wyman v Jones* 400 US 309 (1971).
[175] Justice Marshall's dissent, ibid 339.
[176] F Easterbrook, 'Insider Trading, Secret Agents, Evidentiary Privileges and the Production of Information' 1981 Sup Ct Rev 309, 347; WW Fisher, 'Reconstructing the Fair Use Doctrine' (1988) 101 Harvard L Rev 1659, 1762–65; M Walzer, *Spheres of Justice* (Blackwell: Oxford, 1983) 100–3; G Calabresi and D Melamed, 'Property Rules, Liability Rules and Inalienability: One View of the Cathedral' (1972) 85 Harvard L Rev 1089, 1111–15; Epstein (n 168 above) 12–13; Sullivan (n 114 above) 1486–90.
[177] Sullivan (n 114 above) 1489.
[178] Note 'Another Look at Unconstitutional Conditions' (1968) 117 University of Pennsylvania L Rev 144, 151–58.

is, however, that governments will redefine the criteria for legitimate obstacles. For this reason, the requirements of germaneness and protection of fundamental rights offer a contextual mold for the criterion of reasonableness and assure us that the mechanism of welfare programmes will not be used as a measure of social control. Thus, while the requirement of personal responsibility is not dismissed, using it to coerce poor lone parents towards a particular form of conduct in terms of personal relations and parental obligations cannot be construed as a legitimate objective of welfare-to-work programmes, whether or not clothed as claimants' responsibility. Such measures may violate, to name a few, the right to marry, to bear children or to privacy. Such 'choices', offered through programmes, exploit the mechanism of welfare-to-work and fail to exhibit due regard and *equal respect for the individual's choices*.[179]

By asking how a reasonable person would behave in the claimant's shoes the reasonableness standard allows us to assess both the fairness of the system in its treatment of claimants and the reciprocal behaviour of claimants themselves. This would lead us to conclude, for example, that the British system that allows a person to limit her availability to her usual occupation and to the level of remuneration she is accustomed to while receiving benefits for up to 13 weeks,[180] is closer to treating people with equal concern and respect than a system that requires claimants to receive any job offered to them, as in the United States and Israel, for example. Further, the fact that the 'permitted period' in Britain is contingent upon factors such as the type of usual occupation, the length of training the person has undergone and the availability of employment in that occupation[181] is evidence that the personal responsibility requirement is not abandoned, but is also not used as a pretext for social coercion.

D Deriving the Right to Welfare from Equality

Before explaining how the right to welfare derives from equality, a justification for the project needs to be presented. How can the requirement to treat every individual with equal concern and respect be implemented in the legal realm? To answer this query we need to revert to our previous engagement with concepts of rights. Rights, argues Joel Feinberg, 'are especially sturdy objects to "stand upon", a most useful sort of moral furniture'.[182] Critical approaches of all varieties to the deployment of rights notwithstanding, they are an extremely useful tool in legal discourse and argument. The idea that individuals should be treated with equal concern and respect serves as an important normative baseline, but it

---
[179] Collins (n 25 above) 30.
[180] Jobseeker's Act 1995 ss 6(4), 6(5), 6(6), SI 1996/207 reg 20.
[181] SI 1996/207 reg 16(2).
[182] J Feinberg, 'The Nature and Value of Rights' (1970) 4 J of Value Inquiry 243, 252; Similarly see Holmes and Sunstein (n 54 above) 17.

is one that legal analysis is not accustomed to. Lawyers, however, are quite comfortable inspecting policy and regulation along a platform of rights.

More specifically, rights create a zone of autonomy, a domain of independence that is constructed by dominant norms such as equality and fairness.[183] Liberal equality 'seeks to ensure [individuals] the chance to decide freely, unconstrained by relations of domination'.[184] This section advances the argument that in the modern, Western context, fidelity to equality demands that governments 'guarantee minimum economic welfare in the form of social rights'.[185] Within the framework of welfare-to-work programmes, this would mean recognizing a strong right to welfare and subjecting the conditions placed upon benefits to scrutiny.[186] How does accepting a principle of equal concern and respect justify, within the social and economic context of Western democracies, a legal right to welfare? I conclude this chapter by exploring the argument that contemporary theories of equality demand specific concern for the worst-off in a manner that would necessitate the ascription of a right to welfare. In light of the immediate implications that such a conclusion may entail for social policy, I highlight in the following (and final) chapter, a prominent, and relatively new, social policy ideology—that of social inclusion—and consider its relation with equality and the impact this may have on the establishment of a legal right to welfare.

Before doing so, however, a peculiar obstacle needs to be overcome. It is peculiar because it concerns a question of methodology that one would think should arise more often than it actually does. The question is: how does one go about arguing in favour of a right? In arguments for the recognition of a right, one of the most widely used methods is to link such a right to other recognized rights and values. As Mackie notes, 'rights can be derived from other rights in fairly obvious logical ways'.[187] One need not expect to find one right as the *logical* extension of a more basic core value. Rather, it will be much more common to find the core right as providing strong reasons for the recognition of the right that is reasoned for.[188] This method necessarily entails the existence of gaps between the steps that are ideally (in both senses of the word) governed by a background theory of justice. If someone holds a radically different theory of justice, she may view as question-begging the move from an accepted right to a right that is argued for. This difficulty should be taken into account in the course of the argument.

---

[183] L Williams, 'Welfare and Legal Entitlements: The Social Roots of Poverty' in D Kairys (ed), *The Politics of Law* (3rd edn, Basic Books: New York, 1998) 569, 576.
[184] Fraser (n 28 above) 232.
[185] Honneth (n 7 above) 152–53.
[186] R Plant, H Lesser and P Taylor-Gooby, *Political Philosophy and Social Welfare* (Routledge: London, 1980) 93.
[187] JL Mackie, 'Can There Be a Rights Based Moral Theory?' in Waldron (n 15 above) 168, 170. Black refers, almost with boredom, to the 'ancient methods of analogy and inference'—C Black, 'Further Reflections on the Constitutional Justice of Livelihood' (1986) 86 Columbia L Rev 1103, 1104.
[188] J Raz, 'On the Nature of Rights' (1984) 93 Mind 194, 197–98; J Raz (n 27 above) 168–70.

Though Raz sees the advantage of rights in their ability to form a common culture 'round shared intermediate conclusions, in spite of a great degree of haziness and disagreement concerning ultimate values',[189] it would seem that here the situation is reversed: while liberals and conservatives may agree on various fundamental values, there are rare occurrences where the disagreement is so deep as in the case for and against the right to welfare. This, no doubt, is attributed to a great extent to what Raz referred to as the 'haziness' concerning the ultimate values.[190] Even those that treasure the importance of certain values such as autonomy, dignity, or equality may plausibly disagree on the consequences of their espousal.

With respect to one of the aforementioned values, one cannot ignore the fact that dignity has served as the centerpiece in many modern constitutions, as well as in arguments for social and economic rights.[191] But while dignity refers us to the individual that should be protected from humiliation, exploitation and unnecessary harm, it is equality that is seen by many as sovereign amongst *public* virtues. It is possible, then, to view the concretization of the duty to respect one's dignity as intertwined with, or even emanating from, the obligations that derive from an egalitarian approach. Rawls writes, for example, that 'self-respect is most effectively encouraged by the two principles of justice, again precisely because of the insistence on the equal basic liberties'.[192] The egalitarian paradigm that underlies this claim and the ensuing argument in favour of a right to welfare will be at the centre of this chapter.

Indeed, one of the more natural ways to address the challenge of deriving a right to welfare from equality is by concentrating on the special concern that equality should express towards those who are worst-off. Indeed, Barry makes the more ambitious claim that one thing 'we normally expect a conception of justice to do' is to 'provide some moral basis for the claims of the relatively powerless'.[193] One may argue that some theories of justice (eg utilitarianism) do not see themselves bound to live up to such high expectations. However, the claim is perhaps better suited with regards to *egalitarian* theories of justice (which is, perhaps, what Barry had in mind).

The egalitarian need to care for those who are worst-off, its 'deprivation focus',[194] may be seen as central for egalitarian theories because of the procedure viewed as just when selecting principles and institutions. An egalitarian theory of justice starts from the supposition that the basic institutions of society should reflect the same concern for every person's interest, regardless of caste, creed,

---

[189] Raz 1986 (n 188 above) 181.
[190] R Dworkin, *Taking Rights Seriously* (Duckworth: London, 1977) 93, 128 and Dworkin (n 20 above) 70–72, 90–96.
[191] See eg Gavison (n 23 above) 33, 40; Waldron, 'Introduction' in Waldron (n 15 above) 1, 22; Gewirth (n 27 above) 66.
[192] J Rawls, 'The Basic Liberties and their Priority' in SM McMurrin (ed), *Liberty, Equality and Law* (CUP: Cambridge, 1987) 1, 32; Gewirth (n 27 above) 110–12; but cf S Fredman, *Discrimination Law* (Clarendon: Oxford, 2001) 119–21.
[193] Barry (n 19 above) 46.
[194] Gewirth (n 27 above) 110–13.

gender and so forth. If one permits some form of thought experiment where all are granted veto power on principles and institutions governing their lives, then social institutions 'that did not include the securing of a social minimum, the familiar apparatus of welfare provision...would not command unanimous agreement'.[195] Under the Rawlsian veil of ignorance, some will fear that they will end up being those who are worst off. And if we dismiss this requirement, those who *are* effectively part of the group that is worst-off would demand that their minimal needs would be catered for. All in all, a right to welfare would be one of the principles that would result from such a process.

Thomas Nagel's approach suggests a less abstract connection between equality and consideration of the worst-off. He hypothesizes that he has two children—one healthy and the other disabled.[196] When a change of residence is considered, a choice has to be made between moving to a city where the disabled child will get better schooling and care, and moving to the suburbs where the healthy child may exploit his sporting potential. What should also be considered is that the gain to the disabled child by moving to the city is not as great as the loss to the healthy child, and that in both scenarios the healthy child's welfare will remain greater. In this case, Nagel argues, equality requires granting the welfare of the disabled child greater consideration. Even though a move to the city would reduce the overall welfare of the two siblings combined, equality would be enhanced by edging the welfare of the child who is worst-off closer towards the position of his healthy sibling.[197]

But are we not forcing the healthy sibling to pay for the disabled child's incapacity? Indeed, it is this example that demonstrates why arguments in favour of welfare rights may be perceived as particularly vulnerable to the levelling-down objection. One may argue that if we are anxious that some are not excelling to the same degree as others, maybe we should consider worsening the situation of the latter instead of improving the position of the former? Why do we not shackle the legs of the fastest runners instead of insisting on training those who are lagging behind?[198] This objection, however, can be understood in two different fashions. As a general critique of egalitarianism, I find it to be not much more than a red herring. It is, indeed, true that if equality were the *only* governing principle, noxious results would be the order of the day, such as blinding all sighted people so that nobody would be better off in this respect. A value that would lead to such results if implemented to the full, it is claimed, is not one worth holding, for there can be nothing good about blinding sighted people.

---

[195] Waldron (n 3 above) 305.
[196] T Nagel, 'Equality' in *Mortal Questions* (Canto: Cambridge, 1979) 106, 123–24.
[197] But cf D Parfit, 'Equality and Priority' (1997) 10 Ratio 202; H Frankfurt, 'Equality as a Moral Ideal' in *The Importance of What We Care About* (CUP: Cambridge, 1988) 134, 151.
[198] K Vonnegut, 'Harrison Bergeron' in *Welcome to the Monkey House* (Doubleday: New York, 1998) 7; and less dramatically in Raz (n 27 above) 227, 235; Temkin (n 56 above) 247–48.

As an indictment of egalitarianism as a principle, however, this argument is not difficult to reject. The obvious retort, that equality is never claimed to be the only important value, is not an act of evasiveness. It is simply stating a truism. One need only to browse through chapter 13 of *Leviathan* to understand how life in a community that values only liberty (incidentally, a favoured value of anti-egalitarians) would look like. Indeed, all the egalitarians who I have come across, including those who believe that equality is an intrinsic good and worth tangible sacrifices of utility, assert clearly that equality 'is not all that matters'.[199] An egalitarian need not always prefer, say, a situation where a natural disaster has demolished only the holdings of the rich to the previous state of affairs where there was a significant divide between rich and poor. It is only that *in at least one respect*, the post-disaster situation is held to be more just. However, because most egalitarians are pluralists (ie hold other values as important, in addition to equality) the posterior situation need not win the day all things considered. As a side remark, it is added that when understood as a critique of concrete social policies, leveling-down may be not only non-objectionable, but may actually be mandated. For, if we do care about equality, some unjustified social privileges and advantages that cannot be redistributed, such as hereditary rank or social caste, should indeed be eliminated, even if this would mean only depriving some of their advantage.[200]

The force of the levelling-down objection is most clearly exhibited in cases where equality would require expropriating personal entitlements from people who have a legitimate and otherwise exclusionary claim regarding these entitlements. Blinding all sighted people in the name of equality deprives people of their justified claim for bodily integrity. Public policy matters where future plans are deliberated, however, present the dilemma in a more relevant fashion.[201] Imagine a plan for a museum wing that does not allow access to disabled people on wheelchairs. An egalitarian may argue that we would be better off not building an extra wing at all than building one that would leave members of society excluded. Moreover, we may find her point to be valid. After all, it is not beyond modern society's technical skills to construct a gallery that allows disabled people access. Equality serves here as an important value that affects considerations of public policy, thus avoiding the (presumably) more cost-effective solution. What, however, if the claim would be that the wing should not be constructed at all because it would exacerbate the discrimination against blind people who cannot enjoy exhibitions? Moreover, what if the claim was that equality demands, for the same reason, tearing down all existing museums? Now here, it would seem, our egalitarian has gone too far.

[199] Temkin (n 56 above) 282; Sen (n 63 above) 92–93.
[200] T Scanlon, 'Nozick on Rights, Liberty and Property' (1976) 6 Philosophy and Public Affairs 3, 10.
[201] It should be mentioned that while Parfit states that such cases are the focus of his interest (n 197 above, 203) he later discusses levelling-down scenarios that involve clear loss of entitlements—210–11.

Unlike the claim for bodily integrity mentioned above, it would be difficult to say that the community has a *right* to a new museum wing.[202] It is, naturally, in the community's interest to promote arts and culture, and as such it is not a misguided interest either. However, it is true as well that by doing so, an important value, that of equality, is (further) compromised. The levelling-down objector points to this fact, and I believe she is right in doing so. But she also advances the claim that for an egalitarian to be consistent, he should be opposed to building the new museum wing (or should even support tearing down existing museums). This, however, is not necessarily the case. Cancelling the plan for the new wing is not the only possible solution, and is certainly not the preferable one in this case. Unlike the case of an inaccessible gallery, here it is impossible (we assume) to allow a blind person to enjoy Matisse's colours. This does not entail, however, that sighted people should also be denied the pleasure.

A just solution that takes equality seriously would do two things, then. The first is to *acknowledge* that in building a wing we are violating equality in favour of other values. The second is to *compensate* the community whose situation is (relatively) worsened, redressing 'the bias of contingencies in the direction of equality'.[203] Thus, building a new museum wing should be perceived as catering for the legitimate needs of sighted members of society. Treating all individuals with equal concern and respect would require implementing *parallel* policies to address similar needs of communities who will not be able to enjoy the new cultural gem. This may mean, for example, subsidizing tickets to cultural events that they can enjoy (eg concerts) or building a museum (or museum wing) composed of tactile pictures for the blind in a manner that sighted people cannot enjoy.[204] Such costly solutions that cater for the needs of the blind population may reduce the general level of welfare of the majority, who are sighted. But they do so in a manner that respects the rights and interests of others, avoids the destruction or waste of valuable (human, cultural or material) resources, while seriously addressing the demands of equality. So, in conclusion, we find that the levelling-down objection is not a serious objection to the aim of catering for the needs of those who are worst off.

Returning now to our discussion regarding the right to welfare, we find that prominent egalitarian approaches such as those mentioned in this chapter may be understood to support a legal right to welfare precisely on the grounds noted in this section. Thus, it would seem that a right to welfare would fit neatly within Rawls's structure, as a derivative of his ideal theory[205] as well as under constraints

---

[202] cf Dworkin (n 190) 90.
[203] Rawls (n 16 above) 88; see similarly Jacobs (n 22 above) 64.
[204] This is not at all far fetched. A recent exhibition of 'Earth from the Air' in London featured a huge relief that allowed the blind to share the experience, at least to a certain extent. See <http://www.earthfromtheair.com/blind.html> (23 May 2005).
[205] F Michelman, 'Constitutional Welfare Rights and *A Theory of Justice*' in Daniels (n 6 above) 319.

of a society that is less than well-ordered.[206] First, there is the baseline of an equal distribution of primary goods. Though Rawls distinguishes between inequalities in liberty and inequality in the 'worth' or 'value' of liberty due to unequal economic means, it is clear (even if one accepts this problematic and highly criticized distinction) that though strict equality of liberties may not be required, a 'fair value' of liberties is demanded.[207] Further, as Scanlon suggests, justice for Rawls (and, it seems, for Scanlon as well) 'requires that our institutions be arranged so as to maximize the expectations of the worst-off group in our society'.[208] Since the more affluent members tend to have greater access to basic rights and liberties, to powers and prerogatives of office, to freedom of movement and free choice of occupation and, by nature, to income and wealth,[209] we should construct policies and structures of rights and obligations that would minimize the disparity between rich and poor in these respects.

Similarly, if equality is understood as equal opportunity for welfare[210] or equal opportunity for advantage,[211] it is quite clear that the more encompassing the welfare entitlements the weaker the connection between one's opportunities and her wealth.[212] Thus, if education is free of charge, financial considerations are mitigated to opportunity costs of studying instead of working. And, likewise, an individual who receives subsistence income while unemployed may be able to refrain from accepting the first job offer that comes along, in favour of waiting for one that would increase her enjoyment from a job, maximize her potential and take account of her capabilities. Indeed, research has begun to show that 'by limiting education, particularly postsecondary education, and training activities, TANF may seriously impair welfare mothers' perspective for long-term economic security'.[213] If financial costs potentially cut branches off some opportunity trees, a legal right to welfare may help to hold them in place. Effective choice, as we saw, is dominant in Sen's explanation of equality, and so all of the

---

[206] Also Michelman, 'In Pursuit of Constitutional Welfare Rights' (1973) 121 U of Pennsylvania L Rev 962; J Waldron, 'John Rawls and the Social Minimum' in Waldron (n 3 above) 250.
[207] Rawls (n 16 above) 179, 197–99.
[208] Scanlon (n 6 above) 202.
[209] Rawls (n 92 above) 257. See, similarly, Fried's conception of the right to a 'fair share' of the benefits of social cooperation—Fried, *Right and Wrong* (Harvard UP: Cambridge MA, 1978) 119–31 and by TH Marshall, 'The Right to Welfare' in *The Right to Welfare and Other Essays* (Heinemann: London, 1981) 83, 93.
[210] R Arneson, 'Equality and Equal Opportunity for Welfare' (1989) 56 Philosophical Studies 77.
[211] Cohen (n 32 above) 916.
[212] Raz states that the 'government has an obligation to create an environment providing individuals with an adequate range of options and the opportunities to choose them'—Raz (n 27 above) 418.
[213] S Morel, 'Workfare and *Insertion*: How the U.S. and French Models of Social Assistance Have Been Transformed' in N Gilbert and A Parent (eds), *Welfare Reform: A Comparative Assessment of the French and U.S. Experiences* (International Social Security Series vol 10, Transaction Publishers: London, 2004) 93, 128.

above applies equally to his theory of capabilities.[214] From a slightly different perspective, Dworkin's theory would support the same conclusion. Indeed, when applying equality of resources to the welfare realm, Dworkin remarks that:

> Programs like food stamps, Aid to Families with Dependent Children, and those using federal funds to make higher education available for the poor are the last programs that should be curtailed... If 'targeted' programs like these are thought to be too expensive, or too inefficient, then government must show how alternative plans or programs will restore the promise of participation in the future that these programs offered.[215]

We find, therefore, that fidelity to equality requires recognizing a right to welfare. Such recognition would restrict the range of conditions that may be attached to benefits and would work to change the relationship between claimants, the state and other citizens. This does not, however, conclude our analysis of the central norms and considerations in welfare-to-work programmes. The vivacity of social policy discourse has introduced a new concept to supplement that of equality and it is one that has important implications in the field of welfare-to-work programmes. I refer to the concept of social exclusion addressed in the following chapter.

E Conclusion

The argument advanced in the first section, that equality should be a prime consideration in matters of public policy, and that governments should treat individuals with equal concern and respect, intersects with welfare-to-work programmes at two points, considered in this chapter. The first, the value of personal responsibility, has been frequently presented as an opposition to equality. The second is the right to welfare, here argued to be a derivative of equality.

Should an application for benefits by a chemical engineer be rejected if she refused a job offer as technician, for a third of her previous salary? In the course of the classical era of the welfare state, refusing to accept an offer of employment on such grounds was seen as legitimate. Today, across jurisdictions, the answer of welfare-to-work programmes is quite different. A variety of arguments are employed in favour of the contemporary position including the moral importance of work, the need to be reassured that one is willing to give back for what she receives, and the rejection, for a panoply of reasons, of any form of entitlement. In this chapter, I scrutinized one of the most pervasive arguments in favour of the rejection of entitlements in such cases—one that is based on the concept of personal responsibility. As mentioned in the chapter's opening paragraphs, its

---

[214] See S Deakin, 'The Capability Concept and the Evolution of European Social Policy' in M Dougan and E Spaventa (eds), *Social Welfare and EU Law* (Hart: Oxford, 2005) 3.
[215] Dworkin (n 23 above) 211–12 [emphasis added].

towering presence in the title of the extensive American legislation on the matter confirms its prominence in the public eye. The appeal of the concept of personal responsibility is rarely contested in itself and was not at issue here. What was questioned was the assumption that the ascription of responsibility is a technical matter that takes places in a normative vacuum.

Egalitarians have advanced part of the way towards this conclusion by incorporating responsibility into a theory of equality. However, the initial stages of incorporation have resulted in a certain danger that the new factor that has been introduced into the equilibrium will overpower and undermine the normative structure itself. It is important, therefore, not to be mystified by the ascription of responsibility and to address it without rejecting our fundamental beliefs about a just society. I believe that doing so would lead to some policy decisions that are quite different to those currently in place. This conclusion is strengthened by the idea that equality supports a legal recognition of the right to welfare. As showed, equality includes special concern for the worst-off. Egalitarianism addresses policies, structures and institutions that have an impact on the true opportunities and welfare of the least-fortunate. Among these is the requirement that an egalitarian society should recognize an individual's right to welfare. Such a decision would limit the range of conditions that can be legitimately placed on access to welfare provisions and would enhance respect for one's life choices without necessarily undermining the importance of preserving personal responsibility.

5
Welfare, Work and Social Inclusion

It is time now to close the circle on our investigation. After starting from the descriptive and the factual, we moved to the abstract and the critical, and now we would do well to return and find how the fruits of the journey offer a better understanding of the true purpose of welfare programmes, where they have departed from pursuing just (and often their own declared) objectives and how they can return to take a positive role in the modern welfare state.

To facilitate this endeavour, it will be very useful to employ a new concept—that of social inclusion. Though the concept was mentioned throughout, it is worth explaining its importance for the assessment of welfare-to-work programmes. This is done in the first section of the chapter. It is important to note that this chapter does not intend to add to the growing literature that wishes to shed light on the concept itself. Rather, notwithstanding some of the disagreements and recent suggestions regarding its optimal use, there is a broad consensus that we have at our disposal a complex, multifaceted, multidimensional concept that engages with a variety of disciplines and serves as an excellent transmitter from theory to practice. Moreover, it has become increasingly clear that its main contribution to social policy debates lies in the field of unemployment and labour market policies. It is small wonder that, as noted below, despite being introduced for the first time in France in the late 1970s, the dramatic overhaul of welfare systems all over the Western world has been accompanied by an explosion of literature on social exclusion, especially during the last decade.[1]

Social exclusion, therefore, is employed here in an instrumental fashion, as an intermediary between the theoretical arguments presented to this point and the socio-legal conclusions deriving from them. In addition, it supplements the normative baseline of equality in the analysis of welfare reform. I open this final chapter by briefly explaining how social inclusion is well designed for the task of bringing together the theoretical aspects of welfare-to-work programmes and channeling them into practical exploration. The subsequent sections of the chapter then follow the main themes of the work into an inquiry towards their possible implementation.

---

[1] C Gore, 'Introduction' in G Rodgers, C Gore and J Figueiredo (eds), *Social Exclusion* (ILO: Geneva, 1995) 1.

A Why Social Inclusion?

This book opened with the emphasis placed by welfare-to-work programmes on the ideology of deterrence and on the distinction between deserving and undeserving poor. It may be apt, therefore, that this final chapter addresses what has been perceived as the counterpart of welfare policy: instead of targeted provision that induces stigmatizing and banishing, a policy designed 'to prevent the poor from sliding out of mainstream society and to bring back in those who are already excluded'.[2] Serving as 'the major social phenomenon of our day',[3] the concept of social inclusion encapsulates what welfare-to-work programmes are, or perhaps should be, all about.[4] It is true that few writers neglect mentioning the notorious fluidity and flexibility of the concept. I refer to these traits as 'notorious' because the ambiguity of the concept may divert attention from core problems such as poverty and inequality by turning attention to malleable and open-ended issues. More importantly, perhaps, some warn that it may permit an undue emphasis on personal responsibility by obscuring the distinction between voluntary and involuntary social exclusion.[5]

These insights and worries should not be neglected. However, it is important to note that these are not conceptual objections. Rather, they refer mainly to the policy implications that would derive from embracing such a concept, if not used with care. In this section, however, I would like to briefly identify some of the common traits attributed to the concept by writers of all persuasions. Doing so, I believe, would justify the deployment of social inclusion within the context of welfare-to-work programmes and will pave the path for the subsequent sections.

i) Economic, Social and Moral Perspectives

As preceding chapters made clear, current welfare-to-work discourse is not only about alleviating poverty through paid work. In effect, one may argue that it is not even *primarily* about alleviating poverty. Both advocates and opponents of the programmes find them to be concerned with social norms and moral values. Integration into the workforce is not perceived solely as a mechanism to increase household income. Indeed, this is why individuals are required to enter the workforce, in some cases, despite the fact that this would lead to a *reduction* in household income. Social inclusion permits a multidimensional approach to the

---

[2] J Handler, *Social Citizenship and Workfare in the United States and Western Europe* (CUP: Cambridge, 2004) 79.
[3] P Rosanvallon, *The New Social Question* (Princeton UP: Princeton, 2000) 46.
[4] Handler (n 2 above) 4, 15; P Vincent-Jones, *The New Public Contracting: Regulation, Responsiveness, Relationality* (OUP: Oxford, 2006) 230.
[5] See eg J Hills, 'Does a Focus on 'Social Exclusion' Change the Policy Response?' in J Hills, J Le Grand and D Piachaud (eds), *Understanding Social Exclusion* (OUP: Oxford, 2001) 226, 240–41; G Rodgers, 'What is Special About Social Exclusion?' in Rodgers, Gore and Figueiredo (n 1 above) 43, 53; H Silver, 'Reconceptualizing Social Disadvantage' ibid 57, 60, 78.

problems that welfare-to-work programmes deal with, implicitly or explicitly.[6] Thus, the focus on unemployment as a primary cause of social exclusion does not conflict with the characterization of social exclusion as one's detachment from the 'moral order'.[7]

This also means that the concept is *relational*, in the sense that it takes into account the context within which it is employed including, primarily, the assessment of the interaction between the individual and the state and amongst individuals.[8] Indeed, an influential interpretation of social inclusion objectives refers to the representation of society as a network. The included, then, are those who are connected to others by a multiplicity of bonds. Converesely, the excluded are those whose ties have been severed, and who have been 'relegated to the fringes of the network, where beings lose all visibility, all rationale, and virtually all existence'.[9] The paradigmatic image of the socially excluded individual is the homeless vagrant with no fixed address, deprived of any access to his rights, be they civil or political, economic or social.

The reader may have already guessed that this matrix of bonds indicated by the network metaphor may be, and indeed has been, referred to by some writers on social exclusion using a concept that has been investigated at length above—the social contract. Writers have begun to argue for a new 'type of social contract that can connect work and the right to inclusion'.[10]

Welfare-to-work constructions are paradigmatic examples of such contracts. Indeed, the existence of welfare-to-work spin-offs such as 'healthfare', 'learnfare' and 'wedfare' reveal that impoverished people are expected to change not only their attitude to work, but also to keep within mainstream lifestyles if they wish to receive benefits. Contingent on the way it is construed, social inclusion as a concept may justify or criticize such policies. In both cases it offers a common ground for engaging these issues. Indeed, the questions addressed by the concept of social exclusion assume the existence of a community within which rights are being held, goods are shared and mutual recognition is expressed.[11]

It is thus clear where the theoretical danger lies. Though it is far from being a purely normative concept, social inclusion is definitely a value-laden norm that identifies, first, who is to be included and, second, what it is important to be

---

[6] Hills (n 5 above) 228.
[7] G Room, 'Poverty and Social Exclusion' in G Room (ed), *Beyond the Threshold* (Policy: Bristol, 1995) 1, 6; J Clasen, A Gould and J Vincent, *Long Term Unemployment and the Threat of Social Exclusion* (Policy: Bristol, 1997) 13.
[8] T Burchardt, J Le Grand and D Piachaud, 'Degrees of Exclusion' in Hills, Le Grand and Piachaud (n 5 above) 30, 31. AB Atkinson, 'Social Exclusion, Poverty and Unemployment' in AB Atkinson and J Hills (eds), *Exclusion, Employment and Opportunity* (CASEpaper 4: London, 1998) 1, 13.
[9] L Boltanski, E Chiapello and G Elliot (tr), *The New Spirit of Capitalism* (Verso: London, 2005) 348.
[10] Rosanvallon (n 3 above) 81.
[11] Gore (n 1 above) 1, 8.

included in.[12] In the context of welfare-to-work programmes, the former strikes a familiar chord—the discourse that wishes to distinguish between deserving and undeserving members of the community. The latter question suggests that the concept may assume the moral value attached to work and the importance of inclusion into the work environment. It may thus take for granted that all individuals should be included and, moreover, it may delineate the domain of coerced inclusion.

ii) Bridges Agency and Structural Explanations

Opponents and advocates of current welfare-to-work programmes have, to a frustrating extent, been talking past each other when identifying the matters that need to be addressed by welfare-to-work policies. This observation may be applied to several spheres, but is most evident when commentators wish to assign blame. In the blue corner, neo-liberal thinkers suggest that a claimant *chooses* to live off benefits and therefore should be forced to help herself while bearing responsibility for her life choices and her family's situation. In the red corner, thinkers of the socio-economic left emphasize structural explanations, and the impoverished condition that individuals endure is seen, at worst, as intentionally created so as to facilitate their exploitation or, at best, due to casual indifference.

Social inclusion policies, on the other hand, openly state their objective as transforming the disadvantaged from passive recipients to active agents.[13] Now, some attention has been directed to the distinction between voluntary exclusion and involuntary exclusion.[14] This debate, in itself, reveals the complexity of the notion of exclusion and its sensitivity to causes that led to the situation that is addressed. It also shows that, while a great deal of thought is required in order to integrate concepts that are agency oriented (such as responsibility) with public virtues (such as equality), social inclusion comes with such sensitivities 'built in'. As Atkinson notes, 'in terms of failure to achieve *inclusion*, we may be concerned not just with a person's situation, but also the extent to which he or she is *responsible*'.[15] Indeed, for this reason, critics from the left have warned that exclusion has become the watered-down version of the Marxist notion of exploitation. They argue that it is a 'topic of sentiment' which has replaced a 'topic of denunciation' and that it too easily accepts the poor individual's burden of his or her own responsibility.[16]

The notion of social exclusion, however, is more complicated. It has been said to allow us to collate the ingredients that sociology has always dealt with—history

[12] Rodgers (n 5 above) 44; Silver (n 5 above) 66.
[13] Gore (n 1 above) 33
[14] B Barry, 'Social exclusion, Social Isolation and the Distribution of Income' in Hills, Le Grand and Piachaud (n 5 above) 13; J Le Grand 'Individual Choice and Social Exclusion' (CASEpaper 75; London, 2003).
[15] Atkinson (n 8 above) 14; Also T Burchardt, J Le Grand and D Piachaud, 'Introduction' in Hills, Le Grand and Piachaud (n 5 above) 1, 6.
[16] Boltanski and Chiapello (n 9 above) 347–353.

and biography.[17] It is not that claimants were ever completely passive. As the conditions placed on benefits in past and current programmes show, the welfare state has never, in effect, been content with simply handing out benefits.[18] But the turn to social inclusion polices could be perceived as a third generation in the welfare state's attitude towards the unemployed. The first generation embraced a structural perspective, and envisaged full employment policies and welfare distribution as a mechanism for the treatment of social and economic ills; the second generation experienced an individualistic backlash, blaming welfare as a *cause* for social problems and emphasizing policies of activation;[19] social inclusion discourse may allow, then, for a mediated approach that takes into account both agency and structure.[20] While the importance of choice is central, true integration into the paid labour market requires that structural conditions be met. This would require not only efforts that target the low-wage labour market, but also addressing issues of training, education, health care, child care, social service, transportation and housing.[21]

iii) Strong Connection to the Labour Markets

The dynamics and nature of labour markets are pivotal in understanding the relative importance of, and interrelations between, different dimensions of exclusion.[22] It thus seems natural that contemporary welfare programmes which view social inclusion as one of their objectives also identify paid work to be the most important mechanism towards that end.[23] However, this connection between inclusion and the labour force is not unproblematic, as I explain below. One should ask if the purpose of inclusion into the labour force is an end in itself or an intermediate goal towards greater inclusion in society. Similarly, are *all* inclusions into paid work considered to be on a par with one another, or do some carry greater value than others? Is the border between excluded and included members parallel to the border between unemployed and employed individuals, or can there be workers who are excluded and unemployed people who are included?

These questions cannot be addressed without a better understanding of the objectives lying in the background of social inclusion policies, as well as some of the dynamics of the labour market. For the time being, however, it is noted that while exclusion refers, in the main, to various forms of expulsion from the labour

---

[17] D Byrne, *Social Exclusion* (Open UP: Buckingham, 1999) 1, referring to CW Mills, *The Sociological Imagination* (OUP: New York, 1959) ch 1; See, particularly, Mills' application of this position to unemployment—ibid 9.
[18] Hills (n 5 above) 232–35.
[19] S Deakin and F Wilkinson, *The Law of the Labour Market* (OUP: Oxford, 2005) 185–92.
[20] cf H Silver and F Wilkinson, 'Policies to Combat Social Exclusion' in Rodgers, Gore and Figueiriedo (n 1 above) 283.
[21] Handler (n 2 above) 268–72.
[22] Gore (n 1 above) 32.
[23] Silver and Wilkinson (n 20 above) 286; B Lund, *Understanding State Welfare* (Sage: London, 2002) 192; P Selznick, 'Social Justice—A Communitarian Perspective' in A Etzioni (ed), *The Essential Communitarian Reader* (Rowan and Littlefield: Oxford, 1998) 61, 69.

market,[24] a fresh look into this connection allows us to assess what values are being promoted by policies that promote inclusion into the labour market over other forms of inclusion and what alternative responses can be offered.

iv) A Dynamic Concept

The brief overview offered to this point makes clear that social inclusion reacts to changes in economic, moral and legal contexts. It is, in other words, a concept that encapsulates the dynamics of a process, and has little meaning as an abstract, theoretical and static tool.[25] Its relational aspect means that the way a particular society understands the association amongst individuals and between individuals and the state has an impact on the drawing of borders between excluded and included individuals and the measures that would be employed to facilitate inclusion. The structure of the particular labour market in question should similarly be taken into account when considering the importance of paid work as a central mechanism of inclusion. A further interesting aspect of the dynamic character of social inclusion is tied to the fact that social exclusion is not just a material status but also a mental state. It is not only about one lacking a job or an income, but also about the lack of positive prospects for the future. For this reason, social exclusion has the potential to carry across generations. It is 'not just about ex-post trajectories but also ex-ante expectations'.[26] This would make addressing the matter all the more urgent.

B Social Inclusion Between Equality, Choice and Responsibility

Over the past decade, writers of disparate ideological colours have juxtaposed equality and social exclusion and have highlighted the differences between the concepts. A closer inspection of these arguments, however, finds them to overstate some of the differences, in some cases, or to present a skewed picture of the concepts in question, in other cases.

First, it has been argued that since the objective of social inclusion is to see all individuals participate fully in society, it would presumably be concerned with absolute disadvantages such as truancy, drug abuse and homelessness, while equality addresses relative deprivation.[27] Yet, as indicated, both concepts perceive both absolute *and* relational attributes as highly important. Treating all

---

[24] See eg Boltanski and Chiapello (n 9 above) 346; Clasen, Gould and Vincent (n 7 above) 14.
[25] Hills (n 5 above) 228; Rosanvallon (n 3 above) 46.
[26] Atkinson (n 8 above) 14; R Walker 'The Dynamics of Poverty and Social Exclusion' in Room (n 7 above) 102, 103, 120.
[27] R Lister, 'Strategies for Social Inclusion' in P Askonas and A Stewart (eds), *Social Inclusion* (Macmillan: Basingstoke, 2000) 37; P Robinson, 'Employment and Social Inclusion' ibid 153, 154.

individuals with equal concern and respect demands that the life of one individual would not be considered to be more valuable than the life of another's. But when inspecting particular policies, this would require the alleviation of social ills that affect particular segments of society. Such policies are mandated, inter alia, because a fair and decent society cannot be indifferent to the disparity between the life opportunities that its members enjoy.

On the other hand, policies of inclusion require an analysis of a particular society and the identification of indicators (political participation, employment, crime rates, wealth, etc.) the application of which distinguishes certain groups from others. Though they address particular problems, their relational facets come to the fore when different attributes of different societies require appropriate solutions in each and every case. These points also indicate that there may be situations where *neither* equality nor social inclusion policies are relevant.[28]

Another argument in favor of a strong distinction between the two concepts is that social inclusion policies include an element of coercion that is foreign to the respect that the egalitarian tradition has for individual choice.[29] Since one of the notable factors of recent policies is the harshening of conditions for entitlement, thus narrowing the opportunity for meaningful choice, this factor is especially important for the assessment of contemporary welfare programmes. And, indeed, it would seem that while egalitarians tend to be critical of strict conditions, inclusionists are inclined to see them as a necessary evil. However, it is not at all clear that it is the *egalitarian* tradition which entails respect for individual choice. It is true that *liberal egalitarians*, such as Ronald Dworkin and Brian Barry, hold both equality and individual choice in high regard. However, unlike theories that are based on an ideal of personal autonomy, egalitarian theories do not, as such, entail respect for individual choice.

And turning to inspect the concept of social inclusion, one finds that though coercive measures have been justified by referring to social inclusion, this does not mean that social inclusion objectives are truly advanced by such disregard for an individual's autonomy and her own life choices. In fact, as I argue, the reverse is closer to the truth. It was mentioned above that social inclusion plays a role in bridging the gap between perspectives that place the onus on a person's status and those that focus on her responsibility for that situation. If this potential is to be exploited, it should not allow for easy parallels, such as the one that Giddens draws between the voluntary exclusion of the very rich from society with the (supposedly voluntary) exclusion of the very poor, thus implying that *both* have chosen their condition to the same extent.[30] Rather, egalitarian norms and, moreover, the 'reasonable responsibility' approach, enrich our normative assessment of social inclusion as well.

[28] cf Barry (n 14 above) 16.
[29] H Collins, 'Discrimination, Equality and Social Inclusion' (2003) 66 MLR 16, 31.
[30] A Giddens, *The Third Way* (Polity: London, 1998) 103; cf Lund (n 23 above) 206.

Thus, Brian Barry, in a vein similar to the position outlined in the previous chapter, notes that 'the action chosen appeared to the agent preferable to the alternatives available at the time does not tell us much' if we don't know the quality of choices on offer.[31] And Iris Marion Young finds that a goal of social justice is equality, which 'refers primarily to the full participation and inclusion of everyone in society's major institutions and the socially supported substantive opportunity of all to develop and exercise their capacities and realise their choices'.[32] However, as I note below, Young's proposition, that seeks to combine egalitarian concerns with respect for personal choice, would have been more persuasive if it were to refer to equal *opportunity* for full participation and inclusion. This caveat accounts for those individuals who prefer not to be included at all.

Lastly, critics from the left warn that the new discourse resituates 'the political spectrum by marginalizing or eliminating the issue of equality from the political agenda'.[33] The reason is that while 'exclusion places the problem outside society...inequality inevitably raises the problematic issue of the attainment of equality'.[34] A focus on inclusion, it is suggested, avoids questions concerning the distribution of power in society, in its social space and in its institutions. Writers of different political colours were happy to agree. Thus, Lord Dahrendorf, in a speech in the House of Lords, tried to address some concerns expressed by his peers by explaining that the Dahrendorf Report 'accepts a wide range of inequality as long as the citizen is on board... What matters is not equality but inclusion'.[35] And John Gray, a self-proclaimed 'liberal communitarian', remarks that:

Policies promoting inclusion will sometimes generate inequalities that are regarded by egalitarians as unfair but are viewed by advocates of inclusion as fair. In this latter case—equality and inclusion are not just different. They are rivals.[36]

Similarly, it has been pointed out that the groups targeted by social inclusion policies are not organized by the same criteria that equality laws usually refer to (eg race, ethnicity and gender). Though single parents, old people and unemployed youth may be disproportionately excluded from society, they cut across such traditional categories.[37]

It may be immediately acknowledged that since equality and social inclusion are not identical, it is necessarily the case that there may be policies that would satisfy one objective and not the other. Phrased thus, this is almost an exercise in tautology. Policies based on a different set of principles would naturally

---

[31] Barry (n 14 above) 14; similarly D Attas and A de-Shalit, 'Workfare: the Subjection of Labour' (2004) 21 J of Applied Philosophy 309, 315.
[32] IM Young, *Justice and the Politics of Difference* (Princeton UP: Princeton, 1990) 173.
[33] A Stewart, 'Social Inclusion' in Askonas and Stewart (n 27 above) 1, 4.
[34] G Procacci, 'Against Exclusion' in M Rhodes and Y Meny (eds), *The Future of European Welfare: A New Social Contract?* (Macmillan: Basingstoke, 1998) 63, 74.
[35] R Dahrendorf, 'On the Dahrendorf Report' (1996) 67 Political Q 194, 196.
[36] J Gray, 'Social Inclusion' in Askonas and Stewart (n 27 above) 19, 23.
[37] Collins (n 29 above) 27–28; Rosanvallon (n 3 above) 99.

emphasize different values. Just as egalitarian policies may have to give way to liberty and property (despite all being part of a relatively coherent matrix of social values) so is the case here. Interestingly, however, a stronger relation may exist between equality and inclusion than between equality and liberty. For while, on some understanding, the idea of liberty may be satisfied even in cases of extreme inequality, the same would be difficult to say with regards to social inclusion. An inclusive society would seem incompatible with unjust and excessive inequalities.[38] Indeed, Hugh Collins, in an important attempt to shed light on the relationship between equality and social inclusion,[39] notes (with a touch of the scepticism that political rhetoric is due) that the government paper that discusses the implementation of the Employment and Race Directives states that 'Discrimination usually amounts to exclusion in some form'.[40]

While acknowledging that both equality and social inclusion policies grant considerable importance to assuring access to employment (an understanding, it should be stressed, shared even by those who are most critical of the emphasis placed on labour market inclusion[41]), Collins offers an integrative understanding of the two that places access to employment in its proper, instrumental role and not as the goal itself. Collins dedicates most of his article to the impact that the objective of social inclusion would have on our understanding of equality laws. Thus, a refusal to allow more flexible work patterns is criticized as discriminatory because it would result in the exclusion of many women from the work market.[42] As such, Collins follows Sandra Fredman, who points out that a 'rich idea of equality sees equality as participation and inclusion of all groups, which in turn requires valuing differences and at times treating relevantly different groups differently'.[43] This formulation places social inclusion as an important *interpretation* of equality, as opposed to a conflicting goal, and permits a fresh look at the manner which, inter alia, choice is treated.

Despite its flaws, the purported theoretical distinction between equality and inclusion is carried into the field of welfare proposals. The analysis of social policies in Britain, for example, is increasingly phrased in terms that pose the importance of a cohesive society in opposition to equality.[44] This is unfortunate. Social inclusion may complement the requirement to treat individuals with equal concern and respect, even in the context of welfare reform. Thus, adherence to social

---

[38] Robinson (n 27 above) 154; WJ Wilson, *The Truly Disadvantaged* (Chicago UP: Chicago, 1987) 137–38.
[39] Collins (n 29 above).
[40] Department of Trade and Industry, *Towards Equality and Diversity: Implementing the Employment and Race Directives* (2001) para 1.2 (<http://www.dti.gov.uk/er/equality/consult.pdf> (25 May 2005)); Collins (n 29 above) 21. See A Giddens, *The Third Way and its Critics* (Polity: Cambridge, 2000); A Giddens (ed), *The Global Third Way Debate* (Polity: Cambridge, 2001).
[41] R Levitas, *The Inclusive Society?* (Macmillan: Basingstoke, 1998) 23; Robinson (n 27 above) 153; Lister (n 27 above) 41.
[42] Collins (n 29 above) 30.
[43] S Fredman, 'Equality: A New Generation?' (2001) 30 ILJ 145, 157.
[44] Levitas (n 41 above) 29–48.

inclusion may require asking what structural disadvantages should be addressed so as to promote, for example, the ability of married and unmarried mothers to be included into the labour market. The egalitarian baseline would reject the scenario whereby parents are excluded from the labour market completely because of the unavailability of decent part-time jobs or affordable childcare.

Completing the circle, then, social inclusion objectives offer realistic (and thus reasonable) alternatives to the current state of affairs. This would, in turn, present a concrete realization of what 'treating people as equals' would entail. It would also offer an index for assessing the choices made by individuals (say, not to go to work due to lack of affordable child care). After due account is given to the proper meaning of what just (and successful) social inclusion looks like, one may suggest that welfare-to-work policies should be about *equal opportunity for social inclusion*. This suggestion is posited in contrast to the notion of *equality of responsibility*, which was suggested above to guide many of the current welfare reforms. Social inclusion, as understood here, accounts for important and justifiable social interests without losing sight of the priority that a liberal society should grant to an individual's chosen life-style.

It should be clarified, perhaps, that this chosen life-style may indeed include the choice *not* to be included. Respect for a person's agency and her autonomy necessarily includes the requirement to respect such choices. Equal opportunity for social inclusion does not justify coercive measures that force inclusion on those who prefer to live detached lives. Incorporating social inclusion as part of the egalitarian ideal may result in granting precedence to certain choices that individuals make, even at the expense of existing social norms and patterns. Thus, one may consider the situation of single parents who are excluded from the labour market due to unaffordable child care.[45] The choice not to engage in employment due to financial constraints may seem more legitimate, and the motivation to seek a solution to the structural impediments more pressing, if social inclusion is understood to be part of what treating individuals with equal concern really means.

C. Social Inclusion, Social Contract and the Duty to Work

What is the social structure addressed by theories that employ social inclusion terminology? The concept itself suggests that the observer is able to identify the relevant cleavages, the centre and the periphery, along with the boundaries distinguishing those on one side and those on the other. Social inclusion discourse investigates how the outsiders and insiders should be identified, who is

---

[45] Collins (n 29 above) 31.

responsible for their position, who is responsible for moving outsiders within and what measures are appropriate in doing so.[46]

Ruth Levitas and Hillary Silver have recently offered two typologies of social inclusion. Both have already gained adherents.[47] As I understand Silver, she intended to offer three possible perspectives, all of which are to be employed in the *critique* of current social policy. If this is true, all three perspectives can be categorized as subsets of one of the approaches (the Redistributionist Discourse, discussed below) suggested by Levitas. I shall grant less weight to the censorious facet of the Silver typology, however, and suggest that it be seen as partially overlapping the Levitas typology, addressing some, but not all, of the features that Levitas does.

Levitas finds that three different discourses offer distinct conceptualizations of social inclusion. The traditional understanding of social inclusion, the Redistributionist Discourse (RED), was developed in critical British social policy. Though it is fundamentally preoccupied with the causes and characteristics of poverty, it has branched into a critique of inequality and power structures. The second, Moral Underclass Discourse (MUD), identifies the cause of social exclusion with the moral and cultural delinquency of the excluded themselves— the underclass. And the third, Social Integrationist Discourse (SID) prioritizes economic efficiency and social cohesion and links the two through an emphasis on the integrative function of paid work. Though RED, MUD and SID all posit work as a major factor in social integration and all have moral content, 'they differ', Levitas concludes, 'in what the excluded are seen as lacking. To oversimplify, in RED they have no money, in SID they have no work and in MUD they have no morals'.[48]

It would seem that Silver's exposition begins where Levitas' ends, with what she terms as the *solidarity paradigm*.[49] The correct chronology, as Levitas acknowledges,[50] identifies the first use of social inclusion discourse in French social policy of the late 1970s. These policies covered not only unemployed individuals, but also homeless people, substance abusers, mentally disabled individuals and other 'social misfits'.[51] Most intriguingly, however, it is French *republican* thought that is identified as influencing this policy. Thus, social exclusion is understood as the rupture of the social bond (*lien social*) between the individual and society. The solidarity approach emphasizes the socially constructed cultural and moral boundaries between groups and is contrasted with the liberal ideas of individual rights and state responsibilities. A second paradigm identified

---

[46] Handler (n 2 above) 111–22.
[47] Levitas (n 41 above); Silver (n 5 above) 57. See eg Stewart (n 33 above) 1, 4; Lister (n 27 above); Gore (n 1 above); Rodgers (n 5 above).
[48] Levitas (n 41 above) 27.
[49] The three paradigms are described in Silver (n 5 above) 66–69.
[50] Levitas (n 41 above) 21.
[51] Gore (n 1 above) 1.

by Silver is that of *specialization*. More naturally connected to Anglo-American liberalism, exclusion here is understood to be the result of the economic division of labour and the separation between the public and the private spheres. The social order is conceived as networks of voluntary exchanges between autonomous individuals driven by their own interests and motivations. Lastly, the *monopoly* paradigm identifies exclusion to be a result of group boundaries that are enforced by dominant groups that wish to exclude other groups from the market and to perpetuate inequality by controlling the terms of exchange.

The six perspectives offered by the combined approaches of Levitas and Silver, as I understand them, do not exclude one another nor do they claim to capture the full breadth of policies where social inclusion plays an important role. They are, however, quite helpful in understanding changes of emphasis that take place while the terminology remains the same. Thus, Levitas notes an important shift amongst the discourses advocated by proponents of social inclusion—from RED to SID, with distinct remnants of MUD. Indeed, identified as organically deriving from Anglo-American liberalism, it would be surprising if the specialization paradigm, and the somewhat parallel social integrationist discourse, would not be prominent in contemporary welfare-to-work ideology.

The specialization paradigm understands society to prize the rigid separation of public and private spheres, on the one hand, and to emphasize the contractual exchange of rights and obligations, on the other. Individuals are socially excluded, per the specialization paradigm, because they cannot participate in certain activities and in the aforementioned contractual exchange. It is suggested that removing barriers such as illegal discrimination would allow for the natural inclusionary forces to take hold. In terms of welfare-to-work discourse, this trend fits nicely with the (justified) position that welfare cannot be analyzed without due consideration given to the structure of the relevant labour markets. To complete the portrayal, however, one needs to address the evaluative element of SID, to wit the high currency placed on work *in and of itself*. Tony Blair expresses this sentiment when he writes that 'the best defense against social exclusion is finding a job'.[52] And even more ardently, it has been suggested that 'inclusion through labor should remain the cornerstone of every struggle against exclusion'.[53] This position, of course, serves as one of the prominent rationales for welfare-to-work programmes, that 'having a job is a necessary condition of what has been called social dignity'.[54]

Though even the harshest critics of SID-style policies acknowledge that work cannot be ignored in social inclusion analysis, this is far from saying that forced inclusion into the workforce is a necessary, let alone a sufficient, requirement for

---

[52] T Blair, 'Foreword by the Prime Minister' in Social Exclusion Unit *Bridging the Gap: New Opportunities for 16 18 Year Olds Not in Education, Employment or Training* (Cm 4405, 1999) 6.

[53] Rosanvallon (n 3 above) 65.

[54] A Gutmann and D Thompson, *Democracy and Disagreement* (Harvard UP: Cambridge MA, 1996) 293.

social integration. Unemployment may result in social exclusion but employment does not ensure social inclusion. Whether or not it does so depends on the quality of the work offered.[55] Silver's monopoly paradigm is instructive in explaining why this is the case. The objective of preventing 'exclusion' may be at odds with the use of compulsion if it leads to dropout or to an endless series of work-experience programmes. Where the primary aim of the programme is to reduce public expenditure, dropout may not be considered a problem in the short term. However, this does not take into account the ensuing effects which may result from the need to spend in areas such as health or law enforcement. The 'low-pay-no-pay' cycle is exacerbated by welfare-to-work programmes which reinforce and even perpetuate the boundaries that result in labour market segmentation:

on one side, a stable qualified workforce, enjoying a relatively high wage level and invariably unionized in large firms; on the other, an unstable, minimimally qualified, underpaid and weakly protected labour force in small firms, dispensing subsidiary services.[56]

According to Handler and Hasenfeld, studies of the employment realities of welfare leavers find that they experience substantial periods of unemployment and earnings that leave many families in poverty. Most do not receive health insurance, paid sick leave or child care subsidies.[57] As Deakin and Wilkinson argue, 'rather than attempting to stabilize full-time employment, the state now actively encourages the growth of forms of work which, because they are temporary, part-time or simply low-paid, do not provide subsistence-level wages'.[58] And Lucy Williams argues that 'the structure of low-wage labor often creates and contributes to increased dependency of poor single mother in the workplace'.[59] She adds that focusing on government transfers and programmes to integrate individuals into the worksforce paradoxically reinforces the 'free market' discourse and immunizes it to social and political critique.[60] As a result, Silver finds that such policies 'all call into question existing welfare-state arrangements'.[61] This is a bold statement, so I would like to elaborate somewhat on what it refers to.

---

[55] Atkinson (n 8 above) v, 15.

[56] Boltanski and Chiapello (n 9 above) 229; Hills (n 5 above) 235; Silver (n 5 above) 69. The classic exposition of Dual Market Segmentation is found in RD Barron and GM Norris, 'Sexual Divisions and the Dual Labor Market' in DL Barker and S Allen (eds), *Dependence and Exploitation in Work and Marriage* (Longmans: London, 1976) 47.

[57] J Handler and Y Hasenfeld, *Blame Welfare, Ignore Poverty and Inequality* (CUP: Cambridge, 2007) 63.

[58] Deakin and Wilkinson (n 19 above) 194; see similarly D Finn, 'The Role of Contracts and the Private Sector in Delivering Britain's "Employment First" Welfare State' in E Sol and M Westerveld (eds), *Contractualism in Employment Services* (Aspen: The Hague, 2005) 101.

[59] L Williams, 'Welfare and Legal Entitlements: The Social Roots of Poverty' in D Kairys (ed), *The Politics of Law* (3rd edn, Basic Books: New York, 1998) 569, 576.

[60] L Williams, 'Beyond Labour Law's Parochialism: A Re-envisioning of the Discourse of Redistribution' in J Conaghan, R Fischl and K Klare (eds), *Labour Law in an Era of Globalization* (OUP: Oxford, 2002) 93.

[61] Silver (n 5 above) 77.

While the ideology behind current programmes identifies an 'underclass' that is created as a result of labour market exclusion, the attention of critics is increasingly turned to an 'underclass created by the increasing demands for the unemployed to accept lower benefits and demeaning, low-paid work'.[62] Indeed, welfare-to-work practices, being both conditional and coercive, exhibit not only the opportunity for inclusion, but also the threat of increased exclusion. They may expand opportunities to insiders while arousing only false expectations with those on the outside.[63] First, there is the inevitable exclusion of those who cannot, for whatever reason, comply with the rules.[64] This is why some have followed TH Marshall in insisting that citizenship cannot be based on any but the most general obligations, such as paying taxes.[65] Those who need the most protection (eg part-timers, immigrants, participants in the shadow economy) may be the victim rather than the beneficiaries of regulatory schemes.[66] They are in danger of boarding an 'exclusion trajectory' and suffering even more stigmatization due to their failure to comply with rules that target them. 'The chief concern', then, is that 'sanctions might exacerbate rather than ameliorate the social exclusion' of claimants.[67]

Second, segmentation of the labour market refers to the fact that identifiable groups remain a secondary workforce where jobs are ill-paid, offer no job security and require no skills.[68] Concern that labour markets will be transformed, in effect, into two different labour markets was expressed in the 1994 EU White Paper *Growth, Competitiveness, Employment*.[69] And yet, while exclusion *from* the labour market receives much more attention, exclusion *within* the labour market (or from the 'good' labour market) is not adequately addressed.[70] This is unfortunate, since recent research shows that the 'stickiness' or 'trap' of the low wage labour market is becoming an increasingly troubling phenomenon, especially for welfare leavers. While other participants in the labour market may leave their

---

[62] Clasen, Gould and Vincent (n 7 above) 14.
[63] Boltanski and Chiapello (n 9 above) 233.
[64] R Plant, 'Citizenship and Social Security' (2003) 24 Fiscal Studies 153, 164.
[65] Handler (n 2 above) 265; TH Marshall, 'Citizenship and Social Class' in TH Marshall and T Bottomore, *Citizenship and Social Class* (Pluto: London, 1992); R Dahrendorf, 'The Changing Quality of Citizenship' in B van Steenbergen (ed), *The Condition of Citizenship* (Sage: London, 1994) 10.
[66] For a different aspect of this argument see G Standing, *Global Labour Flexibility* (Macmillan: Basingstoke, 1999) 295–98.
[67] D Finn, 'The "Employment First" Welfare State: Lessons from the New Deal for Young People' (2003) 37 Social Policy and Administration 709, 719.
[68] See Attas and de-Shalit (n 31 above) 313–18.
[69] European Commission, *Growth, Competitiveness, Employment* (Office for Official Publications of the European Communities: Luxemburg, 1994) s 8; see Deakin and Wilkinson (n 19 above) 197.
[70] J Handler, 'Social Citizenship and Workfare in the US and Western Europe: from Status to Contract' (2003) 13 Journal of European Social Policy 229; Rodgers (n 5 above) 44–46; G Rodgers, 'The Design of Policy Against Exclusion' in Rodgers, Gore and Figueiredo (n 1 above) 253, 256; A McKnight, 'Low-Paid Work' in Hills, Le Grand D Piachaud (n 5 above) 97.

initial jobs for higher wages, welfare recipients' job records reveal a weak positive association between the length of labour force participation and earnings.[71] Indeed, one recent study concludes that after two years of leaving welfare, 'the effects of temporary agency placements on the probability of earnings above welfare thresholds are negative'.[72] And yet, 'highlighting the selection process that has gradually made it possible to exclude from stable employment the least qualified...makes it possible to pave the way for a search for policies to counteract exclusion'.[73]

The activation or 'work first' strategy that underlies welfare-to-work programmes assumes that workers will gain skills and knowledge to qualify for better paying jobs. However, requiring claimants to accept any job, including offers for temporary positions, risks exacerbating labour casualisation.[74] Contrary to what some have argued, research has shown that requirements such as workfare have *reduced* participants' capacity and desire to take on training and have interrupted the job search process.[75] Indeed, there is growing evidence that these programmes are proving to be a barrier to employment mobility, as fewer workers are moving up the economic ladder.[76] One study shows that 'the percentage of single parents participating in low waged work in the United States rose from 60.4 per cent to 69 per cent since the social protection reductions in 1996'.[77]

Interestingly, this dynamic has led many to revisit the Marxist conceptualization of the unemployed as an 'industrial reserve army' of labour whose task in a post-industrial, capitalist labour market is to ensure that wage labourers are kept in check.[78] Contemporary writers have even argued that the social and economic position occupied by the unemployed in Marx's analysis is now taken by the socially excluded.[79] Piven and Cloward, in the chapter added to the updated edition of their *Regulating the Poor*, argue that 'desperation pits the unemployed against the still employed, thus weakening labor's market power'.[80]

---

[71] Handler and Hasenfeld (n 57 above) 249.
[72] D Autor and S Houseman, 'Temporary Agency Employment as a Way Out of Poverty?' (2005) 26. <http://www.upjohninstitute.org/publications/wp/05-123.pdf> (25 July 2007)
[73] Boltanski and Chiapello (n 9 above) 235.
[74] Standing (n 66 above) 237.
[75] ibid 330–32.
[76] Handler (n 2 above) 31, 56; Standing (n 66 above) 326–32; B Barry, *Why Social Justice Matters* (Polity: Cambridge, 2005) (n 21 above) 61; R Salais, 'Towards a Capability Approach' in J Zeitlin and DM Trubek (eds), *Governing Work and Welfare in a New Economy* (OUP: Oxford, 2003) 317, 341.
[77] L Williams, 'Poor Women's Work Experience: Gaps in the Work/Family Discussion' in J Conaghan and K Rittich (eds), *Labour Law, Work and Family: Critical and Comparative Perspectives* (OUP: Oxford, 2005) 202–3.
[78] K Marx, *Capital* (S Moore and E Aveling (trans), Swan: London, 1887, rpnt 1938) 642–65; FF Piven and RA Cloward, *Regulating the Poor* (Updated Edition, Vintage, New York, 1993) 5.
[79] Byrne (n 17 above) 44–59; P Ormerod, 'Unemployment and Social Exclusion: An Economic View' in Rhodes and Meny (n 34 above) 23, 32–35; And similarly G Esping-Andersen, *The Three Worlds of Welfare Capitalism* (Polity: Cambridge, 1990) 160.
[80] Piven and Cloward (n 78 above) 355.

However, the monolithic analysis of the unemployed as a 'stagnant pool'[81] of labour is not an accurate description of the modern labour market *as a whole*. The employer, after all, wishes to preserve a reliable, skillful and loyal workforce and avoid the transaction and training costs, along with the break of trust and motivation that are related with frequent changes in personnel.[82]

If the insight of dual market segmentation is employed, however, we find that the above description is accurate only with relation to the primary segment of the workforce. The role of the reserve army of labour, 'constantly changing positions with those in low status employment, and serving to keep the power of the working class in check'[83] is much more plausible insofar as the secondary segment is concerned.[84] In this segment, the use of contingent workers as a strategy to cheapen the workforce, weaken the economic security of workers and to drag down wages is much more accurate a description. While the primary sector consists of permanent employees who enjoy opportunities for promotion, training, pensions and fringe benefits, a periphery of temporary, casual or contract workers is employed in a manner that allows flexible adjusting for change in demand.

In tune with the critical perspective offered by the monopoly paradigm, one may suggest that these policies solidify strategies that serve to exclude people from gaining access to job rents and from a share of benefits from such rents. In a poignant turn of phrase, Barbara Ehrenreich argues that it is not the poor who should feel shame for *their* dependency. Rather, they are the major philantropists of society, and it is the well to do who are dependent on their privation.[85] This accusation is accentuated by a comparison of the distribution of earnings in the United States, Britain and France. Following OECD definitions that view low-paying jobs as two-thirds of the median income and high paying jobs as 50 per cent above the median income, the United States has well over twice the rate of individuals employed in low paying jobs than France (at 33 per cent of the labour force, the United States has doubled the rate measured a decade ago), and a 50 per cent higher rate of individuals employed in high paying jobs, while Britain ranks between the two.[86] As noted below, these data coincide

---

[81] S Webb and B Webb, *The Public Organisation of the Labour Market: Being Part Two of the Minority Report of the Poor Law Commission* (Longmans, Green and Co: London, 1909) 200: 'Every wharfinger, each contractor, each manufacturer, each giver-out of work to be done at home, each builder's foreman, tends thus to accumulate his own reserve of labour, his own "stagnant pool" from which he draws to satisfy the maximum demands of his business'

[82] H Collins, *Justice in Dismissal* (OUP: Oxford, 1992) and citations there; also H Collins, KD Ewing and A McColgan, *Labour Law Text and Materials* (Hart: Oxford, 2001) 479 ff.

[83] Burchardt, Le Grand and Piachaud (n 15 above) 2.

[84] Barry (n 76 above) 205–7; A Paz-Fuchs, 'Welfare Reform Between Capitalism and Patriarchy' (2004) 10 Labor, Society and Law 339 [in Hebrew].

[85] B Ehrenreich, *Nickle and Dimed: On (Not) Getting By in America* (Henry Holt: New York, 2001) 221.

[86] H Boushey and others, *Understanding Low Wage Work in the United States* (CEPR: Washington DC, 2007); G Burtless, 'Social Policy for the Working Poor: U.S. Reform in a Cross-National Perspective' in N Gilbert and A Parent (eds), *Welfare Reform: A Comparative Assessment of the French and U.S. Experiences* (International Social Security Series vol 10,

with the level of coerciveness that characterizes the respective country's welfare-to-work policies.

Without access to the job security awarded to workers in the primary sector, workers in the secondary sectors are systematically marginalized between the secondary labour market and the structure and rules of the benefit system.[87] As Simon Deakin notes, 'deregulation of terms and conditions of employment goes hand in hand with the restriction of the conditions under which social security benefits are made available'.[88] And indeed, it has been pointed out that, in a variety of jurisdictions, workfare participants function as apt replacements for service workers such as nurses and sanitation workers in a manner detrimental for the employment conditions of the original workers.[89] Moreover, the mirror image of this claim is also apparent, if we remember that in the 1960s and 1970s income maintenance had insulated wages from the effects of rising unemployment and workers could consider employing their right to strike without fear of losing entitlements to food stamps. This situation, as noted, changed dramatically when income support contracted and strikers were no longer eligible for food stamps.[90]

It is conceivable that current welfare-to-work programmes will succeed in creating 'economic inclusion and social disinclusion'[91] by moving the boundary from one that exists between the working person and the unemployed to that which separates workers of different status. This assessment is somewhat similar to the conclusion that the Poor Law was exacerbating the problem it was set to deal with by 'reinforcing, and not averting, destitution'.[92]

What of the rationales for work requirements that are not based on labour market analysis? As noted throughout, inclusion into the workforce is never advocated solely by reference to income. Rather, the moral element of welfare-to-work programmes has always granted a sense of urgency to the policies, as if they are not only a vehicle to deal with unemployment, but rather a mechanism through which many of society's ills (drug abuse, teenage and out-of-wedlock pregnancy, ill health, homelessness and so on) may be addressed. If attending to these problems is within society's mandate and interest, one may understand the

---

Transaction Publishers: London, 2004) 3, 21–23; European Foundation for the Improvement of the Living and Working Conditions, *Low-Wage Workers and the Working Poor* (September 2002) <http://www.eurofound.europa.eu/eiro/2002/08/study/tn0208101s.html > (15 April 2007)

[87] B Jordan, *A Theory of Poverty and Social Exclusion* (Polity: London, 1996) 132, 148, 151; Rodgers (n 5 above) 44.

[88] S Deakin, 'The Capability Concept and the Evolution of European Social Policy' in M Dougan and E Spaventa (eds), *Social Welfare and EU Law* (Hart: Oxford, 2005) 3; also S Deakin and F Wilkinson, 'Labour Law, Social Security and Economic Inequality' (1991) 15 Cambridge J of Economics 125, 136–40.

[89] M Diller, 'Working Without a Job: The Social Meaning of the New Workforce' (1998) 9 Stanford L and Society Rev 19, 29–31; Attas and de-Shalit (n 31 above) 319.

[90] Piven and Cloward (n 78 above) 354–62.

[91] Rosanvallon (n 3 above) 93.

[92] Deakin and Wilkinson (n 19 above) 111.

intense moral element in welfare-to-work programmes as some form of return to the French origins of social inclusion rhetoric, as expressed by Silver's solidarity paradigm.

In this context, it is interesting to note that the French scheme, aptly named *Revenu Minimum d'Insertion* (RMI), requires recipients to sign a *'contrat d'insertion'* if they wished to receive residual benefits. As such, this approach seems uncomfortably close to the version of the contractual discourse criticized above.[93] To reach such a conclusion, however, would be premature.

At the moment, the U.S. and France 'present two contrasting, even opposing types of reciprocal approaches in social assistance: the U.S. approach can be described as workfare, while the French approach is *insertion*'.[94] While the former is decentralized, category-based and focuses on the deserving and non-deserving 'dependents', the latter is centralized and essentially unified, and its subject is the insertion of the excluded.[95] While the American model, as noted throughout, is based on the notion that rights carry duties, the French model's approach to poverty and social exclusion 'is addressed not from the perspective of an underclass, but from a general principle of national solidarity',[96] where the contract becomes not a vehicle through which duties are imposed, but rather a 'visible symbol of the state's effective commitment towards the excluded'.[97] Lastly, and fundamentally, while the American welfare-to-work programme targets labour market exclusion, the French model addresses not only professional, but also *social* exclusion.

This process has been enhanced with the adoption of the 1998 *Loi d'orientation sur la lutte contre les exclusions* (LOLE—Orientation Law on the Battle Against Exclusion). LOLE extends new resources to RMI schemes so as to achieve both occupational and social inclusion in a wide range of life aspects: employment, education, health, debt and even culture. The first article of the LOLE is strikingly different when compared to the first article of the PRWORA, cited above: 'The combat against exclusions is a national imperative based on the respect of the equal dignity of all human beings and a priority of all public policies of the nation'.[98]

One may suggest that too much is made of these differences and that the decline in public support for income maintenance in France may advance the country 'further down the road from income maintenance to workfare'.[99] That may well be the case. At the moment, however, it is important to address the (somewhat

---

[93] Ch 1.C above.
[94] S Morel, 'Workfare and *Insertion*: How the U.S. and French Models of Social Assistance Have Been Transformed' in Gilbert (n 99 above) 93.
[95] ibid 95.
[96] S Paugam, 'Poverty and Social Exclusion' in Rhodes and Meny (n 34 above) 41, 58.
[97] Morel (n 94 above) 124; Boltanski and Chiapello (n 9 above) 252.
[98] *Plan National d'Action Français Contre la Pauvreté et l'Exclusion Sociale* (2001) cited in Morel (n 94 above) 115.
[99] N Gilbert, 'Welfare Policy in the United States. The Road from Income Maintenance to Workfare' in Gilbert and Parent (n 86 above) 55, 64; similarly Rosanvallon (n 3 above) 84, 88–89.

ironic) position that stresses the surprising similarities between the two programmes. First, it is suggested that the new universal obligations in American welfare reform, such as the removal of all exemptions from work requirements (such as those that used to be granted to mothers of young children), mark a shift away from the selective model and on towards a universalist, inclusionist logic. And second, that the moral facets in American reform may be viewed as resembling 'social insertion' policies in France.[100]

Though it is quite true that 'more research should be done on the distinct significance of the contract in both countries',[101] it is already clear that the Anglo-American interpretation of the social contract is as remote from its continental version as their historical antecedents were: 'Although contractual language was also used to justify British insertion requirements, it reflected Lockean ideas more than Rousseau's solidarity conception of the social contract'.[102] As noted throughout this book, tying benefits to obligations undermines the role that rights play in practical reasoning and paves the way for behavioral requirements in workfare regimes whose motto is 'rights require duties'.[103] In MUD terminology, the way to force the poor to accept responsibility for themselves and their family is to make welfare authoritative and conditional on training, on accepting low-paid work and on being responsible parents. This is the version of the New Social Contract in Anglo-American social policy that is perceived as the mechanism towards successful social inclusion.[104] Its diluted perception of rights of beneficiaries and duties on the part of the state situate it, at least for the moment, as fundamentally different from its continental counterpart.

It is undeniably true that moral and social norms have to be taken into account when considering work, welfare and family. This is not the same, however, as accepting the *prevailing* norms that pertain to these (and other) institutions as justified.[105] As Hugh Collins argues, the collaboration of equality principles and social inclusion objectives allows one to reassess existing attitudes and patterns.[106] The flexibility of social exclusion permits adaptation to changing realities in society itself such as the increasing rates of women in the workplace, the changes that the 'traditional' family has undergone and the transformation in attitudes to spare time, travel, health and education, to name but a few. All these suggest that though the deep, moral sentiments may be laudable, there is a danger that they will be replaced with a fetishism for their empty shell: the preservation of a marriage for its own sake, the compulsion of work or attendance in education,

---

[100] Morel (n 94 above) 130–31.
[101] ibid 131.
[102] Silver and Wilkinson (n 20 above) 293.
[103] Silver and Wilkinson (n 20 above) 286; Jordan (n 87 above) 206–9; Lund (n 23 above) 195–96.
[104] Jordan (n 87 above) 206; P Agulnik, T Burchardt and M Evans 'Prevention and Response in the British Welfare State' in Hills, Le Grand and Piachaud (n 5 above) 155, 162.
[105] Deakin (n 88 above) 13–15.
[106] Collins (n 29 above)16.

and so on. Commenting on the requirement to compel fathers to assume responsibility and support their children,[107] Christopher Jencks explains:

> Poor mothers often break up with the father of their children because he is physically abusive. Once the break comes, they want him out of their life. If a state agency forces an angry, abusive man to start paying child support, he may reassert his parental rights and begin harassing the mother again. Fanning these embers may not, in fact, be such a good policy.[108]

Apart from shedding light on an unexpected attribute of what may be termed 'enforced responsibility', this remark directs us towards following the true value that should be advanced by the policies, as opposed to placing the intermediate mechanisms on a pedestal. Though the emphasis on education and training distinguishes Britain from the American idea of 'work first', both manifest clear conditionality of benefits and compulsory training and work programmes. Such traits have raised the likelihood that many will opt out of the system and rely on family, friends, begging or crime.[109]

Another point further distinguishes current programmes from the solidarity paradigm. The solidarity paradigm imposed an obligation on the *state* to support the insertion of the excluded.[110] Though it is not suggested here that this paradigm be accepted as a whole, it is important to clarify that an uncritical emphasis placed on existing *social* (moral and cultural) norms, on the one hand, and on *individual* responsibility, on the other hand, was far from what advocates of these social inclusion policies originally intended. Current programmes only superficially embrace the moral underpinnings of the solidarity paradigm while, at the same time, they place a much stronger emphasis on an individualistic, contractual approach. This allows policy-makers to elevate moral standards beyond appraisal, while simultaneously placing the onus on the individual to take the necessary measures to adapt to these norms. Such norms, then, are employed as a vehicle en route to the justification of coercive measures, paramount in welfare-to-work programmes. This is, perhaps, what Goodin refers to when he argues that, in a sense, 'the state, as presently conceived, is *too inclusive*' since it 'claims a monopoly on the power to legitimate any other sources of social succour'.[111]

Therefore, the process may be described in the following manner: moral and cultural norms that putatively underlie the solidarity paradigm identify who are included and who are excluded. It is submitted that the excluded should be brought within society's bounds. Before moving to do so, however, we find

---

[107] See eg *Zablocki v Redhail* 434 US 374 (1978).
[108] C Jencks, 'The Hidden Paradox of Welfare Reform' (1997) 32 American Prospect 36; See S Holmes and C Sunstein, *The Cost of Rights* (WW Norton: London, 1999) chs 9–11; Morel (n 94 above) 129.
[109] Agulnik, Burchardt and Evans (n 104 above) 155, 162.
[110] Silver (n 5 above) 76.
[111] R Goodin, 'Inclusion and Exclusion' (1996) 37 Archives Européennes de Sociologie 343, 363.

that the perception of individuals as rejecting society's shared appreciation for work, family and the like (though, as numerous authors have pointed out, this is often a fallacious assumption)[112] diverts the attention to the personal traits of the excluded, rather than to the structures that lead to that exclusion. This process leads to a lack of empathy that makes it easier to stigmatize and dehumanize excluded groups such as the unemployed.[113] This move is important for, in some cases (the American welfare-to-work programmes being a prominent example) policy-makers prefer, at this point, to employ the individualistic specialization paradigm. As discussed, this paradigm demands a balance between rights offered and duties demanded.

The steps as described assure that welfare claimants arrive at the negotiating table in a precarious position. Their exclusion is not only a descriptive assessment but an evaluative one as well. They are not looked at as having legitimate claims on society's resources, but rather it is the generosity of society that allows for the offer of benefits and job opportunities.[114] If the claimants now refuse the conditions offered to them, they are recategorized as not only excluded, but as also *undeserving* of society's assistance towards inclusion. By making 'exclusion and inclusion entirely a matter of law',[115] this process, as mentioned, leads to the danger of *further* exclusion.

This issue cannot be overemphasized. A decade into the operation of welfare-to-work programmes reveals a disturbing picture. Instead of mitigating social differences and reducing barriers to social mobility, these programmes raise additional difficulties and, in effect, solidify social and class structures. Thus, a close look at reported programme successes reveals that in many cases the clients behind the numbers were those who were already closest to the labour market and required minimum treatment. This process, known as 'creaming', is particularly prevalent where welfare services have been privatized and private companies depend on positive numbers to increase their profits.[116] But creaming is not the only problematic characteristic of programme practices. Indeed, it is quite telling that the mirror practice has been awarded a term of its own. The Australian term 'parking', which has already gained adherents in other countries,[117] refers to the treatment

---

[112] See eg Walker (n 26 above) 116.

[113] Barry (n 14 above) 25–26; Lund (n 23 above) 206.

[114] N Fraser and L Gordon, 'Civil Citizenship Against Social Citizenship? On the Ideology of Contract Versus Charity' in B van Steenbergen (ed), *The Condition of Citizenship* (Sage: London, 1994) 90.

[115] J Shklar, *American Citizenship: The Quest for Inclusion* (Harvard UP: Cambridge, 1991) 92.

[116] M Considine, 'The Reform that Never Ends: Quasi Markets and Employment Services in Australia' in E Sol and M Westerveld (eds), *Contractualism in Employment Services: A New Form of Welfare State Governance* (Kluwer Law: The Hague, 2005) 41; and see my review of the book in (2007) 2 European Rev of Contract L 232.

[117] D Finn, 'The Role of Contracts and the Private Sector in Delivering Britain's 'Employment First' Welfare State' in Sol and Westerveld (n 116 above) 101, 114; L Struyven and K Verhoest, 'The Problem of Agency at Organisational Level and Street Level: The Case of the Flemish Public Employment Service) in Sol and Westerveld (n 116 above) 325, 347.

(or lack thereof) of those deemed unemployable, including refusal of training or other support to overcome acute employment barriers. Thus, workfare schemes seem to have a 'disproportionate impact on disadvantaged groups, especially ethnic minorities' while government data reveal particularly high rates of sanctions in areas of chronic job shortage, 'indicating that those suffering most from the vagaries of the market economy are also those who are the most penalized'.[118] And so, institutional characteristics, distinct from but quite related to the ideological or the administrative facets of welfare-to-work programmes, may well be working against the stated objectives of the programmes and may be exacerbating the situation of the most vulnerable.

Another matter should be mentioned here. Chapter 3 noted that while attention has been given mainly to supposedly high rates of people who fraudulently receive benefits (vertical efficiency), very little notice has been directed at the phenomenon of low take-up rates (horizontal efficiency). This occurrence is all the more intriguing (and troubling) when the causes and effects surrounding it are addressed. By causes, I refer to the fact that the rates of benefit take-up vary according to the characteristic of the benefits in question. Unconditional benefits such as child support, for example, enjoy a take-up rate of close to 100 per cent, while take-up for income maintenance may be as low as 20 per cent. Interviews with deserving claimants clearly show that the stigma that society attaches to these latter benefits serves as a major deterrent in their considerations whether or not to apply for benefits. By effects, I refer to the vicious circle that is thus created: stigma leads to low rates of take-up which, in turn, may exacerbate social exclusion that the benefits themselves are intended to alleviate.[119]

Bringing this section together with the previous one, we find how the analysis of social policy fits neatly within the conceptual platform discussed and criticized hitherto. Instead of relating to equality, social inclusion in its new form highlights reciprocity, contractual obligations and responsibility. SID also entails a different understanding of responsibility than the one that was advocated for in the previous chapter as most befitting egalitarian theory. Since inclusion is achieved through paid work, individuals must actively seek work and hold on to it once acquired. As advocates of the incentive theory of responsibility would argue, successful inclusion turns into a matter of individual responsibility, so the right to be included is transformed into the duty to be included.[120] Thus, Pierre Rosanvallon follows Giddens in arguing for social rights to be 'reinterpreted as a contract articulating rights and obligations'—a 'contract of inclusion'.[121] Under such a conceptualization, social inclusion distances itself not only from equality, but also from the possibility that it would provide a basis for an argument in favour of welfare rights. And, as noted, the duty to be included is tantamount,

---

[118] Vincent-Jones (n 4 above) 242.
[119] Silver and Wilkinson (n 20 above) 288; Atkinson (n 8 above) 18, 22.
[120] Levitas (n 41 above) 178–57.
[121] Rosanvallon (n 3 above) 87–89.

under this paradigm, to the duty to work. Indeed, Guy Standing identifies the 20th century as 'the century of the labouring man'.[122]

> It began with calls echoing around the world for the rights of labour—the right to improved social status, dignity and autonomy...By mid-century...reformers were demanding the right to labour, seeking to ennoble the drudgery of being in a job and hinging everything on 'Full Employment'...The century is ending with libertarians and many others advocating and introducing policies to strengthen the duty to labour, the state-enforced obligation to obtain entitlements and to be treated as citizens and receive state benefits.

But this need not be the case. It may well be argued that under the objectives set *by proponents of social inclusion themselves*, SID (let alone MUD) discourse does not fit the bill. If divisiveness, detachment and disenfranchisement are to be addressed with the seriousness they deserve, it would be difficult to show how forcing individuals to accept low-paying jobs on the periphery of society (albeit within the labour market) would do anything other than cement these problems. Contrariwise, achieving equal opportunity for social inclusion requires structural (legal and social) changes that enhance the individual's real freedom and that affirm society's equal and unconditional commitment to each of its citizens. In the sphere of welfare-to-work, this objective is made viable through the help of recognizing welfare rights.

D Social Inclusion, Poverty and Welfare Rights

The emphasis to this point has been on providing sufficient protection for the individual who is faced with burdensome and potentially unfair choices. It is now important to show why the recognition of welfare rights that would lead to a moderation of the conditions for entitlement would also serve the purposes of social inclusion policies in general which are (justifiably, when understood properly) cited as the prime rationales for welfare-to-work programmes. It is contended that a society that takes account of welfare rights is 'likely to reduce social exclusion, increase individual welfare, promote social justice and, through rendering the opportunities open to all society's members more similar, likely to increase social solidarity'.[123]

1 Basic Needs and Social Inclusion

The traditional understanding of social exclusion emphasized the strong connection to poverty and to the inadequate provision of basic necessities.[124]

---

[122] Standing (n 66 above) 337.
[123] Le Grand (n 14 above) 5.
[124] Room (n 7 above) 4–7.

Indeed, it has been argued that poverty and exclusion 'formed the core logic of welfare-state construction and the creation of various welfare institutions at the regional and national level'.[125] Research has confirmed, even before social exclusion terminology became popular, that certain levels of resources are necessary for playing the roles, participating in the relationships and following the customs expected of members in a society.[126] Indeed, an early proclamation by the European Commission identified persons suffering from poverty as 'persons whose resources...are so limited as to exclude them from the minimum acceptable way of life in the Member State in which they live'.[127] Following the French *contrat d'instertion*, mentioned above, the European Council has recently endorsed a policy document that explicitly views poverty and social exclusion as inseparable.[128] When the employment of social exclusion terminology increased, the Observatory on National Policies to Combat Social Exclusion defined it 'in relation to...a basic standard of living and occupational opportunities of the society'.[129]

It has been argued that without legal rights guaranteed to minimal levels of income, health, housing and decent employment opportunities, individuals born into poverty through no fault of their own 'will interpret the social contract as a giant swindle perpetrated by the well-to do'.[130] We are now closer to an understanding of the strong connection between poverty, social exclusion and limited choices and opportunities that derive from a failure to recognize social rights. Walker sums up this point, arguing that:

It is clear, therefore, that the seeds of social exclusion are inherent within the very experience of poverty: increased social isolation, reduced morale, deviant behaviours and even the experience of ostracism that are all linked more or less directly to the limited choice and restricted opportunities imposed by inadequate resources.[131]

Benefits that are dependent on controversial and stigmatizing requirements lead many individuals to forsake the benefits offered and drop out of the formal labour market and the benefit system, with all the consequences that follow. This premise has led many to argue that an unconditional basic income is the only feasible *inclusive* institutional structure for balancing the market-oriented interests of the better-off with the protection of the poor, and thus linking efficiency

---

[125] Paugam (n 96 above) 45.
[126] P Townsend, *Poverty in the United Kingdom* (Mushroom: Nottingham, 1978) 1; P Townsend, *The International Analysis of Poverty* (Harvester: New York, 1993) 36; Jordan (n 87 above) 93–96.
[127] European Commission, *On Specific Community Action to Combat Poverty* (19 December 1984) cited in Handler (n 2 above) 122.
[128] Rodgers (n 70 above) 258; European Commission, *Joint Report on Social Exclusion: Part I—The European Union Executive Summary* (European Commission: Brussels, 2001) 6 <http://europa.eu.int/comm/employment_social/soc-prot/soc-incl/15223/part1_en.pdf> (7 June 2005).
[129] G Room, *The Observatory on National Policies to Combat Social Exclusion* (2nd Report Commission for European Communities: Brussels, 1992) 14.
[130] Holmes and Sunstein (n 108 above) 193.
[131] Walker (n 26 above) 116.

with social justice.¹³² The arguments for and against complete unconditionality of benefits will take us too far astray and addressing the debate is not necessary here. What should be noted is that if the objectives of social inclusion are to be realized, it is necessary to recognize the importance of legal rights to minimal income, medical care, housing and education. The fact that in many Western societies such basic goods are often allocated through the market suggests that what is needed is a structure that guarantees access to their provision, rather than changing the benefit structure in a manner that emulates the market by focusing on contractual ideology as its central pillar.¹³³

2 Welfare Rights as Strategies Towards Social Inclusion

The strong connection of social exclusion to welfare levels, along with the inherent importance attributed to agency within the idea of social exclusion, permit the consideration of both rights and welfare levels within a single framework.¹³⁴ Some have even suggested interpreting social exclusion as the unequal *access to rights* and that the purpose of social inclusion policies lies in alleviating this disparity.¹³⁵ This line of thought seems to juxtapose the theory developed around the concept of social citizenship with the idea of social inclusion. Thus, one may find the requirement that full members of the community should be 'equal with respect to the rights and duties with which the status [of citizenship] is endowed'¹³⁶ to similarly apply to the objectives of social inclusion policies.

As noted, while civil and political rights are necessary conditions for opening up paths towards participation in the relevant political, social, economic and moral realms, they are not sufficient conditions. Those same rights may be left unused because access to them is hindered by lack of material resources. Elizabeth Anderson argues that 'a just society must assure to all citizens effective access to the social bases of equal standing as citizens'¹³⁷ and that welfare-to-work provisions fail that criterion by victimizing the least advantaged classes in society. A right to welfare that is anchored in the egalitarian ideal may present a joint claim, both to resources and 'to take part in forms of procedural and institutionalised interactions'.¹³⁸

---

[132] Jordan (n 87 above) 149; B Barry, 'Justice, Freedom and Basic Income' in H Siebert (ed), *The Ethical Foundations of the Market Economy* (Mohr: Tobingen, 1994) 75; P van Parijs, 'Competing Justifications for Basic Income' in van Parijs (ed), *Arguing for Basic Income* (Verso: London, 1992); P van Parijs, *Real Freedom for All* (Clarendon: Oxford, 1995); T Walter *Basic Income* (Boyars: London, 1998); Handler (n 2 above) 272.
[133] Barry (n 14 above) 29.
[134] Rodgers (n 5 above) 48, 54.
[135] Gore (n 1 above) 22; Rodgers (n 5 above) 48–50; Room (n 7 above) 6.
[136] TH Marshall, 'Citizenship and Social Class' in Marshall and Bottomore (n 65 above) 18.
[137] E Anderson, 'Welfare, Work Requirements and Dependant Care' (2004) 21 J of Applied Philosophy 243, 251.
[138] Deakin (n 88 above) 17.

So we find that, though it is but one consequence of the inability to exercise rights, social exclusion may be an important manifestation of the denial of social justice in general.[139] This still does not imply, however, that social rights are required in order to ensure that proper inclusion will take place. Some have argued, for example, that coercive and paternalistic approaches would be at least as efficient in achieving these goals.[140] As explained in chapter 2, despite titles such as the 'New Paternalism', this approach is as old as welfare provision itself.[141]

Paternalistic approaches, however, are feasible only if the 'agency' element of social inclusion strategies is minimized to a point of elimination. If any weight is to be given to social contract rhetoric employed by promoters of welfare-to-work policies, welfare rights are necessary to balance out strategies that exclude people from gaining access to jobs and job rents by allowing them to participate in the labour market *on their own terms*, at least to a reasonable extent. Only then can a 'self-enforcing social contract' be established.[142] The requirement that a person accept any job offer, even when it is clear that the reason for refusal is unrewarding pay and conditions, gives the interest society has in filling 'dirty jobs'[143] an immeasurable importance in relation to the claimant's preferences. The multidimensional characteristics of social inclusion allow it to take into account factors beyond social structure or economic situation. Its Janus perspectives—both forward and backward looking—undermine short-term, short-sighted suggestions. These perspectives correspond to the theoretical importance that serious inclusion policy should attribute not only to history, but also to biography; not only to structure, but also to autonomy.

While the individualistic approach has routinely been used (and abused) in an effort to attribute responsibility even when such ascription was misplaced, true respect for autonomy that is at the heart of successful inclusion policies recognizes the importance of respecting the choices that individuals make.[144] Inclusion into various structures—economic, social or moral— is expected to be short-lived and its full potential unfulfilled if it is not achieved by way of mutual effort and consent by both the society and the individual. 'Inclusion contracts', then, will not empower the clients by ignoring their individual needs. In such cases, voices 'become echoes rather than grievances and demands'.[145] This should not be taken to imply, however, that inclusion is irrelevant to empowerment. Quite the contrary. Empowerment requires connectedness, and not only lack of helplessness.

---

[139] Barry (n 14 above) 13–14.
[140] L Mead, *Beyond Entitlement* (Free Press: NY, 1986); L Mead, *The New Paternalism* (Brookings: Washington DC, 1997).
[141] cf Rosanvallon (n 3 above) 103–4 who argues that today the state promotes social forms for financial reasons, while in the past it promoted moral values.
[142] Jordan (n 87 above) 149; Handler (n 2 above) 273.
[143] Mead 1986 (n 140 above) 69, 153.
[144] S White, 'What's Wrong with Workfare' (2004) 21 J of Applied Philosophy 271, 273–79.
[145] Handler (n 2 above) 255.

It entails a person's awareness of her place as an actor within the social and political community and a recognition of her competence within this structure.[146]

It transpires, first, that current efforts to reduce social inclusion into labour market inclusion must be rejected. But, moreover, if inclusion policies are to succeed, they must exhibit an open-minded, flexible and non-coercive approach. Though society may demarcate the legitimate paths to inclusion, it should allow the individual to choose between them. Without guaranteeing an individual's basic security, 'the demand for responsibility seems eminently unfair'.[147] And, as emphasized in previous chapters, institutional respect for an individual's choice is best materialized in this case through the recognition of welfare rights. Doing so would lead to a viable, long-lasting form of social inclusion and to a shift in the emphasis of welfare-to-work policies: away from a focus on moving a person into any job (usually low-paid work supplemented by benefits) and on towards helping individuals move off benefits altogether, into financial independence and participation in the various realms that a society has to offer.

In addition to the impact that a right to welfare has on the conditions that may be placed on benefits, some moral and social consequences are usually seen to derive from the fact that a right is recognized. Significant amongst these is the stigma associated with benefit claiming.[148] In most cases, referring to a right serves as an appropriate counter-argument to moral condemnation, especially (and most trivially) to condemnation that takes the form of 'what right do you have to do that?'.[149] It is evident that pointing to a right should silence the objector. The reason for this is anchored in the idea of the right, as discussed in the first chapter. As proponents of the interest theory of rights have justifiably insisted, rights, in the first instance, are a manifestation of society's conclusion that an individual's interest presents a sufficient reason to hold someone else to a duty. This reasoning would imply that if society recognizes a certain right, it would be paradoxical to charge that a bone-fide use (as opposed to abuse) of the right should give rise to stigma or moral condemnation. Frank Field acknowledged this connection, arguing that 'Welfare should be given as a right and free of any restrictions or stigma'.[150]

The two aspects discussed in this subsection are, unsurprisingly, connected. Social exclusion, as discussed, pays considerable attention to the practical manifestation of rights. The stigma associated with claiming benefits has been shown to lead to low level of take-up. It is argued here, then, that recognition of a right to welfare would result in higher levels of take-up and, consequently, in a more

---

[146] C Keiffer, 'Citizen Empowerment' (1984) 3 Prevention in Human Services 9, 23–32.
[147] Standing (n 66 above) 341.
[148] Walter (n 132 above) 65.
[149] R Plant, H Lesser and P Taylor-Gooby, *Political Philosophy and Social Welfare* (Routledge: London, 1980) 23–25, 52–53, 71
[150] Cited in Lund (n 23 above) 196; see similarly Deakin and Wilkinson (n 19 above) 113.

successful social inclusion policy.[151] In sum, recognizing a right to welfare is effective on two important levels. First, it offers a symbolic recognition that all individuals are of equal value and worth and should be treated with the same levels of concern and respect. All people have a legitimate moral claim to access opportunities denied to them through no fault of their own, and though government administration cannot fully correct all the wrongs delivered by birth and fate, the right to welfare offers a platform on which to lay down such claims and to begin the discourse.

But it is also more than that. Rights to welfare have a second, highly pragmatic element. As such, they represent 'an unsentimental politics of inclusion, mitigating, not abolishing, disparities of wealth incident to a liberal democracy'.[152] The previous section has shown how harsh conditionality and coercive requirements in welfare-to-work programmes lead to labour market structures that exacerbate existing barriers to 'good jobs'. Here we added that social inclusion policies that place an unrestricted emphasis on responsibility potentially deflate motivation and aggravate despair. Both perspectives lead to the conclusion that such compulsion and conditionality leads to increased *exclusion* instead of inclusion.[153]

E Conclusion: Social Inclusion and Conditionality in Welfare-to-Work

Most of the objectives lauded by advocates of welfare-to-work programmes are inherent to social inclusion discourse. While sensitive to the difficulties posed by structural (legal, economic, cultural or other) barriers, an emphasis on social inclusion policies allows one to assess the values that a society cherishes and promotes. Certain social structures, such as family and work, are viewed as important and may be endorsed. Certain lifestyles, such as one that is healthy and educated, are posited as preferable to lifestyles consumed by addiction and ignorance. The fact that numerous individuals live by the wayside of society's preferred values is undisputed. The assignment of blame for their situation is, however, highly disputed—but not here.

This chapter ends a long argument that is forward looking in two respects: first, in asking what policies are expected to alleviate the predicament of impoverished individuals and, second, in considering which amongst these policies are considered legitimate within our current moral and legal framework. If successful, I have shown that the same factors determine our approach to both these matters. While preceding chapters discussed the legitimacy of coercive and harsh conditionality in welfare-to-work programmes, this chapter revisited the

---

[151] Burchardt, Le Grand and Piachaud (n 15 above) 3.
[152] Holmes and Sunstein (n 108 above) 209.
[153] Jordan (n 87 above) 80.

actual consequences in terms of the overriding objective that these programmes (should) have: equal opportunity for social inclusion. For while it is undisputed that labour market inclusion may have positive implications for successful inclusion in general, one should appreciate the limits of a policy that seeks only to insure that individuals work. And while the infusion of moral elements into social inclusion discourse enables consideration of the importance attached to family life, this is not tantamount to coercing a woman to live with her abusive spouse for the purpose of family unity. Further, while the importance of leading a productive, useful life can readily be acknowledged within social inclusion discourse, this does not omit the possibility of revisiting *what* constitutes valuable work, thus reopening the debate regarding the axiomatic (albeit mostly implicit) precedence that society attaches to paid employment, as opposed to child rearing or voluntary work, for example.[154] Treating individuals with equal concern and respect does not conflict with inclusionist goals, if the latter are interpreted with the care and flexibility that the former demands. Only then can equal opportunity for social inclusion be achieved.

But perhaps most importantly, the particular perspective of inclusion policies focuses on achieving social goals, some quantifiable, some less quantifiable. Both types of goals, as we saw, are best achieved through a process of dialogue where mutual respect and trust are necessary. Society has a role in creating the essentials for a fair, just and prosperous commonwealth. At times, such as in the case of education, compulsion is a necessary part of this role. But as TH Marshall has observed, 'it is only the first step that is compulsory. Free choice takes over as soon as the capacity to choose has been created'.[155] Because of fundamental differences in power, the assignment of rights is necessary to open the paths for the excluded individual. When ascription of these rights is awarded and their place in policy formulation recognized, the dialogue can begin.[156]

---

[154] Walter (n 132 above) 104–13.
[155] Marshall (n 136 above) 5.
[156] R Plant, 'Needs, Agency and Welfare Rights' in JD Moon (ed), *Responsibility, Rights and Welfare* (Westview: Boulder, 1988) 55.

6

Conclusion

Prophecy is always dangerous, but there are good chances that this period will one day be termed 'the age of reciprocity' or 'the age of responsibility'. In either case, the title indicates a difficult attitude towards the less fortunate members of society. The idea of reciprocity is currently employed to indicate the fact that the status of an individual's attachment to society—that which has once been referred to as one's 'citizenship'—is contingent upon the fulfillment of obligations. The concept of responsibility is used by most contemporary authors as a counter weight posited against rights in general ('no rights without responsibilities') and against the right to equality in particular. In the latter case, claims for equality are seen to stop at the gate of individual responsibility.

One could justifiably interject at this stage and suggest that such interpretations of the two terms are far from comprehensive. As TH Marshall has shown, one may be in favour of (a very narrow sense of) individual responsibility and still be a strong supporter of equality and, furthermore, of social and economic rights. The moral importance of one's responsibility towards oneself and towards others may be asserted alongside his unconditional rights and alongside the duty to treat him with equal concern and respect. Moreover, while responsibility and reciprocity are relatively modern terms, the concept of the social contract which, in a sense, addresses both the idea of citizenship and that of rights, enjoys a richer tradition. It is even more regrettable, then, that this concept too has been 'hijacked' by those advocating weakening entitlements and undermining the idea of citizenship itself through the shift from status to contract.

The theoretical axis of this book, then, revolved around the ideas of the social contract, responsibility and reciprocity while investigating welfare state ideals of citizenship and rights. The doctrinal material that was found as optimal for this endeavour is that of welfare-to-work programmes. Other cases of conditional entitlement—for housing, health and even voting—are already visible, thus exhibiting the potential scope of the theoretical phenomenon. And yet, it is not coincidental that the antagonism against a putative 'something for nothing' attitude is most explicit in the context of welfare provision. Indeed, it is plausible that in terms of social policy, welfare conditionality is a case-study en route to a deeper change that encompasses a wider range of rights that could be reconfigured as conditional upon obligations.

While concepts such as social contract, reciprocity and responsibility may be employed with intellectual integrity within a liberal philosophy, I have suggested that contemporary use of these terms is problematic, and have offered alternative interpretations. One may argue that in this I am fighting the battle of yesteryear, seeking to unravel the liberal revolution embedded in the phrase 'from status to contract'. Such arguments manifest the need to explain the terminology that is used at any given point. At no point has a return to an age when lords and serfs were separated by birthrights been advocated. In this sense, the move to a liberal structure that postulates someone's ability to enjoy full autonomy and write his or her life-story is most welcome. Moreover, it has been argued here that the change that underlies the coupling of rights and responsibilities is more a counter-revolution than a revolution.

The fetishism of the contract has made the most basic status—that of an equal citizen—contingent upon the fulfillment of certain obligations that relate to the labour market and to moral behaviour. Ironically, financial dependence was historically seen to reflect on one's moral and political stature and thus to potentially deprive him of the right to vote. The circle is now completed, as shown here, by commissioning the mechanism of the contract to the task of disentitling poor individuals and limiting their options instead of emancipating, empowering and allowing one to realize his or her wishes. The ideals that were advanced by the original proponents of the social contract, however, are quite different from those supported by Rawls and Scanlon and different once again from those that underlie current welfare-to-work programmes.

At times, contractual rhetoric is used as a matter of political expediency, overshadowing fiscal, moral or other objectives. At other times, however, social contract is employed to suggest an idea of fairness that is closely related to the approach that views rights as conditional upon the fulfillment of obligations. The danger is, however, that the very objective that underlies the premise of the social contract—that of creating a reasonably cohesive, uniting goal through the *equal* participation of each member—is contradicted by the use of modern contractual measures and conditional rights. Rights will be in the precarious position of potentially being manipulated out of existence and the threat of creating constitutional castes will be real. Rights provide the moral and legal furniture that allows one to access civil society and to have an impact on its direction. Making rights contingent upon obligations leads to a construction of de-facto barriers that obstruct admission to the public arena. Far from being inclusive, such a construction is expected to have *exclusionary* consequences that will hold for generations. Moreover, it is important to note that, notwithstanding some assertions that this structure could encompass the whole field of constitutional law, at the moment it addresses the mechanism of welfare-to-work programmes. The scope of the theory thus makes it clear that the targeted population for inclusion, and those most in danger of permanent exclusion, are identified as the long-term unemployed who experience difficulties entering the labour market.

Alongside the obvious financial costs that unemployment entails, the moral and social facets receive a growing amount of attention. Some arguments in this vein suggest that being out of work is morally problematic in and of itself. Other positions intertwine social explanations for unemployment with social consequences of unemployment and argue that inclusion into the labour market provides a solution to a variety of social and moral ills such as teenage pregnancy, drug abuse and the like. Such attitudes are not new. In fact, one of the important studies of the abolition of begging in 18th century France concluded that 'For a long time we have been seeking the philosopher's stone. It is found, it is work'.[1] Thus, referring to measures such as these as the *New* Paternalism is somewhat misleading. Since the early days of the Poor Law, and perhaps earlier, social policy that targeted the unemployed could at least partially be explained as being motivated by a paternalistic attitude that sought to better the life of the individuals subject to the harsh measures that were attached to welfare relief.

Indeed, the categories of the deserving and the undeserving poor that were employed then are as popular today, and lack of responsibility has been a definitive explanation for the poor's predicament for centuries. If contemporary paternalism is indeed 'new', it is because the context surrounding the measures, rather than the measures themselves, has changed considerably. In some countries, single-parent families are as common as two-parent families. Teenage pregnancy is related to other issues, including changes in society's conception of teenagers' autonomy, education and sexual behaviour, to name but a few. Increased female participation in employment has 'undermined notions of male priority of access to well paid work'.[2] And so, the acknowledgment that the old measures are adapted in a modern context is itself a concession that new justifications are required if such policies are to be judged as fair. It seems that at the moment such justifications are lacking.

The distinction between deserving and undeserving poor conflicts with what could be a reasonable social and legal policy objective: that of equal opportunity for inclusion. Coercive measures, whether paternalism-based or otherwise, have already been shown to lead to further exclusion. This is true with respect of two groups of individuals: first, those who do not manage to conform with the policy regulations that were laid down in the contractual form of 'take it or leave it'; second, those who have been 'successfully' placed in the lowest tiers of a labour market that is characterized by increased rigidity and inhibits opportunity for mobility. It was argued that an alternative approach would be more attractive in terms of living up to the economic, social and philosophical objectives that these programmes proclaim.

Recognizing a true right to welfare has ramifications in several spheres, from the philosophical and symbolic through the social and political and on to the

---

[1] Cited in P Rosanvallon, *The New Social Question* (Princeton UP: Princeton, 2000) 70.
[2] S Deakin and F Wilkinson, *The Law of the Labour Market* (OUP: Oxford, 2005) ch 1, p 3.

legal and practical. On the symbolic level, a right to welfare is a proclamation that the benefits awarded to poor members do not constitute a gratuity or an act of charity. They arise from a duty that, in turn, is rooted in a right held by claimants based on their status as participants in the social endeavour. An established right to welfare, it is asserted, would deflect the stigma associated with claiming benefits. This stigma is a constitutive part of the barrier between the claimants and the rest of society and its erosion is necessary for fruitful inclusion.

Indeed, the socio-political objective of eradicating exclusion, the major social phenomenon of our day, is not antithetic to the traditional values of the classical welfare state. Not only is modern, Western society not required to choose between inclusion and equality, successful inclusion requires considering the values and aspirations of those who are currently excluded with the same care that it treats those members who serve as its core. It is, perhaps, not coincidental that precisely these insights lie at the heart of the humanistic interpretations of the social contract: viewing each citizen as equal (and even endowed with the power of veto) when constructing the nature and institutions of social justice in a given society. Discard this element of equality and the social contract indeed becomes no more than a giant swindle perpetrated by the well-to-do. Lastly, and of prime importance, is the assertion that accepting the importance of a legal right to welfare will impose serious restrictions on the conditions that may be legitimately placed on benefits. If conditions on welfare provision are at all beneficial and fair (leaving aside, for the moment, arguments concerning basic income) the right to welfare would demarcate domains of freedom within which choices made by individuals cannot be subject to interference. A right to welfare and its counter-balance on the unacceptable ease of restricting welfare entitlements would assist in levelling the playing field and increasing the possibility of both successful labour market inclusion and social inclusion.

Needless to say, important though they are, the suggestions that concern the right to welfare and the limits on conditionality cannot be expected to lead, on their own, to a more egalitarian and inclusive society. Numerous other issues have to be considered, some of which I could only allude to here. First, one could submit that following my arguments to their logical conclusion would require the establishment of a basic income scheme. At several points I stated that this is not necessarily the case. Indeed, critics of welfare-to-work programmes tend to express their support for the establishment of such schemes. This support is usually made in passing, as a solution to the many ills identified in the welfare-to-work mechanisms, some of which were highlighted here. However, I believe that the legal, philosophical and economic ramifications of basic income merit more attention than it was possible to grant here and thus prevented me from addressing the issue directly. It is conceivable, however, that the criticisms and suggestions developed here will be transferable when tackling the arguments for and against basic income.

Similar things may be said about the two major realms that reside on both sides of the welfare-to-work trajectory. When inspecting the side of welfare, one finds interesting, if not radical, proposals that concern social services in Western welfare states. Amongst them one need mention the abolition of targeting and means-testing, a reconsideration of the discretion given to field-level agency workers and the suggestion that social service agencies will be relieved of their duties to assess eligibility. The latter point would mean, for example, that employment agencies would focus solely on preparing people for jobs through education and training and on connecting jobseekers with employers.

On the side of work, due attention needs to be given to the labour market in general and the low-wage labour market in particular if clients are expected to exit the no-pay-low-pay cycle. Though the situation of the unemployed is of prime importance, it is important to understand that 'the degradation of the working condition... will ultimately fuel the increase in the number of excluded'.[3] Some of the proposals in the literature focus on financial incentives that would 'make work pay'. These include combining welfare with work (allowing clients to retain eligibility for welfare benefits for a limited period even after entering the labour market), raising (and enforcing) minimum wage, negative income tax, and so forth. Others emphasize different barriers to work, though they too, of course, have financial ramifications. Solutions for matters such as child care, health benefits and transportation could relieve claimants from obligations and difficulties that they confront and that prevent them from accepting job offers.

Lastly, there have been proposals to develop a more flexible low-wage market that includes job-sharing, strengthening rights of temporary workers and equalizing rights of part-time workers with those of full-time workers. Some countries, especially in Europe, are already experimenting with similar measures and the assessments, as one would expect, differ widely. It should be noted, however, that all these suggestions, both on the side of welfare and on the side of work, share the notion that people should work and that society should do its utmost to help them obtain employment. And yet, very few still view government as the employer of last resort. It will be interesting to see, then, how long modern society will hold on to the moral imperative of work in an age when, due to technological and demographic changes, there are not enough jobs to go around. But that, of course, is the subject of a different research altogether.

---

[3] Rosanvallon (n 1 above) 46.

Bibliography

Ackerman B (1980) *Social Justice in the Liberal State* (Yale UP: New Haven).
Adler M and Asquith S (1981) 'Discretion and Power' in M Adler and S Asquith Adler M and Asquith S (eds) (1981) *Discretion and Welfare* (Heinemann: London) 9.
Adriaansens H (1994) 'Citizenship, Work and Welfare' in B van Steenbergen (ed) *The Condition of Citizenship* (Sage: London) 66.
Agulnik P, Burchardt T and Evans M (2001) 'Prevention and Response in the British Welfare State' in J Hills, J Le Grand and D Piachaud (eds) *Understanding Social Exclusion* (OUP: Oxford) 155.
Alexander L (1989) 'Understanding Constitutional Rights in a World of Optional Baselines' 26 San Diego L Rev 175.
Alstott A (1999) 'Work vs. Freedom' 108 Yale LJ 967.
Anderson E (2004) 'Welfare, Work Requirements and Dependant Care' 21 J of Applied Philosophy 243.
Appleby J (1978) *Economic Thought and Ideology in Seventeenth Century England* (Princeton UP: Princeton).
Arneson R (1989) 'Equality and Equal Opportunity for Welfare' 56 Philosophical Studies 77.
Arneson R (1990) 'Is Work Special? Justice and the Distribution of Employment' Am Pol Sci Rev 1127.
Arneson R (1990) 'Liberalism, Distributive Subjectivism and Equal Opportunity for Welfare' 19 Philosophy and Pub Affairs 158.
Ashforth D (1976) 'The Urban Poor Law' in D Fraser (ed) *The New Poor Law in the Nineteenth Century* (Macmillan: Basingstoke) 128.
Atiyah PS (1995) *An Introduction to the Law of Contract* (5th edn, Clarendon: Oxford).
Atkinson AB 'Social Exclusion, Poverty and Unemployment' in AB Atkinson and J Hills (eds) *Exclusion, Employment and Opportunity* (CASEpaper 4: London) 1.
Attas D and de-Shalit A (2004) 'Workfare: the Subjection of Labour' 21 J of Applied Philosophy 309.
Austin J (1880) *Lectures on Jurisprudence* (Murray: London).
Autor D and Houseman S (2005) 'Temporary Agency Employment as a Way Out of Poverty?' <http://www.upjohninstitute.org/publications/wp/05-123.pdf> (25 July 2007).
Baker L (1989) 'The Prices of Rights' 75 Cornell L Rev 1185.
Bamforth N (2001) 'Hohfeldian Rights and Public Law' in M Kramer (ed) *Rights, Wrongs and Responsibilities* (Palgrave: Basingstoke) 1.
Bardach E (1991) 'Implementing a Paternalist Welfare' in L Mead (ed) *The New Paternalism* (Brookings: NY) 251.
Barron RD and Norris GM (1976) 'Sexual Divisions and the Dual Labor Market' in DL Barker and S Allen (eds) *Dependence and Exploitation in Work and Marriage* (Longmans: London 1976).
Barry B (1979) *The Liberal Theory of Justice* (OUP: Oxford).

Barry B (1994) 'Justice, Freedom and Basic Income' in H Siebert (ed) *The Ethical Foundations of the Market Economy* (Mohr: Tobingen) 75.
Barry B (1995) *Justice as Impartiality* (Clarendon: Oxford).
Barry B (2001) 'Social exclusion, Social Isolation and the Distribution of Income' in J Hills, J Le Grand and D Piachaud (eds) *Understanding Social Exclusion* (OUP: Oxford) 13.
Barry B (2005) *Why Social Justice Matters* (Polity: Cambridge).
Barton BH (1996) 'Law and Equality' 94 Michigan L Rev 1993.
Beales HL (1931) 'The New Poor Law' 15 History 308.
Bell W (1965) *Aid to Dependent Children* (Columbia UP: New York).
Ben-Israel R (1997) 'The Ramifications of the Basic Laws on Labor Law and Labor Relations' 4 Labor Law Yearbook 27, 36.
Bennett B and Sullivan K (1993) 'Disentitling the Poor: Waivers and Welfare "Reform"' 26 U of Michigan J of L Reform 741.
Bentham J (1977) 'A Fragment on Government or a Comment on the Commentaries' in JH Burns and HLA Hart (eds) *Collected Works of Jeremy Bentham* (Athlone Press: London) 393.
Bentham J (1996) *An Introduction to the Principles of Morals and Legislation* (Clarendon: Oxford 1996).
Berlin I (1969) 'Two Concepts of Liberty' in I Berlin *Four Essays on Liberty* (OUP: Oxford) 118.
Berlin I (1969) 'Introduction' in I Berlin *Four Essays on Liberty* (OUP: Oxford) 45.
Beveridge W (1942) *Social Insurance and Allied Services* (Cmd 6404).
Black C (1986) 'Further Reflections on the Constitutional Justice of Livelihood' 86 Columbia L Rev 1103.
Boeri T, Layard R and Nickell S (2000) *Welfare-to-Work and the Fight Against Long-Term Unemployment* (Report 206 Department for Education and Employment: London).
Bolen E (2001) 'A Poor Measure of the Wrong Thing: The Food Stamp Program's Quality Control System Discourages Participation by Working Families' 53 Hastings LJ 213.
Boltanski L and Chiapello E (2005) *The New Spirit of Capitalism* (G Elliot—trans, Verso: London).
Bork R (1979) 'The Impossibility of Finding Welfare Rights in the Constitution' 1979 Washington U LQ 695.
Boucher D and Kelly P (1994) 'The Social Contract and its Critics' in D Boucher and P Kelly (eds) *The Social Contract from Hobbes to Rawls* (Routledge: London) 1.
Bou-Habib P and Olsaretti S (2004) 'Liberal Egalitarianism and Workfare' 21 J of Applied Philosophy 257.
Boushey H and others (2007) *Understanding Low Wage Work in the United States* (CEPR: Washington DC).
Brown J (1940) *Public Relief 1929–1939* (Holt: New York).
Brown J, Williams L and Baumann P (1996) 'The Mythogenesis of Gender: Judicial Images of Women in Paid and Unpaid Labor' 6 UCLA Women's LJ 457.
Bryne D (1999) *Social Exclusion* (Open UP: Buckingham) 1.
Bryson A (1995) 'The Jobseeker's Allowance: Help or Hindrance to the Unemployed' 24 ILJ 204.
Buchanan A (1981) 'Deriving Welfare Rights from Libertarian Rights' in PG Brown, C Johnson, P Vernier (eds) *Income Support* (Rowman and Littlefield: Totowa NJ) 233.

Buchanan JM (1975) *The Limits of Liberty* (Chicago UP: Chicago).
Buck T (1989) 'Social Security' 18 ILJ 258.
Burchardt T, Le Grand J and Piachaud D (2001) 'Introduction' in J Hills, J Le Grand and D Piachaud (eds) *Understanding Social Exclusion* (OUP: Oxford) 1.
Burchardt T, Le Grand J and Piachaud D (2001) 'Degrees of Exclusion' in J Hills, J Le Grand and D Piachaud (eds) *Understanding Social Exclusion* (OUP: Oxford) 30.
Burtless G (2004) 'Social Policy for the Working Poor: U.S. Reform in a Cross-National Perspective' in N Gilbert and A Parent (eds) *Welfare Reform: A Comparative Assessment of the French and U.S. Experiences* (International Social Security Series vol 10, Transaction Publishers: London) 3.
Cabinet Office (1991) *The Citizen's Charter* (Cm 1599).
Calabresi G and Melamed D (1972) 'Property Rules, Liability Rules and Inalienability: One View of the Cathedral' 85 Harvard L Rev 1089.
Campbell K (1979) 'The Concept of Rights' (DPhil Thesis: Oxford).
Carney T and Ramia G (2002) *From Rights to Management: Contract, New Public Management and Employment Services* (Kluwer Law: The Hague 2002).
Castiglione D (1994) 'History, Reason and Experience—Hume's Argument Against Contract Theories' in D Boucher and P Kelly (eds) *The Social Contract from Hobbes to Rawls* (Routledge: London) 95.
Castles F and Mitchell D (1993) 'Worlds of Welfare and Families of Nations' in F Castles (ed) *Families of Nations: Patterns of Public Policies in Western Democracies* (Aldershot: Dartmouth).
Castner L and Rosso R (2000) *Characteristics of Food Stamps Households—Fiscal Year 1998* (USDA: Washington DC).
Center on Budget and Policy Priorities (2007) *Implementing TANF Changes and the Deficit Reduction Act* (2nd edn, Washington DC) <http://www.cbpp.org/2-9-07tanf.pdf> (10 July 2007).
Chan J (1995) 'Raz on Liberal Rights and Common Goods' 15 OJLS 15.
Charlesworth L 'The Poor Law' (1999) 6 JSSL 79.
Clasen J, Gould A and Vincent J (1997) *Long Term Unemployment and the Threat of Social Exclusion* (Policy Press: Bristol).
Cohen GA (1989) 'On the Currency of Egalitarian Justice' 99 Ethics 906.
Collins H (1992) *Justice in Dismissal* (Oxford: Clarendon).
Collins H, Ewing KD and McColgan A (2001) *Labour Law—Text and Materials* (Hart: Oxford).
Collins H (2003) 'Discrimination, Equality and Social Inclusion' 66 MLR 16.
Conaghan J (2002) 'Women, Work and Family: A British Revolution?' in J Conaghan, R Fischl and K Klare (eds) *Labour Law in an Era of Globalization* (OUP: Oxford) 53.
Considine (2005) 'The Reform that Never Ends: Quasi Markets and Employment Services in Australia' in E Sol and M Westerveld *Contractualism in Employment Services: A New Form of Welfare State Governance* (Kluwer Law: The Hague).
Corden A (1995) *Changing Perspectives on Benefit Take Up* (HMSO: London).
Cornish W and de N Clark G (1989) *Law and Society in England 1750–1950* (Sweet & Maxwell: London).
Cosenza T (1997) 'Preserving Procedural Due Process for Legal Immigrants Receiving Food Stamps in Light of the Personal Responsibility Act of 1996' 65 Fordham L Rev 2065.

Cox R (1998) 'The Consequences of Welfare Reform' 27 J of Soc Pol 1.
Cranston M (1957) *John Locke* (Longmans: London).
Cranston M (1967) 'Human Rights, Real and Supposed' in DD Raphael (ed) *Political Theory and the Rights of Man* (Macmillan: Basingstoke) 50.
Cranston M (1967) 'Human Rights: A Reply to Professor Raphael' in DD Raphael (ed) *Political Theory and the Rights of Man* (Macmillan: Basingstoke) 95.
Cranston R (1985) *Legal Foundations of the Welfare State* (Weidenfeld and Nicolson: London).
D'Agostino F (2007) 'The Promise of Social Welfare: New Foundations for the Social Contract' (draft, copy with author).
Dahrendorf R (1994) 'The Changing Quality of Citizenship' in B van Steenbergen (ed) *The Condition of Citizenship* (Sage: London) 10.
Dahrendorf R (1996) 'On the Dahrendorf Report' 67 Political Q 194.
Dan-Cohen M (1992) 'Responsibility and the Boundaries of the Self' (1992) 105 Harv L Rev 959.
Daniels N (1975) 'Equal Liberty and Equal Worth of Liberty' in N Daniels (ed) *Reading Rawls* (Blackwell: Oxford) 253.
David D, Macklem P and Mundlak G 'Social Rights, Social Citizenship and Transformative Constitutionalism: A Comparative Assessment' in J Conaghan, R Fischl and K Klare (eds) *Labour Law in an Era of Globalization* (OUP: Oxford) 511.
de Schweinitz K (1961) *England's Road to Social Security: From the Statute of Laborers in 1349 to the Beveridge Report of 1942* (Barnes: New York).
de Tocqueville A (1997) *Memoirs on Pauperism* (S Dreshcer—trans, Dee: Chicago).
de Vita A (2000) 'Individual Preferences and Social Justice' Brazilian Review of Social Sciences 95.
Deacon A (1996) 'Welfare and Character' in A Deacon (ed) *Stakeholder Welfare* (IEA: London) 60.
Deacon A (1997) 'The Case for Compulsion' 98 Poverty 8–10.
Deacon A (2002) *Perspectives on Welfare* (Buckingham: Open UP) 42.
Deacon A (2005) 'An Ethic of Mutual Responsibility? Towards a Fuller Justification for Conditionality in Welfare' in C Beem and L Mead (eds) Welfare Reform and Political Theory (Sage: New York).
Deakin, S (2005) 'The Capability Concept and the Evolution of European Social Policy' in M Dougan and E Spaventa (eds) *Social Welfare and EU Law* (Hart: Oxford) 3.
Deakin S and Morris M (2001) *Labour Law* (3rd edn, Butterworths: London).
Deakin S and Wilkinson F (1991) 'Labour Law, Social Security and Economic Inequality' 15 Cambridge J of Economics 125.
Deakin S and Wilkinson F (2005) *The Law of the Labour Market* (OUP: Oxford).
Dean H and Taylor Gooby P (1992) *Dependency Culture* (Harvester: New York).
DeParle J (2004) *American Dream: Three Women, Ten Kids, and a Nation's Drive to End Welfare* (Viking: New York).
Department of Education and Employment (1998) *A New Contract for Welfare: The Gateway to Work* (Cm 4102).
Department of Employment (1988) *Training for Employment* (Cm 316).
Department of Employment (1988) *Employment for the 1990s* (Cm 540).
Department of Social Security (1997) *Beating Fraud is Everyone's Business* (Cm 4012).

Department of Social Security (1998) *New Ambitions for Our Country: A New Contract for Welfare* (Cm 3805).

Department of Social Security (1998) *A New Contract for Welfare: Principles into Practice* (Cm 4101).

Department of Social Security (1999) *A New Contract for Welfare: Safeguarding Social Security* (Cm 4276).

Department of Social Security (1999) *A New Contract for Welfare: Children's Rights and Parents' Responsibilities* (Cm 4349).

Department of Trade and Industry (2001) *Towards Equality and Diversity: Implementing the Employment and Race Directives* (HMSO: London) <http://www.dti.gov.uk/er/equality/consult.pdf> (25 May 2005).

Department of Work and Pensions (2002) *Income Related Benefits: Estimates of Take Up of Benefits in 2000–2001* (HMSO: London).

Department of Work and Pensions (2006) *Income Related Benefits: Estimates of Take Up of Benefits in 2004–2005* (HMSO: London).

Digby A (1976) 'The Rural Poor Law' in D Fraser (ed) *The New Poor Law in the Nineteenth Century* (Macmillan: Basingstoke) 149.

Diller M (1998) 'Working Without a Job: The Social Meaning of the New Workforce' 9 Stanford L and Society Rev 19.

Diller M (2002) 'New Forms of Governance' 49 UCLA L Rev 1739.

Doron A and Gal J (2000) 'The Israeli Income Support Program in a Comparative Perspective' Social Security 5.

Dunn J (1969) *The Political Thought of John Locke* (CUP: Cambridge).

Drzewsicki K (1995) 'The Right to Work and Rights in Work' in A Eide, C Krauses and A Rosas (eds) *Economic, Social and Cultural Rights* (Dordrecht: London) 169.

Dworkin R (1973) 'The Original Position' 40 U of Chi L Rev 500.

Dworkin R (1977) *Taking Rights Seriously* (Duckworth: London) 365–66.

Dworkin R (1984) 'Rights as Trumps' in J Waldron (ed) *Theories of Rights* (OUP: Oxford) 153.

Dworkin R (1986) *Law's Empire* (Hart: Oxford).

Dworkin R (1986) 'Liberalism' in *A Matter of Principle* (Clarendon: Oxford) 191.

Dworkin R (1986) 'Why Liberals Should Care About Equality' in *A Matter of Principle* (Clarendon: Oxford) 205.

Dworkin R (1988) 'What is Equality? Part 3: The Place of Liberty' 73 Iowa L Rev 1.

Dworkin R (1996) *Freedom's Law* (Harvard UP: Cambridge MA).

Dworkin R (2000) *Sovereign Virtue* (Harvard UP: London).

Dwyer P (2000) *Welfare Rights and Responsibilities* (Policy Press: Bristol).

Easterbrook F (1981) 'Insider Trading, Secret Agents, Evidentiary Privileges and the Production of Information' 1981 Sup Ct Rev 309.

Edelman P (1987) 'The Next Century of Our Constitution' 39 Hastings LJ 1.

Ehrenreich B (2001) *Nickle and Dimed: On (Not) Getting By in America* (Henry Holt: New York).

Ellwood D (1988) *Poor Support* (Basic Books: New York).

Elster J (1988) 'Is There (or Should There Be) a Right to Work' in A Gutmann (ed) *Democracy and the Welfare State* (Princeton UP: Princeton NJ) 53.

Ely J (1986) 'Poor Laws of the Post-Revolutionary South, 1776–1800' Tulsa L J 1.

Epstein R (1985) 'The Uncertain Quest for Welfare Rights' BYU L Rev 201.
Epstein R (1988) 'Foreword' 102 Harvard L Rev 5.
Etzioni A (1995) *The Spirit of the Community* (Fontana: London).
Euben J (1972) 'Walzer's Obligation' 1 Philosophy and Public Affairs 438.
European Commission (1994) *Growth, Competitiveness, Employment* (Office for Official Publications of the European Communities: Luxemburg) s 8.
European Commission (2001) *Joint Report on Social Exclusion: Part I—The European Union Executive Summary* (European Commission: Brussels). http://europa.eu.int/comm/employment_social/soc-prot/soc-incl/15223/part1_en.pdf> (7 June 2005).
European Foundation for the Improvement of the Living and Working Conditions (2002) *Low-Wage Workers and the Working Poor* <http://www.eurofound.europa.eu/eiro/2002/08/study/tn0208101s.html > (15 April 2007).
Fabre C (2000) *Social Rights Under the Constitution* (OUP: Oxford).
Feinberg J (1970) 'The Nature and Value of Rights' 4 J of Value Inquiry 243.
Felstiner W, Abel R and Sarat A (1980) 'The Emergence and Transformation of Disputes: Naming, Blaiming, Claiming...' 15 L and Soc Rev 631.
Field F (1995) *Making Welfare Work* (Institute of Community Studies: London).
Field F (1996) 'A Rejoinder' in A Deacon (ed) *Stakeholder Welfare* (IEA: London) 107.
Finn D (2003) 'The "Employment First" Welfare State: Lessons from the New Deal for Young People' 37 Social Policy and Administration 709.
Finn D (2004) 'Welfare to Work' 13 Benefits 93.
Finn D (2005) 'The Role of Contracts and the Private Sector in Delivering Britain's "Employment First" Welfare State' in E Sol and M Westerveld (eds) *Contractualism in Employment Services* (Kluwer Law: The Hague) 101.
Finnis J (1982) *Natural Law and Natural Rights* (OUP: Oxford).
Fisher WW (1988) 'Reconstructing the Fair Use Doctrine' (1988) 101 Harvard L Rev 1659.
Forsyth M (1994) 'Hobbes's Contractarianism' in D Boucher and P Kelly (eds) *The Social Contract from Hobbes to Rawls* (Routledge: London) 35.
Frankfurt H (1988) *The Importance of What We Care About* (CUP: Cambridge).
Fraser D (1976) 'Introduction' in D Fraser (ed) *The New Poor Law in the Nineteenth Century* (Macmillan: Basingstoke) 13.
Fraser D (2003) *The Evolution of the British Welfare State* (3rd edn, London: Palgrave).
Fraser N (2003) 'Distorted Beyond all Recognition: A Rejoinder to Axel Honneth' in in N Fraser and A Honneth *Redistribution or Recognition?* (Verso: London) 198.
Fraser N and Gordon L 'Civil Citizenship Against Social Citizenship? On the Ideology of Contract Versus Charity' in B van Steenbergen (ed) *The Condition of Citizenship* (Sage: London 1994) 90.
Fredman S (1994) 'A Difference with Distinction' 110 LQR 106.
Fredman S (1999) 'Equality: A New Generation?' 30 ILJ 145.
Fredman S (2001) *Discrimination Law* (Clarendon: Oxford).
Freedland M and King D (2003) 'Contractual Governance and Illiberal Contracts' 27 Cambridge J of Economics 465.
Freeden M (1999) 'The Ideology of New Labour' Political Quarterly 42.
French J (1962) 'Unconstitutional Conditions' 50 Georgetown L Rev 234.
Fried C (1972) 'Book Review—A Theory of Justice' 85 Harv L Rev 1691.
Fried C (1978) *Right and Wrong* (Harvard: Cambridge).

Fullbrook J (1995) 'The Jobseeker's Act 1995' 24 ILJ 395.
Gardner J (1998) 'On the Grounds of Her Sex(uality) 18 OJLS 167.
Gardner J (2001) 'The Mysterious Case of the Reasonable Person' (2001) 51 University of Toronto LJ 273.
Garvey J (1989) 'The Powers and the Duties of Government' 26 San Diego L Rev 209.
Gauthier D (1976) 'The Social Contract as Ideology' 6 Philosophy and Public Affairs 130.
Gauthier D (1979) 'David Hume—Utilitarian' (1979) 88 Philosophical Review 3.
Gauthier D (1984) *Morals by Agreement* (Clarendon: Oxford).
Gauthier D (1999) 'Hobbes's Social Contract' in C Morris (ed) *The Social Contract Theorists* (Rowman & Littlefield: Oxford) 59.
Gauthier D (1999) 'Why Ought One Obey God?' in C Morris (ed) *The Social Contract Theorists* (Rowman & Littlefield: Oxford) 73.
Gauthier D (2000) *The Logic of the Leviathan* (OUP: Oxford).
Gavison R (2003) 'On the Relationship Between Civil and Political Rights and Social and Economic Rights' in JM Coicaud, MW Doyle, AM Gardner (eds) *The Globalization of Human Rights* (United Nations UP: Tokyo) 24.
Gewirth A (1981) 'Are There Any Absolute Rights? 31 Phil Q 1.
Gewirth A (1996) *The Community of Rights* (Chicago UP: Chicago).
Giddens A (1998) *The Third Way* (Polity: Cambridge).
Giddens A (2000) *The Third Way and its Critics* (Polity: Cambridge).
Gilbert N (2004) 'Welfare Policy in the United States: The Road from Income Maintenance to Workfare' in N Gilbert and A Parent (eds) *Welfare Reform: A Comparative Assessment of the French and U.S. Experiences* (International Social Security Series vol 10, Transaction Publishers: London) 55.
Glendon MA (1991) *Rights Talk* (Free Press: New York).
Goodin R (1988) *Reasons for Welfare* (Princeton UP: Princeton).
Goodin R 'Inclusion and Exclusion' (1996) 37 Archives Européennes de Sociologie 343.
Goodin R (1998) 'Social Welfare as a Collective Social Responsibility' in D Schmidtz and Goodin (eds) *Social Welfare and Individual Responsibility—For and Against* (CUP: Cambridge) 97.
Goodin R (2004) 'Support With Strings' 21 J of Applied Philosophy 297.
Gore C (1995) 'Introduction' in G Rodgers, C Gore and J Figueiriedo (eds) *Social Exclusion* (ILO: Geneva) 1.
Gough JW (1957) *The Social Contract* (OUP: Oxford).
Grover C and Stewart J (2002) *The Work Connection* (Palgrave: Houndmills).
Gray J (2000) 'Social Inclusion' in P Askonas and A Stewart (eds) *Social Inclusion* (Macmillan: Basingstoke) 19.
Greenberg M (2001) 'Welfare Reform and Devolution: Looking Back and Forward' (2001) 19 Brookings Review 20.
Gutmann A and Thompson D (1996) *Democracy and Disagreement* (Harvard UP: Cambridge MA).
Haddock B (1994) 'Hegel's Critique of the Theory of Social Contract' in D Boucher and P Kelly (eds) *The Social Contract from Hobbes to Rawls* (Routledge: London).
Hampton J (1986) *Hobbes and the Social Contract Tradition* (CUP: Cambridge).
Hampton J (1991) 'Two Faces of Contractarian Thought' in P Vallentyne (ed) *Contractarianism and Rational Choice* (CUP: Cambridge) 31.

Handler J (1983) 'Discretion in Social Welfare: The Uneasy Position in the Rule of Law' 92 YLJ 1270.
Handler J (1995) *The Poverty of Welfare Reform* (Yale UP: New Haven).
Handler J (2003) 'Social Citizenship and Workfare in the US and Western Europe: from Status to Contract' (2003) 13 Journal of European Social Policy.
Handler J (2004) *Social Citizenship and Workfare in the United States and Western Europe* (CUP: Cambridge).
Handler J and Hasenfeld Y (1997) *We the Poor People* (Yale UP: New Haven).
Handler J and Hasenfeld Y (2007) *Blame Welfare, Ignore Poverty and Inequality* (CUP: Cambridge).
Hare RM (1972) 'Rules of War and Moral Philosophy' (1972) 1 Phil and Pub Affairs 171.
Harel A (2005) 'Theories of Rights' in M Golding and W Edmundson (eds) *Blackwell's Guide to Philosophy of Law and Legal Theory* (Blackwell: Oxford, 2005) 191.
Harris J (1977) *William Beveridge—A Biography* (Clarendon: Oxford).
Harris N (2000) 'The Welfare State, Social Security and Social Citizenship Rights' in N Harris (ed) *Social Security Law in Context* (OUP: Oxford) 3.
Harris N (2000) 'Welfare State and Social Citizenship Rights' in N Harris (ed) *Social Security Law in Context* (OUP: Oxford) 36.
Harel A (1997) 'What Demands are Rights?' 17 OJLS 101.
Harris J (1996) *Justice and Property* (OUP: Oxford).
Hart HLA (1957) 'Positivism and the Separation of Law and Morals' 71 Harv L Rev 593.
Hart HLA (1973) 'Bentham on Legal Rights' in *Oxford Essays in Jurisprudence* (2nd Series, Clarendon: Oxford) 171.
Hart HLA (1973) 'Rawls on Liberty and its Priority' 40 U of Chicago L Rev 534.
Hart HLA (1984) 'Are there any Natural Rights?' in J Waldron (ed) *Theories of Rights* (OUP: Oxford) 77.
Hart HLA (1994) *The Concept of Law* (2nd edn, Clarendon: Oxford).
Hegel GWF (1991) *Elements of the Philosophy of Right* (CUP: Cambridge).
Hegel GWF (2000) *Elements of the Philosophy of Right* (CUP: Cambridge).
Held V (1993) *Feminist Morality: Transforming Culture, Society, and Politics.* (Chicago UP: Chicago).
Hills J (2001) 'Does a Focus on 'Social Exclusion' Change the Policy Response?' in J Hills, J Le Grand and D Piachaud (eds) *Understanding Social Exclusion* (OUP: Oxford) 226.
Himmelfarb G (1984) *The Idea of Poverty* (Faber: London).
Hirschman AO (1991) *The Rhetoric of Reaction: Pervisity, Futility, Jeopardy* (Havard UP: Cambridge).
Hobbes T (1992) *Leviathan* (CUP: Cambridge).
Hoke C (1998) 'State Discretion Under New Federal Welfare Legislation' 9 Stanford L and Society Rev 115.
Holmes S and Sunstein C (1999) *The Cost of Rights* (WW Norton: London).
Honneth A (2003) 'Redistribution as Recognition: A Response to Nancy Fraser' in N Fraser and A Honneth *Redistribution or Recognition?* (Verso: London) 110.
Holmes E (2005) 'Anti-Discrimination Rights Without Equality' 68 Modern L Rev 175.
Home Office (2002) *Justice for All* (Cm 5563).
Howe L (1985) 'The "Deserving" and "Undeserving"' 14 J of Soc Pol 49.

Hubin D and Lambeth M (1991) 'Providing for Rights' in P Vallentyne (ed) *Contractarianism and Rational Choice* (CUP: Cambridge) 112.
Hume D (1978) *Treatise of Human Nature* (OUP: Oxford 1978).
Hume D (1987) 'On the Original Contract' in *Essays Moral, Political and Literary* (Liberty Classics: Indianapolis) 485.
Hurley S (2003) *Justice, Luck and Knowledge* (Harvard UP: London).
Jencks C (1992) *Rethinking Social Policy* (Harvard UP: Cambridge MA).
Jencks C (1997) 'The Hidden Paradox of Welfare Reform' 32 American Prospect 36.
Jennings J (1994) 'Rousseau, Social Contract and the Modern Leviathan' in D Boucher and P Kelly (eds) *The Social Contract from Hobbes to Rawls* (Routledge: London) 115.
Jacobs L (1993) 'Realizing Equal Life Prospects: The Case for a Perfectionist Theory of Fair Shares' in G Drover and P Kerans (eds) New Approaches to Welfare Theory (Elgar: Brookfield) 49.
Jolls C, Sunstein C and Thaler R (1998) 'A Behavioral Approach to Law and Economics' 50 Stanford L Rev 1471.
Jones C and Novak T (1999) *Poverty, Welfare and the Disciplinary State* (Routledge: London).
Jordan B (1996) *A Theory of Poverty and Social Exclusion* (Polity: London).
Kant I *Metaphysics of Morals* (CUP: Cambridge).
Karger H (1999) 'The International Implications of U.S. Welfare Reform' (1999) 55 Social Security 7.
Keiffer C (1984) 'Citizen Empowerment' 3 Prevention in Human Services 9.
Kelsen H (1949) *General Theory of Law and State* (A Wedberg (tr) Harvard UP: Cambridge MA).
King D (1995) *Actively Seeking Work* (Chicago UP: Chicago).
King D (1999) *In the Name of Liberalism* (OUP: Oxford).
Kramer M (1998) 'Rights Without Trimmings' in M Kramer, N Simmonds and H Steiner *A Debate Over Rights* (Clarendon: Oxford) 1.
Kramer M (2001) 'Getting Rights Right' in M Kramer (ed) *Rights, Wrongs and Responsibilities* (Palgrave: Basingstoke) 28.
Kreimer S (1983) 'Allocational Sanctions' (1983) 132 Pennsylvania L Rev 1293.
Kymlicka W (1989) *Liberalism, Community and Culture* (Clarendon: Oxford).
Labour Commission on Social Justice (1994) *Social Justice—Strategies for National Renewal* (Vintage: London).
Lawes K (2000) *Paternalism and Politics* (Macmillan: Basingstoke).
Le Grand J (2003) 'Individual Choice and Social Exclusion' (CASEpaper 75: London).
Leibfried S (1992) 'Towards a European Welfare State: On Integrating Poverty Regimes into the European Community' in Z Ferge and J Kohlberg (eds) *Social Policy in a Changing Europe* (Westview Press: Boulder) 245.
Lessnoff M (1986) *Social Contract* (Macmillan: Basingstoke).
Levin-Epstein J (2003) *Lifting the Lid off the Family Cap* (CLASP) <http://clasp.org/publications/family_cap_brf.pdf> (28 July 2007).
Levin-Epstein J and Hutchins J *Teens and TANF: How Adolescents Fare Under the Nation's Welfare Program* (Kaiser Family Foundation). <http://www.clasp.org/publications/Teens_TANF.pdf>
Levine-Clark M (2000) 'Engendering Relief' 11 J of Women's History 107.

Levitas R (1998) *The Inclusive Society?* (Macmillan: Basingstoke).
Lister R (2000) 'Strategies for Social Inclusion' in P Askonas and A Stewart (eds) *Social Inclusion* (Macmillan: Basingstoke) 37.
Locke J (2000) 'The Second Treatise' *Two Treatises of Government* (CUP: Cambridge).
Lodemel I and Trickey H. (2000) 'A New Contract for Social Assistance' in I Lodemel and Trickey (eds) *'An Offer You Can't Refuse': Workfare in International Perspective* (Policy Press: London).
Lund B (2002) *Understanding State Welfare* (Sage: London).
Lundy L (2000) 'From Welfare to Work? Social Security and Unemployment' in N Harris (ed) *Social Security Law in Context* (OUP: Oxford) 291.
Lurie I (1973) 'Major Changes in the Structure of the AFDC Program Since 1935' 59 Cornell L Rev 825.
Mabbott JD (1973) *John Locke* (Macmillan: Basingstoke).
Macarov D (1980) *Work and Welfare—The Unholy Alliance* (Sage: London).
MacCormick N (1977) 'Rights in Legislation' in PMS Hacker and J Raz (eds) *Law, Morality and Society* (Clarendon: Oxford) 189.
Mackie JL (1984) 'Can There Be a Rights Based Moral Theory?' in J Waldron (ed) *Theories of Rights* (OUP: Oxford) 168.
Macklem P and Scott C (1992) 'Constitutional Ropes of Sand or Justiciable Guarantees Social Rights in a New South African Constitution' 141 U of Pennsylvania L Rev 1.
Macneil I (1974) 'The Many Futures of Contract' 47 Southern California L Rev 691.
Macneil I (1980) *The New Social Contract* (Yale UP: London).
Macneil I (1983) 'Values in Contract' 78 Northwestern U L Rev 340.
Macpherson CB (1962) *The Political Theory of Possessive Individualism* (OUP: Oxford).
Mann K and Roseneil S (1994) 'Some Mothers Do 'Ave 'Em: Backlash and the Gender Politics of the Underclass Debate' 3 J of Gender Studies 317.
Marshall D (1937) 'The Old Poor Law 1662–1795' 8 Economic History Review 38.
Marshall TH (1964) *Class, Citizenship and Social Development* (Doubleday: New York).
Marshall TH (1981) 'The Right to Welfare' in *The Right to Welfare and Other Essays* (Heinemann: London) 83.
Marshall TH and Bottomore T (1992) *Citizenship and Social Class* (Pluto: London).
Marshall WP (1989) 'Towards a Nonunifying Theory of Unconstitutional Conditions' 26 San Diego L Rev 243.
Marx K *Capital* (S Moore and E Aveling—tr, Swan: London 1938).
McConnell M (1989) 'Unconstitutional Conditions' 26 San Diego L Rev 255.
McKeever G (1999) 'Detecting, Prosecuting and Punishing Benefit Fraud' 62 MLR 261.
McKeever G (1999) 'Fighting Fraud: An Evaluation of the Government's Social Security Fraud Strategy' 21 J of Social Welfare and Family Law 357.
McKnight A (2001) 'Low-Paid Work: Drip Feeding the Poor' in J Hills, J Le Grand and D Piachaud (eds) *Understanding Social Exclusion* (OUP: Oxford) 97.
Mead L (1997) 'The Rise of Paternalism' in L Mead (ed) *The New Paternalism* (Brookings: Washington DC) 1.
Mead L (1997) 'Welfare Employment' in L Mead (ed) *The New Paternalism* (Brookings: Washington DC) 39.
Mead L (1986) *Beyond Entitlement* (Free Press: London).
Melden AI (1981) 'Are There Welfare Rights?' in PG Brown, C Johnson, P Vernier (eds) *Income Support* (Rowman and Littlefield: Totowa NJ) 259.

Michelman F (1969) 'On Protecting the Poor Through the Fourteenth Amendment' 83 Harvard L Rev 7.
Michelman F (1973) 'In Pursuit of Constitutional Welfare Rights' 121 U of Pennsylvania L Rev 962.
Michelman F (1975) 'Constitutional Welfare Rights and *A Theory of Justice*' in N Daniels (ed) *Reading Rawls* (Blackwell: Oxford) 319.
Michelman F (1979) 'Welfare Rights in a Constitutional Democracy' 1979 Washington U LQ 659.
Michener H and Delamater JD (1994) *Social Psychology* (3rd edn, Harcourt: Orlando).
Mill JS (1977) *Principles of Political Economy* (CUP: Cambridge).
Miller D (1976) *Social Justice* (Clarendon: Oxford).
Miller D (1992) 'Distributive Justice: What the People Think' 102 Ethics 555.
Miller D (1999) *Principles of Social Justice* (Harvard UP: Cambridge MA).
Mills CW (1959) *The Sociological Imagination* (OUP: New York).
Monaghan HP (1978) 'The Constitution Goes to Harvard' 13 Harvard CR–CL L Rev 117
Morel S (2004) 'Workfare and *Insertion*: How the U.S. and French Models of Social Assistance Have Been Transformed' in N Gilbert and A Parent (eds) *Welfare Reform: A Comparative Assessment of the French and U.S. Experiences* (International Social Security Series vol 10, Transaction Publishers: London) 93.
Moss J (2004) 'Introduction' 21 J of Applied Philosophy 239.
Mundlak G (2000) 'Social-Economic Rights in the New Constitutional Discourse' 7 Labor Law Yearbook 65.
Murphy J (1977) 'Rights and Borderline Cases' 19 Arizona L Rev 228.
Murphy L and Nagel T (2002) *The Myth of Ownership* (OUP: New York).
Murray C (1984) *Losing Ground* (Basic Books: New York).
Murray C (1990) *The Emerging British Underclass* (IEA: London)
Murray C (1994) *Underclass: The Crisis Deepens* (IEA: London).
Nagel T (1973) 'Rawls on Justice' 82 Philosophical Review 220.
Nagel T (1979) 'Equality' in *Mortal Questions* (Canto: Cambridge) 106.
Nagel T (1986) *The View from Nowhere* (OUP: New York).
Nagel T (1991) *Equality and Partiality* (OUP: New York).
National Research Council (2001) *Evaluating Welfare Reform in an Era of Transition* (National Academy Press: Washington DC).
Noble C (1997) *Welfare as We Know It* (OUP: Oxford).
Note (1960) 'Unconstitutional Conditions' 73 Harvard L Rev 1595.
Note (1968) 'Another Look at Unconstitutional Conditions' 117 University of Pennsylvania L Rev 144.
Note (1969) 'Welfare Due Process' 3 Georgia L Rev 459.
Note (1997) 'Recent Legislation' 110 Harv L Rev 983.
Nozick R (1974) *Anarchy, State and Utopia* (Basic Books: New York).
Nussbaum N (2004) 'Beyond the Social Contract' 24 *Tanner Lectures on Human Values* (University of Utah Press: Salt Lake City).
Oaxley G (1974) *Poor Relief in England and Wales 1601–1834* (David & Charles: London).
OECD (2002) *Benefits and Wages—OECD Indicators* (OECD Publications: Paris) <http://www1.oecd.org/publications/e-book/8102091E.pdf>
O'Connor A (2004) 'Cracking Under the Pressure? It's Just the Opposite, for Some' New York Times (10 September 2004).
O'Hagan T (1999) *Rousseau* (Routledge: London).

O'Neil O (2003) 'Constructivism v. Contractualism' 16 Ratio 319.
O'Neil RM (1966) 'Unconstitutional Conditions' California L Rev 443.
Ormerod P (1998) 'Unemployment and Social Exclusion: An Economic View' in M Rhodes and Y Meny (eds) *The Future of European Welfare: A New Social Contract?* (Macmillan: Basingstoke) 23.
Orshansky M (1965) 'Counting the Poor' (1965) 28 Social Security Bull 3.
Page S and Larner M (1997) 'Introduction to the AFDC Program' 7 The Future of Children 20.
Palmer E (2000) 'Resource Allocation, Welfare Rights' 20 OJLS 63.
Parfit D (1984) *Reasons and Persons* (Clarendon: Oxford).
Parfit D (1997) 'Equality and Priority' 10 Ratio 202.
Parry G (1964) 'Individuality, Politics and the Critique of Paternalism in John Locke' 12 Political Studies 163.
Paugam S (1998) 'Poverty and Social Exclusion: A Sociological View' in M Rhodes and Y Meny (eds) *The Future of European Welfare: A New Social Contract?* (Macmillan: Basingstoke) 41.
Paz-Fuchs A (2004) 'Welfare Reform Between Capitalism and Patriarchy' (2004) 10 Labor, Society and Law 339.
Paz-Fuchs A (2007) 'Book Review: E Sol and M Westerveld (eds) *Contractualism in Employment Services*' 2 European Rev of Contract L 232.
Paz-Fuchs (2008) 'Rights, Duties and Conditioning Welfare' 21(1) Canadian J of Law and Jurisprudence (forthcoming).
Peck J and Theodore N (2000) 'Beyond Employability' 24 Cambridge J of Economics 729.
Peffer R (1978) 'A Defense of Rights to Well-Being' 8 Phil and Pub Affairs 65.
Peters R (1956) *Hobbes* (Penguin: London).
Pitkin H (1965) 'Obligation and Consent—I' 59 Am Pol Sci Rev 990.
Piven, FF and Cloward RA (1993) *Regulating the Poor* (Updated Edition, Vintage: New York).
Pogge T (1989) *Realizing Rawls* (Cornell UP: Ithaca).
Plant R (1990) 'Citizenship and Rights' in R Plant and N Barry *Citizenship and Rights in Thatcher's Britain: Two Views* (IEA Health and Welfare Unit: London).
Plant R (1988) 'Needs, Agency and Welfare Rights' in JD Moon (ed) Responsibility, Rights and Welfare (Westview: Boulder) 55.
Plant R (1993) 'Free Lunches Don't Nourish: Reflections on Entitlement and Citizenship' in G Drover and P Kerans (eds) *New Approaches to Welfare Theory* (Elgar: Brookfield) 33.
Plant R (2003) 'Citizenship and Social Security' 24 Fiscal Studies 153.
Plant R, Lesser H and Taylor-Gooby P (1980) *Political Philosophy and Social Welfare: Essays on the Normative Provision of Welfare Provision* (Routledge: London).
Polanyi K *The Great Transformation* (Beacon: Boston).
Porter E 'Stretched to Limit, Women Stall March to Work' New York Times (2 March 2006).
Posner R (1981) *The Economics of Justice* (Harvard UP: Cambridge MA).
Powell T (1916) 'The Right to Work for the State' 16 Columbia L Rev 99.
Procacci G (1998) 'Against Exclusion' in M Rhodes and Y Meny (eds) *The Future of European Welfare: A New Social Contract?* (Macmillan: Basingstoke) 63.
Puttick K (1999) 'Social Security. 2020: A Welfare Odyssey' 29 ILJ 190.
Quigley W (1990) 'Backwards into the Future. How Welfare Changes in the Millenium Resemble English Poor Laws of the Middle Ages' 9 Stanford L and Society Rev 101.

Raphael DD (1967) 'Human Rights, Old and New' in DD Raphael (ed) *Political Theory and the Rights of Man* (Macmillan: Basingstoke) 54.
Rawls J (1971) *A Theory of Justice* (OUP: Oxford).
Rawls J (1980) 'Kantian Constructivism in Moral Theory' 77 J of Phil 545.
Rawls J (1982) 'Social Unity and Primary Goods' in A Sen and B Williams (eds) *Utilitarianism and Beyond* (CUP: Cambridge) 159.
Rawls J (1985) 'Justice as Fairness: Political Not Metaphysical' 14 Philosophy and Public Affairs 223.
Rawls J (1987) 'The Basic Liberties and their Priority' in SM McMurrin (ed) *Liberty, Equality and Law* (CUP: Cambridge).
Rawls J (1988) 'The Priority of the Right and Ideas of the Good' 17 Philosophy and Public Affairs 251.
Rawls J (1993) *Political Liberalism* (Columbia UP: New York).
Rawls J (1999) *A Theory of Justice* (Revised Edition Harvard UP: Cambridge MA).
Raz J (1975) *Practical Reasons and Norms* (Clarendon: Oxford).
Raz J (1977) 'Promises and Obligations' in PMS Hacker and J Raz (eds) *Law, Morality and Society* (Clarendon: Oxford) 210.
Raz J (1984) 'On the Nature of Rights' 93 Mind 194.
Raz J (1986) *The Morality of Freedom* (Clarendon: Oxford).
Raz J (1994) *Ethics in the Public Domain* (Clarendon: Oxford).
Reich C (1963) 'The New Property' 73 Yale LJ 733.
Reich C 'Individual Rights and Social Welfare' (1965) 74 Yale LJ 1245.
Riley P (1999) 'A Possible Explanation of Rousseau's General Will' in C Morris (ed) *The Social Contract Theorists* (Rowman & Littlefield: Oxford) 167.
Ripstein A (1999) *Equality, Responsibility and the Law* (CUP: Cambridge).
Ripstein A (1999) 'The General Will' in C Morris (ed) *The Social Contract Theorists* (Rowman & Littlefield: Oxford) 219.
Ripstein A (2004) 'Justice and Responsibility' 17 Can J of L and Jurisp 361.
Roberts D (1979) *Paternalism in Early Victorian England* (Croom Helm: London).
Roberts D (1995) 'The Only Good Poor Woman: Unconstitutional Conditions and Welfare' 72 Denver L Rev 931.
Robinson P (2000) 'Employment and Social Inclusion' in P Askonas and A Stewart (eds) *Social Inclusion* (Macmillan: Basingstoke) 153.
Rodgers G (1995) 'What is Special About Social Exclusion?' in G Rodgers, C Gore and J Figueiriedo (eds) *Social Exclusion* (ILO: Geneva) 43.
Rodgers G (1995) 'The Design of Policy Against Exclusion' in G Rodgers, C Gore and J Figueiriedo (eds) *Social Exclusion* (ILO: Geneva) 253.
Roemer J (1986) 'The Mismarriage of Bargaining Theory and Distributive Justice' 97 Ethics 88.
Roemer J (1995) 'Equality and Responsibility' *Boston Review* <http://bostonreview.net/BR20.2/Roemer.html> (30 July 2004).
Roemer J (1996) *Theories of Distributive Justice* (Harvard UP: Cambridge MA).
Room G (1992) *The Observatory on National Policies to Combat Social Exclusion* (2nd Report Commision for European Communities: Brussels).
Room G (1995) 'Poverty and Social Exclusion' in G Room (ed) *Beyond the Threshold* (Policy: Bristol) 1.
Rosanvallon P (2000) *The New Social Question* (Princeton UP: Princeton).

Rose M (1976) 'Settlement, Removal and the New Poor Law' in D Fraser (ed) *The New Poor Law in the Nineteenth Century* (Macmillan: Basingstoke) 25.

Rose N (1995) *Workfare or Fair Work* (Rutgers UP: New Brunswick NJ).

Rosenbaum A (1981) *The Philosophy of Human Rights* (Aldwych: London).

Ross WD (2002) *The Right and the Good* (Clarendon: Oxford).

Rousseau JJ (1998) *The Social Contract* (Wordsworth: Ware Hertfordshire).

Rowlingson, K (1997) *Social Security Fraud: The Role of Penalties* (DSS Research Report 64: London).

Salais R (2003) 'Towards a Capability Approach' in J Zeitlin and DM Trubek (eds) *Governing Work and Welfare in a New Economy* (OUP: Oxford) 317.

Scanlon T (1973) 'Rawls's Theory of Justice' 121 U of Pennsylvania L Rev 1020.

Scanlon T (1975) 'Preference and Urgency' 72 J of Philosophy 655.

Scanlon T (1976) 'Nozick on Rights, Liberty and Property' 6 Philosophy and Public Affairs 3.

Scanlon T (1982) 'Contractualism and Utilitarianism' in A Sen and B Williams (eds) *Utilitarianism and Beyond* (CUP: Cambridge) 103.

Scanlon T (1998) *What We Owe to Each Other* (Harvard UP: Cambridge MA).

Schauer F (1991) *Playing by the Rules* (Clarendon: Oxford).

Scheffler S (1992) 'Responsibility, Reactive Attitudes and Liberalism in Philosophy and Politics' 21 Philosophy and Public Affairs 299.

Schirm A and Castner L (2000) *Reaching Those in Need: State Food Stamps Participation Rates in 2000* (United States Department of Agriculture Washington DC) <http://www.fns.usda.gov/oane/MENU/Published/FSP/FILES/Participation/Reaching2000.pdf> (2 July 2003).

Schneider P (1967) 'Social Rights and the Concept of Human Rights' in DD Raphael (ed) *Political Theory and the Rights of Man* (Macmillan: Basingstoke) 81.

Selznick P (1994) *The Moral Commonwealth* (U of California: Berkeley).

Selznick P (1998) 'Social Justice—A Communitarian Perspective' in A Etzioni (ed) *The Essential Communitarian Reader* (Rowan and Littlefield: Oxford).

Sen A (1982) *Choice, Welfare and Measurement* (Blackwell: Oxford).

Sen A (1992) *Inequality Reexamined* (Clarendon: Oxford).

Shakespeare W (1600 rpnt 1995) *The Merchant of Venice* (Penguin: London).

Shapiro I (1986) *Evolution of Rights in Liberal Theory* (CUP: Cambridge).

Shklar J (1991) *American Citizenship: The Quest for Inclusion* (Harvard UP: Cambridge)

Shue H (1988) 'Mediating Duties' 98 Ethics 687.

Siaroff A (1994) 'Work, Welfare and Gender Equality: A New Typology' in D Sainsbury (ed) *Gendering Welfare States* (Sage: London) 82.

Silver H (1995) 'Reconceptualizing Social Disadvantage' in G Rodgers, C Gore and J Figueiriedo (eds) *Social Exclusion* (ILO: Geneva) 57.

Silver H and Wilkinson F (1995) 'Policies to Combat Social Exclusion' in G Rodgers, C Gore and J Figueiriedo (eds) *Social Exclusion* (ILO: Geneva) 283.

Simmonds N (1998) 'Rights at the Cutting Edge' in M Kramer, N Simmonds and H Steiner *A Debate Over Rights* (Clarendon: Oxford) 112.

Simmons AJ (1992) *The Lockean Theory of Rights* (Princeton UP: Princeton).

Simmons AJ (1999) 'Political Consent' in C Morris (ed) *The Social Contract Theorists* (Rowman & Littlefield: Oxford) 121.

Simon WH (1983) 'Legality, Bureaucracy and Class in the Welfare System' 92 YLJ 1198.

Simon WH (1986) 'Rights and Redistribution in the Welfare System' (1986) 38 Stanford L Rev 1431.
Simons K (1989) 'Offers, Threats and Unconstitutional Conditions' 26 San Diego L Rev 289.
Sinfield A (2005) 'The Goals of Social Policy: Context and Change' in J Andersen and others (eds) *The Changin Face of Welfare* (Policy: Bristol).
Smart JJC 'An Outline of Utilitarian Ethics' in JJC Smart and B Williams *Utilitarianism: For and Against* (CUP: Cambridge) 54.
Smith IT (2000) *Industrial Law* (7th edn, Butterworths: London).
Social Exclusion Unit (1999) 'Foreword by the Prime Minister' in *Bridging the Gap: New Opportunities for 16–18 Year Olds Not in Education, Employment or Training* (Cm 4405).
Sommer H (1997) 'The Non-Enumerated Rights' 28 Hebrew U L Rev.
Standing G (1999) *Global Labour Flexibility* (Macmillan: Basingstoke).
Stanley A (1992) 'Beggars Can't Be Choosers' in C Tomlins and A King (eds) *Labor Law in America* (Johns Hopkins UP: Baltimore) 128.
Steiner H (1984) 'A Liberal Theory of Exploitation' 94 Ethics 225.
Steiner H (1998) 'Working Rights' in M Kramer, N Simmonds and H Steiner *A Debate Over Rights* (Clarendon: Oxford) 233.
Steiner H (2001) 'Choice and Circumstance' in M Kramer (ed) *Rights, Wrongs and Responsibilities* (Palgrave: Basingstoke) 225.
Stewart A (2000) 'Social Inclusion' in P Askonas and A Stewart (eds) *Social Inclusion* (Macmillan: Basingstoke) 1.
Staff of House Committee on Ways and Means, 102d Congress, 2d Session *Overview of Entitlements Programs: Background Material and Data on Programs Within the Jurisdiction of the Committee of Ways and Means* (1992).
Struyven L and Verhoest K (2005) 'The Problem of Agency at Organisational Level and Street Level: The Case of the Flemish Public Employment Service) in E Sol and M Westerveld *Contractualism in Employment Services: A New Form of Welfare State Governance* (Kluwer Law: The Hague).
Sullivan K (1989) 'Unconstitutional Conditions' 102 Harvard L Rev 1413.
Sullivan K (1989) 'Unconstitutional Conditions and the Distribution of Liberty' 26 San Diego L Rev 327.
Sumner LW (1987) *The Moral Foundations of Rights* (Clarendon: Oxford).
Sunstein C (1989) 'Is There an Unconstitutional Conditions Doctrine' 26 San Diego L Rev 337.
Sunstein C (1991) 'Preferences and Politics' 20 Philosophy and Public Affairs 3.
Swirski B (2000) *From Welfare to Work—Government Plan to Reduce Income Support Benefits* (Adva: Tel Aviv).
Temkin L (1993) *Inequality* (OUP: Oxford).
Thatcher M (1993) *The Downing Street Years* (HarperCollins: London).
Timmins N (1995) *Five Giants—A Biography of the Welfare State* (Fontana: London).
Townsend P (1978) *Poverty in the United Kingdom* (Mushroom: Nottingham).
Townsend P (1993) *The International Analysis of Poverty* (Harvester: New York).
Tushnet M (2002) 'State Action, Social Welfare Rights and the Judicial Role: Some Comparative Observations' 3 Chi J International L 435.

USDA (2003) *Food Stamp Participation Rates and Benefits* (United States Department of Agriculture Washington DC) <http://www.fns.usda.gov/oane/MENU/Published/FSP/FILES/Participation/PartDemoGroup.pdf> (2 July 2003).
Vallentyne P (1991) 'Gauthier's Three Projects' in P Vallentyne (ed) *Contractarianism and Rational Choice* (CUP: Cambridge) 1.
van Alstyne WV (1968) 'The Demise of the Right-Privilege Distinction in Constitutional Law' 81 Harvard L Rev 1439.
van Hoof GJH (1984) 'The Legal Nature of Economic, Social and Cultural Rights' in P Alston and K Tomasevski (eds) *The Right to Food* (Dordrecht: Boston) 97.
van Oorschot W (1995) *Realizing Rights* (Avebury: Aldershot).
van Oorschot W (1999) 'Troublesome Targeting: On the Multi-Level Causes of Non-Take-Up' (1999) 56 Social Security 193.
van Oorschot W and L Halman L (2000) 'Blame or Fate, Individual or Social' 2(1) European Societies 1.
van Parijs P (1992) 'Basic Income Capitalism' 102 Ethics 465.
van Parijs P (1992) 'Competing Justifications for Basic Income' in P van Parijs (ed) *Arguing for Basic Income* (Verso: London).
van Parijs P (1997) *Real Freedom for All* (Clarendon: Oxford).
van Parijs P (1998) 'Why Surfers Should be Fed' 20 Philosophy and Public Affairs 101.
Vincent-Jones P (2000) 'Contractual Governance' 20 OJLS 317.
Vincent-Jones P (2006) *The New Public Contracting: Regulation, Responsiveness, Relationality* (OUP: Oxford).
Vonnegut K (1998) *'Harrison Bergeron'* in *Welcome to the Monkey House* (Doubleday: New York).
Waldron J (1984) 'Introduction' in J Waldron (ed) *Theories of Rights* (OUP: Oxford) 1.
Waldron J (1989) 'Rights in Conflict' 99 Ethics 503.
Waldron J (1993) *Liberal Rights* (CUP: Cambridge).
Waldron J (1994) 'John Locke—Social Contract versus Political Anthropology' in D Boucher and P Kelly (eds) *The Social Contract from Hobbes to Rawls* (Routledge: London).
Waldron J (1999) *Law and Disagreement* (OUP: Oxford).
Walker R (1995) 'The Dynamics of Poverty and Social Exclusion' in G Room (ed) *Beyond the Threshold* (Policy: Bristol) 102.
Walter T (1998) *Basic Income* (Boyars: London).
Walzer M (1981) 'Philosophy and Democracy' 9 Political Theory 379.
Walzer M (1983) *Spheres of Justice* (Blackwell: Oxford).
Warren E and Brandeis L (1890) 'The Right to Privacy' 4 Harvard L Rev 193.
Warrender H (1957) *The Political Philosophy of Hobbes* (OUP: Oxford).
Wax A (2000) 'Welfare Rights' 63 Law and Contemporary Problems 257.
Wax A (2001) 'A Reciprocal Welfare Programme' 8 Va J Soc Pol 477.
Wax A (2003) 'Something for Nothing' 52 Emory LJ 1.
Webb S and Webb B (1909) *The Public Organisation of the Labour Market: Being Part Two of the Minority Report of the Poor Law Commission* (Longmans, Green and Co: London).
Webb S and Webb B (1963) *English Poor Law History: Part I—The Old Poor Law* (Cass: London).

Webb S and Webb B (1963) *English Poor Law History—Part II: The Last Hundred Years* (Cass: London).
Webb S and Webb B (1963) *English Poor Law Policy* (Cass: London).
Weber G (1988) 'The Striker Amendment to the Food Stamp Act' 22 Ga L Rev 741.
Wellman C (1982) *Welfare Rights* (Rowman and Allanheld: Totowa).
Weil A (2004) 'Assessing Welfare Reform in the United States' in N Gilbert and A Parent (eds) *Welfare Reform: A Comparative Assessment of the French and U.S. Experiences* (International Social Security Series vol 10, Transaction Publishers London) 145.
Westen P (1980) 'Incredible Dilemmas' 66 Iowa L Rev 741.
White S (2000) 'Social Rights and the Social Contract' (2000) 30 British Journal of Political Science 507.
White S (2004) 'What's Wrong with Workfare' 21 J of Applied Philosophy 271.
Wikeley N (1989) 'Unemployment Benefit, the State and the Labour Market' 16 J of L and Society 291.
Wikeley N and Ogus AI (2002) *The Law of Social Security* (5th edn, Butterworths: London).
Williams B (1973) 'A Critique of Utilitarianism' in JJC Smart and B Williams *Utilitarianism: For and Against* (CUP: Cambridge) 93.
Williams H (1994) 'Kant on the Social Contract' in D Boucher and P Kelly (eds) *The Social Contract from Hobbes to Rawls* (Routledge: London) 132.
Wilson H (1986) *Memoirs: The Making of a Prime Minister 1916–1964* (Weidenfeld & Nicolson: London).
Williams L (1992) 'The Ideology of Division: Behavior Modification Welfare Reform Proposals' 102 Yale LJ 719.
Williams L (1994) 'The Abuse of Section 1115 Waivers: Welfare Reform in Search of a Standard' 12 Yale L and Policy Rev 8.
Williams L (1998) 'Welfare and Legal Entitlements: The Social Roots of Poverty' in D Kairys (ed) *The Politics of Law* (3rd edn, Basic Books: New York) 569.
Williams L (2002) 'Beyond Labour Law's Parochialism: A Re-envisioning of the Discourse of Redistribution' in J Conaghan, R Fischl and K Klare (eds) *Labour Law in an Era of Globalization* (OUP: Oxford) 93.
Williams L (2005) 'Poor Women's Work Experience: Gaps in the Work/Family Discussion' in J Conaghan and K Rittich (eds) *Labour Law, Work and Family: Critical and Comparative Perspectives* (OUP: Oxford).
Wilson WJ (1987) *The Truly Disadvantaged* (Chicago UP: Chicago).
Wintemute R (1995) *Sexual Orientation and Human Rights* (OUP: Oxford).
Wolf S (1990) *Freedom Within Reason* (OUP: Oxford).
Wolff J (2004) 'Training, Perfectionism and Fairness' 21 J of Applied Philosophy 285.
Wyne E (1980) *Social Security* (Westview: Boulder, Colorado).
Young IM (1990) *Justice and the Politics of Difference* (Princeton UP: Princeton).

Index

agency approach
  the role of equality and individual
    responsibility, 141–6
  social inclusion, 175–6

Beveridge, William, 104–5
Blair, Tony, 14, 46, 183
budgetary capabilities, 26–8

Clinton, Bill, 96, 102, 132
communitarianism, 53–4, 133, 179
competency of courts, 25–6
conditionality
  conclusions, 201–5
  contemporary programmes in GB, 103–7
  contemporary programmes in US
    current themes, 110
    legislative background, 99–100
  'illegitimate condition' theory
    discrimination based on immutable
      characteristics, 155–8
    fundamental rights, 161–2
    germaneness requirement, 159–61
    importance, 152–5
  intersection with social contract and
    welfare state
    choice theory, 51–3
    interest theory, 50–3
    theoretical background, 49–50
  introduction, 1, 5–6
  Poor Law relief
    conclusions, 92–3
    deterrence, 77–80
    efficiency, 86–9
    historical significance, 75–7
    quid-pro-quo, 89–92
    social control, 80–6
  quid-pro-quo
    contemporary programmes, 107–8,
      120–2, 126–9
    introduction, 5
    Poor Law relief, 76–7, 89–92
    transformation of social contract theory
      to policy, 47
  reciprocity
    collective interests, 62–4
    conclusions, 201–5
    introduction, 1, 5–6
    transformation of social contract theory
      to policy, 43

  recognition of legal right to welfare
    importance, 162–3
    justification for outcome, 163–70
  rights-based approach
    consequences, 62–4
    constructing welfare rights, 57–62
    reciprocity and collective interests, 53–7
  social inclusion, 199–200
contemporary programmes
  conclusions, 130–1
  current themes
    Great Britain, 122–30
    overview, 107–10
    United States, 110–22
  legislative background
    Great Britain, 102–7
    United States, 98–102
  overview, 94–8
control
  changing social attitudes, 83–4
  contemporary programmes in GB, 105
  justifications, 80–1
  moral correction, 81–3
  paternalism, 84–6

Deakin, Simon, 188
deserving poor
  conclusions, 203
  Poor Law relief, 72–4
  significance, 45–6
deterrence
  contemporary programmes, 108–10
  contemporary programmes in GB,
    123–5
  contemporary programmes in US
    current themes, 111–13
    legislative background, 101–2
  introduction, 5
  policy measures in US, 58
  Poor Law relief, 76–7, 77–80
discretion
  contemporary programmes, 72
  Poor Law relief, 69–72
Dworkin, Ronald, 7, 33, 62, 133–4, 135, 137,
  142, 147, 148, 150, 170, 178

economics
  conclusions, 203
  contemporary programmes in GB, 103
  contemporary programmes in US, 117–19

economics (cont.)
　discrimination based on immutable
　　characteristics, 156
　germaneness requirement, 160
　introduction, 5
　overview, 108
　Poor Law relief, 76–7, 86–9
　social inclusion, 173–5
egalitarianism. *see* equality
equality
　conclusions, 170–1, 204–5
　contemporary programmes in GB, 104–5
　'expensive taste' objections, 147
　'illegitimate condition' theory
　　discrimination based on immutable
　　　characteristics, 155–8
　　fundamental rights, 161–2
　　germaneness requirement, 159–61
　　importance, 152–5
　importance within general theory, 133–7
　incentive-based approach, 138–41
　introduction, 6–8
　recognition of legal right to welfare
　　importance, 162–3
　　justification for outcome, 163–70
　the role of choice and individual
　　responsibility
　　agency approach, 141–6
　　incentive-based approach, 138–41
　　overview, 137–8
　　reasonableness, 146–52
　role of co-dependence, 21
　social contract theory, 36, 38–42
　social inclusion as a justification for coercive
　　programmes, 177–81

Field, Frank, 43, 54, 188
financial capabilities, 26–8
Food Stamps, 11–12, 44, 110–113, 117, 188
fraud
　contemporary programmes in GB, 125
　contemporary programmes in US, 113
　transformation of social contract theory to
　　policy, 46–7

Gauthier, David, 40, 59
germaneness requirement, 159–61
Giddens, Anthony, 59, 178, 193

Handler, Joel, 108, 114
Hart, HLA, 50, 51, 65
Hobbes, Thomas, 29, 30, 33–4, 38–42

'illegitimate condition' theory
　discrimination based on immutable
　　characteristics, 155–8
　fundamental rights, 161–2

　germaneness requirement, 159–61
　importance, 152–5
individual responsibility
　see also personal responsibility
　conclusions, 201–5
　contemporary programmes
　　current themes in US, 121–2
　　overview, 108
　'no rights without responsibilities', 59
　Poor Law relief, 68–9
　recognition of legal right to welfare
　　importance, 162–3
　　justification for outcome, 163–70
　role within egalitarianism
　　agency approach, 141–6
　　incentive-based approach, 138–41
　　overview, 137–8
　　reasonableness, 146–52
　social inclusion
　　importance, 175–6
　　justification for coercive
　　　programmes, 177–81
　transformation of social contract theory to
　　policy, 44–5

Jobseeker's Allowance, 61, 122, 124

King, Desmond, 16, 67, 90

less eligibility principle
　contemporary programmes in GB, 124–5
　Poor Law relief, 74–5
levelling-down objections, 167
Locke, John, 30, 31, 34–5
luck, 141–7

morality
　conclusions, 203
　contemporary programmes in GB,
　　129–30
　contemporary programmes in US, 99
　　current themes, 113–17
　　legislative background, 100–1
　'free and equal moral persons', 149
　introduction, 5
　'no rights without responsibilities', 59
　Poor Law relief, 76–7
　social contract theory, 33–8, 39–40
　social control and correction, 81–3
　social inclusion, 173–5
mothers
　lone / single parents, 69, 99, 114, 116, 181
　teenage mothers, 102
　welfare mothers, 100, 169, 191

New Deal for Lone Parents (NDLP),
　129, 130

Index

New Deal for Young Persons (NDYP), 129, 130

paternalism, 84–6
personal responsibility, 6, 7, 8, 46, 59, 83, 93, 122, 132–3, 140, 163, 170, 171, 173, 201
  introduction, 6–8
  see also **individual responsibility**
Poor Law relief
  administration
    importance, 68
    local control, 69–72
    responsibility, 68–9
  beneficiaries
    deserving and undeserving poor, 72–4
    less eligibility principle, 74–5
    overview, 72
  conditionality
    conclusions, 92–3
    deterrence, 77–80
    efficiency, 86–9
    historical significance, 75–7
    quid-pro-quo, 89–92
    social control, 80–6
  historical significance, 67–8
  introduction, 4–5

quid-pro-quo
  contemporary programmes
    in GB, 126–9
    in US, 120–2
    overview, 107–8
  introduction, 5
  Poor Law relief, 76–7, 89–92
  transformation of social contract theory to policy, 47

Rawls, John, 31–7, 39–41, 65, 133, 135, 146–9, 150, 158, 165, 169, 202
reasonable responsibility, 138, 146–52, 162–3, 178
reciprocity
  collective interests, 62–4
  conclusions, 201–5
  introduction, 1, 5–6
  transformation of social contract theory to policy, 43
rights
  assumption of co-dependence, 20–1
  choice theory of rights
    see also **individual responsibility**
    introduction, 4
    role, 51–3
  conclusions, 203–4
  conditionality
    consequences, 62–4

  constructing welfare rights, 57–62
  reciprocity and collective interests, 53–7
  contemporary programmes in US, 101
fundamental rights
  'illegitimate condition' theory
    fundamental rights, 161–2
    germaneness requirement, 156
  interest theory of rights, 50–3
  protection of rights, 22–7
  realization of rights, 22–7
  recognition of legal right to welfare
    importance, 162–3
    justification for outcome, 163–70
  respect, 22
  right to welfare, 12, 20, 21, 28, 29, 36–7, 50, 57, 62, 64, 67–8, 93, 131, 132–171, 196, 198, 199, 203–4
  significance, 18–20
  social and economic rights, 18–26, 28, 37, 54, 64, 132, 165
    court competency argument, 25–6
    pragmatic dimensions, 24–9
    realization, 23
    separation of powers argument, 25–6
    theoretical dimension, 21–4
    vagueness argument, 24–5
  social contract theory, 33–8
  social inclusion
    basic needs, 194–6
    rationales, 194
    strategic approaches, 196–9
Rousseau, Jean-Jacques, 30, 34, 53

Scanlon, Thomas, 36–41, 133, 169, 202
self-respect, 32, 36–7, 40, 84, 136, 185
social contract
  conclusions, 201–5
  contemporary programmes in GB, 104–5
  intersection with welfare state
    conclusions, 64–5
    conditionality, 49–64
    modern programmes, 10–18
    rights-based approach, 18–29
    theoretical traditions and their development, 29–48
  introduction, 3–4
social control
  changing social attitudes, 83–4
  justifications, 80–1
  moral correction, 81–3
  paternalism, 84–6
social inclusion
  alternative perspectives, 181–94
  conclusions, 204

social inclusion (cont.)
  conditionality, 199–200
  importance
    bridge between agency and structural approaches, 175–6
    connection with labour markets, 176–7
    dynamic concept, 177
    economic social and moral perspectives, 173–5
  introduction, 8
  justification for coercive programmes, 177–81
  meaning, 172
  Moral Underclass Discourse (MUD), 182–3, 194
  poverty and welfare rights
    basic needs, 194–6
    rationales, 194
    strategic approaches, 196–9
  Redistribution Discourse (RED), 182–3
  Social Integrationist Discourse (SID), 182–3, 194
social policy, 1, 4, 10, 12–15, 29, 39, 42, 43, 45, 46, 60, 61, 98, 105, 110, 139, 151, 164, 170, 172, 182, 185, 187, 190, 193, 201

Temporary Assistance for Needy Families (TANF), 11, 45, 97, 110–113, 115–20, 169
transformation of social contract theory to policy, 47–8

undeserving poor
  conclusions, 203
  Poor Law relief, 72–4
  significance, 45–6

United States
  contemporary programmes
    current themes, 110–22
    legislative background, 98–102
    overview, 95–7
  creating legal rights, 58
  intersection with social contract and welfare state, 10–18
  Poor Law relief
    deterrence as a driving force, 77
    quid-pro-quo, 89–92
  recognition of legal right to welfare
    fundamental rights, 161–2
    most important moment, 132
    'personal responsibility with a vengeance', 140
  transformation of social contract theory to policy
    dominant paradigm, 43
    morality, 47–8
    quid-pro-quo, 47
universality, 28–9

welfare
  defined, 2–3
  reform, 2–3, 10–11, 14, 43–4, 46, 49, 53, 54, 57, 58, 61, 62, 83–4, 86, 87, 89, 95, 101, 112, 123, 125, 131, 132, 138, 142, 172, 180–1, 190
welfare states
  intersection with social contract
    conclusions, 64–5
    conditionality, 49–64
    modern programmes, 10–18
    rights-based approach, 18–29
    theoretical traditions and their development, 29–48
  introduction, 4